A NEW CRITIQUE
OF THEORETICAL THOUGHT

A NEW CRITIQUE
OF
THEORETICAL THOUGHT

BY

HERMAN DOOYEWEERD Dr jur.
Professor of Philosophy of Law, Free University of Amsterdam
Fellow of the Royal Dutch Academy of Sciences

TRANSLATED BY

DAVID H. FREEMAN
Assistant Professor of Philosophy, Wilson College

AND

WILLIAM S. YOUNG
Assistant Professor of Philosophy, Butler University

VOLUME I

THE NECESSARY PRESUPPOSITIONS
OF PHILOSOPHY

PAIDEIA PRESS LTD.
1984

This book was originally published in four volumes.

First published by The Presbyterian and Reformed Publishing Company in 1969.
This edition published in 1983 by special arrangement.

Paideia Press Ltd., P.O. Box 1000, Jordan Station, Ontario, Canada L0R 1S0.

ISBN 0-88815-152-7
Third printing, 1984.

Printed in the United States of America.

FOREWORD (ABREVIATED) TO THE FIRST EDITION

The appearance of this first systematic presentation of my philosophy fills me with a deep sense of appreciation to God for the strength He granted me to overcome innumerable difficulties. I would also like to acknowledge my indebtedness to the Board of Directors of the Dr Kuyper Foundation (Kuyperstichting) whose support made the publication of this work possible.

The first rudimental conception of this philosophy had ripened even before I came to the Kuyper-foundation (1921).

Originally I was strongly under the influence first of the Neo-Kantian philosophy, later on of HUSSERL's phenomenology. The great turning point in my thought was marked by the discovery of the religious root of thought itself, whereby a new light was shed on the failure of all attempts, including my own, to bring about an inner synthesis between the Christian faith and a philosophy which is rooted in faith in the self-sufficiency of human reason.

I came to understand the central significance of the "heart", repeatedly proclaimed by Holy Scripture to be the religious root of human existence.

On the basis of this central Christian point of view I saw the need of a revolution in philosophical thought of a very radical character. Confronted with the religious root of the creation, nothing less is in question than a relating of the whole temporal cosmos, in both its so-called 'natural' and 'spiritual' aspects, to this point of reference. In contrast to this basic Biblical conception, of what significance is a so-called 'Copernican' revolution which merely makes the 'natural-aspects' of temporal reality relative to a theoretical abstraction such as KANT's 'transcendental subject'?

From a Christian point of view, the whole attitude of philosophical thought which proclaims the self-sufficiency of the latter, turns out to be unacceptable, because it withdraws human thought from the divine revelation in Christ Jesus.

The first result of the Biblical point of view with respect to the root of all temporal reality was a radical break with the philosophical view of reality rooted in what I have called the immanence-standpoint [1].

The discovery of the transcendental ground-Idea at the foundation of all philosophical thought, made it possible to display the different theoretical views concerning the structure of reality, as developed by the dominant immanence-philosophy, in their dependence upon a supra-theoretical a priori. It made the inauguration of criticism possible upon a much more deeply lying plane than a supposed merely theoretical one.

If temporal reality itself cannot be *neutral* with respect to its religious root, if in other words the whole notion of a static temporal cosmos *'an sich'*, independent of the religious root of mankind, rests on a fundamental misconception, how can one any longer seriously believe in the religious neutrality of theoretical thought?

One of the fundamental principles of this new philosophy is the cosmological basic principle *of sphere-sovereignty*. Its development was suggested by (the famous Dutch thinker and statesman) ABRAHAM KUYPER, but depends upon the introduction of a religious Christian foundation into philosophy. On this principle rests the *general theory of the modal law-spheres* developed in Volume II. The first conception of this theory was gained after the discovery of the inner structure of the modal aspects of human experience which I could explain even in my inaugural address *The Significance of the Cosmonomic Idea for Jurisprudence and Philosophy of Law* (1926). In the elaboration of this theory difficulties arose, not only because it could nowhere find a point of contact in the immanence-philosophy, but also because it cannot become fruitful apart from a close contact with the *special theory of the modal law-spheres*, which investigates the basic problems of the various special sciences in the light of the Christian transcendental ground-Idea.

For this reason in my earlier publications I discussed the theory of the modal law-spheres always in connection with my own field of special science, i.e. jurisprudence. I wished to assure myself that this philosophical theory has a principial

---

[1] *Translator's note.* The meaning of this terminology will become clear in the course of the discussion. D. H. F.

value for special scientific thought before I drew any provisional systematic conclusions.

The theory of the structures of individuality which I have developed in the third volume has also given rise to many systematic problems. Even in my work *The Crisis in the Humanistic Theory of the State* (1932) I have not only indicated the importance of this theory with respect to the view of the structure of naïve experience, but I have also shown its significance for sociology and jurisprudence.

In its earlier stage this theory had not yet been worked out to a sufficient degree. Its significance is not limited to the sciences, but it touches the fundamental structures of empirical reality.

I am strongly convinced that for the fruitful working out of this philosophy, in a genuinely scientific manner, there is needed a staff of fellow-labourers who would be in a position independently to think through its basic ideas in the special scientific fields. It is a matter of life and death for this young philosophy that Christian scholars in all fields of science seek to put it to work in their own specialty.

I am also very thankful that from the outset I found at my side my colleague Dr VOLLENHOVEN, professor of Philosophy at the Free University of Amsterdam, whose name has been inseparably joined to my own. It was a great joy to both of us to find an enthusiastic independent fellow-worker in Prof. Dr H. G. STOKER, whose publications made our movement known in South Africa, and who in his profound constructive criticism has called attention to various points which require further working out.

And although I cannot see through STOKER's peculiar concepts in their full compass, and at first sight have certain objections to them, yet this does not prevent me from rejoicing greatly over the fact that STOKER is making his philosophical gifts, of which he already gave evidence in the circle of MAX SCHELER, serviceable to a further independent construction of this new philosophy. His cooperation is to be esteemed of great value, particularly in his own special field of psychology.

And finally I am further encouraged by the rise of a circle, though it be still modest, of scientific adherents, each of whom endeavours in his own department to make the newly developed philosophy fruitful.

Bound by one and the same Christian faith, equally inspired by the stimulating effect of the Christian root of life in the practice of science, a first circle of scientific workers has thus attached itself to this philosophy. God grant that this modest group may grow and that many that should be our adherents, but who still resist the Christian Idea of science, may be convinced that the question is not a matter of a 'system' (subject to all the faults and errors of human thought) but rather it concerns the *foundation* and the root of scientific thought as such.

In conclusion let me make two final remarks. The first is addressed to my opponents on grounds of principle. I am fully conscious that any method of criticism which tries to penetrate to the religious motives of a thinker is in danger of causing an emotional reaction and giving offense. In tracking down a philosophical train of thought to its deepest religious foundations I am in no way attacking my adversaries personally, nor am I exalting myself in an ex cathedra style. Such misunderstanding of my intention is very distressing to me. An act of passing judgment on the personal religious condition of an adversary would be a kind of human pride which supposes it can exalt itself to God's judgment seat. I have continually laid emphasis on the fact that the philosophy which I have developed, even in the sharp penetrating criticism which it exercises against non-Christian immanence-philosophy, constantly remains within the domain of *principles*. I wish to repudiate any self-satisfied scientific attitude in confronting immanence-philosophy. The detailed criticism of the Humanistic immanence-philosophy in the second part of the first volume, must be understood as self-criticism, as a case which the Christian thinker pleads *with himself*. Unless this fact is understood, the intention of this philosophy has not been comprehended. I should not judge immanence-philosophy so sharply were it not that I myself have gone through it, and have personally experienced its problems. I should not pass such a sharp judgment on the attempts at synthesis between non-Christian philosophy and the Christian truths of faith, had I not lived through the inner tension between the two and personally wrestled through the attempts at synthesis.

My second observation is of a more formal character. Many have been deterred from the study of this new philosophy by its supposed obscurity and complexity, and especially by its new terminology. They desire a popular form which makes a direct appeal without requiring effort. To these and similar objections I have but one reply to make. This philosophy, to be sure, is difficult and complicated, just because it breaks with much traditional philosophical views. He who will make it his own must try to follow step by step its turns of thought, and penetrate behind the theoretical structure to the religious basic attitude of this whole mode of philosophizing. To those who are not ready in reading to free themselves from the traditional views of reality and epistemology and who look at merely isolated sub-sections of the work, this philosophy will not open its meaning.

But nobody can get rid of this view by ignoring it. As little as Christian thought can isolate itself in an attitude of negation toward non-Christian philosophy, so little may the latter adopt such an attitude toward this trend of Christian philosophy.

It has always been a law of human knowledge that the truth is gained only in the conflict of opinions. May then the conflict about this philosophy be carried on merely for the sake of truth, and thus in a chivalrous fashion.

I do not consider it to be a disadvantage if this philosophy does not enjoy a rapid and easy success. No one less than KANT declared in the foreword of his *Prolegomena zu einer jeden künftigen Metaphysik:* 'allein Popularität hatte ich meinem Vortrage (wie ich mir schmeichele) wohl geben können, wenn es mir nur darum zu tun gewesen wäre, einen Plan zu entwerfen und dessen Vollziehung andern anzupreisen, und mir nicht das Wohl der Wissenschaft, die mich so lange beschäftigt hielt, am Herzen gelegen hätte; denn übrigens gehörte viel Beharrlichkeit und auch selbst nicht wenig Selbstverläugnung dazu, die Anlockung einer früheren, günstigen Aufnahme der Aussicht auf einem zwar späten, aber dauerhaften Beifall nachzusetzen.'

If the elaboration of the Kantian philosophy was deemed worthy of this self-denial it is certainly obvious that those interested in the Christian foundation of theoretical thought should not be concerned with personal success, which is after all of no value. Rather they should be willing to carry on a long and difficult labour firmly believing that something permanent can be achieved with respect to the actualization of the idea concerning an inner reformation of philosophy.

For, as a matter of fact the precarious and changing opinion of our fellow-men is not even comparable with the inner happiness and peace that accompanies scientific labour when it is based upon Christ, Who is the Way, the Truth and the Life!

Amsterdam, 1935   THE AUTHOR.

FOREWORD TO THE SECOND (THE ENGLISH) EDITION

The first (Dutch) edition of this work, published in the years 1935 and 1936, has been long out of print. I am pleased to see that both in the Netherlands and in other countries the lively interest manifested in the philosophy expounded in it has necessitated a second edition, this time in the English language. To me as well as to the translators the new edition has given very difficult problems to solve.

Naturally, the evolution of my conceptions has not been at a standstill since 1936, so that on various points important additions and far-reaching alterations proved to be unavoidable. On the other hand, the book being designed as a rigorously self-contained whole, there was but little scope left for this revision. I had to restrict any changes to what was absolutely necessary, if I did not want to write an entirely new work. The same limitations also apply to the digestion of recent literature on the subject. Notwithstanding all these restraints, however, it proved to be inevitable to increase the volume of the original work considerably.

The translators were up against great difficulties in rendering the phrasing and unusual terminology of the Dutch text in correct, current English; they had to remain in contact with me throughout. The greatest difficulties, however, will have to be overcome in the next two volumes, which contain the positive exposition of the Philosophy of the Cosmonomic Idea. I thank them sincerely for the devotion with which they have accomplished the translation of the first volume now published. In these thanks I want to include especially Mr H. DE JONGSTE, who will be the co-translator, together with Mr FREEMAN, of volumes II and III, and who will draw up the Index of authors and subjects dealt with. He has already taken an intensely active share in the revision of the English text of the first volume.

Finally, I tender my sincerest thanks in the first place to the Nederlandse Organisatie voor Zuiver Wetenschappelijk Onderzoek, whose considerable support in the form of a subsidy has made the revised edition of this voluminous work possible; and in the second place no less to my publishers H. J. Paris of Amsterdam and The Presbyterian and Reformed Publishing Company, who undertook substantial risks and have brought out such an excellently produced work.

THE AUTHOR.

Amsterdam, July 1953.

TRANSLATORS' PREFACE

The year 1926 marks a milestone in the development of Christian philosophy. On October 15th Dr HERMAN DOOYEWEERD became professor of philosophy and history of law in the Free University of Amsterdam. In his inaugural address, DOOYEWEERD, seeking a distinctively Christian foundation for his own special field of Jurisprudence, found himself involved in more general philosophical questions. Between 1926 and the present, DOOYEWEERD has been instrumental in the founding of a new movement in Christian philosophy. A rather extensive literature has appeared during these years, the chief works being DOOYEWEERD's *De Wijsbegeerte der Wetsidee*, 3 Volumes (1935—36), (of which this work is a translation with the author's revisions), a small work in English, *Transcendental Problems of Philosophic Thought* (1948), and the first volume of a new trilogy, *Reformatie en Scholastiek in de Wijsbegeerte (Reformation and Scholasticism in Philosophy)* (1949), several works by Prof. Dr H. TH. VOLLENHOVEN, including *De Noodzakelijkheid eener Christelijke Logica (The Necessity of a Christian Logic* (1932) and *Het Calvinisme en de Reformatie van de Wijsbegeerte (Calvinism and the Reformation of Philosophy)* (1933) and the first volume of a series on the History of Philosophy (1950), a quarterly journal *Philosophia Reformata* (1936—1953), as well as a number of smaller works, including J. M. SPIER's splendid introduction to the philosophy of DOOYEWEERD, which has been translated into English under the title, *An Introduction to Christian Philosophy*, published by the Presbyterian and Reformed Publishing Company.

Though Dutch in its inception, this new Christian philosophy has proved itself to be international in character. Its adherents are to be found throughout the world. But up until now only those who read the Dutch language could acquire a substantial knowledge of the movement.

The publication of Volume 1 is to be followed by Volumes 2,

3 and 4. Volume 2 is devoted to an analysis of the inter-relationships of the various aspects of our world and to a detailed treatment of epistemology. Volume 3 sets forth an elaborate theory of individual things and social structures. Volume 4 will contain an extensive index of the entire work.

DOOYEWEERD was a student at the Free University of Amsterdam, under Professors FABIUS, ANEMA and P. A. DIEPENHORST. He received the doctor's degree in jurisprudence at the age of 22, with a thesis on "The Cabinet in Dutch Constitutional Law."

Before his acceptance of his post at the Free University he served as manager of the Abraham Kuyper Foundation and established the political quarterly, *Antirevolutionaire Staatkunde*. As a systematic philosopher DOOYEWEERD displays tremendous intellectual powers which assure him a place among the leading contemporary philosophers.

American and English philosophers of many persuasions, who are often annoyed by the disparagement of science on the part of some contemporary continental philosophers, will find DOOYEWEERD's respect for science refreshing. Students of modern philosophy will be interested in his historical analysis of the development of modern Humanistic thought. DOOYEWEERD's own positive contribution will be of special interest to those concerned with the problems of Christian philosophy and the philosophy of religion. But not to these only, since it has raised new problems in ontology, epistemology, anthropology and science which are of great concern to every thinker generally. From the standpoint of the history of ideas anyone who wishes to know the significant tendencies of current modern thought, must take cognizance of this movement.

In translating we have sought, in compliance with the wishes of the author, to give as literal a translation as is in keeping with ordinary English usage. The presence of new philosophical terms in the original has led us occassionally to coin words in English which are not a part of a general philosophic vocabulary. Part I and chapters 5 and 6 of part II have been translated by Professor YOUNG. The remainder of part II and part III have been translated by Professor FREEMAN. Inasmuch as the translators are indebted to each other for advice and aid, the work is a joint undertaking in its entirety.

The support of the Dutch Government, in the form of a subsidy given by the Nederlandse Organisatie voor zuiver Wetenschappelijk Onderzoek, greatly encouraged the publication of this

English edition. Grateful acknowledgement is also due to Dr SAMUEL G. CRAIG, President of the Presbyterian and Reformed Publishing Company, whose interest in the work has been cultural rather than mercenary.

The translators are under great obligation to Professor DOOYEWEERD, for reading the rough draft of the translation and making many suggestions and corrections; to Professor WILLIAM WELMERS, of Cornell University, to Professor GEORGE P. RICE, GEORGE BARBER and GORDON H. CLARK, of Butler University, to Professor ELIZABETH FLOWER, of the University of Pennsylvania, to Mr JOSEPH ZIMBROLT, for their advice and criticism on matters of English style; to Mr H. DE JONGSTE, for his assistance in proof reading; to Rev. HAROLD ANDERSEN and Miss GLORIA ERICKSON for their help with the typing; and to Mrs FREEMAN, for her aid with certain Dutch idioms.

The Translators:
DAVID HUGH FREEMAN,
Wilson College.
WILLIAM YOUNG,
Butler University.

1953

CONTENTS

	Page
FOREWORD (ABREVIATED) TO THE FIRST (DUTCH) EDITION	v
FOREWORD TO THE SECOND (ENGLISH) EDITION	x
TRANSLATORS' PREFACE	xii
CONTENTS	xv

PART I - PROLEGOMENA

INTRODUCTION - THE FIRST WAY OF A TRANSCENDENTAL CRITIQUE OF PHILOSOPHIC THOUGHT	3
Meaning as the mode of being of all that is created	4
The direction of philosophical thought to the totality of meaning implies critical self-reflection	5
The supposed reduction of the selfhood to an immanent, subjective pole of thought	6
The transcendence of our selfhood above theoretical thought. The so-called transcendental subject of thought cannot be self-sufficient as a theoretical abstraction	7
How does philosophical thought attain to the Idea of the totality of meaning?	7
The Archimedean point of philosophy and the tendency of philosophical thought towards the Origin	8
The opposition between so-called critical and genetic method is terminologically confusing, because it is not clearly defined in its sense	9
The restlessness of meaning in the tendency of philosophic thought towards the origin	11
The three requirements which the Archimedean point must satisfy	12
The immanence-standpoint in philosophy	12
The immanence-standpoint does not in itself exclude the so-called metaphysical way to that which transcends human thought	13

	Page
We employ the term immanence-philosophy in the widest possible sense	13
The inner problematic situation of the immanence-standpoint	15
Why totality of meaning cannot be found in the coherence of the modal aspects	15
The Archimedean point as concentration-point for philosophic thought	16
Does the so-called transcendental subject of thought satisfy the requirements for the Archimedean point?	16
The theoretical synthesis supposes the modal diversity of meaning of the logical and the non-logical which is its opposite	18
The pitfall in the conception of the so-called transcendental subject of thought as Archimedean point: cosmic diversity of meaning and diversity in the special logical meaning	19
Misunderstanding of the intermodal synthesis of meaning as a transcendental-logical one	19
The necessary religious transcending in the choice of the immanence-standpoint	20

CHAPTER I - THE TRANSCENDENTAL CRITICISM OF THEORETICAL THOUGHT AND THE CENTRAL SIGNIFICANCE OF THE TRANSCENDENTAL GROUND-IDEA FOR PHILOSOPHY . 22

§ 1 - THE PROBLEM OF TIME 22

RICKERT's conception of the self-limitation of thought	23
The immanence of all modal aspects of meaning in time	24
The influence of the dialectical ground-motives upon the philosophical conception of time	25
The integral character of cosmic time. The correlation of temporal order and duration, and the subject-object relation in the latter	28
All structures of temporal reality are structures of cosmic time	29
The transcendental Idea and the modal concepts of time. The logical aspect of temporal order and duration	30
No static conception of the supra-temporal. Is the acceptance of a central trans-cosmic time desirable?	32
The eschatological aspect of cosmic time in faith	33
Naïve and theoretical experience of time	33

§ 2 - THE TRANSCENDENTAL CRITICISM OF THEORETICAL THOUGHT AND THE DOGMA CONCERNING THE AUTONOMY OF THE LATTER. THE SECOND WAY TO A TRANSCENDENTAL CRITICISM OF PHILOSOPHY . 34

The dogmatic positing of the autonomy of theoretical thought	35

Contents XVII

	Page
The different views of the autonomy of theoretical thought and the origin of this difference	35
The dogma concerning the autonomy of theoretical thought as an impediment to philosophical discussion among the various schools	36
The necessity of a transcendental criticism of the theoretical attitude of thought as such. The difference in principle between transcendent and transcendental criticism	37

§ 3 - THE FIRST TRANSCENDENTAL BASIC PROBLEM OF THEORETICAL THOUGHT. THE "GEGENSTAND-RELATION" VERSUS THE SUBJECT-OBJECT-RELATION 38

The *antithetical structure of the theoretical attitude of thought in its purely intentional character and the origin of the theoretical problem*	39
A closer confrontation of the naïve attitude with the theoretical	41
The subject-object-relation in naïve experience	42
The consequences of ignoring the first transcendental basic problem in the traditional conception as to the relation of body and soul in human nature	44

§ 4 - THE SECOND TRANSCENDENTAL BASIC PROBLEM: THE STARTING-POINT OF THEORETICAL SYNTHESIS 45

The impasse of the immanence-standpoint and the source of the theoretical antinomies	45
The various -isms in the theoretical vision of reality	46
The problem of the basic denominator for the theoretical comparison and distinction of the modal aspects	47
The rôle of the -isms in pure mathematics and in logic	47
Provisional delimitation of the moral aspect	48
The starting-point of theoretical synthesis in the Kantian critique of knowledge	49
The problem of the starting-point and the way of critical self-reflection in theoretical thought	51

§ 5 - THE THIRD TRANSCENDENTAL BASIC PROBLEM OF THE CRITIQUE OF THEORETICAL THOUGHT AND KANT'S TRANSCENDENTAL UNITY OF APPERCEPTION 52

The alleged vicious circle in our transcendental criticism	56
What is religion?	57
The impossibility of a phenomenology of religion. The existent character of the ego as the religious centre of existence	57
The supra-individual character of the starting-point	59
The meaning of the central command of love	60

		Page
The spirit of community and the religious basic motive		61
The Greek form-matter-motive and the modern Humanistic motive of nature and freedom		61
Sin as privatio and as dynamis. No dialectical relation between creation and fall		63
The dialectical character of the apostate ground-motives. Religious and theoretic dialectic		64
The uncritical character of the attempts to bridge the religious antithesis in a dialectical starting-point by a theoretical dialectic		64
The religious dialectic in the scholastic motive of nature and grace		65
The ascription of the primacy to one of the antithetic components of the dialectical ground-motive		66
The meaning of each of the antithetic components of a dialectic ground-motive is dependent upon that of the other		68
§ 6 - THE TRANSCENDENTAL GROUND-IDEA OF PHILOSOPHY		68
The three transcendental Ideas of theoretical thought, through the medium of which the religious basic motive controls this thought		68
The triunity of the transcendental ground-Idea		69
The transcendental critique of theoretical thought and the dogmatic exclusivism of the philosophical schools		70
The metaphysical-analogical concept of totality and the transcendental Idea of the totality of meaning. Transcendental critique of the metaphysical conception of the *analogia entis*		71
The so-called logical formalizing of the concept of totality and the philosophical Idea of totality		73
The principle of the Origin and the continuity-principle in COHEN's philosophy		74
Being and Validity and the critical preliminary question as to the meaning of these concepts		76
Levelling of the modal diversity of meaning in the generic concept rests upon an uncritical misjudgment of the special meaning in the logical aspect		77
The masking of the transcendental ground-Idea by the so-called dialectical logic. THEODOR LITT		77
Modal diversity and radical identity of meaning. Logical identity has only model meaning. PARMENIDES		79
§ 7 - THE TRANSCENDENTAL GROUND-IDEA AS HYPOTHESIS OF PHILOSOPHY		82

Contents XIX

	Page
The theoretical character of the transcendental ground-Idea and its relation to naïve experience	82
The datum of naïve experience as a philosophical problem	83
The naïve concept of the thing and the special scientific concept of function	83
Philosophy, special science, and naïve experience	84
"Reflexive" thought versus "objective" thought in recent philosophy. The confusion of "object" and "Gegenstand" in this opposition	86
The transcendental ground-Idea as hypothesis of philosophy	86
The relation of transcendent and transcendental points of views and the original meaning of the transcendental motive	88
KANT's opinion concerning the transcendental Ideas. Why did KANT fail to conceive of these Ideas as ὑπόθεσις of his critiques	89
It was FICHTE who tried to remove the difficulties involved in the Kantian dualistic conception	90
The decline of the transcendental motive in the Marburg methodological logicism, in LITT's conception of reflexive thought, and in HUSSERL's "egology"	91
The basic Idea of philosophy remains a subjective ὑπόθεσις The criterion of truth and relativism	91
The transcendental limits of philosophy and the criterion of speculative metaphysics	92
CALVIN's verdict against this metaphysics	93

§ 8 - THE TRANSCENDENTAL GROUND-IDEA OF PHILOSOPHY AS COSMONOMIC IDEA (WETSIDEE) 93

The Origin of this terminology	93
Objections against the term "cosmonomic Idea" and the grounds for maintaining it	94
Misunderstanding of the philosophy of the cosmonomic Idea as meaning-idealism	96
Cosmonomic Idea, modal concept of laws and modal concept of subject and object	97
The dependence of the modal concepts of law, subject and object upon the cosmonomic Idea	98

§ 9 - THE SYMBOL OF THE REFRACTION OF LIGHT. THE COSMIC ORDER OF TIME AND THE COSMOLOGICAL PRINCIPLE OF SOVEREIGNTY IN ITS PROPER ORBIT. THE MODAL ASPECTS OF REALITY AS MODAL LAW-SPHERES 99

The lex as boundary between the "Being" of God and the "meaning" of the creation	99

		Page
The logical function of thought in apostasy		100
The re-formation of the cosmonomic Idea by the central motive of the Christian religion		101
The modal law-spheres and their sphere-sovereignty		102
Christian religion does not allow of any absolutizing with respect to its fulness of meaning		104
Sphere-sovereignty of the modal aspects in their inter-modal coherence of meaning as a philosophical basic problem		104
Potentiality and actuality in cosmic time		105
Cosmic time and the refraction of meaning. Why can the totality of meaning disclose itself in time only in refraction and coherence of modalities?		105
The logical function is not relative in a logical but in a cosmic sense		106
The elimination of cosmic time-order in KANT's *Critique of Pure Reason*		107

§ 10 - THE IMPORTANCE OF OUR COSMONOMIC IDEA IN RESPECT TO THE MODAL CONCEPTS OF LAWS AND THEIR SUBJECTS 108

Modal concepts of the lex and its subject. The subject as subject to laws 108

The disturbance of the meaning of the concepts of the modal laws and their subjects in the Humanistic immanence-philosophy 108

Rationalism as absolutizing of the general rule, irrationalism as absolutizing of individual subjectivity 110

The concept of the subject in the irrationalistic phenomenology and philosophy of existence 111

The concept of the lex and the subject in ancient Greek thought and its dependence on the Greek form-matter-motive 112

CHAPTER II - PHILOSOPHY AND LIFE- AND WORLD-VIEW 114

§ 1 - THE ANTITHETIC POSITION OF THE PHILOSOPHY OF THE COSMONOMIC IDEA IN RESPECT TO THE IMMANENCE-PHILOSOPHY AND THE POSTULATE OF THE HISTORICAL CONTINUITY IN PHILOSOPHICAL THOUGHT CONTAINED IN THE IDEA OF THE "PHILOSOPHIA PERENNIS" 114

The basis of cooperation between Christian thought and the different trends of immanence-philosophy 114

A popular argument against the possibility of Christian science and philosophy 115

Partial truths are not self-sufficient. Every partial truth is dependent upon truth in its totality of meaning 116

	Page
The undeniable states of affairs in the structure of temporal reality	116
The idea of the perennial philosophy	117
How is the idea of the "philosophia perennis" to be understood? Philosophic thought and historical development	118
What is permanent, and what is subjected to the historical development of thought. The scholastic standpoint of accommodation forever condemned	119
The conception of the antithesis of standpoints in the immanence-philosophy as "Weltanschauungslehre" (theory of life- and world-views)	120
The consequence of our transcendental critique for the history of philosophy	122
The only possible ultimate antithesis in philosophy	123

§ 2 - THE DISTINCTION BETWEEN PHILOSOPHY AND LIFE- AND WORLD-VIEW AND THE CRITERION 124

The boundaries between philosophy and a life- and world-view as seen from the immanence-standpoint. Disagreement as to the criterion 124

Life- and world-view as an "individual impression of life", THEODOR LITT and GEORG SIMMEL 126

The relationship as seen from the Christian transcendence-standpoint 127

§ 3 - THE NEUTRALITY-POSTULATE AND THE "THEORY OF LIFE AND WORLD-VIEWS" 128

RICKERT's defence of the neutrality-postulate 129

Criticism of the fundamentals of the "Weltanschauungslehre" 134

Immanent antinomy in RICKERT's philosophy of values . . . 135

The test of the transcendental ground-Idea 136

The philosophy of the cosmonomic Idea does not judge about matters over which no judgment belongs to man, but leads to fundamental self-criticism of the thinker 137

§ 4 - SEQUEL: THE PRETENDED SELF-GUARANTEE OF THEORETICAL TRUTH 138

LITT's argument concerning the self-guarantee of theoretical truth 138

Critique of LITT's conception 141

The first pitfall in LITT's demonstration: the unconditional character of the 'transcendental cogito' 142

The second pitfall: the opposition of transcendental thought and full reality 143

	Page
The "self-refutation of scepticism" reduced to its true proportion	144
The test of the transcendental ground-Idea	147

§ 5 - THE TRANSCENDENTAL GROUND-IDEA AND THE MEANING OF TRUTH ... 148

The impossibility of an authentic religiously neutral theory of the life- and world-views. The concept of truth is never purely theoretical with respect to its meaning	148
Immanence-philosophy recognizes no norm of truth above its transcendental ground-Idea	150
The distinction between theoretical and a-theoretical judgments. The inner contradiction of a restriction of the validity of truth to the former	151
Theoretical and non-theoretical judgments. The latter are never a-logical, but merely non-"gegenständlich"	153
LITT's distinction between theoretical and "weltanschauliche" truth and the self-refutation of this distinction in the sense in which LITT intends it	154
The inner contradiction of this dualism. The meaninglessness of judgments, which are alleged not to be subjected to the norm of truth	154

§ 6 - CLOSER DETERMINATION OF THE RELATION BETWEEN PHILOSOPHY AND A LIFE- AND WORLD-VIEW ... 156

The life- and world-view is no system and cannot be made a system without affecting its essence	157
What is the meaning of the concept "universal-validity"? The Kantian conception is determined by the critical Humanist immanence-standpoint	158
The possibility of universally valid judgments depends on the universal supra-subjective validity of the structural laws of human experience	160
The universal validity of a correct judgment of perception	161
The criterion of universal validity of a judgment concerning supra-theoretical states of affairs and the unconditional validity of the religious law of concentration of human experience	162
The so-called "transcendental consciousness" as hypostatization of theoretical human thought in its general apostasy from the fulness of meaning of truth	163
Impurity of the opposition "universal-validity" and individuality as a contradictory one	164
Neither life- and world-view, nor philosophy is to be understood individualistically	164

PART II - THE DEVELOPMENT OF THE BASIC ANTINOMY IN THE COSMONOMIC IDEA OF HUMANISTIC IMMANENCE-PHILOSOPHY

CHAPTER I - THE BASIC STRUCTURE OF THE HUMANISTIC TRANSCENDENTAL GROUND-IDEA AND THE INTRINSIC POLARITY BETWEEN THE CLASSICAL SCIENCE-IDEAL AND THE IDEAL OF PERSONALITY 169

§ 1 - INTRODUCTION. HUMANISTIC PHILOSOPHY AND THE HUMANISTIC VIEW OF LIFE AND THE WORLD 169

The undermining of the personal sense of responsibility in the religious commitment 170

The synthetic standpoint of Thomistic philosophy and the disruption of this synthesis by the nominalism of late scholasticism 172

The Aristotelian-Thomistic philosophy and medieval culture 173

The integral and radical character of the religious ground-motive of creation, the fall and redemption in the Biblical sense 173

Sin and the dialectical conception of guilt in Greek and Humanistic philosophy 175

Once again the inner reformation of philosophic thought . . 176

The speculative logos-theory 177

Philosophy as ancilla theologiae in Augustinian scholasticism 177

The scholastic character of AUGUSTINE's cosmonomic Idea . . 178

The entrance of the dialectical ground-motive of nature and grace in Christian scholasticism 179

Creation as a natural truth in THOMAS' *theologia naturalis* . . 180

The elimination of the integral and radical meaning of the Biblical motive of creation in THOMAS' metaphysics 180

The elimination of the radical meaning of fall and redemption. The neo-Platonic Augustinian trend in THOMAS' natural theology 181

The Aristotelian cosmonomic Idea 181

The content of the Thomistic cosmonomic Idea 182

The intrinsic dialectic of the scholastic basic motive of nature and grace and the nominalism of the fourteenth century . . 183

The "primacy of the will" in the nominalistic school of thought versus the "primacy of the intellect" in the realistic metaphysics of THOMAS AQUINAS. There is no essential connection between realism and the primacy of the intellect . . 185

Contents

	Page
The primacy of the will in the cosmonomic Idea of Augustine	185
The potestas Dei absoluta in Duns Scotus and William of Occam	186
The nominalistic conception of the potestas Dei absoluta entirely contrary to its own intention places God's Creative Will under the boundary-line of the lex	187
The nominalistic critique effectuated a radical disruption between the Christian and pagan motives in medieval scholasticism	187
Secularization of nominalism in late scholasticism	188

§ 2 - THE RISE OF HUMANISTIC PHILOSOPHICAL THOUGHT 188

The collapse of the ecclesiastically unified culture 189

A closer consideration of the religious ground-motive of Humanism: the motive of nature and freedom 190

The ambiguity of the Humanistic motive of freedom 190

The new ideal of personality of the Renaissance 191

The motive of the domination of nature and the ambiguity of the nature-motive 192

The πέρας and the ἄπειρον. The antithesis with the ancient ideal of life 194

The Cartesian "Cogito" in contra-distinction to the theoretical nous as the Archimedean point of Greek metaphysics 195

There is no relationship between Descartes' and Augustine's Archimedean point. The misconception of the Jansenists of Port Royal on this issue 196

The connection between Descartes' methodological scepticism and the discovery of analytical geometry. The creation-motive in the Cartesian "cogito" 197

The polar tension between the ideal of personality and the ideal of science in the basic structure of the Humanistic transcendental Idea 198

The tendency towards infinity in Giordiano Bruno's pantheism 199

§ 3 - THE POSTULATE OF CONTINUITY IN THE HUMANISTIC SCIENCE-IDEAL AND THE BASIC ANTINOMY IN THE HUMANISTIC COSMONOMIC IDEA 200

The concept of substance in the new Humanistic metaphysics is quite different from the Aristotelian-Thomistic or Platonic one 201

The lex continui in Leibniz and the Marburg school of Neo-Kantians 204

The fundamental antinomy in the basic structure of the Humanistic transcendental ground-Idea 204

Contents XXV

The supposed solution of this antinomy in transcendental thought 205
The tendency of continuity in the freedom-motive of the ideal of personality 206

§ 4 - A DIORAMA OF THE DIALECTICAL DEVELOPMENT OF HUMANISTIC PHILOSOPHY AFTER KANT. THE PROCESS OF RELIGIOUS UPROOTING AND THE ACTUALITY OF OUR TRANSCENDENTAL CRITIQUE 207

The origination of a new historical science-ideal out of an irrationalistic and universalistic turn in the freedom-motive . 207
The polar tension between the historistic ideal of science and the idealistic dialectic of HEGEL's freedom-idealism 208
The rise of positivistic sociology and the transformation of the historical method of thought into a natural scientific one . . 209
The transformation of historicism into naturalistic evolutionism 210
The first expression of the spiritual disintegrating process in Historicism. NIETZSCHE's religion of power 210
The rôle of neo-Kantianism and neo-Hegelianism in the crisis of historicism 212
The classic ideal of science and the development of 20th century physics. The neo-positivism of the Vienna school . . . 212
HUSSERL's eidetic logic and phenomenology 213
The attitude of decline in SPENGLER's philosophy of history and in Humanistic existentialism 214
The actuality of our transcendental critique of theoretical thought 215

CHAPTER II - THE IDEAL OF PERSONALITY AND THE NATURAL SCIENCE-IDEAL IN THE FIRST TYPES OF THEIR MUTUAL POLAR TENSION UNDER THE PRIMACY OF THE FORMER 216

§ 1 - THE NATURALISTIC-MONISTIC AND THE DUALISTIC TYPE OF TRANSCENDENTAL GROUND-IDEA UNDER THE PRIMACY OF THE SCIENCE-IDEAL. ITS CONNECTION WITH THE PESSIMISTIC AND SEMI-PESSIMISTIC VIEW OF LIFE 216

The conflict between DESCARTES and HOBBES as the first expression of the basic antinomy in the Humanistic cosmonomic Idea 216
HOBBES' pessimism and its connection with his ascription of primacy to the science-ideal. Virtue and necessity in MACCHIAVELLI 217

	Page
The dualism between thought and extension in Descartes	218
The background of the ideal of personality in this dualism	218
The metaphysical problem concerning the relation between soul and body acquires a new significance in the light of the transcendental Humanist ground-Idea	219
The deeper ground of Descartes' partial indeterminism	220
The antinomy in Hobbes' naturalistic conception of thought in the light of the deterministic ideal of science. The *ideae innatae* of Descartes	221

§ 2 - THE MATHEMATICAL-IDEALISTIC TYPE OF HUMANIST TRANSCENDENTAL GROUND-IDEA 223

The supposed Thomistic-Aristotelian traits in Leibniz' philosophy 223

The secularization of the motive of nature and grace in Leibniz' philosophy 226

The refinement of the postulate of continuity in the science-ideal by means of Leibniz' mathematical concept of function. The discovery of differential and integral calculus 227

The two roots of Leibniz' philosophy. The misunderstanding in Schmalenbach concerning the Calvinistic origin of Leibniz' individualism 229

Leibniz' concept of force and the *motive of activity* in the ideal of personality 230

Primacy of the mathematical science-ideal in Leibniz' transcendental ground-Idea 232

Leibniz' Humanistic theism 234

Logicization of the dynamical tendency in the ideal of personality 234

Leibniz' intellectual determinism and his doctrine of innate Ideas in the light of the lex continui 236

§ 3 - THE MODERATE NOMINALISM IN LEIBNIZ' CONCEPTION OF IDEAS. THE IDEA AS SYMBOL OF RELATIONS AND AS THE CONCEPT OF LAW OF THE RATIONALISTIC IDEAL OF SCIENCE 240

The apparent fight against nominalism in the third book of Leibniz' *"Nouveaux Essais"* 241

Leibniz' nominalistic standpoint in his treatise concerning the philosophical style of Nizolius (1670) 244

The notion of the logical alphabet and the symbolical conception of ideas 245

Contents

		Page
§ 4 -	THE MODAL ASPECTS OF REALITY AS MODI OF MATHEMATICAL THOUGHT	247
	Phenomenon and noumenon in LEIBNIZ' metaphysics; "verités de raison" and "verités de fait". LEIBNIZ' mathematical idealism	249
	SPINOZA and LEIBNIZ. WOLFF's eradication of the distinction between necessary and contingent truths	250
§ 5 -	THE BASIC ANTINOMY IN THE HUMANISTIC TRANSCENDENTAL GROUND-IDEA IN ITS MATHEMATICAL-IDEALISTIC TYPE AND THE RELATION OF THIS TYPE TO THE OPTIMISTIC LIFE- AND WORLD-VIEW	252
	The Theodicy with its apparent reconciliation of the ideals of science and personality. The optimism of LEIBNIZ	252
	The deceptive formulation of the polar tension between the ideal of science and that of personality in the terminology of the Christian doctrine of faith	253
	The basic antinomy in the Humanistic transcendental ground-Idea acquires in LEIBNIZ the mathematical form of the antinomy of the actual infinity	255
	"Metaphysical evil" as an eternal necessary truth in creative mathematical thought	256
	Metaphysical evil as the root of physical and moral evil (sin!)	258
	How LEIBNIZ attempted to resolve metaphysical evil into the continuity of infinite mathematical analysis	259
	LEIBNIZ and BAYLE	260

CHAPTER III - THE IDEAL OF PERSONALITY AND THE IDEAL OF SCIENCE IN THE CRITICAL TRANSITION TO THE PRIMACY OF THE IDEAL OF PERSONALITY 262

§ 1 -	THE PSYCHOLOGICAL TURN IN THE SCIENCE-IDEAL AND ITS TRANSCENDENTAL IDEA OF ORIGIN	262
	The psychological turn in the ideal of science in empiricism since LOCKE	262
	The inner antinomy in LOCKE's psychological dualism	264
	LOCKE maintains the mathematical science-ideal with its creation-motive, though in a limited sphere	267
	The tendency toward the origin in LOCKE's opposition to the innate Ideas, and the transcendental Idea of origin in LOCKE's epistemology	268
	The distinction between the knowledge of facts and the knowledge of the necessary relations between concepts	269

§ 2 - THE MONISTIC PSYCHOLOGICAL TYPE OF THE HUMANISTIC TRANSCENDENTAL GROUND-IDEA UNDER THE PRIMACY OF THE SCIENCE-IDEAL 271

The psychologized conception of the science-ideal in HUME. Once again the nominalistic trait in the ideal of science . . 272

HUME and Pyrrhonic scepticism. SEXTUS EMPIRICUS 275

Sceptical doubt in HUME, as in DESCARTES, has only methodological significance 275

The criterion of truth 276

The natural and philosophical relations. The laws of association 277

§ 3 - THE TRANSITION OF THE CREATION-MOTIVE IN THE SCIENCE-IDEAL TO PSYCHOLOGICAL THOUGHT. HUME'S CRITICISM OF MATHEMATICS 280

Contradictory interpretations of HUME's criticism of mathematics 280

The method of solving this controversy 282

HUME drew the full consequences of his "psychologistic" nominalism with respect to mathematics 283

HUME's psychologistic concept of space. Space as a complex of coloured points (minima sensibilia) 284

Psychologizing of the mathematical concept of equality . . 285

The position of arithmetic in HUME's sensationalism . . . 287

HUME's retrogression into the Lockian conception of mathematics remains completely inexplicable on the sensationalistic basis of his system 288

§ 4 - THE DISSOLUTION OF THE IDEALS OF SCIENCE AND OF PERSONALITY BY THE PSYCHOLOGISTIC CRITIQUE 289

HUME's criticism of the concept of substance and his interpretation of naïve experience 289

The creative function of imagination and the way in which the creation-motive of the Humanistic ideal of science is transmitted to psychological thought 292

HUME destroys the metaphysical foundation of the rationalist ideal of personality 294

The radical self-dissolution of the ideals of science and of personality in HUME's philosophy 296

§ 5 - CONTINUATION: THE CRITICISM OF THE PRINCIPLE OF CAUSALITY AS A CRITIQUE OF EXPERIENCE 297

The problem pertaining to the necessary connection of cause and effect is to HUME the problem of the origin of natural laws as such 298

According to Hume, the law of causality is only to be maintained as a psychical law of association. Nevertheless, every legitimate foundation for the ideal of science in a mathematical physical sense is lacking 299

The way in which Hume's *Critique* finally undermines the foundations of his own psychological science-ideal 299

Hume disregards the synthesis of logical and psychical meaning in his psychological basic denominator 300

§ 6 - THE PRELUDE TO THE SHIFTING OF THE PRIMACY TO THE IDEAL OF PERSONALITY 302

The extension of the psychologized science-ideal over the modal boundaries of meaning of the aesthetic, juridical, moral and faith-aspects 302

The cooperation between the associations of ideas and those of passions 304

The way in which Hume's psychologized ideal of science destroys the conception of freedom of the will in the sense of the mathematical ideal of science 305

The prelude to the shift of primacy to the ideal of personality 306

Hume withdraws morality from the science-ideal. Primacy of the moral feeling 307

Hume's attack upon the rationalistic theory of Humanist natural law and upon its construction of the social contract. Vico and Montesquieu 310

§ 7 - THE CRISIS IN THE CONFLICT BETWEEN THE IDEAL OF SCIENCE AND THAT OF PERSONALITY IN ROUSSEAU 313

Rousseau's religion of sentiment and his estrangement from Hume 316

Optimism and pessimism in their new relation in Rousseau 317

Locke and Rousseau. The contrast between innate human rights and inalienable rights of the citizen 318

The ideal of personality acquires the primacy in Rousseau's construction of the social contract 319

The antinomy between the natural rights of man and the rights of citizen. Rousseau's attempt to solve it 321

The origin of this antinomy is again to be found in the tension between the ideal of science and that of personality 323

CHAPTER IV - THE LINE OF DEMARCATION BETWEEN THE IDEALS OF SCIENCE AND OF PERSONALITY IN KANT. THE (CRITICAL) DUALIST IDEALISTIC TYPE OF TRANSCENDENTAL GROUND-IDEA UNDER THE PRIMACY OF THE HUMANIST IDEAL OF PERSONALITY 325

§ 1 - INTRODUCTION. THE MISCONCEPTION OF KANT'S TRANSCENDENTAL IDEALISM AS THE PHILOSOPHIC EXPRESSION OF THE SPIRIT OF REFORMATION 325

KRONER's view of the relation of KANT's transcendental idealism to the Christian religion 325

Is KANT the philosopher of the Reformation? PRZYWARA . . 326

The Idea of freedom as both the religious totality and origin of meaning: HÖNIGSWALD 328

§ 2 - THE DEVELOPMENT OF THE CONFLICT BETWEEN THE IDEAL OF PERSONALITY AND THAT OF SCIENCE IN THE FIRST PHASE OF KANT'S THOUGHT UP UNTIL HIS INAUGURAL ORATION OF 1770 . . 330

The motives of the preceding Humanistic philosophy. The manner in which KANT wrestles with their mutual tension. The influence of Pietism 330

In his natural scientific conception, KANT remained a faithful adherent of the ideal of science; his reverence for the spirit of the "Enlightenment" 331

The influence of ROUSSEAU and HUME 332

KANT's first period: KANT as an independent supporter of the metaphysics of LEIBNIZ and WOLFF. The primacy of the mathematical science-ideal in the first conception of his transcendental ground-Idea 335

KANT's second period: the methodological line of demarcation between mathematics and metaphysics. The influence of NEWTON and English psychologism 336

The rupture between the metaphysics of the science-ideal and moral philosophy in this period of KANT's thought 338

Influence of CRUSIUS 339

Third period: the dominating influence of HUME and ROUSSEAU. Complete emancipation of the ideal of personality from the metaphysics of the science-ideal 340

The transitional phase in KANT's thought until 1770 341

The problem of the mathematical antinomies. LEIBNIZ' and NEWTON's conception of space and time 343

§ 3 - THE FURTHER DEVELOPMENT OF THIS CONFLICT AND THE ORIGINATION OF THE REAL CRITICAL PHILOSOPHY 344

	Page
The separation of understanding and sensibility in Kant's inaugural address of 1770	344
The development of Kant's new conception of the ideal of personality. Earlier optimism is replaced by a radical pessimism with respect to the sensory nature of man	346
The new conception of the ideal of personality as ὑπόθεσις in the transition to the critical standpoint	351
The "Dialectic of Pure Reason" as the heart of Kant's *Critique of Pure Reason*	353

§ 4 - The antinomy between the ideal of science and that of personality in the critique of pure reason 354

The deepest tendencies of Kant's Copernican revolution in epistemology are brought to light by the ascription of primacy to the ideal of personality resulting in a new form of the Humanistic ground-Idea	355
The dualistic type of the Kantian transcendental ground-Idea	357
In Kant's transcendental dualistic ground-Idea the basic antinomy between the ideals of science and of personality assumes a form which was to become the point of departure for all the subsequent attempts made by post-Kantian idealism to conquer this dualism	358
The expression of this dualism in the antithesis of natural laws and norms	359
The form-matter schema in Kant's epistemology as an expression of the inner antinomy of his dualistic transcendental ground-Idea	360
The function of the transcendental Ideas of theoretical reason	362
Kant's shifting of the Archimedean point of Humanist philosophy is clearly evident from his critique of metaphysical psychology, in which self-consciousness had identified itself with mathematical thought	365
Kant's criticism of "rational cosmology" (natural metaphysics) in the light of the transcendental trend of the cosmological Ideas	367
The intervention of the ideal of personality in Kant's solution of the so-called dynamical antinomies and the insoluble antinomy in Kant's dualistic transcendental ground-Idea	369
Within the cadre of Kant's transcendental ground-Idea the natural "Ding an sich" can no longer be maintained. The depreciation of the theoretical Idea of God	372

§ 5 - The development of the basic antinomy in the "critique of practical reason" 372

Autos and nomos in Kant's Idea of autonomy	373

The dualistic division between the ideal of science and the ideal of personality delivers the latter into the hands of a logical formalism 374

The precise definition of the principle of autonomy through the Idea of personality as "end in itself" 376

In the application of KANT's categorical imperative to concrete actions, the dualism between "nature" (ideal of science) and "freedom" (ideal of personality) becomes an antinomy . 378

KANT's characterization of LEIBNIZ' conception of free personality as "automaton spirituale" 380

KRONER's conception of the origin of the antinomy in KANT's doctrine of "pure will" as "causa noumenon" 381

The antinomy between nature and freedom in KANT's concept of the highest good 381

KANT formulates the antinomy between the ideal of science and that of personality as it is implied in the concept of the highest good as the "antinomy of practical reason" 383

In KANT's Idea of God the ideal of personality dominates the ideal of science 384

§ 6 - THE DEVELOPMENT OF THE BASIC ANTINOMY IN THE CRITIQUE OF JUDGMENT 385

The attempt to resolve the dualism between the ideal of science and that of personality in the *Critique of Judgment*. The problem of individuality 385

KANT's rationalistic conception of individuality 387

The idea of teleology in nature 388

The law of specification as the regulative principle of the transcendental faculty of judgment for the contemplation of nature 389

The reason why the *"Critique of Judgment"* cannot resolve the basic discord in KANT's Archimedean point 390

The same antinomy which intrinsically destroys the Idea of the "homo noumenon" recurs in the principle of teleological judgment 393

The fictitious character of the teleological view of nature follows directly from KANT's transcendental ground-Idea . . 395

The origin of the antinomy of the faculty of teleological judgment in the light of KANT's cosmonomic Idea 396

The basic antinomy between the ideals of science and personality in KANT is everywhere crystallized in the form-matter schema. A synopsis of the development of this antinomy in the three Critiques 400

KANT's dualistic transcendental ground-Idea lacks an unequivocal Archimedean point and an unequivocal Idea of the totality of meaning 402

CHAPTER V - THE TENSION BETWEEN THE IDEAL OF SCIENCE AND THAT OF PERSONALITY IN THE INDENTITY-PHILOSOPHY OF POST-KANTIAN FREEDOM-IDEALISM 403

§ 1 - THE TRANSITIONAL PERIOD BETWEEN CRITICAL IDEALISM AND MONISTIC FREEDOM-IDEALISM. FROM MAIMON TO FICHTE . . . 403

MAIMON's attempt at a solution of the antinomy in KANT's form-matter scheme by means of LEIBNIZ' principle of continuity 404

MAIMON's falling away from the veritable transcendental motive. How the transcendental Idea loses for him its direction toward KANT's ideal of personality 405

MAIMON's mathematical Criticism and the Marburg school among the Neo-Kantians 406

The problem as to the relation between the universal and the particular in knowledge within the domain of KANT's apriori forms of consciousness. MAIMON's cosmonomic Idea 408

In the explanation of his "principle of determinability" MAIMON starts from three fundamentally different ways in which thought can combine a manifold of "objects of consciousness" into a logical unity 409

The break between form and sensory matter of knowledge. MAIMON's later critical scepticism with respect to KANT's concept of experience 410

Within the limits of the critical standpoint, the mathematical science-ideal appears unable to overcome KANT's dualism between sensibility and reason 412

§ 2 - THE CONTINUITY-POSTULATE IN THE NEW CONCEPTION OF THE IDEAL OF PERSONALITY AND THE GENESIS OF THE DIALECTICAL PHILOSOPHY IN FICHTE's FIRST "THEORETISCHE WISSENSCHAFTSLEHRE" (1794) 413

The ground-motive of FICHTE's first "Wissenschaftslehre". The creative moment in the personality-ideal 413

The Archimedean point in FICHTE's transcendental groundIdea 415

FICHTE's "absolute ego" as origin and totality of all cosmic diversity of meaning is nothing but the hypostatization of the moral function 416

FICHTE's attempt at a transcendental deduction of the Kantian forms of thought from the self-consciousness 418

	Page
Dialectical thought, dominated by the ideal of personality, usurps the task of the cosmic order	420
To FICHTE the "absolute ego" remains outside the dialectical system. The Idea of the absolute ego as ethical task	422
FICHTE attempts to give an account of the possibility of theoretical knowledge by referring the latter to the selfhood. Why this attempt cannot succeed on FICHTE's immanence-standpoint	423
Transcendental deduction of the Kantian categories of relation from self-consciousness. The science-ideal is here derived from the ideal of personality	424
The domination of the continuity-postulate of the ideal of personality. The Humanist transcendental ground-Idea in its transcendental monist-moralistic type	426
Productive imagination is to FICHTE the creative origin of sensory matter	426
FICHTE conceives of the productive imagination as an unconscious function of reason	429
In his concept of the productive imagination, FICHTE does not penetrate to pre-theoretical cosmic self-consciousness but remains involved in KANT's functionalistic view of knowledge	431
FICHTE's doctrine of the productive imagination and HEIDEGGER's interpretation of KANT	434

§ 3 - THE TENSION BETWEEN THE IDEALS OF SCIENCE AND PERSONALITY IN FICHTE'S "PRAKTISCHE WISSENSCHAFTSLEHRE" (1794) . . 435

FICHTE refers the impulse toward sensory experience to the moral function of personality, in which the ideal of personality is concentrated	436
The infinite and unlimited ego as moral striving. Elimination also of KANT's practical concept of substance. The ego as infinite creative activity is identified with KANT's categorical imperative	437
The "fatalism" so keenly opposed by FICHTE is nothing but the science-ideal of the "Aufklärung", dominating the ideal of personality	440
The dialectical line of thought of the practical doctrine of science: feeling, intuition, longing, approbation, absolute impulse (categorical imperative)	442
The categorical imperative as the absolute impulse that is grounded in itself	446
FICHTE's dithyramb on the ideal of personality: "Ueber die Würde des Menschen" (On the dignity of man)	447

Contents

	Page
The passion for power in FICHTE's ideal of personality. The science-ideal converts itself into a titanic ideal of culture	448
The antinomy between the science-ideal and personality-ideal has actually converted itself in FICHTE's first period into an antinomy between Idea and sense within the personality-ideal itself	450

CHAPTER VI - THE VICTORY OF THE IRRATIONALIST OVER THE RATIONALIST CONCEPTION OF THE HUMANISTIC TRANSCENDENTAL GROUND-IDEA. THE IDEAL OF PERSONALITY IN ITS IRRATIONALIST TURN IN THE PHILOSOPHY OF LIFE 451

§ 1 - THE TRANSITION TO IRRATIONALISM IN FICHTE'S THIRD PERIOD UNDER THE INFLUENCE OF THE MOVEMENT OF THE "STURM UND DRANG" ("STORM AND STRESS") 451

FICHTE's relation to "Sturm und Drang" 451

The irrationalist view of the individuality of genius. The irrationalist turn in the ideal of personality 453

Tension between the irrationalist conception of freedom and the science-ideal in its Leibnizian form in HERDER. The antinomy is sought in "life" itself. The Faust- and the Prometheus-motif 453

The irrationalist Idea of humanity and the appreciation of individuality in history 454

FICHTE's third period and the influence of JACOBI. Transcendental philosophy in contrast with life-experience. The primacy of life and feeling 455

HEGEL as opposed to the philosophy of life and feeling . . . 457

KANT's sensory matter of experience is now the "true reality" to FICHTE 457

Recognition of the individual value of the empirical as such. FICHTE's estimation of individuality contrasted with that of KANT. Individualizing of the categorical imperative 460

No radical irrationalism in FICHTE's third period 461

§ 2 - AESTHETIC IRRATIONALISM IN THE HUMANISTIC IDEAL OF PERSONALITY. THE IDEAL OF THE "BEAUTIFUL SOUL". ELABORATION OF THE IRRATIONALIST FREEDOM-MOTIVE IN THE MODERN PHILOSOPHY OF LIFE AND ITS POLAR TENSION WITH THE SCIENCE-IDEAL . . . 462

SCHILLER and KANT's "Critique of aesthetic Judgment". Aesthetic idealism. The influence of SHAFTESBURY 462

The ideal of "the beautiful soul" 463

	Page
The "morality of genius" in early Romanticism	465
The tension of the ideals of science and personality in Nietzsche's development. Biologizing of the science-ideal (Darwin)	465
The relationship of αὐτός and νόμος in the irrationalist ideal of personality. Dialectical character of the philosophy of life. Modern dialectical phenomenology	466
The types of the irrationalist cosmonomic Idea of Humanistic thought	467

§ 3 - THE GENESIS OF A NEW CONCEPT OF SCIENCE FROM THE HUMANISTIC IDEAL OF PERSONALITY IN ITS IRRATIONALIST TYPES. FICHTE'S FOURTH PERIOD 467

Orientation of a new science-ideal to the science of history	468
Fichte in his fourth period and the South-West-German school of Neo-Kantianism	469
Hegel's supposed "rationalism"	470
"Intellectual intuition" in Schelling	471
Hegel's new dialectical logic and its historical orientation	472
The problem of the "Realität der Geisterwelt" (reality of the world of spirits)	473
Trans-personalist turn in the ideal of personality. The new conception of the "ORDO ORDINANS" in Fichte's pantheistic metaphysics	474
Fichte's basic denominator for the aspects of meaning becomes historical in character. Fichte's philosophy of history	476
Natural individuality must be annihilated in the historical process by the individuality of the spirit	478
Individuality and Society	478
Abandonment of the Critical form-matter schema	479
Fichte's logic of historical thought	481
Fichte's new historical concept of time	485
In the "Staatslehre" of 1813, Fichte anticipates the "cultural-historical" method of the South-West-German school of Neo-Kantianism. The synthesis of nature and freedom in the concept of the "free force"	486
The "hidden conformity to law" of historical development. The irrationalist concept of the law	488
Irrationalizing of the divine world-plan	489
The concept of the "highly gifted people" (das geniale Volk)	491
The inner antinomies in this irrationalist logic of history	492

Law and individuality 493

The "historical nationality" as "true reality" contrasted with the state as conceptual abstraction 494

PART III - CONCLUSION AND TRANSITION TO THE DEVELOPMENT OF THE POSITIVE CONTENTS OF THE PHILOSOPHY OF THE COSMONOMIC IDEA

CHAPTER I - THE ANTITHETICAL AND SYNTHETICAL STANDPOINTS IN CHRISTIAN PHILOSOPHICAL THOUGHT . . . 499

§ 1 - A SYSTEMATIC PRESENTATION OF THE ANTITHESIS BETWEEN THE BASIC STRUCTURE OF THE CHRISTIAN AND THAT OF THE VARIOUS TYPES OF HUMANISTIC TRANSCENDENTAL GROUND-IDEA 499

Schema of the basic structure and the polar types of the Humanistic cosmonomic Idea, in confrontation with the Christian ground-Idea 501

§ 2 - THE ATTEMPTS TO SYNTHESIZE CHRISTIAN FAITH WITH IMMANENCE-PHILOSOPHY BEFORE AND AFTER THE REFORMATION . . . 508

The consequences of the synthetic standpoint for Christian doctrine and for the study of philosophy in patristic and scholastic thought 508

The cleft between "faith" and "thought" is only a cleft between the Christian faith and immanence-philosophy . . 509

The false conception concerning the relationship between Christian revelation and science. Accommodated immanence-philosophy as ancilla theologiae 510

The consequence of the Reformation for scientific thought . 511

The after-effect of the nominalistic dualism in LUTHER's spiritualistic distinction between the Law and the Gospel . . 511

The scholastic philosophy of MELANCHTON. MELANCHTON and LEIBNIZ 513

MELANCHTON did not break radically with immanence-philosophy 515

Why a radical Christian philosophy can only develop in the line of CALVIN's religious starting-point 515

The cosmonomic Idea of CALVIN versus the Aristotelian-Thomistic one 518

CALVIN's Idea of the Law versus BRUNNER's irrationalistic and dualistic standpoint 519

There is no dualism between "gratia communis" and "gratia particularis" 523

Abraham Kuyper and his often misunderstood idea of antithesis 523

Why I reject the term "Calvinistic philosophy" 524

The philosophy of the cosmonomic Idea and Blondelism .. 525

The significance of the philosophy of the cosmonomic Idea for a philosophic contact between the different schools .. 526

CHAPTER II - THE SYSTEMATIC PLAN OF OUR FURTHER INVESTIGATIONS AND A CLOSER EXAMINATION OF THE RELATION OF THE PHILOSOPHY OF THE COSMONOMIC IDEA TO THE SPECIAL SCIENCES 528

§ 1 - THE SO-CALLED DIVISIONS OF SYSTEMATIC PHILOSOPHY IN THE LIGHT OF THE TRANSCENDENTAL GROUND-IDEA 528

The fundamental significance of the transcendental ground-Idea for all attempts made in Humanistic immanence-philosophy to classify the problems of philosophy 528

WINDELBAND's opinion concerning the necessity of dividing philosophy into a theoretical and a practical section 531

The distinction between theoretical and practical philosophy in Greek thought 532

The sophistic distinction between theoretical and practical philosophy in the light of the Greek motive of form and matter 533

The axiological turn of this distinction. The primacy of theoretical philosophy versus the primacy of practical philosophy 536

The primacy of practical knowledge in the naturalistic-nominalistic trends of Greek immanence-philosophy 538

In Greek immanence-philosophy, the necessity of ascribing primacy to the theoretical or to the practical reason is connected with the dialectical form-matter motive 539

Why we cannot divide philosophy into a theoretical and a practical 540

§ 2 - THE SYSTEMATIC DEVELOPMENT OF THE PHILOSOPHY OF THE COSMONOMIC IDEA IN ACCORDANCE WITH INDISSOLUBLY COHERING THEMATA 541

The philosophy of the cosmonomic Idea does not recognize any dualistic division of philosophy. The themata develop the same philosophical basic problem in moments which are united in the transcendental ground-Idea, in its relation to the different structures of cosmic time. These moments are inseparably linked together 542

The philosophy of the cosmonomic Idea does not recognize any other theoretical foundation than the transcendental critique of philosophical thought 543

§ 3 - A CLOSER EXAMINATION OF THE RELATIONSHIP BETWEEN PHILOSOPHY AND THE SPECIAL SCIENCES 545

The separation of philosophy and the special sciences from the standpoint of modern Humanism 546

The intrinsic untenability of a separation between science and philosophy 548

The impossibility of drawing a line of demarcation between philosophical and scientific thought in mathematics, in order to make this special science autonomous with respect to philosophy 549

The positivistic-nominalistic conception of the merely technical character of constructive scientific concepts and methods 550

The positivistic view of reality versus the jural facts . . . 551

The modal-functional and the typical structures of reality . . 552

The absolutization of the concept of function and the illegitimate introduction of a specific structural concept of individuality as a functional one 555

The dependence of empirical sciences upon the typical structures of individuality. The revolution of physics in the 20th century 556

The defence of the autonomy of the special sciences from the so-called critical-realist standpoint 559

Experiments do not disclose a static reality, given independently of logical thought; rather they point to the solution of questions concerning an aspect of reality which, under the direction of theoretical thought, is involved in a process of enrichment and opening of its meaning 561

The appeal to reality in scientific investigation is never philosophically and religiously neutral. Historicism in science 562

The conflict between the functionalistic-mechanistic, the neovitalistic and holistic trends in modern biology 564

PART I
PROLEGOMENA

INTRODUCTION

THE FIRST WAY OF A TRANSCENDENTAL CRITIQUE OF PHILOSOPHIC THOUGHT

If I consider reality as it is given in the naïve pre-theoretical experience, and then confront it with a theoretical analysis, through which reality appears to split up into various modal aspects[1] then the first thing that strikes me, is the original *indissoluble interrelation* among these aspects which are for the first time explicitly distinguished in the theoretical attitude of mind. A indissoluble inner coherence binds the numerical to the spatial aspect, the latter to the aspect of mathematical movement, the aspect of movement to that of physical energy, which iself is the necessary basis of the aspect of organic life. The aspect of organic life has an inner connection with that of psychical feeling, the latter refers in its logical anticipation (the feeling of logical correctness or incorrectness) to the analytical-logical aspect. This in turn is connected with the historical, the linguistic, the aspect of social intercourse, the economic, the aesthetic, the jural, the moral aspects and that of faith. In this inter-modal cosmic coherence no single aspect stands by itself; every-one refers within and beyond itself to all the others.

The coherence of all the modal aspects of our cosmos *finds its expression in each* of them, and also *points beyond* its own

---

[1] Here are meant the fundamental universal modalities of temporal being which do not refer to the concrete "what" of things or events, but are only the different modes of the universal "how" which determine the aspects of our theoretical view of reality. For instance, the historical aspect of temporal reality is not at all identical with what actually happened in the past. Rather it is the particular mode of being which determines the historical view of the actual events in human society. These events have of course many more modal aspects than the historical. There does not exist a purely historical reality. The same holds good for all other modal aspects.

limits toward a central totality, which in its turn is expressed in this coherence [1].

Our ego expresses itself as a totality in the coherence of all its functions within all the modal aspects of cosmic reality. And man, whose ego expresses itself in the coherence of all its temporal modal functions, was himself created by God as the *expression* of His image [2].

Meaning as the mode of being of all that is created [3].

This universal character of *referring* and *expressing*, which is proper to our entire created cosmos, stamps created reality as *meaning*, in accordance with its dependent non-self-sufficient nature. *Meaning* is the *being* of all that has been *created* and the nature even of our selfhood. It has a *religious root* and a *divine origin*.

Now philosophy should furnish us with a theoretical insight into the inter-modal coherence of all the aspects of the temporal world. Philosophy should make us aware, that this coherence is a coherence of *meaning that refers to a totality*. We have been fitted into this coherence of meaning with all our modal functions, which include both the so-called "natural" and the so-called "spiritual". Philosophy must direct the theoretical view of totality over our cosmos and, within the limits of its possibility, answer the question, "Wie alles sich zum Ganzen webt".

Philosophical thought in its proper character, never to be disregarded with impunity, is theoretical thought directed to the *totality of meaning* of our temporal cosmos.

These single introductory theses contain in themselves the entire complex of problems involved in a discussion of the possibility of genuine philosophy.

---

[1] We shall subsequently see why this deeper totality necessarily transcends the mutual coherence of all modal aspects of temporal reality, just as our selfhood transcends the coherence of its functions in these aspects.

[2] This was wiped out when man intended to be something *in himself*. Cf. the splendid pronouncement in CALVIN's *Épître à tous amateurs de Jésus Christ* 1535, (ed. J. Pannier, Paris; 1929) p. 36: „Car il lavoit formé à son image et semblance, telleme(n)t que la lumière de sa gloire reluysoit clairement en lui... Mais le malheureux voulant estre q(uel)que chose en soymesme... son image et semblance en estoit effacée..."

[3] *Translator's note:* In the original Dutch text this passage reads: "De zin is het zijn van alle creatuurlijk zijnde". "Het zijn van het zijnde" has no more an equivalent in English than MARTIN HEIDEGGER's "das Sein des Seienden," which is its German equivalent.   W. Y.

Philosophical thinking is an actual activity; and only at the expense of this very actuality (and then merely in a theoretic concept) can it be abstracted from the thinking self.

This abstraction from the actual, entire ego that thinks may be necessary for formulating the concept of philosophical thought. But even in this act of conceptual determination it is the self that is actually doing the work. That ego is actually operating not merely in its *thought*, but in *all* the functions in which it expresses itself within the coherence of our temporal world. There is no single modal aspect of our cosmos in which I do not actually function. I have an actual function in the modal aspect of number, in space, in movement, in physical energy, in organic life, in psychical feeling, in logical thought, in historical development, in language, in social intercourse with my fellowmen, in economic valuation, in aesthetic contemplation or production, in the juridical sphere, in morality and in faith. In this whole system of modal functions of meaning, it is I who remain the central point of reference and the deeper unity above all modal diversity of the different aspects of my temporal existence.

The direction of philosophical thought to the totality of meaning implies critical self-reflection.

Can philosophy — which ought to be guided by the Idea of the totality of meaning — then ever be possible without critical self-reflection? Evidently not. A philosophy which does not lead to this reflection must from the outset fail to be directed to the *totality of meaning* of our cosmos. Γνῶθι σεαυτόν, "know thyself", must indeed be written above the portals of philosophy.

But in this very demand for critical *self*-reflection lies the great problem.

To be sure, the ego is actually active in its philosophical thought, but it necessarily transcends the philosophical concept. For, as shall appear, the self is the *concentration-point of all* my cosmic functions. It is a subjective *totality* which can neither be resolved into philosophical thought, nor into some other function, nor into a coherence of functions. Rather it *lies at the basis* of all the latter as their presupposition. Without conceptual determination, however, we cannot think in a theoretical sense, and consequently we cannot philosophize.

How then can *self*-reflection be possible, if it does not transcend the concept and consequently the limits of philosophical thought?

However, there seems to be a way out of this difficulty.

There is no sense in requiring philosophical thought to exceed its immanent limits in order to attain to self-reflection.

If it be granted, that in philosophical thought the ego is active when actually thinking, it follows that this thinking must be concentrated from the outset upon the selfhood, only in so far as the latter functions in the logical sphere as a subjectivity which is no longer to be eliminated. This thinking ego then is the residue of a methodical elimination of all those moments in the concrete "individual self" functioning in "time and space" which I can still make into a "Gegenstand"[1] of the ultimate subjective logical function of thought.

The supposed reduction of the selfhood to an immanent, subjective pole of thought.

That which remains is a so-called "transcendental-logical subject". It no longer has anything individual in itself and does not *transcend* the boundaries of our logical function. It is conceived of as an immanent, subjective pole of thought, in opposition to which the entire experienceable reality recedes into the counter-pole of "Gegenständlichkeit". As such it is considered to be a transcendental pre-requisite of all concrete theoretical knowledge. For all knowledge is necessarily related to an ultimate "I think". And the latter is nothing but the ultimate logical unity of the epistemological subject.

However, in taking cognizance of this experiment of thought, there appears to us the ghost of the "blessed Münchhausen". For, in point of fact, the so-called transcendental logical subject of thought is here again abstracted from the ego which is actually operative in its logical function. It is even isolated to the greatest conceivable degree of abstraction, since it is the product of a methodical process of elimination by which the thinker imagines, he is able, ultimately, to set the logical function of thought apart as a self-sufficient activity.

---

[1] *Translator's note:* "Gegenstand": this German term commonly translated by "object" in epistemological discussions, is used by DOOYEWEERD in the sense of the non-logical aspects of reality which in the theoretical attitude of thought are opposed to the logical function. It is sharply contrasted by him with the "object", the meaning of which will be explained in a later context. W. Y.

> The transcendence of our selfhood above theoretical thought. The so-called transcendental subject of thought cannot be self-sufficient as a theoretical abstraction.

But this entire reduction of the thinking ego to the would-be "transcendental logical subject", *executed in the process of thought,* can be performed only by the selfhood. This latter, which thinks theoretically, cannot *itself* in turn be the *result of the abstraction formed by thought.* The "transcendental logical subject," in the supposed sense of universal subjective logical pole of thought, is, in the final analysis, nothing but the bare *concept* of the subjective logical unity of thought which presupposes the thinking ego. Besides, this is a pseudo-concept, since it is supposed to be incapable of analysis.

Philosophical thought, however, cannot isolate itself in its subjective logical function, because it has no *selfhood* as mere thought, as so-called *"reines Denken."* All actuality in the act of thinking issues from the ego, which transcends thought. The actual "transcendental-logical subject" remains an abstraction, produced by the thinking ego. And it is, moreover, a *meaningless abstraction involved in internal contradictions.* For the actual logical function of thought never can be "an sich". Apart from the transcending ego, it simply is not actual, or rather has no existence at all.

Philosophical self-reflection then supposes in any case, that our ego, which transcends the limits of theoretical thought, should direct its reflecting act of thought toward *itself.* Philosophical thought does not return to itself, in the process of reflecting, but it is the ego which in the process of philosophical thinking should return to itself. And this actual return to oneself in the reflecting act of thought must finally transcend the limits of philosophical thought, if indeed the desired self-reflection is to be arrived at. This same conclusion may be reached along a different road. It may be drawn from the idea of philosophical thought as theoretical thought of the totality.

> How does philosophical thought attain to the Idea of the totality of meaning?

The proper character of philosophical thought, as we have said, may never be disregarded with impunity. Philosophical thought is theoretic thought *directed* towards the *totality* of *meaning.*

Therefore, I must first give my thought a fixed direction in the *idea* of the totality of meaning.

If this *idea*[1] is not to remain completely without content, if it is to succeed in showing a direction to my philosophical thought, then it must be possible that I, who am to practise philosophy, should *choose my standpoint in this totality of meaning of our temporal cosmos*. For, unless such a standpoint can be found, the latter will remain strange to me. In my central selfhood I must participate in the totality of meaning, if I am to have the *idea* of it in my philosophical thought.

To speak in a figure: In the process of directing my philosophical thought in the idea towards the totality of meaning, I must be able to ascend a lookout-tower above all the modal speciality of meaning that functions within the coherence of the modal aspects. From this tower I must be able to survey this coherence with all the modal diversity of meaning included in it. Here I must find the point of reference to which this modal diversity can be related, and to which I am to return in the process of reflecting thought. In other words, if I am not to lose myself in the modal speciality of meaning during the course of philosophic thought, I must be able to find a standpoint which transcends the special modal aspects. *Only by transcending the speciality of meaning, can I attain to the actual view of totality by which the former is to be distinguished as such.*

The Archimedean point of philosophy and the tendency of philosophical thought towards the Origin.

This fixed point from which alone, in the course of philosophical thought, we are able to form the idea of the totality of meaning, we call the *Archimedean point* of philosophy.

However, if we have found this Archimedean point, our selfhood makes the discovery that the view of totality is not possible apart from a view of the origin or the ἀρχή of both totality and speciality of meaning.

The totality in which our selfhood is supposed to participate, may indeed transcend all speciality of meaning in the coherence of its diversity. Yet it, too, in the last analysis remains *meaning*,

---

[1] *Translator's note:* "Idea" is used here in the technical sense of a "limiting concept" which refers to a totality not to be comprehended in the concept itself.　　　　　　　　　　　　　　　　　　　　　W. Y.

which cannot exist by itself, but supposes an ἀρχή, an *origin which creates meaning.*

All meaning is *from, through,* and *to* an origin, which cannot itself be related to a higher ἀρχή.

The genetic relativity of meaning, the fact that it is not self-sufficient, lies in its very character. And if it is impossible that philosophical thought be something different from theoretical thought directed to the totality of meaning of our cosmos, then the direction toward the ἀρχή is necessarily included in its tendency to totality.

All genuine philosophical thought has therefore started as thought that was directed toward the origin of our cosmos. From the outset, non-Christian philosophy sought this origin within the realm of meaning itself, although it gave many exalted names to it. However, for the present I am not concerned with this fact. My sole concern at this moment is to place in the forefront the basic genetic tendency of philosophical thought as thought *directed to the origin.*

The introduction of the critical question as to the limits of our knowledge would be premature at this stage. The epistemological problem: What are the limits to our knowledge? presupposes, in fact, some insight into the meaning of knowledge as necessarily related to the ego. So long as this insight has not been achieved, the appeal to the epistemological inquiry is premature; it may seemingly banish the whole of the basic genetic tendency from philosophical thought, but this verdict can never be peremptory.

> The opposition between so-called critical and genetic method is terminologically confusing, because it is not clearly defined in its sense.

For the basic tendency mentioned above is so essential to philosophy that it makes its appearance at the heart of all epistemological questions. In its reference to the *apriori conditions* of all human knowing, the critical question how universally valid knowledge of our cosmos is possible may need to be sharply distinguished from all questions relating to the non-apriori moments of our knowledge. Yet it is to a high degree terminologically confusing to speak of a *critical*, in opposition to a *genetic* mode of thought, as is usual in certain currents of the neo-Kantian philosophy.

For the critical question, after a little reflection, necessarily leads to the genetic: What is the *origin* of our knowledge and of knowable reality?[1]

The only thing that matters is the question about the meaning of the genetic problem, and no sooner has this question been raised, than it is seen to imply the problem of how a theory of knowledge is at all possible.

Meaning, as we said, constantly points *without* and *beyond* itself toward an origin, which is itself no longer *meaning*. It remains within the bounds of the *relative*. The true *Origin,* on the contrary, is *absolute* and *selfsufficient!*

Suppose now, that one or more of our cognitive functions in their apriori structure are from the outset theoretically *regarded as independent,* i.e. thought of apart from all further possible *determinedness* (as is done by a certain idealistic trend of philosophic thought, which is falsely called *critical*). In that case these functions are necessarily elevated to the rôle of apriori origin of our knowable cosmos.

If philosophic thought comes to a halt at this assumed ἀρχή, the question as to the *meaning of our knowledge* is automatically precluded. For the ἀρχή is *transcendent* to all meaning. In this case, the *knowable cosmos* rather derives all its meaning from the supposedly self-sufficient apriori structure of the cognitive functions.

At this stage of the preliminary fundamental questions which concern the *foundation of philosophy*, philosophic thought has come to rest in the pretended origin of all knowable meaning.

Thus for example, from the standpoint of the neo-Kantian of the Marburg School, there is no sense in inquiring after the origin of transcendental-logical meaning, in which this philosopher supposes he can understand the whole of cosmic reality. According to him, the very *origin* of our knowable world is transcendental-logical in nature. Thus reality derives all its possible meaning from transcendental-logical thought!

If, however, the thinker finds *no* rest in logical meaning, he is necessarily driven further into preliminary philosophical questions. The pretended ἀρχή appears not to be the true origin, but rather to exist merely as meaning, which points beyond itself towards its true origin.

---

[1] The 'critical' Marburg school, for instance, even speaks of an origin of being in a *transcendental-logical* sense. "Nur das Denken kann erzeugen, was als Sein gelten darf" (COHEN). Here one can clearly see how critical and genetic problems coincide in a transcendental logical sense.

Thought will not be set at rest in the preliminary philosophical questions, until the ἀρχή is discovered, which alone gives meaning and existence to philosophic thought itself.

Philosophic thought cannot withdraw itself from this tendency towards the origin.

It is an immanent conformity to law for it to find no rest in *meaning*, but to think from and to the *origin* to which meaning owes its ground and existence. Only after the raising of questions ceases to be meaningful, does philosophic thought attain to the Origin, and is it set at rest.

> The restlessness of meaning in the tendency of philosophic thought towards the origin.

This restlessness, manifests itself in the *tendency* of philosophic thought to move *toward the origin*. It is essentially the restlessness of our ego which is actually operative in philosophic thought. It issues from our own selfhood, from the root of our existence. This restlessness is transmitted from the selfhood to all temporal functions in which this ego is actually operative.

Inquietum est *cor* nostrum et mundus in corde nostro!

Our selfhood is actually operative in philosophic thought. As certainly as philosophic self-reflection is impossible apart from the direction towards the ego, so certainly does it require to be directed towards the ἀρχή of our selfhood and of the totality of meaning. The ego must participate in this totality, if genuine thinking in terms of totality is to be possible.

Philosophic thought as such derives its actuality from the ego. The latter restlessly seeks its origin in order to understand its own meaning, and in its own meaning the meaning of our entire cosmos!

It is this tendency towards the origin which discloses the fact, that our ego is subjected to a central *law*. This law derives its fulness of meaning from the origin of all things *and limits and determines the centre and root of our existence*.

Thus, a two-fold pre-supposition of philosophic thought is discovered at the outset. In the first place, philosophic thought pre-supposes an *Archimedean point* for the thinker, from which our ego in the philosophic activity of thought can direct its view of totality over the modal diversity of meaning. Secondly, it presupposes a choice of position in the Archimedean point in the face of the ἀρχή, which *transcends all meaning* and in which our ego comes to rest in the process of philosophic thought.

For, if the attempt is made to go beyond this ἀρχή, the formulating of any question has no longer any meaning.

The three requirements which the Archimedean point must satisfy.

The Archimedean point should satisfy these three conditions: First - It may not be divorced from our own *subjective self*. For it is our self that is actually operative in philosophic thought. And only in this centre of our existence can we transcend the modal diversity of meaning.

Second - It may not be divorced from the concentric *law* of the ego's existence. Without this law the subject drops away into chaos, or rather into *nothingness*. Only by this law is the ego *determined* and *limited*.

Third - It must transcend all modal diversity of meaning and be found in the totality and radical unity of the latter. Our ego must participate in this totality, if it is to have an idea of it in the process of philosophic thought.

The immanence-standpoint in philosophy.

The prevailing conception accepts the self-sufficiency of philosophic thought in accomplishing its task, notwithstanding the fact, that for the rest there exists a great divergence of opinion about the nature, task and methods of philosophy. While regarding this autonomy of reason as the alpha and omega of philosophic insight, many thinkers are sure to concede the necessity of the Archimedean point. DESCARTES in his *"cogito"* supposed that he had found the only fixed point in the universal methodical scepticism with respect to all reality present in experience. Since this great thinker the necessity of an Archimedean point has generally been recognized by modern philosophy, at least so far as the latter realizes the necessity of critical self-reflection. But modern philosophy will have to rise with might and main against our position, that this Archimedean point cannot be sought in philosophic thought itself. In regard to the Archimedean point of philosophy, it must cling tightly to the immanence-standpoint. Consequently it rejects every support that is found in something which transcends the immanent boundaries of theoretic thought, as *such*. At the utmost it will agree that — within the latter — the theoretic intuition ("Wesensschau") is the ultimate ground of philosophical certainty.

Every attack against this immanence-standpoint will mean

an attack on the scientific character of philosophy itself. Or — in so far as the very field of philosophic inquiry is considered to be of a supra-scientific character — it will be regarded as an attack on the freedom of philosophic thought.

> The immanence-standpoint does not in itself exclude the so-called metaphysical way to that which transcends human thought.

In itself the acceptance of the immanence-standpoint does not in any way imply the rejection of the so-called *metaphysical* way to that which transcends *human* thought. Classical immanence-philosophy was even entirely based upon a metaphysical *prima philosophia*.

This metaphysical road to the totality of meaning and the ἀρχή, at least in the rationalistic currents, involves the attempt to overstep the boundaries of philosophic thought in the idea of an absolute deified thought. The latter should comprise in itself the fulness of being, it should be the νόησις νοήσεως, the *"intellectus archetypus"* in a purely logical sense.

In other words, the rationalistic-metaphysical way to an ἀρχή that transcends human thought absolutizes the logical function of thought.

Deified thought, the νόησις νοήσεως, becomes the ἀρχή; human thought in its assumed participation in divine reason, is understood to be the Archimedean point. The totality of meaning is sought in the system of the Ideas immanent in thought.

The immanence-standpoint, however, does not necessarily imply belief in the self-sufficiency of the logical function of human thought, in *contradistinction to the rest of the immanent functions of consciousness.*

The age-old development of immanence-philosophy displays the most divergent nuances. It varies from metaphysical rationalism to modern logical positivism and the irrationalist philosophy of life. It is disclosed also in the form of modern existentialism. The latter has broken with the Cartesian (rationalistic) "cogito" as Archimedean point and has replaced it by existential thought, conceived of in an immanent subjectivistic historical sense [1].

> We employ the term immanence-philosophy in the widest possible sense.

Thus we do not take the term immanence-philosophy in the

---
[1] We are only referring to the *Humanistic* philosophy of existence.

usual narrow meaning of philosophy which sees all reality as immanent in consciousness and has broken every bridge between the functions of human consciousness and an extra-mental "Ding an sich". Rather we mean it in the wide sense of all philosophy that seeks its Archimedean point in philosophic thought itself, irrespective of its further understanding of this latter, whether in a rationalistic, irrationalistic, metaphysical, transcendental-logical, vitalistic, psycho-logical or historical sense.

On this standpoint, the task of philosophy can be viewed more broadly or more narrowly. Thus there exists in modern immanence-philosophy a current which stresses the purely *theoretical* character of philosophic inquiry and recognizes, that the theoretical is merely one of the many aspects from which we may view the cosmos, *even though it be the only one from which we can really grasp it in the view of totality.*

Alongside of the theoretical cosmos, the religious, the aesthetic, the moral and other a-theoretical "worlds" are recognized. To philosophy is expressly denied the right to claim the monopoly of value for its "theoretical cosmos".

So much the more powerfully, however, does this school of philosophy bring to the fore the self-sufficiency of "transcendental" thought as Archimedean point for philosophy and at the same time as ἀρχή of the "theoretical cosmos".

The theoretical cosmos, on this standpoint, is really the "creation" of philosophic thought. The latter must first of all demolish methodically everything a-theoretical, leaving a chaotic material of consciousness, which is to be ordered as a cosmos in the creative forms of philosophic thought (RICKERT).

The immanence-philosopher has the sincere conviction, that the *scientific* character of philosophic thought can only be maintained in this conception of philosophy. What would become of the "objectivity", of the "universal validity", of the controllability of philosophic thought, if philosophy were to bind itself to presuppositions which go beyond its own immanent boundaries? Religious and "weltanschauliche" convictions may be highly respectable; indeed, a philosophy that understands its limits, will guard against attacking them. But, within the domain of philosophy, their claims cannot be recognized. Here it is not a matter of believing in what exceeds "the limits of our cognitive faculty". But it is solely a question of objective theoretical truth, valid alike for everyone who wants to think theoretically.

Observe the presence in this same connection of the so-called *neutrality-postulate* in respect to religious conviction and personal life-view. However, this postulate is in no sense inherent in the immanence-standpoint. It is accepted only by those currents in immanence-philosophy which deny to the latter any dominion over personal life.

All the acumen which the advocates of this standpoint have at their disposal is brought to bear on the demonstration of the correctness of this neutrality-postulate. When later on we enter upon a more special discussion of the relation of philosophy to a life-and-world-view, we shall have to face two of the most acute modern pleas in its behalf, those of HEINRICH RICKERT and THEODOR LITT.

The inner problematic situation of the immanence-standpoint.

In this Introduction it suffices for us to bring to the fore *the inner problematic nature of the immanence-standpoint*. It will suffice to show, how the choice of this standpoint is not possible, unless the limits of philosophic thought are actually transcended.

At this point we proceed from that which we learned above to be essential to the Archimedean point of philosophy. The latter, as we demonstrated, must be elevated above the modal diversity of meaning. Should the Archimedean point itself be enclosed in this diversity, then it would be per se unsuitable as a point of reference, from which the view of totality must be directed over the different modal aspects of our cosmos.

Furthermore, the Archimedean point, as we previously observed, must also transcend the *coherence* in the diversity of the modal aspects. Of this thesis we are now to render a further account.

Why the totality of meaning cannot be found in the coherence of the modal aspects.

Why can the totality of meaning not be found in the *immanent coherence* of meaning among the different modal aspects? Because the immanent *coherence* among all special aspects of meaning of our cosmos lacks in itself the inner concentration-point in which these latter meet in a radical unity. This truth becomes immediately evident to us in the act of self-reflection.

In this Introduction we began by observing, that our ego expresses itself in all special modal aspects of our existence. This is possible only because the latter find their *concentration-*

point in the ego. Now the self is elevated above the modal diversity of meaning and is thus *transcendent* with respect to it. Our selfhood does not coalesce with the mutual *coherence* among all functions which we have in the cosmos.

The modal diversity of meaning exists only in the coherence of all modal aspects, but it is the *expression* of a totality of signification which through the medium of time is broken up into a modal diversity of aspects.

The totality or fulness of meaning is the necessary transcendent centre where, in their mutual coherence, all modal aspects converge into *the unity of direction towards the Origin, towards the 'Ἀρχή of all meaning.*

The Archimedean point as concentration-point for philosophic thought.

Thus, in connection with the preceding, the Archimedean point of philosophy must truly be the concentration-point for *philosophic thought* and as such it must transcend the modal diversity of meaning *even in its coherence.* Can this concentration-point be found in philosophic thought itself? In other words, can we discover anywhere in theoretical thought a point that really transcends the modal diversity of meaning?

Does the so-called transcendental subject of thought satisfy the requirements for the Archimedean point?

With all sorts of terms not properly analysed in their meaning, the attempt is made to suggest to us, that we possess such a unity beyond the diversity of meaning in philosophic thought. The "transcendental consciousness", the "transcendental cogito", the "transcendental unity of apperception", the "transcendental logical ego" and such like are conceived of as the subjective pole of thought, to which the empirical world is related as "Gegenstand".

This unity is thought of as a logical unity of the thinking consciousness which does not imply any multiplicity or diversity of moments. Instead, every special synthesis of a multiplicity of perceptions should be necessarily related to this unity.

Consequently, the latter should also transcend the coherence of the modal aspects. For, indeed, this inter-modal coherence of meaning, too, presupposes the transcendental subject of thought as central logical point of reference.

However, this argument rests upon a serious misunderstanding which is caused by the pitfall concealed in the conception of the "transcendental cogito" itself.

For the latter neglects the basic transcendental problem concerning the relation of the ego and its logical function of thought [1].

It may be true that I myself transcend the coherence of all modal aspects of meaning, but this does not hold good for my logical function of thought. The unity of the ego which thinks cannot be of a transcendental logical character. For the ego is the concentration-point not only in respect to my logical, but to all of my modal functions. The logical unity of the thinking subject remains a unity within a multiplicity of moments. For the logical aspect together with all other aspects is also bound to the inter-modal coherence of meaning. As we shall show in detail in a later context of our inquiry, this coherence is expressed in its own modal structure, and the latter is the very transcendental condition of our logical function of thought. Consequently, the logical function of the act of thought does not transcend the modal diversity of meaning, and therefore it must lack that unity above all multiplicity which characterizes the central ego. But, it will be objected, is not the very diversity of meaning which is in view, a state of affairs that is meaningful only for thought that makes distinctions? Thus it may be true, that the logical function of thought, so far as it is still conceived of as an aspect of experienced reality, is confined to the diversity of meaning. But this does not prove, that the *transcendental-logical* subject of thought (understood as the ultimate subjective pole of thought) is unable to transcend the coherence of the modal aspects. On the contrary, does it not appear, just at this point, that all modal diversity of meaning is irreversibly dependent upon this transcendental subject of thought, and does it

---

[1] "Pure transcendental thought" is always meant in a logical sense. For the other modal aspects of the real act of theoretical thinking e.g. the psychical or the historical, do not satisfy the requirements of "pure thought" in the sense which is meant here. Only the linguistic aspect is usually comprehended in it, but in a strict conception of "pure thought" that aspect, too, should be eliminated, because it cannot be "pure" in the sense ascribed to "transcendental reflexive thought", "Linguistic signification", taken in its modal meaning, remains always bound to time, and to the coherence with the other modal aspects of temporal reality. Only by reducing the linguistic aspect of meaning to a purely logical one can it be maintained as belonging to supposed "pure thought". However, we shall see, that the logical function of thought itself is nothing without the inter-modal coherence of meaning.

not appear that in respect to the latter we can in fact speak of a "Transcendenz in der Immanenz"? At this juncture we have indeed approached a very fundamental point in our discussion with the adherents of the so-called "transcendental" inmanence-standpoint.

In the last objection we meet a new pitfall, which we have to lay bare carefully, in order that it shall not catch us again and again.

We must attribute logical meaning to the subjective pole of thought under discussion in so far as it is conceived of as an ultimate *logical* unity of our thinking self-consciousness; and more precisely, in so far as it is presented as a subjective logical pole of *philosophical* thought, we must attribute *theoretical* logical meaning to it.

Now in the sequel, we shall demonstrate in still further detail, that in theoretical thought we are constantly active in an opposition of the non-logical aspects to the logical aspect of meaning. It is from this very opposition that the theoretical *problem* is born.

The theoretical synthesis supposes the modal diversity of meaning of the logical and the non-logical which is its opposite.

In this process of theoretical thought, characterized by its antithetical attitude, every correct formation of concepts and judgements rests upon a sharp distinction among the different aspects of meaning and upon a synthesis of the logical aspect with the non-logical aspects of our experience which are made into a "Gegenstand" [1]. This synthesis is in itself a basic problem of philosophy.

However, in every case it supposes the inter-modal coherence as well as the modal diversity of logical and non-logical meaning.

Consequently, the logical meaning of the assumed subjective pole of thought is different from all non-logical aspects of meaning. But at the same time it is fitted with the latter in an indissoluble *coherence.*

Now there is a logical diversity which is immanent in the logical meaning of thought, but which could not exist apart from a cosmic modal diversity of meaning, within which the

---

[3] We must observe that the modal aspects of our experience are at the same time the modal aspects of *all* reality in its *integral* empirical sense. Empirical reality is by no means exhausted in sensory perceptions. We shall have to return to this point in different later contexts.

logical side itself functions. A closer discussion of this state of affairs will follow in a later context.

> The pitfall in the conception of the so-called transcendental subject of thought as Archimedean point: cosmic diversity of meaning and diversity in the special logical meaning.

The pitfall in the last objection made by the adherents of transcendental logicism consists in the identification of cosmic diversity of meaning with diversity in its logical or analytical sense.

How could the fundamental modal diversity of meaning, to which the logical function of thought necessarily remains bound, itself be of logical origin? If this supposition were dealt with seriously, it should destroy itself at the outset in the following antinomy: the proclamation of logical meaning as the origin of the cosmic diversity of meaning is tantamount to the elimination of the modal diversity, and consequently to the abandoning of theoretical thought itself. For the latter is possible only in the process of analysis and inter-modal synthesis of meaning. This consequence was inferred by some Sophists from the logicism of PARMENIDES.

The so-called transcendental subject of thought cannot be maintained, unless, from the start, the inter-modal synthesis is introduced into the logical aspect itself. But, as soon as this occurs, the "transcendental-logical subject of thought" is thrown back into the midst of the modal diversity of meaning. For the inter-modal synthesis presupposes the modal diversity and the mutual coherence of the logical and non-logical aspects of meaning. Consequently how could an Archimedean point be given within theoretical thought?

> Misunderstanding of the intermodal synthesis of meaning as a transcendental-logical one.

Transcendental logicism can be maintained apparently only by a curious *shift of meaning*, which interprets the truly intermodal synthesis as a so-called transcendental-logical one, as an act of the would-be self-sufficient transcendental subject of thought.

What really happens in this first choice of a position is an *absolutizing* of the *transcendental-logical function* of theoretical thought and this absolutization is not to be explained in terms of a purely theoretical conclusion from the inner nature of reflecting thought itself. Consequently, ἀρχή and Archimedean point coincide in this transcendental logicism.

The rationalistic metaphysics which distinguished ἀρχή and Archimedean point absolutized the logical aspect of actual thought only in the ἀρχή, regarded as Intellectus Archetypus.

The necessary religious transcending in the choice of the immanence-standpoint.

By this original choice of a position, the attempt is made to detach the logical function of theoretical thought (whether only in the ἀρχή or in the ἀρχή and Archimedean point alike) from the inter-modal coherence of meaning and to treat it as independent. *In the nature of the case, this choice is no act of a "transcendental subject of thought", which is merely an abstract concept. It is rather an act of the full self which transcends the diversity of modal aspects.*

And it is a *religious* act, just because it contains a choice of position *in the concentration-point* of our existence in the face of the Origin of meaning.

In the choice of the immanence-standpoint in the manner described above, I myself elevate philosophic thought, whether in the transcendental-logical or in the metaphysical-logical sense, to the status of ἀρχή of the cosmos. This ἀρχή stands as origin, beyond which nothing meaningful may be further asked, and in my view no longer occupies the heteronomous mode of being which is *meaning*. It exists in and through itself.

This choice of a position in the face of the ἀρχή transcends philosophic thought, though in the nature of the case it does not occur *apart* from it. It possesses the fulness of the central selfhood, the fulness of the *heart*. It is the first concentration of philosophic thought in a unity of direction. It is a religious choice of position in an idolatrous sense.

The proclamation of the self-sufficiency of philosophic thought, even with the addition of "in its own field", is an absolutizing of meaning. Nothing of its idolatrous character is lost by reason of the thinker's readiness to recognize, that the absolutizing κάτ᾽ ἐξοχήν which he performs in the *theoretical* field is by no means the only rightful claimant, but that philosophy should allow the religious, aesthetic or moral man the full freedom to serve other gods, outside the theoretical realm.

The philosopher who allows this freedom to the non-theoretician is, so to speak, theoretically a *polytheist*. He fights shy of proclaiming the theoretical God to be the only true one. But, within the temple of this God, no others shall be worshipped!

Thus the first way of our critique of philosophical thought has for a provisional conclusion:

Even on the immanence-standpoint the choice of the Archimedean point proves to be impossible as a *purely theoretical* act which prejudices nothing in a religious sense.

In truth the selfhood as the religious root of existence is the hidden performer on the instrument of philosophic thought. Only, it is *invisible* on the basis of the immanence-standpoint.

Actually, philosophic thought in itself offers us no Archimedean point, for it can function only in the cosmic coherence of the different modal aspects of meaning, which it nowhere transcends.

The immanent Ideas of the inter-modal coherence of meaning and of the totality of meaning are transcendental *limiting* concepts. They disclose the fact, that theoretical thought is not self-sufficient in the proper field of philosophy, a point to which we shall have to return in detail.

No other possibility for transcending the inter-modal coherence and the modal diversity of meaning is to be found, except in the religious root of existence, from which philosophic thought also has to receive its central direction.

CHAPTER I

THE TRANSCENDENTAL CRITICISM OF THEORETICAL THOUGHT AND THE CENTRAL SIGNIFICANCE OF THE TRANSCENDENTAL GROUND-IDEA FOR PHILOSOPHY

§ 1 - THE PROBLEM OF TIME

In our "Introduction" we argued that no philosophical thought is possible without a transcendent starting-point. We contended that even the philosopher who believes, that he can find such a point in theoretical thought itself, despite all his protestations to the contrary, must exceed the limits of theoretical thought in order to discover its true Archimedean point [1].

---

[1] RICKERT (*System der Philosophie*, p. 241) observes: „Gewisz zeigt das heterologische Princip" (in our train of thought, the requirement that *the modal diversity of meaning be distinguished theoretically*) „bei der Frage nach der letzten Welteinheit die *Grenze* unseres Denkens, aber gerade dadurch eröffnet es uns zugleich die Möglichkeit, uns von seinen Fesseln zu befreien. Sind wir imstande, durch Denken die Grenze des Denkens *fest zu stellen,* so müssen wir auch imstande sein, diese *Grenze* zu überschreiten." [It is certain, that the heterological principle marks the limits to our thought in the problem of the ultimate unity of the world. But in this way it creates the possibility of liberating ourselves at the same time from its fetters. If we are able to determine the boundaries of thought through thinking, we must be able, too, to exceed these limits].

On the *immanence standpoint,* this conclusion contains an overt contradiction: Thought determines its own boundaries and is thereby able to exceed these limits! Can it under these conditions continue to be pure transcendental thought? It is here unavailing to distinguish with RICKERT between a merely "heterological" and a "heterological-monological" thought, in which the latter would exceed the limits of the former alone. Where this sort of monological thinking autonomously attempts to conceive of the unity of the cosmos in the subjective *meaning* connecting "reality" and "value", it exceeds the immanent limits of the activity of thought qua talis. And it involves itself in the antinomy which RICKERT himself honestly lays bare in his pronouncement (op. cit. p. 260): „So bringen wir das in einem Begriff, was wir streng genommen in *einem* Begriff

This apriori transcends the immanent limits of philosophic thought.

Rickert's conception of the self-limitation of thought.
Rickert, one of the leading thinkers of the South-West German school of neo-Kantians, holds, that we can never become conscious of the limits of thought by taking a stand beyond the latter and, looking down from that point upon thought, learn to know it in its limitedness: "As soon as we are beyond thought, we do not know anything" [1]. Indubitably correct. We can even go further and say: it is entirely impossible for us, in the actuality of our self-consciousness, to stand beyond our thought; for, apart from thought, our human selfhood cannot disclose itself in the temporal coherence of our world. But Rickert on the immanence-standpoint lacks an appreciation of the transcendence of our *selfhood*. And our selfhood, as we have seen, is never to be eliminated from the act of thinking [2].

To be sure — if we want to learn the limits of our thought — we must, while thinking, come to a transcendental theoretic

---

nicht fassen können." [Thus we form a concept of that which, strictly speaking, cannot be contained in a concept.]

[1] *System der Phil.*, p. 247: „Sobald wir auszerhalb des Denkens sind, erkennen wir nichts."

[2] See also his essay: *Wissenschaftliche Philosophie und Weltanschauung* in *Logos*, Bnd. XXII, Heft I (1933), pp. 56f: „Wer das, was er als theoretische Erkenntnis der Welt in ihrer Ganzheit nicht nur logisch zwingend zu begründen vermag, sondern es zugleich abzugrenzen gelernt hat gegen die Lebensüberzeugungen, die seine auszerwissenschaftliche Weltanschauung formen, der wird auf Grund seiner universalen Erkenntnis, die als Philosophie notwendig auch den *ganzen Menschen* mit zum „Gegenstande" macht, indem sie sich über ihn stellt zugleich am besten einsehen, weshalb die auszerwissenschaftliche Stellungnahme zur Welt, so lange sie nicht, wie die theoretische Wahrheit, den Anspruch auf Geltung für a l l e erhebt, neben der wissenschaftlichen Philosophie unangefochten bestehen bleiben kan." [Anyone who is able not only to establish stringently on a logical foundation that which he has learnt as theoretical knowledge of the world in its totality, but also to delimit it at the same time from those views of life that form his non-scientific view of the world, will be best in a position to understand, why the non-scientific attitude towards the world, so long as it does not claim universal validity for all, like theoretical truth, can hold its own by the side of scientific philosophy. For his universal knowledge which as philosophy necessarily makes the entire man also its object, transcends man himself.].

Idea of the limits. But on this account, it is not to be supposed, as RICKERT does, that these limits are set by thought. Nor can they be known by a thought which would be abstracted from its religious root and from the inter-modal coherence of meaning.

After we have recognized the necessity of transcending, we may advance another step.

The intent of philosophy is to give us a theoretical insight into the coherence of our temporal world as an inter-modal coherence of meaning. Philosophic thought is bound to this coherence, within which alone it has meaning.

It is a *temporal* coherence. Man transcends it in his *selfhood*, it is true, — but within this coherence he exists in a *status of being-universally-bound-to-time*. Man is bound to time together with all creatures that are fitted with him in the same temporal order.

The immanence of all modal aspects of meaning in time.

As we observed in the Introduction, within this temporal coherence reality displays a great diversity of modal aspects which are essentially modalities of cosmic *meaning*. We mentioned the aspects of number, space, motion, energy, organic life, feeling and sensory perception, the logical analytical and historical aspects, the aspect of symbolic signification, that of social intercourse (ruled by norms of fashion, courtesy, ceremony etc.) the economic, aesthetic, jural, moral, and faith aspects.

This is a very rough preliminary schema of the fundamental modalities of meaning, not yet investigated in the refined theoretical analysis of their modal structures. But it may serve as a provisional orientation into the modal diversity of our temporal cosmos.

All these modal aspects are interwoven with one another in a cosmic order of time which guarantees their coherence of meaning. As we shall see below, time-*order* is necessarily related to factual time-*duration*. And only this indissoluble correlation of order and duration can be called *cosmic time*, in distinction from all its special modal aspects. Nowhere else do we actually transcend this cosmic time, except in the religious centre of our existence. Neither in the *concept* as to its intentional meaning, nor even in the *transcendental Idea* as a limiting concept *qua talis*.

In the first orientation into the modal diversity of our cosmos, we see ourselves compelled to set this conception in contrast to that of immanence-philosophy. For, in consequence of its starting-point, the latter has lost the insight into the universal inter-modal character of time and into the coherence of meaning among its different modal aspects.

I have treated the problem of time in detail in a separate work [1]. In the present connection some introductory remarks may suffice to prepare our further investigations.

The influence of the dialectical ground-motives upon the philosophical conceptions of time.

Here I am obliged to anticipate for a moment the results of later critical investigations in order to make clear the influence of the dialectical ground-motives upon the philosophical view of time from the immanence-standpoint.

Even in classical Greek thought this view was entangled in a falsely posed dilemma, i.e. whether time has a subjective mental or rather an objective physical character. In the brief treatise that ARISTOTLE devotes to this question in his *Physics* IV 10, 217 b. 29ff, he develops the conception that time is the measure (the number or rather the numerability) of motion according to the ὕστερον καὶ πρότερον; the problem is posed here in the framework of the *Greek form-matter motive,* the dialectical religious character of which will be explained presently. According to ARISTOTLE, motion (which is treated here exclusively in the sense of change of place) is a striving of matter after form and from potentiality to actuality. As long as it has not attained its form, it is a flowing plurality of earlier and later. It is without unity and consequently without actual being, because being implies unity. The *psychè*, however, can give unity to this plurality in the subjective synthesis of the act of counting. Therefore, time cannot actually exist outside the soul. Does it then, in the local movement of things, have only a potential existence in the plurality of phases of the earlier and later? ARISTOTLE's exposition fails to provide a clear answer to this question.

[1] *Het tijdsprobleem in de Wijsbegeerte der Wetsidee* (The problem of time in the philosophy of the cosmonomic idea). This treatise is also published in the review *Philosophia Reformata* (publisher J. H. Kok, Kampen), 5th year 1940, pp. 160ff. and pp. 193ff.).

A quite different view from the Aristotelian was found in the old Ionian nature-philosophers. Whereas ARISTOTLE deified the form-motive in identifying deity with pure Form, the latter, on the contrary, deified the matter-motive of the ever flowing Stream of life which cannot fix itself in any form. Time is viewed here, especially in Anaximander, as a divine order of *dikè* avenging the injustice of things which have originated in an individual form, by dissolving this latter in pure matter and carrying back all things to their form-less Origin.

The dilemma posed by ARISTOTLE could not arise here, since the Ionian thinkers made no difference between the physical and the mental spheres. According to them "matter" was animated. ARISTOTLE, on the contrary, held that the *psyché* is the form of the material body and that "matter" is only a potentiality. It cannot have actual being without a form which guarantees the unity of being.

In consequence of the inner dialectic of the form-matter-motive, medieval Aristotelian scholasticism was also broken up into diametrically opposed trends with respect to its view of time. ALBERT THE GREAT, in his commentary on the *Physics*, defended an objective physical conception and ascribed to the movement of things, independently of the soul, a form and structure of its own, in the so-called *numerus formalis* [1]. THOMAS AQUINAS veers toward the opposite subjectivistic psychological position. In this he follows AUGUSTINE [2]. Time as the numerical measure of motion can have real existence only in the soul, although THOMAS concedes, that it has a *fundamentum in re* in the motion of matter [3].

---

[1] ALBERTUS MAGNUS, *Physicorum* L. IV tr. 3 c. 16: "Ad numerare tria exiguntur, scilicet *materia* numerata, et *numerus formalis,* et *anima* efficienter et formaliter *numerans:* ergo si non est anima adhuc numerus est secundum esse formale et secundum numerum numeratum; ergo, quo numeratur est duplex, scilicet quo numeratur efficienter, et quo numeratur formaliter." Time is such a *numerus formalis.*

In modern times the same conception is found again in the neo-Thomist P. HOENEN S.J., in his *Philosophie der anorganische natuur* [Philosophy of inorganic nature] (Antwerpen-Nijmegen) 1940, p. 284.

[2] AUGUSTINUS, *Confessiones* L. XI, 33: "Inde mihi visum est nihil alium esse tempus quam distentionem: sed cuius rei nescio, et mirum, si non ipsius animae."

[3] THOMAS, *De Instantibus*, Cap. I. Opusc. XXXVI. Cf. on this point my treatise: *De idee der individualiteits-structuur en het Thomistisch*

In modern Humanistic philosophy, the problem of time is posed in the framework of the Humanistic ground-motive of *nature and freedom*. The latter is to be subjected to a detailed investigation in the second part of this volume.

The inner dialectic of this basic motive drives philosophical thought at the outset toward a conception of time orientated rationalistically toward mechanical motion as it was conceived of by classical physics. And subsequently it drives it toward an irrationalistic vitalistic, psychological or historical view (dominated by the freedom-motive). Here too, one comes across the opposition of objectivistic and subjectivistic views.

In KANT's *Critique of Pure Reason,* time is viewed as a transcendental form of intuition of sense experience, in which the objective-physical as well as the subjective-psychical impressions of consciousness are ordered in succession. Time is coordinated here with space as the other form of intuition.

In the twentieth century, the philosophical discussion is set in motion once more by the development of EINSTEIN's relativity-theory, which views time as a fourth dimension of the physical world-space (the ordering system x, y, z, t).

BERGSON alleges against EINSTEIN that in the theory of relativity time is denatured to a spatial line. "True time", according to him, is the *psychical duration of feeling,* in which we immediately enjoy a living experience of the creative freedom of the "élan vital" (inaccessible to natural-scientific thought). This actual "durée" is of inner psychical character and lacks mathematical uniformity of successive parts. All moments here penetrate one another qualitatively.

Psychical "'durée", according to BERGSON, is the *absolute* time.

Modern phenomenology also speaks of "true time" as an "Erlebnisstrom", in opposition to the objectivistic conception of time in modern mathematical natural science. DILTHEY and HEIDEGGER conceive of time in an irrationalistic historical sense, but in HEIDEGGER historical time has a dialectical existential meaning.

In all these philosophical discussions of the subject, it strikes us again and again that time is unwittingly identified with one

---

substantie-begrip, II [The idea of the individuality-structure and the Thomistic concept of substance] (Philosophia Reformata 9th and 10th years, 1944/5), pp. 1f.

of its modal aspects or modalities of meaning. As long as philosophical thought proceeds from a dialectical ground-motive and is caught in a religious dualism, an *integral* conception of time is excluded.

The integral character of cosmic time. The correlation of temporal order and duration, and the subject-object relation in the latter.

The idea of cosmic time [1] constitutes the basis of the philosophical theory of reality in this book. By virtue of its integral character it may be called new.

According to this conception, time in its cosmic sense has a *cosmonomic* and a *factual* side. Its cosmonomic side is the temporal *order* of succession or simultaneity. The factual side is the factual *duration*, which differs with various individualities.

But the *duration* remains constantly subjected to the *order*. Thus, for example, in the aspect of organic life, the temporal order of birth, maturing, adulthood, aging and dying holds good for the more highly developed organisms.

The duration of human life may differ considerably in different individuals. But it always remains subject to this biotic order of time. No man can come into this world as an adult. Temporal order and duration are each other's correlata and so they may not be dissociated. Consequently, the opposition between rationalistic and irrationalistic conceptions has lost its foundation for us. For the former absolutizes the cosmonomic side and the latter the factual-subjective side of time.

The duration discloses itself further in a subject-object relation, which will be subjected to a detailed analysis in volumes II and III, and to which we shall return presently in a provisional way.

For the moment, we must be satisfied with the observation that the *objective* duration can never *actually* exist independently of the *subjective* in the subject-object-relation. This is of essential importance for the problem of the "measurement of time". Consequently, the polar opposition between subjectivistic and objectivistic conceptions is also meaningless from our standpoint.

---

[1] The term "cosmic" may not of course be understood in a natural-scientific sense.

> All structures of temporal reality are structures of cosmic time.

We must further observe, that all the basic structures which we shall discover in temporal reality in the course of our inquiry (in vol. II and III), the modal structures of the various aspects as well as the typical totality-structures of individuality, are grounded in the order of cosmic time. They are all specific structures of time and as such necessarily related to the factual duration of transitory beings, events, processes, acts, social relationships and so on.

The entire empirical reality in its overrich diversity of structures is enclosed and determined by universal cosmic time. In each of its modal aspects, the latter expresses itself in a specific modality of meaning with respect to temporal order as well as duration.

But its *cosmic* character discloses itself precisely in the indissoluble inter-modal coherence of meaning into which it fits the modal aspects.

As a matter of fact we shall see, in the second volume of this work, that the modal aspects are bound by cosmic time in an order of before and after, which is expressed in their very internal modal structure.

This order discloses its *temporal* character, namely, in the empirical *opening-process* of the modal aspects of reality (to be investigated more closely in vol. II). In this process, anticipatory structural moments come to be developed; and these moments disclose their inner coherence of meaning with the modal aspects that are later in order. The complex of anticipatory structural moments is, for example, lacking in the as yet closed structure of the logical aspect as we discover it in the pre-theoretical attitude of thought. Anticipatory structural moments find expression within this aspect only in the theoretical attitude of thought. Only in the latter is disclosed the inner connection with the historical, linguistic, economic and later aspects. Thus — to give another instance — in a closed primitive jural order, the anticipating connection with morality — as expressed in the principles of equity, good faith, good morals, punishment according to guilt etc. — is absent.

The opening-process, intended here, has *temporal duration* and comes about according to the inter-modal temporal order of the aspects. We shall go into all these points in detail in vol. II.

The transcendental Idea and the modal concepts of time. The logical aspect of temporal order and duration.

We can form a theoretical concept of the separate modal *aspects* of time. But time itself, in its all-embracing cosmic meaning can never be comprehended in a concept, because the former alone makes the concept possible. It can only be *approximated* in a theoretical *limiting-concept* in critical self-reflection as to the necessary pre-supposita of the theoretical attitude of thought. We then get a transcendental idea of cosmic time-order in the theoretical discontinuity of its different modal aspects. This discontinuity is caused by logical analysis.

In the logical or analytical aspect, itself, cosmic time discloses a *modal-analytical sense*.

The logical order of simultaneity and of prius and posterius is as much a modal aspect of the integral order of time as the physical. It has meaning only within the cosmic time-order in the coherence of *all* its modal aspects. Therefore, it is meaningless to set the *logical* prius and posterius in opposition to the *temporal* before and after, as if the former had no authentic meaning as time-aspect.

The theoretical concept joins in logical simultaneity the analyzed characteristics of that which is defined in it. It is thereby subjected to the logical principles of identity and contradiction, which give expression to the analytical (normative) temporal order of simultaneity in the sense of logical implication and exclusion. Likewise the theoretical logical movement of thought follows the analytical temporal order of prius and posterius (the premises are logically prior to the conclusion), as being subjected to the principle of the sufficient ground [1].

---

[1] The logical movement of thought has subjective duration in the real act of thought and is subjected to the logical order of *prius et posterius* with respect to the logical aspect of this act. From the side of psychologists it is objected that actually the process of logical concluding does not follow explicitly the logical order of prius et posterius. However, it is at least not to be doubted that it does so, when we draw a syllogistic inference in theoretic logical form. This is only possible in a real act of theoretical thought, which does disclose explicitly the logical aspect of time which is present only implicitly in pre-theoretic logical conclusions and which has also a logical aspect of duration. It must be observed, that the logical order of succession differs fundamentally from that of mathematical movement in its original modal sense. For in the analytical succession of thought the former stages do not disappear, be-

Nowhere, hence not in the logical aspect either, does cosmic time in itself offer a concentration-point that could serve as a point of departure for philosophic thought.

In time, meaning is broken into an incalculable diversity, which can come to a *radical* unity only in the religious centre of human existence. For this is the only sphere of our consciousness in which we can transcend time [1].

---

cause the inference implies its premises. Besides, the analytical order of prius, et posterius is a normative one, which ought to be followed in a theoretical logical syllogism if the inference is to be correct.

[1] It has become apparent to me that some adherents of my philosophy are unable to follow me in this integral conception of cosmic time and its relationship to the concentration-point of philosophic thought.

Some seek the concentration-point of human existence *in* time and suppose, that this religious centre must certainly be pre-functional but not supra-temporal.

But, at least within the horizon of *cosmic* time we have no single experience of something "pre-functional", i.e. of anything that would transcend the modal diversity of the aspects. We gain this experience only in the religious concentration of the radix of our existence upon the absolute Origin. In this concentration we transcend cosmic time. How could man direct himself toward eternal things, if eternity were not "set in his heart"? Even the idolatrous *absolutizing* of the temporal cannot be explained from the temporal horizon of human existence. For the latter nowhere provides a point of contact for an idea of the absolute, unless it be related apriori to the supra-temporal. This act of concentration presupposes a supra-temporal starting-point in our consciousness.

This, however, is not to say that the religious centre of human existence is found in a rigid and static immobility. That is a metaphysical-Greek idea of supra-temporality. It found, for example, sharp expression in PARMENIDES' conception of the eternal divine form of being and in PLATO's original conception of the transcendental world of the εἰδή and of the immortal soul, enclosed entirely in the pure form of theoretical thought (cf. PLATO's *Phaedo*).

In the case of the founder of the Eleatic school, this conception originated from an absolutizing of the modal spatial aspect, an aspect bound to the horizon of time. The eternal being, which has no coming into being nor passing away is in his view enclosed in the ideal static-spatial form of the sphere. In his dialectical dialogue *Parmenides*, PLATO himself has laid bare the inner antinomies involved in this absolutization.

The spatial is not in the least supra-temporal since it implies *simultaneity* in the modal meaning of continuous dimensional extension, and the spatial relations in temporal reality have subjective-objective duration of time. So far as the spatial relationships in abstract geometry are viewed apart from transitory things and events, i.e. according to their

Only from this supra-temporal concentration-point are we in a position to gain a veritable notion of time. Beings that are entirely *lost* in time lack that notion.

> No static conception of the supra-temporal. Is the acceptance of a central trans-cosmic time desirable?

If we say, that we transcend cosmic time in the root of our existence, we must guard against metaphysical Greek or Humanistic conceptions of the "supra-temporal". We shall later on see, that the central sphere of human existence is in the full sense of the word a *dynamic* one. Out of it the dramatic conflict between the civitas Dei (city of God) and the civitas terrena (earthly city) takes its *issue* in the history of the world. We can even call it the central sphere of *occurrence*, for *that which occurs* cannot be distinguished too sharply from the *historical aspect* of cosmic time, which is only one of its temporal *modalities of meaning*.

I have considered whether — in order to cut off all misunderstanding respecting the term "supra-temporal" — it would be recommendable to introduce the expression "central transcosmic" time.

But this would lead to a duplication of the temporal horizon,

---

modal structure alone, they, nevertheless, always continue to express the spatial *temporal order* of greater and less *in simultaneity*. A spatial order of time, can exist only in the coherence of meaning with all other aspects. The same holds good for the + and — order of numbers, which is no less a modal aspect of the order of time and is in temporal reality continually related to factual *duration*, because the numerical relations as well as the spatial ones are, in reality, constantly subjected to change. The + and the — directions in the order of numbers, however, maintain themselves in every factual temporal duration of numerical relationships, because they express an arithmetical *order* of time, which determines the place and value of each of the numbers.

This must be my answer, if other adherents of my philosophy are of the opinion that cosmic time does not find expression in the numerical and spatial aspects as such. This would even spell a regress in face of the view of KANT, who made number originate from a schematizing of the logical category of quantity in time; also in face of the insight of HAMILTON who defined arithmetic as the *science of pure time or order in progression*. (Cf. J. ALEXANDER GUNN, *The Problem of time* (London, 1939), p. 92); also in face of the intuitionalistic school in mathematics, which makes all natural numbers originate from a synthesis of the original intuition of time and the original ideas of one and addition.

in connection with which it would become necessary to use the word in two fundamentally different senses. Furthermore, the general explanation "duration determined by the order of succession or simultaneity" would no longer prove serviceable to cover both meanings. I would not know what criterion would have to be accepted for a "trans-cosmic" time. Consequently, the meaning of this term would remain entirely in the dark. For these reasons, I still prefer to reserve the term "time" for the cosmic one and its different modal aspects.

The eschatological aspect of cosmic time in faith.

To be sure, cosmic time has its limiting aspect in faith and there is a temporal order and duration in the special meaning of the latter. The modal meaning of faith, as we shall see in the second volume, is by its nature related to divine revelation. In this eschatological aspect of time faith groups the "eschaton" and, in general, that which is or happens beyond the limits of cosmic time. In this special sense are to be understood the "*days of creation*", the initial words of the book of Genesis, the order in which regeneration *precedes* conversion etc.

Theology will always need this limiting aspect of time in which the cosmic temporal order is indissolubly connected with the revealed supra-temporal realm. However, I cannot agree with the tendency of some modern Christian theologians, who identify the eschatological aspect of time with the historical and reject the supra-temporal central sphere of human existence and of divine revelation.

Naïve and theoretical experience of time.

In the naïve pre-theoretical attitude of experience, we have an immediate integral experience of cosmic time in the uninterrupted coherence of all its modal aspects, inclusive of the normative ones, and in concentric relatedness to the selfhood. If I hasten to my work and look at my watch, then time has for me *not only an abstract objective aspect of movement*, but I experience it in the continuous coherence of its aspects of number, space and movement, with the stream of organic life, duration of feeling and the normative social aspects. When I let a person go first who is ranked higher in the social scale, intuitively, I am aware of the temporal aspect of symbolic significance and of the social intercourse-aspect of temporal order. This holds likewise for the economic and juridical aspects of time, when I spend the scanty time that I have at my disposal in a definite economic manner or guard myself against mora in the performance of my legal obligations. The implicit experience of normative aspects of the temporal order in the notion of being "too late" is one of the most evident indications of the integral character of the naïve consciousness of time.

But it is no less certain, that in naïve experience the different modal aspects do not explicitly come to consciousness, but only implicitly and conjointly. The continuity of cosmic time here completely covers the modal boundaries of its aspects.

In the philosophical-theoretical attitude of thought, on the contrary, we can approximate time — and temporal reality — only in an analytical setting-asunder of its modal aspects, which nevertheless continue to express their coherence of meaning in their very intrinsic structure.

§ 2 - THE TRANSCENDENTAL CRITICISM OF THEORETICAL THOUGHT AND THE DOGMA CONCERNING THE AUTONOMY OF THE LATTER. THE SECOND WAY TO A TRANSCENDENTAL CRITICISM OF PHILOSOPHY

Here a second way is opened to subject philosophic thought to a transcendental criticism. In the "Introduction" we chose the way from above: we started from the position that it is the nature of philosophy to be directed to the totality of meaning of temporal reality and to the selfhood, and we then came immediately to the problem of the Archimedean-point and to that of the ἀρχή.

But in this line of thought, we had to start from a supposition about the character of philosophy, which is not at all universally accepted in philosophical circles. Besides, it might seem, that a due account of the transition from the theoretical basic problem of philosophy to the central religious sphere was lacking.

Therefore, since the appearance of the first (i.e. the Dutch) edition of this work, I have directed all my attention to a sharpening of the method of transcendental criticism, whereby the objection, mentioned above, might be met. The conceptions of the task of philosophy are extremely divergent and every apriori choice of a position in this matter may be esteemed dogmatic. Consequently, if our transcendental critique is actually to embrace every possible conception of the philosophic task, it must necessarily examine the *theoretical attitude of thought as such*. For no veritable philosophy whatsoever can escape this attitude[1].

The dogmatic positing of the autonomy of theoretical thought.

Immanence-philosophy in all its nuances stands or falls with the dogma of the autonomy of theoretical thought. However, hitherto it has been simply *posited*, that this autonomy follows from the nature of such thought, without justifying this assertion by means of a really critical investigation of the inner structure of the theoretical attitude of thinking itself. Not only traditional metaphysics, but also Kantian epistemology, modern phenomenology and phenomenological ontology in the style of NICOLAI HARTMANN continued in this respect to be involved in a theoretical dogmatism. Essentially supra-theoretical prejudices were thus treated as theoretical axioms, and no account was given of the fundamental significance of these prejudices for the whole theoretical vision of empirical reality.

The different views of the autonomy of theoretical thought and the origin of this difference.

There was, however, actually every reason to make the so-called autonomy of theoretical thought a critical problem. In the first place, it cannot be denied, that in Greek philosophy it had a meaning entirely different from that in Thomistic scholasticism. In both of these, again, it was viewed entirely otherwise than in modern Humanistic thought. As soon as one penetrates to the root of these fundamentally different conceptions, one encounters a difference in religious starting-point, which is at the basis of the pretended autonomy of thought.

When Greek philosophy begins to claim its autonomy over against popular faith, *it does so because, in its estimation, theoria is the true way to the knowledge of God. Pistis* (faith), which continues to cling to the sensory mythological representations, gives only a doxa, an uncertain opinion. As early as the time of PARMENIDES' didactic poem, these two ways are set sharply in opposition to one another. PLATO said, that it is exclusively destined for philosophers to approach the race of the gods.

---

[1] In a later context we will explain the fact, that so-called *existential* philosophical thought also retains a theoretical character.

But the whole philosophical theoria of the Greeks, as I have shown in detail from the sources in the first volume of my *Reformation and Scholasticism in Philosophy*, continues to be dominated by the same religious ground-motive which was also at the bottom of the popular faith and which, since the time of ARISTOTLE, was called the *form-matter motive.*

On the other hand, the Thomistic vision of the autonomy of the naturalis ratio is unintelligibile, unless its religious background is apprehended, namely, the scholastic *basic motive of nature and grace*. This motive was entirely foreign to Greek thought. Similarly one cannot approach the modern Humanistic conception of autonomy in its fundamental difference from Thomism, without having understood its religious background in the Humanistic ideal of science and personality. This religious background finds expression in the ground-motive which since KANT has been called that of *nature and freedom*.

The Thomist claims that, in the proper use of natural reason, philosophy can never come into contradiction with the supernatural truths of grace in the church doctrine. This standpoint implies an *accomodation* to the ecclesiastical dogma of the Aristotelian metaphysics and view of nature (accepted as a product of natural reason). The Kantian or Hegelian will show as little understanding for this typical scholastic striving after accomodation as would have been the case with ARISTOTLE himself, had he been acquainted with Thomism. Thus the dogma concerning the autonomy of theoretical thought can never account for the fundamentally different conceptions of it. Thereby it loses its right to serve as an unproblematic starting-point of philosophy.

> The dogma concerning the autonomy of theoretical thought as an impediment to philosophical discussion among the various schools.

It appears again and again, that this dogma impedes a mutual understanding among philosophic schools that prove to be fundamentally opposed in their true (though hidden) starting-point. This is a second ground for doubting its character as a purely theoretical axiom.

For if all philosophical currents that *claim* to choose their standpoint in theoretical thought alone, actually had no deeper presuppositions, it would be possible to convince an opponent of his error in a purely theoretical way.

Prolegomena 37

But, as a matter of fact, a Thomist has never succeeded by purely theoretical arguments in convincing a Kantian or a positivist of the tenability of a theoretical metaphysics. Conversely, the Kantian epistemology has not succeeded in winning over a single believing Thomist to critical idealism.

In the debate among these philosophical schools, one receives the impression that they are reasoning at cross-purposes, because they are not able to find a way to penetrate to each other's true starting-points. The latter are masked by the dogma concerning the autonomy of theoretic thought. The same holds, for example, in the debate conducted by a positivist of the Vienna school with a Hegelian thinker or a Spinozist.

This simple fact of experience, in the nature of the case, does not yet prove the impossibility of autonomous theoretical reflection in philosophy. But it is quite sufficient to show, that it is necessary to make the autonomy of theoretical thought a *critical problem* and no longer to pass it off as a scientific *axiom*.

This problem should be posed as a *quaestio iuris*. It touches the empirical sciences as well as philosophy, since both imply the theoretical attitude of thought.

> The necessity of a transcendental criticism of the theoretical attitude of thought as such. The difference in principle between transcendent and transcendental criticism.

The proper answering of the question raised above requires a transcendental criticism of the theoretical attitude of thought as such. By this we understand a critical inquiry (respecting no single so-called theoretical axiom) into the *universally valid conditions which alone make theoretical thought possible, and which are required by the immanent structure of this thought itself*. In this latter restriction lies the difference in principle between a *transcendent* and a *transcendental* criticism of science and philosophy.

The former does not really touch the inner character and the immanent structure of the theoretical attitude of thought, but confronts, for instance Christian faith with the results of modern science and with the various philosophical systems, and thus ascertains, whether or not factual conflicts exist.

It remains *dogmatic*, however, as long as it fails squarely to face the primary question, whether the theoretical attitude of thought itself, with reference to its inner structure, can be independent of supra-theoretical prejudices. With such a dogmatic, merely *transcendent* criticism, one constantly runs the risk of regarding as the result of unprejudiced science and philosophical reflection, something that appears upon critical inquiry to be the consequence of a masked religious prejudice and an anti-Christian attitude of faith. Besides, there is another ever present danger. What is actually a complex of philosophical ideas dominated by unbiblical motives, may be accepted by dogmatic theology and accomodated to the doctrine of the church. The danger is, that this complex of ideas will be passed off as an article of Christian faith, if it has inspired the terminology of some confessions of faith. Transcendent criticism, in other words, is valueless to science and philosophy, because it confronts with each other two different spheres whose *inner point of contact is left completely in the dark.* One can then just as well proceed to exercise criticism of science from the standpoint of art or politics!

In order to guarantee from the outset a really critical attitude in philosophy, transcendental criticism of theoretical thought should come *at the very beginning* of philosophical reflection.

§ 3 - THE FIRST TRANSCENDENTAL BASIC PROBLEM OF THEORETIC THOUGHT. THE "GEGENSTAND-RELATION" VERSUS THE SUBJECT-OBJECT-RELATION.

How is the theoretical attitude of thought characterized, in contrast with the pre-theoretical attitude of naïve experience?

Our introductory survey of the problem of time has shown us the way which must necessarily lead to the solution of this question.

It became evident, that in the theoretical attitude of thought we analyze empirical reality by separating it into its modal aspects. In the pre-theoretical attitude of naïve experience, on the contrary, empirical reality offers itself in the integral coherence of cosmic time. Here we grasp time and temporal reality in typical total-structure of individuality, and we do not become aware of the modal aspects unless *implicitly*. The aspects are not set asunder, but rather are conceived of as being together in a continuous uninterrupted coherence.

The antithetical structure of the theoretical attitude of thought in its purely intentional[1] character and the origin of the theoretical problem.

Theoretical thought has a typically antithetic attitude in all of its positive forms. Here we oppose the logical, i.e. the analytical function of our real act of thought, to the non-logical aspects of our temporal experience. The latter thereby becomes "Gegenstand" in the sense of *"opposite"* (Widerstand) to our analytical function [2]. These non-logical aspects, as well, belong to our *real* act of thought in its temporal concreteness and are consequently not to be sought exclusively *outside* the full temporal structure of the latter. In other words, *the antithetic structure of the theoretical attitude of thought can present itself only within the temporal total-structure of the act of thinking.*

The first structure is only an *intentional* one; it does not have an *ontical*[3] character.

The non-logical aspects stand in an intentional antithesis to the logical function of thought. Any attempt to grasp the former in a logical concept is met with resistance on their part. From this resistance the theoretical problem originates.

In logical analysis the aspect which is opposed to the logical is distinguished theoretically from the remaining aspects. Con-

---

[1] *Translator's Note:* The term "intentional" is used here in the sense of a merely mental directedness towards the "Gegenstand", a sense akin to that of the phenomenological usage (BRENTANO, HUSSERL).   W. Y.

[2] By the logical aspect of our act of thought, we understand the aspect of analytical distinction; distinction in the sense of setting apart what is given together.

At this juncture I must once more mention, that logical analysis is not the only mode of distinction. Secondly, I must recall, that logical or analytical diversity supposes a cosmic diversity of meaning which is at the basis of all analysis. So far as the first point is concerned, it is sufficient to refer to animals distinguishing their mates, food, etc. The distinction made by animals is certainly not of a logical nature. So far as the second point is concerned, we must observe, that logical analysis would have nothing to distinguish apart from a previously given cosmic diversity of meaning. In other words, logical analysis would in this case become meaningless. For we may not forget, that the logical aspect can reveal its logical sense only in the coherence of meaning with all other aspects.

[3] *Translator's Note:* The term "ontical" is not intended in the sense in which HEIDEGGER employs it, nor in a metaphysical sense in general. It is exclusively related to empirical reality in its integral sense which includes all modal aspects and individuality-structures.   W. Y.

sequently, if we designate the opposed aspect by the symbol "x" and the remaining aspects by the symbol "y", then "x" will also stand in an antithetic relation to "y".

This theoretical antithesis does not correspond to the structure of empirical reality. It is only a consequence of the necessary theoretical abstraction of the modal aspects from cosmic time. This latter links up the aspects in a continuous coherence of meaning and can never be eliminated *from reality*.

Now we have seen, that the non-logical aspects of experience offer resistance to a logical analysis of their structure. This resistance arises from the fact that, even when theoretically abstracted, the modal structure of the non-logical aspect x which is made into a "Gegenstand" continues to express its coherence (of meaning) with the modal aspects y which have not been chosen as the field of inquiry.

Theoretical abstraction of the modal aspects from cosmic time is necessary for a theoretical insight into the modal diversity of meaning as such [1].

As soon as we have realized, however, that the theoretical attitude of thought arises only in a theoretical abstraction, we can no longer consider theoretical reason as an *unproblematic datum*.

---

[1] In this context, I must remark, that the modal structure of the analytical aspect itself is given as a whole and not in analyzed moments. However, in the theoretical attitude of thought we can analyze the structure of the analytical aspect; but only in its theoretical abstraction and opposition to the non-logical aspects. For the analytical aspect, like all others, expresses in its modal structure the temporal order into which the different aspects are fitted. Consequently, this structure is a unity in a multiplicity of analyzable moments. The theoretical act in which we perform this analysis is, of course, not identical with the abstracted modal structure of the logical aspect. The subjective analytical function of this concrete act remains bound to its modal structure in its temporal coherence with the other aspects. In its theoretical abstraction this modal structure has only an intentional existence in our act of thought, and can be made into the "Gegenstand" of our actual logical function. It is, consequently, not the latter which can be made a "Gegenstand", but only the abstracted, purely intentional, modal structure of the logical function. We never arrive at a "transcendental logical subject" which can be detached from all modal structures of time and can be sovereign and "absolute" in this sense.

The first transcendental basic problem as to the theoretical attitude of thought.

The first transcendental basic problem with which we are confronted is exactly the theoretical "gegenstand-relation".

We can formulate this problem as follows: *"What do we abstract in the antithetic attitude of theoretic thought from the structures of empirical reality as these structures are given in naïve experience? And how is this abstraction possible?"*

Those who reject the integral conception of cosmic time developed above must seek another solution to the critical problem we have proposed. But if we seriously confront the theoretical attitude of thought with the pre-theoretical attitude of naïve experience, the problem itself can no longer be brushed aside.

A closer confrontation of the naïve attitude with the theoretical.

The naïve attitude of thought in principle lacks an intentional antithetic structure. Consequently, it knows of no theoretical problems. This subject cannot be treated in its full scope prior to the third volume. Nevertheless, in our Prolegomena, we must elucidate more closely some essential states of affairs with relation to the attitude of naïve experience in so far as this is demanded by our present transcendental criticism of theoretical thought.

We have previously observed, that in the naïve attitude of experience, our logical function of thought, so far as its intentional content is concerned, remains entirely accommodated to the continuous coherence of cosmic time. In this respect, our logical function, like all other functions of consciousness, remains completely *within* this coherence.

In naïve experience we grasp reality in the typical total structures of individual things and concrete events. All modal aspects are grouped and typicalized [1] in a characteristic manner and in an unbroken coherence of time within an individual totality. This occurs without involving any analytical distinction of the modal aspects. The naïve process of concept-formation is not directed toward the latter, but toward *things* or *concrete events*

---

[1] *Translator's Note:* For the Dutch term "getypiseerd" Prof. DOOYE-WEERD himself has coined the English term "typicalized", which could be rendered "ordered according to types". It should be noted, that a "typical" structure is never identical with the full "individuality" of reality. W. Y.

as *individual totalities*. It is not concerned with abstract relations of number or space, nor with the effects of energy as such, but with things which are countable, spatial and subjected to physical-chemical changes. In the total structure of naïve experience, the logical aspect is joined with the non-logical aspects in an *indissoluble coherence*. Consequently, the logical aspect is conceived of as an inherent, but implicit component of concrete reality itself. The same is true of the aspect of sensory perception, the historical culture-aspect, the aesthetic, and so on. But how is this to be understood?

The subject-object relation in naïve experience.

Naïve experience can have this integral character only by virtue of the *subject-object relation* inherent in it. In this relation, *objective* functions and qualities are unreflectingly ascribed to things and to so-called natural events within modal aspects in which it is not possible for them to appear as *subjects*.

Thus, as adult men who have outgrown animistic representations, we know perfectly well, that water itself does not *live*. Nevertheles, in the aspect of organic life, we ascribe to it the objective function of being a necessary means for life. We know that a bird's nest is not alive, but we can conceive of it meaningfully as a thing only in relation to the subjective life of the bird. Thus we conceive of a bird's nest as a typical *object* of life. We know, that a rose does not feel or think or engage in aesthetic valuation as a subject. Nevertheless we ascribe to it respectively, objective qualities of sensory colour and odour, objective logical characteristics, objective cultural qualities and objective beauty. Further, this subject-object relation in the attitude of naïve experience and thought is grasped as a *structural relation of reality itself*. That is to say, the objective functions belong to things themselves in relationship to *possible subjective functions* which the things do not possess in the aspects of reality involved.

The sensory colour red is ascribed to a rose, not in relation to *my*, or *your*, individual sense-perception, but in relation to any possible normal human perception of colour. Similarly water is a means of life for every possible living organism. But then too, when the subject-object relation in the biotic aspect is wholly individualized, as in the case of the bird's nest, naïve experience still ascribes the objective functions in question to the things *themselves*. It ascribes these objective functions to them in structural relation to the subjective life of the animal concerned. The objective qualities which are ascribed to this thing in the logical and post-logical aspects are undoubtedly related to subjective functions of human nature. But they are related in such a manner that, here too, the typical structure of individuality of the thing, which is characterized by a specific relation to animal life, finds expression. The bird's nest remains a bird's nest with respect to its objective logical characteristics. It remains a bird's nest, even though it is a possible object of human culture and has an objective symbolic signification expressed in its name, and objective aesthetic qualities.

The metaphysical substance-concept, the concept of a "Ding an sich" is in principle foreign to naïve experience. So is also the abstract enclosing of the reality of things in those modal aspects which form the field of inquiry of physics, chemistry and biology.

Through the subject-object-relation we consequently experience reality in the total and integral coherence of all its aspects, as this is *given* within the temporal horizon of human experience. Naïve experience leaves the typical total structures of this reality *intact*.

The antithetic relation of the theoretical attitude of thought, on the contrary, sets reality apart in the diversity of its modal aspects.

Dogmatic theory of knowledge, which considered the theoretical attitude of thought as an unproblematic datum, consequently eradicated the fundamental difference between the theoretical and the pre-theoretical attitude of thought, and finally identified the *subject-object-relation* with the antithetic *gegenstand-relation*.

Thus naïve experience itself was misinterpreted as a *theory about reality,* and identified with the uncritical theory of "naïve realism" or the "copy theory". Then, in alliance with modern natural science and the physiological theory about the "specific energies of the senses", modern epistemology undertook the task of refuting this "naïve realism"! At present, it is not necessary to enter further into this fundamental misconception. We will deal with it more fully in the third volume.

For the moment it is sufficient, that we have made clear the fundamental difference between the naïve and the theoretical attitude of thought, so that we can fully realise the in-escapability of the *first* transcendental problem with respect to the latter.

The consequences of ignoring the first transcendental basic problem in the traditional conception as to the relation of body and soul in human nature.

The dogmatic ignoring of this problem has had far-reaching consequences for the entire vision of temporal reality. Even in philosophical and theological anthropology these consequences may be demonstrated. For example, the traditional dichotomistic conception of human nature as a composition of a material body and an immortal rational soul is doubtless connected with the misconception, that the antithetic relation in the theoretical attitude of thought answers to reality itself.

ARISTOTLE, in accord with PLATO, tried to prove, that the theoretical activity of thought (the *nous poiètikos,* i.e. active intellect) in forming logical concepts must be wholly independent of and separated from the organs of the material body. The active intellect must be separate from the body, because it can grasp everything other than itself in logical universality and abstraction. The theoretical activity of thought is here hypostatized in its *logical aspect* as an immortal *ousia* or substance.

THOMAS AQUINAS accepted this Aristotelian argument, but accommodated it in scholastic fashion to the doctrine of the church. Consequently, he held, that the entire rational soul, which was considered to be characterized by the theoretical activity of thought, must be an immortal and purely spiritual substance!

A direct conclusion is here drawn from the purely intentional antithetic structure of the attitude of theoretical thought to a *real* separateness of the logical function from all pre-logical aspects of the body! This conclusion was directed by the dualistic form-matter motive, which impeded an integral view of empirical reality.

But it is of no avail to ignore the problem implied in the theoretical antithesis. For new transcendental problems arise, as soon as we try to account for the way we follow, in the theoretical attitude of thought, in order to overcome the intended antithesis.

We cannot stop at the theoretical *problem,* born out of the resistance offered by the non-logical "Gegenstand" to our logical function in its analytical activity. We must proceed from the theoretical *antithesis* to the theoretical *synthesis* between the logical and the non-logical aspects, if a logical concept of the non-logical "Gegenstand" is to be possible.

§ 4 - THE SECOND TRANSCENDENTAL BASIC PROBLEM: THE STARTING-POINT OF THEORETICAL SYNTHESIS

Now, however, a second transcendental problem arises which can be formulated as follows:

From what standpoint can we reunite synthetically the logical and the non-logical aspects of experience which were set apart in opposition to each other in the theoretical antithesis?

This question touches the kernel of our inquiry. By raising this second basic problem, we subject every possible starting-point of theoretical thought to a fundamental criticism. In this way we must finally settle the question whether the dogma of the autonomy of theoretical reason is compatible with the intentional structure of the theoretical attitude of thought.

Now it is evident, that the *true* starting-point of theoretical synthesis, however it may be chosen, is in no case to be found in one of the two terms of the antithetic relation. It must necessarily transcend the theoretical antithesis, and relate the aspects that theoretically have been set asunder to a deeper radical unity (or in the case of a dualistic standpoint, perhaps to a pair of assumed radical unities). For one thing is certain: the antithetic relation, with which the theoretical attitude of thought stands or falls, offers in itself no bridge between the logical thought-aspect and its non-logical "Gegenstand". We saw earlier, that even cosmic time, which guarantees the indissoluble *coherence* among the modal aspects, does not present an Archimedean point to theoretical thought.

This seems to imply at the same time, that the latter has in itself no *starting-point* for the theoretical synthesis.

Even here the dogma as to the autonomy of theoretical reason appears to lead its adherents into an inescapable *impasse*.

The impasse of the immanence-standpoint and the source of the theoretical antinomies.

In order to maintain the pretended self-sufficiency of theoretical thought, the advocates of this dogma are compelled to seek their starting-point in theoretical reason itself.

But the latter, by virtue of its very antithetic structure, is obliged to proceed in a synthetical way. Now there are as many modalities of theoretical synthesis possible as there are modal aspects of a non-logical character belonging to temporal experience.

There is a synthetic thought of mathematical, physical, biological, psychological, historical, and other character. In which of these possible special scientific points of view may the theoretical vision of empirical reality seek its starting-point? No matter how the choice is made, it invariably amounts to the *absolutizing* of a special synthetically grasped modal aspect.

The various -isms in the theoretical vision of reality.

This is the source of all *-isms* in the theoretical image of reality. The attempt must constantly be made to reduce all other aspects to mere modalities of the absolutized one. These -isms play their confusing rôle in the different branches of science as well as in philosophy.

Now such *-isms* (as materialism, biologism, psychologism, historicism etc.) are uncritical in a double sense. In the first place they can never be justified *theoretically*. The antithetic structure of the theoretical attitude of thought offers resolute resistance against every attempt to reduce one of the aspects to another. It avenges the *absolutizing* by involving theoretical thinking in internal antinomies. In the entire theoretical sphere there is no place for the *absolute,* because the theoretical attitude of thought is itself grounded in an antithetical *relation.*

Theoretical synthesis cannot cancel this relation. Such would be tantamount to the cancellation of the theoretical attitude of thought itself. In every theoretical synthesis, logical analysis remains bound to the modal structure of the opposite non-logical aspect. And the synthesis is, consequently, partly of a logical and partly of a non-logical character. The theoretical synthesis is, to be sure, a *union,* but not the deeper *unity* of the logical and non-logical.

It pre-supposes a supra-theoretical starting-point which must transcend theoretical diversity.

Consequently, what we have said also holds for every special scientific synthetic point of view. And with this we touch the second ground of the uncritical character of all -isms in the theoretical conception of reality.

In each of them the second transcendental basic problem returns unsolved. The absolutizing itself cannot issue from the theoretical attitude of thought. It points to a supra-theoretical starting-point, from which the theoretical synthesis is performed.

But, the objection will be raised, we sought after a starting-point for the *theoretical synthesis*.

Imperceptibly this problem has been identified with that of a starting-point for the *theoretical vision of reality*. Has not the problem been entirely shifted in this way? Does science indeed require a theoretical vision of *reality*? Is this, for example, necessary for pure mathematics, for logic, for ethical theory?

> The problem of the basic denominator for the theoretical comparison and distinction of the modal aspects.

In order to answer this question, I may first recall, that the theoretical attitude of thought consists in setting apart the modal aspects of temporal reality in opposition to one another. It consists primarily in the opposition of the logical aspect of our act of thinking to all aspects which are of a non-logical character. Every theoretical distinction of the latter aspects supposes an insight into their *mutual relationships and coherence*. Or, in other words, it supposes a basic denominator, under which the non-logical aspects can be brought in order to be *compared* with one another. For they could not be distinguished, unless they have something in common. On our own standpoint, the modal aspects have no other common denominator than the cosmic time-order. From our point of view, the latter expresses itself in the modal structure of each of the aspects, and is the guarantee of its coherence of meaning with all the rest. On the immanence-standpoint, another denominator of comparison must be sought, for example, in the way already discussed, by reducing all other aspects to modalities of a special (absolutized) one, or, as was usual in Greek and scholastic metaphysics, by accepting the metaphysical concept of being as a so-called "analogical unity", lying at the basis of the diversity of special aspects. Now, the theoretical vision of the mutual relationships and coherence of the aspects in every case implies a theoretical vision of reality. For the latter is nothing but the vision of the abstracted modal aspects in the totality of their coherence.

> The rôle of the -isms in pure mathematics and in logic.

Neither a special science nor philosophy can escape such a theoretical vision of reality.

In pure mathematics, the problem immediately arises: How is one to view the mutual relationship between the aspects of number, space, movement, sensory perception, logical thought and symbolical signification? Different schools in pure mathematics such as *logicism, symbolistic formalism, empiricism and intuitionism* arise in accordance with their respective theoretical visions on this basic problem. These differences are not restricted to the philosophy of mathematics. The famous Dutch mathematician, BROUWER, the chief representative of the intuitionistic school abolished an entire branch of special scientific work which had been built up by the logicist and formalist theories (the theory of the so-called transfinite numbers).

The first three schools, logicism, symbolistic formalism and empiricism, try to reduce the aspects of number and space to the logical, the linguistic and the sensory-perceptual aspects respectively.

Even in logic itself we observe the rise of a great diversity of theoretical schools. Here, too, this difference as to the nature and limits of the field of inquiry is determined by a theoretical vision of reality in its modal aspects. It is determined by a theoretical conception of the place that the logical aspect occupies in the entire order and coherence of the modal aspects (psychologism, mathematicism, symbolistic-conventionalism, dialectical historism, etc.). Invariably the starting-point which is chosen for theoretical synthesis in general, remains decisive for the vision of the mutual relationship and coherence of the modal aspects.

That this is also the case in normative ethics, aesthetics and theology, may be demonstrated convincingly. Yet we would have to anticipate too much of our later inquiries, were we now to elaborate all these points. Especially the current conceptions as to the field of inquiry for ethics are still vague. They are ill-defined to such a degree, that an adequate discussion of ethics would require a detailed exposition, which would exceed the compass of our transcendental criticism of the theoretical attitude of thought.

Provisional delimitation of the moral aspect.

In the present context, therefore, we will only establish the fact that ethics, so far as it lays claim to a field of inquiry distinct from theology and the philosophy of law, can have no other "Gegenstand" than the *moral aspect* of temporal reality. This aspect is characterized as that of the temporal relationships of love as differentiated more precisely by the typical structures of temporal society as conjugal love, love of parents and children, love of country, social love of one's fellow-man, and so on[1]. It is again evident, that this aspect has its own modal meaning only in the coherence with all other modal aspects of temporal reality. The theoretical vision of this coherence is then again decisive for the conception which one has of the moral norms, and this vision, in its turn, is dependent upon the *starting-point* of the theoretical-ethical reflection.

From the above it is quite evident, that each special realm of theoretical inquiry, whether or not it is called "empirical" in the narrower sense, pre-supposes a theoretical vision of temporal reality. And such a theoretical vision of reality must necessarily exceed the boundaries of any special science and exhibit a *philosophical* character. Consequently it appears at the same time, *that no single special science can possess an essential autonomy with respect to philosophy in the sense of a theory of reality.* For the rest we shall revert to this subject in he last part of this volume.

But have we at all proved definitely, that theoretic thought itself, with respect to its inner character, is dependent on a supra-theoretical starting-point, by which the autonomy of this thought is excluded? We may not accept this too hastily. For KANT, the father of the so-called critical-transcendental philosophy, supposed that he could lay bare a starting-point in theoretical reason itself, which *would rest at the basis of every possible theoretical synthesis,* and consequently would not be gained by the absolutizing of a special scientific point of view. Can the autonomy of theoretical thought be actually demonstrated along the way of KANT's critique of knowledge?

The starting-point of theoretical synthesis in the Kantian critique of knowledge.

This was the question which in our Introduction was raised at the very outset of the first way of our transcendental critique. Here we argued, that philosophical thought, as theoretical thought directed to the totality of meaning of our temporal cosmos, cannot arrive at a transcendental idea of this totality without critical self-reflection. But the very critical problem appeared to be

---

[1] The "disposition of the heart", which is rationalized by KANT and proclaimed as the criterion of morality in his "Gesinnungsethik", is actually of a *central-religious* character and so can, as such, never be related exclusively to the moral aspect; KANT's conception in this matter hangs together with his religious absolutizing of morality.

the relation between the thinking ego and its theoretical-logical function of thought. At first sight, it might seem, that the problem is here formulated in an unsatisfactory functionalistic manner. Why must we direct our attention solely to the logical function and why not to the integral act of theoretical thinking? To be sure, the latter may be characterized by its theoretical-logical aspect, but it can by no means be identified with the latter. We are now able to reply to this question, since in the second way of our transcendental critique we have engaged in an enquiry with respect to the inner structure of the theoretical attitude of thought. It is precisely the antithetic structure of the latter which obliged KANT and his followers to oppose the logical function to the other modal aspects of the integral act of thought. The only, but fundamental, mistake in their argument was the identification of the real act with a purely psychical temporal event, which in its turn could become a "Gegenstand" of the ultimate transcendental-logical "cogito". For we have seen, that the "gegenstand-relation" can only be an intentional relation *within* the real act of theoretic thought between its logical and its non-logical aspects. The real act itself can never be made the "Gegenstand" of its logical function, since the latter can be actual only within a real act of our consciousness, and does not have any actuality in a theoretical abstraction. But the identification of this real act with its psychical aspect is not tenable, and is an indicant of a dualistic view of reality. And the latter cannot be explained in terms of a purely theoretical epistemology.

The second way of our transcendental critique of philosophy involves resuming the investigation of KANT's conception concerning the transcendental cogito, notwithstanding the fact that, already in our *Introduction,* we did lay bare the pitfalls concealed in it.

The second investigation seeks to arrive at a critical formulation of the third transcendental basic problem. This problem is involved in the theoretical attitude of thought with respect to critical self-reflection. In this inquiry we wish to account critically for our transition from the theoretic to the central religious sphere. This involves also a deeper critical inquiry into the transcendental problem of the origin in philosophical thought. For, in our Introduction, it could appear, that this problem was introduced as a "deus ex machina", the necessity of which was unaccounted for in the course of our first critical inquiry. Finally our second investigation seeks to arrive at the ultimate stage of our transcendental critique, which was not yet reached by the first way explained in our Introduction.

The problem of the starting-point and the way of critical self-reflection in theoretical thought.

In order to discover the immanent starting-point of all special synthetic acts of thought in which these latter find their deeper unity, we must, according to KANT, look away from the "Gegenstände" of our knowledge and exercise critical self-reflection in theoretical thought. It must be granted, that this hint indeed contains a great promise. For it may not be doubted that, as long as theoretical thought in its logical function continues to be directed merely to the opposed modal aspects of temporal reality which form its "Gegenstand", it remains dispersed in a theoretical *diversity*. Only when theoretical thought is directed to the thinking *ego*, does it acquire the concentric direction towards an ultimate unity of consciousness which must lie at the root of all modal diversity of meaning. If you ask the special sciences active in the field of anthropology: What is *man*? you will obtain a diversity of items from physical-chemical, biological, psychological, cultural-historical, linguistic, ethnological and sociological points of view. These items are valuable. But no special science, nor an encyclopaedic sociology, can answer the question, what man *himself* is in the unity of his selfhood. Human I-ness *functions*, to be sure, in all modal aspects of reality. But it is, nevertheless, a *central and radical unity*, which as such *transcends* all temporal aspects [1]. The way of critical self-reflection is, consequently, the only one that can lead to the discovery of the true starting-point of theoretical thought. Even SOCRATES realised this, when he gave the Delphic maxim, Γνῶθι

---

[1] As soon as this transcendent character of the ego is overlooked, and the ego is conceived of as a merely immanent centre of its acts, its radical unity disappears and the ego is viewed as a merely *structural* unity in the diversity of its mental acts.

This is clearly seen from SCHELER's explanation of human personality in his *The place of man in the cosmos* („Die Stellung des Menschen im Kosmos", p. 75) as a "monarchical arrangement of acts, one of which at every turn takes the lead" („eine *monarchische Anordnung von Akten*, unter denen je e i n e r die Führung und Leitung besitzt"). As a matter of fact, the central position of the ego as to its temporal acts is not to be maintained in this way. The selfhood is dissolved in the structure of its acts.

σέαυτον (know thyself), a new introspective meaning and raised it to a primary requisite of philosophic reflection.

§ 5 - THE THIRD TRANSCENDENTAL BASIC PROBLEM OF THE CRITIQUE OF THEORETICAL THOUGHT AND KANT'S TRANSCENDENTAL UNITY OF APPERCEPTION

But here there arises a new transcendental problem, which we can formulate as follows:

How is this critical self-reflection, this concentric direction of theoretical thought to the I-ness, possible, and what is its true character?

It cannot be doubted, that an authentic transcendental problem resides here, if it is borne in mind, that the theoretical attitude of thought, with respect to its internal structure, is bound to the previously investigated antithetic relation.

Neither phenomenology, founded by EDMUND HUSSERL, nor modern existentialism has been able to dissociate its theoretical attitude of thought from this "Gegenstand-relation".

Phenomenology, following in the footsteps of FRANZ BRENTANO, has even posited the intentional relatedness of *every* act of consciousness to a "Gegenstand". However, this view is not our immediate concern now.

For it is evident, that the term "Gegenstand" cannot be meant in our sense, when BRENTANO and HUSSERL ascribe also to *feeling* an intentional relation to a "Gegenstand" (for instance a melody!).

However, the intentional antithetical structure, inherent in all theoretical thought, is doubtless present in the phenomenological attitude itself, which opposes the absolute "cogito" (in the sense of the "absolute transcendental consciousness") to the "world" as its intentional "Gegenstand" which is dependent on the former [1].

SCHELER considers the "gegenstand-relation" (by which the human mind can oppose itself not only to the "world", but can even make into "Gegenstand" the physiological and psychical aspects of human existence itself) as the most formal category of the logical aspect of mind (GEIST) [2].

---

[1] Cf. HUSSERL, *Ideen zu einer Phänomenologie and phänomenologischen Philosophie*, p. 92.

[2] SCHELER, *Die Stellung des Menschen im Kosmos*, p. 58. „Gegenstand-Sein ist also die formalste Kategorie der logischen Seite des

Modern Humanistic existentialism, too, can grasp existence as the free historical *ex-sistere* only in its theoretical *antithesis* to the "given reality of nature" (for HEIDEGGER, "Dasein" as the "ontological" manner of being against the "given world" as the "ontical"; for SARTRE, "le néant" as against "l'être"). Indeed, HEIDEGGER, too, is a phenomenologist, although his phenomenological method is an irrationalistic one in the hermeneutical sense of DILTHEY's historicism; and phenomenology, as we have seen, implies the theoretical antithesis.

In the face of this antithetical attitude of existential thought, it is of no consequence, that the philosophy of existence wishes to create a great distance between existential thinking as authentically *philosophical* on the one hand, and all scientific thought which is directed to a "Gegenstand" on the other. For the term "Gegenstand" has in our critique another meaning than that here intended, viz. "given object" („das Vorhandene"), although *naturally science, too, is bound to the "gegenstand-relation"*.

For the present, then, it is not to be understood, how the concentric direction of theoretical thought to the ego could arise from the theoretical attitude of thought itself.

KANT, however, did not wish to abandon the autonomy of theoretical reason. He supposed, as we have seen, that in the logical function of thinking (the "Verstand") a *subjective pole of thought* may be demonstrated, which is opposed to all empirical reality, and which, as the *transcendental-logical unity of apperception*, lies at the basis of all synthetic acts of thought as their *starting-point*. The "I think", so he says, must be able to accompany all my representations (KANT means here doubtles "synthetic concepts of empirical "Gegenstände"), if they are to be *my* representations. This was to be a final transcendental-*logical* unity of consciousness, which itself can never become a "Gegenstand", because every theoretical act of knowledge must proceed from this "I think". It is the "transcendental-logical subject of thought", which would have to be viewed as the universally valid condition of every scientific synthesis. It is, consequently, in no way identical with our empirical, real act of thought, which, according to him, can be again made a "Gegenstand" of this "transcendental subject". It is only a merely-*logical* point of unity of the consciousness, which lacks

---

Geistes" [Being a "Gegenstand" is therefore the most formal category of the logical side of the mind].

all empirical individuality. KANT denies also, that we would possess real self-*knowledge* in this transcendental-logical *concept* of the thinking ego. For, according to his epistemological conception, human *knowledge* can have relation only to impressions, given in sensory perception ("Empfindung"), which have been received in the transcendental forms of intuition of space and time and are ordered by logical categories to an "objective reality of experience".

Has KANT now succeeded in demonstrating a starting-point, immanent in "theoretical reason" itself, which satisfies the requirements of a genuine transcendental criticism of theoretical thouht? In our *Introduction* we answered this question negatively.

In the second way of our critical inquiry we can strengthen the grounds for this reply. For we saw, that the true starting-point for the theoretical synthesis is never to be found *within* the antithetical relation which characterizes the theoretical attitude of thought. KANT's transcendental-logical ego remains caught in the *logical* pole of this relation, which, according to his own conception, finds its counterpole in the non-logical aspect of sense perception. If, as he himself explains emphatically, the logical aspect of thought and the aspect of sense perception are not reducible to each other, then it follows in a stringent way, that in the former no starting-point can be found for their theoretical union.

As we shall show in still greater detail in the epistemological part of the second volume, KANT, in consequence of his axiom that every synthesis should proceed from the logical function of thought, has abandoned the critical way of inquiry and has *eliminated* the authentic problem of synthesis by means of a dogmatic statement. The dogma as to the autonomy of "theoretical reason" forced him to do so. But, by reason of this theoretical dogmatism, the *true* starting-point of his theory of knowledge remained hidden.

The third basic problem formulated by us is, just as the first, ignored by KANT. As a result he was unable to bring the second problem to a critical solution.

If then, in theoretical thought as such, no starting-point for the inter-modal synthesis is to be found, the concentric direction of this thought, necessary for critical self-reflection, cannot have a *theoretical* origin. It must spring from the ego as the individual centre of human existence.

We have said in our *Introduction*, that the selfhood cannot give this central direction to its theoretical thought without concentrating itself upon the true, or upon a pretended absolute origin of all meaning. That is to say, that self-knowledge in the last analysis appears to be dependent upon knowledge of God, which, however, is quite different from a theoretical theology. Can we account for this statement?

In the first place, we must grant, that both self-knowledge and knowledge of the absolute origin or pseudo-origin, exceed the limits of theoretical thought, and are rooted in the "heart" or the religious centre of our existence.

Nevertheless, this central supra-theoretical knowledge does not remain enclosed in the heart, but must by its very nature penetrate the temporal sphere of our consciousness. Theoretical thought, too, is concerned in this central knowledge, in the transcendental process of self-reflection, in the concentric direction of the theoretically separated aspects of the gegenstand-relation to the thinking self.

For we have seen, that without veritable self-*knowledge* the true starting-point of theoretical synthesis cannot be discovered, and that theoretic self-reflection in thought presupposes this central knowledge, since the concentric direction of theoretical thought can start only from the ego. KANT as well as modern phenomenology, has overlooked this truth. The empirical fact, that selfknowledge appears to be dependent on knowledge of God is established by ERNST CASSIRER in the second volume of his *Philosophie der symbolischen Formen,* on the basis of a wealth of anthropological and ethnological data [1].

But a real account of this fact is rendered only by the Biblical Revelation concerning the creation of man in the image of God. God reveals Himself as the absolute Origin excluding every independent counter-power which may be His opposite. He has expressed His image in man by concentrating its entire temporal existence in the radical religious unity of an ego in which the totality of meaning of the temporal cosmos was to be focused upon its Origin.

The fundamental dependence of human self-knowledge upon the knowledge of God has consequently its inner ground in the essence of religion as the central sphere of our created nature.

---

[1] We shall return to this point in detail in the second volume in the discussion of the problem concerning the relation between faith and history.

The alleged vicious circle in our transcendental criticism.

The question could now be raised, whether our transcendental criticism in its third stage does not make an unwarranted leap by explaining the concentric direction of theoretical thought as an effect of the central religious sphere of consciousness. Has this in fact been proved stringently, and what then is here understood by religion?

Finally, if our criticism should actually prove something stringently, does it not move in a vicious circle? For does a *proof* not suppose this very autonomy of theoretical thought, the impossibility of which our criticism tried to demonstrate?

To these questions I must reply as follows:

What is stringently proved, in my opinion, is the thesis, that the concentric direction of thought in its self-reflection cannot originate from the theoretical attitude of thought itself, and that it can issue only from the ego as a supra-theoretic individual centre of human existence.

It would be an uncritical petitio principii to pretend, that our criticism even at this point moves in a vicious circle by abandoning the autonomy of theoretical self-reflection. Up to now it has remained strictly within the theoretical sphere, and has laid bare structural states of affairs which had been ignored under the very influence of the dogma as to the autonomy of theoretical reason. However, these states of affairs, once they have been discovered, may no longer be ignored by anyone who appreciates a veritably critical standpoint in philosophy.

It is of course impossible, that this transcendental criticism — although up to the question of self-*knowledge* being of a strictly theoretical character — itself should be unprejudiced. For in this case it would refute its own conclusions. But what shall we say, if the very supra-theoretical presuppositions hold here, which free theoretical thought from dogmatic "axioms" standing in the way of a veritable critical attitude? If, as we have demonstrated, theoretical synthesis is *possible* only from a supra-theoretical starting-point, then only the *contents* of the supra-theoretical presuppositions implied thereby, can be questionable, but not the very necessity of them.

Hitherto, however, the demonstrative force of our critique has been *negative* in character, so far as it, taken strictly, can only demonstrate, that the starting-point of theoretical thought cannot be found in that thought itself, but must be supra-theoretical in character. That it is to be found only in the central religious sphere of consciousness, is no longer to be proved *theoretically*, because this insight belongs to self-*knowledge*, which as such transcends the theoretical attitude of thought. We can only say, that this self-*knowledge* is necessary in a critical sense, because without it the true *character* of the chosen starting-point remains hidden from us. And this would be fatal for the critical insight into its true significance in respect to the inner direction of philosophic thought.

What is religion?

To the question, what is understood here by religion? I reply: the innate impulse of human selfhood to direct itself toward the *true* or toward a *pretended* absolute Origin of all temporal diversity of meaning, which it finds focused concentrically in itself.

This description is indubitably a theoretical and philosophical one, because *in philosophical reflection* an account is required of the meaning of the word "religion" in our argument. This explains also the formal transcendental character of the description, to which the concrete immediacy of the religious experience remains strange.

If, from out of the central religious sphere, we seek a theoretical approximation of it, we can arrive only at a transcendental *idea*, a limiting concept, the content of which must remain abstract, as long as it is to comprehend all possible forms in which religion is manifested (even the apostate ones). Such an idea invariably has the function of relating the theoretical diversity of the modal aspects to a central and radical unity and to an Origin.

The impossibility of a phenomenology of religion. The ex-sistent character of the ego as the religious centre of existence.

There is one thing, however, on which we cannot lay too much stress. As the absolutely central sphere of human existence, religion transcends all modal aspects of temporal reality, *the aspect of faith included*. It is not at all a temporal phenomenon which manifests itself within the temporal structure of human act-life. It can be approximated only in the concentric direction of our consciousness, not in the divergent one, not as a "Gegenstand" [1].

Therefore, with respect to its inner essence, religion can never be described "phenomenologically". It is no "psychological phenomenon", it is no emotional feeling-perception; it is not to be charactized, as is done by RUDOLPH OTTO, as experience of the "tremendum". It is the *ex-sistent* condition [2] in which the ego is bound to its true or pretended firm ground.

Hence, the mode of being of the ego itself is of a religious character and it is nothing *in itself*.

Veritable religion is absolute *self-surrender*. The apostate man who supposes, that his selfhood is something in itself, loses himself in the surrender to idols, in the absolutizing of the relative. However, this absolutizing itself is a clear manifestation of the *ex-sistent* character of the religious centre of our existence, which, to be sure, *expresses* itself in all modal aspects of time, but never can *be exhausted* by these [3]. Even in the religious

---

[1] This does not hold as to belief and its different contents. For we have seen, that the faith-function is bound to cosmic time and to the temporal coherence of meaning with the other modal functions of our existence. It should not be identified with the religious centre of this latter. Nevertheless, the direction and contents of faith are not to be understood apart from the religious ground-motive by which it is directed and from a divine Revelation, no matter whether the latter is understood in its true meaning or is misinterpreted in an apostatic sense.

[2] I use here a term well known in modern existence-philosophy. However, it is evident, that it is not meant here in the Humanistic sense.

[3] Therefore, modern existence-philosophy, so far as it considers time to be an existential trait of the "authentic" human ego, remains entangled in the diversity of meaning of the terms 'ego' and 'selfhood' which comes to light, as soon as we lose sight of the religious radix of human existence.
We can project an idol of our "true ego" and elevate this idol to an "ideal selfhood" which is placed over against our "empirical" I-ness, considered as the "objectivation" of our self in the "past" and subjected to the natural law of causality. If in this case our "ideal selfhood" is related to the freedom of the "present" and the "future", there is born a dialectical time-problem in the existential conception of the ego, due to the dialectical ground-motive of *nature and freedom*. But the "authentic", the "fundamental" I-ness (or whatever you will name it) will ever recede from our view, as long as this latter is dispersed in time. A truly critical hermeneutic method in philosophical anthropology has the task to lay bare the origin of these dialectical problems as to the ego and true selfhood of man, and to unmask the temporal idols projected about it. A purely *temporal* ex-sistere may never be identified with the ex-sistent

absolutizing of the historical aspect of our existence in the self-surrender to an aspect of time, we transcend the latter.

Nevertheless, the *autonomous ex-sistere* of the ego which has lost itself in the surrender to idols, must be broken down by the *divine ex-trahere* from the state of apostasy, if man is to regain his true ex-sistent position.

After having given an account of what we understand by religion, we can establish the fact that the concentric direction in theoretical thought must be of religious origin. It must be of a religious origin, even though it always remains theoretical in character, because of its being bound to the antithetic gegenstand-relation. It springs from the tendency to the origin in the centre of human existence, which tendency we previously discovered in the *Introduction*. But now we have made clear the inner point of contact between philosophic thought and religion from the intrinsic structure of the theoretical attitude of thought itself. Critical self-reflection in the concentric direction of theoretical thought to the ego necessarily appeals to self-knowledge (which goes beyond the limits of the theoretical gegenstand-relation). Consequently we may establish the fact, that even the theoretical synthesis supposes a religious starting-point. *Furthermore, we have now explained, that it is meaningless to ask for a theoretical proof of its religious character, because such a proof presupposes the central starting-point of theoretical thought.*

The supra-individual character of the starting-point.

We must now proceed to the final and decisive stage of our transcendental critique.

We have established the necessary religious nature of the starting-point and have learned of the intrinsically *ex-sistent* character of the selfhood. Therefore, we can no longer seek the true point of departure of philosophic thought in the individual ego alone. We observed in our Introduction that the I-ness must share in the Archimedean point, but that in this latter must be concentrated the total meaning of the temporal cosmos.

The ego, however, is merely the concentration-point of our individual existence, *not* of the entire temporal cosmos. Moreover, philosophy is as little as science in the narrower sense

---

character of the religious centre of human nature which is implied in its tendency towards its divine Origin.

merely a matter of the individual. It can be cultivated only in a *community*. This, too, points to the necessity of a *supra-individual* point of departure.

Critical self-reflection in theoretical thought is, to be sure, the necessary way to the discovery of the starting-point of philosophy. It is indeed the individual ego which gives to its thought the concentric direction. However, true self-*knowledge* discovers the ex-sistent character of the selfhood also in the fact that the ego is centrally bound with other egos in a religious community. The central and radical unity of our existence is at the same time individual and supra-individual; that is to say, in the individual I-ness it *points beyond* the individual ego toward that which makes the whole of mankind spiritually *one in root* in its creation, fall and redemption.

According to our Christian faith, all humanity is spiritually included in Adam. In him the whole human race has fallen, and in mankind also the entire temporal cosmos, which was concentrated in it. In Jesus Christ, the entire *new* humanity is one in root, as the members of one body.

Our I-ness is, in other words, rooted in the spiritual community of mankind. It is no self-sufficient "substance", no "windowless monad", but it lives in the spiritual community of the *we*, which is directed to a Divine *Thou*, according to the original meaning of creation.

The meaning of the central command of love.

This is the deep meaning of the central command of love: Thou shalt love God above all and thy neighbour as thyself. This command in its indivisible unity is of a *religious* and not of a moral character. For the moral relations of love to our fellowmen are merely a modal aspect of temporal society. In their modal speciality of meaning, they have sense only in the coherence with all other aspects of this society. They are also differentiated necessarily according to the diversity of social relationships in conjugal love, parent- and children-love, social love of the neighbour, love of the fatherland, and so on. But the *religious* command of love understands the neighbour as a member of the radical religious community of mankind in its central relationship to God, who created man after His image. Therefore, it is in truth the *radix* of all modal aspects which unfolds the divine law in temporal reality.

The spirit of community and the religious basic motive.

Now a religious community is maintained by a common spirit, which as a *dynamis*, as a central motive-power, is active in the concentration-point of human existence.

This spirit of community works through a *religious ground-motive*, which gives contents to the central mainspring of the entire attitude of life and thought. In the historical development of human society, this motive will, to be sure, receive particular *forms* which are historically determined. But in its central religious meaning it transcends all historical form-giving. Every attempt at a purely historical explanation of it, therefore, necessarily moves in a vicious circle. For, by virtue of the inner structure of the theoretical attitude of thought, the historical explanation itself supposes a central and supra-theoretical starting-point, which is determined by a religious basic motive or ground-motive.

Since the fall and the promise of the coming Redeemer, there are two central main springs operative in the heart of human existence. The first is the dynamis of the Holy Ghost, which by the moving power of God's Word, incarnated in Jesus Christ, re-directs to its Creator the creation that had apostatized in the fall from its true Origin. This dynamis brings man into the relationship of sonship to the Divine Father. Its religious ground-motive is that of the Divine Word-Revelation, which is the key to the understanding of Holy Scripture: the motive of *creation, fall, and redemption by Jesus Christ in the communion of the Holy Ghost*.

The second central main spring is that of the spirit of apostasy from the true God. As religious dynamis (power), it leads the human heart in an apostate direction, and is the source of all deification of the creature. It is the source of all absolutizing of the relative even in the theoretical attitude of thought. By virtue of its idolatrous character, its religious ground-motive can receive very diverse contents.

The Greek form-matter motive and the modern Humanistic motive of nature and freedom.

In Western thought, this apostate spirit has disclosed itself chiefly in two central motives, namely, (1) that which has dominated the classical Greek world of culture and thought, and which has been brought (since the time of ARISTOTLE) under the fixed designation of the *form-matter motive*, and (2) that of the modern Humanistic life- and world-view, which, since the time of IMMANUEL KANT, has been called the motive of *nature and freedom*. Since the 18th century, this latter motive came more and more to dominate the world of Western culture and thought.

The former motive originated from the encounter of the older pre-Homeric Greek *religion of life* (one of the different nature-religions) with the later *cultural religion* of the Olympic gods. The older religion of life deified the eternally flowing Stream of life, which is unable to fix itself in any single individual form. But out of this stream there proceed periodically the generations of transitory beings, whose existence is limited by an individual form, as a consequence of which they are subjected to the horrible fate of death, the *anangkè* or the *heimarmenè tychè*. This motive of the form-less eternally flowing Stream of life is the *matter-motive* of the Greek world of thought. It found its most pregnant expression in the worship of DIONYSUS, which had been imported from Thrace.

On the other hand, the form-motive was the main spring of the more recent Olympian religion, the religion of form, measure and harmony, which rested essentially upon the deification of the cultural aspect of Greek society (the Olympian gods were personified cultural powers). It acquired its most pregnant expression in the Delphic Apollo as law-giver.

The Olympian gods leave mother earth with its ever flowing Stream of life and its threatening *anangkè*. They acquire Olympus for their seat, and have an immortal individual form, which is not perceptible to the eye of sense. But they have no power over the fate of mortals.

The form-matter motive itself was independent of the mythological forms which it received in the old nature-religions and the new Olympian culture-religion. It has dominated Greek thought from the outset.

The autonomy which philosophic theoria demanded, in opposition to popular belief, implied, as we have observed in an earlier context, only an emancipation from the mythological forms which were bound to sensory representation. It did not at all imply a loosening of philosophic thought from the central religious ground-motive which was born out of the encounter of the culture-religion with the older religion of life.

The modern Humanistic ground-motive of *nature and freedom*, which we shall presently subject to a detailed investigation in the transcendental criticism of Humanistic philosophy, has taken its rise from the religion of the free autonomous human personality and that of modern science evoked by it, and directed to the domination of nature. It is to be understood only against the background of the three ground-motives that formerly gave the central direction to Western thought, namely, the form-matter-motive, the motive of creation, fall and redemption, and the scholastic motive of nature and grace. The last-named motive was introduced by Roman-Catholicism and directed to a religious synthesis between the two former motives.

It is not surprising, that the apostate main spring can manifest itself in divergent religious motives. For it never directs the attitude of life and thought to the true *totality of meaning* and the true radix of temporal reality, because this is not possible without the concentric direction to the true Origin.

Idolatrous absolutizing is necessarily directed to the *speciality* of meaning, which is thereby dissociated from its temporal *coherence,* and consequently becomes *meaningless* and *void.* This is the deep truth in the time-honoured conception of the fall as a *privatio*, a deprivation of meaning, and as a *negation*, a *nothingness*.

Sin as privatio and as dynamis. No dialectical relation between creation and fall.

However, the central *dynamis* of the spirit of apostasy is no "nothing"; it springs from the creation, and cannot become operative beyond the limits in which it is bound to the divine order of meaning. Only by virtue of the religious concentration-impulse, which is concreated in the human heart, can the latter direct itself to idols. The dynamis of sin can unfold itself only in subjection to the religious concentration-law of human existence. Therefore, the apostle PAUL says, that without the law there is no sin and that there is a *law* of sin.

Consequently, there can be no inner contradiction between creation and fall as long as they are understood in their Biblical sense. A contradiction would exist, if, and only if, sin were to have not merely an imaginary but a *real* power in *itself,* independent of creation.

The dialectical character of the apostate ground-motives.
Religious and theoretic dialectic.

On the contrary, it belongs to the inner nature of the idolatrous ground-motives, that they conceal in themselves a religious antithesis.

For the absolutizing of special modal aspects of meaning, which in the nature of the case are *relative*, evokes the *correlata* of these latter. These correlata now in religious consciousness claim an absoluteness opposed to that of the deified aspects.

This brings a religious dialectic into these basic motives, that is to say, they are in fact composed of two religious motives, which, as implacable opposites, drive human action and thought continually in opposite directions, from one pole to the other. I have subjected this religious dialectic to a detailed investigation in the first volume of my new trilogy, *Reformation and Scholasticism in Philosophy*. And I demonstrated, that this dialectic is quite different from the *theoretical* one which is inherent in the intentional antithetical gegenstand-relation of theoretic thought.

For *theoretical* antithesis is by nature *relative* and requires a theoretical synthesis to be performed by the thinking "self". On the other hand, an antithesis in the religious starting-point of theoretical thought does not allow of a genuine synthesis. In the central religious sphere the antithesis necessarily assumes an absolute character, because no starting-point beyond the religious one is to be found from which a synthesis could be effectuated.

The uncritical character of the attempts to bridge the religious antithesis in a dialectical starting-point by a theoretic dialectic.

Every philosophical effort to bridge such a religious antithesis in the starting-point by means of a theoretical logical dialectic is fundamentally *uncritical*. This was the way, however, of all so-called dialectical philosophy, from HERACLITUS up to the Hegelian school, in so far as it aimed at an ultimate synthesis of its opposite religious motives.

The theoretical syntheses which pretend to fulfil this task, are merely illusory at the very point here mentioned. They are subjected to the intrinsic law of all religious dialectic, that is to say, as soon as philosophy returns to the path of critical self-reflection, they are necessarily dissolved again into the polar antithesis of their starting-point. Against HEGEL's synthetical dialectic which attempted to think together the antithetic motives of nature and freedom, PROUDHON directs the verdict, earlier pronounced by KANT and later repeated by KIERKEGAARD: "L'antinomie ne se résout pas" (The antinomy cannot be solved).

Even in Greek antiquity the efforts to reconcile the religious antithesis between the form- and the matter-motive by means of a dialectical logic were dissolved in a later evolution of Greek thought into a polar antithesis [1].

The religious dialectic in the scholastic motive of nature and grace.

A more complicated religious dialectic is exhibited by the scholastic basic motive of nature and grace, introduced in philosophy and theology by Roman Catholicism, and taken over by Protestant scholasticism.

It originally aimed at a synthesis between the central motive of the Word-revelation and that of the Greek (especially the Aristotelian) view of nature (the form-matter motive). But it lends itself as well to a combination of the former with the Humanistic ground-motive of nature and freedom. In this attempt at synthesis, the Christian basic motive necessarily loses its radical and integral character.

For nowhere in the scholastic vision of human nature is there a place for the Biblical revelation of the *heart* as religious centre and radix of temporal existence. Therefore, Thomistic scholasticism could proclaim the autonomy of natural reason in the "natural sphere" of knowledge, without being aware of the fact that in so doing it handed philosophy over to domination by another religious motive. And the latter could not be rendered harmless by a simple *accommodation* to the doctrine of the church.

The Greek or the Humanistic basic motive, which here dominates the vision of nature, has in its turn undergone a certain scholastic accommodation to the Christian doctrine of creation or to that of creation and fall, respectively. In the dialectical tension between "nature" and "grace" is concealed, as a component, the inner dialectic of the Greek or Humanistic basic motive, respectively.

In scholastic anthropology this component finds a clear expression in the dichotomist conception of the relation of body

---

[1] See my analysis of the Platonic dialectic in my *Reformation and Scholasticism in Philosophy*, vol. I.

and soul. The latter is dominated either by the motive of "matter" and "form" or by that of "nature and freedom".

The inner dialectic of the ground-motive of nature and grace drove scholastic thought in the 14th century from the Thomistic (pseudo-) synthesis (Natura praeambula gratiae) to the Occamist antithesis (no point of contact between nature and grace according to WILLIAM OF OCCAM, the leader of the nominalist scholasticism of the 14th century).

In the most recent time it has disclosed its polar tendencies in the "dialectical theology". The conflict between KARL BARTH and EMIL BRUNNER was entirely dominated by the question whether in "nature" there may be accepted a "point of contact" for "grace". Against BRUNNER's "yes", going in the synthetic direction, BARTH set his inexorable "no" [1].

The development of the religious dialectic of the form-matter motive in Greek philosophy and the dialectic unfolding of the motive of nature and grace in the scholastic Christian philosophy have been investigated in detail in the first and second volumes of my *Reformation and Scholasticism in Philosophy*. The second part of book I of the present work will be dedicated completely to a transcendental criticism of modern Humanistic philosophy, in which the dialectical development of the motive of *nature and freedom* will be traced.

The ascription of the primacy to one of the antithetic components of the dialectical ground-motive.

In default of a basis for a real synthesis between the antagonistic religious mainsprings which are operative in a dialectical ground-motive, there remains only a single way out, viz. that of ascribing the "primacy" or the religious precedence to one of the two.

In so far as a philosophic current has become conscious of the religious antithesis in its starting-point, such an ascription will increasingly go hand in hand with a depreciation of and withdrawal of divine attributes from the other mainspring. The ancient Ionian natural philosophy held to the primacy of the matter-motive. It originated in the archaic period in which the old nature- and life-religion, which had been pushed back by the public Olympian religion of the polis broke forth again

---

[1] This extremely antithetical conception as to the relation of nature and grace is no longer maintained in BARTH's *Kirchliche Dogmatik*.

openly in religious revivals, in the remarkable Dionysian and Orphic movements.

Consequently, the Ionian thinkers must have been fully aware of the religious conflict in the form-matter motive. The form-principle in this philosophy is entirely deprived of its divine character. According to these thinkers the true God is the form-less, eternally flowing stream of life, generally represented by a "moveable element" (water, fire, air), but in ANAXIMANDER conceived of as an invisible "apeiron", flowing in the stream of time and avenging the injustice of the transitory beings which have originated from it in an individual form, by dissolving them in their formless origin. The deepest conviction of these philosophers may perhaps be expressed by quoting in a typical Greek variant the famous words of Mephisto in GOETHE's Faust:

„Denn alles was (in Form) besteht,
„Ist wert das es zu Grunde geht."

With ARISTOTLE, on the contrary, in whose philosophy — in accordance with SOCRATES and PLATO — the primacy has passed over to the form-motive, the deity has become "pure Form", and "matter" is completely deprived of any divine quality by becoming the metaphysical principle of imperfection and "potentiality".

In the late-medieval scholasticism of WILLIAM OF OCCAM, which had become keenly conscious of the antagonism between the "nature"- and the "grace-motive", "natural reason" has become entirely tarnished. There is no longer place here for a metaphysics and a natural theology, although the autonomy of natural reason is maintained to the utmost. The grace-motive retains the primacy, but not in a synthetic hierarchical sense as in Thomism.

In the modern Humanistic philosophy there is originally wanting the clear notion of the religious antithesis between the motive of dominating nature by autonomous science and that of the autonomous freedom of human personality. But scarcely had this notion awakened in ROUSSEAU, when he depreciated the ideal of science and ascribed the primacy to the freedom-motive which is the mainspring of his religion of feeling. KANT, who follows ROUSSEAU in this respect, deprived "nature" (in the natural-scientific sense) of all divine character and even denied its divine origin. God is, according to him, a postulate of practical reason, i.e. a postulate of autonomous morality which is completely dominated by the Humanistic freedom-motive.

In modern philosophy of life as well as in the Humanistic existence-philosophy, there is seen a still deeper depreciation of the motive of the autonomous control of nature. The freedom-motive here has the absolute religious primacy, even though in a form which is quite different from what it possessed in ROUSSEAU and KANT.

The meaning of each of the antithetic components of a dialectic ground-motive is dependent upon that of the other.

Finally we must observe, that the meaning of each of the antithetic components of a dialectic ground-motive is dependent upon that of the other.

Consequently, it is not possible to understand the meaning of the Greek matter-motive apart from that of the form-principle, and reverse. In the same way, the signification of the scholastic nature-motive and that of the grace-motive determine one another mutually. And so do the Humanistic nature-motive and the freedom-motive.

It is of great consequence for a critical study of the history of philosophic thought that one does not lose sight of this state of affairs. In Greek thought the term "nature" had a very different sense from that which it has in modern Humanistic philosophy. In a Thomistic discussion of the problem of freedom and causality the term freedom may not be understood in the Humanistic sense; as little as the Thomistic concept of causality may be conceived in the sense of the classical-Humanistic motive of nature-domination.

§ 6 - THE TRANSCENDENTAL GROUND-IDEA OF PHILOSOPHY

The three transcendental Ideas of theoretical thought, through the medium of which the religious basic motive controls this thought.

With the exposure of the religious ground-motives as the true starting-points of philosophy our general transcendental criticism of the theoretical attitude of thought has completed its chief task.

At present, there remains only the question as to the way in which these religious motives control the immanent course of philosophic thought.

To this question the answer must be: through the medium of a triad of transcendental Ideas, which correspond to the three transcendental basic problems of the theoretical attitude of thought. Theoretical thought hereby gains successively its concentric direction to the presupposita which alone make it possible, no matter if a thinker has become aware of them in a really critical way of self-reflection.

For while the theoretical *concept* of a modal aspect is directed to the modal *diversity* of meaning and *separates* the aspect concerned from all the others, the transcendental theoretical *Idea* is directed to the *coherence*, the *totality* and the *Origin* of all meaning, respectively.

This theoretical Idea does not cancel the theoretical separation and antithesis of the modal aspects, and thus it retains a theoretical character. But within the theoretical attitude of thought itself, it relates the analytically separated and opposed aspects concentrically to their mutual relationship and coherence of meaning, to their integral — or else dialectically broken — radical unity and Origin. It relates them in other words to the presupposita which alone make possible the theoretical concept of the modal speciality and diversity of meaning.

The triunity of the transcendental ground-Idea.

The transcendental Ideas, which are related to the three stages of critical self-reflection in theoretical thought described above, form an *indissoluble unity*.

For the question, how one understands the mutual relation and coherence of meaning of the modal aspects as theoretically set apart and opposed to one another, is dependent on the question whether or not one accepts the integral religious unity in the root of these aspects, which brings their totality of meaning to concentric expression. Furthermore, this last question is dependent upon the following: how the idea of the Origin of all meaning is conceived of, whether this idea has an integral or rather a dialectically broken character, i.e., whether only one Archè is accepted, or whether two principles of origin are opposed to one another.

Therefore, we can view the three transcendental Ideas, which contain the answer to these fundamental problems, as three directions of one and the same transcendental *ground-Idea*.

This is the basic Idea of philosophy, but indirectly it also lies at the basis of the various special sciences. The latter ever remains dependent on philosophy in their theoretical conception of reality, and in their method of forming concepts and problems.

The contents of this Idea, so far as it is directed to the Origin and to the unity (or duality respectively) in the root of the temporal diversity of meaning, is directly determined by the religious basic motive of theoretical thought.

The transcendental critique of theoretical thought and the dogmatic exclusivism of the philosophical schools.

What now is the fruit of this transcendental critique of thought for the discussion among the philosophical schools?

It can pave the way for a real contact of thought among the various philosophical trends. For — paradoxical as it may sound — this contact is basically excluded on the dogmatic standpoint of the autonomy of theoretical reason. Our transcendental critique wages a merciless war against the masking of supra-theoretical prejudices as theoretical axioms which are *forced* upon the opponent on penalty of his being viewed as an outsider in philosophical matters. In other words, it aims its attack against the *dogmatic exclusivism* of the schools, all of which fancy themselves to possess the monopoly on philosophical truth.

A sharp distinction between theoretical judgments and the supra-theoretical pre-judgments, which alone make the former possible, is a primary requisite of critical thought.

To this end a painstaking investigation is necessary, as to the transcendental ground-Idea of a philosophical line of thought, with which one intends to enter upon a serious discussion.

An apriori which is binding on all philosophic thought is undoubtedly contained in this basic Idea of philosophy. But what does it avail immanence-philosophy to withdraw from critical self-reflection with respect to this transcendental ground-Idea, if after all this latter manifests its apriori influence in the formulation of every philosophic problem?

Every philosophic thinker must be willing to account critically for the *meaning* of his formulation of questions. He who really does so, necessarily encounters the transcendental ground-Idea of meaning and of its origin.

The metaphysical-analogical concept of totality and the transcendental Idea of the totality of meaning. Transcendental critique of the metaphysical conception of the *analogia entis*.

Thomistic metaphysics will deny the religious foundation of the transcendental Idea of totality and origin of the modal diversity of meaning in its inter-modal coherence. As to the transcendental Idea of totality, it will argue, that our thought does have an immanent and autonomous transcendental concept of totality, as of a whole that is more than the sum of its parts. Granted, but in what *sense* is this concept to be understood? Does there not hide in this very concept the whole transcendental problem concerning the relation of modal diversity to the totality and radical unity of meaning? Is not the geometrical concept of totality quite different from the physical-chemical (e.g. that of the atom), from the biological, the psychological, the linguistic, etc.?

The totality in its relation to the modal diversity and intermodal coherence of meaning cannot be truly approximated by such essentially special scientific concepts which are bound to the modal aspects of meaning, unless I am willing from the outset to steer my philosophic thought into the channels of the different -isms which our transcendental critique has unmasked.

I think, Thomistic metaphysics will agree with this argument. However, it will say, that the transcendental concept of totality is implied in the metaphysical concept of being, which is not of a generic and specific but of an analogical character. Consequently, when we say, that being is a whole in which everything participates, we must conceive of the concept of the whole in this transcendental analogical sense. It is as such a metaphysical pre-supposition of all generic and specific concepts of totality. However, it does not satisfy the requirements of a transcendental Idea in the true critical sense. For, a purely analogical concept of totality lacks as such the concentric direction which is inherent in the transcendental ground-Idea of meaning. It *does not* direct the modal diversity of meaning in theoretic thought to its unity of root, but remains dispersed by this diversity. For this very reason it cannot replace the transcendental ground-Idea. Moreover, the metaphysical concept of being in its Aristotelian sense is not at all an autonomous concept of theoretical thought, as is pretended here. As soon as we subject it to a radical transcendental critique, it appears to be ruled by the dialectical form-matter motive, which is of a religious character.

Pure matter and pure Form are the two poles in the first (so-called transcendental) distinction of being. Pure matter is the principle of potentiality and imperfection; pure Form is identified with God as pure actuality and unmoved Mover of material nature. This Aristotelian concept of deity is of course accommodated to the Christian doctrine of creation. Here the metaphysical Idea of being and totality results in a transcendental Idea of the Origin which lies at the foundation of a "natural theology". The existence of God as unmoved Mover is proved in various ways, all of which apparently start from empirical data in nature, but which — besides their logically untenable leap from the relative to the absolute — pre-suppose the very conception of God which should be proved. The Ionian philosophers of nature and HERACLITUS, who deified the matter-principle of the eternally flowing stream of life, could never ask for an unmoved Mover as prime cause of empirical movement. This was not a logical mistake on the part of these thinkers, but is to be explained only in terms of their holding to the religious precedence of the matter-motive.

In the Thomistic system autonomous metaphysics should replace the transcendental critique of theoretical thought. However, all its metaphysical axioms and "proofs" are nothing but religious pre-suppositions in a dogmatical theoretical elaboration, masked by the dogma concerning the autonomy of natural reason.

It may be supposed, that ARISTOTLE himself was fully aware of the religious character of his form-matter motive, as can be seen from the truly religious manner in which in his *Metaphysics* he speaks about the mystical moments of union of human thought with the divine pure Form through theological theoria.

THOMAS could not be aware of this, because his view of the autonomy of natural reason (ruled by the scholastic motive of nature and grace) implied a meaning of autonomy quite different from that of the Aristotelian conception.

Our conclusion must be, that the metaphysical concept of the whole and its parts, implied in the analogical concept of being, is a pseudo-concept. It does not explain in what manner the theoretic diversity of meaning can be concentrated on a deeper unity. A purely analogical unity, as implied in the analogical concept of being, is no unity at all, but remains dispersed in the diversity of the modal aspects of meaning.

It cannot even explain the coherence in this modal diversity, because this coherence is the very pre-supposition of a true analogy [1].

An analogical concept cannot be useful in philosophy, unless it is qualified by a non-analogical moment of meaning which determines its special modal sense. But this state of affairs cannot be explained before the development of our theory of the modal aspects of meaning. And this is reserved for the second volume of this work.

The so-called logical formalizing of the concept of totality and the philosophical Idea of totality.

Now EDMUND HUSSERL has supposed in his *Logische Untersuchungen* (II, 1 p. 284 fl.) that one could pass beyond the modal diversity [of meaning] of the totality-concept by means of the *logical formalizing* of the latter.

In this way he arrived at the "formal logical" relation, "whole and its parts", which is to be purified from all non-logical speciality of meaning. And in regard to this formal relation there can, according to him, be formulated different purely logical propositions and definitions by means of the formal concept of "logical foundation" (logische Fundierung). I must reserve basic criticism of these so-called purely analytical definitions and propositions until, in the course of the discussion of the problem of knowledge in vol. II, KANT's distinction between synthetic and analytic judgments is subjected to a critical investigation [2]. I must,

---

[1] I have not discussed here the theological use of the analogia entis. For this subject I may refer to my recent treatise in the quarterly review "*Philosophia Reformata*", 17th year (1952) entitled: "*The transcendental critique of theoretical thought and the Thomistic theologia naturalis.*"

There is no place in our philosophy for an analogical concept of being in its metaphysical-theological sense.

Being is only to be ascribed to God, whereas creation has only *meaning*, the dependent mode of reality or existence. A true concept of being is impossible. The *word* being has no unity of meaning. When, in our Introduction, we called meaning the being of all that has been created, the word "being" designed only "essence", which does not transcend the boundaries of meaning. Only the transcendental ground-Idea which is ruled by the central motive of the divine Word-Revelation, can relate the different modal aspects of meaning to the divine Being of the Origin. But this Idea is not an autonomous concept, and it is incompatible with every form of natural theology.

[2] That the proposition: "the whole is more than its parts" should be purely analytic, is to be disputed on good grounds. It can even be disputed

however, even in the present context observe, that even a logically formalized concept "whole", granted that it has any sense, would remain ultimately enclosed in the modal speciality of signification, namely in that of the *modal-analytical aspect,* which itself supposes the inter-modal coherence of meaning, especially that between the analytical and the linguistic aspect.

For this very reason, this concept is unfit to occupy the place of the transcendental Idea of totality. On the contrary, it must be dependent on a transcendental Idea of meaning.

Only the latter can, as a limiting concept, point beyond the modal diversity to the temporal coherence and the supra-temporal totality of meaning. Yet, this transcendental Idea is nothing apart from a content which philosophic thought is incapable of deriving from itself.

Every attempt at a sufficient determination of the meaning of philosophical concepts necessarily discloses, in the process of critical self-reflection, the transcendental ground-Idea of the philosophical course of thought.

The principle of the Origin and the continuity-principle in Cohen's philosophy.

Hermann Cohen, the founder of the Marburg neo-Kantian School, for example, starts by interpreting philosophic thought (the "Vernunft") as self-sufficient "thinking of being" and of its origin. To this thought, as thought *of the origin* („Ursprungs-denken"), he sets the task of creating reality from this thought itself, namely, in a transcendental-logical process according to the "principle of continuity". With reference to such a program the following critical problems must be raised: *Where* do you actually find your Archimedean point in that "Vernunft", which you yourself *break up* into the modal diversity of logical,

---

on the basis that the question whether *every* whole implies the existence of parts is not to be answered in terms of pure logic. Even the linguistic meaning of the term "whole" is not of purely logical character. The term may in itself very well be used in opposition to "existing in parts". This holds in particular for a concentric whole as the human I-ness, in which the entire temporal human existence is concentrated.

For the rest, it appears from Husserl's explanation that his formalized concept of the whole is conceived in the special sense of pure mathematics and that, according to him, the latter is to be reduced to pure logic. Consequently, his logical formalization of the concept "the whole and its parts" is based upon a transcendental Idea of the relation and coherence of the modal aspects of meaning.

ethical, and aesthetic reason?[1] What *meaning* do you ascribe to the *principle of the origin* and to that of *continuity*, with which you intend to bridge the modal diversity of meaning referred to?

These questions are not to be evaded in philosophic thought! COHEN's system suggests to us, that the "principle of truth" („Grundsatz der Wahrheit") implies a *continuous* coherence between logos and ethos. Nonetheless, thought and volition are to have different meanings. Therefore, it is no use transferring the principles of "origin" and "continuity" from the "Logic of Pure Knowledge" to the "Ethics of Pure Will". The *coherence* in the *diversity of meaning* may not be sought in the *speciality of meaning*. To be sure one can strike on the anvil of the "unity of reason"[2]. But, as long as this unity is not shown to us in a totality *beyond the diversity* of meaning, implied in its different functions, the "unity of Reason" remains an ASYLUM IGNORANTIAE[3]. As soon as COHEN's principle of continuity itself is reduced to its origin, it turns out to be a principle with a

---

[1] COHEN himself recognizes this question as a *special* problem of philosophy. See his *Logic of pure Knowledge (Logik der reinen Erkenntnis)*, 3rd Ed., p. 17. Actually it is rather the *basic* problem of his philosophy, with respect to which only critical self-reflection as to his logicistic ground-Idea could bring clarity. For, apart from a transcendental ground-Idea, the unity of consciousness cannot be grasped philosophically.

[2] Remarkably we find this sort of mystification in the strongest degree in KANT, who in his criticism has contributed most toward the dissolution of this would-be unity in the dualism of *theoretical* and *practical* reason, which *in substance (essence)* he never bridged. In the Preface of the *Kr. der R. V.* (1st. Ed.) he writes: „In der Tat ist auch reine Vernunft eine so volkommene Einheit, dasz, wenn das Prinzip derselben auch nur zu einer einzigen aller der Fragen, die ihr durch ihre eigene Natur aufgegeben sind, unzureichend wäre, man dieses immerhin nur wegwerfen könnte, weil es alsdann auch keiner der übrigen mit voller Zuverlässigkeit gewachsen sein würde." ["Indeed, pure reason is a perfect unity to such an extent, that, if the principle presented by it should prove to be insufficient for the solution of even a single one of those questions to which the very nature of reason gives birth, we must reject it, as we could not be perfectly certain of its sufficiency in the case of the others"].

In the Preface, p. 19, of his *Grundl. zur Metaphysik der Sitten*, he speaks of „am Ende nur eine und dieselbe Vernunft, die blosz in der Anwendung unterschieden sein mag" ["ultimately it is one and the same Reason that may show diversity only in its application"].

[3] As in COHEN's expression: „Das Denken, das die Bewegung mit sich führt, verwandelt sich selbst in Wollen und Handlung." [*Ethics of Pure Will;* 4th Ed., p. 110: "Thinking in which movement is inherent, transforms itself into will and action."] *Ethik des Reinen Wollens*, 4th

special mathematical sense [1], which is absolutized to an transcendental Idea of the inter-modal coherence in the modal diversity of meaning! Here a supra-theoretical motive manifests itself and also determines the contents of COHEN's Idea of totality.

Theoretical thought remains imprisoned in the modal diversity of meaning and therefore does not become truly *philosophic thought*, so long as it not directed by a transcendental Idea of the totality which is dependent on a supra-theoretical basic-motive.

Being and Validity and the critical preliminary question as to the meaning of these concepts.

The so-called South West German School in neo-Kantian philosophy proceeds to introduce into philosophic thought the opposition between *being* and *validity*, *reality* and *value*. Behind this opposition there crops up anew the transcendental problem as to the mutual relations of modal speciality, inter-modal coherence, and totality of meaning. For the question arises: In what *sense* are *being* and *validity* understood here? Are they intended as transcendental logical determinations, originating from thought, as *basic categories*? If so, can a basic category of "being" in its transcendental-*logical* sense bridge the modal diversity of the different aspects which, even in an abstract naturalistic conception of empirical reality as defended by KANT, cannot be eliminated? In KANT's epistemology "reality" was only one of the "categories of modality". Is "validity" also to be understood in the sense of such a category? If so, can it bridge in this logical sense the fundamental diversity of meaning in the "realm of values"?

It is of no avail for RICKERT to reserve the term "meaning" exclusively for "culture", as a subjective relating of "reality" to "values". The fundamental philosophical distinction between "being" and "validity" pretends to have a meaning. The critical question is whether these "categories" embrace the totality of meaning of empirical reality and of the realm of values, respectively, or only their logical aspect.

Ed., p. 110. COHEN seeks the deeper unity in the „*Methode der Reinheit*", but this method can bridge the fundamental diversity of meaning only for a logicistic outlook.

[1] In fact derived from the infinitesimal calculus.

Prolegomena

Genericity of meaning versus totality of meaning.

If the category does not possess this totality of meaning, what then is its relation to the totality and to the coherence of meaning among the modal aspects? By ascribing a mere *generic meaning* to the "logical categories", I do not advance a single step.

Levelling of the modal diversity of meaning in the generic concept rests upon an uncritical misjudgment of the special meaning in the logical aspect.

In a special science, to be sure, one may form so-called generic concepts (class-, genus-concepts, etc.) in order to join together the individual phenomena *within* a special modal aspect of reality. But the irreducible *modal meaning* of the different aspects themselves does not permit itself to be levelled down logically by any generic concept. This levelling out always implies, that the specific meaning of the logical aspect is ignored. In theoretical thought every attempt by means of a "generic concept" to gloss over the diversity of meaning of the logical aspect of thought and the modal aspects set in opposition to it, betrays the influence of a transcendental ground-Idea. For, in such a generic concept, I ascribe to the special modal meaning of logic the power to bridge the modal diversity of meaning in the theoretical *gegenstand-relation*. This exceeds the limits of genuine logic and attributes to a pseudo-logical concept the function of a transcendental Idea of totality.

The most seductive way in which the transcendental ground-Idea of philosophy is masked is that of dialectical logic. This may finally be illustrated by the philosophical standpoint of another famous German thinker in respect to the relation of logic and reality.

The masking of the transcendental ground-Idea by the so-called dialectical logic. THEODOR LITT.

THEODOR LITT, who in this respect intends to continue the tradition of post-Kantian idealism, supposes, that he has found the Archimedean point of his philosophic thought in the "pure reflection" of theoretical thought on its own activity. In the course of his inquiries he proceeds to introduce a dialectical identity of the "thinking ego" (the "pure thought in its self-reflection") and the "concrete ego" (the ego as real individual "totality" of all its physical-psychical functions "in space and time").

However, in the critical consideration of this dialectical conception, we are obliged to raise the following questions: *In what sense* do you understand this "dialectical identity" and *in what sense* the "concrete ego"?

Then it appears forthwith, that the "dialectical identity" is intended in a transcendental-*logical* sense; for LITT teaches us: "In the unity of the thinking I and the concrete I, the former gains the mastery" [1].

The "thinking ego" is conceived here in the reflexive-logical sense of FICHTE's „Wissenschaftslehre". It is the "transcendental-logical subject of KANT's epistemology which has its "Gegenstand" in the "empirical ego in time and space", but, in a second reflexion should overcome this antithesis which in KANT was definitive. Only in "pure thought", according to LITT, does the "concrete ego" come to itself. For the latter does not transcend the former. The relation is just the reverse "It" (i.e. the concrete ego) "has the standpoint of possible self-assurance absolutely *beyond* itself, and is thus absolutely *not* „übergreifend" (i.e. capable to conceive the transcendental ego) [2].

The critical question is, however, whether the "pure" (i.e. abstracted) logical function of human thought can transcend the modal limits of its aspect in a dialectical way, and whether the deeper unity *beyond* the modal diversity of meaning can be of a dialectical-logic character. Here we again touch the transcendental problem of the "Archimedean point", discussed in our Introduction.

In this "Archimedean point" the modal diversity of meaning, which at first sight is confusing, must be overcome. For from this point our selfhood must direct the philosophical view of totality over the modal and typical diversity of meaning in its theoretical distinction.

In LITT, however, the theoretic relating of the modal diversity of meaning to its integral unity of root has become impossible as a result of the hidden dualism in his religious ground-motive. Therefore he introduces a *dialectical* idea of unity which must relate this modal diversity to the two antithetic motives, each of which for itself pretends to express an ultimate unity of meaning (scl. *nature and freedom*).

---

[1] „In der Einheit von denkendem und konkretem Ich eignet dem ersteren die übergreifende Macht."

[2] *Einleitung in die Philosophie* (1933), p. 162: „Es hat den Standort möglicher Selbstvergewisserung durchaus *jenseits* seiner selbst, ist also durchaus *nicht* übergreifend."

Modal diversity and radical identity of meaning. Logical identity has only modal meaning, PARMENIDES.

All *diversity* of meaning in temporal reality supposes a temporal *coherence* of meaning and the latter in its turn must again be the expression of a deeper *identity*. We have seen, that the transcendental Idea of coherence of meaning is the necessary basic denominator, under which I must theoretically bring the modal aspects in order to be able to *compare* them with one another in their diversity.

For if they were to have nothing *in common* with each other, they could not even be *distinguished* from one another. On our own standpoint, as I have previously observed, only the transcendental *Idea of time* can serve as such a basic denominator. For the cosmic order of time expresses itself alike in the modal structure *of all aspects, and brings them into indissoluble* coherence of meaning, without derogating from their mutual irreducibility.

But the temporal coherence of meaning of the aspects supposes their deeper identity in a religious unity of root. For we have seen, that without this latter, there would still be lacking the necessary *starting-point* for the comparison, and consequently for theoretical synthesis. The denominator of comparison cannot itself furnish us with this point of departure.

But the unity-and-identity, taken in its dialectical-*logical* sense, is not the unity-and-identity to which the transcendental ground-idea of philosophy can be directed.

For, the *logical* or *analytical* unity-and-identity, on which PARMENIDES supposed he could build his entire metaphysical doctrine of being, is not the unity-identity sought for *beyond the temporal diversity of meaning.*

It is only by a metaphysical identification of "pure" reflexive logical thought and being that LITT assumes a dialectical unity-and-identity of the "concrete ego" and the "transcendental logical ego".

Here LITT disagrees fundamentally with KANT but is in keeping with FICHTE and HEGEL. By means of a dialectical logic he attempts to overcome the dualism in his *hidden* starting-point: the dialectical ground-motive of nature and freedom. The "concrete ego" is conceived here as a "physical-psychical individual" belonging to the realm of nature. The "pure thinking ego", or the "reflexive-logical subject" is nothing but the theoretical expression of the freedom-motive, in the pure reflexive act of thought[1]. It has the free and autonomous power of opposing itself to the whole "concrete ego" which is dispersed in the diversity of its functions. It has also the sovereign power of transcending the modal limits of the logical aspect and its analytical laws. Consequently, it is identical with the "concrete ego", but identical in a *dialectical-logical* sense.

However, this dialectical Idea of unity-and-identity is a pseudo-logical one. It is nothing but a masked transcendental ground-Idea, expressing the supra-theoretical presuppositions of LITT's philosophy. It is conceived in an uncritical synthetic form, which in the transcendental process of critical self-reflection must necessarily be reduced to an antithetic one. For the dialectical ground-motive of *nature and freedom* does not allow of a real synthesis of its antagonistic components. Nevertheless, the freedom-motive has the inner tendency to absorb the opposite one, just as the motive of the domination of nature has the tendency to absorb the freedom-motive. This is also demonstrated

---

[1] See op. cit. p. 74: „Das seelische Leben so der umfassenden Kausalität des Naturgeschehens einordnen — das heiszt dieses Seelenleben aufs offenkundigste "vergegenständlichen". Geht man von diesem Aspekt in die Tiefen der Reflexion zurück, so sieht man die genannte Schwierigkeit alsbald in nichts zergehen. Denn einmal erweist sich hier die Ansicht, die das seelische Leben dem gegenständlichen Denken darbietet, als durchaus bedingt und der Korrektur sowohl fähig als auch bedürftig, womit an Stelle der „Freiheit" die angeblickte „Notwendigkeit" höchst zweifelhaft zu werden beginnt. Diese Anzweiflung aber verwandelt sich in Verneinung, sobald ein Weiteres bedacht wird: das unanfechtbarste Zeugnis dafür, das das seelische Leben der Erhebung über jede Art von „Notwendigkeit" fähig ist, liegt — in eben dem Denken selbst, das sich in der Reflexion seiner bewuszt wird... „Freiheit", die alle Verkettung von Ursache und Wirkung unter sich läszt, ist überall da verwirklicht, wo gedacht wird, also u.a.auch da, wo „Notwendigkeit", „Kausalität" gedacht wird." ["The inclusion of psychic life into the comprehensive causality of natural events is most manifestly objectivizing psychic life. If from this aspect we turn back to the depths of reflection, the difficulty just mentioned passes into nothingness. For here it appears, that the aspect that psychic life presents to objectivizing thought, is always and in every respect one of being conditioned and capable of correction as well as needing it, so that instead of "freedom" it is the so-called "necessity" which begins to be most doubtful. This doubt turns into a denial, as soon as a further thought presents itself: The most irrefutable evidence of the fact that psychic life is capable of transcending any kind of "necessity" is to be found in thought itself which becomes conscious of itself in reflection... "Freedom", leaving all manner of connection between cause and effect behind, is realized wherever there is thought, hence a.o. also there where "necessity", "causality" is thought."]

by LITT's important sociology, in which the pattern of thought of natural-science is completely replaced by a dialectical phenomenological one.

Dialectical logic is an uncritical attempt to solve the transcendental basic-problem of the theoretical synthesis. It intends to overcome the theoretical antithesis by a dialectical-logical Idea of unity, which turns out to be no unity at all. For LITT does not actually solve the transcendental problem concerning the unity in the root of the modal diversity of meaning in its theoretical distinction. He does not and cannot explain how the "pure thinking ego" and the "concrete ego" which is its theoretic opposite (Gegenstand), can be one and the same. This identity cannot be a logical one. For in this case the "gegenstand-relation" would be eliminated, whereas LITT wants to maintain this latter emphatically. Now we saw, that in default of a transcendental idea of the integral unity in the root of human selfhood — which is excluded by LITT's dialectical ground-motive —, dialectical logic furnishes philosophy with an apparently autonomous dialectic Idea of unity. However, the transcendental critique of philosophic thought does not permit itself to be led astray by theoretical dogmatism. Dialectic logic, no more than scholastic metaphysics, can replace it.

Logic itself is to be set by philosophy within the complex of problems involved in the relation between modal speciality, diversity, temporal coherence and totality of meaning.

Whoever does not want to fall into the uncritical error of logicism, should admit, that the logical aspect of thought is itself enclosed within the modal diversity and the inter-modal coherence of meaning and — at least in that respect — has no philosophic advantage above the other aspects. At this very point, the Biblical religious conception of the centre of human existence unfolds its full critical signification for philosophy.

LITT intends not only a *logical* but a *real* identity of the pure thinking and the concrete ego, in order to save the real identity of the selfhood in the antithesis of the gegenstand-relation.

However, he cannot accept the religious transcendence of the I-ness in respect to its pure logical thought. He holds to the opinion, that the ego by elevating itself to the abstracted function of "pure thought" has reached the ultimate limit of its inner possibilities [1].

---

[1] Op. cit. p. 162/3: „Damit ist schon gesagt, dasz das Ich erst, indem es

Consequently, according to him, the real identity of the "concrete" and the "pure thinking" ego must be a dialectical-logical one, because the concrete ego "comes to itself" only in pure reflexive thought. This is a dialectical-metaphysical logicism, although LITT emphatically rejects the metaphysical Aristotelian conception of pure thought as a substance which is absolutely separate from the "concrete ego".

§ 7 - THE TRANSCENDENTAL GROUND-IDEA AS HYPOTHESIS OF PHILOSOPHY

The theoretical character of the transcendental ground-Idea and its relation to naïve experience.

The question may now be raised, why I conceived the contents of the transcendental ground-Idea of philosophy only as a fundamental determination of the relation between origin, totality and modal diversity of meaning in the coherence of the different modal aspects. Is this not much too abstract a conception of this basic Idea?

We have seen, that naïve experience has not yet arrived at the level of theoretical analysis of the different modalities of meaning; therefore it does not explicitly conceive the modal aspects of temporal reality. Reality presents itself to the pre-theoretic view exclusively in the typical total-structures of individuality, which encompass all modal aspects together; but the latter are not conceived here in theoretical distinction. Now it appeared, that naïve experience is in no way inconsequential for philosophy. Therefore, it seems insufficient to point the transcendental ground-Idea only toward the theoretical anti-thesis of the modal aspects of temporal reality.

---

sich zum Ich des reinen Denkens zuspitzt und emporsteigt, das Äuszerste und Letzte seiner inneren Möglichkeiten erreicht: denn erst als solches wird es Subjekt der Reflexion und damit mächtig der „übergreifenden" Denktat. In seinen Gesichtskreis fällt von nun an grundsätzlich alles, was das konkrete Ich nur immer tun und erleiden mag; es ist im Besitz der Souveränität, die es ihm gestattet, sich dem Ganzen seines konkreten Erlebens, dieses sein denkendes Tun eingeschlossen, gegenüberzustellen." ["This is to say that only in rarefying and elevating itself into the -I- of pure thought can the -I- reach the utmost limits and the last of its inner possibilities — for only as such does it become the subject of reflection and consequently able to "comprehensive" thinking. Everything that the concrete -I- can ever do or suffer, falls within its range of vision; it is in possession of the sovereignty that enables it to oppose to itself the whole of its concrete experience, that of its thinking act included."]

Every philosophic view of empirical reality ought to be confronted with the datum of naïve experience in order to test its ability to account for this datum in a satisfying manner. Therefore, is it not also necessary to direct the contents of the transcendental ground-Idea toward the diversity and coherence of meaning in the typical structures of individuality?

The datum of naïve experience as a philosophical problem.

This question I will answer as follows.

Philosophy must convert the datum of naïve experience into a fundamental philosophic problem. For it is evident, that by maintaining the attitude of naïve experience one would never be able to account for that datum philosophically. Consequently, since philosophy is bound to the theoretic attitude of thought, its transcendental ground-Idea is also bound to the theoretical gegenstand-relation in which temporal reality is set asunder in its modal aspects.

Therefore, philosophy cannot examine the typical structures of individual totality without a theoretical analysis of their given unity. These structures, too, must be made a philosophical problem, and this problem can be no other but that of their temporal unity in the modal diversity of meaning, manifesting itself in the different aspects of reality. Their typical character and their relation to concrete individuality does not derogate from this state of affairs.

Besides, the transcendental ground-Idea of meaning implies a relation to the cosmonomic side as well as to the factual subject-side of temporal reality. And the latter is by nature individual. In other words, this transcendental Idea is also a ground-Idea of type and individuality, but it is always bound to the theoretical gegenstand-relation.

The naïve concept of the thing and the special scientific concept of function.

On the level of modern scientific thought the naïve concept of the thing is in the process of being broken up into functional concepts. This is done in order to gain knowledge of the functional coherence of the phenomena within a special modal aspect. Under the influence of the classic Humanistic ideal of science, which we shall examine presently in detail, there was even an evident tendency to eliminate the typical structures of individuality and to dissolve the entire empirical reality into a continuous functional system of causal relations. This was, to be sure, an absolutizing of the scientific concept of function and it could only lead philosophical thought astray. However, this consideration does not derogate from the value of the concept of function as such.

The gain accruing from its application in the different branches of science was enormous. One by one, the modal aspects of temporal reality, especially the mathematical and physical ones, opened to penetrating scientific analysis the secret of their immanent functional relations and laws.

But the more deeply special scientific thought penetrated into its "Gegenstand" (i.e. the abstracted special aspect of reality which limits its field of research), the more sharply was revealed the fundamental deficiency of theoretical thought in comparison with naïve experience.

By being bound to a special scientific viewpoint, a special science loses the vision of the whole with respect to empirical reality, and consequently the integral empirical reality itself is lost from its grasp. If special science were to be entirely autonomous, this void could never be filled and special science would be impossible for lack of a veritable view of reality. For temporal reality is not given in abstracted modal aspects; it does not give itself „*gegenständlich*". Special science is never in a position to account for our naïve experience of things; it cannot even render an account of its own possibility.

Naïve experience has an integral vision of the whole, so far as it conceives of temporal things and events in their typical structures of individual totality. Furthermore, so far as it is rooted in the ground-motive of the Christian religion, naïve experience also has the radical and integral view of temporal reality by which the latter is concentrically conceived in its true religious root and in its relation to its true Origin. But its view of the whole is a naïve one, which for lack of a theoretical insight into the modal diversity of meaning does not satisfy the requirements of the transcendental ground-Idea as hypothesis of philosophic thought. The concrete unity of things is not a problem to naïve experience.

Philosophy, special science, and naïve experience.

Only philosophy has the task of grasping in the view of totality the different modal aspects of meaning as they are set asunder by theoretic thought. In this way, philosophy has to account for both naïve experience and special science.

Therefore, even where naïve experience is made into a theoretic problem of philosophy, the transcendental ground-Idea of the latter can have no other contents but that which we have found in our transcendental critique.

Methodically, philosophic inquiry as to the modal structures of the abstracted aspects of temporal reality must necessarily *precede* the philosophic analysis of the typical structures of individual totality. For the latter imply the theoretical problem of the structural temporal unity in the diversity of its modal aspects. Special science, as such, in its different branches can neither have an autonomous conception of the modal structures of the different aspects nor of the typical structures of individual totality.

For, a theoretical analysis of these temporal structures requires the theoretic view of totality which is in the nature of the case a philosophic one.

The modal structure of a special aspect is a temporal unity in a diversity of modal structural moments, which can display their modal meaning only in their structural coherence and totality. Besides, we have seen, that within the modal structure of a special aspect there is expressed the inter-modal coherence of cosmic time-order, so that the former cannot be conceived of theoretically without a transcendental idea of its coherence with all other modal aspects and of the radical unity of the modal diversity of meaning. Special sciences — with the exception of pure mathematics — are pointed to the examination of the functional coherence as well as the typical character (and in diffferent branches of science also the individuality) of transitory phenomena *within* a special modal aspect of temporal reality. The very modal structures of temporal reality are not to be conceived theoretically by means of special scientific concepts, which in their turn must be made a philosophic problem. When, for instance, EINSTEIN's theory of relativity handles the concepts of time and space, the special synthetic meaning of these concepts in relation to those of other special sciences as biology, psychology, history, etc. remains hidden.

This meaning can be made clear only in a philosophic inquiry as to the modal structure of the physical aspect, which requires the theoretical view of totality.

Nevertheless, a philosophic conception of this modal structure is an implicit hypothesis of physics, because its special branch of inquiry is limited in principle by the structure of the physical aspect of experience and empirical reality.

"Reflexive" thought versus "objective" thought in recent philosophy. The confusion of "object" and "Gegenstand" in this opposition.

It is not right, that philosophy must or can abandon the antithetic relation (gegenstand-relation) which we found to be inherent in the theoretic attitude of thought. This is supposed by that current in modern immanence-philosophy which opposes philosophy (as reflexive thought, introverted to the "transcendental logical subject of pure thinking") to all „gegenständliches Denken". This latter should be the "naïve" manner of thought proper to special science, entirely lost in the study of its "objects" without reflecting about the activity of the pure thinking ego, which can never be made into a "Gegenstand". We have met this conception of the difference between philosophical and "objective" scientific thought in the discussion of THEODOR LITT's standpoint as to the relation of "thinking ego" and "concrete ego".

It is evident, that it is based upon a fatal confusion of "object" and "Gegenstand" and of the really "naïve" and the theoretical attitudes of thought. In fact, it appeared, that LITT's "pure thinking ego" could not be detached from the *gegenstand-relation*.

What distinguishes philosophy from special science cannot be the abandoning of the antithetical relation, but rather the focusing (of the former) towards the totality and unity in the root of temporal meaning. We have seen, that this concentric direction of theoretic thought is possible only by means of truly critical self-reflection which must break through the theoretic horizon in order to gain religious self-knowledge.

The transcendental ground-Idea as hypothesis of philosophy.

Consequently, we arrive again and again at the transcendental ground-Idea as the real *hypothesis* of philosophic thought. The supposition, that philosophy might refrain from giving an account of the conditions of its possibility has appeared to be uncritical in the highest degree.

In the first place, philosophy itself requires its transcendental foundation, its ὑπόθεσις. A vicious circle is involved in making special science a philosophic (epistemological) problem, while withdrawing from a critical consideration of the pre-suppositions of philosophical thought itself. For the main transcendental problem involved in special science, viz. the possibility of an inter-modal synthesis of meaning, is implied a fortiori in philosophic thought. The latter is immediately confronted at every stage of its inquiry with the fundamental problems concerning the relation of origin, totality, modal diversity, and inter-modal coherence of meaning.

Now since philosophic thought cannot become its own "Gegenstand", philosophy, in the basic critical question as to its own possibility, encounters its immanent limits within cosmic time. These limits can be accounted for only in the concentric direction of theoretical thought to its supra-theoretic pre-suppositions.

Truly *reflexive* thought, therefore, is characterized by the critical self-reflection as to the transcendental ground-Idea of philosophy, in which philosophic thought points beyond and above itself toward its own apriori conditions within and beyond cosmic time.

As soon as reflexive theoretic thought is conceived of as a "free" act which transcends all structural limits, because the latter can belong only to the "gegenständliche" world, we arrive once more at the illusory conception of the sovereignty and autonomy of philosophic reflection.

The pitfall in this conception appeared to be the identification of *"Gegenstand"* and "temporal reality", due to the lack of insight into the true character of the "gegenstand-relation" and of cosmic time as hypothesis of the latter. The structural limits of philosophic thought transcend the gegenstand-relation, because they are founded in cosmic time, which cannot be determined by thought, since it is the very pre-supposition of the latter.

Only in reflection on its transcendental ground-Idea is philosophy urged on to its insurmountable apriori limits which give philosophic thought its ultimate well-defined character in the universal cosmic coherence of meaning. It is not philosophic thought that determines its apriori conditions in self-sufficiency, but the very reverse: philosophic thought is determined and limited by its transcendental focusing toward its presupposita. It is limited by being bound to its intentional as well as to its ontical structure in cosmic time.

In the basic Idea of philosophy we are engaged in reflection *while thinking* to the limits of philosophic thought. This Idea is therefore in the full sense of the word, a *limiting*-concept "par excellence", the final transcendental *foundation* or ὑπόθεσις of philosophy, in which we retire into ourselves when thinking. We can reflect critically upon the limits of philosophic thought, only because *in our selfhood* we transcend them as limits of *philosophic* knowledge. The pre-supposita of philosophy, toward which the basic idea of philosophy points, are themselves infinitely more than *Idea*. Idealism, which elevates the Idea itself as totality of meaning, is possible only upon the immanence-standpoint. But its *transcendental foundation*, its philosophic *ground-Idea* continues to point *beyond the Idea* to that which exceeds the transcendental limits of philosophy, inasmuch as it alone *makes philosophic idealism possible*. The immanence-standpoint merely prevents philosophic thought from proceeding to this last stage of critical self-reflection.

The relation of transcendent and transcendental points of view and the original meaning of the transcendental motive.

We can thus provisionally summarize our point of view with reference to the limits of philosophy:

The religious pre-suppositon of philosophy, toward which the ground-Idea as transcendental foundation of philosophy is directed in its contents, toward which as Idea it *points*, is of a *transcendent* nature, whereas philosophic thought is itself of a *transcendental* character. The choice of the Archimedean point necessarily crosses the boundary line of the temporal coherence of our world. Philosophy itself, *though directed* by its ground-Idea, remains within this boundary line, *because it is possible only by virtue of the temporal order of the world.*

Transcendent and *transcendental*, taken in this sense, are thus no "either-or". For the actually transcendental direction of theoretic thought pre-supposes the transcendent and central sphere of our consciousness from which this direction starts, since this starting-point is not be found in theoretic thought itself.

Only in this view as to the relation of transcendent and transcendental conditions of philosophy is the original *critical meaning* of transcendental thought given its due.

KANT's opinion concerning the transcendental Ideas. Why did KANT fail to conceive of these Ideas as ὑπόθεσις, of his critiques.

The real transcendental direction of KANT's epistemology in this original critical sense does not disclose itself until the necessary function of the transcendental Ideas of theoretical reason are discussed in the "transcendental dialectic". Here KANT clearly explains, that these Ideas point to an absolute totality which transcends the immanent limits of "objective experience", and at the same time in their theoretical knowledge remain bound to the immanent limits of theoretical knowledge itself. Here, also emerge the three transcendental Ideas which in their triunity must be considered as the transcendental ground-Idea and the real ὑπόθεσις of every possible philosophy, namely, the Idea of the universe which — although in KANT restricted to the sphere of "nature" — corresponds to our Idea of the integral coherence of meaning in cosmic time, the Idea of the ultimate unity of human selfhood and that of the absolute Origin (Urwesen).

Nevertheless, KANT does not accept these transcendental Ideas in their triunity as the real hypothesis of his "critical" philosophy. He does not see that, in their very theoretical use, they must have a real content which necessarily depends upon supra-theoretic pre-suppositions differing in accordance with the religious ground-motives of theoretic thought. He restricted their significance theoretically to a purely formal-logical one; they have, according to him, only a regulative, systematic function in respect to the use of the logical concepts (categories) which are related apriori to sensory experience. Why did KANT at this critical point abandon the real transcendental motive?

Naturally one could answer: because he held to the autonomy of theoretic thought, and this would not be incorrect. But the deeper reason is to be found in the fact that he had become aware of the unbridgeable antithesis in the *ground-motive of nature and freedom,* and now rejected every attempt at dialectical synthesis.

Nevertheless, he did not see, that his theoretical epistemology itself remained bound to a transcendental ground-Idea, whose contents were determined by this very religious basic motive. His conception of the autonomy and spontaneity of the transcendental logical function of thought is doubtless ruled by the Humanistic freedom-motive, whereas the nature-motive finds clear expression in his conception of the purely receptive character of the sensory function of experience, and of its subjection to the causal determinations of science. KANT accepted the synthesis between natural necessity and freedom in his epistemological conception concerning the apriori relatedness of the transcendental categories to sensory experience, whereas he rejected this synthesis in his ethics. Nevertheless, we shall see in the more detailed investigation of his theory of knowledge, that he could not account for the possibility of the synthesis between the logical and the sensory function of consciousness, because of his dualistic starting-point. This is consequently not to be explained in terms of a purely theoretical critique of human knowledge. But it is dependent on the fundamental dualism in his religious ground-motive.

> It was FICHTE who tried to remove the difficulties involved in the Kantian dualistic conception.

In the first edition of his „Wissenschaftslehre", FICHTE made "*practical* freedom" the hypothesis of his theoretical epistemology and introduced a dialectical logic for the sake of bridging the Kantian gulf between epistemology and ethics. This, too, is not to be understood from a purely theoretical standpoint, but only from FICHTE's new conception of the transcendental ground-Idea of Humanistic thought. In this conception the postulate of continuity, implied in the freedom-motive, broke through the boundaries which in the Kantian conception were accepted with respect to the theoretical use of the transcendental Idea of freedom.

Anyhow, the very transcendental motive implies the focusing of theoretic thought by self-reflection on its transcendental ground-Idea which points beyond and above its own theoretical limits to its transcendent pre-supposita.

In KANT's "dialectic of pure reason" the transcendental Ideas within their theoretical limits do point, indeed, to a transcendent realm of the "noumenon", in which at least the Ideas of free autonomous will and of God have "practical reality". KANT did not accept limits of theoretical thought which are not set by thought itself, except its being bound to sensory perception. The transcendental Idea of freedom in its dialectical relation to the category of causality is, in fact, the *hypothesis* of his transcendental logic, although he did not acknowledge it as such. This is the same Idea which in KANT's "Critique of Practical

Reason" obtains "practical, reality" for "reasonable belief".

If this essential function of the transcendental idea as *hypothesis* in its pointing beyond the limits of theoretical thought is lost sight of, the very transcendental motive hidden in KANT's criticism cannot be understood.

The decline of the transcendental motive in the Marburg methodological logicism, in LITT's conception of reflexive thought, and in HUSSERL's "egology".

In the (so-called critical) logicistic idealism of the Marburg School this motive fades away into the merely methodological postulate of logical purity and continuity in the system of knowledge.

When COHEN says, that the transcendental Idea is nothing but the "self-consciousness of the (logical) concept", this pronouncement lacks the very transcendental meaning of KANT's conception, because in COHEN, the pointing of this Idea towards a transcendent sphere has disappeared. The tendency toward the origin on the part of philosophic thought, which in his „*Logik des Ursprungs*" (Logic of Origin) is very evident, here fails to lead to critical self-reflection in the true sense of the word. The same must be said with respect to LITT's conception of the pure self-reflection of theoretical thought and with respect to EDMUND HUSSERL's so-called *"ego-logy"*, both of which exclude the existence of limits for the "transcendental cogito" ("I think"). No matter how these latter conceptions of the "cogito" may differ from one another, both deny the transcendence of the ego in respect to transcendental thought or transcendental (phenomenologically purified) consciousness, respectively. The very transcendental Idea, pointing beyond and above itself to the pre-suppositions of philosophical thought, has no sense here.

The basic Idea of philosophy remains a subjective ὑπόθεσις. The criterion of truth and relativism.

In its entire transcendental function the basic Idea of philosophy remains only a *subjective* — although necessary — ὑπόθεσις (hypothesis) of philosophy. This hypothesis may not dominate truth in a relativistic fashion. The truth of this hypothesis, on the contrary, is *accountable* to the forum of an ultimate judge.

In the very inquiry as to the universally-valid criterion of truth, we shall have to fight the decisive battle with those currents in immanence-philosophy which suppose, that only the immanence-standpoint guarantees such a criterion.

If we succeed in proving, that it is in fact the immanence-standpoint that leads to a complete relativizing of this standard, then these currents in the immanence-philosophy, by way of immanent criticism, are ejected from their position as guardians of "objective truth".

In the present context, in which we are discussing the necessary apriori function of the basic Idea of philosophy, we intend only by anticipation to cut off the misunderstanding to the effect that our philosophy would turn over the criterion of truth to relativism.

The transcendental limits of philosophy and the criterion of speculative metaphysics.

Philosophic thought, in its transcendental direction toward the totality and Origin of meaning, remains bound to cosmic time. Cosmic time is its pre-supposition, and in this time, philosophy is bound to a cosmic order (to be explained later).

Every philosophy which fails to appreciate this limit, necessarily falls into *speculative metaphysics*. In all its varieties, the latter characteristically seeks the absolute and supra-temporal *within* the cosmic time-order through the absolutizing of special modes of meaning.

In the above mentioned sense, every form of absolutizing the theoretical-logical function of thought is speculative-metaphysical. A speculative metaphysical character also belongs to the position that the laws of special modal aspects of our cosmos, (e.g. laws of number, space, logic, morality, aesthetics) possess absolute universal validity, even for God. What we have said applies both to the ancient Platonic doctrine of Ideas and to the modern theory of absolute values, the doctrine of "truths in themselves" and "Sätze an sich", and the "absolute consciousness" in HUSSERL's phenomenology. It is equally applicable to the traditional metaphysical doctrine of the immortal soul (viz. as complex of truly temporal functions!). The modern hypostatization of the „Geist" in the higher (non-sensory) psychical, logical, and post-logical functions of mental acts is also speculative and metaphysical irrespective as to whether this hypostatization unfolds itself in a rationalist or irrationalist sense.

All such speculative and consequently uncritical theories fail to appreciate the immanent limits of philosophic thought. They rest upon an absolutizing of modal aspects abstracted by theoretical thought from the temporal coherence of meaning. They disturb the absolutized realm of meaning by ascribing to it the mode of subsistence of the 'Ἀρχή, regardless of whether this mode of subsistence is thought of as "being" or as non-substantial actuality, or as "validity" and regardless of whether the absolutizing respects the actual-individual *subject-side* or indeed the *cosmonomic side* of the special realm of meaning. When we proceed to examine more closely the inseparable coherence of all special aspects of meaning of our temporal cosmos, the inner hollowness of such metaphysical speculations will become completely clear to us.

CALVIN's verdict against this metaphysics.

CALVIN's judgment: "DEUS LEGIBUS SOLUTUS EST, SED NON EXLEX", ("God is not subject to the laws, but not arbitrary") touches the foundations of all speculative philosophy by laying bare the limits of human reason set for it by God in His temporal world-order. This is the alpha and omega of all philosophy that strives to adopt a critical position not in name but in fact.

I have laid all emphasis upon the transcendental character of authentic critical philosophy, because I wish to cut off at the root the interference of speculative metaphysics in the affairs of the Christian religion. An authentic critical philosophy is aware of its being bound to the cosmic time-order. It only points beyond and above this boundary line to its pre-supposita. Its task, worthy of God's human creation, is great; yet it is modest and does not elevate human reason to the throne of God.

§ 8 - THE TRANSCENDENTAL GROUND-IDEA OF PHILOSOPHY AS COSMONOMIC IDEA (WETSIDEE)

The Origin of this terminology.

From the start, I have introduced the Dutch term *wetsidee (idea legis)* for the transcendental ground-Idea or basic Idea of philosophy. The best English term corresponding to it seems to be "cosmonomic Idea", since the word "law" used without further specification would evoke a special juridical sense which, of course, cannot be meant here.

This term was formed by me, when I was particularly struck by the fact that different systems of ancient, medieval and modern philosophy (like that of LEIBNIZ) *expressly* oriented philosophic thought to the Idea of a divine world-order, which was qualified as lex naturalis, lex aeterna, harmonia praestabilita, etc.

In this cosmonomic Idea, which implied a transcendental Idea of subjectivity, an apriori position was actually chosen with respect to the transcendental basic problems of philosophic thought.

In the systems we have in mind this cosmonomic Idea was generally conceived of in a large measure in a rationalistic and metaphysical manner. Hence it became a very attractive task to show, that each authentic system of philosophy is actually *grounded* in a cosmonomic Idea of this or that type, even when its author does not account for it; and the execution of the task intended here was bound to succeed. For it is not possible, that philosophic thought, which is intrinsically subjected to the temporal world-order, should not be burdened with an apriori view as to the origin and totality of meaning of this cosmic order and its correlative *subject*. And philosophy must have an apriori view with respect to the mutual relation and coherence of the different aspects of meaning in which the divine order and its subject disclose themselves.

Objections against the term "cosmonomic Idea" and the grounds for maintaining it.

Yet it may not be denied, that the choice of the term "cosmonomic Idea" can lead to misunderstanding.

Thus Dr H. G. STOKER, professor of philosophy at the University of Potchefstroom, in his interesting writings, *The New Philosophy at the Free University* (1933) and *The philosophy of the Idea of Creation* (1933), thought he had to contrast the cosmonomic Idea as a narrower basic Idea with the Idea of creation as the all-embracing. Later on the famous Dutch philosopher and scientist Dr PHILIP KOHNSTAMM joined this opinion after his transition to the philosophy of the cosmonomic Idea.

Nevertheless, there are special reasons for maintaining the first term as a designation for the transcendental basic Idea of philosophy. In the first place, in pointing to the *preliminary questions* of philosophic thought, the basic Idea of philosophy must be so conceived, that it actually catches the eye as a necessary condition for *every philosophic system*. This implies, that the universal term by which this basic Idea is designated may not include special contents derived from the ground-motive of the Christian religion. The determination of the *contents* of the transcendental basic Idea is to be a subject of subsequent discussion.

A cosmonomic Idea is actually at the basis of every philosophical system. On the other hand, an Idea of creation will be rejected as a transcendental basic Idea of philosophy by each thinker who denies creation, or in any case supposes, that it must be eliminated from philosophic thought.

Besides, if one wants to determine the *contents* of the *Christian* basic Idea for philosophic thought, the term "Idea of creation" is certainly insufficient to this end.

For in the central motive of Christian religion, which dominates these contents, the fall and redemption through Jesus Christ in the community of the Holy Ghost also play an essential rôle.

In the second place the term "cosmonomic Idea" has in its favour the fact, that in its pointing to the origin and meaning of the cosmic *nomos* or order, and to its relation to *subjectivity*, it gives expression from the outset to the *limiting* character of the basic transcendental Idea.

For the *nomos* is, as even SOCRATES argued in PLATO's famous dialogue *Philebus,* EX ORIGINE, *limitation* of a subject.

Viewed thus, the term "cosmonomic Idea", because of its critical focusing of the preliminary questions concerning meaning (in its origin, totality, and modal diversity) toward the relation of the cosmic order (nomos) and its subject, really designates the central criterion for the fundamental discrimination of the different starting-points and trends in philosophy. In the transcendental basic Idea of cosmic order there runs the boundary line between the immanence-philosophy in all its nuances and the Christian-transcendence position in philosophy. It is here that the criterion for truly *transcendental* philosophy resides, which recognizes its immanent cosmonomic boundaries, and speculative metaphysics, which supposes it can transgress the latter. Here, within immanence-philosophy is to be found the criterion of rationalism which absolutizes the natural and ethical laws at the expense of individual subjectivity, and irrationalism which, on the contrary, attempts to reduce the nomos to a dependent function of individual creative subjectivity.

Finally the misunderstanding as to the import of the term "cosmonomic Idea" may easily be cut off by a short explanation of its meaning.

Considered from the linguistic point of view, it may appear to refer only to the *nomos-side* of the cosmos. However, it actually occupies a position just as much with reference to the *subject-side* of reality in all its individuality. For the cosmic *"nomos"* has meaning only in indissoluble correlation with the *subject-side* of the cosmos.

In other words, the cosmonomic Idea implies the *Idea of the subject,* which points toward the *factual-side of reality* according to the basic relation among totality, diversity and coherence of meaning.

For the rest, I can attach no very great value to a discussion about the name that is to be given to the transcendental basic Idea of philosophy. In the last analysis, what matters is not the *term,* but that which is *signified* by it.

Let anyone then who has an objection against the term "cosmonomic Idea" avoid it and use the term "transcendental ground-Idea" or "transcendental basic Idea".

In the Netherlands, however, it has become quite current to indicate this whole philosophic movement by the term „Wijsbegeerte der Wetsidee" (Philosophy of the cosmonomic Idea) [1].

As yet the question raised especially by STOKER (who otherwise accepts the philosophy of the cosmonomic Idea) remains open as to whether created reality is not more than *meaning*.

Misunderstanding of the philosophy of the cosmonomic Idea as meaning-idealism.

Here there is the threat of a possible misunderstanding to the effect that the philosophy of the cosmonomic Idea, in its concentration upon the problem of meaning might drift into the water of an "idealism of meaning" (STOKER). In this context, I am not yet able to cut off this serious misunderstanding by the roots. To this end it is first necessary to confront our conception of meaning with that of immanence-philosophy.

From the start, however, our inquiries should make clear the ultimate character of meaning as the mode of reality of the

---

[1] *Translator's Note.* The author is referring to a school of philosophy which has developed in the Netherlands and elsewhere, and which was inspired by the publication of the Dutch edition of this work in 1935-36. This school has already exerted influence in Holland and special chairs devoted to the study of the *Philosophy of the Cosmonomic Idea* have been established at the Universities of Utrecht, Leiden, Groningen, at the School of Economics in Rotterdam, and the Technical School at Delft. D. H. F.

whole of creation, which finds no rest in itself. Meaning-idealism, as we are able to note it, for example, in RICKERT, issues from a distinction between meaning (*Sinn*) ascribed to reality *subjectively* by the absolutized transcendental consciousness by means of reference to values („Wertbeziehung"), and reality as such that is meaningless in itself. But RICKERT views "reality" only in the abstract sense of its psycho-physical aspects. From our point of view, meaning is universally proper to all created things as their restless *mode of existence*. As *meaning*, reality points toward its Origin, the Creator, without Whom the creature sinks into nothingness.

It is objected, that *meaning* cannot *live, act,* or *move*. But is not this life, this action, this movement, with respect to the mode of existence of created reality, itself meaning, pointing beyond itself, not *coming to rest in itself?* Only God's Being is not *meaning,* because He alone exists by and through Himself.

Hence, even the *totality* of meaning, which transcends philosophic thought, necessarily has its correlate in the Being of the Ἀρχή and in every transcendental basic Idea a position is taken with reference to this Ἀρχή.

In fact, nobody who speaks about modal aspects of reality, or even about concrete things, can understand them otherwise than in their *meaning,* that is in their relative mode of reality which points to their temporal coherence, to a totality in the root, and to the Origin of all relative things. If the pre-logical aspects of temporal reality were not aspects of *meaning,* standing in relation to the logical aspect, then thought could not even form a *concept* of them.

Such is the preliminary justification of our terminology.

Cosmonomic Idea, modal concept of laws and modal concept of subject and object.

The special modal concepts of laws and of subject and object used in the different branches of science depend upon the cosmonomic Idea in its broad import, including the transcendental Idea of subjectivity and objectivity.

The modal concepts of laws and of subject and object are essentially limited to a special aspect. Unlike the cosmonomic Idea, these modal concepts do not in themselves point beyond the diversity of meaning toward the transcendent origin and totality. But, whatever special meaning these concepts may possess, according to the modal aspects of reality comprehended by theoretical thought, they are always dependent upon a cosmonomic Idea.

The dependence of the modal concepts of law, subject and object upon the cosmonomic Idea.

In pure mathematics, for example, the logicistic trend conceives of the numerical and spatial laws as purely analytical, and the series of real numbers is considered to be continuous by reason of the logical continuity of the principle of progression; this concept of mathematical laws is grounded on a cosmonomic Idea of a logicist and rationalist type. The mechanist trend in biology conceives of the special laws of organic life merely as physical-chemical ones; this concept of biotic law is entirely dependent on a cosmonomic Idea founded upon the deterministic Humanist ideal of science in its classical form.

In the so-called „*reine Rechtslehre*" (pure theory of law) of the neo-Kantian scholar HANS KELSEN, the legal rule is identified with a logical judgment in the form: "If a... there ought to be b" and the juridical subject and its subjective right are dissolved into a logical complex of legal rules; this juridical concept of law is grounded on a cosmonomic Idea of a dualistic Humanistic type: according to this Idea there is an unbridgeable gulf between two ultimate kinds of laws, namely natural laws and norms, originating from fundamentally different logical categories of transcendental thought which "create" the scientific fields of research. This dualistic cosmonomic Idea is ruled by the dialectical ground-motive of nature and freedom in a typical antithetic conception which, however, does not agree with the genuine Kantian view.

Besides, it may be observed, that the three special scientific concepts of laws, mentioned above, are of a rationalistic type: the subject-side of reality within the special modal aspects is reduced to the nomos-side.

The laws of the special aspects concerned in biological and juridical investigation are conceived of in a purely *functionalistic sense*. There is no room here for *typical* laws corresponding to the structures of individuality [1]. This, too, finds its ground in

---

[1] In pure mathematics the typical structures of individuality are, of course, not yet in order, because typical numerical and spatial relations are to be found only in concrete reality.

Nevertheless, the question concerning the relation between the law-side and the subject-side of the numerical and spatial aspects cannot be eliminated in pure mathematics. Numbers and spatial figures are subject

the cosmonomic Idea which lies at the base of these special scientific concepts.

We shall return to this state of affairs in a later context.

§ 9 - THE SYMBOL OF THE REFRACTION OF LIGHT. THE COSMIC ORDER OF TIME AND THE COSMOLOGICAL PRINCIPLE OF SOVEREIGNTY IN ITS PROPER ORBIT. THE MODAL ASPECTS OF REALITY AS MODAL LAW-SPHERES

Now what positive content does the transcendental ground-Idea of philosophy receive from the central motive of the Christian religion?

The Archimedean point of philosophy is chosen in the new root of mankind in Christ, in which by regeneration we have part in our reborn selfhood.

The lex as boundary between the "Being" of God and the "meaning" of the creation.

The *totality of meaning* of our whole temporal cosmos is to be found in Christ, with respect to His human nature, as the *root* of the reborn human race. In Him the *heart*, out of which are the issues of life, confesses the Sovereignty of God, the Creator, over everything created. In Christ the heart bows under the lex (in its central religious unity and its temporal diversity, which originates in the Creator's holy will), as the *universal boundary (which cannot be transgressed)* between the *Being* of God and the *meaning* of His creation [1]. The transcendent

---

to their proper laws, and they may not be identified with or reduced to the latter. This distinction is the subject of the famous problem concerning the so-called "actual infinity" in pure mathematics. The principle of progression is a mathematical *law* which holds good for an infinite series of numbers or spatial figures. But the infinite itself cannot be made into an actual number.

[1] From the theological side some have raised an objection against the conception of the lex as the *boundary* between God and the creation. This objection can arise only from a misunderstanding. The term "boundary" merely intends to indicate an essential distinction between God and the creature with respect to their relation to the lex.

As sovereign Origin, God is not *subjected* to the law. On the contrary this *subjectedness* is the very characteristic of all that which has been created, the existence of which is limited and determined by the law. Christ Jesus also, with respect to His human nature, was *under* the law, but not with respect to His Divine nature.

But if every creature is *under* the law, then the limit which the latter sets for the creature's existence can never be transgressed.

CALVIN has expressed the same conception as to the relationship of

totality of meaning of our cosmos exists only in the religious relation of dependence upon the absolute *Being* of God. It is thus no *eidos* in the sense of the speculative Platonic metaphysics, no *being* set by itself, but it remains in the ex-sistential mode of *meaning* which points beyond itself and is not sufficient to itself.

Sin is the revolt against the Sovereign of our cosmos. It is the *apostasy* from the fulness of meaning and the deifying, the absolutizing of *meaning*, to the level of God's *Being*. Our temporal world, in its temporal diversity and coherence of meaning, is in the order of God's creation bound to the religious root of mankind. Apart from this root it has no meaning and so no reality. Hence the apostasy in the heart, in the religious root of the temporal world signified the apostasy of the entire temporal creation, which was concentrated in mankind.

Thus the disruption of the fall permeated all temporal aspects of meaning of cosmic reality. There is no single one of them that is excepted in this respect, neither the pre-logical aspects of temporal reality, nor the logical, nor the post-logical ones.

This becomes evident, as soon as we have seen, that they are fitted by the cosmic time-order in an indissoluble coherence of meaning which is related to a radical religious unity. The semblance of the contrary can only originate, when we have lost sight of this coherence.

The logical function of thought in apostasy.

In this context the Biblical conception must be especially maintained against every effort to exempt the logical function from the fall. For in every effort in this direction Christian thought leaves open a wide door of entry to the dialectical ground-motives of immanence-philosophy. We shall return to this point in a later context.

By the fall of man, human thought (νοῦς), according to St Paul's word, has become νοῦς τῆς σαρκός, the "carnal mind" (Colos. II : 18), for it does not exist apart from its apostate religious root. And thought includes its logical function.

Of course the logical *laws of thought* or the modal structural law of the logical aspect are not affected by sin. The effects of

---

God to the law in his earlier quoted statement "Deus legibus solutus est, sed non exlex"; in which he intended at the same time to refute any notion that God's sovereignty is despotic arbitrariness.

apostasy disclose themselves only in the subjective activity of thought, which is *subjected* to these laws. In the apostate attitude, we are continually inclined to make the logical aspect of meaning independent, and to set it apart from its coherence with all other modal aspects, which implies a lack of appreciation of its modal boundaries.

The re-formation of the cosmonomic Idea by the central motive of the Christian religion.

From the Christian starting-point the cosmonomic Idea of our philosophy obtains the following contents: To the ultimate transcendental question: What is the Ἀρχή of the totality and the modal diversity of meaning of our cosmos with respect to the cosmonomic side and its correlate, the subject-side? it answers: the sovereign holy will of God the Creator, who has revealed Himself in Christ. To the second transcendental question, with respect to its cosmonomic-side: What is the totality of meaning of all modal aspects of the cosmic order, their supra-temporal unity beyond all modal diversity of meaning? it answers: the requirement grounded in God's sovereignty, of the love and service of God and our fellow-creatures with our whole heart. To the same question, with respect to its subject-side, it answers: the new religious root of the human race in Christ (in which, indeed, nothing of our created universe can be lost) in subjection to the fulness of meaning of the divine law. To the third transcendental question: What is the mutual relation between the modal aspects of reality? it answers: *sphere-sovereignty*, that is to say: mutual irreducibility, yet in the all-sided cosmic coherence of the different aspects of meaning, as this is regulated in God's temporal order of the world, in a cosmic order of time.

In order to bring this cosmonomic Idea, *in its theoretical focusing upon the modal aspects of meaning* of our cosmos, nearer to the vision of those not schooled in philosophy, I use a very old symbol, which of course should not be interpreted in a physical sense.

The light of the sun is refracted through a prism, and this refraction is perceived by the eye of sense in the seven well-known colours of the spectrum. In themselves all colours are dependent refractions of the unrefracted light, and none of them can be regarded as an integral of the colour-differentiation. Further, not one of the seven colours is capable of existing in the spectrum apart from the coherence with the rest, and by the interception of the unrefracted light the entire play of colours vanishes into nothing.

The unrefracted light is the time-transcending totality of meaning of our cosmos with respect to its cosmonomic side and its subject-side. As this light has its origin in the source of light, so the totality of meaning of our cosmos has its origin in its Ἀρχή through whom and to whom it has been created.

The prism that achieves the refraction of colour is *cosmic time*, through which the religious fulness of meaning is broken up into its temporal modal aspects of meaning.

As the seven colours do not owe their origin to one another, so the temporal aspects of meaning in face of each other have *sphere-sovereignty* or *modal irreducibility*.

In the religious fulness of meaning, there is but one law of God, just as there is but one sin against God, and one mankind which has sinned in Adam.

But under the boundary line of time this fulness of meaning with reference to its cosmonomic-side as well as to its subject-side separates, like the sunlight through the prism, into a rich variation of modal aspects of meaning. Each modal aspect is sovereign in its own sphere, and each aspect in its modal structure reflects the fulness of meaning in its own modality.

The modal spheres of laws and their sphere-sovereignty.

Every modal aspect of temporal reality has its proper sphere of laws, irreducible to those of other modal aspects, and in this sense it is sovereign in its own orbit, because of its irreducible modality of meaning.

The acceptance of the basic philosophic principle of modal sphere-sovereignty consequently has an indissoluble coherence with the Christian transcendence-standpoint ruled by the religious ground-motive of creation, fall into sin, and redemption.

The immanence-standpoint is incompatible with this cosmonomic principle.

This incompatibility is not due to an inability of immanence-philosophy to recognize, that the totality and deeper unity of meaning must transcend its modal diversity, and that the modal aspects *which it admits as such* cannot originate from one another.

For every scientific thinker must necessarily distinguish different modal aspects of temporal reality, and guard against jumbling them together.

However, we have seen in our transcendental critique of theoretic thought, that the immanence-standpoint must necessarily lead to an absolutizing of the logical function of thought, or to an absolutizing of a special theoretical synthesis.

The theoretically abstracted modal aspect which is chosen as the basic denominator for all the others or for a part of them, is torn out of the inter-modal coherence of meaning of temporal reality. It is treated as independent and elevated to the status of an ἀρχή which transcends meaning. This occurs whether or not the thinker realizes it. Over against this unrestricted sovereign authority, the remaining aspects of meaning of our cosmos are unable to validate any sphere-sovereignty. Mathematical logicism will admit only logical realms of thought with relative autonomy. Psychologism allows only psychological realms (whether or not understood transcendentally) which are not reducible to one another [1]; historicism accepts only different realms of historical development, etc. etc. [2]. If the thinker has become aware of the implacable antithesis in his hidden religious starting-point, his philosophic system will exhibit an overt dualism. Instead of one single basic denominator there will be chosen two of them, which will be conceived of in an antithetic relation. The transcendental ground-Idea in all its three directions will disclose the dualistic character of the religious basic motive without any attempt to bridge this dualism. But in this case, too, there will be no acceptance of a modal sphere-sovereignty of the different aspects and their proper law-spheres.

Because of the choice of its Archimedean point immanence-philosophy is forced to construct various *absolutizations* of modal aspects. In our analysis of the modal structures of the different spheres of laws, we shall show why these absolutizations can seemingly be carried out. On the immanence standpoint, now, the Christian starting-point may be reproached conversely with an absolutizing of *religious meaning*. But this objection, upon somewhat deeper reflection, is not tenable even on the standpoint of immanence-philosophy.

---

[1] See e.g. the typical instance of HEYMANS' psycho-monism with its elaboration on all realms of meaning of our cosmos. *Einführung in die Metaphysik* (Introduction into metaphysics), p. 33ff. and pp. 334ff.

[2] Cf. SPENGLER's *Untergang des Abendlandes* (Decline of the Occident).

> Christian religion does not allow of any absolutizing
> with respect to its fulness of meaning.

In the first place, the Christian religion, by virtue of its fulness of *meaning*, does not admit of any absolutizing: it is *religio*, i.e. connection between the *meaning* of creation and the *Being* of the 'Ἀρχή, the two of which may not be brought on the same level.

He who tries to make the religious totality of meaning independent of its *Archè*, becomes guilty of a contradiction in terms. But any one who should contend, that at any rate God is absolutized does not know, what he says.

In the second place, there is usually at the basis of the said reproach the confusion between the *temporal meaning of the faith-aspect*, which is actually contained within a modal sphere, and the *fulness of meaning of religion*, which transcends the boundary of cosmic time and cannot possibly be enclosed in a modality of meaning.

Let it be borne in mind, finally, that also unsuspected opponents of the Christian transcendence-standpoint in philosophy, such as HEINRICH RICKERT, admit, that religion within its fulness of sense does not tolerate a coordination with special realms of meaning as law, morality, science and so on. It can hardly be denied, that the view of religion as an "autonomous categorial realm of thought" destroys its meaning. On the other hand, the contention, that a recognition of necessary religious pre-suppositions of philosophical thought would destroy the meaning of this latter, ought to be demonstrated more stringently by immanence philosophers. Their (religious) confession of the self-sufficiency of theoretic reason is not sufficient in this respect.

> Sphere-sovereignty of the modal aspects in their
> inter-modal coherence of meaning as a philosophical
> basic problem.

As a transcendental basic principle the sphere-sovereignty of the modal aspects therefore stands in indissoluble connection with our transcendental Ideas of the Origin and of the totality and radical unity of meaning. Moreover, this principle is indissolubly linked up with our transcendental Idea of cosmic time. For this latter implies, as we have seen, a cosmic coherence of meaning among the modal aspects of temporal reality. And this coherence is regulated, not by philosophic thought, but by the divine temporal world-order.

It is, however, a highly remarkable state of affairs which is disclosed in the sphere-sovereignty of the modal aspects of meaning. For it might appear, as if sphere-sovereignty were incompatible with the inter-modal coherence of meaning guaranteed by the cosmic order of time.

In fact there is hidden a philosophic basic problem of the first rank, which cannot be solved, before our general theory of the modal structures in the second volume has been developed.

In the present context we can say only, that the key to this solution is to be found in the modal structure of the different aspects, which is of a cosmonomic character.

The same cosmic time-order which guarantees the modal sphere-sovereignty does in fact also guarantee the inter-modal coherence of meaning between the modal aspects and their spheres of laws.

Potentiality and actuality in cosmic time.

We have said in an earlier context, that all structures of temporal reality are structures of cosmic time. As structural *laws* they are founded in cosmic time-order and are principles of temporal *potentiality* or *possibility*. In their realization in individual things or events they have time-duration and *actuality* as transitory factual structures.

Everything that has real existence, has many more potentialities than are actualized. Potentiality itself resides in the factual subject-side; its *principle*, on the contrary, in the cosmonomic-side of time. The factual subject-side is always connected with individuality (actual as well as potential), which can never be reduced to a general rule. But it remains bound to its structural laws, which determine its margin or latitude of possibilities.

Cosmic time and the refraction of meaning. Why can the totality of meaning disclose itself in time only in refraction and coherence of modalities?

Prof. Dr H. G. STOKER, and lately also Prof. Dr PH. KOHNSTAMM[1] have raised the question, why it should be precisely

---

[1] Prof. Dr PH. A. KOHNSTAMM, in his essay, *Pedagogy, Personalism, and Philosophy of the Cosmonomic Idea* (in the anniversary papers in honour of Prof. Dr J. WATERINK, Amsterdam 1951), pp. 96f., in which the author, an outstanding Dutch thinker who died shortly thereafter, made known for the first time his adherence to the *Philosophy of the*

in cosmic time that the totality of meaning is refracted into coherent modal aspects. The reason is, in my opinion, that the fulness of meaning, as totality and radical unity, is not actually given and cannot be actually given in time, though all temporal meaning refers beyond itself to its supra-temporal fulfilment.

It is the very signification of cosmic time in its correlation of order and duration to be successive refraction of meaning into coherent modal aspects.

Sphere-sovereignty of modal aspects and their modal spheres of laws makes no sense in the fulness and radical unity of meaning.

In the religious fulness of meaning love, wisdom, justice, power, beauty, etc. coincide in a radical unity. We begin to understand something of this state of affairs in the concentration of our heart upon the Cross of Christ. But this radical unity of the different modalities is impossible in time considered as successive refraction of meaning.

Hence, every philosophy that tries to dissolve this totality of meaning into Ideas of reason, or absolute values, always ensnares itself in antinomies by which the cosmic order of time avenges itself on theoretic thought which tries to transgress its boundaries.

The logical function is not relative in a logical but in a cosmic sense.

Also the attempt to approximate cosmic time otherwise than in a *limiting* concept must necessarily lead to antinomies, because cosmic time is the very pre-supposition of the concept. With regard to its fundamental analytic aspect the concept is necessarily *discontinuous,* and is incapable of comprehending the cosmic *continuity* of time, which exceeds the modal boundaries of its aspects. The logical function in its modal speciality of meaning is indeed *relative,* but its relativity is not itself of a *logical,* but of a *cosmonomic temporal* character. If philosophy should attempt to interpret the *cosmonomic coherence* of

---

Cosmonomic Idea. He had a reservation, however, so far as the conception of time was concerned.

This hangs together with his thought, in itself altogether correct, that the Bible ascribes not even to God any supra-temporality in the Greek metaphysical sense. But the conception of the supra-temporal defended by myself is radically different from the Greek, as I have previously established with emphasis.

meaning in a *dialectical-logical* sense, it must begin in each case with a *logical* relativizing of the fundamental principles of logic, and thereby sanction the antinomy.

The elimination of cosmic time-order in KANT's *Critique of Pure Reason*.

By the hypostatization of "theoretical reason" as the self-sufficient Archimedean point of philosophy, the cosmic order of time is eliminated from philosophic thought, particularly from epistemology. In this way the critical basic question of all philosophy, namely: How is it itself *possible?* is relegated to the background. This elimination was also a source of subjectivism in the development of philosophic thought.

KANT's so-called Copernican revolution in epistemology (or, should one accept HEIDEGGER's interpretation of KANT, which in our opinion is by no means convincing, — in "ontology") is the direct proof of the *impossibility* of a truly *critical* critique of theoretic reason apart from a transcendental insight into the cosmic order of time. In his *Prolegomena zu einer jeden künftigen Metaphysik* § 4 (W.W. Cass. IV, p. 23) the philosopher of Königsberg writes of *The Critique of Pure Reason:* „Diese Arbeit is schwer und erfordert einen entschlossenen Leser, sich nach und nach in ein System hinein zu denken, *das noch nichts als Gegeben zum Grunde legt, auszer die Vernunft selbst*" (I italicize) „und also, ohne sich auf irgendein Faktum zu stützen, die Erkenntnis aus ihren ursprünglichen Keimen zu entwickeln sucht" [1].

What the reader is asked to do here is simply an abdication from the preliminary questions of critical thought. "Theoretic reason", according to KANT's transcendental conception a manifest product of theoretical abstraction, should be accepted as *given*. The question as to how philosophic thought is possible is thereby cut off. For the cosmic order of time, by which the relations of meaning of this thought are guaranteed, is lost sight of.

---

[1] KANT's *Prolegomena to every future Metaphysics* (Works, Cass. Ed. IV, p. 23).

["This work is difficult and requires a resolute reader to think his way gradually into a system, which sets at its foundation nothing as given except reason itself, and thus, without supporting itself upon any fact, seeks to develop knowledge from its original seeds."]

§ 10 - THE IMPORTANCE OF OUR COSMONOMIC IDEA IN RESPECT TO THE MODAL CONCEPTS OF LAWS AND THEIR SUBJECTS

Modal concepts of the lex and of its subject. The subject as subject to laws.

Through the cosmonomic Idea grounded in the Christian starting-point which we have set at the basis of our philosophic thought, the *concepts of laws and their subjects,* with which we shall operate further in their *modal speciality of meaning,* acquire their pregnant content. We have seen, that in this transcendental ground-Idea the lex is recognized as originating from God's holy creative sovereignty, and as the absolute *boundary* between the Being of the 'Ἀρχή and the *meaning* of everything created as "subject", *subjected* to a law.

Consequently, this transcendental meaning of the relation between the divine law and its subject will find expression in every concept of a modal aspect with respect to its special cosmonomic- and its special subject-side.

The fundamental importance of this conception will disclose itself in the second and the third volumes of this work.

In the present context I must remind the reader emphatically of my earlier explanation, that the subject-side of cosmic time implies the subject-object relation which we have discussed provisionally in connection with naïve experience.

The question whether this cosmic relation finds expression in all of the modal aspects or in a part of them only, cannot be investigated before the development of our general theory of the modal structures of the aspects and their modal law-spheres.

In every case I must establish the fact that in every modal aspect where this relation is to be found, the subject-side embraces both the subjective and the objective functions, which temporal reality discloses in this aspect.

The disturbance of the meaning of the concepts of the modal laws and their subjects in the Humanistic immanence-philosophy.

In the Humanistic immanence-philosophy, in its rationalistic as well as in its irrationalistic trends, this concept of the modal subject in its relation to the modal laws has been entirely lost and must *necessarily* be lost — to the incalculable injury of the philosophic analysis of reality.

The subject becomes *sovereign* — either in the metaphysical sense of "substance" (noumenon), or in a transcendental logical or phenomenological sense.

In KANT's "theoretical" philosophy, for example, the subject is only subject in an epistemological sense, and as such ἀρχή of the *form* of the theoretical laws of nature; the "transcendental subject" is itself the *law-giver of nature* in a transcendental-logical sense.

The pre-psychical aspects of reality were, after the destruction of the traditional metaphysics of nature, dissolved into a synthesis of logical and sensory functions of consciousness; their modal structural-laws were replaced by a-priori transcendental *forms* of *theoretical understanding* and of *subjective sensibility* in an apriori synthesis.

That numbers, spatial figures, energy-effects and biotic functions are really *modal subjects,* subjected to the laws of their own modal spheres, is a conception far removed from modern immanence-philosophy.

In KANT's so-called "practical" philosophy, the subject in the metaphysical sense of *homo noumenon* (pure will) becomes the autonomous law-giver for moral life. In accordance with the dualistic conception of his transcendental ground-Idea he does not accept a radical unity of the order of creation above the polar opposition between laws of nature and norms.

Two features typify the theoretical concept of the subject in immanence-philosophy, since it gave up the earlier metaphysics of nature.

1 - It is conceived only in the special sense of the epistemological and ethical functions of consciousness. The empirical things and events are taken into consideration only as *objects* of sensory perception and of theoretical or practical thought. This was the necessary consequence of the resolution of so-called "empirical" reality into the logical and psychical aspects of consciousness abstracted by theoretical thought from the cosmic temporal coherence of meaning. This resolution was attended by the elimination of the cosmic order of time, and by the proclamation of the so-called critical „Satz des Bewustseins", to be discussed later on, according to which the possibility of our knowledge is limited to our subjective and objective *contents of consciousness,* received merely by sensory perception and formed by logical apperception.

2 - In this view, the subject lacks its original meaning of

"sujet", being *subjected* to a law which does not originate from this subject itself. In the last analysis, in its function as a "transcendental subject" or "ideal subject" respectively, it has received the crown of autonomous, self-sufficient law-giver in accordance with the Humanistic ideals of science and of personality (to be discussed later).

In the classical rationalist conception, the *empirical* subject is reduced to a complex of causal relations by which it should be completely determined.

The "laws" are identified here with the "objective". Consequently the *empirical* subject is conceived of as an "object", which in its turn is identified with "Gegenstand" of the ultimate "transcendental subject of thought".

Modern so-called "realistic" positivism understands the concept of the lex (in relation to norms as well as to the so-called laws of nature) in the sense of a scientific judgment of probability. Here, too, this concept is completely dissociated from the modal structures of the different spheres of laws and from the typical structures of individuality, which are founded in the cosmic time-order.

This positivism conceives of laws as "autonomous" products of scientific thought, which tries to order by way of a "logical economy" the "facts", understood as merely sensory data.

Quite different from the rationalist concepts of the laws and their subjects are those of the irrationalist trends of Humanistic thought.

Rationalism as absolutizing of the general rule, irrationalism as absolutizing of individual subjectivity.

We have seen in an earlier context, that the *rationalist* types of immanence-philosophy tend to dissolve *the individual subjectivity into a universally valid order of laws*, the origin of which is sought in *sovereign reason*.

The irrationalist Humanistic types did not tamper with the conception of the "laws" as a product of thought or reason, but fell into the opposite extreme of seeing in this "theoretical order" merely a pragmatical falsification of *true* reality. The latter in its creative *subjective individuality*, is not bound to universally valid laws and mocks at all "concepts of thought". *Thus the absolutizing of the laws in the rationalist types is replaced by the absolutizing of the subjective individuality in the irrationalist types of the Humanistic immanence-philosophy.* This irrationalism is ruled by an irrationalist turn of the freedom-motive.

The concept of the subject in the irrationalistic phenomenology and philosophy of existence.

As a typical phenomenon in the philosophy of most recent times, we point to the conceptions of subject and selfhood in the modern irrationalist trend in phenomenology (SCHELER), and in the philosophy of existence (HEIDEGGER, and a number of others).

Here the reproach is made against KANT, that he still conceived of selfhood or "personality" as law-giving *subject in substantial terms* and consequently did not yet penetrate to the pure actuality of the selfhood.

As HEIDEGGER expresses it in his *Being and Time* (1927, a Reprint from Yearbook for Philosophy and Phenomenological Research, Vol. 8, p. 320): "For the ontological concept of the subject does not characterize the *selfhood of the Ego qua self, but the sameness and constancy of something already extant.* To determine the Ego ontologically as *Subject,* means to estimate it as something already extant. The being of the Ego is understood as the reality of the res cogitans (thinking substance)" [1].

SCHELER also in his standard work, *Der Formalismus in der Ethik und die materiale Wertethik (Formalism in Ethics and the Material Ethics of Value,* 3rd Ed., 1927, p. 397ff.), in a manner that leaves nothing to be desired as to clarity, has qualified personality as "pure actuality" which as such is transcendent to the *cosmos* as "world of things" (resolved into the abstract physical-psychical aspects of temporal reality!).

In discussing *"the place of man in the cosmos"* we shall find occasion to enter more closely into these conceptions. We shall see that the *actuality* which is brought again so sharply to the fore by modern phenomenological thought, does not stand in opposition to *subjectivity,* but rather constitutes its very kernel. In other words, it belongs in all modal aspects of our cosmos

---

[1] HEIDEGGER: *Sein und Zeit,* p. 320: „Denn der ontologische Begriff des Subjects charakterisiert *nicht die Selbstheit des Ich qua Selbst, sondern die Selbigkeit und Beständigkeit eines immer schon vorhandenen.* Das Ich ontologisch als *Subject* bestimmen, besagt es als ein immer schon Vorhandenes ansetzen. Das Sein des Ich wird verstanden als Realität der res cogitans."

(even the pre-logical) to the subject-functions (functioning in them) with respect to their *meaning*. For the entire conception to the effect that temporal reality should be something *statically* given, a fixed "Vorhandenes", rests upon a fundamental failure to appreciate the *dynamic* character of reality in the whole coherence of its different modal aspects. In our view, this dynamic character is guaranteed by the mode of ex-sistence of all created things as meaning, finding no rest in itself, and by the opening-process of temporal reality which will be explained in vols. II and III.

On the other hand SCHELER as well as HEIDEGGER accept the static conception of reality with respect to the "given world of things" and do reject this conception only as to "free personality" or "free human existence" respectively.

From this very view of the concept of the subject and of the "Dingwelt" in general, it appears, that also modern phenomenology and Humanistic existentialism move in the paths of immanence-philosophy. By choosing their Archimedean point in the "transcendentally purified actual consciousness" or in "existential thought", respectively, they make the "transcendental ego" sovereign.

It is the Humanistic ground-motive of nature and freedom whose dialectical character is responsible for the different conceptions of the laws and their subjects hitherto discussed.

> The concept of the lex and the subject in ancient Greek thought and its dependence on the Greek form-matter-motive.

Quite different from the Humanistic conceptions of the lex and the subject were those of ancient Greek thought, dominated by the form-matter-motive in its original religious sense. The modern concept of causal natural law, as well as the modern concept of the autonomous subject, conceived in the Kantian sense of law-giver, are unknown here.

At the outset, under the primacy of the matter-motive, the law of nature has the juridical sense of justice (*dikè*): every individual form must be dissolved into "matter" according to a standard of proportionality. This *dikè* is conceived of as an *Anangkè*, an unescapable fate to which the form-things are subjected.

Under the primacy of the form-motive of the later culture-religion the concept of the law in its general sense of order assumes a teleological sense in respect to all "natural subjects".

This conception is introduced by SOCRATES and elaborated in a metaphysical way by PLATO and ARISTOTLE. It was opposed to the extreme Sophistic view of the purely conventional character of the nomos in human society and the complete lack of laws in "nature" as a stream of flowing becoming.

In ARISTOTLE's *Metaphysics* the subject is identified with "substance", composed of form and matter. Natural law rules the striving of every matter to its proper substantial form. In PLATO's *Philebus*, the natural law is conceived of as the *peras*, setting a limit to the *apeiron*, the formless stream of becoming, which thereby receives the character of a *genesis eis ousian*, a becoming to being. This Pythagorean conception is maintained also with respect to ethical law.

Just as the Humanistic motive of nature and freedom, the Greek form-matter-motive, in view of its dialectical character, could never lead philosophic thought to a transcendental cosmonomic Idea in which the divine law was conceived in its radical religious unity. For the same reason there was no room here for a radical unity of the human subject above all of its temporal functions in their modal diversity. The transcendental Idea of the origin, too, remains bound to the polar dualism of matter and form. It lacks the integral character founded in the Biblical creation-motive. Therefore, according to the Greek conception, the subject can never be viewed as "sujet", subjected to divine law in the integral Biblical sense. In PLATO and ARISTOTLE the teleological law of the form-principle finds its original opposite in the *'Anangkè* of the matter-principle. At the utmost, "natural law" in its Greek sense, is conceived of as a subjective participation of the rational material substances in divine thought, as the origin of all cosmic forms. But this conception is, properly speaking, rather a Thomistic interpretation of the original Aristotelian view.

Finally, the Christian-scholastic concepts of the lex and the subject in the modal diversity of meaning, are dominated by the dialectical ground-motive of nature and grace. They rest upon an accommodation of the Greek or the Humanistic conceptions, respectively, to the Christian ones. We shall return to this scholastic view in the first part of this volume in the explanation of the rise of Humanistic thought.

CHAPTER II

PHILOSOPHY AND LIFE- AND WORLD-VIEW

§ 1 - THE ANTITHETIC POSITION OF THE PHILOSOPHY OF THE COSMONOMIC IDEA IN RESPECT TO THE IMMANENCE-PHILOSOPHY AND THE POSTULATE OF THE HISTORICAL CONTINUITY IN PHILOSOPHICAL THOUGHT CONTAINED IN THE IDEA OF THE "PHILOSOPHIA PERENNIS".

The philosophy of the cosmonomic idea requires, as we have seen, a radical self-critique on the part of those who engage in philosophic inquiry.

By its transcendental critique of theoretic thought it leads to the discovery of a radical antithesis between the transcendental ground-Idea of a philosophy which is entirely ruled by the central motive of the Christian religion, and that of immanence-philosophy in all its various trends. This antithesis may not be bridged by any compromise and runs along a line of separation entirely different from what has hitherto been supposed.

The necessity of this radical break with the immanence-standpoint could not be understood, before our transcendental critique had laid bare the all-controlling position of the transcendental ground-Idea in respect to the inner development and direction of philosophic thought.

Genuine Christian philosophy requires a radical rejection of the supra-theoretical pre-suppositions and "axioms" of immanence-philosophy in all its forms. It has to seek its own philosophic paths, prescribed by its proper transcendental ground-Idea. It cannot permit itself to accept within its own cadre of thought problems of immanence-philosophy which originate from the dialectic ground-motives of the latter.

The basis of cooperation between Christian thought and the different trends of immanence-philosophy.

Nevertheless, this radical rupture with the starting-points and transcendental ground-Ideas of immanence-philosophy does not mean, that an intrinsically re-formed Christian philosophy should intend to break off philosophical contact with Greek, scholastic, and modern Humanistic philosophy. On the contrary, because of its radical-critical standpoint, the Christian philosophy developed in this work is enabled to enter into the most inward contact with immanence-philosophy. It will never break the community of philosophical thought with the other philosophical trends, because it has learned to make a sharp distinction between philosophical judgments and the supra-theoretic prejudices which lay the foundation of every possible philosophy. The danger of breaking this community of thought is, as we saw in an earlier context, always caused by the philosophical dogmatism, which makes its religious pre-suppositions into theoretic "axioms", and makes the acceptance of the latter the necessary condition for philosophical discussion.

Meanwhile, the question remains: On what basis can philosophical trends, differing radically in their religious ground-motive and their transcendental ground-Idea, cooperate within the framework of one and the same philosophical task? What can be the *common basis for this cooperation?* As regards this point we will in the first place consider a popular argument against the entire Idea of a Christian science and philosophy, an argument which could just as well be raised against the general result of our transcendental critique of theoretical thought focused in the thesis, that theoretical thought is always dependent upon a religious ground-motive.

A popular argument against the possibility of Christian science and philosophy.

The popular argument, referred to here, runs as follows: $2 \times 2 = 4$, no matter whether a Christian or a heathen passes this judgment.

Doubtless, this argument is a poor affair, if it should be brought up against the results of our transcendental critique of theoretic thought. Nevertheless, at the same time it draws our attention to undeniable states of affairs that must necessarily form the basis for a cooperation of the different philosophical schools and trends in the accomplishment of a common task. Let us for a moment consider these two aspects of the argument more closely.

> Partial truths are not self-sufficient. Every partial truth is dependent upon truth in its totality of meaning.

The proposition: $2 \times 2 = 4$ is not "true in itself", but only in the context of the laws of number and the logical laws of thought. This context is, as we have seen, possible only in the all-sided coherence of meaning of all modal law-spheres and supposes a totality of meaning of which both the numerical and the logical aspects are special modal refractions in cosmic time. There exists no partial truth which is sufficient to itself. Partial *theoretical* truth is truth only in the coherence of the theoretical truths, and this coherence in its relativity pre-supposes the fulness or the totality of truth.

Consequently, also the philosophical view of the mutual relation and coherence of the numerical and the logical aspects — and thereby of the modal meaning of number and of logical concepts — is influenced from the start by the transcendental ground-Idea of philosophical thought and by the religious ground-motive which determines its content.

> The undeniable states of affairs in the structures of temporal reality.

On the other hand, however, it must of course be granted, that the judgment $2 \times 2 = 4$ refers to a state of affairs in the numerical relations which is independent of the subjective theoretical view and its supra-theoretical pre-suppositions. Not in the sense, however, that this "state of affairs" is a "truth in itself" and has an "absolute validity". For just like the proposition by which it is established, this "state of affairs" is dependent upon the cosmic order of time and the inter-modal coherence of meaning guaranteed by the latter. It has no meaning outside of this temporal order.

Nevertheless, it is founded in this *order*, and not in a theoretical view of the numerical aspect and its modal laws. Well then, this cosmic order with all temporal laws and structural states of affairs founded in it, is, indeed, the same for every thinker, no matter whether he is a Christian, a pagan or a Humanist. Structural states of affairs, as soon as they are discovered, force themselves upon everybody, and it does not make sense to deny them. It is the common task of all philosophic schools and trends to account for them in a philosophic way, that is to say in the light of a transcendental ground-Idea. They must learn from one another, even from fundamental mistakes made in the theoretical interpretations of the laws and the structural states of affairs founded in the temporal order of our cosmos. Immanence-philosophy can discover many states of affairs which had up to now been neglected in a philosophy directed by an intrinsically Christian transcendental ground-Idea, and vice versa.

In the philosophical effort to account for them in the context of a theoretical view of totality, there may be a noble competition between all philosophical trends without discrimination. We do not claim a privileged position for the Christian philosophy of the cosmonomic Idea in this respect. For even the Christian ground-motive and the content of our transcendental ground-Idea determined by it, do not give security against fundamental mistakes in the accomplishment of our philosophical task. On the contrary, for the very reason that in the Christian ground-motive the fall into sin is an essential factor, the possibility is excluded that a veritable Christian philosophy should lay claim to infallibility in the respect. The danger of ascribing infallibility to results of philosophic investigation is much greater on the immanence-standpoint, especially on the Humanistic, insofar as it seeks the ultimate standard of truth in theoretic thought itself. We shall return to this point presently in the discussion of the problem of truth.

The Idea of the perennial philosophy.

Meanwhile, there remains another objection against our conception concerning the radical antithesis between the Christian and the immanence-standpoint in philosophy, an objection which is not yet entirely refuted by our previous argument. For the question may be raised, what then is left — in the cadre of our philosophy — of the time-honoured Idea concerning the "philosophia perennis" which even modern Thomistic thought, in its relative isolation, zealously maintains?

By adopting an antithetic attitude against the entire immanence-philosophy in its evolution from Greek thought to the latest time, is not, for an authentically Christian philosophy, all connection with the historical development of philosophic thought cut off? That is to say, does not the latter place itself outside this historical development? If this were really so, then at once the sentence of doom would be pronounced over the attempt undertaken in this work at a *reformation* of philosophic thought from the Christian point of view. Reformation is not creation out of nothing.

> How is the Idea of the "philosophia perennis" to be understood? Philosophic thought and historical development.

But if an appeal is made to the Idea of the "philosophia perennis", one should know, what is to be understood by it. Philosophic thought as such stands in an inner relationship with historical development, postulated by our very philosophical basic Idea, and no thinker whatever can withdraw himself from this historical evolution. Our transcendental ground-Idea itself requires the recognition of the "philosophia perennis" in this sense and rejects the proud illusion that any thinker whatever, could begin as it were with a clean slate and disassociate himself from the development of an age-old process of philosophical reflection. Only let not the postulate of the "philosophia perennis" be turned against the religious ground-motive of philosophy with the intention of involving it (and not only the variable *forms* given to it) in historical relativity.

For he who does so, will necessarily fall into a historical relativism with respect to truth, as is encountered in DILTHEY's philosophy of the life- and world-views or, in a still more striking manner, in the case of an OSWALD SPENGLER.

Whoever takes the pains to penetrate into the philosophic system developed in this work, will soon discover, how it is wedded to the historical development of philosophic and scientific thought with a thousand ties, so far as its immanent philosophic content is concerned, even though we can nowhere *follow* the immanence-philosophy.

The philosophical elaboration in this book of the basic principles of sphere-sovereignty for example would not have been possible apart from the entire preceding development of modern philosophy and of the different branches of modern science. Nevertheless, it is just with the philosophic Idea of sphere-sovereignty that we turn on principle against the Humanistic view of science. In like manner it can be said, that our transcendental critique of theoretic thought has an inner historical connection with KANT's critique of pure reason, notwithstanding the fact that our critique was turned to a great extent against the theoretical dogmatism in KANT's epistemology.

What is permanent, and what is subjected to the historical development of thought. The scholastic standpoint of accommodation forever condemned.

The elaboration of our philosophy of the cosmonomic Idea is thus necessarily bound to historical development. Insight into the wealth of meaning of the cosmic order may grow, even through the work of schools of thought against which our own is set in an irreconcilable antithesis. Nevertheless, the *religious starting-point,* and consequently the whole direction which philosophic thought acquires thereby by means of its threefold transcendental ground-Idea, remains consistent. *This starting-point may no longer be abandoned by any single phase of Christian philosophic thought, if it is not to fall back into a scholastic standpoint of accommodation which has proved to be fatal to the idea of a philosophia christiana reformata.*

Every serious philosophic school contributes to the development of human thought to a certain extent, and no single one can credit itself with the monopoly in this respect.

No single serious current of thought, however apostate in its starting-point, makes its appearance in the history of the world without a task of its own, by which, even in spite of itself, it must contribute to the fulfilment of the Divine plan in the unfolding of the faculties which He makes to perform their work even in His fallen creation. In the development of the basic features of our philosophy of history we shall further elaborate this point.

We cannot discuss the immanent historical meaning of God's guidance in history, until we are engaged in the philosophical analysis of the modal structure of the historical aspect. Our opinion concerning the historical task of immanence-philosophy pre-supposes indeed the acceptance of this guidance, but this acceptance involves very complicated problems for philosophical thought which we cannot yet solve at this stage of our inquiry.

We can only say, that it implies the biblical-Augustinian idea of the continuous struggle in the religious root of history between the *civitas Dei* and the *civitas terrena.* This Idea shall guide us, when we enter into the confusing labyrinth of the history of philosophic thought. It can indeed guide us, since we have gained insight into the all-controlling influence of the religious starting-points in respect to the inner development of philosophic theories.

The conception of the antithesis of standpoints in the immanence-philosophy as "Weltanschauungslehre" (theory of life- and world-views).

In itself, the Idea of the antithesis of standpoints is not at all foreign to immanence-philosophy, namely in its modern form of "*Weltanschauungslehre*" (theory of life- and world-views).

On the contrary, many antitheses are constructed here, of which that between *idealism* and *naturalism* belongs to the most ancient. In this matter, curiously enough, idealism, in its Kantian and post-Kantian forms of transcendental "critical" idealism, insists on the opinion that this antithesis may be resolved in its favour by way of pure theory of knowledge. Consequently, no freedom-belief transcending the boundaries of theoretical reason need be called in aid at this point. For one need only reflect on the very operation of thought in order to see immediately, that every effort to reduce theoretical thought to a natural object pre-supposes a "transcendental subject of thought" or a "transcendental consciousness", without which objective experience of natural phenomena would be impossible [1].

Besides, various modern thinkers have tried to neutralize the conflict of the different standpoints within philosophic thought by making philosophy itself into a neutral "theory of the life- and world-views", without allowing it to take sides in the various antitheses.

Thus DILTHEY [2] came to set up three types of "philosophic world-views" which he holds to recur repeatedly in the historical development, viz.: 1. *Materialistic positivism* (Democritus, Epicurus, Hobbes, the Encyclopaedists, Comte, Avenarius); 2. *Objective idealism* (Heraclitus, the Stoics, Spinoza, Leibniz, Shaftesbury, Goethe, Schelling, Schleiermacher, Hegel); 3. *Freedom-idealism* (Plato, the Christian philosophy, Kant, Fichte, Maine de Biran).

Much more differentiated is RICKERT's [3] classification of the

---

[1] It must be evident in the light of our transcendental critique of theoretic thought, that this pretended purely epistemological refutation of naturalism is based on supra-theoretic pre-suppositions. We have seen in an earlier context, that the so-called "transcendental subject" is nothing but an absolutization of the logical function of thought, and that this absolutization is inspired by the Humanistic freedom-motive implying the autonomy of human thought.

[2] DILTHEY: *Die Typen der Weltanschauung* in "Weltansch." Berlin 1911.

[3] *System der Philosophie.* In the South-West German school of the

"life- and world-views", oriented to the Neo-Kantian philosophy of values.

He offers us a detailed outline in which the following types are analysed from the philosophic point of view of value: 1. Intellectualism. 2. Aestheticism. 3. Mysticism. 4. Moralism. 5. Eudemonism. 6. Eroticism. 7. Theism, Polytheism.

What is typical of these and similar classifications of the "life- and world-views" is that they, being construed from the immanence-standpoint, obliterate the only really radical antithesis, i.e. that between the immanence- and the Christian transcendence-standpoint, and attempt to subsume the Christian starting-point in philosophy under one of the many -isms of immanence-philosophy. At the same time, so far as the thinker who makes such groupings does not present himself as a complete relativist with respect to a life- and world-view, the relative oppositions on the immanence-standpoint are proclaimed as *absolute*.

The first insight that the philosophy of the cosmonomic Idea gives us with respect to the "Weltanschauungslehre" of the immanence-philosophy is that all "weltanschauliche" oppositions on the immanence-standpoint are completely relative, and that they become irreconcilable only by religious absolutizing, due to a dialectical ground-motive.

We shall learn to recognize idealism and naturalism in modern Humanistic philosophy as a polar opposition which lay hidden from the outset in the basic structure of its common transcendental ground-Idea, and originates from the antithesis in its central religious motive as an inner antinomy between the ideals of science and personality — nature and freedom.

Aestheticism and moralism are not even *polar* oppositions, but originate simply from the hypostatization of special modal aspects of meaning, which in the Humanistic basic motive are only different manifestations of the free and autonomous human personality.

Even in the so-called "theistic" type, the immanence-standpoint is only apparently abandoned. This appears clearly from the fact that "theistic philosophy" from the start was built upon a metaphysical *Idea of God,* which found its origin in the hypostatization of the NOUS. Consider only ARISTOTLE's theistic philo-

---

Neo-Kantians, even WINDELBAND had proclaimed philosophy to be the science of the life- and world-view („Wissenschaft der Weltanschauung"). See his *Einleitung in die Phil.* (2d Ed. 1920), pp. 19ff.

sophy. The divine νοῦς as actus purus, ("pure actuality") and "pure Form", first transcendent cause, unmoved mover and final end of the cosmos, is nothing but the hypostatization of theoretical thought, ruled by the Greek form-motive, and concealed behind a theistic disguise. It is the *idol-Idea* of this immanence-philosopher.

Things are not different in the case of the "theistic" philosophy of DESCARTES or LEIBNIZ. However, with these thinkers the hypostatization of theoretical thought is ruled by the Humanistic ground-motive of nature and freedom, which gives an entirely different character to their "theism".

Finally, what has such a philosophic "theism", ruled by the religious ground-motives of ancient Greek or modern Humanistic thought, respectively, in common with the radical Christian attitude with regard to the philosophic questions of life and the world?

The consequence of our transcendental critique for the history of philosophy.

It must be very confusing in the study of the history of philosophic thought to classify ancient Greek, medieval scholastic and modern Humanistic thinkers after the abstract schematisms presented by DILTHEY and RICKERT without considering the different religious ground-motives of the philosophic systems.

The philosophical meaning of terms as idealism, materialism, intellectualism, mysticism and so on, is entirely dependent upon the different transcendental ground-Ideas of philosophic thought and the religious ground-motives which rule the contents of the latter. Greek idealism for instance, ruled by the primacy of the religious form-motive, is completely different from the mathematical idealism of LEIBNIZ which is ruled by the modern Humanistic science-ideal, implied in the dialectical motive of nature and freedom. The terms "matter" and "nature" have in Greek thought a sense entirely different from that in modern Humanistic philosophy. ANAXIMANDER and ANAXIMENES were materialists in the sense of the Greek matter-motive, not at all in the sense of HOBBES, whose materialistic metaphysics was ruled by the mechanistic science-ideal of pre-Kantian Humanism. DEMOCRITUS was not at all a materialist in the modern Humanistic sense. His "atoms" were "ideal forms" in the sense of the Greek form-motive which was only conceived here in a mathematical sense. The Greek ideal of the καλοκἀγαθον (the beautiful and good) cannot be identified with the modern Humanist aestheticism of a SCHILLER, which is ruled by the religious motive of nature and freedom, as little as the Kantian moralism has a deeper affinity with SOCRATES' ethical thought.

There is a great danger hidden in a pretended purely theoretical analysis of ancient Greek or medieval philosophical trends after general schemes of classification which are construed apart from the religious ground-motives of Western thought. For, unawares, ancient and medieval thinkers are interpreted in this case after a pattern of thought prescribed by the modern Humanistic ground-motive of nature and freedom. Neither DILTHEY nor RICKERT have escaped this pitfall.

Thus, our transcendental critique of philosophic thought is of great importance also for the history of philosophy.

The only possible ultimate antithesis in philosophy.

In the light of the transcendental ground-Idea, there exists only one ultimate and radical anti-thesis in philosophy, viz. that between absolutizing, i.e. deifying of *meaning*, in apostasy from God *on the one hand*, and, *on the other hand*, the return of philosophic thought in Christ to God, which leads to the insight into the complete relativity and lack of self-sufficiency of all that exists in the created mode of meaning.

If, however, this antithesis is the ultimate one, there is no further room alongside of it for equivalent antitheses of another kind.

Naturally, it is true, that there is a radical difference between the religious ground-motives of ancient Greek and modern Humanistic thought. However, it can hardly be said, that these motives could have an antithetical relation to one another in the same final and radical sense as that between the Christian and apostatic ground-motives. As to the religious antithesis which we have discovered within each of the dialectical ground-motives themselves, we were able to establish that they had the character of a *polar tension* between the two components, which is quite different from the relation between the Christian and the apostatic starting-points.

Such polar tensions are radically excluded in the transcendental ground-Idea of every really Christian philosophy. Therefore, in all philosophy that is rooted in the Christian transcendence-standpoint, there can be no question on principle of idealism or naturalism, moralism or aestheticism, rationalism or irrationalism, theism or mysticism; for all such -isms can be grounded only in the immanence-standpoint.

Consequently, so far as such -isms have actually gained access to Christian philosophic thought, for lack of an integral Christian cosmonomic Idea, they appear as *atavisms* in the literal sense of the word, rudiments of apostatic thought, which can in no way prove to be compatible with the basic Christian attitude.

§ 2 - THE DISTINCTION BETWEEN PHILOSOPHY AND LIFE- AND WORLD-VIEW AND THE CRITERION

Must then the life- and world-view really be blended with philosophic thought? Is the relation between philosophy and life- and world-view perhaps this, that philosophy is nothing but an elaborate life- and world-view, perhaps an „Anweisung zum seligen Leben" (a guide to the blessed life) under the disguise of philosophic theory? Granted, that for the life- and world-view the absolute antithesis, as above formulated, is really inescapable, must not philosophy, if it is to maintain its theoretical character, for that very reason refrain from a choice of position, lest it should obliterate its boundaries with respect to the former?

In such questions we once again find on our path the dogma concerning the autonomy of theoretic thought. They compel us to form a clearer Idea of the relation between philosophy and a life- and world-view.

> The boundaries between philosophy and a life- and world-view as seen from the immanence-standpoint. Disagreement as to the criterion.

Meanwhile, it is very difficult indeed to enter into discussion with the immanence-philosophy on this point. For from its point of view there are strenuous divergences of opinion concerning the question: What exactly do you mean by a life- and world-view, and does it stand in opposition to philosophy? For example, HEINRICH RICKERT wants to approach the nature of the life- and world-view axiologically from his theoretical philosophy of values, and sees the essential characteristic in the personal a-theoretical commitment with respect to the question: What is for you the highest value? Another defender of the autonomy of theoretic philosophy, THEODOR LITT, upbraids RICKERT for having transgressed the very limits of philosophy in his *theoretical* philosophy of values. According to him, value is ex origine a-theoretical, and consequently all foundation of theoretical truth, as to its absolute validity, in a value (as RICKERT does), is to be rejected. LITT seeks the criterion between philosophy and a life- and world-view in this very point, that in philosophic thought no single valuation may be "either one of the determining factors or even the decisive factor;" that *valuations* put in a word is for him, "conclusive evidence for the fact that the subject has not sacrificed its concretely personal relation to the totality of reality to the striving after pure knowledge" [1].

Measured by this criterion, immanence-philosophy in its age-long development was full of life- and world-views, and the process of purification is still scarcely begun in any proper sense. In NIETZSCHE's philosophy of life, however, just the reverse is the case. To philosophy is ascribed the task of determining the practical "ordering of values according to rank". In his *Genealogy of Morals* (p. 38) the philosophers are called „Befehlende und Gesetzgeber" (commanders and law-givers). Philosophy thus becomes an "art of living", which merely shares the expression in concepts with theoretical science.

Also the modern so-called "existential philosophy", strongly influenced by SÖREN KIERKEGAARD, proceeds along the same line in its conception of the relation between philosophy and a life- and world-view.

According to KARL JASPERS, philosophy was from the start more than a mere "universal theory". "It gave impulses, drew up tables of values, made human life meaningful and purposive, it gave him the world in which he felt safe, in a word it gave him: a view of life and the world" [2]. Only "prophetic philosophy" that gives a world-view, in that it constructs tables of value as norms, in his esteem deserves the name of *philosophy*. But this name, according to him, has at present become customary for that which can better and more clearly be called universal logic, sociology and psychology, which as theory refrain from all

---

[1] *Einleitung in die Philosophie* (Leipzig und Berlin 1933) p. 261: „der bündige Beweis dafür, dasz das Subjekt sein konkret-persönliches Verhältnis zum Ganzen der Wirklichkeit nicht dem Willen zu reiner Erkenntnis aufgeopfert hat."

[2] „Sie gab Impulse, stellte Werttafeln auf, gab dem Menschenleben Sinn und Ziel, gab ihm die Welt, in der er sich geborgen fühlte, gab ihm mit einem Wort: Weltanschauung."

valuation. For this very reason, JASPERS calls his well-known book that intends to give only a *theory* of possible life- and world-views, and to *understand* the meaning of these latter psychologically, not a "philosophy", but a *"Psychology of the Life- and World-views"* [1].

We can thus establish the fact that, on the one hand, philosophy and life- and world-views are distinguished most sharply according to an axiological criterion, while, on the other hand, they are identified with one another. Within the first school of thought, again, there is a dispute over the question, whether philosophy may orient itself at any rate to a theoretical value, or whether every attitude of valuation must be excluded.

However this may be, we continue for the moment to stand somewhat aloof from such an axiological criterion as has been referred to, for, as we shall see, it is heavily burdened with the *transcendental basic-idea* of the thinkers in question.

A "concept of value", taken in an objective idealistic, or indeed in a subjective-psychologistic sense, betrays its origin in immanence-philosophy. How shall the "philosophy of the cosmonomic Idea", which starts by raising the question as to the possibility of philosophy and thereby urges to critical self-reflection as to the transcendental ground-Idea, accept off-hand a criterion that has originated from a philosophy which is not aware of the importance of its own transcendental ground-Idea?

LITT calls it "a lack of logical integrity", to require for a life- and world-view the "universal validity", which ex origine belongs only to "theoretical truth" [2]. But even this "argument ad hominem" is not capable of making an impression, when it appears that LITT's conception of the *meaning* of theoretical truth bears the stamp of a transcendental basic Idea which is born of a supra-philosophical choice of position, according to his own view, perhaps from a *life- and world-view!*

Life- and world-view as an "individual impression of life", THEODOR LITT and GEORG SIMMEL.

Each man, thus says LITT, has his individual "life- and world-

---

[1] *Psychologie der Weltansch.* 3d Ed. 1925, pp. 1—7.

[2] The opposition: life- and world-view, on the one hand, and theoretical truth on the other is, in addition, impure and misleading. The true opposition must be: life- and world-view and philosophy, both of which are subjected to a norm of truth.

view". The latter is nothing but an individual impression of life, which arises in closest contact with the conception of *experienced reality*, formed by the community, in which the man lives. All community-life creates an atmosphere of common convictions which make themselves felt, wherever something of importance is said, thought or done, without such convictions being subjected to any criticism. Such community-conceptions of the problem of world and life display the most varied forms from the image-world of the myths to the dogmas of religion and the profane wisdom of the popular outlook on life. In its origin, philosophy is undoubtedly still interwoven most closely with such life- and world-views. To preserve a pure scientific conscience, however, it must distinguish itself most sharply from them. For it is concerned with the universally valid theoretical truth which finds its place only in the realm of theoretical thought.

Curiously enough, LITT's characterization of the *life- and world-view* as an "individual impression of life" agrees rather well with GEORG SIMMEL's characterization of *philosophy* as "a temperament, seen through a picture of the world", and as the revelation of "what is deepest and final in a personal attitude toward the world in the language of a picture of the world" [1].

We notice this agreement for the present with special interest, since SIMMEL is an adherent of the historicistic and relativistic *philosophy of life*, to which LITT, as we shall see, also exhibits a strong approximation, in spite of the semblance of the contrary.

LITT's vision on life- and world-views, too, does not help us any further, since, as we shall see in the sequel, the same prejudices are again brought into play here as in the case of the criterion of value. In other words, the determination of the relationship between philosophy and a "life- and world-view" is ruled by a transcendental ground-Idea, of whose importance the thinker has not been fully aware in critical self-reflection.

The relationship as seen from the Christian transcendence-standpoint.

How shall we then from our standpoint, determine the relationship between philosophy and a life- and world-view?

We begin by setting on the foreground that the concept "life-

---

[1] *Hauptprobleme der Philosophie (Chief Problems of Philosophy)*, pp. 23, 28.

and world-view" is raised above the level of vague representations burdened either with resentment or with exaggerated veneration only if it is understood in the sense that is necessarily inherent in it *as a view of totality*. An individual *impression of life*, fed from a certain sphere of convictions, is no "life- and world-view."

The genuine life- and world-view has undoubtedly a close affinity with philosophy, because it is essentially directed towards the totality of meaning of our cosmos. A life- and world-view also implies an Archimedean point. Like philosophy, it has its religious ground-motive. It, as well as philosophy, requires the religious commitment of our selfhood. It has its own attitude of thought. However, it is not, as such, of a theoretical character. Its view of totality is not the *theoretical*, but rather the *pre-theoretical*. It does not conceive reality in its abstracted modal aspects of meaning, but rather in typical structures of individuality which are not analyzed in a theoretical way. It is not restricted to a special category of "philosophic thinkers", but applies to everybody, the simplest included. Therefore, it is entirely wrong to see in Christian philosophy only a philosophically elaborated life- and world-view. To do so would be a fundamental misunderstanding of the true relationships. The Divine Word-revelation gives the Christian as little a detailed life- and world-view as a Christian philosophy, yet it gives to both simply their *direction* from the starting-point in their central basic motive. But this direction is really a *radical* and *integral* one, determining everything. The same holds for the direction and outlook which the *apostate religious* motives give to philosophy and a life- and world-view.

Therefore philosophy and a life- and world-view are *in the root* absolutely united with each other, even though they may not be identified.

Philosophy cannot take the place of a life- and world-view, nor the reverse, for the *task* of each of the two is different.

They must rather understand each other mutually from their common religious root. Yet, to be sure, philosophy has to give a theoretical account of a life- and world-view, of which something will be said later.

§ 3 - THE NEUTRALITY-POSTULATE AND THE "THEORY OF LIFE AND WORLD-VIEWS"

It is intensely interesting to trace in the neutrality-postulate, the influence of the *personality-ideal*, which we shall discuss later on as a basic factor in the transcendental Humanistic ground-Idea. We have repeatedly established the fact that by means of this postulate various modern currents in immanence-philosophy attempt to avoid self-reflection as to the transcendental ground-Idea of their philosophic system. It finds its origin in KANT's sharp separation between theoretical and practical reason and in his attempt at the emancipation of the free and autonomous personality from the tyranny of the Humanistic ideal of science, which was itself evoked by the religious freedom-motive of Humanism. The intended postulate is really not of a *theoretical*, but of a *religious* origin.

First of all, the theoretical arguments which have been introduced for the defence of this neutrality-postulate will be faced.

RICKERT's defence of the neutrality-postulate.
RICKERT has indeed developed them in the greatest detail in his *System der Philosophie* ("System of Philosophy")[1]. Accor-

---

[1] From the same author there has appeared: *Grundprobleme der Philosophy (Basic Problems of Philosophy*, 1934), which to a large extent treats of the same problems.

No new points of view are opened by RICKERT's essay *Wissenschaftliche Philosophie und Weltanschauung* (Scientific Philosophy and World-view) in *Logos*, Vol. 22 (1933), pp. 37ff., which is aimed against the modern existence-philosophy of HEIDEGGER, JASPERS, etc. RICKERT's opponents demand an existential mode of philosophical thinking in opposition to a purely theoretical one.

The essay referred to intends to demonstrate that the totality of the cosmos is accessible only to theoretical thought, while from the total man, seen by RICKERT — in the strain of all immanence-philosophy — as an individual complex of functions, this cosmic totality must remain hidden.

This whole argumentation stands or falls with the immanence-standpoint itself and with its transcendental ground-Idea for which RICKERT does not account, in consequence of which his standpoint becomes uncritically dogmatic, or rather "doctrinaire".

That the selfhood as totality of human existence cannot be sought in the temporal coherence of its functions remains hidden from him.

"Individual man in the totality of his existence necessarily restricts his interest to one or more parts of the cosmic totality. Any one who tries to think in a universal way and notwithstanding this wishes at the same time to philosophize as an *"existing thinker"*, badly understands himself and his own existence. Only after he has detached himself from it, with the aid of philosophy, his view is able to be free

ding to him, philosophy, so far as its inner nature is concerned, is the theoretical science which has to understand the entire cosmos theoretically as a totality, even though this cosmos is sharply separated by theoretical thought into the two spheres of temporal-spatial (sensibly perceptible) *nature-reality* and *timeless values* which *have absolute validity*.

It has no life- and world-view to preach as "persuasion", or "faith" or "imperative". It must restrict itself scrupulously to a theoretical attitude of knowledge. Imperatives, norms are not the business of theory. The concept of a normative science is internally contradictory.

"Reality" (for RICKERT exhausted in its psycho-physical aspects) is not considered by philosophy in the objectivizing sense of the special sciences. The special sciences must establish what reality is as "mere reality". Philosophy has nothing to say about that. Reality studied by the special sciences is the *immanent*, conscious, given reality, the "psycho-physical". No other reality exists (loc. cit. p. 179).

Yet reality to RICKERT is more than "mere reality". As theoretical *form*, in which the understanding conceives an empirical sensory material of consciousness, reality is a *category of thought*, which is not itself *real*, but *has validity* ("*Geltung*") *only*.

KANT adopted this "critical" standpoint with respect to reality, when he proclaimed the "universally-valid" transcendental subject, stripped of all individuality, in the synthesis of its forms of thought and intuition to be the formal origin of the real "Gegenstand" of knowledge. Only the sort of "validity" or "value", on the basis of which the subject builds up his "world" epistemologically, is decisive for the "objectivity" of reality gained on the basis of critical philosophy (loc. cit. p. 175).

Still more clearly does the theoretical Idea of the *totality of*

---

and wide enough to comprehend the totality of the cosmos in his vision and in his truthful judgment."

[„Der ganze Mensch beschränkt sich mit seinen Interessen notwendig auf einen oder mehrere ihrer Teile. Wer universal zu denken sich bemüht und trotzdem gleichzeitig als ganzer Mensch oder als existierender Denker philosophieren möchte versteht sich selbst und seine eigene Existenz schlecht. Erst wenn er sich von ihr mit Hilfe der Theorie losgemacht hat, kann sein Blick frei und weit genug werden, um das Ganze der Welt überschauend und wahr urteilend zu erfassen."]

reality, viewed by KANT essentially as an *infinite task* for thought, show its *value-character*. What makes this totality to be "absolute totality" is only the value that holds (p. 175).

For the problem of the "totality of reality" to be susceptible of philosophical solution, it must be understood as an epistemological *problem*. Philosophy does not deal with reality as "mere reality", but with the problem of the *knowledge of reality*. It seeks to understand the theoretical values which *are* not really, but which *hold good* and which lead the knowledge of reality so that this latter thereby acquires anchorage and coherence. The philosophic problems of reality, in other words, are to be understood only as questions of the theory of knowledge, as theoretical *problems of meaning and value*. Theoretical philosophy of reality is an epistemology. It wants to interpret the *meaning* of knowledge and this is possible only on the basis of *values*.

Meanwhile, it would be altogether inadmissable to restrict the task of philosophy to the investigation of these merely theoretical values. Philosophy, which is essentially *a theory of values*, must be directed toward the "Voll-endung" (fulfilment), toward the totality, and must thus necessarily include the *universe of values* in its horizon. It must strive after a philosophic *system* of values. Consequently, it must also investigate the *a-theoretical* ones, which, according to the traditional view, are distinguished as morality, beauty, and holiness, in order to be able to interpret the meaning of all of life theoretically.

According to RICKERT's view, the system of values with respect to its material content cannot be deduced from general axiological *forms*. To set up such a system, one needs a *material*, in terms of which for the first time we have to gain an insight into the *multiplicity* of the "values". How is philosophy to track down this multiplicity? To this end it must orient itself to the *historical life of culture*.

To understand this line of thought, we must observe that, according to RICKERT, *philosophy*, as the theory of totality, has the task of re-uniting in thought the "worlds" of "natural reality" and "values that hold", which "worlds" by theoretical thought were absolutely separated at first. When we are not thinking, we immediately experience this unity "free from concepts" and philosophy would not veritably become philosophy of the "Vollendung" (fulfilment), if it stopped with an unreconciled dualism in theoretical thought.

So there is needed a theoretical connecting-link between values and reality, a *third realm*, which joins the two into one. This third realm is understood theoretically in the concept of *meaning*, which to RICKERT is "logically prior" to the theoretical separation into reality and value. Meaning is itself neither real nor effective value, but the synthetic union of both, constituted in the valuating act of the subject. Meaning, "significance" ("Bedeutung"), belongs to all "acts", so far as the subject chooses a position in them with respect to values. In the "immanent meaning of the act", value and reality are synthetically together. The immanent meaning is not itself *value,* but reality is here *related to values* by meaning. It is reality to which "values cling" in meaning.

In the concept of *meaning,* the distinction between values and reality has not been dropped, but they are joined in a higher synthetic unity. "Value", too, for RICKERT is *meaning,* but *transcendent, timeless* and *absolute* in character. *Meaning* as the intermediate link between value and reality is, on the contrary, "immanent meaning". Only in this third realm of immanent meaning does the subject find its place in RICKERT's view. "Reality" is merely the *object* of the transcendental epistemological subject, and in the realm of values there is no subjectivity at all.

Well then, for the discovery of the multiplicity of the values, philosophy must orient itself to the realm of immanent meaning which has precipitated itself solely in the *historical life of culture* in the cultural goods as "the truly objective" and which is understood by historical science theoretically and objectively.

The science of history has to do with *culture* as "reality to which values cling" („wertbehaftete Wirklichkeit"), although in its procedure, it looks away from the absolute values. Thus it presents philosophy the matter which the latter requires for its systematic value-theory. From the historical cultural "goods", philosophy must abstract the general *values,* in order to delimit the problems which arise for philosophy as a doctrine of the *meaning of life.* In so doing, it must necessarily work with an "open system", which leaves room for new values which were not previously discovered.

Now the absolute universal validity of the theoretical value of truth alone can be demonstrated in a manner convincing to all thinking beings. It alone possesses a self-guarantee for this validity. The relativistic view of this value cancels itself theoretically, because it must require absolute truth for its own standpoint, if it is to be taken seriously.

On the contrary, the a-theoretical values, such as RICKERT conceives them in his open system (beauty, personal holiness, impersonal holiness, morality, and happiness) are not to be proved in their universal validity just because proof resides in the theoretical realm. Philosophy as theoretical science of totality must suffice with providing us with theoretical insight with respect to these values. It can bring them only into a *theoretical* system, whereby nothing is said as to the practical priority of one of these values, but only *a formal order* of the "stages of value" is given.

As theoretical science of totality it cannot proclaim a certain value to be the highest. It would thereby fall into a "prophetism" which would be incompatible with its un-prejudiced theoretical starting-point. It would become a life- and world-view, even if it declared the theoretical values which dominate its own field of research to be in this sense the highest, dominating all of life. In this case, instead of thinking philosophically in theoretical style, it would preach an intellectualism, such as was the case in the philosophy of the Enlightenment.

Nevertheless, philosophy must really include the life- and world-views in its theoretical inquiry. For the object of philosophy is the *totality of the cosmos* and to this totality also belongs the subject, i.e. the whole man and his relation to the cosmos, the subject that chooses a position in life with respect to values. Hence philosophy necessarily becomes also a theory of the life- and world-views, "Weltanschauungslehre" or theory of the *total meaning of life* („Theory des vollendeten Lebens"), and in this very capacity is it philosophy of values.

As "Weltanschauungslehre", philosophy has simply to develop theoretically the various possible types of life- and world-views, that is to say, to point out the consequences of elevating one of the various values *to the highest rank*. It has, in other words, only to furnish us with theoretical clarity as to the meaning of each life- and world-view. "For the rest it leaves to the individual man to choose that view of life and the world that suits his personal extra- or super-scientific nature best"[1].

---

[1] „Im übrigen wird sie es dann dem einzelnen Individuum überlassen die Weltanschauung zu *wählen,* die am besten zu seiner persönlichen auszer- oder überwissenschaftlichen Eigenart paszt" (op. cit., p. 407).

Criticism of the fundamentals of the "Weltanschauungslehre".

It would lead us too far and would also be superfluous in the present context to pursue the development of the method of RICKERT's "Weltanschauungslehre" further.

We are here concerned only with rendering a critical appraisal of its fundamentals and its critical arguments.

These fundamentals seem to be strongly grounded. RICKERT appears zealously to defend the boundaries of theoretical philosophy against all attempts at usurpation which wish to make of theory something more than theory. In the rejection of an intellectualistic foundation for philosophy, the separation between philosophy and a life- and world-view appears to be really maintained consistently. Furthermore, RICKERT shows himself so little confined by intellectualistic prejudices, that he theoretically recognizes the necessity for religion to penetrate the whole of life and never to allow itself to be satisfied with a coordination of other values and the value that dominates it. He recognizes, too, that the axiological point of view cannot exhaust the essence of religion.

Nevertheless, a pitfall, fatal to RICKERT's entire conception of the essence, task and place of philosophy, is concealed in his plea for the theoretical neutrality of philosophy.

The neutrality-postulate would have meaning and in that case also have *complete* meaning, only if the "theoretical truth-value", which — according to RICKERT — solely and exclusively is to dominate philosophy, possessed validity in itself, independent of a cosmic temporal order, independent also of the other values, independent namely of the religious *fulness* of truth.

Now the pitfall lies concealed in the apriori identification of "truth" with *theoretical correctness* and in the further apriori pre-supposition that truth thus interpreted rests in itself as an absolute "value": "We see in philosophy a theoretical attitude of mind, and seek in it nothing but that which we call truth. We thereby pre-suppose, that truth possesses a value of its own, or that there is a meaning in striving after truth for the sake of truth. In this lies the further pre-supposition, that there is truth that is timelessly valid, and even this pre-supposition will arouse opposition in our times. It includes the conviction that there is truth resting in itself or absolute truth, by which all philosophical views of the universe are to be measured"[1].

---

[1] RICKERT, loc. cit., p. 39: „Wir sehen in der Philosophie ein theoreti-

It would be trifling to play off the word "conviction" against the author and to object, that, according to his own conception, "convictions" are not a matter of philosophy but of a life-view. For RICKERT is indeed of opinion that the truth-value is the only one in the realm of values, the absolute universally-validity of which may be proved theoretically.

Yet the opinion that the absolute validity of the "theoretical truth-value" can be proved theoretically is hardly to be sustained. For does not every theoretical proof suppose a norm for its correctness? (I would not like to say an absolute truth-value, possessing its validity in itself!).

How can that be proved which is pre-supposed in the proof? To this point, however, I shall devote separate attention below.

> Immanent antinomy in RICKERT's philosophy of values.

For the present I will only demonstrate, that the absolutizing of theoretical truth to an absolute value, resting in itself, viewed from RICKERT's own standpoint, leads to an insoluble antinomy.

RICKERT himself desires to relate philosophic thought to the "totality of values." In contradistinction to this totality, the "truth-value", according to RICKERT's own *theoretical* view, is only a species of transcendent meaning in the (transcendent) diversity of values. That being granted, the theoretical truth-value is in no case to be *set by itself*. In any case, it supposes the *totality* of values. The Idea of an absolute theoretical "truth-value" resting entirely in itself is thus internally contradictory and dissolves itself.

Furthermore, the diversity of values supposes a coherence of meaning among them.

For how could they otherwise belong to the same totality of values? That being granted again, what meaning is to be ascribed to the postulate of "theoretical purity" for my philosophic

---

sches Verhalten und suchen in ihr nichts anderes als das, was wir Wahrheit nennen. Dabei setzen wir voraus, dasz die Wahrheit einen Eigenwert besitzt, oder dasz es einen Sinn hat, nach Wahrheit um der Wahrheit willen zu streben. Darin steckt die weitere Voraussetzung, dasz es Wahrheit gibt, die zeitlos gilt, und schon diese Voraussetzung wird in unserer Zeit Anstosz erregen. Sie schliesz die Überzeugung ein, dasz es in sich ruhende, oder absolute Wahrheit gibt, an der alle philosophischen Ansichten vom Weltall zu messen sind."

thought, if the "theoretical truth-value" which alone could give meaning to this thought, cannot satisfy this postulate without cancelling itself?

For, can a special value, torn out of the coherence of meaning with all the others and set by itself, escape from becoming meaningless?

If not, then the postulate of the self-sufficiency of theoretical thought is also reduced AD ABSURDUM and in this way too, it is demonstrated that in "pure" theoretical thought the true Archimedean point of immanence-philosophy cannot be found.

The test of the transcendental ground-Idea.

If we apply the *test of the transcendental ground-Idea*, then RICKERT's metaphysical concept of value immediately turns out to be ruled by a specific supra-philosophical choice of position with respect to Ἀρχή and totality of meaning of the different modal laws, especially of the modal norm-spheres. The line of thought is as follows: the norm *as lex* (imperative) is necessarily related to a subject, is thus *relative* and consequently cannot be the absolute Ἀρχή of meaning. Since the referring of the norms to God's sovereignty comes into conflict with the secret religious proclamation of the sovereignty of human personality, an Idea of reason must be hypostatized as a value sufficient to itself. This value now appears to be elevated to the position of Ἀρχή of the laws. In truth, however, the apostate selfhood in the Idea of value proclaims the so-called "practical reason" to be the souvereign Ἀρχή.

The absolute "value", sufficient to itself, is, as we saw, nothing but the hypostatization of the norm (in its modal speciality of meaning), which to this end is dissociated from the subject on the one hand and from God as Ἀρχή on the other hand and now rests in itself as a Platonic Idea. However, this "value" is not conceived of, as by PLATO, as a "being", a pattern-form in respect to the perceivable cosmos, but as a "holding good" [1].

---

[1] AUGUST MESSER, *Deutsche Wertphilosophie der Gegenwart* (German Value-Philosophy of the Present), 1926, pp. 2ff., supposes that he can satisfactorily cut off the reproach of hypostatization, directed against the philosophy of values, by pointing to the sharp distinction between value and reality. Only a "realism of values", such as was recognized in PLATO's doctrine of Ideas could be said to rest upon hypostatization. But we noticed previously, that the hypostatization is in itself independent of the

The true root of this metaphysical axiological theory is the *Humanistic ideal of personality* as a *basic factor* in the central religious motive of Humanism, which ideal of personality in KANT's "primacy of the practical reason", after a long struggle, gained the ascendency over the *Humanistic science-ideal* of the intellectualistic "Aufklärung" (Enlightenment), about which our further discussion will follow in the next part. Theoretic philosophy may not dominate the autonomous freedom of human personality in the choice of its life- and world-view.

A religious ground-motive is at the basis of RICKERT's postulate of theoretic neutrality, a ground-motive which has expressed itself in a transcendental ground-Idea; the apriori influence of the latter upon RICKERT's thought can be demonstrated in his concept of the law and the subject, his view of reality, his metaphysical idea of value, his conception of time, and so on.

> The philosophy of the cosmonomic Idea does not judge about matters over which no judgment belongs to man, but leads to fundamental self-criticism of the thinker.

As one sees, the referring of a philosophic system to its transcendental ground-Idea leads to a radical sharpening of the anti-thesis in philosophic thought and to the discovery of really stern truths. But immanence-philosophy may not complain about this, for it, too, requires of philosophic thought to seek the truth and nothing but the truth. On its part, it offers sharp opposition to every attack upon the self-sufficiency of theoretical thought. Moreover, it should be kept in mind, that the radical criticism which the philosophy of the cosmonomic Idea exercises may in no part be understood as a judgment as to the personal religious condition of a thinker. Such a judgment does not belong to man and lies entirely outside the intention of our philosophy. We know, after all, that in the heart of the Christian himself the apostate selfhood and the selfhood redirected to God wage a daily warfare.

But this *full* truth will be impressed by the radical self-criticism which the philosophy of the cosmonomic Idea requires of the thinker: The proclamation of the self-sufficiency of philosophic thought signifies the withdrawal of that thought from Christ as the new religious root of our cosmos. This *cannot* proceed from

---

question, whether it is understood in terms of "being" or rather of "holding good".

Him, but necessarily issues from the root of existence which has fallen away from God.

§ 4 - SEQUEL: THE PRETENDED SELF-GUARANTEE OF THEORETICAL TRUTH

LITT's argument concerning the self-guarantee of theoretical truth.

We may not stop at RICKERT's plea for the neutrality-postulate. Indeed, it has not escaped other defenders of this postulate, that RICKERT's very foundation of the notion of neutrality in his *philosophy of values* exceeds the limits of "purely theoretical" thought. In an earlier context we pointed to THEODOR LITT, who reckons the value-Idea as such to the territory of a "life- and world-view."

We must, therefore, try to penetrate to the gist of the argument which is adduced in support of the neutrality-postulate, and which in fact is not necessarily connected with the conception of philosophy as a theory of values. This gist is to be found in the pretended self-guarantee of "theoretical truth" in respect to its absoluteness. We saw, that RICKERT, too, pointed his entire demonstration in the direction of this "self-guarantee", but showed his weak side by reason of the axiological turn of his argument. We will therefore pay no further notice to this axiological turn, and devote our attention exclusively to the question, whether in some other manner the "self-guarantee of theoretical truth" is to be maintained as the basis of a "purely theoretical" conception of philosophy.

We previously observed, that this pretended self-guarantee *can* in no case *be proved theoretically*. THEODOR LITT, too, has discovered the pitfall which is hidden from the defenders of the absoluteness and self-guarantee of "theoretical truth" in the conception, that *it should be possible to demonstrate it in a theoretical way*.

Nay, he goes so far as to charge those who consider this "self-guarantee" to be demonstrable, with *relativism*, in as much as they attempt to refer "truth" to something that is not yet itself truth, something other than truth, if possible *more than truth*.

The only point really capable of theoretical demonstration in his view is the internal contradiction in which every form of a relativistic view of truth must involve itself.

This would really signify not much, or rather nothing, for the defence of the self-sufficiency of theoretical thought, if LITT did not also start from an aprioristic identification of the absolute self-guaranteeing truth with *theoretical correctness.*

For if truth is not regarded as being exhausted in its relation to theoretical thought, but in "theoretical verity" there is seen only a refraction of meaning (not sufficient to itself) of the fulness of all truth, i.e. of its *religious fulness,* then the demonstration that "relativism" is self-destructive turns immediately against such as deny this fulness of verity.

LITT, however, has armed himself at the very outset against all misunderstanding of his opinion on this point by making self-sufficient truth hold good exclusively in correlation to the "cogito", to the "I think (theoretically)".By this means he intends also expressly to cut off all "hypostatization" of verity as an Idea or "value" which has *being* or *validity* apart from all subjectivity.

In other words, the "absolute, self-sufficient truth" holds only in and for theoretical thought! Yet this judgment is ostensibly self-contradiction incarnate! How can a truth be absolute and self-sufficient, the validity of which is relativized to *theoretical thought?*

The philosophy of values, at any rate, escaped from *this* contradiction by hypostatizing truth as an absolute *value,* elevated in itself above all relationship to subjectivity. By restricting the validity of truth from the outset to the theoretical thought-relation, LITT falls here into a fundamental *relativism,* which he supposed he had just cut off at the root in his absolutizing of *theoretical* truth.

It is interesting to see how LITT now seeks to justify himself against the reproach of *relativism* as to verity.

Such a *relativism* for him is in all its possible forms an internally contradictory scepticism, which in its argumentation must simultaneously pre-suppose and annihilate the authentic concept of truth: "Annihilate: for that which they call 'truth' in express words is not truth; pre-suppose: for the act of annihilating is a spiritual deed, which is meaningful only if 'truth' in the original sense is accepted as possible and attainable" [1].

This antinomy would remain hidden from scepticism, only

---

[1] *Einleitung,* p. 29: „Vernichten: denn das, was sie expressis verbis „Wahrheit" *nennen,* ist nicht Wahrheit; voraussetzen: denn dieser Akt der Vernichtung ist ein geistiges Tun, das nur dann sinnvoll ist, wenn „Wahrheit" im ursprünglichen Sinne als möglich und erreichbar angenommen wird."

because it has not advanced to the last stage of self-reflection on the part of theoretical thought. It asks only reflectively after the claim to validity which is inherent in the judgments of thought directed to "Gegenstände", but forgets that the judgments of this reflective thought also make a claim of absolute validity as to truth! In other words, it has not attained to the reflective introspection of thought, wherein thought is directed exclusively toward itself and not toward its "Gegenstände".

If biology, psychology, and even anthropology investigate the thought-function scientifically, then they can examine it only as a special aspect of reality in full relativity to the other aspects. They remain then in the sphere of "objective thought", for which thought itself signifies a piece of "reality", a "Gegenstand".

But in all biological, psychological and anthropological thought the actual "I think", which can never be made into a "Gegenstand" of thought, remains hidden. It is pre-eminently the task of philosophical thought, as thought directed to self-reflection, to set in the light this *subjective antipole* of all *objective reality;* it is its very task to demonstrate how the *validity of truth,* which the judgments of objectivizing scientific thought claim for themselves, remains dependent upon the absolute validity of truth of the pronouncements of reflective thought.

Well then, if the binding of the absolute validity of truth to the thought-relation really were to signify, that truth was limited to *real* thinking beings, then, but only *then*, according tot LITT, would his conception of truth have slipped down into the paths of sceptical relativism. But this is not the case. For by the "cogito" (I think), to which absolute truth in its validity is restricted, there is here to be understood only "pure thought", i.e. "that thought of which we said above, that it 'springs back' again and again into the counter-position to the 'Gegenstand' thought of." This "thought" is no longer an aspect of concrete temporal reality. It is the transcendental subject of thought, itself universally valid, the self-consciousness that has arrived at determinateness in reflective thought, which is not inherent in individual reality, but in "Denken schlechthin" (mere thought as such). For all temporal and spatial reality, the *full concrete ego* (self) as individual experiential reality included, is in the epistemological relation only the *"objective antipole"* of this transcendental "I think", so that the "cogito" in this transcendental sense can never be subsumed under it.

The introduction of absolute truth into the thought-relation thus conceived of should not actually lead to the consequences of relativism, since the attempt is not here made *to deduce* "truth" from something else. Rather there is accepted, in LITT's view, a strict *correlation* between truth and (transcendental) "cogito". "Here there is consequently a strict balance between the members, which are united by this relation: just as 'truth', is determined in view of the 'thinking being', so the 'thinking being' is determined in view of 'truth', and only in view of it"[1]. A *correlation* of this absoluteness should not allow the least scope to "relativism".

Critique of LITT's conception.

We have deliberately reproduced LITT's conception of the absoluteness and self-guarantee of theoretical truth in as detailed a fashion as possible, and as far as possible in his own words, in order to do full justice to his argument. Every link in the argument actually counts, if in our criticism we are not to pass our opponent and find merely a *fancied* refutation.

We again plan to begin with *immanent* criticism.

Let us hold to the strict correlation in which the author sets theoretical thought and truth. It is clear, that the *relativizing of the fulness [of meaning] of verity* to a *merely theoretical truth*, which beyond possible contradiction is involved in the intended correlation, at best could not detract from the absoluteness and pretended self-guarantee of verity only in case the "transcendental cogito" could lay claim to the same absoluteness as *truth itself*. This would mean, that they are one and the same, identical in a logical sense. Indeed the argument must result into such an identification. After all, the entire demonstration respecting the self-guarantee of "theoretical truth" must serve to save the unconditional, "purely theoretical" character of philosophic thought itself. For what is involved here in the first place, is not the self-sufficiency of "truth", but the self-guarantee, the *self-sufficiency of philosophic thought*. LITT may emphatically reject the Idea that he would *deduce* the "truth" from philosophic thought. Yet he will not be able to deny, that the supposed absoluteness and self-sufficiency of theoretical verity stands or falls with that of philosophic thought itself.

---

[1] „Hier besteht also ein strenges *Gleichgewicht* zwischen den Gliedern, die durch die Relation verbunden sind: wie die „Wahrheit" im Hinblick auf das „denkende Wesen", so ist das „denkende Wesen" im Hinblick auf die „Wahrheit" und *nur* im Hinblick auf sie bestimmt."

It is entirely in Litt's line, that we seek to approximate the meaning of the *correlation* intended by him from the subjective philosophic pole of thought. For, according to him, it does not make sense to speak about that which I cannot grasp in a *concept* when thinking *subjectively*. Consequently, this holds also with regard to "absolute truth". However, it may not be denied, that in this very way a serious danger has arisen for the absoluteness of verity, and that in the course of further reasoning this absoluteness threatens to be dissolved into the absoluteness of philosophic thought. For now "absolute truth" appears also to require theoretical logical determination by philosophic thought. Otherwise, how could it be "purely theoretical"?

In contradistinction to this, the determination which philosophic thought would have to receive from the side of "absolute truth" appears to be logically *un-determined* to the highest degree.

If "absolute verity" does not appear to be identical with the "absolute cogito" in its dialectical development of thought, it sinks back in Litt's own line of thought to the level of the "Gegenstand" of thought, which must receive all its determination from *thought* itself.

The first pitfall in Litt's demonstration: the unconditional character of the 'transcendental cogito'.

However, when we pass on to the *subjective pole of thought*, to the 'transcendental cogito' — which in Litt's Kantian opinion maintains itself in contradistinction to all *reality* as its absolute opposite — then, in the conception of the "unconditional character" of this pole of thought, the pitfall laid bare in our Introduction reappears.

For the "cogito" is nothing but the *selfhood* in its logical thought-activity. It is altogether impossible to dissolve this *selfhood* in the modal meaning of *its logical function*, unless we have left a bare *concept*, which is itself merely a product of the thinking *ego*.

This pitfall was, indeed, observed by Fichte, the father of the entire dialectical-reflective way of thinking, when he spoke of a necessary tension between "absolute ego"[1] and "thinking ego."

Litt, on the contrary, who intends to follow in Fichte's foot-

---

[1] This is something entirely different from Litt's *"full concrete ego"*, intended as "object" of thought.

steps, has not observed the antinomy of "unconditioned thought", for he hypostatizes theoretical thought in the Humanistic sense of *value-free* reflection. FICHTE, in his Kantian phase, refused to do so, because he did not seek the *root* or the *selfhood* of human existence in "theoretical", but in the so-called "practical reason", i.e. in KANT's "homo noumenon" as synthetic hypostatization of the ethical function of personality. In other words, to him theoretical thought was *ethically determined* from the outset. In LITT, the *full ego* is identical with the concrete, individual complex of *its functions in temporal-spatial reality* and so can be determined only by the transcendental absolute thought! However, in *this so-called "full, concrete ego" the selfhood which transcends all thought is not really to be found.*

Thus LITT's conception of the absolute self-guarantee of the "merely-theoretical truth" dissolves itself into a speculative hypostatization of thought; this latter disintegrates into internal contradictions and cannot again be rendered harmless by a dialectical turn of thought by which it recognizes itself in the last analysis as logically identical (in the opposition) with the "full ego". With the acceptance of the unconditioned character, the self-sufficiency of philosophic thought, the actual I-ness falls. This I-ness persists in its *religious actuality which determines all thought,* in contradistinction to all logical concepts. With the denial of the actual I-ness or self-hood, however, the possibility of knowledge and the possibility of forming concepts must be lost. LITT would actually have to come to these destructive consequences in his system, if in it he had consistently followed the postulate of the purity of philosophic thought. The fact that he has nonetheless developed a philosophical system, proves that he was far from thinking "purely theoretically"!

The second pitfall: the opposition of transcendental thought and full reality.

A second pitfall in LITT's conception of the transcendental "cogito", already laid bare in an earlier context of our transcendental critique, is the supposition that, in the antithetic relation of theoretic thought *full temporal reality* — in opposition to the subjective pole "I think" — would spring back into the antipole of "Gegenständlichkeit" (for LITT, identical with *objectivity!*).

This supposition is completely incorrect and contradictory, since it neglects the temporal coherence of meaning, to which the logical function of thought remains bound even in its ultimate actuality which may not be objectivized.

In our transcendental critique of theoretical thought we have shown, that the antithetical relation from which alone the epistemological problem of the "Gegenstand" can arise does not correspond to reality. Consequently, reality itself, can never be made into a "Gegenstand" of thinking in its actual logical function, but is only a merely intentional abstraction performed *within* the real theoretical act of our consciousness. In the absolutizing of the "transcendental logical subject" it is entirely overlooked that theoretical thought is possible only in an inter-modal synthesis which pre-supposes the cosmic coherence of meaning in time, and consequently cannot be of a purely logical character.

The second misconception, however, which we must lay bare in Litt's argument, grounded in the first, is, that the selfhood should be determined only by "pure" thought, i.e. by dialectical logic.

The "self-refutation of scepticism" reduced to its true proportion.

So the self-refutation of scepticism, in which Rickert and Litt alike focus the force of their argument, can actually have nothing to do with a pretended self-guarantee of merely theoretical truth.

Let us try to reduce it to its true proportions. Then the state of affairs appears to be that logical thought in its subjectivity is necessarily subjected to the logical laws, in casu — the "principium contradictionis" (principle of contradiction).

If anybody is to think theoretically, he ought to begin by recognizing the validity of this principle, which is in no sense absolute and "unconditioned", but rather of a cosmic-temporal character. Does this mean, that other creatures, or God Himself, could set aside the principle of non-contradiction in their thought? If this question is to have a *meaning,* one must proceed from the supposition that God Himself, or e.g. the angels, also would *have to think* in a cosmic temporal fashion. For, as a matter of fact, human thought is able to proceed in setting aside the principle of non-contradiction; e.g. the whole "dialectic logic" does so. But whoever would suppose this "thought" in the case of God and the angels, supposes at the same time, that they are included in the cosmic temporal order and that they are subjected to the laws that rule therein, although they can transgress them in so far as they have a norm-character. Quod *absurdum!* and with respect to the sovereign God: *Quod blasphenium!*

From the time of Greek *Sophism*, sceptical relativism has been characterized by its primary denial that thought is subjected to a *norm* of truth. It is an *irrationalism* in the epistemological field.

Actually this denial must necessarily lead to antinomy, so far as the judgment: "There is no truth" must itself be tested by the norm of verity. Does, however, this judgment in its claim to truth, imply the validity of an absolute, self-sufficient *theoretical* verity? In no way! He who says: "There is no truth", intends this statement in the first place against the validity of a norm of verity in the temporal coherence of meaning. Furthermore, he directs it in the most absolute sense also against the supratemporal *totality* and *Origin* of truth. Thereby, he necessarily entangles himself in the antinomy, that his very judgment makes claim to a verity, which must be the *full* one.

LITT's proclamation of the self-sufficiency of *theoretical truth*, however, must lead to the same sceptical relativism and consequently to the same antinomy. Consistently thought out, it can recognize no norm which dominates the absolutized "transcendental-logical subject", since it declares the subjective 'cogito' to be sovereign and proclaims it to be the ἀρχή of all meaning and order.

How could subjective theoretical thought still be viewed as self-sufficient, if it were acknowledged, that it is *subject* to a law, *which it has not itself imposed?*

In LITT's line of thought, the "transcendental cogito" does not belong to the full temporal reality *in its indissoluble correlation of cosmonomic side and subject-side.* Reality in the "Gegebenheitskorrelation" [i.e. the datum-correlation] is seen only in the absolutized individuality, which is ascribed to the "concrete ego" itself. It is as little subjected to laws, as the "transcendental ego", but is understood as the absolute irrational which can be *objectivized* only in the "Erkenntniskorrelation" (correlation of knowledge) and conceived by the "transcendental-logical ego" in universally valid thought forms.

Nowhere in LITT's philosophy does the cosmic law really have a place in its original inseparable correlation to the individual *subjectivity* that is subjected to it. The "pure thinking subject" with its reflective and objectivizing thought-forms is itself the "universally valid" and the origin of all universal validity.

The *"theoretical universal validity"* originating from the "autonomous" selfhood (which identifies itself with its transcendental-logical function in the will to "pure thought") is the substitute for the cosmic order and its different modal law-spheres to which all individual subjectivity is subjected according to God's law of creation.

However, here arises a dialectical tension, a veritable antinomic relation between *universal validity* and *individuality;* between absolutized theoretical thought with its would-be self-sufficient absolute truth and individual subjectivity in the 'datum-correlation' ("Gegebenheitskorrelation"); between "thinking ego" and "living (experiencing) ego"; between *philosophy as a universally valid theory, and a life- and world-view as an entirely individual impression of life* on the part of the sovereign personality, not *subjected to any norm of truth!*

In its *dialectical thought* philosophy has, according to LITT, eventually to establish this *lawlessness of individuality*. In the irrationality of life, it has to recognize *its* dialectical *other* which possesses no universal validity. It has to establish in a "universally valid manner" the individual law-lessness of personality in its life- and world-view, in order eventually to understand its *dialectical unity-in-the-opposition* with that life- and world-view! For actually, dialectical "purely theoretical thought" and a "life- and world-view" as a norm-less "individual impression of life" are, in the light of LITT's transcendental ground-Idea, two dialectical emanations from the same *ego,* which lives in a relativistically undermined *Humanistic ideal of personality.*

The absolutizing of the "transcendental cogito" to a self-sufficient, "unconditioned", "sovereign" instance implies, that "pure thought" is not subjected to a *cosmic order,* in which the laws of logical thought too, are grounded. Since theoretical reason also tries to create the coherence of meaning between its logical aspect and the other modal aspects of our cosmos, the result is a dialectical mode of thought, which relativizes in an expressly *logical* way the basic laws of logic as norms and limits of our subjective logical function.

How can such "dialectical thought" subject itself to a veritable norm of truth that stands *above* it? The absolutizing of theoretical truth, which amounts to the dissolution of its *meaning,* is the work of the apostate selfhood, that will not subject itself to the laws established by the Ἀρχή of every creature, and therefore ascribes to its dialectical thought a sovereignty surmounting all boundaries of laws. To LITT, the criterion of all relativism resides in the denial of the self-sufficiency of "purely theoretical" truth. By this time, we have seen how the proclamation of this self-sufficiency is *in truth* nothing but the primary absolutizing of theoretical thought itself, *which is the fountain of all relativism*, since it denies the fulness of meaning of verity and up-roots theoretical thought.

The "self-refutation of scepticism" is at the same time the self-refutation of the neutrality-postulate and of the conception of theoretical thought as self-sufficient!

But that self-refutation may not be overestimated in its proportion. For, in the last analysis, it proves no more than that whoever will think theoretically has to subject himself to a theoretical norm of truth which cannot have originated from that thought itself; for this norm has *meaning* only in the *coherence of meaning* and in relation to the totality of truth, to the *fulness* of verity, which, exactly as *fulness, must transcend theoretical thought itself*, and thus can never be "purely theoretical".

That self-refutation which manifests itself in the contradiction, in which logical thought turning against its own laws necessarily entangles itself, cannot of itself lead us to the positive knowledge of verity.

It is merely a *logical* criterion of truth, which is not self-sufficient.

For in the conception of the full material meaning of truth, philosophy exhibits its complete dependence upon its transcendental basic Idea as the ultimate theoretical expression of its religious ground-motive.

The test of the transcendental ground-Idea.

In applying the test of the transcendental ground-idea to LITT's philosophical system, we come to the surprising result, that there is still less question of an authentic rationalistic bent with him than with RICKERT. In his dialectical thought, LITT rather inclines to the pole of the *irrationalist philosophy of life*, which he has simply brought under dialectical thought-forms. The absolutizing of dialectical thought that is considered to be elevated above a "borniertes gegenständliches Denken" (a narrowly restricted kind of objective thought holding itself to the principle of non-contradiction) points, in the light of LITT's conception of individuality, to the opposite of a rationalistic hypostatization of universal laws. In this respect Litt actually exhibits a strong kinship with Hegel, whose so-called "pan-logism" is as little to be understood rationalistically, but discloses its true intentions only against the background of the irrationalist turn of the Humanistic ideal of personality in Romanticism! In general, dialectic thought has an anti-rationalist tendency.

Litt's dialectical philosophy, measured by its own criterion, is an "irrationalist life- and world-view" in the would-be universally-valid forms of dialectical thought, an *irrationalistic logicism*, oriented historically.

But we, who apply another criterion, can recognize no dialeclical unity of philosophy and a life- and world-view, but rather find the deeper unity of the two in their religious ground-motive. The content of Litt's transcendental ground-Idea is determined by an irrationalist turn of the Humanistic freedom-motive in its dialectical tension with the motive of scientific domination of nature, which has undergone a fundamental depreciation in his philosophy.

§ 5 - THE TRANSCENDENTAL GROUND-IDEA AND THE MEANING OF TRUTH

> The impossibility of an authentic religiously neutral theory of the life- and world-views. The concept of truth is never purely theoretical with respect to its meaning.

On account of its immanent theoretical character philosophy has to give a theoretical account of a life- and world-view, with which it is, however, united in its religious root. It cannot accomplish this task, however, until it attains to critical self-reflection with respect to its transcendental ground-Idea.

As little as it can be religiously neutral itself, so little can it give a neutral theory of the life- and world-views.

No single philosophic "Weltanschauungslehre" is neutral, inasmuch as it cannot be neutral with respect to the material meaning of truth, not even in a sceptical relativism that upsets all foundations of philosophic theory.

Litt considers life- and world-views, as bound in "a dialectical unity" with philosophy (loc. cit. pp. 251ff) and interprets them as concrete personal confessions of the individual struggle between person and cosmos. Philosophy, which should remain a science of a *universally valid character*, must, according to him, surmount the content of these confessions regarded as "something merely concrete, i.e. purely individual and limited", although the *impulse* to philosophic thought has originated out of this same concrete "view of life". The irrationalist Humanistic ideal of personality which is the basic factor in the *transcendental Idea* of LITT's dialectical system at once discloses itself in this secularized irrationalist and personalist outlook on a life- and world-view.

To be sure, LITT may in this manner interpret his own life- and world-view; but if he claims "universal validity" and "absolute truth" for this philosophic outlook on every life- and world-view, then in the nature of the case there is no question of "theoretical neutrality", and there *can* be no question of it, since otherwise he would have to abandon his own Humanistic vision as to the meaning of truth.

The whole hypostatization of "pure" dialectical thought serves only to release human personality, in its interpretation of life, from every norm of truth, and to loosen its individuality from the bond of a law. Hence the conflict against all "universally-valid norms and values" by which a rationalistic or semi-rationalistic Humanism still wished to bind that individuality in the human person.

We find as little neutrality in RICKERT's theory of life- and world-views.

In him, too, there exists a religious unity in the meaning that he ascribes to his theoretical concept of truth, and in his proclamation of the sovereignty of personality loosed from the norm of truth in the choice of its life- and world-view. Only he stops half-way on the road to irrationalism, and still holds fast to formal universally-valid values and norms of reason.

By wresting the life- and world-views into the theoretical scheme of his philosophy of values, in the nature of the case he theoretically *falsifies* the meaning of every life- and world-view that rejects the religious starting-point of this philosophy.

How can one, for example, interpret the Calvinistic life- and world-view theoretically as a "theistic" one, grounded in the choice of the "value of holiness" as "highest value", to which as subjective commitment ("Subjectsverhalten") "piety" answers and as "good" the "world of gods" (thus RICKERT's sixth type!)?

It is evident, that here, in a religious aprioristic manner, a Humanistic-idealist meaning is inserted in the transcendental theoretical Idea of truth, which in advance cuts off an unprejudiced understanding of a life- and world-view with a different religious foundation.

The dependence of the meaning which a philosophic system reads into in the theoretical concept of truth, upon the *transcendental ground-Idea* appears from a confrontation of the various conceptions of verity, which immanence-philosophy has developed. By way of illustration, compare the *nominalist* view of HOBBES with the *realistic* and *metaphysical* conception of ARISTOTLE. In HOBBES truth and falsehood are considered only as attributes of language and not of "things". According to HOBBES the exact truth consists only in the immanent agreement of concepts with each other on the basis of conventional definitions (cf. LEVIATHAN. Part I, 4). In ARISTOTLE truth consists in the agreement of the judgment with the metaphysical *essence* of the things judged. Also compare KANT's *transcendental-logical, idealistic concept of truth* with HUME's psychologistic one; or the *mathematical* concept of truth of a DESCARTES with the *dialectical* view of a HEGEL or LITT, to say nothing of the pragmatic concept of scientific verity in the modern Humanistic philosophy of life, and in existentialism [1].

The supposition that, if the validity of truth is but restricted to pure theory, the meaning of verity can be determined in a "universally-valid fashion", is based on self-deception.

The consequence of the postulate of neutrality would actually have to be the allocation of the concept of truth to a personal choice of a life- and world-view.

Immanence-philosophy recognizes no norm of truth above its transcendental ground-Idea.

Actually, immanence-philosophy recognizes no norm of truth above its transcendental ground-Idea. In fact, the dogma concerning the autonomy of theoretical reason — especially in its Humanistic sense — hands truth over to the subjective commitment of the apostate personality. Therefore it is in vain that transcendental idealism attempts a refutation of the relativistic view of verity by means of *logical* arguments only.

Truth admits of no restriction to 'the theoretical-logical sphere

---

[1] He who desires a more complete picture of the confusing diversity in conceptions of the meaning of truth, need only consult EISLER's *Wörterbuch der Philos. Begriffe.* Vol. III (4th Ed. 1930) Sub voce *Wahrheit* (pp. 450—471).

as regards its fulness and temporal coherence of meaning. The validity of truth necessarily extends as far as the realm of judgments extends.

The distinction between theoretical and a-theoretical judgments. The inner contradiction of a restriction of the validity of truth to the former.

The consequence of LITT's conception (which RICKERT also had to take, although he persisted in calling all judgments theoretical [1]) is, that a sharp distinction must be made between *theoretical judgments* on the one hand, and *a-theoretical judgments of valuation* on the other, and that only the former can lay claim to universal validity of truth. Measured by this criterion, the judgment "This rose is beautiful", for example, or the judgment "This action is immoral" is withdrawn from this universal validity.

This entire distinction, however, (which goes back to KANT's dualistic transcendental ground-Idea with its cleavage between theoretical knowledge and apriori rational faith) is untenable and cancels itself when it is thought out.

For there exists no meaningful judgment of valuation, which does not at once, as a *judgment,* lay claim to validity of truth. An aesthetic or moral judgment as formulated above, with respect to its full intention must run as follows: "This rose is *in truth* beautiful" and "This action is *in truth* immoral", respectively. For these judgments imply the supposition: there exists a universally valid standard of aesthetic and moral valuation and to this rose and this action, respectively, the predicates "beautiful" and "immoral" are truly ascribed in my judgment [2].

---

[1] Cf. e.g. *System der Phil.*, p. 388. But it may not be denied that, for example the expression: "Truth is the highest value" is a *judgment*, which, in RICKERT's own view, can never be called a *theoretical* judgment, because it proceeds from a life- and world-view. Besides, as is well known, for RICKERT the theoretical judgments too are oriented to a (theoretical) *value*.

[2] RICKERT, loc. cit. p. 388 supposes that the explicit assertion that something is beautiful, insofar as we seek to found this judgment theoretically, should be a theoretical judgment about the "aesthetic value", and that in such a judgment the characteristic aesthetic attitude, which according to him lacks a universally valid standard, is in fact abandoned. The art lover, however, who is not at all related theoretically to the work of art, but who, in the full contemplation of the work, asserts the judgment "This work of art is beautiful" wants just as well, and necessarily so,

This is the case, even though he who asserts the judgment is incapable of rendering a theoretical account of this supposition.

Whoever denies this state of affairs, which is rooted in the fact, that no single modal aspect of our temporal cosmos is self-sufficient (but rather each refers to the inter-modal *coherence of meaning)*, denies thereby the *meaning* of aesthetic and moral judgments themselves. He cuts through the coherence of meaning among the logical, the aesthetic and the moral law-spheres and can no longer allow even the principle of contradiction to be valid for the so-called "a-theoretical" judgments.

If a man standing before REMBRANDT's *"Night-Watch"*, in opposition to the predominant conception, were to call this masterpiece *un-aesthetic, un-lovely* and at the same time would claim: "There exists no universally valid norm for aesthetic valuation", he would fall into the same contradiction as the sceptic who denies a universally-valid truth. He can try to defend himself, by making the reservation: I for one think this painting unlovely. But then it has no meaning to set this subjective impression against the generally predominant view. If this critic should also concede this, and so refrains from pressing his opinion upon others, then his judgment becomes *meaningless* as an *aesthetic* judgment. In other words, it is then no longer an aesthetic judgment, since it lacks aesthetic *qualification and determinateness.*

Every subjective valuation receives its *determinateness* by being subjected to a norm, which determines the subjectivity and defines it in its *meaning!* There exists no *aesthetic* subjectivity apart from a universally valid aesthetic norm to which it is subjected.

Let it not be objected here, that the beauty of the "Night-Watch" is so thoroughly individual, that it cannot be exhausted in universally valid aesthetic norms.

For individuality is proper to the subjective as such, and the "Night-Watch", without possible contradiction, is the objective realization of a completely individual, *subjective*-aesthetic conception. But this is not the point here. The question is only

---

to imply the *truth* of his assertion in this non-theoretical judgment. To claim, with RICKERT, that such a non-theoretical aesthetic judgment is impossible, is simply untenable. Besides, if aesthetic valuation were to know no tension between norm and aesthetic object, as RICKERT pretends, why then do I distinguish beautiful and ugly in my a-theoretical appreciation of art?

whether the judgment: "The "Night-Watch" is beautiful", really has a universally-valid *meaning* or not. If not, then it does not make sense either to say, that the "Night-Watch" is a great work of art. If so, then the judgment must necessarily make claim to universally-valid truth. Tertium non datur!

> Theoretical and non-theoretical judgments. The latter are never a-logical, but merely non-"gegenständlich".

As we have shown before in our transcendental criticism of theoretic thought, the matter stands thus: theoretical judgments are abstract, distinguishing and combining modal meanings. They embody theoretical knowledge, which exists in an intermodal synthesis of meaning between the logical aspect of thought and the modal meaning of an a-logical aspect of our experience which has been made into a "Gegenstand".

These judgments are subjected to the norm of theoretical truth, which holds for scientific knowledge.

The non-theoretical, so-called "practical" judgments are not *a-logical* — no judgment can be a-logical — but merely *non-"gegenständlich"*, i.e. not grounded in the theoretical attitude of knowledge, which *sets* the logical aspect of thought *in contrast* to the abstracted a-logical aspect of experience.

They are subjected to the norm of pre-theoretical truth, which holds for pre-scientific knowledge but possesses *universal validity* as well as the norm of theoretical truth [1].

As all temporal truth is based on the temporal coherence of meaning of the logical and the non-logical aspects of reality, it points out beyond itself to the fulness of meaning of verity, which is given only in the religious totality of meaning of our cosmos in its relation to the Origin.

With respect to its meaning every judgment appeals to the fulness of truth, in which no temporal restriction any longer has meaning. For verity does not allow any limitation as to its *fulness of meaning*.

He who thus relativizes its validity to a would-be "pure" theoretical thought, and at the same time recognizes that the theoretical scientific judgments do not exhaust the realm of judgments, falls into the logical self-refutation of scepticism.

---

[1] In our treatment of the problem of knowledge, we shall show, that theoretical truth cannot stand alongside of the pre-theoretical, but that they make appeal to each other in a deeper sense.

For, on the one hand, he denies the *fulness* of truth by *relativizing* this latter to the special realm of the *theoretical*, in distinction from the *non*-theoretical. Yet, on the other hand, he requires for his conception *full* validity of truth without any restriction [1].

> LITT's distinction between theoretical and "weltanschauliche" truth and the self-refutation of this distinction in the sense in which LITT intends it.

LITT makes a sharp distinction between truth in its *proper sense* of *theoretical universally valid* verity and the "so-called" "truth of a life- and world-view". In itself, this distinction might make good sense, were it not that LITT actually *denies* all "weltanschauliche Wahrheit".

For, used with the latter signification, the word "truth" in his view would be merely a predicate, applied to assertions of a life- and world-view, in order thereby to express: "the unmutilated integrity with which a thinker makes confession of his interpretation of life to himself and to others, the inner consistency with which he develops it, the convincing force, with which he knows how to represent and support it and... the agreement between it and his actual behaviour in life" [2].

> The inner contradiction of this dualism. The meaninglessness of judgments, which are alleged not to be subjected to the norm of truth.

However, as soon as we attempt seriously to carry through this conception, it appears to dissolve itself in inner contradiction. For, if the judgments which a life- and world-view provides are not subjected to a universally-valid norm of truth,

---

[1] This antinomy goes back to a basic antinomy in the transcendental idea of the thinker. For, on the one hand, he can*not* locate the *totality of meaning* in the theoretical, because, in that case, the personality-ideal with its a-theoretical "values" would be relegated to a corner. But, on the other hand, he supposes he can find his Archimedean point in theoretical thought. A merely logical antinomy does not exist, as we shall see later.

[2] loc. cit., p. 255: "Die ungeschminkte Aufrichtigkeit, mit der ein Denker sich vor sich selbst und anderen zu seiner Lebensdeutung bekennt, die innere Folgerichtigkeit mit der er sie entwickelt, die überzeugende Kraft, mit der er sie vorzutragen und zu begründen weisz und... die Übereinstimmung zwischen ihr und seiner tätigen Bewährung im Leben."

they lose all meaning. They are really no judgments, and so cannot contain an individual "interpretation of life".

For a subjective "interpretation of life" which is expressed in a series of judgments, makes sense only, if our temporal cosmos in which we live, actually exists as a coherence of meaning. If this is the case, the judgments in which that interpretation is given are necessarily subjected to a universally valid norm of truth, in accordance with which my subjective interpretation should agree with the true state of affairs; in other words, the question is whether or not the judgment is true with respect to the meaning of our cosmos. However, if there is no universally-valid truth with respect to the latter, then I can give no subjective "interpretation of life" either. For I can *interpret* only that of which I can judge *truly* that *it has a meaning, even though I should personally leave undecided the verity of my individual interpretation.*

LITT now supposes, that he can escape these destructive consequences of his standpoint by making theoretical truth in its universal validity the judge as to essence, meaning and *limits* of the so-called "weltanschauliche Wahrheit". Thus the judgments of the life- and world-view again appear to be subjected to the really mysterious "universally valid theoretical truth" — but only in order immediately to release them again from every norm of verity. For, the universally valid truth in this respect turns out to be that the judgments of the life- and world-view, as assertions of a merely individual impression of life, are situated "beyond truth and falsity".

For LITT, by reason of the transcendental basic Idea of his philosophical system, is, as we saw, still more averse to an intellectualistic philosophy than RICKERT. "Truth" must be restricted to the theoretical realm, if theoretical thought is not again, in the old intellectualistic way, to dominate the life- and world-view of the sovereign personality.

If, however, he persists in the view that, for example, the judgments: "God is the Creator of the world, which He has created to His glory", and indeed: "Religion has to give way to science", are situated "beyond truth and falsity", because they comprise merely individual interpretations of life, then it is necessary to draw the full consequences of this conception. For in this case there cannot even exist any universally valid truth with respect to the totality of meaning of our temporal world either (which indeed according to LITT's own admission is *more* than *merely theoretical*) and its relation to the modal diversity of meaning.

If this consequence too is accepted, then the meaning of a life- and world-view as well as that of philosophic theoretical thought must be denied together with the meaning of "theoretical truth". Theoretical thought has then annihilated its own foundations.

For philosophic thought is directed to the totality of meaning. However, if there exists no universally valid truth as to the relationship of totality, particularity and coherence of meaning, then philosophic thought has no norm of truth either, by which it may be tested.

The pole of absolute scepticism is hereby attained, and consequently the pole of complete self-refutation.

The concept of an "absolute merely theoretical truth" dissolves itself in inner contradiction. Our transcendental critique, however, penetrates behind the *logical* contradictions, in which the doctrine of the self-sufficiency of "pure theoretical truth" is entangled, to the root of this doctrine and exposes the relativistic bottom on which it builds its theoretical system. Only on the basis of its relativistic *religious* attitude, can the emphasis be explained, with which this school in modern times tries to safeguard at least theoretical truth against the invasion of relativism, which for a long time has undermined its life- and world-views.

An intrinsically Christian philosophy does not need to learn from the Humanistic ideal of personality, that theoretical thought cannot dominate religion and a life- and world-view. But Humanistic philosophy may learn from our transcendental criticism that, on the contrary, philosophic thought is dependent upon the religious ground-motive of the thinking ego.

§ 6 - CLOSER DETERMINATION OF THE RELATION BETWEEN PHILOSOPHY AND A LIFE- AND WORLD-VIEW

In what sense does philosophy have to give an account of the life- and world-view?

It has to bring the latter to theoretical clarity by rendering a theoretic account of its pre-theoretic picture of the world. So far as it includes in its horizon life- and world-views which possess another religious foundation than that which finds expression in its own transcendental ground-Idea, it must try to approximate this foundation in a transcendental ground-Idea, which is equal to the task of the theoretical illumination of these life- and world-views. This is the only way in which it is really possible to do justice to the various types of life- and world-views.

> The life- and world-view is no system and cannot be made a system without affecting its essence.

At this juncture, the problem also necessarily emerges, why philosophy will never be in a position to replace the life- and world-view. It cannot do so for the same reason that prevents it from replacing naïve experience by theoretical knowledge. There is left a residue of living immediacy in every life- and world-view, which must necessarily escape theoretical concepts.

An authentic life- and world-view is never a system; not that it should be lost in *faith* or *feeling*, but because in it thought must remain *focused* in the full concrete reality. This is exactly what *theoretical, systematic thought* as such cannot do.

As soon as a life- and world-view is made into a *system*, it loses *its proper* universality, it no longer speaks to us out of the fullness of reality. It now speaks out of the distance which scientific abstraction must preserve in opposition to life, if it is to furnish us with theoretical knowledge.

A life- and world-view has no universality in the sense of a (philosophic) system. It does not bear a "closed" character, as LITT supposes. It must rather remain continuously *open* to each concrete situation of life, in which it finds itself placed. Its deeper unity lies only in its religious root.

To the Calvinistic life- and world-view, as developed by Dr A. KUYPER in the Netherlands since the last decades of the nineteenth century, belongs undoubtedly also the radical Christian view of science. But how is this view of science born? Not from a philosophical or systematic tendency, but rather in the midst of a concrete situation of life. The pressure of the scholastic notion of science on the one hand, the necessity for defence against the ruling Humanistic view of science on the other, stimulated young neo-Calvinism to a consideration of its religious calling in the realm of science.

While Christianity in the Roman Empire was still being persecuted with fire and sword, its attitude with respect to politics and wordly culture in general was, in the main, a negative one. There could be a positive commitment with respect to the task of the Christian in this territory, only when the possibility of exercising influence in these realms had been created.

Apart from the concrete influence of the rationalistic thought of the "Enlightenment" upon all realms of life, the reaction of the ideal of personality would never have disclosed itself in Humanistic circles. This reaction has been an important turning-point in the development of the Humanistic life- and world-view. That is to say, the requirement of the neutrality of science with respect to personal commitment in a life- and world-view would never have been born apart from this concrete situation.

Many more instances may be adduced in favour of our thesis. We constantly find the development of a life- and world-view in immediate contact with concrete situations in the fulness of life. These things will remain so, because this immediate relation to the latter is essential to the life- and world-view.

On this account we must repeat, that it is entirely erroneous to conceive of Christian philosophy as nothing but a theoretical elaboration of a Christian life- and world-view.

A life- and world-view may not be "elaborated" philosophically. It must elaborate itself in the sequence of immediate life- and world-situations.

Is it then peculiar to the concrete individuality and so prevented from laying claim to "universal validity"?

> What is the meaning of the concept "universal-validity"? The Kantian conception is determined by the critical Humanist immanence-standpoint.

For this question to be answered satisfactorily, it is first necessary to render an account of the correct *meaning* of the concept "universal validity". Up to the present, we came to know this concept only in the dogmatic cadre of a pretended "unconditioned pure thought" in which it really took the place of a standard of truth.

KANT, as is well known, was the first to give to it an apriori epistemological meaning. "Universally valid" means to him: independent of all "empirical subjectivity", valid for the "transcendental consciousness", the "transcendental cogito", which is itself in its apriori syntheses the *origin* of all universal validity in the field of experience. In this sense, the *synthetic apriori, which makes objective experience possible,* is universally valid.

On the other hand, perception has merely "subjective validity", since it is dependent upon sensory impressions, on which no objective, necessary validity can be grounded.

KANT has applied this contrast to *judgments,* by distinguishing the latter into *mere judgments of perception and judgments* of experience. "So far as empirical judgments have objective validity, they are JUDGMENTS OF EXPERIENCE. Those, however, which are *only subjectively valid*, I call mere JUDGMENTS OF PERCEPTION. The latter require no pure concept of the understanding, but only the logical connection of perceptions in a thinking subject. The former, however, at all times require, in addition to the representations of the sensory intuition, special *concepts originally produced in the understanding*, which bring it about, that the judgment of experience is objectively valid" [1].

KANT illustrates this distinction with the following examples: The judgments "The room is warm, the sugar is sweet, wormwood is revolting" and "The sun heats the stone" are merely subjectively valid judgments of perception [2].

The last-named judgment, however, becomes a *judgment of experience*, with a genuine claim to universal validity, if I say, "The sun causes the heat of the stone", for here "to perception is added the concept of the understanding, i.e. causality, which *necessarily* connects the concept of the sunshine with that of heat, and the synthetic judgment becomes necessarily universally valid, consequently objective, and is transformed from a perception into experience" [3].

This whole view of universal validity stands or falls with the critical Humanist immanence standpoint and with the vision which it determines as to the structure of experience and of temporal reality.

---

[1] *Prolegomena zur einer jeden künftigen Metaphysik (Prolegomena to any future metaphysics)* W. W. GROSSHERZOG WILHELM ERNST Ausg. IV, S. 422 (*Works*, GROSSHERZOG WILHELM ERNST ed. IV, p. 422): „*Empirische Urteile, so fern sie objektive Gültigkeit haben*, sind E r f a h r u n g s - u r t e i l e; die aber, so *nur subjektiv gültig* sind, nenne ich blosze W a h r n e h m u n g s u r t e i l e: Die letztern bedürfen keines reinen Verstandesbegriffs, sondern nur der logischen Verknüpfung der Wahrnehmungen in einem denkenden Subjekt. Die ersteren aber erfordern jederzeit über die Vorstellungen der sinnlichen Anschauung noch besondere, *im Verstande ursprünglich erzeugte Begriffe*, welche es eben machen, dasz das Erfahrungsurteil *objektiv gültig* ist."

[2] ib. p. 423 j° note p. 426.

[3] note p. 426: „kommt über die Wahrnehmung noch der Verstandesbegriff der Ursache hinzu, der mit dem Begriffe des Sonnenscheins den der Wärme *notwendig* verknüpft, und das synthetische Urteil wird notwendig allgemeingültig, folglich objektiv, und aus einer Wahrnemung in Erfahrung verwandelt."

The break with this immanence standpoint makes necessary also a break with this view of the universally valid. In the light of our transcendental basic Idea the universal validity to which a judgment lays claim, can merely be conceived in the sense of the agreement of the judgment with the divine law for the cosmos in its modal diversity, inter-modal coherence and fulness of meaning, apart from the validity of which no judgment would have meaning.

> The possibility of universally valid judgments depends on the universal supra-subjective validity of the structural laws of human experience.

The possibility of *universally valid judgments* rests only and exclusively on the *universal validity* (raised above all individual subjectivity) *of the structural laws of human experience.*

"Universal validity" is a normative qualification, which supposes, that the judging subject is subjected to laws which can never take their origin from a so-called transcendental-logical subject, and with which the judging subject can *come into conflict.* As such it is connected very closely with the *structure of truth.*

Consequently, we can investigate the problem of universal validity in an all-sided manner only in the more particular treatment of the *problem of knowledge.* In the present connection we must still be content with introductory observations.

In the first place, then, we observe, that universal validity cannot be limited to the judgments of theoretical thought, for the very reason that the laws of theoretical thought do not hold "an sich", but only in the cosmic coherence of meaning and in dependence on the religious root-unity of the divine law.

Universal validity is ascribed to every judgment to which each judging subject *ought* to assent, so not to a judgment that has meaning only for the individual subject who judges. The judgments, "I do not believe in God" and "I do not think the Night Watch of REMBRANDT beautiful", can never have universal validity, because they express only a subjective opinion, which is restricted *in the subjective function of the judgment to the individual ego.*

On the other hand, it is indifferent for the universal validity of a judgment, whether it makes an assertion about a concrete individual state of affairs *beyond the subjective function of the judgment,* or indeed about abstract theoretical states of affairs.

The judgment of naïve experience, "This rose which stands on my table is red", if it is to be taken seriously, at once lays claim to concrete truth and universal validity for every human subject of judgment perceiving at this moment, since it is not restricted in the subjective function of the judgment to the individual ego, but has an objective sense.

Its universal validity depends, however, on the structural laws of pre-theoretical experience, in which thought lacks the intentional "gegenstand-relation".

Undoubtedly, there are *structural differences* in the universal validity of judgments. In the first place, between theoretical and pre-theoretical ones.

The universal validity of a correct judgment of perception.

The validity of a judgment of perception, as formulated above, does not depend on the concrete hic et nunc (here and now) of the subjective-sensory aspect of perception.

If this were the case, then indeed, as KANT taught, the judgment of perception would be of merely *subjective* validity, and could not lay claim to universal validity. As we observed previously, however, the structural laws of naïve experience (at the same time structural laws of temporal reality itself, as will appear to us in the discussion of the problem of knowledge) are the laws that guarantee the universal validity of a correct judgment of perception.

These structural laws also regulate the subject-object relations in naïve experience, which we have to investigate more amply in a later context. They guarantee the plastic structure of the experience of things, *also with respect to its subjective-objective sensory and logical aspects*, and only make the universal validity of a concrete judgment of perception possible.

That KANT can ascribe only subjective validity to these judgments, finds its ground in his construction — which falsifies the entire structure of naïve experience — of the datum of experience as a chaotic sensory material, which must first be *formed* by a transcendental consciousness to an objective coherent reality, ordered in a universally valid manner. It is further grounded on the old — indeed metaphysical — prejudice that the so-called secondary qualities of things (i.e. the sensory qualities which cannot be measured and weighed) are merely subjective in character and do not belong to the "objective" reality of things[1]. Above all it is rooted in the circumstance that, from his criticistic standpoint, KANT has totally wiped out the structural differences between theoretical knowledge and naïve experience.

In the nature of the case, we cannot elaborate all these points in detail until later.

The criterion of universal validity of a judgment concerning supra-theoretical states of affairs and the unconditional validity of the religious law of concentration of human experience.

There is, in the second place, a fundamental difference between a judgment concerning a supra-theoretical religious state of affairs as: "God is the Creator of the world" or "All laws are grounded in absolute Reason", *on the one hand*, and the judgments which make an assertion about cosmic or cosmological states of affairs within the temporal boundary of the universe, *on the other hand*.

The universal validity to which the first judgments lay claim, depends on their agreement or disagreement with the central religious unity of the divine law, as it is revealed in the Word of God, and to which the judging *self-hood* in the heart of its existence is *subjected, as to the religious concentration-law of its temporal existence*.

All universal-validity to which a judgment lays claim depends, *in the final instance, upon the universal, unconditional validity of this religious law of concentration*. No single modal law, not

---

[1] Cf. *Prolegomena* (Ed. cit.) § 19 Note, where KANT observes with reference to the examples of judgments of perception given by him: "I gladly confess, that these examples do not represent such judgments of perception as could ever become judgments of experience, even if a concept of the understanding were to be added, since they are related merely to feeling, which everyone recognizes to be merely subjective and which consequently can never be attributed to the object, and so can never become objective." ("Ich gestehe gern, dass diese Beispiele nicht solche Wahrnehmungsurteile vorstellen, die jemals Erfahrungsurteile werden könnten, wenn man auch einen Verstandesbegriff hinzu täte, weil sie sich bloss auf Gefühl, welches jedermann als bloss subjektiv erkennt und welches also niemals dem Objekt beigelegt werden darf, beziehen und also auch niemals objektiv werden können.")

This subjectivistic view of the so-called secondary qualities we cannot refute until in the 2d Book we deal more closely with the subject-object relation.

even the cosmic order of time itself (which maintains the coherence of meaning between the modal law-spheres) is *self-sufficient* to guarantee the universal validity of any human judgment, since the universal validity of these laws has *meaning*-character and the law is *nothing* apart from the bond with its Origin. It must consequently be clear, in the light of the Christian cosmonomic Idea, that the universal validity of a religious judgment of the Christian life- and world-view cannot be dependent upon the greater or smaller circle that assents to it; nor can it be derogated from by the circumstance that through apostasy, human thought is withdrawn subjectively from the fulness of meaning of truth and that man is incapable *by himself* of directing his thought again toward the absolute verity.

> The so-called "transcendental consciousness" as hypostatization of theoretical human thought in its general apostasy from the fulness of meaning of truth.

By the hypostatization of the so-called "transcendental consciousness" as Origin of universal validity, the basis of the validity of truth is really undermined.

For in this hypostatization, truth is made dependent upon the really *general apostasy* of thought in the immanence-philosophy.

It makes no sense to suppose, that the immanent laws of human knowledge should draw theoretical thought away from the religious fulness of meaning of verity. It is rather the apostate self-hood in the grip of its dialectical religious ground-motive that attempts to dissociate these laws from their coherence of meaning and from their religious root and thereby subjectively falsifies their signification in the judgment. The concept "normal consciousness' is not identical with the "norm of consciousness".

The truth and universal validity of a judgment do not find their criterion in an apo-state "normal-consciousness".

The great diversity and divergence of life- and world-views is, according to LITT, an indication that they are only individual impressions of life, and that they lack a universally valid standard of truth. But any one who sets out in this way renders no service with his arguments to the view, that only judgments of theoretical thought can make claim to universally valid truth. A simple reference to the dividedness of philosophical and even of special scientific theories among themselves may be a sufficient stimulus to hastily abandon this by-way.

Impurity of the opposition "universal-validity" and individuality as a contradictory one.

For the rest, in dealing with the *problem of knowledge*, we shall show, that the opposition: universal-validity in theoretical thought versus concrete individuality in the life- and world-view, is impure, since even in theoretical thought the individuality of the thinker may in no way be eliminated. The view that in theoretical thought there should be no place for the individual is a remnant of the rationalistic view of science of the period of the "Enlightenment".

We pointed out, that a life- and world-view can follow no systematic tendency in its development, but must remain in immediate proximity to the concrete situations of life, even though it rightly gives a general formulation to its judgments. Focused in the full temporal reality, it, or rather its adherent, directs the religious vision of totality toward the reality of life in its concrete structure. Historical evolution, too, the tempo of which it ought to follow in its thought, is not conceived by it in scientific style, but in its continuous involvement in full temporal reality as a not yet theoretically distinguished component of the latter.

In this way, LITT's thesis as to the unscientific individual character of the life- and world-view is reduced to its proper proportions.

But how do matters stand with regard to his view, that a life- and world-view, in distinction from philosophy, lives in a sphere of *common convictions?*

Neither life- and world-view, nor philosophy is to be understood individualistically.

A life- and world-view is not individualistic, but truly social in origin. It is ex-origine the common conviction, subjected to the norm of the full truth, of a human community bound together by a central religious motive.

We have seen, however, in our transcendental criticism of the theoretical attitude of thought, that philosophy, too, necessarily issues from such a religious ground-motive, which rests at the basis of a particular philosophical community of thought.

In philosophy as well as in a life- and world-view, social

prejudices of an illegitimate character can show themselves, which hang together with the limitation of vision (view) of the social environment and consequently should be overcome (class- and racial prejudices, prejudices of a limited church group, etc., etc.). Modern sociology of thought (SCHELER, KARL MANNHEIM, JERUSALEM and others) has cast a penetrating light on this state of affairs. But since philosophy, by reason of its theoretical attitude of thought in general, comes sooner to a critical standpoint with respect to such illegitimate prejudices, it can at this point exercise a wholesome influence on the pre-theoretical reflection. For it is impossible, that philosophy and a life- and world-view should not influence each other mutually.

Philosophic thought should find in the life- and world-view of the thinker a continuous actual stimulus to religious self-reflection. Conversely, a life- and world-view should come to theoretical clarity in philosophic thought.

But as little as philosophy may fall with impunity into the concrete tone of the life- and world-view, as little may the life- and world-view accept with impunity the distance from the full reality which is suitable to theoretical thought.

One in root, making mutual appeal to each other, and influencing each other, they, nevertheless, should remain sharply distinguished, each according to its own task and essential character.

PART II

THE DEVELOPMENT OF THE BASIC ANTINOMY IN THE COSMONOMIC IDEA OF HUMANISTIC IMMANENCE-PHILOSOPHY

CHAPTER I

THE BASIC STRUCTURE OF THE HUMANISTIC TRANSCENDENTAL GROUND-IDEA AND THE INTRINSIC POLARITY BETWEEN THE CLASSICAL SCIENCE-IDEAL AND THE IDEAL OF PERSONALITY

§ 1 - INTRODUCTION. HUMANISTIC PHILOSOPHY AND THE HUMANISTIC VIEW OF LIFE AND THE WORLD

At least in its dominating trends modern Western immanence-philosophy is rooted in a common Humanistic ground-motive of a religious character, which we learned to know in our Prolegomena as the motive of *nature and freedom*. The various forms of the transcendental ground-Idea of the different schools in which this central religious motive has found its theoretical expression may at first sight seem somewhat confusing by their great diversity. Nevertheless, this transcendental Idea possesses a fixed basic structure, which can be seen in each variation.

Of course historical connections between modern Humanistic philosophy and medieval and ancient systems are present everywhere. However, the former displays a *new character*, which is not to be explained in terms of a purely historical development of human thought.

In this philosophy the connection between the basic structure of the transcendental ground-Idea, and that of the pre-theoretic Humanistic world- and life-view has gradually developed to such an extent, that the boundaries between the theoretic and the pre-theoretical attitude of thought seem to have been wiped out. As a result, in most instances, the Humanist is unable to account for his *cosmonomic Idea* in philosophy. He thinks it is possible to philosophize in an unprejudiced fashion, because his religious presuppositions are accepted by the world- and life-view of Humanism, as self-evident and indubitable.

The autonomy of human reason was not — as in the ancient Greek world — a postulate of theoretic philosophy only. It was from the outset proclaimed by the Humanistic life- and world-view, itself. The dogmatic reliance on theoretical thought was not undermined until the modern crisis in the foundations of the Humanistic world- and life-view began to cast its shadow upon philosophical reflection. Modern existentialism was born out of this crisis. It broke with the scientific conception of philosophy and sought to play the same rôle that had previously been filled by the now uprooted world- and life-view.

Ancient and medieval philosophy respectively were balanced by the counter poise of the religious world- and life-view of the people and the church. The latter could criticize and stimulate philosophical thought from the practical, pre-theoretical point of view. Humanistic philosophy, on the other hand, does not find any counterpoise in its own world- and life-view. At the time of the Enlightenment and of the natural scientific positivism of the last century, Humanistic philosophy invaded the latter in popular form and imprinted upon it its quasi-scientific mask.

This theoretization of the world- and life-view of Humanism led to the serious eradication of the boundary between the scientific and naïve attitude of thought which we noticed above; and it undermined all sense of responsibility in the personal religious commitment implied in every philosophic standpoint. Modern existentialism has sharply taken exception to this impersonal attitude of philosophic reflection.

The undermining of the personal sense of responsibility in the religious commitment.

During the Enlightenment the Humanistic world- and life-view appealed to science as the crown-witness of sovereign reason. The personal responsibility involved in the choice of one's religious position was shifted without question upon the shoulders of "Reason", the impersonal divinity which had been elevated to the throne.

Here could be observed a noteworthy interaction between the rationalistic philosophy and the world- and life-view of Humanism. At its beginning, at the time of the Renaissance, the latter was completely aware of its real religious motive. However, in the eighteenth century when Humanistic philosophy had been popularized, this notion gradually began to fade away. The Humanistic world- and life-view lost the impulse to arrive at religious self-consciousness in its pre-theoretical attitude. It now believed in the impartiality and sovereign infallibility of theoretical thought. Even when philosophy chose to express itself in a metaphysical theology, it had lost the stimulus to religious self-consciousness. For it no longer had a counter-poise in a Humanistic world- and life-view which was conscious of its religious ground-motive [1].

The Humanistic world- and life-view allowed itself to be deprived of its initial vitality without offering the slightest opposition. It lost the notion of the irreplaceable significance of the naïve attitude toward reality. It preferred to be quasi-scientific and became static and abstract. No longer did it retain any proximity to life, but it made its pronouncements as from a theoretical distance. Neither did the Humanistic view of the world and of life protest against the falsification of naïve experience by the theoretical interpretation of rationalistic philosophy. This was only possible, because the Humanistic world- and life-view had itself been made into a theory.

It is true, that in the period of *Sturm und Drang*, and in the subsequent period of Romanticism, the Humanistic ideal of personality strongly reacted against rationalistic philosophy. But, this reaction was too much drenched with theoretical philosophical motives to keep a sufficient distance from Humanistic philosophy. And, just as the Renaissance, this reaction was too aristocratic in character to find any real echo among the larger classes of society. Its failure to appeal to the masses was most times the weak point of the Humanistic world- and life-view, and in this respect the latter was at a positive disadvantage, when compared with the Christian view.

Undoubtedly Humanism acquired an influence on the masses during the Enlightenment and in the period of natural scientific positivism by popular scientific literature, *belles lettres*, and other means of propaganda. However, this influence came from above, viz. from philosophy which was popularized. This was also the case at the time of the French revolution and in the rise of socialism as a mass-movement. Humanistic philosophy has never found a fruitful and deep inner religious contact with a life- and world-view which, as the Christian one, lives sponta-

---

[1] To be sure, in so far as the Christian world- and life-view had not been unduly influenced by immanence philosophy, it vehemently opposed the latter. However, Humanistic philosophy does not have a common root with the Christian world- and life-view.

neously in the heart of the simple man and calmly retains its pious certainty against all errors of theoretical thought.

The Dutch Christian statesman and thinker, Dr ABRAHAM KUYPER, discovered this weak point in the relationship between the philosophical theory and the life- and world-view of Humanism. And, in his struggle against the enligthened liberalism of the last century, he concentrated his attack upon this very point.

It is true that, in the first decades of the XXth century, especially under the influence of the KANT-renaissance, a strong impulse was revealed to delineate the boundary between philosophical theory and a life- and world-view. We have paid full attention to this tendency in the latter part of the Prolegomena. In this very period, however, the undermining influence of philosophical historicism and relativism had penetrated into the latter. And this relativism has led to the modern crisis in Humanism. A historistic philosophy of life was born out of this crisis. And especially in the period after the first world war, it began to produce a new *outlook* [1] in syndicalistic and fascistic movements. This new *outlook* was concerned with the suggestion of the masses rather than with questions of truth.

The synthetic standpoint of Thomistic philosophy and the disruption of this synthesis by the nominalism of late scholasticism.

To gain an insight into the basic structure of the cosmonomic idea of Humanistic thought we must go back to the period of the origination of the latter. I treated the genesis of the Humanistic outlook in detail in my study-series entitled, *In den Strijd om een Christelijke Staatkunde (In the struggle for a Christian Politics)* [2]. Here I described the way in which the religious starting-point of Humanism was gradually applied to philosophic thought in the basic structure of a new cosmonomic Idea. Consequently, I shall now confine myself to a very short sketch of the main lines of this historical development.

---

[1] *Translator's note:* Henceforth the term "*outlook*" shall be used instead of the longer expression *world- and life-view*.   D. H. F.

[2] I began this series in the first issue of the review „Anti-Revolutionaire Staatkunde" (published by the Dr A. Kuyper foundation). The gradual clarification of my insights in this study will not escape the reader. I am no longer in complete agreement with what I have written in the first part of this study; it is too strongly under the influence of TROELTSCH's and DILTHEY's view of the Middle Ages and the Reformation.

The Aristotelian-Thomistic philosophy and medieval culture.

The Renaissance, which displayed such a varied picture in the different countries, began as a spiritual movement of a modern Humanistic character. It began when the medieval ecclesiastically unified culture [1] had collapsed. The latter had found its best philosophical expression in Aristotelian-Thomistic philosophy.

Following his teacher ALBERTUS MAGNUS, THOMAS AQUINAS sought to adapt to Christian doctrine the speculative Aristotelian philosophy in interrelation with neo-Platonic, Augustinian, and other philosophical motives that had already become the common property of Christian thought in the patristic period. He sought to effectuate this accomodation by curtailing the excessive pagan branches of speculative Greek philosophy. By so doing he followed the example given by AVICENNA and MAIMONIDES who similarly sought to effect a synthesis between Aristotelianism and the doctrines taught in the Koran and in the Old Testament, respectively.

In his transcendental basic Idea, the "lex aeterna", with its subjective counterpart in the "lex naturalis", Christian and pagan Ideas were brought to a seemingly complete convergence. Through the "lex naturalis", the creation, in its essential nature, has a subjective part in the eternal law of reason of the divine worldplan.

The integral and radical character of the religious ground-motive of creation, the fall and redemption in the Biblical sense.

In order to enable the reader to understand, that this convergence is not actual, it is necessary to give a more detailed account of the integral and radical character of the central ground-motive of the Christian religion in its Biblical sense, *the motive of creation, the fall into sin, and the redemption through Jesus Christ in communion with the Holy Ghost*. To this end I may first recall the chief points of the explanation devoted to this subject in the Prolegomena.

As the Creator, God reveals Himself as the Absolute and Integral Origin of the "earthly world", concentrated in man, and of the world of the angels. In the language of the Bible He is the Origin

---

[1] This term is frequently used by TROELTSCH; it designates the period in which the Church directed all human activity in the family, political life, science and art, school and business. It refers to the period in which all of culture bore an ecclesiastical stamp.

of heaven and earth. There is no original power which is *opposed to* Him. Consequently, in His creation we cannot find any expression of a dualistic principle of origin.

The integral character of the Biblical motive of creation is superbly expressed in the majestic 139th psalm:

"Wither shall I go from thy spirit? or whither shall I flee from thy presence?

If I ascend up into heaven, thou art there: if I make my bed in hell, behold, thou art there.

If I take the wings of the morning, and dwell in the uttermost parts of the sea;

Even there shall thy hand lead me, and thy right hand shall hold me.

If I say, Surely the darkness shall cover me; even the night shall be light about me.

Yea, the darkness hideth not from thee; but the night shineth as the day: the darkness and the light are both alike to thee."

This is certainly the radical opposite of the Greek dualism of the form- and matter motive.

In the revelation that God created man according to His image, He discloses man to himself, in the religious radical unity of his created existence, and in the religious solidarity of mankind, in which was integrally concentrated the entire meaning of the temporal cosmos.

The integral Origin of all things according to God's plan of creation has its created image in the *heart of man* participating in the religious community of mankind. The latter is the integral and radical unity of all the temporal functions and structures of reality, which ought to be directed in the human spirit toward the Absolute Origin, in the personal commitment of love and service of God and one's neighbour.

This Christian view cut off at the very roots the religious dualism of the Greek motive of form and matter, which came to a head in anthropology in the dichotomy between a material body and a theoretical rational substance of a pure *form*-character.

Moreover, the creation implies a providential worldplan, which has its integral origin in the Sovereign Will of the Creator. We have indicated this world-plan in the transcendental Idea of the cosmic temporal order. Naturally, Divine Providence is not restricted to the law-side of the temporal world. However, in so far as it embraces also the factual side, this Providence is hidden from human knowledge, and therefore not accessible to a Christian philosophy.

The revelation of the fall into sin is inseparably connected with that of creation. Sin, in its radical Biblical sense, does not play any rôle in the dialectical basic motives of Greek and Humanistic thought. It cannot play such a part here, because sin can only be understood in veritable radical self-knowledge, as the fruit of Biblical Revelation.

Sin and the dialectical conception of guilt in Greek and Humanistic philosophy.

The Greek religious consciousness only recognized the conflict between the principles of form and matter in man. Humanism only acknowledged the conflict between sensory nature (determined by the mechanical law of causality) and the "rational autonomous freedom" of human personality. This latter opposition, even in its Kantian conception, only arrived at the recognition of an evil moral inclination of man to substitute in place of the moral law (the categorical imperative) the sensory desires as a motive for action.

Both the Greek and the Humanistic oppositions do not touch the religious root of human existence, but only the temporal branches of human life. They are only absolutized here in a religious sense. Their concept of guilt, in consequence, is of a merely dialectical character. It consists of a depreciation of an abstract complex of functions of the created cosmos over against an other abstracted and deified complex.

In its revelation of the fall, however, just like in that of creation, the Word of God penetrates to the root, to the religious centre of human nature.

The fall is the apostasy of this centre, of this *radix* of existence, it is the falling away from God. This was spiritual death, because it is the apostasy from the absolute source of Life. Consequently the fall was radical. It involved the whole temporal cosmos, since the latter had its religious root only in mankind. Every conception which denies this radical sense of the fall, (even though it uses the *term* "radical" as in KANT's conception of the "radical evil" in man), is diametrically opposed to the basic motive of Holy Scripture. Since, as we have seen, the revelation of the fall does not in any way mean the recognition of an antithetic principle of origin which is opposed to the Creator, sin cannot be thought of as standing in a *dialectical relation to the creation*.

And because of the radical character of sin, redemption in Christ Jesus must also be radical.

The Divine Word, through which, according to the pronouncement of John's gospel, all things were made, became flesh in Jesus Christ. The Word has entered into the root and the temporal ramifications, in body and soul, of human nature. And therefore it has brought about a radical redemption. Sin is not *dialectically* reconciled, but it is *really* propitiated. And in Christ as the new root of the human race, the whole temporal cosmos, which was religiously concentrated in man, is in principle again directed toward God and thereby wrested free from the power of Satan. However, until the return of Christ, even humanity which is renewed in Him still shares in the apostate root of mankind. Consequently, the struggle of the Kingdom of God continues to be waged against the kingdom of darkness until the "consommatio saeculi".

God maintains the fallen cosmos in His gratia communis (common grace) by His creating Word. The redeemed creation shall finally be freed from its participation in the sinful root of human nature and shall shine forth in a higher perfection.

Once again the inner reformation of philosophic thought.

When the central motive of the Christian religion, which we have just described, rules theoretical thought, this must, as we stated in the Prolegomena, necessarily lead to an inner reformation of the theoretical vision of temporal reality. The integral and radical character of this ground-motive destroys at its very roots any dualistic conception of the coherence and mutual relation of the theoretically abstracted modal aspects.

There is no longer room for a so-called dichotomy between the pre-logical aspects on the one hand, and the logical and post-logical on the other. There is no place for a dichotomy between "sensory nature" and "super-sensory freedom" or for a hypostatizing of the so-called natural laws in opposition to norms which are set in contrast with each other without any mutual coherence and deeper radical unity.

On the contrary, in the structure of every aspect of reality is expressed the unbreakable integral coherence with all the others. This is explained by the fact that the aspects are one in their religious root and Origin, in accordance with the Biblical motive of creation.

And this motive will constantly stimulate theoretical thought to the discovery of the irreducible peculiar nature of the modal aspects, as well as of the total structures of individuality, because God also created the former according to their own nature.

The motives of the fall and redemption, which cannot be understood apart from the creation, shall then operate in the theoretical vision of reality, in the struggle against every absolutizing of the relative, by which the apostate religious motives withdraw thought from the radical unity and integral Origin of the temporal cosmos. They shall also find expression in the complete recognition of the conflicts in temporal reality which exist because of sin, and which cannot be cloaked or reasoned away by any rationalistic theodicy.

However, these conflicts shall never be ascribed to the *cosmic order*, as is done by dialectical irrationalism under the influence of an irrationalist turn of its dialectic ground-motive. The law of creation has remained the same in spite of sin. In fact, without the lex, sin would not be able to reveal itself in the temporal cosmos.

And finally the motive of sin will guard Christian philosophy from the ὕβρις (pride) which considered itself to be free of theoretical errors and faults, and which believes itself to have a monopoly on theoretical truth.

Because of the solidarity of the fall and of the conserving operation of common grace, philosophical schools dominated by apostate ground-motives must be taken seriously. And in general the Biblical ground-motive will stimulate philosophic thought to an extremely

cosmonomic Idea of Humanistic immanence-philosophy 177

critical attitude against the disguising of apostate super-theoretical prejudices by clothing them in the form of universally valid theoretical axioms.

If the central ground-motive of creation, the fall and redemption is to have the above-sketched reforming influence upon philosophical thought, this motive must, as we have shown in our transcendental critique, determine the content of our cosmonomic Idea and must exclude all *dialectical motives* which lead thought in an apostate direction.

However, Christian philosophy did not follow this course in the patristic or medieval period.

In the very first centuries of the Christian church, the latter had to wage a life-and-death struggle in order to save the Biblical ground-motive from being strangled by that of the Greeks. In this struggle was formulated the dogma of the Divine essential unity (homoousia) of the Father and the Son (this was soon to include the Holy Spirit) and the dangerous influence of gnosticism in Christian thought was broken.

The speculative logos-theory.

Before this period, we find in various apologists, especially in the Alexandrian school of CLEMENS and ORIGEN, a speculative logos-theory derived from the Jewish Hellenistic philosophy of PHILO. This logos-theory basically denaturalized the Biblical motive of creation (and so also the motives of the fall and redemption). It conceived of the divine creating Word (Logos) as a lower divine being which mediates between the divine unity and impure matter. The Alexandrian school thereby actually transformed the Christian religion into a high ethical theory, into a moralistically tinged theological and philosophic system, which as a higher *gnosis* was placed above the faith of the Church. Similarly, Greek philosophical theology had placed itself above the *pistis* of the common people.

It is in this period that the Church maintained unequivocally the unbreakable unity of the Old and New Testament in opposition to the gnostic division (which was also defended by MARCION in the second century A.D.). It thus overcame the gnostic religious dualism which had driven a wedge between creation and redemption, and thereby had fallen back into a dualistic principle of origin.

Philosophy as ancilla theologiae in Augustinian scholasticism.

In the orthodox patristic period philosophical thought reached its highest point in AURELIUS AUGUSTINUS, who left his stamp upon Christian philosophy until the 13th century, and who even since then has exerted an important influence.

However, no one was yet able to express the central motive of the Christian religion in the transcendental ground-Idea of philosophy without the interference of the Greek form-matter motive. Besides, the relation between philosophy and dogmatic theology was not clarified, because the inner *point of contact* between the religious ground-motive and philosophic thought had not yet been accounted for.

The Christian character of philosophy was sought in its subservient attitude toward dogmatic theology [1]. Philosophy was to be the "ancilla theologiae". All philosophic questions were to be handled in a theological framework. Philosophy was denied an independent right to exist.

This denial is included in AUGUSTINE's famous statement: *"Deum et animam scire volo. Nihilne plus? Nihil omnino."* AUGUSTINE's denial of the autonomy of philosophy with respect to the divine light of revelation is in this way robbed of its critical significance. For philosophic thought itself was not intrinsically reformed by the Biblical ground-motive of the Christian religion, but in its theoretical vision of temporal reality it remained orientated to Greek philosophy (especially toward the Neo-Platonists and the Stoics). AUGUSTINE did not clearly see the religious character of the ground-motive of Greek philosophy, and therefore started on the path of *scholastic* accommodation of Greek thought to the doctrine of the Christian church.

The scholastic character of AUGUSTINE's cosmonomic Idea.

Even in the Augustinian cosmonomic Idea (the lex aeterna with its expression in the lex naturalis) we encounter the neo-Platonic conception of the descending progression of degrees of reality accommodated to the Idea of the divine Sovereignty of the Creator [2]. This latter, however, was again joined with the neo-Platonic logos-theory, after this theory had been accommodated to the dogma of the divine Trinity. In this way theology itself was encumbered with Greek philosophy. Even Genesis 1 : 1 was interpreted by AUGUSTINE in the cadre of the Greek form-matter motive!

In spite of all this, however, the integral and radical character of the central ground-motive of the Christian religion remained fore-

---

[1] This conception of philosophy as "ancilla theologiae" is not Christian in origin, but is derived from ARISTOTLE's *Met.* B. 996 b 15 where the Greek thinker proclaimed metaphysical theology (as the science of the end of all things and of the supreme good) to be the queen of the sciences. The other sciences are thus "the slaves of theology and may not contradict it". This Aristotelian conception is now simply taken over and applied to the relationship between Christian theology and philosophy.

[2] Cf. *De Civitate Dei,* x11, 3: *"Naturas essentiarum gradibus ordinavit"* and his neo-Platonic theory of the "esse" and "minus esse". Cf. also his neo-Platonic theory of the different levels of the mystical elevation of the soul to God.

most in the *theological* conceptions of the great church-father. This motive found expression in the strong emphasis which he laid upon the absolute creative Sovereignty of God, and in his rejection of any position which would attribute original power to evil. The central motive of Christian religion is also in evidence in AUGUSTINE's acceptance of the radical character of the fall and in his rejection of the autonomy of theoretical thought, because of the insight that the Word of God is the only firm ground of truth. However, this insight was only won from the central religious standpoint. It could, as we observed above, not yet lead to an inner reformation of philosophical thought for lack of a critical insight into the inner point of contact between religion and theoretical thinking.

AUGUSTINE's increasing reserve with respect to Greek philosophy is also to be explained in terms of his growing understanding of the radical character of the Christian religion. At the very least, the great Church-father regarded Greek philosophy as a natural foundation for a "super-natural revealed knowledge". In his conception of world-history, developed in his famous work *De Civitate Dei*, an undeniably original Christian line of thought is followed. The central theme: the conflict between the *civitas Dei* and the *civitas terrena*, is entirely dominated by the Biblical ground-motive.

The radical antithesis between the Christian religion and the ancient heathen world is openly and sharply laid bare, so that there is not the slightest suggestion of a religious synthetic point of view.

However, here too, the Christian ground-motive could not yet find expression in a genuine philosophy of history. To be sure, AUGUSTINE was the first to break radically with the Greek Idea of time, and to pave the way for an authentic Idea of historical development. But the periods of this development were not conceived in an intrinsically historical sense: rather they were construed from sacred history in a speculative theological way!

The entrance of the dialectical ground-motive of nature and grace in Christian scholasticism.

The situation became quite different when the dialectical ground-motive of nature and grace made its entry into Christian scholasticism. This occurred in the period of the Aristotelian Renaissance, in which, after a bitter struggle, the Augustinian-Platonic school was pushed out of the dominating position that it had hitherto enjoyed. Roman Catholicism now strove consciously to effect a religious synthesis between the Greek view of nature (especially the Aristotelian) and the doctrines of the Christian faith.

This synthetic standpoint found its most powerful philosophical and theological expression in the system of THOMAS AQUINAS. The two foundational tenets of this system were the positing of the autonomy of natural reason in the entire sphere of natural knowledge, and the thesis that nature is the understructure of super-natural grace.

THOMAS took over the Augustinian pronouncement that philosophy is the *ancilla theologiae*, however, he gave it an entirely different meaning. For he considered that philosophy belonged to the sphere ruled by the natural light of reason, and ascribed to it independence of revealed theology. This would have been a gain for Christian philosophy, if THOMAS had not withdrawn "natural thought" from the central ground-motive of the Christian religion. The latter was now replaced by the form-matter-motive in its Aristotelian conception, but not without an accommodation of this pagan religious motive to the ecclesiastical doctrine of creation.

In this scholastic way of accommodation, required by the Roman-Catholic ground-motive of nature and grace, the form-matter motive lost its original religious sense. But at the same time the Biblical creation-motive was deprived of its original integral and radical character.

Creation as a natural truth in THOMAS' *theologia naturalis*.

Creation is proclaimed to be a natural truth, which can be seen and proven by theoretical thought independent of all divine revelation. And we have seen in the Prolegomena, that the five ways of this proof pre-supposed the axioms of the Aristotelian metaphysics, and especially the Aristotelian idea of God as "pure Form" opposed to the principle of "matter".

This signified, ultimately, the elimination of creation in its Biblical sense as the *religious motive* of theoretical thought.

The elimination of the integral and radical meaning of the Biblical motive of creation in THOMAS' metaphysics.

The Greek form-matter motive in all its different conceptions excludes in principle the Idea of creation in its Biblical sense. *The sum total of Greek wisdom concerning the Origin of the cosmos is: "ex nihilo nihil fit" (from nothing nothing can originate)*. At the utmost, Greek metaphysical theology could arrive at the Idea of a divine demiurg, who gives form to an original matter as the supreme architect and artist. Therefore, the scholastic accommodation of the Aristotelian concept of God to the Church-doctrine of creation could never lead to a real reconciliation with the Biblical ground-motive. The unmoved Mover of Aristotelian metaphysics, who, as the absolute theoretical nous, only has himself as the object of his thought in blessed self-contemplation, is the radical opposite of the living God Who revealed Himself as Creator. THOMAS may teach, that God has brought forth natural things according both to their form and matter, but the *principle* of matter as the principle of metaphysical and religious imperfection cannot find its origin in a pure form — God.

Nor could the Aristotelian conception of human nature be reconciled to the Biblical conception concerning the creation of man in the image of God. According to THOMAS, human nature is a composition of a material body and a rational soul as a substantial form, which, in contradistinction to ARISTOTLE's conception, is conceived of as an immortal substance. This scholastic view has no room for the Biblical conception of the radical religious unity of human existence. Instead of this unity a natural and a supranatural aspect is distinguished in the creation of man. The supranatural side was the original gift of grace, which as a *donum superadditum* was ascribed to the rational nature.

The elimination of the radical meaning of the fall and redemption. The neo-Platonic Augustinian trend in THOMAS' natural theology.

In accordance with this conception of creation, the view of the fall was also deprived of its radical meaning. Sin merely caused the loss of the supernatural gift of grace, and did not lead to a corruption of human nature. The latter was simply injured by its loss of the donum superadditum.

Redemption in Christ Jesus can no longer have a relation to the very religious root of the temporal cosmos, but it can only bring nature to its supra-natural perfection.

In his natural theology THOMAS connected the Aristotelian Idea of God with the neo-Platonic-Augustinian Idea of creation. Just as he took over the Augustinian doctrine of the logos with its eternal Ideas, so he strongly developed the metaphysical theory, with respect to the analogical concept of Being *(analogia entis),* in the direction of *negative theology.* All this only led to new antinomies, because this trend of thought came into conflict with the foundations of Aristotelian metaphysics [1].

The Aristotelian cosmonomic Idea.

According to the scholastic ground-motive of nature and grace, the Thomistic cosmonomic Idea has a natural and a supra-natural side.

The former rules THOMAS' philosophy, the latter his theology of revelation. The natural component is the Aristotelian transcendental ground-Idea, accommodated to the Augustinian Idea of the lex aeterna.

According to the Aristotelian cosmonomic Idea all of nature is dominated by a dual teleological order: every natural substance strives according to its nature toward its own perfection, which is enclosed in its *essential form.*

In their relationship to each other the substantial forms are arranged in a hierarchical order in which the lower is the

---

[1] See my treatise in *Philosophia Reformata* (vol. 8, 9, 10), "*De idee der individualiteits-structuur en het Thomistisch substantiebegrip*", (The idea of the structure of individuality and the Thomistic substance-concept).

matter of a higher form. This is the content of the lex naturalis. As pure actual form the deity can be accepted as the origin of the motion which proceeds from matter toward form as its goal. However, there is no way in which the deity can be considered as the origin of the principle of matter, with its blind arbitrary ἀνάγκη. Even the Aristotelian theory of categories is permeated with the dualism of its dialectical ground-motive. It makes a fundamental distinction between the specific categories of matter (spatiality, number) and those of form. The concept of substance, as the central category of being, pretends to unite into an absolute unity the form and matter of natural beings. But it cannot accomplish this union, because it lacks a real starting-point for this synthesis. To attain this desired result it would be necessary to have a deeper radical unity above the opposed principles of form and matter [1]. And, as we saw in the Prolegomena, the metaphysical (transcendental) concept of being can only bring them into an *analogical* unity.

The content of the Thomistic cosmonomic idea.

In THOMAS' cosmonomic Idea the Aristotelian lex naturalis, which is immanent to natural substances, is related to a transcendent lex aeterna as the plan of creation in the divine Mind.

The latter is the Origin of the former. In conformity with the Aristotelian Idea of God, the lex aeterna was now considered identical with *divine reason*. As a compromise with the Augustinian conception, only the *obligating force* of the lex naturalis (what is here thought of is only the natural ethical law) is derived from the sovereign will of the Creator. The Christian Idea of divine providence in the order of creation is now transformed into the Aristotelian Idea of the teleological natural order, with its hierarchy of substantial forms, which conforms to the religious form-matter motive.

In the typical transcendental ground-Idea of Thomism the divine Origin of the natural order was conceived of as the

---

[1] Apparently ARISTOTLE tried to relativize the absolute contradiction between the two poles of the Greek ground-motive by conceiving of them in the modal meaning of the cultural aspect. In this modal aspect form-giving is related to a material which as "cultural object" has a potentiality to cultural shapes. The orientation of the relation between matter and form to culture is entirely in keeping with the ascription of religious primacy to the form-motive of the culture-religion.

first cause and final goal of the whole temporal movement in nature from matter to form, from means to end. And the supra-natural sphere of grace, in which the divine Origin is conceived in the light of Revelation and in which the lex naturalis finds its supra-natural complement in the lex charitatis et gratiae, was placed above the natural order as a higher level. It is this view that became the speculative philosophic expression of the Idea of synthesis which typified the entire ecclesiastically unified culture.

The intrinsic dialectic of the scholastic basic motive of nature and grace and the nominalism of the fourteenth century.

However, the intrinsic dialectic of the motive of nature and grace in scholastic philosophy soon became evident.

As long as the Roman Catholic church was strong enough, the artificial synthesis between the Christian and Greek world of Ideas could be maintained, and the polar tendencies in the ground-motive of nature and grace could not develop freely. Ecclesiastical excommunication was sufficient to check the development of these tendencies in philosophy and in every day affairs.

In the critical period of the Late Middle Ages however, as we shall see in the following paragraph, the ecclesiastically unified culture began to collapse. One secular sphere after another began to wrest itself free from ecclesiastical domination.

Since the 14th century the nominalism of the late scholasticism under the leadership of WILLIAM OF OCCAM, turned against the artifical compromise between Christian and pagan lines of thought in the Thomistic system. This reaction commenced after the Averroistic PETRUS AUREOLI and DURANDUS of St. Porcain, in a somewhat different philosophical and theological orientation, had taken up the nominalistic tradition of earlier centuries.

Before the 14th century nominalism had been always suppressed by realistic scholasticism with its doctrine of the reality of the universal forms ("universalia"). It had repeatedly received the official condemnation of the church. In the 14th century, however, nominalism became a cultural factor of world-significance. It was able to pave the way for modern philosophical thought, since the church had lost its dominating influence on philosophy.

The Thomistic cosmonomic Idea required the realistic-metaphysical conception of the Aristotelian "substantial forms". As soon as this conception would be abandoned, the whole Thomistic-Aristotelian Idea of the natural order, as an understructure of the supra-natural order of grace, was doomed to break down. And the same holds good in respect to natural theology as an understructure of the sacred theology of revelation.

At this very point Thomism was subjected to the criticism of OCCAM's nominalism, which, in the last analysis, was founded on an extremely nominalistic conception of the "potestas Dei absoluta". It cut off every metaphysical use of natural reason by denying that the universal concepts of thought have a "fundamentum in rē"[1].

It joined forces with the so-called terministic suppositional logic as presented in the seventh treatise[2] of the "*Summulae*" of PETRUS HISPANUS and conceived of "universalia" as only being "signs", which in the human mind stand for *(supponunt)* a plurality of individual things, but which themselves possess no reality "in" or "before" the latter. In so far as they do not rest upon arbitrary convention, as the *"voces"*, the *"universalia"* are *"conceptus"* or *"intentiones animae"* formed by the understanding. They function merely as copies of the corresponding traits of individual things and only have a subjective value for knowledge. When OCCAM limited scientific knowledge to the logical judgment and the universalia, he thereby intended to depreciate science and not the Christian faith.

Faith, in a positivist manner bound to Holy Scripture — here conceived in a pseudo-juridical sense, as an ecclesiastical law book — and to the tradition of the Church, may maintain the

---

[1] It may be observed in this connection that OCCAM started from the traditional metaphysical opposition between the logical thought-function and "reality in itself"; and that the only sources of our knowledge are to be found in sensory perception and logical understanding. We have seen in the Prolegomena, that this metaphysical pre-supposition excludes the insight into the integral horizon of our temporal experience.

[2] Under the title *"de terminorum proprietatibus"*, later expanded to a separate textbook under the title *"Parva Logicalia"*. This part of the *Summulae* did not stem from Aristotelian logic. And in opposition to PRANTL, recent investigations have established, that it was even less of Byzantine origin. The "Moderni" grounded themselves just on this treatise, whereas e.g. Duns Scotus chose the *whole* book of PETRUS HISPANUS as the foundation of his logic, and joined the 7th treatise with realistic metaphysics.

realistic conception of "substantial forms". But philosophical thought can only hold to a completely sceptical attitude with respect to the reality of universals. This position destroyed the realistic metaphysical concept of truth.

> The "primacy of the will" in the nominalistic school of thought versus the "primacy of the intellect" in the realistic metaphysics of THOMAS AQUINAS. There is no essential connection between realism and the primacy of the intellect.

The brunt of the attack upon the Thomistic conception of the "lex aeterna" lay in the nominalistic turning of the doctrine of the primacy of the will against the Thomistic doctrine of the primacy of the intellect. This whole controversy can only be understood in the light of scholastic and patristic syncretism. It is meaningless in a philosophy which in its transcendental ground-Idea holds to the integral and radical ground-motive of the Christian religion.

The conflict between the primacy of the will and the primacy of the intellect was originally unrelated to the conflict between realism and nominalism. Realists of the Augustinian school had contended for the primacy of the will. And JOHANNES DUNS SCOTUS, the great opponent of THOMAS AQUINAS, was essentially a more consistent realist than THOMAS. Nevertheless, in his doctrine of the *Potestas Dei Absoluta,* he gave a new stimulus to the conception of the primacy of the will.

> The primacy of the will in the cosmonomic Idea of AUGUSTINE.

We have seen, that even in the cosmonomic Idea of AUGUSTINE the risky attempt was made to reconcile the Christian conception of the Absolute Sovereignty of God's Creative Will with the neo-Platonic *basic Idea* of the hierarchical ordination of reality in higher, more real and lower, less real spheres, in which pure matter formed the lowest level [1]. In AUGUSTINE's later period we find priority being given to the Christian conception of God's Will als Creator and to the insight into the obfuscation of human reason by the fall. This Christian conception became involved in the proclamation of the "primacy of the will", because it had

---

[1] Cf. *De civitate Dei* XII, 2: "naturas essentiarum gradibus ordinavit" and his neo-platonic doctrine of the *"esse"* et *"minus esse".* Compare also his neo-platonic levels of the mystical elevation of the soul to God.

to wrestle with the competitive realistic metaphysics which sought its Archimedean point in theoretic reason.

Nominalism was related to the Augustinian tradition by way of Franciscan thought. However, Occam changed the doctrine of the primacy of the will in a radically irrationalistic manner. He totally deformed the Christian confession of God's Sovereignty as Creator.

The potestas Dei absoluta in Duns Scotus and William of Occam.

In Duns Scotus the *potestas Dei absoluta*, as distinguished from the *potestas Dei ordinata*, was bound to the unity of God's holy and good *Being* (essence). According to him, the *lex aeterna* also originates in the essence of God. And absolute goodness and truth are grounded in the divine Being[1]. Consequently, the Scotist conception of the *potestas absoluta* cannot have any nominalistic purport. It had no further intention than to account for the fact that sometimes in the Old Testament God seems to give "dispensation" of some commands of the second table of the Decalogue. This was doubtless a scholastic-juridical conception of the latter. However, in Duns the potestas Dei absoluta, too, is always the expression of God's holy and good Being.

William of Occam abandoned the idea of a lex aeterna and a potestas absoluta "being bound to God's Being". In Aristotelian fashion the speculative-metaphysical theology had viewed the essence of God as pure *Form*. Nominalism now conceived of the potestas Dei absoluta in a sense which had some affinity with the unpredictable *Anangkè* of the Greek matter-motive. And by so doing, it separated itself from the integral Self-Revelation of

---

[1] Cf. the following statements of Scotus: "Intelligere non est primum in Deo, sed PRIMUM DANS ESSE EST IPSUM ENS, tum quia potentia non potest esse prima ratio essendi, tum quia intellectus praesupponit rationem objecti et potentiae sicut per se causas ejus vel principia" (R. P. I d. viii q. 1). "Deus est agens rectissima ratione" (R. P. iv d. 1 q. 5, n. 9).

"Quidquid Deus facit, propter se facit — omnia enim propter seipsum operatus est Altissimus — et ex charitate perfectissima quae ipse est, facit; ergo ejus actus est ordinatissimus, tame ex fine quam ex principio operativo" (Ox. II d. xxvii, q. I, n. 2).

"Nomine legis aeternae intelligimus judicium divini intellectus, qui producens omnia in esse intelligibile, subinde dat unicuique primum esse intelligibile, atque in eis omnes veritates relucent, adeo ut intellectus pervadens terminos necessario intelligat veritates omnes in illis involutas, tam speculativas, quam practicas" (Ox. I, d. iii q. 4).

God in His Word, to an even greater degree than the Thomistic realism had done in its theologia naturalis. It abstracted the Will of God from the Fulness of His Holy Being and conceived of His sovereign power as an orderless tyranny. In his *De Trinitate* AUGUSTINE had expressly warned against isolating the Will of God and the "ratio divina".

> The nominalistic conception of the potestas Dei absoluta entirely contrary to its own intention places God's Creative Will under the boundary-line of the lex.

This functionalistic, theoretical mode of contemplation is only possible under the boundary-line of the cosmic temporal order. Consequently, God's will was actually placed under the lex; a result entirely in conflict with the intention of OCCAM. In relation to religious and ethical laws we can only speak of "arbitrariness" in the sense of an anti-normative behaviour, which supposes a norm. This is exactly what OCCAM does, when he allows for the possibility that God could have just as well sanctioned with His Will an "egoistic" ethics, and when he even conceives of the central religious commandment included in the first table of the decalogue, as a mere product of divine arbitrariness. Idolatry, too, presupposes a religious norm, which is transgressed by it.

As we observed in the Prolegomena, the concept "possibility" only has a reasonable sense, if we pre-suppose the necessity of a law in relation to which subjective individuality retains its full latitude but nevertheless remains subject to the necessary determinations and limitations imposed by it.

> The nominalistic critique effectuated a radical disruption between the Christian and pagan motives in medieval scholasticism.

Nevertheless, nominalistic thought served as a liberator at least in one respect. Under its sharp critique the Christian and pagan motives, which had apparently been most effectively synthesized in the Thomistic transcendental ground-Idea, were radically disrupted. "Nature" and "grace" were completely separated. Thus after a short time, Humanism could consistently develop the line of "autonomous natural thought". This it did in a new manner based upon the dialectical ground-motive of nature and freedom. It might be expected, that the Reformation would have developed an essentially Christian philosophy, based upon the central ground-motive of Holy Scripture. That this did not occur for several centuries, is due solely to the fact that the Reformation was quickly captured by the scholastic ground-motive of nature and grace. This latter motive again led theological and philosophic thought along a scholastic path. We shall return to this point in part three of this volume. For the present we need only concern ourselves with the significance of late medieval nominalism as a condition for the rise of modern Humanistic thought.

As long as nominalistic scholasticism subjected itself in a positivistic faith to the dogma of the Church, it rested in an unreconciled dualism between faith and natural knowledge. In the late Middle Ages, however, some representatives of nominalism gave it a form which prepared the way for a complete secularization of the life- and world-view.

Secularization of nominalism in late scholasticism.

This process of secularization was introduced by JOHN OF JANDUN and MARSILIUS OF PADUA, which, just as PETRUS AUREOLI at an earlier period, belonged to the school of Averroistic nominalism [1].

§ 2 - THE RISE OF HUMANISTIC PHILOSOPHICAL THOUGHT

In the meanwhile the ecclesiastically unified culture broke down. It was no longer dominated by the high medieval conception of the "*Corpus Christianum*". This breakdown was partially prepared by the powerful influence of nominalistic spheres of culture. They undermined the medieval hierarchical Idea of social life and they revealed individualistic tendencies wherever they unfolded [2].

---

[1] In my work entitled *In den Strijd om een Christelijke Staatkunde (In the Struggle for a Christian Politics)*, Chap. I, XII (A.R. Staatk. Ist year, pp. 617 and following), I have established in detail the fact that we may speak of an Averroistic nominalism in these thinkers. In my analysis of the document *Defensor Pacis* I also showed the secularization of nominalistic thought.

[2] In this connection see the important study of PAUL HÖNIGHEIM, *Zur Soziologie der mittelalterlichen Scholastik* (Die soziologische Bedeutung der nominalistischen Philosophie) in *Hauptprobleme der Soziologie*, Erinnerungsgabe für MAX WEBER (1923), S. 173—221. [On Sociology of Medieval Scholasticism (The Sociological Significance of Nominalistic Philosophy, in Chief Problems of Sociology, Memorial Gift for MAX WEBER (1923), pp. 173—221].

The hierarchical institutional Roman Catholic Church had undermined its own influence by secularization. Political life and economy now broke loose from its unifying grasp. And science, art, ethics, and the faith of the individual soon followed suit.

The collapse of the ecclesiastically unified culture.
National states began to form which re-conquered piece by piece the terrain lost by the Church. They employed the most unscrupulous means to strengthen and maintain their power. Economic life emancipated itself by all sorts of evasion of the canon law's prohibition of interest and of the doctrine of the *justum pretium*. Supported by the discovery of the new gold- and silvermines, finance assumed an increasingly central position. The rise of large-scale industry and business brought about an expanded establishment of credit. An early capitalism arose with all of its social problems. And the discovery of the sea routes to America and India opened unlimited perspectives for the future.

Medieval society, impregnated with the organic guild-idea, saw its foundations methodically undermined. The process of social differentiation and individualization began: the individual began to feel free and independent in all spheres. The contact with the East, established by the Crusades, brought contact with other religions. Presently, when in the general process of secularization, the absoluteness of the Christian religion was relativized by philosophy to the highest stage in the development from natural religion, this contact became the stimulus of a strongly neo-Platonic and mystic-theosophically tinged "universal theism". In Italy the prophet of this theism was GEORGIUS GEMISTHOS PLETHON, the spiritual father of the Platonic academy at Florence. In Germany, the movement was led by MUTIANUS RUFUS, the Erfurter humanist.

After the discovery of the pure sources of Greek and Roman culture an additional resentment was present in the struggle against the barbarian linguistic forms of scholasticism. This resentment arose against the mutilation of the ancient world- and life-view due to its synthesis with Christianity. Especially in Italy, the first cradle of the Humanistic Renaissance, the side of the ancient world-view was often taken without reserve.

The transition to a new historical period announced itself in this revolutionary ferment. A great Humanistic spiritual movement arose. It soon methodically built its secularized outlook upon a new cultural basis and impressed its own religious mark upon philosophy.

In Germany, and especially in the Netherlands, the paths of a so-called Biblical Humanism and Reformation temporarily crossed; yet the tendencies to complete the secularization of Christian doctrine were present from the start in a preponderatingly moralistic interpretation of the Holy Scripture, as it was found in ERASMUS and other Biblical Humanists. In my previously cited work, *"In the struggle for a Christian politics"*, this whole development has been treated in detail. In the present context it was only necessary, that we should prepare our inquiry into the basic structure of the transcendental ground-Idea of Humanistic thought.

A closer consideration of the religious ground-motive of Humanism: the motive of nature and freedom.

We have seen, that this transcendental Idea is determined by the religious ground-motive which since KANT must be designated as the motive of nature and freedom. We must now pay closer attention to the latter.

This new dialectical motive rests upon an absolute secularization of the Biblical motive of creation and Christian freedom (as a fruit of redemption). After introducing a fundamental change in their original religious meaning, it assimilated also the central motives of Greek and scholastic philosophy. We shall subsequently discover the form-matter motive and the motive of nature and grace in an entirely new Humanistic sense in the philosophy of LEIBNIZ and KANT.

The ambiguity of the Humanistic motive of freedom.

Unlike that of the Greeks and the scholastic thinkers, the inner dialectic of the Humanistic ground-motive is not born out of a conflict between two different religions. The deepest root of its dialectical character lies in the ambiguity of the Humanistic freedom-motive. The latter is the central driving force of the modern religion of human personality. And from its own depths it calls forth the motive to dominate nature, and thus leads to a religion of autonomous objective science in which there is no room for the free personality. Nevertheless, the religious self-surrender to autonomous science is, in the last analysis, nothing but the religion of autonomous human personality itself, which splits itself up into two opposite directions, not to be reconciled in a really critical Humanistic self-reflection. This is the result of the Humanistic secularization of the Christian motives of creation and freedom in Jesus Christ. By this secularization the insight into the religious *radical unity* of human personality is entirely lost.

In its motive of freedom, Humanism requires *absolute autonomy* for human personality. This implies a rejection of all faith in authority and of any conception according to which man is subject to a law not imposed by his own reason. However, this secularized freedom-motive displayed various tendencies which came into conflict with one another.

Modern man wished to have his destiny in his own hands, and therefore he wished to free himself from all faith in "supernatural" powers. Humanism applied the Copernican revolution in astronomy to the sphere of religion. The latter must concentrate on man and his religious needs. It must no longer require man to surrender completely to a Sovereign Creator and Redeemer, it could no longer be based upon a "heteronomous" Divine Revelation.

The Idea of a personal God could be accepted only in so far as the autonomous personality has need of it. This Idea could be accepted as a metaphysical foundation for the truth of mathematical thought (DESCARTES), as a postulate of practical reason (KANT), or as a requirement of religious feeling (ROUSSEAU). It may be accepted in any other Humanistic form, but it may never be held to be the fruit of the self-revelation of a sovereign God.

The new ideal of personality of the Renaissance.

In the Renaissance the new religion of personality also secularized the Christian idea of regeneration. The ideal of personality preached by the Renaissance in its first appearance in Italy required a *renascimento* of man which should ring in a new period. This ideal of personality is permeated with an unquenchable thirst for temporal life and with a Faustian desire to subject the world to itself.

The individualistic orientation of the new Humanistic freedom-motive during the first phase of its development led the nominalistic tendencies of late scholasticism in a new direction. The Occamist depreciation of natural reason was replaced by a truly religious confidence in its liberating power.

The new ideal of personality expressed itself originally in a strongly aristocratically tinted life- and world-view. And it scarcely wished to mask its antithesis with the ecclesiastically bound outlook of the Middle Ages.

In Italy in the 15th century this ideal of personality had become the watchword of the new period which, as we observed above, expected a "*renascimento*" in a Humanistic sense. The Idea of the "*uomo universale*" is voiced in Leo Battista Alberti's autobiography as well as in the figure of Leonardo Da Vinci. This new ideal was soon to spread over all the lands which were bearers of the culture of the Renaissance [1]. And even at the start it was filled with a Faustian spirit, which looked forward to the progress of culture, and sought this progress in the subjugation of nature by scientific investigation which knows no authority higher than science.

The motive of the domination of nature and the ambiguity of the nature-motive.

For from the very beginning the Humanistic motive of freedom led to a revolution in the modern view of nature.

The Greek vision of *physis* was, as we saw, dominated by the religious motive of matter and form. In the light of the form-motive nature bears a teleological character, and gives expression to the Greek Idea of the good, the true, and the beautiful.

The motive of matter with its unpredictable and orderless *anangkè* led the Greek view of nature to the extreme counter-pole of the super-sensory form: the mysterious depths of life and death in the eternal process of growth and decay.

The Biblical Christian view of nature was dominated by the central motive of creation, fall, and redemption. The revelation of the radical depravity of nature due to sin casts an infinitely darker shadow over the temporal cosmos than that of the Greek motive of matter.

Humanism broke in principle with both the Greek and the Christian view of nature. It had intended to free human personality from all faith in super-natural powers. It also intended to emancipate nature from the bonds of this faith. Modern autonomous man considers the "immeasurable nature" external to himself in the same way that he thinks of himself. That is to

---

[1] See Jacob Burckhardt's *Kultur der Renaissance in Italien*. Ch. II in 1⁴, pp. 143 ff.

say, the same ambiguity which is inherent in the Humanistic motive of freedom will also reveal itself in the motive of nature.

"Unmeasurable nature" can be viewed as a macrocosmic reflection of the autonomous freedom of human personality. In this case Humanism yields to an aesthetic enjoyment of the "creating freedom" which reveals itself in nature. But nature can also be viewed as a reflection of the Faustian *domination-motive*, which permeated the Humanistic ideal of personality from the very beginning. In this case nature can only be viewed as an object that can be *dominated* by autonomous science.

The motive of nature now becomes a new motive of domination, which can only lead to a deterministic theoretical view of reality. GALILEO and NEWTON laid the foundations for modern mathematical natural science. Grasping the phenomena of nature, according to their mathematical aspects and their aspects of movement and energy, in a system of functional causal relations, natural science actually pointed towards the way which would enable us to rule natural phenomena.

After these foundations had been laid, Humanism embraced this new scientific method with a religious passion, and elevated it to a universal model for thought. All of reality should be construed in terms of this new method. To this end, all modal structures of individuality, which are grounded upon the divine order of creation, must be methodically demolished. Autonomous theoretical thought will now recreate the cosmos by means of the exact concepts of mathematical natural science. It will bring forth a structureless view of reality, in which all phenomena are ordered in a continuous causal series. At this point the dialectical tension between the motive of nature and that of freedom is directly in evidence.

Nature conceived of in this way does not have any place for an autonomous freedom of human personality.

This religious dialectic was henceforth to dominate Humanistic philosophy. In our transcendental critique of theoretical thought we have become familiar with the general lines of this process. We have seen how primacy is alternatively ascribed to either of the antagonistic motives, and how the attempt is made to draw a line of demarcation between their two separate spheres of validity while recognizing their polar antithesis. We have become familiar with the attempts to bridge over this religious antithesis by means of a dialectic manner of thought, and we are acquainted with the subsequent disruption of this apparent synthesis.

The Renaissance did not explicitly develop the model of thought of modern natural science. Nevertheless, it displayed, in its developed ideal of personality, the germ of the ambiguity that we have indicated above. At least, we are safe in saying, that it contained the tendencies of a new science-ideal, which was directed toward the domination of nature. Naturally, as long as this motive of domination did not lead to a deterministic view of nature, the conflict with the motive of freedom was not in evidence. But this domination-motive was predisposed to a deterministic view of reality according to its *religious meaning*, and in time could only develop with an inner necessity in this direction.

Late scholasticism had lost itself in endless conceptual distinctions. The rising Humanism turned away from such "formalistic hairsplitting" and wished to show its sovereign power over the cosmos. The watchword "to the things themselves" was given; not only in critical philology, but also in the research of endless nature, in which, since COPERNICUS' introduction of the heliocentric view of the world, the earth had lost its central position. The autonomous human personality wished to test its unlimited power of expansion in the endless spaces of the universe.

The πέρας and the ἄπειρον. The antithesis with the ancient ideal of life.

For modern man the πέρας, the limited, is no longer the highest principle that it was for the contemplative classical metaphysics of Greece. The highest principle is rather the ἄπειρον, the endless, the Platonic μῆ ὄν. Modern man is obsessed and enticed by the *endless*, and believes, that he can rediscover himself in it, in his boundless impulse of activity (CUSANUS, BRUNO).

This tendency towards the infinite is not a passing attitude of the Renaissance. It became more deeply entrenched in the following period. In LEIBNIZ, the limited even became "metaphysical evil"[1].

---

[1] In this connection the comparison is interesting which WINDELBAND makes in his *Geschichte der neueren Phil.* I, 508, between the metaphysics of LEIBNIZ and that of PLATO, ARISTOTLE and Neo-Platonism: *"das Chaos der Kosmogonien, das μὴ ὄν des* PLATON, *die ὕλη des* ARISTOTELES, *das βάθος des Neu-platonismus — sie sind in der rationalistischen Philosophie*

Even though the difference on this point remains within the immanence-standpoint and therefore is relative, this characteristic of the modern ideal of personality cannot be explained in terms of the conception of personality found in antiquity.

In the flourishing period of Greek and Roman culture, personality was considered as being harmoniously bound to an objective rational world-order. And in accordance with its appointed destiny it was dedicated to the all embracing state. Nominalistic subjectivism and individualism are here phenomena of decadence which were viewed as a mortal danger to the polis.

The Humanistic ideal of personality, however, was born in close contact with the Christian Idea of freedom. Humanism secularized the latter and animated its ideal of the free autonomous man with a strong belief in a great future of mankind.

The Cartesian "Cogito" in contra-distinction to the theoretic *nous* as the Archimedian point of Greek metaphysics.

After much preparation in various sorts of directions (especially in the system of NICOLAUS CUSANUS) the principles of Humanistic philosophical thought received their first clear formulation in the system of DESCARTES. The cogito in which this thinker supposed he had found his Archimedean point, is in no sense identical with the "logos" or "nous" of classic Greek philosophy. In the latter, human reason was conceived of as bound to an objective metaphysical order of being, in which the thinking subject only has a part. This metaphysical order was considered as the standard of truth in respect to theoretical thought. Quite different from this Greek conception of reason is that of the founder of Humanistic philosophy.

By means of the "cogito", DESCARTES called to a halt the universal methodical scepticism with respect to all the data of experience. The given world should be broken up in a methodical theoretical way in order to reconstruct it from autono-

---

zu der "région des vérités éternelles" als der bindenden Möglichkeit der Weltschöpfung geworden." ["The "Chaos" of the cosmogonies, the μὴ ὄν of PLATO, the ὕλη of ARISTOTLE, the βάθος of Neo-Platonism — therefore, in rationalistic philosophy, have become the "région des vérités éternelles" (the region of eternal truths), as the binding possibility of the creation of the world"]. And yet WINDELBAND in an inconceivable manner speaks of a "Platonic idealism" in LEIBNIZ.

mous mathematical thought. It is the new ideal of personality which is active behind this philosophical experiment. It does not accept any order or law that the sovereign personality of man had not itself prescribed in rational thought. Although DESCARTES substantialized this cogito to a "res cogitans" and thereby seemed to fall back upon scholastic metaphysics, no one should fail to recognize, that in his new regulatives for methodical thought the Humanistic motive of freedom and of the domination of nature is the driving force.

From his *"cogito, ergo sum"* the French thinker directly proceeds to the Idea of God, and therein discovers the foundation of all further knowledge. This Idea of God is nothing but the absolutizing of mathematical thought to divine thought, which cannot mislead us. The whole Idea of God serves to imprint upon the new mathematical method the mark of infallibility.

The Jansenists of Port Royal who accepted Cartesianism as an exact method of thinking, supposed they had found an inner affinity between DESCARTES' founding of all knowledge in self-consciousness and the immanent Idea of God, and AUGUSTINE's "Deum et animam scire volo". This was a grave error.

There is no relationship between DESCARTES' *and* AUGUSTINE's *Archimedean point. The misconception of the Jansenists of Port Royal on this issue.*

For this inner affinity does not exist, in spite of the appearance of the contrary. In an unsurpassed manner CALVIN expounded in his *Institutio* the authentic Christian conception of AUGUSTINE which made all knowledge of the cosmos dependent upon self-knowledge, and made our self-knowledge dependent upon our knowledge of God. Moreover, CALVIN dissociated this conception from AUGUSTINE's scholastic standpoint with regard to philosophy as "ancilla theologiae". This view is radically opposed to the conception of DESCARTES. In his "cogito", the latter implicitly proclaimed the sovereignty of mathematical thought and deified it in his Idea of God, in a typically Humanistic attitude towards knowledge.

Consequently, there is no inner connection between AUGUSTINE's refutation of scepticism by referring to the certainty of thought which doubts, and DESCARTES' "cogito, ergo sum". AUGUSTINE never intended to declare the *naturalis ratio* to be autonomous and unaffected by the fall.

The connection between DESCARTES' methodological scepticism and the discovery of analytical geometry. The creation-motive in the Cartesian "cogito".

Let us not forget, that DESCARTES' universal scepticism with respect to the reliability of all experience except selfconsciousness, was very closely connected with his discovery of analytical geometry. The latter became for him the methodological model of all systematic philosophy. By the introduction of coordinates it became possible to determine every point of space by three numbers and every spatial figure by an equation between the coordinates of its points. In this way geometrical propositions were proven by means of arithmetical calculation apparently without any pre-supposition other than the laws of arithmetic. And the origin of the latter was sought in sovereign thought.

DESCARTES found the original pattern for clear and distinct thought in this method. According to the latter, thought does not take as its foundation anything which it did not itself produce in a supposed logical process of creation. In the *Preface* to his *De Corpore* the English thinker THOMAS HOBBES describes, completely in terms of the story of creation in the first chapter of the book *Genesis*, the methodological demolition of all given reality executed by human reason in order to reconstruct the cosmos out of the simplest elements of thought. The logical activity of the philosopher must create, just like the artist or as God, Who gives order to chaos[1]. This motive of logical creation — inspired by the deification of mathematical thought in the Idea of the intellectus arche-typus — was continually carried through in the first phase of Humanistic philosophy, especially by LEIBNIZ.

This motive is modern and Humanistic. It is not found in ancient, patristic, or medieval philosophy. It can only be explained in terms of a secularization of the Christian Idea of creation in the Humanistic ideal of personality.

Modern philosophy proclaimed sovereign reason to be the origin of the theoretically construed cosmos. But, in this conception of sovereign reason, the two mutually antagonistic motives of "nature" and "freedom" were active. And the polar tension between them reveals itself evermore intensively in the further dvelopment of Humanistic thought.

---

[1] *Opera latina*, Vol. I, *De Corpore Praef*. The biblical conception of creation is evidently confused here with the Greek Idea of the divine demiurge.

The polar tension between the ideal of personality and the ideal of science in the basic structure of the Humanistic transcendental Idea.

As we observed above, the ideal of personality is itself the religious root of the classical naturalistic science-ideal. As soon as the former began to unfold its tendency to dominate nature, it evoked this philosophical science-ideal with an inner necessity. However, the latter soon became the bitterest enemy of the ideal of personality.

To be sure, at the outset Humanism borrowed many motives of its life- and world-view from the Stoic ideal of the self-sufficient sage, from Epicurean ethics (VALLA) and from other sources. But because of its inherent Faustian impulse to dominate nature, it had an inner predisposition to a deterministic view of the world of an entirely new character. Since the rise of mathematical natural science, the new mathematical ideal of knowledge became the *transcendental ideal of cosmic order*. It appeared to endow philosophical thought with the scepter of legislator of the world. In this way the new science-ideal *only gradually* became a basic factor in the Humanistic transcendental ground-Idea. It is true, that the thirst after the newly discovered infinite nature, with all its mysteries, had from the very first manifested itself in the painting and poetry of the Renaissance.

It is true also, that before the rise of the new natural science, the Faustian passion to dominate had revealed itself in a flourishing growth of alchemy, by which it was hoped, that the mysteries of nature could be laid bare.

The French thinker PETRUS RAMUS had even developed a new semi-Platonic mathematical method in logic in which — in contradistinction to the Aristotelian syllogism — "invention" should play a main part. This Ramistic method, which soon acquired a great influence, doubtless manifested a new spirit in scientific thought.

Nevertheless, originally, nature was not in any way conceived of as a mechanical system, but as filled with beauty, force, and life. Even LEONARDO DA VINCI, who anticipated GALILEO's mathematical-mechanical analysis of empirical phenomena, conceived of nature as a teleological whole animated with life.

LORENZO VALLA had deified nature as the sphere of expansion of the ideal of personality: *"Idem est natura, quod Deus, aut fere idem" (De Voluptate I,* 13).

Since the Copernican revolution in astronomy unlimited possibilities seemed to be opened to the investigating mind. Modern man discovered in nature a macrocosmos which found its reflected image in his own personality as microcosmos [1].

The tendency towards infinity in GIORDIANO BRUNO's pantheism.

GIORDANO BRUNO, in his pantheistic philosophy, joined NICOLAUS CUSANUS' doctrine of the infinite and his metaphysical mathematical doctrine of the *coincidentia oppositorum;* he religiously interpreted COPERNICUS' theory in a dithyrambic glorification of the infinity of the universe, and of its reflection in human personality as a monadic microcosmos. Here we see how the Humanistic ideal of personality becomes conscious of its power of expansion. The immeasurable space of the cosmos waited to be ruled by man. "Nature" as "natura naturata" is the self-development of God (natura naturans). The new ideal of personality here discloses itself in the original aesthetic character of the Italian Renaissance. It does not yet experience the close oppression of the deterministic science-ideal. The seeds of modern-astronomical thought are still shrouded in the aesthetic phantasy of the poet. BRUNO's system is only a prelude to the development of the classic Humanistic ideal of science. The new ideal of personality assumes the new view of "infinite nature" without perceptible tensions.

The entire opposition between the "Jenseits" and the "Diesseits" of Christian dogmatics was considered here as anthropocentric (in the sense of the astronomical theory which had been refuted by COPERNICUS) and ascribed to the standpoint of sensory appearance and imagination, a standpoint that ought to be conquered by philosophic consciousness.

In this view the religious freedom-motive is still in complete accordance with the nature-motive.

The former permeated the new Humanistic view of nature which as yet betrayed nothing of its later mechanization. The future tension between the ideal of science and the ideal of personality is at best intimated in BRUNO by the trouble he takes to reconcile the unity and homogeneousness of infinite nature in all its parts to the Idea of the creating individuality

---

[1] Compare what CASSIRER in his *Erkenntnisproblem* I, 18 and following, observes concerning the relation between the new Humanistic concept of the ego and the new concept of nature.

of the monads, in which Idea the new ideal of personality is concentrated.

The decisive turn did not come before the mathematical conception of natural phenomena, which the Renaissance ascribed to PLATO and DEMOCRITUS, was made fruitful in an exact method of analysis and synthesis capable of dominating nature by means of the functional concept of mechanic causality.

Henceforth, the ideal of the free self-sufficient personality acquired a veritable counter-pole in the mechanical view of nature.

The proclamation of the creative sovereignty of the mathematical method implied the intention to logically construct the coherence of the world out of the continuous movement of thought. Directly after the rise of mathematical natural science the latter became the sheet-anchor of the new ideal of knowledge, which originally had been entirely orientated to this methodical pattern.

§ 3 - THE POSTULATE OF CONTINUITY IN THE HUMANISTIC SCIENCE-IDEAL AND THE BASIC ANTINOMY IN THE HUMANISTIC COSMONOMIC IDEA

The new mathematical and naturalist science-ideal was typified by a particular postulate of continuity.

We have pointed out how the cosmic time-order grounds the modal aspects of reality in their sphere-sovereignty and brings them, at the same time, into a continuous *temporal coherence* [1]. However, this cosmic order is eliminated, if mathematical thought is declared to be unconditionally sovereign in philosophy. For, if mathematical thought is sovereign, it can itself construc the *coherence* in the *modal diversity* of aspects. It need only eliminate the obstacles which the inner structures of the modal aspects of reality place in its way.

The cosmic temporal continuity in the inter-modal *coherence* of these aspects is then replaced by the mathematical-logical continuity in the movement of thought.

The same postulate of continuity of the mathematical ideal of science hides behind DESCARTES' universal methodical scepticism

---

[1] *Tranlator's note:* Since meaning is the mode of being of all created existence, a *temporal coherence* is a *coherence of meaning.* However, for stylistic reasons I shall use the abreviated form *"temporal coherence"* in italics.   D. H. F.

and HOBBES' experiment of thought mentioned above. Both sought theoretically to demolish the cosmos to a chaos, in order that it should be reconstrued, in a continuous procedure of mathematical and natural scientific thought, as a theoretical cosmos.

This postulate of continuity pre-supposed that, by virtue of its methodical sovereignty, mathematical thought has the power to surpass the modal boundaries of the diverse aspects of experience and temporal reality.

Modern natural science, founded by KEPPLER, GALILEO and NEWTON, turned away from the Aristotelian-Thomistic concept of substance which was rooted in the Greek form-matter motive. Such in order to scientifically investigate the physical aspect of reality by means of analytical and synthetical mathematical thought. With its concept of function, modern science wished to grasp the functional coherence of physical phenomena in mathematically formulated natural laws.

It had — correctly in its own field — cleared away the old obstacles that had impeded the application of mathematical methods in natural-scientific research. Modern natural science discarded the Ptolemaic-Aristotelian view of the universe with its distinction between the sublunary and supra-lunary world. It also discarded the Aristotelian "qualitates occultae" and it proclaimed the universality of the laws of motion for the entire physical aspect of the cosmos[1]. The Humanistic science-ideal, however, could not accept the limitation of this special scientific postulate of continuity to the field of physics.

GALILEO's postulate for the modern physical method implied a reduction of all qualitative distinctions, in the sense of scholastic "qualitates occultae", to mathematically determined differences of motion. According to its science-ideal, Humanistic philosophy now sought to apply this postulate to all other aspects of reality in order to construe a continuous mechanical image of the world.

> The concept of substance in the new Humanistic metaphysics is quite different from the Aristotelian-Thomistic or Platonic one.

In its first phase the science-ideal pointed towards the development of a new metaphysics. It was supposed that the true essence,

---

[1] For the details of the genesis of this new concept of science compare my *In the Struggle for a Christian Politics*, Chapter I, VI and VII (A.R. Staatkunde, Vol. I). See also the literature cited in this series.

the super-temporal substance of "reality in itself" could only be grasped by the new mathematical method of thought. However, even in the Monadology of LEIBNIZ, this new concept of substance does not have anything to do with the substantial forms of Aristotelian-Thomistic metaphysics, which were grounded in a lex aeterna.

The new concept of substance, if it is viewed in the light of the new Humanistic science-ideal, has in essence a nominalistic background. It is nothing but the hypostasis of the concept of function of the new scientific method. And this concept of function specifies the common denominator under which the science-ideal wishes to bring the different modal aspects of reality. It is, as it was defined by LEIBNIZ, the hypostasis of the modern functional concept of law. The functional coherence between variant phenomena, construed by thought, becomes the "invariant", the substance of reality [1].

Do not let us forget, that the new mathematical natural science had its precursor in the Occamistic school at the University of Paris during the 14th century. Remember, that before GALILEO the new concept of the law of motion was formulated in full mathematical precision by NICOLAUS OF ORESME who also anticipated the discovery of COPERNICUS and invented the method of analytical geometry before DESCARTES. The whole functionalistic conception of reality was rooted in a nominalistic tradition.

The fact, that the "substance" of nature was still conceived of as *"Ding an sich"*, in spite of the choice of the Archimedean point in the mathematical cogito, proves, that before KANT Humanist philosophy had not yet arrived at critical self-refection and was unaware of the very root of its science-ideal. It proves, that Humanistic thought was still formally wed to ancient and medieval thought; but it proves nothing against the new character of this concept of substance!

Therefore, one must be extremely careful in drawing consequences from an external agreement in the scholastic-Aristotelian and modern-Humanistic definition of this concept.

When DESCARTES defines substance as "res quae ita existit, ut nulla alia rē indigeat ad existendum" (*Princ.* I, 51), this definition sounds rather the same as the one we find, for example, in JOHANNES DAMASCENUS (*Dial.* 4, 1 p. 538) and later on in

---

[1] Thus, explicitly in LEIBNIZ' *Hauptschr.* 11 S., 292f. and 340, where substance is defined as the "abiding law for a series of changes".

SUAREZ (*Disp.*, xxx, p. 299). And the definition which DESCARTES gives in his *Rationes more geometrico dispositae* (p. 86 V and VI): "omnis res cui inest immediate, ut in subjecto, sive per quam existet aliquid quod percipimus, ... vocatur substantia," is to be found again in rather the same formulation in ARISTOTLE's *Categ.*, c. 5, a 12.

In itself this agreement only indicates, that the metaphysical concept of substance ever rests upon the hypostatization of theoretical abstractions. But, even in view of this, we may not close our eyes to the new peculiar sense which the concept of substance acquires in Humanistic philosophy. It is the basic structure of the Humanistic transcendental ground-Idea which is responsible for this new meaning. In this Humanistic philosophy the criterion of truth is not sought in an agreement between thought and "the essence of reality outside of our mind." It is sought in thought itself with the "*more geometrico*" attained clearness and distinctness of concepts [1]. This thought no longer finds its supposed fulcrum in a transcendent world of ideas reposing in itself, nor in the Aristotelian entelechies, which in a teleological world-order are inherent in the world of material things as its substantial forms. Thought now granted to itself a logically creating sovereignty. According to its own intention, it only rests upon a mathematical method which freely rules over "empirical" reality. The clear mathematical concept is above everything else.

Besides, the metaphysical concept of substance is absolutely not essential to the Humanistic ideal of science. When the Humanistic metaphysics of nature collapsed under the critique of BERKELEY, LOCKE, HUME and KANT, the mathematical concept of function or the transcendental form of thought rendered the same service as the common denominator under which philosophical thought could subsume the aspects of reality. In keeping with the Humanistic ideal of science reason must employ the method of continuity as the scepter of its absolute sovereignty. It must exceed all modal boundaries.

---

[1] Even in NICOLAUS CUSANUS this changed attitude toward knowledge is evident. See my *In the Struggle for a Christian Politics*. In DILTHEY I have encountered a relative agreement with my conception of the modern "cogito" as Archimedian point. (See A. METZGER, *Phänomenologie und Metaphysik*, 1933, pp. 17ff.). Hower, DILTHEY sees a Christian metaphysical background behind this "cogito".

The lex continui in Leibniz and in the Marburg school of Neo-Kantians.

Leibniz, still entirely caught in the pre-critical Humanistic metaphysics, even elevated this method to a metaphysical law: the lex continui. He gave it a scientific foundation in the differential calculus, his great discovery in mathematics. In the XXth century the anti-metaphysical neo-Kantian Marburg school, radically broke with the Ding an sich, but, nevertheless,. elevated the "lex continui" to the basic law of philosophical thought.

The Humanistic ideal of science can call into play its postulate of continuity in various forms; in the form of Humanistic metaphysics, in that of the transcendental "critical" thought, and also in the form of the positivistic philosophy of the last century (Comte). It can ground this postulate in a metaphysical concept of substance, but also in the continuity of the movement of thought which arises out of a basic correlation of abstracting and combining (Natorp), or in a positivistically conceived natural scientific method.

In all these forms this postulate of continuity opposes the subjection of philosophical thought to the cosmic-temporal order originating in the Divine plan of creation. However, the sphere-sovereignty of the modal aspects did not permit itself simply to be eliminated by the supposed continuity of a scientific method. The Humanistic science-ideal has led philosophy into a maze of antinomies. Every time philosophical thought tried to surpass the modal boundaries of the different aspects by means of a mathematical or mechanistic method, it punished itself by becoming involved in antinomies. In tracking down these intrinsic antinomies we shall later on discover a method of testing the correctness of our theory of the modal aspects of experience.

The fundamental antinomy in the basic structure of the Humanistic transcendental ground-Idea.

At this stage we only wish to point out, that the consistent following out of the naturalistic ideal of science must reveal a fundamental antinomy in the basic structure of the Humanistic transcendental ground-Idea. This science-ideal, evoked by the ideal of personality, acknowledged no limits to the application of the new natural scientific method. Had not scientific thought been emancipated from the cosmic order and declared "unconditionally" sovereign?

But the moment must come when personality, the new sovereign in the Humanistic ground-motive which had glorified itself in its absolute freedom, must itself fall a prey to this ideal of science. Personality had been absolutized in its temporal functions of reason. The physical and biological functions had been subjected to the domination of the mathematical and mechanical method of thought. The postulate of logical continuity implied, that the psychical, logical, historical, linguistical, social, economic, aesthetic, juridical, ethical, and faith-functions of personality must also be subjected to the naturalistic science-ideal. Thereby, the latter dealt a death blow to the sovereignty of the ideal of personality! *"Die ich rief, die Geister, Werde ich nun nicht los!"*

In the consistent carrying out of its postulate of continuity, the ideal of science must abolish the ideal of personality and unmask the Idea of its unconditional freedom as an illusion.

The supposed solution of this antinomy in transcendental thought.

As we saw in an earlier context, the transcendental-idealistic trend in Humanistic philosophy thinks, that since KANT and FICHTE this fundamental antinomy has been solved in a definitive way.

The discovery of the transcendental cogito had opened the way to self-reflection of thought, and had brought to light the absolute dependence of all natural scientific syntheses upon the transcendental-logical function of the ego. And the latter can never be made into a *Gegenstand*. Therefore, was it not true, that this discovery had established insurmountable boundaries for the naturalistic science-ideal, and fully guaranteed the absolute freedom of the rational functions over against the natural law of causality?

However, we have seen, that the conception of the *"Unbedingtheit"* of the "transcendental cogito" involves Humanistic philosophy in new antinomies. "Reason" in its supposed autonomy should here appoint the boundaries of the ideal of science. In fact, it was nothing but the reaction of a threatened ideal of personality which established the illusive conviction, that by means of "pure thought" the absolutism of the nature-motive in its transcendental ground-Idea could be bridled.

Let us grant, that the Humanist thinkers, who consistently followed the classical science-ideal, were guilty of a primitive naturalism, insofar as they supposed it to be possible to comprehend actual thought in a natural scientific manner. But the Kantian transcendental philosophy in no way denounced the expansion of the natural scientific method over the total concrete act of thinking in its empirical temporal character. It subsumed this latter without the least scruple under a naturalistically conceived, psychological common denominator of the ideal of science. Modern transcendental philosophy only wished to limit the science-ideal by means of a hypostatization of a "transcendental-logical subject", which should be elevated above the inter-modal coherence of meaning between the different aspects of the concrete act of thought. As soon as the untenability of this presupposition is seen, it must become evident, that transcendental idealism is helpless in the face of the absolutistic pretension of the naturalistic science-ideal.

In keeping with the latter, this idealism can in fact only accept a cosmic determinateness of the empirical act of thought in the specific sense of a natural scientific relation of causality. Only the flight into an idealistic absolutization can procure to the Humanistic ideal of personality an apparent security against the consequences of the science-ideal with its postulate of continuity.

Consequently, we must establish the fact, that the transcendental ground-Idea of Humanistic thought in its basic structure discloses the irreconcilable conflict inherent in its religious ground-motive.

By the latter Humanistic philosophy seems to be placed in the face of an inexorable "either-or".

A new struggle for primacy, this time for the ideal of science, and then for the ideal of personality, was unchained. And in this struggle no objective judge was present.

The tendency of continuity in the freedom-motive of the ideal of personality.

The ideal of personality, too, sought support in rational functions (which were isolated by theoretical thought in an inter-modal synthesis of meaning). And its freedom-motive possesses the same tendency of continuity as the science-ideal which did not recognize heteronomous limits.

The attempt, soon to be made by KANT, to delineate the boundaries of each must lead to new antinomies, which we shall examine more closely in their proper places. After he had ascribed the primacy to the freedom-motive, the dialectical development of Humanistic thought offers a really fascinating spectacle.

I think, the more detailed exposition in the following chapters, which begins with the conflict between DESCARTES and HOBBES, and must be concluded with the last phase of FICHTE's idealism, will gain perspective by letting precede a brief diorama of the whole dialectical development of the Humanistic ground-motive in post-Kantian thought up to the most recent phase.

§ 4 - A DIORAMA OF THE DIALECTICAL DEVELOPMENT OF HUMANISTIC PHILOSOPHY AFTER KANT. THE PROCESS OF RELIGIOUS UPROOTING AND THE ACTUALITY OF OUR TRANSCENDENTAL CRITIQUE.

German freedom-idealism in the Restoration period no longer recognized the line of demarcation KANT had drawn between nature and freedom, between the ideal of science and that of personality. The attempt was now made to synthesize both antithetical motives in a dialectical mode of thought, and it was thought, that the hidden traces of freedom could be found in nature itself.

The freedom-motive and the ideal of personality, rooted therein, in this phase receive a new irrationalist and universalistic[1] form. The philosophy of the Enlightenment, and even KANT, had conceived them in a rationalist and individualistic sense.

> The origination of a new historical science-ideal out of an irrationalistic and universalistic turn in the freedom-motive.

In our further exposition of the dialectical development of Humanistic philosophical thought we shall see, how there arose out of this new conception of the freedom-motive a new scientific mode of thought, namely, the historical. And we shall see, how the latter, in opposition to the natural scientific and rationalistic method of the Enlightenment, was elevated to the rank of a new ideal of science and a new universal thought-model. This led to an historicistic vision of reality which also permeated the view of nature. In the long run this historicism proved to be much a more dangerous opponent to the Humanistic freedom-motive than the science-ideal based upon classic physics.

As soon as it began to follow its own inner tendencies it under-

---

[1] The term "universalistic" is meant here in contrast to "individualistic".

mined the religious foundations both of the classical Humanistic science-ideal and of the ideal of personality. This led to the final phase in the development of the dialectical ground-motive of nature and freedom in philosophic thought: that of a spiritual uprooting.

In the first (Dutch) edition of this work my transcendental critique of Humanistic thought did not include any sketch of this further development of the religious dialectic in the transcendental *ground-Idea* of Humanistic philosophy since the historicizing of the science-ideal. I now feel the need of briefly sketching this final phase. For since the appearance of the Dutch edition it has become evident, that the phenomena of spiritual uprooting in Humanistic thought were not merely of a passing nature, but reflect a crisis in the very spiritual foundations of western culture.

For, since the time of the Enlightenment, Humanism has been the leading power in this culture.

As soon as historicism permeated the view of nature in the dialectical method of freedom-idealism, "natural history" was conceived of as the basis of human cultural history.

In SCHELLING's speculative nature-philosophy the process of development moves in a series of lower and higher potentialities from the pole of mechanical necessity (inert matter) to the pole of creative freedom (the living organism).

But, according to him, there is also to be found in the history of culture a dialectical union of necessity and freedom.

Necessity is implied here in the individual nature of a nation, in its individual spirit ("Volksgeist") and tradition, which rule man to a great extent unconsciously. Freedom discloses itself in the awakening of historical consciousness. And in the work of art the polar tension between necessity and freedom should find its ultimate reconciliation.

The polar tension between the historicistic ideal of science and the idealistic dialectic of HEGEL's freedom-idealism.

Now the historicistic ideal of science could not reveal its radical relativistic consequences so long as it was inspired and held in check by post-Kantian freedom-idealism. In this phase it remained bound to the irrationalistic and universalistic mode of thought in the Restoration-period. HEGEL's dialectical logicizing of the historical process as a dialectical unfolding of the Absolute

Idea in the *objective spirit* ("objectiven Geist") signified at the very least a return to the rationalistic and individualistic view of history of the Enlightenment.

Indeed it must contribute considerably to bringing the inner tension to light between the true historical science-ideal and the dialectical-metaphysical logic, inspired in the last analysis by the religious dialectic of necessity and freedom. For, it was impossible to conceive in a satisfactory manner historical development in its unpredictable course in the apriori dialectical thought-forms of the Hegelian system.

This idealistic dialectic must become unbearable to those who had welcomed the historical mode of thought as a new turn in the science-ideal. It bound empirical investigation to an apriori schematicism in which the "creative freedom" of man in the historical process was reduced to the rôle of a puppet of the World-Reason.

Even the fact that HEGEL had a deep historical insight and could fill up his dialectical-idealistic schematicism with a rich historical material, could not save this schematicism itself.

The rise of positivistic sociology and the transformation of the historical method of thought into a natural scientific one.

Even in the first half of the 19th century freedom-idealism was confronted with a dangerous competitor in the positivistic sociology of de ST SIMON and AUGUST COMTE. These thinkers sought to unite the historical manner of thought of the Restoration with the natural scientific view of the Enlightenment. They tried to transform into a rationalistic Idea of progress, the irrationalistic idea of development, as it was conceived of in the Romantic and Historical school.

It is in this very period that the new historical mode of thought in the rising sociology began to relativize the Ideas which de ST SIMON and COMTE — doubtless still under the influence of freedom-idealism — considered to be leading in the historical dynamic of society.

In his famous "law of the three stages" (in passing formulated even by TURGOT) COMTE tried to conceive the historical development of Western society in terms of a necessary causal process. Historicist relativism, however, was not yet carried out here up to its ultimate consequences. Therefore, this first attempt at a historical relativizing of the leading Ideas of Western culture was still an inconsistent one. It is true, that the Ideas of the first two stages, viz. the theological and the metaphysical, were completely abandoned to historical relativity. The Ideas of the third stadium, however, as the embodiment of the classic science-ideal and its domination-motive in a positivistic form, are elevated to the rank of final goal of the entire historical process, and to the standard by which the latter is to be judged. This was nothing but the old faith in the freeing power of science, as we encountered it in the Enlightenment. This positivistic historicism is still firmly rooted in the religious basic motive of Humanism. Later on it proclaimed itself to be a new religion, "un nouveau christianisme".

The transformation of historicism into naturalistic evolutionism.

At about the middle of the 19th century historicism took a new turn in evolutionism. The *dogma* of evolution spread from biology to all the branches of science. Thus there began a new triumphal march of the classic deterministic science-ideal in its historical transformation. Since ROUSSEAU and KANT religious primacy had been ascribed to the motive of freedom. But now the religious dialectic again led Humanistic thought to the acceptance of the primacy of the nature-motive. Freedom-idealism began to collapse. Marxist sociology transformed the idealistic dialectic of HEGEL into a historical-materialism. The latter explained the ideological super-structure of society in terms of a reflection of the economic mode of production. Marxism and Darwinism united, but they, too, did not carry historicism to its extreme relativistic conclusions. Both still believed in a final goal of development which is itself outside of the historical relativity. The religious ground-motive of Humanism dominates the trust of both in objective science and in its freeing activity for humanity.

The first expression of the spiritual disintegrating process in Historicism. NIETZSCHE's religion of power.

However, in the latter half of the 19th century the process of spiritual uprooting began to reveal itself in historicism in an almost pathological form. NIETZSCHE's gospel of the super-man is the first manifestation of this process.

In his first period NIETZSCHE was under the influence of German Romanticism and idealism from which he fell under the domination of Darwinian evolutionism. In the third and final phase of his thought, however, he developed a religion of power which completely broke away from the Humanistic motive of nature and freedom in its original religious sense.

The view of NIETZSCHE is based upon the Darwinian basic tenets and upon a radical historistic vision of reality. Proceeding on this foundation he views man only as an "animal", which is not yet "fixed", and whose sole superiority to other species of animals consequently consists in the fact that man is not bound to static instincts and to a statically circumscribed *"Umwelt"*.

In the historical development of culture man has his destiny in his own hands, and thereby displays an absolutely dynamic nature. NIETZSCHE wishes to build his anthropology exclusively upon the positive data of "nature and history". He fulminates against the fact that man overestimates his own importance, views the whole cosmos as related to himself, and imagines himself to be a free rational personality, radically elevated above the animals.

Man is a "phantastic animal" that from time to time has the need of reflecting upon the goal of his existence and thus posits ideologies concerning God and morality. However, science has progressed so far, that man has killed his gods, and now only retains his own historical future. But history — in spite of all Christian and Humanistic ideologies — is nothing but a struggle for power [1].

Thus the *"Wille zur Macht"* is the only existential escape for man from the nihilism to which historicism leads.

The kingdom of the *"super-man"*, of the "blond beast", in which this *will to power* will assume super-human forms, can only be established through an "Umwertung aller Werte" (transvaluation of all values) on the ruins of Christian and Humanistic ideologies.

The ideal of science and the ideal of personality of Humanism are both rejected. NIETZSCHE considers science only as a biological aid in the struggle for existence. It only has a pragmatic value. Consistent historicism can no longer have faith in scientific *truth*. Nor can it believe any longer in the Idea of humanity

---

[1] In our analysis of the modal structure of the historical aspect in Vol. II, we shall see that domination or power is indeed the nuclear moment of this aspect.

which was rooted in the religious motive of freedom. Thus NIETZSCHE introduced into Humanistic philosophy the great process of religious decay. And this would soon enough lead to a radical spiritual crisis in the culture of the West, accelerated by the two world-wars.

The rôle of neo-Kantianism and neo-Hegelianism in the crisis of historicism.

This inner decay even revealed itself in the philosophic movements which in the first decades of the 20th century sought to revive Kantian or Hegelian philosophy.

The neo-Kantians (the Marburg school and that of RICKERT, WINDELBAND and LASK) and the neo-Hegelians both tried to check the absolutism of naturalistic positivism, and to arrest the nihilistic consequences of historicism.

Under the influence of RICKERT and his follower, MAX WEBER, historicism began to turn away from naturalistic evolutionism. In its apriori construction of the development of human society the latter could not keep its ground against an accurate cultural-historical investigation of the ethnological facts. The hypnosis of the "dogma of evolution", wherein the XIXth century was dying away, again began to make room for the epistemological reflection upon the methodological difference between natural science and cultural science. For a time it seemed as though Humanistic thought would return to the great figures of German idealism. But the religious root of this idealism was too strongly undermined in Neo-Kantianism and Neo-Hegelianism by the all conquering historical relativism.

Consequently, they could not check the spiritual crisis. The rôle of Neo-Kantianism in Germany was in fact at an end with the rise of national socialism. And German neo-Hegelianism interpreted HEGEL's dialectical freedom-idealism preponderately in a relativistic sense, so that it was soon a docile instrument of the Hitler-regime.

The classic ideal of science and the development of 20th century physics. The neo-positivism of the Vienna school.

On the other hand, a return to the old deterministic science-ideal was no longer possible. The development of micro-physics in the 20th century revealed, that the deterministic conception of the laws of nature could not be maintained. Quantum-mechanics dethroned the classical concept of causality. Neo-positivism, proceeding from MACH, acquired its centre in the Vienna school. At the very least, it expected from modern natural science, a more adequate approach to reality.

It viewed the formulas and concepts of physics as mere conventional symbols, which only had value for the economy of thought, but could never lay claim to truth.

HUSSERL's eidetic logic and phenomenology.

The *"eidetic"* logic which EDMUND HUSSERL established, sought to rejuvenate the Idea of *mathesis universalis*. But faith had been lost in the creative power of autonomous mathematical thought. So HUSSERL's introduction of an "eidetic method" in his pure logic is to be understood only from the general decay of former certainties; it was an attempt at founding logical thought-itself on a direct intuition of the essences ("Wesensschau") which would not need a criterion of truth. The phenomenology which he developed later on was, to be sure, formally connected with the cogito of DESCARTES in its broad sense of reflecting self-consciousness. However, it was developed into a transcendental idealism in which both DESCARTES' mathematical ideal of science and KANT's faith in the practical reality of the Idea of freedom fell under the phenomenological *epochè* (ἐποχή)[1].

With this development the so-called transcendental Ego-logy was placed in a religious vacuum.

Radical historicism had denatured the central ground-motive of Humanism to a historical phenomenon. HUSSERL reduced it to a "phenomenon" that is constituted by the transcendental ego itself. The transcendental-phenomenological consciousness becomes an "uninterested observer"; the phenomenologist believes, that in the theoretical epochè (ἐποχή) he can give an adequate *essential description* of the entire act-life of man in its intentional relation to the world. In this way phenomenology, as a universal philosophical science of the "essences" (Wesenswissenschaft), should have to found all empirical sciences [2]. But behind the absolutized transcendental the-

---

[1] See *Die Pariser Vorträge*, Works, Vol. I edited and introduced by Prof. Dr S. STRASSER (publ. M. Nijhoff, The Hague, 1950), p. 9.

[2] Cf. *Cartesianische Meditationen* II § 15. *Works*, Vol. 1, 1950, p. 72 and following.

oretical consciousness yawns the abyss of nothingness, and this in spite of the fact that a degenerate religious motive of autonomous freedom still operates in this very absolutizing. For, in fact, there is no religious neutrality in the seemingly purely theoretical attitude of this "Ego-logy".

The second main trend in phenomenology which directly arose out of historicism and was established by Wilhelm Dilthey in his last period, was of an irrationalistic origin. It was assimilated by Heidegger in his philosophy of existence, after Sören Kierkegaard had laid the foundations of existential thought in strong opposition to the Hegelian idealism.

Besides, since Nietzsche, a strongly variegated philosophy of life was born out of historicism. It agreed with existentialism in its deep depreciation of the science-ideal and of the Humanistic freedom-idealism.

A general devalution of Reason here made its entrance. The "cogito" was replaced by the "vivo", the Absolute Idea by the mythos and the "stream of life". In the latter the Humanistic freedom-motive sought its refuge after the decay of its religious ideal of personality. This ideal seemed to receive the death-blow from the side of depth-psychology. In the analytical way of the mechanicist science-ideal Freud had laid bare the dark depths of the unconscious.

Human consciousness seemed to be dethroned and with it the autonomous standards of Humanistic ethics and religion.

The attitude of decline in Spengler's philosophy of history and in Humanistic existentialism.

Since the first world-war the spiritual crisis of Western culture is expressed in Humanistic philosophy in an attitude of decline. Spengler's *Der Untergang des Abendlandes*, Heidegger's *Sein und Zeit* and Sartre's *l'Être et le Néant*, are in this respect three extremely representative works. Modern man has gone through two world wars. Historicism only permits him to retain the insight into the meaninglessness of his existential freedom in the face of nature in which he is "thrown". Western culture is doomed to decline (Spengler) and the freedom of human existence is a "freedom towards death" (Heidegger), a nothingness (Sartre).

Since Roman Catholicism and the Reformation had been pushed away from their dominating position, Humanism had played the leading rôle in Western culture for two centuries.

But now because of this intrinsic process of decay it has lost its monopolistic position of power. Anti-Humanistic spiritual movements (national socialism, fascism and bolshevism) have arisen out of the pathological degeneration of its religious freedom-motive caused by the radical consequences of historicism. Humanism was thus placed on the defensive.

A chaotic struggle for leadership in the future development of the West has now broken out. The older cultural forces, Roman Catholicism and Protestantism, have also re-awakened out of their philosophical and cultural lethargy, and with a new force now seek in philosophy to take part in the gigantic struggle for the future of our culture.

The actuality of our transcendental critique of theoretical thought.

It is precisely in the light of this whole development of Humanistic philosophy that a radical transcendental critique of theoretical thought is highly necessary and actual. The foundations upon which our culture had sought to build have been shaken everywhere by the storms of a tremendous transitional period. Therefore, the autonomy of theoretical thought can no longer properly be posited as a philosophic axiom. It is understandable, that this has been done in the period in which the Humanistic ground-motive was practically unchallenged in philosophy. However, in the present spiritual crisis anyone who thinks he can take refuge on this dogmatic standpoint, in order to block the way to a radical critical self-reflection in philosophy, thereby displays the fact that he has understood nothing of the deepest causes of this crisis.

The following more detailed transcendental critique of Humanistic philosophy only wishes to show the development of the latter in the light of the dialectical tensions in its own transcendental ground-Idea. This is, in my opinion, the only way to do justice to the different movements within this philosophy.

CHAPTER II

THE IDEAL OF PERSONALITY AND THE NATURAL SCIENCE-IDEAL IN THE FIRST TYPES OF THEIR MUTUAL POLAR TENSION UNDER THE PRIMACY OF THE FORMER

§ 1 - THE NATURALISTIC-MONISTIC AND THE DUALISTIC TYPE OF TRANSCENDENTAL GROUND-IDEA UNDER THE PRIMACY OF THE SCIENCE-IDEAL. ITS CONNECTION WITH THE PESSIMISTIC AND SEMI-PESSIMISTIC VIEW OF LIFE

The basic antinomy in the Humanistic cosmonomic Idea found its first expression in the violent philosophical conflict between the "semi-idealism" of DESCARTES and the mechanistic naturalism of THOMAS HOBBES [1].

DESCARTES and HOBBES, two great thinkers, were at one in their faith in the modern ideal of personality. And they both had an unlimited trust in the new scientific method as the instrument of the philosophical science-ideal. Nevertheless, they combated each other bitterly in the *actio finium regundorum* between the two basic factors in the *transcendental ground-Idea* of Humanistic thought.

> The conflict between DESCARTES and HOBBES as the first expression of the basic antinomy in the Humanistic cosmonomic Idea.

Saturated with GALILEO's conception of mathematical mechanics, HOBBES would not recognize any limits to the continuity of the natural science-ideal. He wished to found this postulate of continuity in a monistic metaphysical ontology. To this end it was necessary that even in its psychical, logical, linguistic, juridical and moral functions all reality be brought under one and

---

[1] For a detailed analysis of HOBBES' philosophical and political theories see my "*In the Struggle for a Christian Politics*, Chap. I, XV in *Antirevolution. Staatkunde*, Vol. I (1927) p. 142—195.

the same metaphysical basic denominator, viz. the *"moving body"*.

This system may be called materialism up to a certain point, but then — however contradictory this may sound — an *"idealistic materialism"*. For HOBBES did not really comprehend the "moving body" in a narrow physical sense. Rather it was conceived of by him as a neutral metaphysical-mathematical basic denominator, created by sovereign thought. "Body" is everything that is capable of mathematical analysis. HOBBES even considered the state to be a body, although an artifical one. In a genuinely nominalistic manner, by means of a social contract, the state is construed in mathematical thought out of its simplest elements, viz. the individuals and their psychical emotions of fear. It is a "Leviathan", a perfect instrument of domination, the synthesis of all natural power of its "elements", viz. the individuals. The domination-motive of the science-ideal has completely absorbed the freedom-motive. In the same way the autonomous freedom of the human will is sacrificed to the mechanistic conception of the human soul.

HOBBES' pessimism and its connection with his ascription of primacy to the science-ideal. Virtue and necessity in MACCHIAVELLI.

HOBBES' "pessimistic" view of human nature was very closely connected with his ascription of primacy to the science-ideal in its mechanistic form. However, this did not at all affect his enthusiastic faith in the ideal of personality. He even sought to elevate the latter to the throne of unlimited dominion by means of the new science. The Faustian consciousness of power in the Humanistic ideal of personality has perhaps never found a more optimistic expression than in HOBBES' *Leviathan,* where he deals with the "kingdom of darkness" which is destroyed by the light of reason.

Did not MACCHIAVELLI, the man of the Renaissance, previously display a similar tension between pessimism and optimism when he combined the ideas of *virtue* and *necessity*? The former was to advance mankind. But the latter was conceived of as a mechanical law which gave dominating power to the lower passions in human nature.

In Humanistic philosophy even "pessimism" and "optimism" turn out to be based on the polar tensions within the basic structure of its transcendental ground-Idea. They are another expression of the polar tension in the latter.

The dualism between thought and extension in DESCARTES.

Why did DESCARTES hypostatize the "thinking soul" and the "extended body" as "finite substances", the one incapable of being reduced to the other? And why did he elevate the sole attributes of these finite substances, viz. extension and thought, to the two basic denominators for the pre-logical and the so-called spiritual aspects of reality, respectively? Why did he, in sharp contradistinction to his British contemporary, maintain this dualism (irreconcilable to the science-ideal) between body and soul?

Had not DESCARTES enthusiastically welcomed HARVEY's discovery of the double circulation of the blood as a new victory of the modern Idea of science over the scholastic doctrine of the substantial forms? Had he not abandoned the entire biotical aspect of experience to the domination of the mechanistic viewpoint? Whence then the requirement that science must view the "thinking substance" as if no matter existed, and the "extended substance" (with "filled space" as the basic denominator for the pre-logical aspects of reality) as if no 'spirit" existed? This can only be explained by the polarity of his cosmonomic Idea.

The background of the ideal of personality in this dualism.

The ideal of personality, rooted in the Humanistic motive of freedom, had retired in the theoretical ideal of clear and distinct thought. If — as HOBBES supposed — mathematical thought itself should be subjected to a causal determination from the side of the movements of the material body, there would be left no freedom at all in the supposed root of human personality. Nay, the mathematical science-ideal would in this way dissolve itself. There would not remain a standard of theoretical truth, if thought were subjected to the laws of mechanical movement.

In the Cartesian type of transcendental ground-Idea, too, the idea of a given cosmic order had been totally eliminated. Therefore, DESCARTES must choose an arbitrary boundary in order to bridle the absolutism of the science-ideal. In fact, the ideal of personality was elevated to the rank of referee. But the ideal of personality had become infected by rationalism and identified itself with mathematical thought. It now sought to save the latter from being reduced to an object of natural science.

The tension between the ideal of science and the ideal of personality gradually became acute in the basic structure of the Humanistic transcendental Idea.

But in its first manifestation its true character remained hidden in the rationalistic metaphysics of the science-ideal.

Actually Humanism had not yet arrived at critical self-reflection in philosophical thought as to the very root of the latter. The mere coordination of the "res extensa" and the "res cogitans" in DESCARTES' metaphysics clearly bears witness to this state of affairs.

> The metaphysical problem concerning the relation between soul and body acquires a new significance in the light of the transcendental Humanist ground-Idea.

The mathematical science-ideal retained the primacy even in DESCARTES' attempt at a solution of the insoluble metaphysical problem concerning the relation of "soul and body". This problem had an important previous history in Greek and scholastic immanence-philosophy. It now acquired a peculiar character in modern Humanistic thought because of the basic structure of the transcendental ground-Idea of the latter.

DESCARTES accepted a metaphysical dualism between body and rational soul. Nevertheless, in an intrinsically contradictory manner this dualism is partly abandoned by his conception of an *influxus physicus* which was assumed to enter human consciousness from a small gland (parva glandula) in the brain. In this way he thought consciousness could be stimulated to sensory perceptions and affects which have a disturbing influence upon the logical function of thought.

This partial break with the dualism became for DESCARTES the way to extend the mathematical and natural scientific method to the psychological sphere. It now became possible to construe a purely naturalistic theory of the affects and passions.

However, if the foundations of the mathematical science-ideal and of the ideal of personality (which had sought refuge in clear and distinct thinking) were to be preserved, then an "influxus physicus" could not be accepted in mathematical thought itself and in the pure volition directed by it. This consideration led to an epistemology and ethics which met the demand of the ideal of science and exalted the mathematical method as the norm of metaphysical truth and the standard of the moral good.

For, according to Descartes, the imperfection and constraint of the spirit proceed from the passive influencing of the soul by the body in sensory perceptual impressions and in emotions. The perfect free personality ought to conquer the confusion of sensory perception by the pure concept formed *more geometrico*. And it ought to rule the emotions by means of the moral will which only acts according to clear and distinct Ideas.

The deeper ground of Descartes' partial indeterminism.

I do not at all wish to deny, that there exist external ties between Descartes and medieval philosophy. But in the final analysis Descartes' partial "indeterminism" has outgrown the problems of the Middle Ages, because it is ruled by another transcendental ground-Idea. This also holds good for the scholastic conflict concerning the primacy of the will or that of the intellect. In the Cartesian indeterministic conception of the process of the will, an absolute freedom ("liberum arbitrium indifferentiae") is ascribed to the will over against the inadequate sensorily obscured Ideas. Is this to be understood in the sense of the Scotist conception of the primacy of the will? In my opinion this would be a fundamental misunderstanding. In Descartes the only motive for this indeterministic conception is to be found in his care not to undermine the foundations of the ideal of science. However, according to him, the "will" is just like fantasy and sensory perception only a "modus" of thought. In the face of the clear and distinct concepts of the latter, the will does not possess freedom of choice [1].

Error in theoretical knowledge must be explained as an apostasy of the will from the mathematical attitude of thought. Because of this apostasy the will involves us in sensorily obscured Ideas. In the field of ethics, immorality is also due to

---

[1] In spite of his partial indeterminism Descartes can write: "Nam si semper quid verum et bonum sit clare viderem, numquam de eo quod esset iudicandum vel eligendum deliberarem; atque ita, quamvis plane liber, numquam tamen indifferens esse possem" (*Meditationes* IV p. 28). [For if I always clearly saw what is true and good, I would never deliberate how I must judge or choose; and thus, although being entirely free, I could, however, never be indifferent]. If the problems in Descartes had not changed it would be very easy to see a connection here with Thomas' intellectual determinism. Just as Windelband has tried to relate Descartes' partial indeterminism to the views of Duns Scotus).

this apostasy. Here the impure will involves us in the causal processes of affects and passions. According to the rationalist ideal of science, the mathematical "cogito" can never err. The statement, "God cannot make our thought to err", is only the religious expression of the conviction that "the mathematical method of the thinking ego is infallible." Error and moral wickedness equally result from the constraint of the soul which arises from the influence of the body. This constraint must be conquered by self-reflection upon the absolute freedom and sovereign self-sufficiency of mathematical thought.

Yet the inner antinomy in the basic structure of the transcendental ground-Idea of Humanistic thought revealed itself both in DESCARTES' breaking through the metaphysical dualism between thought and extension and in the self-refutation of HOBBES' monistic naturalist metaphysics. In HOBBES, the normative foundations of truth and moral goodness were undermined by his elaboration of the mechanistic view in epistemology and ethics. Thereby both the science-ideal and the ideal of personality fell a prey to logical self-dissolution.

The antinomy in HOBBES' naturalistic conception of thought in the light of the deterministic ideal of science. The IDEAE INNATAE of DESCARTES.

HOBBES' sensationistic theory of knowledge is in conflict with his nominalistic mathematical concept of truth[1]. In the last analysis it reduces thought to a movement explicable in terms of natural causality. The sole motive for this theory is to be found in the wish to satisfy the postulate of continuity implied in the mechanistic science-ideal. For that reason biotic stimulus, psychical emotion, logical thought and social process were subsumed under the basic denominator of GALILEO's mechanics, and the modal boundaries of meaning between the different aspects were levelled for the sake of a methodical monism.

On the other hand, to save the very foundations of the science-ideal, DESCARTES accepted a metaphysical dichotomy between mathematical *thought* and mechanistically determined *spatial nature*. He must conceive of the mathematical-metaphysical

---

[1] This concept of truth stands or falls with the validity of the normative PRINCIPIUM CONTRADICTIONIS which can never be explained in terms of natural causality.

Ideas as "ideae innatae"[1]. And he had to render account of the origin of these concepts exclusively in terms of natural causality.

However, at bottom DESCARTES' metaphysics is no less modern and nominalistic than that of HOBBES[2]. Both refuse to subject mathematical thought to a cosmic order which the former has not itself posited. Both resolve the ideal of personality into the ideal of science, which thereby obtains a strong ethical impetus. In the case of both, the apostate religious root of personality has identified itself with mathematical thought, which in creative freedom wants to choose its own metaphysical basic denominators for temporal reality.

In DESCARTES, we can only speak of a primacy of the ideal of personality within the science-ideal itself. In this connection it is merely of secondary significance that the basic denominator

---

[1] Not as innate concepts present at birth. DESCARTES made this clear in his polemic with REGIUS. The latter conceived of the *ideae innatae* as being present at birth, but for DESCARTES innate concepts are only an in-born *capacity* to think them: "Non enim unquam scripsi vel judicavi, mentem indigere ideis innatis, quae sint aliquid diversum ab ejus facultate cogitandi" (*Notae*, pp. 184 and 185. Ed. 1698). ["For I have never written or judged, that the mind has need of innate ideas which are something different from its faculty of thought".].

[2] DESCARTES' nominalistic standpoint is sharply formulated in his *Principia Philosophiae* I, 58 ff. He qualifies universals as mere "modus cogitandi" and general names. In the French translation, *Méditations Métaphysiques* (in Oeuvres Choises, Nouvelle ed., Paris, Garnier Frères, p. 97) the intended passage reads thus: "mais on doit savoir que toute idée étant un ouvrage de l'esprit, sa nature est telle qu'elle ne demande de soi aucune autre réalité formelle que celle qu'elle reçoit et emprunte de la pensée ou de l'esprit, dont elle est seulement un mode, c'est à dire une manière ou une façon de penser." ["However, because every Idea is a work of the mind, it is to be understood, that its nature is such that it does not demand any other formal reality than that which it receives and borrows from thought or mind; it is only a mode of the latter, that is to say a manner or fashion of thinking"].

In the sequel of his argument DESCARTES calls the Ideas in me a representation, an "imago" of the first and principal causes of these Ideas in God. But this does not signify a return to the realistic „Abbildtheorie". We must never forget, that in his methodical scepticism, DESCARTES primarily understands the cogito in a subjective and individual sense, and therefore has to struggle with solipsistic arguments. The Idea of God must serve in the first place to refute these arguments: "et par conséquent, je ne puis moi-même être seul dans le monde" [and consequently I cannot be alone in the world"]. Thus the bridge is built to an absolute mathematical thought which, elevated above all fallible subjectivity, creates the real RES EXTENSIVA.

which HOBBES accepts for all knowable reality is different from that which DESCARTES chooses for the pre-logical aspects of reality. DESCARTES conceives movement only as a modus of filled space. For HOBBES space is merely a subjective "PHANTASMA REI EXISTENTIS" just as time is merely "a PHANTASMA MOTUS"; HOBBES' basic denominator is not space but mathematically determined movement.

§ 2 - THE MATHEMATICAL-IDEALISTIC TYPE OF HUMANIST TRANSCENDENTAL GROUND-IDEA

It is not our intention to write a history of modern philosophy. Consequently, we shall not discuss the Cartesian circle of Jansenist at Port Royal, which soon united Cartesian philosophy with Christian-Augustinian and neo-Platonic-Augustinian motives. Nor shall we discuss the similar attempts at synthesis undertaken by the Occasionalists, which encountered strong opposition from orthodox Cartesians.

Our purpose is only to investigate the development of the polar tensions within Humanist philosophy itself in a few of its most representative systems. Consequently, we shall examine these tensions separately and apart from the complications which arise by the intrinsically contradictory union of the Humanist with the scholastic-Christian "realist" standpoint in philosophy.

We must then first fix our attention upon the great refinement of the polar tension between the mathematical science-ideal and the ideal of personality in the philosophy of LEIBNIZ.

The supposed Thomistic-Aristotelian traits in LEIBNIZ' Philosophy.

It is usual to speak of a reconciliation in LEIBNIZ between the new mathematical and mechanical view of nature and the teleological Aristotelian-Thomistic doctrine of substantial forms. Indeed, in many respects LEIBNIZ himself has provided the occasion for this misunderstanding. In his copious letter to JACOB THOMASIUS (April 20/30 1669) he spoke of such a reconciliation and up till the last period of his life we find statements in this same strain. The letter that he sent to REMOND DE MONTMORT in the year 1715 (Philos. Schriften ed. by ERDMANN[1], p. 701 f.) is note-worthy

---

[1] For the most part my own quotations will be taken from this edition of LEIBNIZ' works. The quotations from GERHARDT's edition are only supplementary and refer to papers which are not in ERDMANN. Even though

in this connection. And also by continually emphasizing the Idea of the "perennis philosophia" he seems to be pointing in this direction. Did not LEIBNIZ intend to unite in his system all the philosophical motives of his predecessors? WINDELBAND even speaks of a "Platonic idealism" in LEIBNIZ' doctrine of the "eternal verities". Actually one can find in LEIBNIZ the seemingly realist idealistic thesis that the "eternal verities" [1] exist *"in quadam regione idearum"*, namely in God. And in his letter concerning Platonic philosophy (1797 Erdm. p. 445), he identifies this very conception with the Platonic doctrine of an intelligible world.

Nevertheless, there is absolutely no evidence of an actual realistic conception of Ideas in LEIBNIZ' metaphysics. His transcendental ground-Idea recognizes no other Ἀρχή but mathematical thought in its deified form.

As appears from his paper *De Rerum Originatione radicali* (p. 148) written in 1697, the origin of the cosmos is sought by him in a *"mathesis quaedam divina sive mechanismus metaphysicus"* which is incomprehensible only to the finite mind, but functions in God as creative thought.

Even in his doctor's thesis, *Disputatio metaphysica de principio individui* (defended by LEIBNIZ in 1663 when seventeen years old) he chose the side of nominalism. In this thesis he only gave evidence of a rather superficial knowledge of scholastic philosophy. In his *Dissertatio de stilo philophico Nizolii* (1670) he called the sect of nominalists *"omnium inter scholasticas profundissima"* and considered it to be in absolute agreement with the modern way of philosophizing [2]. It will subsequently

---

GERHARDT's edition contains much additional material, it is sometimes inaccurate.

[1] LOCKE's nominalist standpoint is not doubted. Yet he, too, speaks of "eternal relations between the Ideas" *(Essay concerning human understanding* iv, 1 para. 9). He is only referring to ethical and mathematical Ideas which are created by thought itself. This conception of the Ideas as a creation of thought itself is incompatible with a *veritable realism of Ideas*.

[2] ERDMANN, p. 68: "secta Nominalium, omnium inter scholasticas profundissima, et hodiernae reformatae philosophandi rationi congruentissima; quae quum olim maxime floreret, nunc, apud scholasticos quidem, extincta est. Unde conjicias decrementa potius quam augmenta acuminis." A little further on, however, LEIBNIZ observes: "Idem dicendum est de nostri temporis philosophicae Reformatoribus, eos si non plusquam Nominales tamen Nominales esse fere omnes".

become evident that LEIBNIZ remained a nominalist in his entire further course of development. In speaking of nominalism here we mean the type, dominated by a modern Humanistic ground-Idea, which starts from the primacy of the classical Humanistic science-ideal and holds to supra-arbitrary fundamentals of the latter. This moderate nominalism — in contrast with the extreme kind of HOBBES — maintains the intrinsic (supposedly supra-temporal) necessity of the logical relations of thought [1]. In his *Dissertatio de stilo philosophico Nizolii*, quoted above, LEIBNIZ testified that nearly all thinkers of his day who aimed at a "reformation" of philosophy, were nominalists in this sense. If they were not nominalistic in this sense they were "plusquam Nominales", that is to say they went further than WILLIAM OF OCCAM, GREGORIUS OF RIMINI, GABRIEL BIEL and a number of thinkers of the Augustinian order who adhered to nominalism in its moderate form [2]. It was this moderate nominalism which maintained itself in LEIBNIZ' mature thought in the doctrine of *"vérités éternelles"*, in the sense of eternal logical possibilities which reside in the creative mathematical thought of God. We shall discuss this later.

It is no reconciliation between the modern science-ideal and a scholastic doctrine of substantial forms, which lies at the foundation of LEIBNIZ' philosophical endeavour. Rather his system manifests the increasing tension between the two factors of his Humanistic ground-motive. This tension puts its stamp upon his metaphysics; and the solution which he attempted to give to the fundamental antinomy in his Humanistic ground-Idea must be considered as the greatest that Humanistic thought was able to attain during the phase of the primacy of the science-ideal. This will become evident from our further analysis.

The fact that in his metaphysics LEIBNIZ again introduced

---

[1] LEIBNIZ' treatise concerning the philosophical style of NIZOLIUS, to which we have referred, contains a veritable panegyric of the basic tenets of nominalism. In it he opposed the extreme nominalism of HOBBES according to whom truth would only be a property of language and "qui, ut verum fatear, mihi plusquam nominalis videtur." "Non contentus enim cum Nominalibus universalia ad nomina reducere, ipsam, rerum veritatem ait in nominibus consistere." [which, to be true, seems to me to be more than nominalist." "For, not being satisfied by reducing, in accordance with the nominalists, the universalia to names, he contends that the very truth of things consists in the latter"].

[2] ERDMANN p. 69.

Aristotelian terms such as: entelechy, materia prima et secunda, potentiality and actuality, actus purus, causa efficiens and causa finalis, should not lead us astray and make us oblivious of the modern Humanistic sense which he ascribed to these terms. Let us not forget, that, by virtue of his education in the scholastic philosophy of MELANCHTON, he had become familiar with this terminology.

The secularization of the motive of nature and grace in LEIBNIZ' philosophy.

Even the scholastic contrast between the sphere of nature and the sphere of grace and the Idea of the subservience of the former to the latter reappears in LEIBNIZ. But he ascribes to this dialectical motive a completely different meaning. Even from this it is clearly evident, that his philosophy is not grounded in a scholastic accommodation of the Greek basic motive to that of Christian thought (as in THOMAS), but that it is rooted solely in the Humanistic immanence-standpoint.

In LEIBNIZ the sphere of grace never means anything but the realm of rational creatures who are in possession of freedom by clear and distinct thought. And the sphere of nature is only the realm of creatures who lack this freedom. In the former the deity (pure reason) displays itself as the most wise monarch; in the latter, as the most perfect architect. In the first, laws are ethical, and in the second, mechanical [1]. In this way also AUGU-

---

[1] *Principes de la nature et de la grâce* (1714) 15 (ERDMANN 717): "C'est pourquoi tous les esprits, soit des hommes, soit des génies entrant en vertu de la raison et des vérités éternelles dans une espèce de société avec Dieu, sont des membres de la Cité de Dieu, c'est à dire, du plus parfait état, formé et gouverné par le plus grand et le meilleur des Monarques, où il n'y a point de crime sans châtiment, point de bonnes actions sans récompense proportionnée; et enfin, autant de vertu et de bonheur qu'il est possible; et cela, non pas par un dérangement de la Nature comme si ce que Dieu prépare aux âmes troubloit les loix des corps; mais par l'ordre même des choses naturelles, en vertu de l'harmonie préétablie de tout temps entre les R è g n e s d e l a N a t u r e e t d e l a G r â c e." [*Principles of nature and grace:* "Therefore all spirits, either of men or of genii, entering by means of reason and the eternal verities into a sort of society with God, are members of the City of God, that is to say of the most perfect state, formed and governed by the greatest and the best of monarchs; where there is not ony crime without punishment, not any good deed without proportionate recompense; and finally as much virtue and happiness as is possible; and such

STINE's Christian conception of the Civitas Dei becomes denaturated in LEIBNIZ' speculative metaphysics. AUGUSTINE's conception is reduced to an Idea of a constitutional kingdom in which the deity reigns by the grace of metaphysical-mathematical thought. The creative will of the deity is bound to the eternal metaphysical verities of the latter. LEIBNIZ' Humanistic secularization of the Christian religion received its most evident expression in his conception of sin as a privatio. At first sight this conception seems to be orientated to that of AUGUSTINE, but actually it is entirely Cartesian. LEIBNIZ holds sin to be a lack of (mathematical) distinctness and clearness in conception, because of which the will does not arrive at a correct judgment.

> The refinement of the postulate of continuity in the science-ideal by means of LEIBNIZ' mathematical concept of function. The discovery of differential and integral calculus.

Let me now point out the intensive enrichment which the mathematical Humanistic science-ideal acquires in LEIBNIZ by the application of the mathematical concept of function which he introduced.

This concept, discovered in the differential and integral calculus, afforded an extremely fruitful and fine instrument of thought [1]. It was assimilated into the Cartesian science-ideal. Consequently, by infinitesimally small transitions of thought it became possible to carry through the postulate of continuity of this science-ideal across the boundaries of the modal aspects. And, in addition, the crass materialism of HOBBES and the crass dualism of DESCARTES could thereby be avoided.

---

not by means of a disarrangment of Nature, as if that which God prepares for the souls should disturb the laws of the bodies; but by the very order of natural things, by virtue of the harmony preestablished for all times between the Realms of Nature and of Grace."]

[1] As it appears from GERHARDT's publication of LEIBNIZ' scientific writings, the discovery of differential and integral calculus took place during LEIBNIZ' stay in Paris in the years 1673—76. He first published the basic principles of this new calculus in 1684 and 1686 in two treatises entitled *Nova methodus pro maximis et minimis* and *De geometria recondita et analyse indivisibilium atque infinitorum*. As is generally known these publications involved him in an unpleasant controversy with NEWTON, who had designed his fluctional calculus in 1665/6. The dispute centered around the priority of both discoveries. It is established, that LEIBNIZ' discovery is entirely independent of NEWTON's.

The principle of continuity that LEIBNIZ indicates as the final basis of his analysis is everywhere presented by him as a regulative principle and a logical method of thought.

If we view two series of values of variable magnitudes which are joined with each other by a fixed law, then, if we approach the limits of both, the functional relation, existing among the members of the two series, may not be viewed as abolished.

From a sensory viewpoint these limiting cases, in contrast to the remaining elements, may appear as entirely heterogeneous, just as rest and motion, equality and inequality, parallellism and intersection of lines must appear as irreconcilable contradictions in the direct sensory intuition. But this cleft, existing for our sensory perception, must be bridged over by thought. When two isolated elements are contrasted with each other, it may seem, that the one is utterly dissimilar to the other. Yet, if the former can be deduced and developed from the latter in a continuous logical process, their connection gains a higher and more securely grounded character, than any sensory perceptible agreement would have made possible [1].

LEIBNIZ himself formulated the main principle of this new calculus as follows: "If a continuous transition is given which ends in a final term, then it is always possible to introduce a common rational calculus (rationationem communem instituere) which likewise includes the final term" [2].

This brilliant discovery which was made in the infinitesimal calculus was to become one of the strongest foundations for the progress of modern physics. However, at the same time it became a metaphysical instrument of the Humanistic mathematical science-ideal.

The concept of function and the principle of continuity become metaphysical, when employed in the attempt logically to bridge over the modal boundaries of *meaning* of the different law-spheres and to reduce in the last analysis the whole cosmic coherence in the modal diversity of meaning to a logical and mathematical one. This was attempted according to the ideal that had animated Humanistic philosophy since DESCARTES,

---

[1] CASSIRER, *Das Erkenntnisproblem (The problem of knowledge)* vol II, p. 158.

[2] In his treatise: *Cum prodiisset atque increbuisset Analysis mea infinitesimalis* (Historia et Origio Calc. differ. ed. by GERHARDT, p. 40, quoted in CASSIRER, loc. cit.).

viz. the "mathesis universalis", as a universal method of thought.

The two roots of LEIBNIZ' philosophy. The misunderstanding in SCHMALENBACH concerning the Calvinistic origin of LEIBNIZ' individualism.

In LEIBNIZ' metaphysics this attempt was undertaken in a truly masterly manner. SCHMALENBACH, in his extensive study of LEIBNIZ, examined the logicistic-arithmetical basic Idea which is the primary root in LEIBNIZ' metaphysics [1].

However, under the influence of MAX WEBER, he wrongly thought, that the root of this arithmeticism itself — by means of which the science-ideal now rationalized *individuality* — is to be found in "Calvinistic religiosity". This was a fundamental misunderstanding both of the latter and of the true religious ground-motive of LEIBNIZ' arithmeticism. Rather this religious motive is to be sought in the individualistic and rationalistic Humanistic ideal of personality at the inception of the „Aufklärung".

The differential-number became a monad in a metaphysical sense; it became the true noumenal unity of reality which lies at the foundation of all compound phenomena. These monads

---

[1] HERMAN SCHMALENBACH, *Leibniz* (Drei Masken-Verlag, München, 1921). In the meanwhile one should bear in mind that "arithmeticism" is here used in the sense of the concept of function of differential calculus. LEIBNIZ comprehended the latter as a universal method of analysis. He applied it with equal facility to number, space and motion, and to the field of biology and psychology.

In his work *"Meditationes de cognitione, veritate et ideis"* (Meditations on knowledge, truth and ideas), LEIBNIZ still defended the conception that number, as a sum of static units, is the metaphysical basic Idea of the cosmos and arithmetic is a sort of "statica of the universum". Later on he abandoned this view and held that a discrete element is only a function of the mathematical principle of progression, and number itself is only the simplest instance of the general relation of thought. Thus LEIBNIZ is actually a logicist in his mathematical conception.

It is, however, incorrect to suppose that he thereby abandoned in his *metaphysics* the arithmetical standpoint as such. In his book *Leibniz' System in seinen wissensch. Grundlagen* (1902) and in the second vol. of his *Erkenntnisproblem*, CASSIRER erroneously arrives at this conclusion on the basis of his own epistemological conception of the calculus of infinity. LEIBNIZ' monadology actually arose, as SCHMALENBACH has shown in detail, in conscious opposition to metaphysical space-universalism, just as much as to materialistic atomism. It rests upon the hypostatization of the differential-number.

fill the noumenal cosmos in gapless density. They were thought of as animate beings which in their representations reflect, each in its proper way, the *universe,* but which, with respect to each other, sustain an absolutely closed, self-sufficient existence. Just as such they come to be the expression of the Humanistic ideal of personality in its individualistic and rationalist conception.

In this way the noumenal metaphysical cosmos was resolved into an infinite multitude of "windowless" monads, spaceless, animated points of force. The lex continui which originates out of mathematical thought maintains a continuous coherence of meaning between them and between the different modal aspects of their inner world. In LEIBNIZ' system this result was attained without it being necessary to subsume the entire cosmos under a mechanistic basic denominator.

BRUNO's aesthetically tinted individualism in his conception of the monad as a microcosmos was transformed by LEIBNIZ into a mathematical one. The Idea of microcosmos, the Idea of the *"omnia ubique"* in the Humanistic ideal of personality as it was conceived during the Renaissance, was rationalised. The mathematical science-ideal reduced the individual with its qualitative individuality to a function of the principle of progression and thereby made the individual accessible to rational calculation. In this way, by the lex continui, the self-sufficient individuality of the monads [1], as an expression of the ideal of personality, was reconciled to the ideal of science.

LEIBNIZ' concept of force and the *motive of activity* in the ideal of personality.

The individual self-sufficiency of personality and the motive of infinite activity had from the very beginning been predominant in the Humanistic ideal of personality as it was conceived of the during the Renaissance. And now both of these moments could be expressed in the metaphysics of the science-ideal. In the Cartesian system the tendency of activity in the ideal of

---

[1] *La Monadologie* (1714): "On pouvroit donner le nom d'Entéléchies à toutes les substances simples ou Monades créées, car elles ont en elles une certaine perfection (ἔχουσι τὸ ἐντελές), il y une suffisance (αὐτάρκεια), qui les rend sources de leur actions internes..." (ERDMANN, 706). [The name of Entelechies might be given to all simple substances or created Monads, for they have a certain perfection in themselves, a kind of self-sufficience *(autarky)* which enables them to be the sources of their own internal activity...].

personality could not, as in BRUNO, penetrate the Idea of the cosmos itself. The "res extensiva" as a natural substance is, in DESCARTES, a part of absolutized static space of which motion is only a modus.

In contrast with this, LEIBNIZ hypostatized the concept of force, introduced by NEWTON in physics, and made it into the essence of the monad-substance, which as a self-sufficient microcosmos does not permit any outside influence. In LEIBNIZ this metaphysical concept of force appears in the outward Aristotelian form of "entelechy" and "causa-finalis", but is not actually to be interpreted in an Aristotelian sense [1]. Rather it is penetrated by the motive of activity in the Humanistic ideal of personality. In this modern sense it is opposed to Cartesian metaphysics. Continuous static space is no longer considered to be the essence of nature, but instead its essence is sought in the *working force*.

Space and time are in LEIBNIZ only ideal arrangements of phenomena. The first is an arrangement or relation of coexistence; the second is an arrangement or relation of succession. Space is, as LEIBNIZ wrote in his fourth letter to CLARKE: *"Cet ordre qui fait que les corps sont situables, et par lequel ils ont une situation entre eux en existant ensemble"* [2].

Regulated by the laws of physical motion, mechanical matter (LEIBNIZ called it "materia secunda") is only the mode of appearance of the metaphysical force which belongs to the essence of the monad, "un phénomène, mais bien fondé, résultant des Monades" [3].

---

[1] In his *Système Nouv. de la Nature* (1695) LEIBNIZ observed: "Il fallut donc rappeller et comme réhabiliter les formes substantielles, si decriées aujourd'hui; mais d'une manière qui les rendit intelligibles, et qui sépara l'usage qu'on en doit faire de l'abus qu'on en a fait" (ERDMANN, pag. 124). ["It was thus necessary to recall and as it were to rehabilitate the substantial forms which have been so much reviled nowadays; but in a manner which rendered them intelligible and separated the use which is to be made of them from the abuse which has been made of the same"].

[2] ERDMANN, p. 758. ["This order which makes it possible for bodies to be localized and by which in their coexistence they have a situation in relation to one another"].

[3] It is again evident that LEIBNIZ uses the scholastic-Aristotelian terms *materia prima et secunda* in a totally modified sense. *Materia prima* has become the substantial force of the monads which is the metaphysical cause of inert matter in the world of appearance: the *materia secunda*. Compare LEIBNIZ' letter to REMOND DE MONTFORT (ERDMANN, p. 124): "Quant à l'inertie de la matière, comme la matière elle même n'est autre

In this fashion the dynamical motive of the ideal of personality penetrated infinite nature itself. There is no trace of a real revival of the Aristotelian concept of entelechy in LEIBNIZ. The Idea of the autarchy, of the self-sufficiency of the monad is entirely in conflict with Aristotelian metaphysics, especially with the Aristotelian conception of the relation between soul and body. Moreover, LEIBNIZ' concept of force has essentially nothing to do with the Aristotelian doctrine of entelechies which is dominated by the Greek ground-motive of form and matter, and to which the titanic *dunamis* of the Humanistic ideal of personality and science is wholly foreign.

Meanwhile, in LEIBNIZ' metaphysics the ideal of personality reached a position of extremely intensive tension with the mathematical science-ideal. This tension was due to the fact that he tried to express the basic tendencies of the former in a metaphysics derived from the latter. LEIBNIZ did not for a moment wish to derogate from the primacy of the science-ideal. On the contrary, the Faustian motive of dominating nature by mathematic thought ruled him perhaps even more than it had his rationalistic predecessors.

Primacy of the mathematical science-ideal in LEIBNIZ' transcendental ground-Idea.

In LEIBNIZ' transcendental ground-Idea, the construction of the relation between totality and modal diversity in the coherence of meaning is completely left to the mathematical science-ideal.

This is evident in the first place from the theoretical common denominator under which he subsumes all modal aspects of experience, namely, the representation (perception) which he conceives as "représentation du composé, ou de ce qui est dehors, dans le simple" [representation of the composite or what is outward, in the simple substance][1].

---

chose qu'un phénomène, mais bien fondé, résultant des Monades: il n'en est de même de l'inertie, qui est une propriété de ce phénomène." ["Just like matter itself is nothing but a phenomenon, but a well-founded one, resulting from the Monads, the same holds good in respect to the inertness of matter, which is a property of this phenomenon"].

[1] ERDMANN, p. 714. Also compare *Monadologie*, 14 (ERDMANN, p. 706): "L'état passager qui enveloppe et représente une multitude dans l'unité ou dans la substance simple, n'est autre chose que ce qu'on appelle la perception qu'on doit distinguer de l'apperception ou de la conscience." [The transitory state which envelopes and represents a multitude in a

In LEIBNIZ' metaphysics, all monads, also the material ones have become perceiving points of force, which only in their representations reflect the coherence of the cosmos in its modal diversity of aspects. And once this rationalistic basic denominator had been established for the modal diversity of meaning, the mathematical lex continui of the science-ideal had gained complete control. For in LEIBNIZ' metaphysical conception of the world-order, all monads were arranged in a mathematically conceived progression [1]. The monads do not differ because of a fundamental specific nature. The realistic Aristotelian conception of species is totally abandoned in LEIBNIZ' metaphysics. In fact, the qualitative difference between the monads has been quantified: it consists only in the degree of clarity of their perceptions in which the cosmos reflects itself and in the degree of the tendency to pass from one perception to the other: "And consequently a Monad in itself, and in the moment, could *not* be distinguished from another except by the properties and internal actions which can be nothing but these perceptions (that is to say, the representations of the composite, or of what is outward, in the simple) and *its* appetitions (that is to say, its tendencies to pass from one perception to the other) which are the principles of change" [2].

A continuous ascending progression breaks through the dis-

---

unity or in the simple substance, is nothing but what is called the perception which is to be distinguished from the apperception or the consciousness]. Every monad is thus a unity in the multiplicity of its perceptions: "Car la simplicité de la substance n'empêche point la multiplicité des modifications, qui se doivent trouver ensemble dans cette même substance simple." *Princ. de la Nat. et de la Grâce* 2. [For the simplicity of the substance does not prevent the multiplicity of the modifications which must be found together in this same simple substance];

[1] This transcendental Idea of world-order outwardly reminds us of ARISTOTLE's two-fold lex naturalis. It is, however in essence a mathematical construction. It arranges both the material and rational monads in a continuous progression, after the pattern of the calculus of infinity. And, proceeding from the lower to the higher, it places the deity, the central monad, at the apex.

[2] ERDMANN, p. 714: "Et par conséquent une Monade en elle même, et dans le moment, ne sauroit être discernée d'une autre que par les qualités et actions internes, lesquelles ne peuvent être autre chose que ces perceptions (c'est à dire, les représentations du composé, ou de ce qui est dehors, dans le simple) et de ses appétitions (c'est à dire, ses tendances d'une perception à l'autre), qui sont les principes du changement."

continuity of the monads by passing from the unconscious perceptions (the so-called *"petites perceptions"* [1]) of the material monads, via the conscious, but confused representations of the sensory soul-monads, to the clear and distinct apperceptions of the limited spiritual monads. And from thence it passes to the infinite creative mathematical thought of the deity, which is pure thought without sensory perceptions.

In this mathematical world-order man has his place between the two poles: matter and deity. In man, intelligence (mathematical thought) and sensation, activity and passivity, spontaneity, and receptivity occur together. Therefore, the human mind is limited in its thought, a limitation which is lacking in the deity, as "actus purus".

Leibniz' Humanistic theism.

Ostensibly, an Aristotelian theism is here adhered to; however, in essence, the deity has become identical with the final hypostasis of the mathematical science-ideal. Theism passes — nearly imperceptibly — into a logical-mathematical pantheism: *"Harmonia universalis, id est Deus."*

The infinite analysis of the entire cosmos is accomplished in God's thought alone; on this ground the world-order is in essence qualified as a purely mathematical coherence of meaning. This is true even though human thought, on account of its limitedness (that is, its metaphysical imperfection), cannot gain insight into the absolute mathematical necessity of a seemingly contingent event within the world of phenomena.

Logicization of the dynamical tendency in the ideal of personality.

Even though it more or less continued to be an irrationalistic residue in Leibniz' system, the metaphysical concept of force, as an expression of the activity-motive in the ideal of personality, was rationalized as much as possible. The individualistic ideal of personality of the early "Enlightenment" did not permit any violation of the self-sufficiency of the *individuum*. And for the sake of the mathematical science-ideal, the entire activity of all the monads was subsumed under the basic denominator of

---

[1] The "unconscious perception" is thus conceived of as an infinitesimal degree of consciousness.

representation (Vorstellung). Consequently, the metaphysical concept of force had to be accommodated to the latter [1]: the autarchical activity of the monad was interpreted in the sense of a tendency (appétition) to pass from the one representation to the other. This tendency, in scholastic formulation conceived of as a "causa finalis", brings in motion, in every monad alike, the system of representations in which the universe is reflected [2].

This logicization of the concept of force was not a "deus ex machina" in LEIBNIZ' monadology.

As we have seen, the monad is primarily the hypostatized differential in the infinitesimal calculus [3]. Now the differential

---

[1] This concept of force which arose from the ideal of personality, was a stumbling block for the neo-Kantians of the Marburg school because of its irrationalist predisposition. They deemed it to be in conflict with the postulate of continuity of pure thought. See COHEN, *Logik der reinen Erkenntnis*, 3e Aufl., p. 263/4.

[2] *Monadologie* 15: "L'action du principe interne, qui fait le changement, ou le passage d'une perception, à une autre, peut être appellé A p p é t i t i o n; il est vrai, que l'appétit ne sauroit toujours parvenir entièrement à toute la perception, où il tend, mais il en obtient toujours quelque chose, et parvient à des perceptions nouvelles." ["The activity of the internal principle which effects the change or the passing of a perception into another, may be called A p p e t i t i o n; it is true, that the appetite cannot always entirely reach the perception to which it tends, but it always attains something of the same, and arrives at new perceptions."]

Ib. 79: "Les âmes agissent selon les lois des causes finales par appétitions, fins et moyens." ["The souls act according to the laws of the final causes by appetitions, aims and means"].

[3] LEIBNIZ called them metaphysical points, and according to him mathematical points are their "point de vûe", which enables them to express the universe. See his *Syst. Nouv.* 11 (ERDM. p. 126): "Il n'y a que les a t o m e s d e s u b s t a n c e, c'est à dire, les unités réelles, et absolument destituées de parties, qui soient les sources des actions, et les premiers principes absolus de la composition des choses, et comme les derniers élémens de l'analyse des substances. On les pourroit appeler, p o i n t s m é t a p h y s i q u e s: ils ont q u e l q u e c h o s e d e v i t a l, et *une espèce de* p e r c e p t i o n, et les points mathématiques sont leur p o i n t d e v u e, pour exprimer l'Univers... Ainsi les points physiques ne sont indivisibles qu'en apparence; les points mathématiques sont exacts, mais ce ne sont que des modalités: il n'y a que les points métaphysiques ou *de substance... qui soient exacts et réels*; et sans eux il n'y auroit rien de réel, puisque sans les véritables unités il n'y auroit point de multitude." ["There are no other atoms but the substantial ones, that is to say the real units which absolutely lack parts; they are the very sources of the actions, and the first absolute principles of the composition of things, and the last elements of the analysis of the substances.

number, as we shall explain in our analysis of its modal meaning in the following volume, anticipates the modal meaning of motion [1]. Meanwhile, the original meaning of motion is logicized by LEIBNIZ; it is transformed into an Idea of mathematical *thought*-movement and is then laid as ὑπόθεσις at the foundation of natural science [2]. This also paved the way for the logicizing of the concept of force which in LEIBNIZ' monadology is the necessary prerequisite for the movement of thought and of the lower perceptions.

Insofar as it must guarantee the closed autarchy of the monadic individuals, "force", as a tendency, only continued to be the expression of LEIBNIZ' individualistic personality-ideal, because it never becomes active through functional causes outside the monads.

LEIBNIZ' intellectual determinism and his doctrine of innate Ideas in the light of the lex continui.

DESCARTES had utilized a partial indeterminism to explain both the possibility of ethical faults and error in thought. This is no longer necessary in LEIBNIZ' system. In fact it is even impossible here.

For this partial indeterminism implied the acceptance of an "influxus physicus". As we have seen the latter was intrinsically contradictory in DESCARTES' system; nevertheless, it was necessary to explain the origin of sensorily confused perceptions. The will possesses a *liberum arbitrium indifferentiae* with respect to these confused perceptions. If one allows himself to be influenced by them, one turns away from the path of clear and distinct thought, and error and "sin", respectively, arise in the theoretical and practical realm.

In LEIBNIZ' metaphysics, on the contrary, the Idea of the

They might be called m e t a p h y s i c a l   p o i n t s: they have a k i n d of v i t a l i t y and a kind of p e r c e p t i o n, and the mathematical points are their v i e w-p o i n t in order to express the Universe... Consequently, the physical points are indivisible only in appearance; the mathematical points are exact but they are nothing but modalities; only the metaphysical or substantial points... are both exact and real; and without them there would be nothing real, because without the veritable units, there would be no multitude at all."}

[1] Here is meant motion in its original exact pre-physical sense, as it was viewed by GALILEO and is made the "Gegenstand" of an apriori mathematical science, viz. the phoronomy (KANT).

[2] See GERHARDT's edition V, 437, 10.

absolute windowlessness, the absolute inner self-sufficiency of the monads, excludes any "influxus physicus". Even the sensory perceptions in the human soul-monad are produced in absolute autarchy, entirely from the inside [1].

On the other hand, the sharp antithesis between sensibility and logical thought had disappeared. Consequently, error of thought and "sin" acquire a less accentuated significance than they had in DESCARTES.

The proclamation of a "primacy of the will", even if only partial, has become superfluous because of the lex continui. The *irrational gap between sensory perception and the clear concept is bridged over by the logical mathematical principle of continuity*. Both sin and error of thought are in LEIBNIZ only the consequence of the metaphysical imperfection of the finite rational monads, through which clear mathematical thought is again and again obscured by sensory "perceptions". They are only gradual conditions, since from the sensory perceptions the clear mathematical concept can develop itself in a continuous transition.

In this way even DESCARTES' doctrine of innate ideas has been relativized by the lex continui. In a noteworthy manner the latter bridged over the antithesis between sensationalistic and rationalistic trends in epistemology. In his work, *Nouveaux Essais sur l'Entendement*, published posthumously in 1765, LEIBNIZ explained the "idées innées" as dormant, virtual representations which are not yet "connues" [of which we are not yet aware]. Potentially present in sensory perceptions, they gradually develop themselves *into clear and distinct concepts*.

Since all monads in their perceptions equally represent the

---

[1] *Monadologie* 51 (ERDMANN, p. 709): "Mais dans les substances simples ce n'est qu'une influence idéale d'une Monade sur l'autre, qui ne peut avoir son effet que par l'intervention de Dieu, en tant que dans les idées de Dieu une Monade demande avec raison, que Dieu en réglant les autres dès le commencement des choses, ait regard à elle. Car puisqu'une Monade créée ne sauroit avoir une influence physique sur l'intérieur de l'autre, ce n'est que par ce moyen, que l'une peut avoir de la dépendance de l'autre." [But in the simple substances it is only an ideal influence of a Monad over the other, an influence which cannot have its effect but by the intervention of God; namely, in so far as in the Ideas of God a Monad demands in good reason that, in arranging the others since the beginning, God has regard to it. For, because a created Monad cannot have a physical influence over the inner life of the other, it is only in this way that one can be dependent on the other].

entire cosmos, in every moment the result of the movement of representations must be the same in each of them; each monad only lives in itself. As we saw, it has no windows by which it can experience anything of the other monads; all of them experience the same things: their representations are in exact correspondence with each other by means of a pre-established harmony, and in this way it appears as though they continually influence each other.

Here LEIBNIZ' cosmonomic Idea clearly discloses itself in the Idea of Harmonia Praestabilita. In keeping with the mathematical science-ideal the latter implies the most stringent determinism in the process of development of the representations. Not the least margin is allowed in this process. For, if a single monad could arbitrarily deviate from the universally identical course of representations, the harmony in the whole cosmos would be disturbed. Every momentary condition of a monad is a natural consequence of its preceding condition: "the present is pregnant with the future" [1]. LEIBNIZ' standpoint in the problem of freedom of the will — the stumbling block between the science-ideal and the ideal of personality in Humanistic philosophy — is thereby implicitly determined.

This German thinker rejected the *liberum arbitrium indifferentiae* that DESCARTES maintained with respect to the sensory representations. He called this conception of the freedom of the will an *indifferentia aequilibrii* by which, in the last analysis, action would be able to occur *without any ground*.

In his short essay *De Libertate*, first published by ERDMANN,

---

[1] *Monadologie* 22 (ERDMANN, p. 706), Compare also the well-known place in the *Principes de la Nature et de la Grâce:* "Car tout est réglé dans les choses une fois pour toutes avec autant d'ordre et de correspondance qu'il est possible; la suprême Sagesse et Bonté ne pouvant agir qu'avec une parfaite harmonie. Le présent est gros de l'avenir: le futur se pourroit lire dans le passé; l'éloigné est exprimé dans le prochain. On pourroit connaître la beauté de l'Univers dans chaque âme, si l'on pouvoit déplier tous ses replis, qui ne se développent sensiblement qu'avec le tems." ["For everything is regulated in the things once for all with as much order and correspondence as possible: the highest Wisdom and Goodness being unable to act without a perfect harmony. The present is pregnant with the future: the future would permit itself to be read in the past; the distant is expressed in the proximate. One would be able to know the beauty of the Universe in every soul, if one could lay bare all its secrets which do not develop themselves perceptively but in course of time"].

LEIBNIZ asserted, that all actions of substances are determined: "*Nihil fit sine ratione*"[1].

The Idea of the harmonia praestabilita implies the acceptance of a "praedispositio rerum ex causis aut causarum series"[2]. The spiritual monad is a sort of *automaton spirituale:* everything in man is predetermined[3]. But, according to LEIBNIZ, this stringent determinedness of the will is in no way in conflict with the freedom of the rational personality. It may not be understood in the sense of mechanical coercion. The determining causes are only "inclinantes, non necessitantes". Insofar as the principle of action lies in the one who acts, the action is voluntary. Naturally, for the monad is autarchical; it has no windows. The freedom of man is greater in proportion to the degree in which he acts in accord with reason; he becomes a slave when he allows his actions to be determined by blind emotions and passions.

The ideal of personality was still conceived of individualistically. It required that the monads be thought of as autarchical and active individuals. However, in the philosophic basic Idea of "harmonia praestabilita" the individuality of the monads is brought under the absolute domination of the mathematical science-ideal. This subjugation was accomplished by means of the lex continui, the principle of universal order and coherence in the cosmos (principium quoddam generale).

The lex continui, as well as the harmonia praestabilita in which it is encompassed, owe their origin to the deity. The deity, in turn, is, as we observed, only the hypostasis of pure creative mathematical thought, *which is no longer troubled by sensory representations.* Volition is only a modus of thought. The deity

---

[1] ERDMANN, p. 669: "O m n e s t a m e n a c t i o n e s s u n t d e t e r m i n a t a e e t n u n q u a m i n d i f f e r e n t e s, quia semper datur ratio inclinans quidem nontamen necessitans, ut sic potius, quam aliter fiat. Nihil fit sine ratione. L i b e r t a s i n d i f f e r e n t i a e e s t i m p o s s i b i l i s." ["All actions, however, are determined and never indifferent, because there is always given some directing, although not compelling reason, that it happens rather in this way than otherwise. Nothing happens without reason. A libertas indifferentiae is impossible."]

[2] Compare *Causa Dei asserta per justitiam eius* (ERDMANN, p. 660): "Neque etiam praedispositio rerum aut causarum series nocet libertati." [For also the predestination of things or the series of causes does not harm freedom].

[3] *Theodicée* 1, 52 (ERDMANN, p. 517).

is at the outset identified with world-harmony. In LEIBNIZ' the Spinozistic "Deus sive natura" becomes the "Harmonia universalis, id est Deus"[1]. The kernel of this Idea of world-harmony is actually the functionalistic mathematical lex continui.

§ 3 - THE MODERATE NOMINALISM IN LEIBNIZ' CONCEPTION OF IDEAS. THE IDEA AS SYMBOL OF RELATIONS AND AS THE CONCEPT OF LAW OF THE RATIONALISTIC IDEAL OF SCIENCE

The veritable realistic metaphysics had always viewed the well-founded generic and specific concepts of thought as copies („Abbilder") of the eternal *eidè* or as the abstracted substantial forms of reality, respectively.

Such a realistic view was from the very beginning in conflict with the creation-motive in the mathematical science-ideal of Humanism. As CASSIRER[2] rightly has shown, there is, indeed, no trace of a realistic form-theory in LEIBNIZ. In true nominalistic fashion, in him, the ideas become symbols of reality; they only represent the proportions, the relations which exist between the individual elements of reality. Very characteristic of this conception is LEIBNIZ' treatise *Quid sit Idea,* in which he employs almost word for word OCCAM's distinction between conventional voces and the universal symbols which are grounded in nature. LEIBNIZ writes: "it further appears that some expressions possess a "fundamentum in natura", while the others, e.g. the words of language or arbitrary signs, at least partially rest upon an arbitrary convention. Those which are grounded in nature require a certain sort of similitude as that which exists between a cer-

---

[1] Compare LEIBNIZ' letter to the Duke JOHANN FRIEDRICH v. BRAUNSCHWEIG (1671), Gerh. I, 61.

[2] *Erkenntnisproblem* 11, 166 ff. See also p. 189 where CASSIRER gives expression to the inner sympathy of neo-Kantianism (of the Marburg school) with LEIBNIZ' ideal of science. "Die überlieferte Metaphysik der "substantiellen Formen" erfährt indessen hier nur eine scheinbare Erneuerung... Die oberflächliche Ansicht dasz die "Formen" der Dinge es sind, die in den Geist eindringen und in ihm die Erkenntnis der Objekte erzeugen, wird van LEIBNIZ in allen Phasen seines Denkens gleich rückhaltlos verworfen." ["Meanwhile, the traditional Metaphysics of "substantial Forms" is here only apparently revived... In all phases of his thought LEIBNIZ rejected with equal consistency the superficial view, that it would be the "forms" of things which penetrate into mind and produce in the latter the knowledge of the objects."]

tain region and its geographical map. At least they require a connection of the kind which exists between a circle and its perspective reflection in an ellipse. For every point of the ellipse there is a point of the circle which corresponds to it in accordance with a fixed specific law. The fact that there is an Idea of things in us, consequently only means, that God (who in like manner is the origin of spirit and of things) has given such power of thought to the human mind, that the latter can produce results from its own activity which completely agree with the actual results in things"[1]. So the functional law of motion also becomes an Idea which does not proceed from reality, but which is laid by reason at the foundation of the experience of reality: "That in nature everything occurs in a mechanical manner is a principle, that one can guarantee by pure thought only and never by experience"[2].

The apparent fight against nominalism in the third book of LEIBNIZ' *"Nouveaux Essais".*

Only in the light of this whole course of thought, can we understand the exact meaning of LEIBNIZ' apparent fight against nominalism[3] in the third book of his *Nouveaux essais sur l'entendement humain.* I must acknowledge, that the reading of this book caused me to waver in my opinion that LEIBNIZ' standpoint can be qualified as nominalistic. And when I now explain my hesitation in retrospect, I can only find the ground for it in LEIBNIZ' remarkable art of clothing his modern Humanistic conception in the guise of the traditional terminology of realistic scholasticism. In the vivid dialogue between PHILALETHE and THEOPHILE, the former defends the philosophy of LOCKE and the latter that of LEIBNIZ. The chief concern of the dialogue is, in the final analysis, only to maintain the eternal truths (in LEIBNIZ' logicistic mathematical sense of "logical possibilities") in oppositon to an extreme nominalism that holds all universal Ideas to be arbitrary creations of language. And as we shall see later on, this last conception was in no sense the view of LOCKE, but rather that of HOBBES.

---

[1] Gerh. VII, 263 sqq.
[2] Gerh. V, 437, 10.
[3] In this sense the third book of LEIBNIZ' *Nouveaux essais* was understood in the last but one ed. of UEBERWEG's *Hist. of Phil.* III (revised edition of Frischeischen-Köhler and Moog, p. 332).

Let me call attention to the fact, that in the beginning of the second book, where the question is raised concerning the character of Ideas in general, the spokesman for LEIBNIZ' conception expressly establishes the fact, that the Idea as an object of thought is only an object that is immanent to thought and, as such, is an expression of the character or the qualities of things [1].

This standpoint is continually maintained in the third book, which treats the entire controversy concerning the reality of universals in a most remarkable manner, under the subject of language or words. In the treatment of the "names of substances" the supporter of LEIBNIZ' own standpoint observes, that formerly there were two axioms adhered to by philosophers, that of the realists and that of the nominalists. "Both", says THEOPHILE, "are good, provided that one understands them correctly" [2].

The simple Ideas and those of substance (according to the affirmations of LEIBNIZ' mouthpiece in the treatment of the "names of the simple Ideas") are not grounded in any real existence but only in the possibility of thought: "il n'y auroit donc rien qui oblige ces Idées d'etre fondées dans quelque existence réelle" [3]. Even our most clear and distinct concepts do not have any model in nature of which they could be the copy. Even the universalia do not have such a model in natural reality [4].

Finally, the essentiae, the general essential characteristics of things, are identified by LEIBNIZ with the logical possibilities or "eternal truths" in creative mathematical thought [5]. We shall subsequently examine this point in detail.

---

[1] ERDMANN, 222: "Ph. Après avoir examiné, si les Idées sont innées, considérons leur nature et leurs différences. N'est il pas vrai, que l'Idée est l'object de la pensée? Ph. Je l'avoue, pourvu que vous ajoutez, que c'est un objet immédiat interne, et que cet objet est une expression de la nature ou des qualités des choses." [Ph. "After having examined whether the Ideas are innate, let us consider their nature and their differences. Is it not true, that the Idea is the object of thought?
Th. I admit it, provided that you add that it is an immediate internal object, and that this object is an expression of the properties of things."]

[2] ERDMANN, p. 320.

[3] ERDMANN, p. 307. ["Consequently, there could be nothing which obliges these Ideas to be founded in some real existence."]

[4] Ibid., p. 320.

[5] Ibid.: "les Essences sont perpétuelles, parce qu'il ne s'y agit que du

cosmonomic Idea of Humanistic immanence-philosophy   243

On this ground alone the advocate of LEIBNIZ' philosophy opposed the qualification of these essentialia generalia as arbitrary symbols. "The essentiae" are not imaginary, *their reality is that of thought itself*.

The distinction between nominal and real definitions must also be considered in this connection. By means of it LEIBNIZ opposed extreme nominalism.

According to this nominalistic conception, definitions only exist in an arbitrary union of symbols which function in thought as "counters".

LEIBNIZ observes, that this view only comprehends nominal definitions. A real definition must grasp the essence of the thing, which essence is identical with the logical possibility of the thing defined. The real definition must cause us to know this possibility apriori *by discovering the logical principle of the origin of the thing in question*[1].

In other words, LEIBNIZ' whole fight against nominalism only touched the extreme wing of it, which he had already rejected in 1670. It did not strike at the nominalist basic tenet, that Ideas (conceived of as essential structural principles of reality) *do not possess any real existence outside of thought*.

LEIBNIZ' metaphysics only recognized real monads. The Ideas belong to the representations of the latter. And eternal truths

---

possible." p. 305: "L'essence dans le fond n'est autre chose que la possibilité de ce qu'on propose. Ce qu'on suppose possible est exprimé par la définition; mais cette définition n'est que nominale, quand elle n'exprime point en même tems la possibilité, car alors on peut douter si cette définition exprime quelque chose de réel, c'est à dire de possible, jusqu'à l'expérience vienne à notre secours pour nous faire connaître cette réalité a posteriori, lorsque la chose se trouve effectivement dans le monde." ["The essences are perpetual, because they are nothing but possibilities." p. 305: "At bottom the essence is nothing but the possibility of that which is proposed. That which is supposed to be possible is expressed by the definition; but this definition is only a nominal one, if at the same time it does not express the possibility; for otherwise it may be doubted, whether this definition does express something real, that is to say possible, until experience comes to our aid in order to make us know this reality a posteriori, when the thing is really present in the world."]

[1] *Ibid.*, p. 306, where the advocate of LEIBNIZ' opinion says of reason, that it enables us "connaître la réalité apriori en exposant la cause ou la génération possible de la chose définie." ["to know reality a priori by exposing the cause or the possible generation of the defined thing"].

Also see *Ibid.*, p. 138 *(Réflexions sur l'Essai de Locke)*.

are only the virtually innate logical and mathematical relations which are in these representations, and which come to our clear consciousness in mathematical and metaphysical thought.

These "ideal eternal truths" do not lie at the foundation of empirical reality as Platonic Ideas, but only as necessary principles of origin inherent in mathematical thought itself. They are nothing but the foundations of the Humanistic science-ideal in its mathematical-logical conception. It is this that LEIBNIZ seeks to defend against the naturalistic nominalism of HOBBES [1].

LEIBNIZ' nominalistic standpoint in his treatise concerning the philosophical style of NIZOLIUS (1670).

This is not my own arbitrary hypothesis, rather it is explicitly confirmed by LEIBNIZ himself in his treatise *De Stilo Philosophico Nizolii*. We have seen, that in this work he took with great emphasis the side of moderate nominalism, as the latter was defended in the Occamistic school. And at the same time he fought against NIZOLIUS' conception of the universalia.

MARIUS NIZOLIUS (1489—1576) a nominalistic thinker of an extremely sensationalistic orientation, had conceived of the universalia as mere collectives, in which all individual things which are symbolically implied in them, are simultaneously comprehended.

A concept is only an abbreviated summation of many sensorily perceived individuals which are signified by a common name. This conception of universalia does not do justice to the Humanistic science-ideal with its creation-motive: "Non vero error hic Nizolii levis est", writes LEIBNIZ, "habet enim magnum aliquid in recessu. Nam si universalia nihil aliud sunt quam singularium collectiones, sequetur, *scientiam nullam haberi per demonstrationem* (quod et infra colligit NIZOLIUS) sed collectionem singularium, seu inductionem. *Sed ea ratione prorsus evertantur scientiae* et sceptici vicere" [2].

---

[1] *Ibid.*: "Il dépend donc pas de nous de joindre les Idées comme bon nous semble, à moins que cette combinaison ne soit justifiée ou par la raison qui la montre possible, ou par l'expérience, qui la montre actuelle, et par conséquent possible aussi." ["Consequently it does not depend on us to join the Ideas as we like, unless this combination is justified either by reason which shows its possibility, or by experience which shows its actuality and consequently its possibility too."].

[2] ERDMANN, p. 70. ["This error of NIZOLIUS is not really unimportant, for it conceals a great consequence. For if the universals are nothing but

The conception of "universalia" which LEIBNIZ here opposes to NIZOLIUS is in its very nature not realistic. It conceives of the universal concept as a *totum distributivum,* as an apriori totality comprehended in the definition, which is independent of the sensory perception of a particular instance. According to LEIBNIZ, the real significance of the universal is to be sought *in the universal validity of the judgment.* This universal validity is not and cannot be founded in any great quantity of sensory perceptions of particular instances, but only and exclusively *"in the universal Idea or definition of terms".*

Even at this stage, this "universal idea" is conceived of in the sense of a "real definition" in which we indicate the apriori possibility of the genetic construction or the method of "logical creation". A real definition is grounded in the logical postulate of the universal conformity of all events to laws. It is the rationalist Humanistic concept of the law, as it is implied in the mathematical science-ideal that is defended here by LEIBNIZ against extreme nominalism. It is this concept of the law that he defended against NIZOLIUS as well as against THOMAS HOBBES. The latter, according to LEIBNIZ, had even begun to doubt the theorem of PYTHAGORAS "that has been deemed worthy of the sacrifice of a hecatomb" [1].

The notion of the logical alphabet and the symbolical conception of Ideas.

All that we have said becomes clearer, if we view it against the background of LEIBNIZ' Idea of a logical alphabet, a "universal symbolical characteristic". This Idea was first developed by RAYMUNDUS LULLUS (1235—1315). Since the Renaissance it had been advocated by the adherents of the mathematical science-ideal. LEIBNIZ gave a primitive form to it in his *De Arte Combinatoria,* which he wrote at an early age (1666). In the further development of his thought, he continually enlarged this primi-

---

collections of individuals, then it follows, that science has nothing by demonstration (which is also NIZOLIUS' conclusion) but only a collection of individual instances or induction. In this manner, however, the sciences are completely destroyed and the sceptics have gained the victory."]

[1] ERDMANN, p. 71. This must be a misunderstanding in LEIBNIZ. HOBBES considered geometry as an apriori science, because the conditions of its constructions depend on our will. He did not draw the destructive consequences from his extreme nominalism with respect to mathematics.

tive conception by elaborating his discovery of the analysis of the infinite. His intention was to create a logical instrument which should make it possible to construct all of knowledge from a relatively small number of elements. The "Ars Combinatoria" would then consist in determining the number of possible combinations of simple logical elements. It would thus contain the schema required in order to answer all the questions that could arise with respect to reality.

In the primitive form in which LEIBNIZ had developed this idea in his youth, it was still entirely orientated to arithmetic as the theory of discrete quantity. Insofar as it is not a prime, every number allows itself to be comprehended as a product of prime numbers. For each number it is possible, on the basis of this analysis, to establish two numbers, with or without a common divisor. In the same fashion, complex concepts must first be arranged in specific basic classes, before the question regarding their mutual possibility of combination will allow itself to be answered in a systematic way.

A true judgment should consequently pre-suppose that subject and predicate possess a common logical factor, or that the predicate is entirely implied in the concept of the subject.

The discovery of the infinitesimal analysis, however, led LEIBNIZ to a fundamental modification of this criterion of truth. In a discourse concerning the distinction of necessary and contingent truths, he wrote, that it was geometrical knowledge and the infinitesimal analysis that first illuminated his mind and taught him to see, that concepts also can be subjected to an infinitesimal analysis [1]. The truth of a judgment cannot depend upon the fact, that the predicate is entirely implied in the concept of the subject, but is dependent upon the question, whether we can discover a general rule for the movement of thought, from which we can conclude with certainty, that the distinction between subject and predicate in the prolonged analysis must approach zero [2]. Thus the lex continui (the principle of continuity discovered in the infinitesimal calculus) now penetrated the Idea of the mathesis universalis, in which Idea the mathematical science-ideal finds its pregnant expression.

The factual contingent phenomena must in the prolonged

---

[1] *Opuscula*, p. 18.

[2] *Generales Inquisitiones de Analyse Notionum et Veritatum*, 1686, *Opusc.*, p. 374, quoted by CASSIRER II, 181.

analysis approach infinitesimally close to "eternal truths" of mathematical thought. Once again, as CASSIRER has brought to light, the central significance of LEIBNIZ' view of universal Ideas, as symbols of real relations, discloses itself in this context. Empirical reality cannot be at once grasped by mathematical thought. It can only be approached by it in continually more perfect symbols, in the process of a continuous methodical transition from the simplest to the more complicated phases of empirical reality: "It is not an accident," observes CASSIRER, "which urges us to replace the conceptual relations by relations of "symbols"; for in essence the concepts themselves are nothing but more or less perfect symbols by virtue of which we try to gain insight into the structure of the universe" [1].

This is in accordance with LEIBNIZ' conception, provided one does not interpret the symbolic function of Ideas in the extreme nominalistic sense [2]. In LEIBNIZ the Ideas have their foundation in a mathematical order of thought, which in its hypostatization as the thought of the intellectus archetypus is the sphere of the "vérités éternelles".

§ 4 - THE MODAL ASPECTS OF REALITY AS MODI OF MATHEMATICAL THOUGHT

LEIBNIZ' transcendental ground-Idea is not conceived of in an objective idealist sense as in the realist metaphysics of PLATO, ARISTOTLE and THOMAS AQUINAS. It bears the (no longer medieval) nominalistic stamp of subjective idealism that seeks its Archimedean point in the "cogito". Here we do not find a realism of ideas but an hypostatizing of individuals. The monads are not merely hypostases of the differential number and nothing more. As we have seen, they are thought of as animate, perceiving points of force, as subjective mirrors of the universe. Creative mathematical thought is deified in the "central monad". Consequently, when in his monadology, LEIBNIZ ascribes reality

---

[1] Op. cit., p. 187: „Es ist kein Zufall der uns dazu drängt die Verhältnisse der Begriffe durch Verhältnisse der „Zeichen" zu ersetzen; sind doch die Begriffe selbst ihrem Wesen nach nichts anderes als mehr oder minder volkommene Zeichen, kraft deren wir in die Struktur des Universums Einblick zu gewinnen suchen."

[2] Once again LEIBNIZ combated this extreme nominalistic conception in his early work *Dialogus de connexione inter res et verba, et veritatis realitate* (1677), ERDMANN, p. 76ff.

to the "essentiae" or "possibilitates" or "eternal truths" in the divine thought, even this is not to be understood in a realistic sense. For we must remember again and again, that in LEIBNIZ divine thought is nothing else but creative thought in the sense of the mathematical science-ideal. It is creative thought in which mathematical possibility and reality coincide[1]. Here the radical difference between the Leibnizian and the Platonic conception of eternal Ideas should be obvious to everyone. The creation-motive in the absolutized mathematical thought is entirely foreign to the realistic Platonic conception of the divine *nous* as the demiurge, who gives form to a matter after the pattern of the eternal Ideas[2]. The creation-motive in LEIBNIZ' conception is the Humanistic secularization of the Christian

---

[1] *Monadologie* 43 and 44 (ERDMANN, p. 708): "Il est vrai aussi qu'en Dieu est non seulement la source des existences mais encore celle des essences, en tant que réelles, ou de ce qu'il y a de réel dans la possibilité. C'est parce que l'entendement de Dieu est la Région des vérités éternelles, ou des idées dont elles dépendent, et que sans lui il n'y auroit rien de réel dans les possibilités, et non seulement rien d'existant, mais encore rien de possible.

Cependant il faut bien que s'il y a une réalité dans les Essences ou possibilités, ou bien dans les vérités éternelles, cette réalité soit fondée en quelque chose d'existant et d'actuel, et par conséquent dans l'existence de l'Être nécessaire, dans lequel l'essence renferme l'existence, ou dans lequel il suffit d'être possible pour être actuel." ["It is also true, that in God is not alone the source of the existences but, besides, that of the essences, in so far as they are real, or of that which is real in the possibility. This is due to the fact, that the understanding of God is the realm of the eternal truths or of the Ideas on which they depend, and that without this there would not be anything real in the possibilities, and not only nothing that exists but nothing that is possible either.

However, if there is a reality in the Essences or possibilities, or in other words in the eternal truths, this reality must necessarily be founded in something existent and actual, and consequently in the existence of the necessary Being in which the essence includes the existence, or in which it suffices to be possible for being actual."]

[2] It is true, that in his famous dialogue *Politeia* 509b PLATO seems to say that the *eidè* originate from the ἰδέα τοῦ ἀγαθοῦ (Idea of the good) and that in 597b the θεός (deity) as demiurge is said to be the origin of the εἶδος of a couch (κλίνη).

However, this is not to be understood in the sense of a divine creation of the κόσμος ὁρατός (the phenomenal world). Even in the *Politeia* the divine mind (νοῦς) is only conceived of as the origin of the eternal *forms*, never of "*matter*". Besides, in the later dialogues the conception of the divine *Nous* as the origin of the eternal forms (*eidè*) is abandoned. See my *Reformation and Scholasticism in Philosophy*, vol. I (the Greek prelude), p. 231 ff. and p. 361 (the conception of the *Timaeus*).

cosmonomic Idea of Humanistic immanence-philosophy 249

view with its confession of God's sovereignty as Creator. In LEIBNIZ' transcendental ground-Idea the totality of meaning is sought in free mathematical thought. This corresponds to the mathematical science-ideal, whose domain had been extended by the infinitesimal calculus. The different modal aspects of temporal reality are conceived of as modi of a mathematical order, and the lex continui maintains the coherence of meaning between these aspects.

It is extremely interesting to follow the application of this transcendental basic idea in LEIBNIZ' epistemology, aesthetics, ethics and theology.

Phenomenon and noumenon in LEIBNIZ' metaphysics: "vérités de raison" and "vérités de fait". LEIBNIZ' mathematical idealism.

The universe in the representation of the monads is sensory *phenomenon*, so far as this representation has not attained to the clarity of the mathematical concept which is orientated to the infinitesimal calculus [1].

In their pre-established mutual harmony as the metaphysical differentials of mathematical thought, the representing monads are the root of reality, the *noumenon* [2]. And, at the same time,

---

[1] LEIBNIZ' pronouncement concerning the phenomenon is characteristic: "Nihil aliud de rebus sensibilibus aut scire possumus, aut desiderare debemus, quam ut tam inter se, quam cum indubitatis rationibus consentiant...*Alia in illis veritas aut realitas frustra expetitur, quam quae hoc praestat*." (Phil. Schr. hrg. von GERHARDT, IV S. 356, quoted by CASSIRER *Erkenntnisproblem* I, 410 note 1). ["Concerning the perceptible things we neither can know, nor ought to desire anything except that they agree both among themselves and with indubitable grounds... it is vain to seek in them another truth or reality than that which this provides."]

[2] *Nouveaux Essais* Livre, IV (ERDMANN, p. 346): "Il faut considérer... que tout a m a s r é e l suppose des Substances simples ou des Unités réelles et quand on considère encore ce qui est de la nature de ces unités reélles, c'est à dire la p e r c e p t i o n et ses suites, on est transféré pour ainsi dire dans un autre monde, c'est à dire dans l e m o n d e i n t e l l i g i b l e d e s S u b s t a n c e s, au lieu qu'au paravant on n'a été que parmi les p h é n o m è n e s d e s s e n s." ["It is to be considered... that every real composite supposes simple substances or real units, and when in addition one considers, what belongs to the nature of these real units, namely the p e r c e p t i o n and its effects, one is, so to say, transferred into another world, that is to say into the intelligible world of the substances, whereas before one has only been among the sensory phenomena."]

insofar as they belong to the spiritual monads, they are the autarchical individuals of the ideal of personality.

This contrast between the noumenon and phenomenon (which is relativized by the lex continui) has a very close connection with LEIBNIZ' distinction between the "vérités de raison" and the "vérités de fait". The "vérités de raison" are eternal necessary truths. The "vérités de fait" are contingent truths determined by temporal and factual grounds and consequences. The former are of a purely noumenal nature; they owe their origin exclusively to pure thought. Hence they are analytical truths. They rest entirely and exclusively upon the logical basic law of non-contradiction as the norm of logical possibility. In a rationalistic line, mathematical judgments thereby become analytical. From this it appears, that LEIBNIZ was not conscious of the inter-modal synthesis of meaning in his supposed Archimedean point.

The factual contingent truths are of an empirical character. They do not permit themselves to be deduced from eternal truths by finite human thought. They can only be established by thought in confrontation with sensory experience. The judgments in which they are formulated are subject to the *principium rationis sufficientis,* to which LEIBNIZ ascribed a natural scientific causal meaning. In the deity, the central monad, this entire contrast between "vérités de raison" and "vérités de fait" completely disappears. For, the deity, as absolute creative thought (intellectus archetypus), is able to accomplish the infinite mathematical analysis of reality and this analysis makes evident the metaphysical or eternal necessity of the "verités de fait".

SPINOZA and LEIBNIZ. WOLFF's eradication of the distinction between necessary and contingent truths.

SPINOZA[1] had a geometrical conception of the root of the cosmos. From it he concluded, that as modi within the two attri-

---

[1] I shall not here pass judgment on the question as to whether or not SPINOZA actually belongs in the cadre of Humanistic philosophy. It is certain, that the documented investigation of S. VON DUNIS BORKOWSKY in his work *Spinoza* has cast new doubt upon the Cartesian-Humanistic interpretation of SPINOZA's system. The mystical-religious trait in his thought is doubtless not Cartesian. The mystical interpretation prevails in the Dutch neo-Spinozism of the XXth century, in opposition to the rationalist interpretation of the XIXth century Spinozist VAN VLOTEN.

butes (thought and extension) of the sole substance (the deity), all things must be understood as an eternal mathematical consequence, derived from the essence of the deity.

Because empirical investigation would not increase our knowledge of eternal and unchangeable geometrical truths, SPINOZA intended to exclude the empirical changes of things from his mathematic ideal of science.

On the basis of his monadology and epistemology, which bridged over empiricism and rationalism, LEIBNIZ rejected this consequence in conscious opposition to SPINOZA.

LEIBNIZ' popularizer, CHRISTIAN WOLFF, no longer understood the inventive, or "creative" character of Cartesian and Leibnizian mathematical logic. WOLFF again reduced the *principle of sufficient reason* to the logical *principium contradictionis* and thereby abolished the distinction between "necessary" and "contingent truths". In doing so, WOLFF meanwhile only drew a consequence which lay hidden in LEIBNIZ' Humanistic theology. According to LEIBNIZ, the "eternal" or "metaphysical truths" are vaguely present in the *"petites perceptions"* of material monads. And they are hidden in the human soul as "unconscious" representations which, in the apperceptions, become clear and distinct concepts. These latter are not, as LOCKE supposed, themselves derived from sensory experience. They are rather initially contained in experience as a logical apriori, of which we gradually become conscious.

In the human mind the "contingent truths", whose discovery rests upon sensory experience, in this way become a preliminary step to the eternal mathematical truths. Thus LEIBNIZ' transcendental basic Idea contains indeed a mathematicistic Idea of the Origin.

According to LEIBNIZ, the psychical sensory aspect of reality is only a phenomenal expression of the eternal mathematical relations of thought. No other reality than this can meaningfully be ascribed to it.

And the same thing is true of the remaining modal aspects of cosmic reality. Even the aesthetic aspect is brought under the basic denominator of mathematical thought: "Music charms us", writes LEIBNIZ in his *Principes de la Nature et de la Grâce"*, although its beauty consists in nothing but the proportions of numbers and in the calculation (of which we are unaware but which is, nevertheless, performed by the soul) of the vibrations of the sounding objects which meet one another at fixed intervals. The pleasures which the eye finds in the proportions, are of the same nature: and those which are caused by the other senses, will come to something like it, although we are not able to explain it so clearly" [1].

Even perfection, as the basic principle of the Leibnizian ethics, is logicized in the sense of the mathematical ideal of science. Perfection is the freedom which consists in the fact that the will obeys the reason. The goal of the moral endeavour of the spiritual monad is rational self-determination, in which man acts only according to clear and distinct concepts.

Man elevates himself above the animal by this rational freedom. The latter is obtained by the logical understanding of the adequate representations of the other monads, and by the insight into the harmonia praestabilita as the rational order, which places the individual in a universal coherence with all other individuals. The moral fruit of this enlightenment of consciousness would be the love (pietas) which includes the appreciation of the good of our fellow-men as our own well-being.

§ 5 - THE BASIC ANTINOMY IN THE HUMANISTIC TRANSCENDENTAL GROUND-IDEA IN ITS MATHEMATICAL-IDEALISTIC TYPE AND THE RELATION OF THIS TYPE TO THE OPTIMISTIC LIFE- AND WORLD-VIEW

The Theodicy with its apparent reconciliation of the ideals of science and personality. The optimism of LEIBNIZ.

This Humanistic metaphysics was crowned by a rationalistic theodicy, a justification of God's world-government by means of a reconciliation of the evil reality (with its mechanical laws and moral depravity) and the ethical ideal of modern man: the perfection and free self-determination of the individual.

Here LEIBNIZ concentrated the tremendous power of his intellect on the attempt to resolve the continually intensified anti-

---

[1] ERDMANN, p. 717/8: "La Musique nous charme, quoique sa beauté ne consiste que dans les convenances des nombres, et dans le compte, dont nous ne nous apercevons pas, et que l'âme ne laisse pas de faire, des battements ou vibrations des corps sonnans, qui se rencontrent par certains intervalles. Les plaisirs que la vue trouve dans les proportions, sont de la même nature; et ceux que causent les autres sens, reviendront à quelque chose de semblable, quoique nous ne puissons pas l'expliquer si distinctement."

nomy between the mathematical science-ideal and the ideal of personality. This is the very motive that lay hidden in his Theodicy. And this attempt is that which lay behind the formal scholastic reconciliation of the *"causae efficientes"* and *"causae finales"* in the divine worldplan. It lay behind the speculations concerning the relationship between metaphysical and logical possibility, empirical reality, and mathematical necessity. And the radical optimism expressed by it is typical of the faith of the entire "Enlightenment" in the final unity of these antagonistic factors in the Humanistic transcendental ground-Idea. It typifies the faith that finally scientific thought will make humanity free.

But it was not before the great progress of mathematical thought due to LEIBNIZ' discovery of the infinitesimal analysis, that this optimistic faith could find its "philosophical justification". In HOBBES it was still in an overt contradiction to his "pessimist scientific" view of human nature.

In LEIBNIZ' *Theodicy* the intrinsic antinomy between the ideal of science and that of personality is arrayed in the scholastic form of the contrast between nature and grace.

The reconciliation between these two spheres, their deeper identity, as LEIBNIZ called it, was sought in the creative mathematical thought of the deity. The latter utilized the metaphysical possibilities in its creation of the world in order to choose the reality which, in the light of the Humanistic ideal of personality, appears as the best and therefore as the ethically necessary. Not long after, KANT reduced the metaphysical Leibnizian categories of possibility, reality and necessity to transcendental categories of modality, which are strictly bound to the sensory experience of natural phenomena. This indicates, that the mathematical science-ideal had lost its primacy in KANT; it also marked the end of the rationalistic optimism of the philosophy of the "Enlightenment".

The deceptive formulation of the polar tension between the ideal of science and that of personality in the terminology of the Christian doctrine of faith.

By reading LEIBNIZ' *Essais sur la Bonté de Dieu, la liberté de l'Homme et l'Origine du Mal*, one at first gains the impression that the German thinker is actually concerned with the difficulties which arise in Christian dogmatics, when it sets forth the doctrine of God's sovereignty as Creator, His eternal predestination, and man's original sin, and at the same time maintains the personal responsibility and guilt of man.

In the first part of the *Essais*, LEIBNIZ divides these difficulties into two classes: The first originates from the freedom of man which seems to be incompatible with the omnipotent Divine nature; the second is concerned with the government of God: even if man should be free in his actions, an eternal predestination would seem to impute to the Divine Creator too large a share of the responsibility for the existence of both physical and moral evil.

Extremely deceptive in this whole formulation of the problem is the fact that in the light of LEIBNIZ' Idea of God the problem acquires a sense which is absolutely different from that which it possesses in Christian doctrine.

One need only remember that this idea of God is in essence only the final hypostasis of creative mathematical thought: the existing cosmos is only the realized choice out of an infinite possibility of worlds and such a choice demands a rational cause: "The cause of the world must have had regard or relation to all these possible worlds in order to determine one of them. And this regard or relation of an existent substance to simple possibilities cannot be anything else but the u n d e r s t a n d-
i n g which has the Ideas of them; and determining one of them cannot be anything else but the act of the w i l l which chooses. And it is t h e p o w e r of this substance which renders the will efficient"[1].

In other words the divine substance is the creative mathematical thought that itself is only bound to the "vérités éternelles". Will and power belong to the essence of this thought as the creative origin of the cosmos.

This final hypostasis of the mathematical ideal of science now clashed with the postulate of the ideal of personality. It clashed with the autarchical self-sufficiency and absolute freedom of the finite spiritual monads and with the postulate of

---

[1] ERDMANN, p. 506: "Il faut que la cause du Monde ait eu égard ou relation à tous ces Mondes possibles; pour en déterminer un. Et cet égard ou rapport d'une substance existante à de simples possibilités, ne peut être autre chose que l' e n t e n d e m e n t qui en a les idées; et en déterminer une, ne peut être autre chose que l'acte de la v o l o n t é qui choisit. Et c'est la p u i s s a n c e de cette substance, qui en rend la volonté efficace."

the happiness and perfection of man, who by means of pure thought ought to participate in this good.

The apparent solution of this antinomy is construed by mathematical thought itself in the speculations concerning the metaphysical relation of possibility, reality, and necessity, and in the synthesis between "nature" and "grace".

In order to understand the course of LEIBNIZ' argument as it is related to the transcendental basic Idea of his mathematical idealism, it is necessary to return for a moment to his discovery of the differential and integral calculus. This discovery, according to LEIBNIZ' own testimony, is connected with the most basic foundations of his entire philosophy.

> The basic antinomy in the Humanistic transcendental ground-Idea acquires in LEIBNIZ the mathematical form of the antinomy of actual infinity.

The basic antinomy in the Humanistic cosmonomic Idea in LEIBNIZ' metaphysics was formulated, as it were, as a mathematical problem. It was formulated as the reduction of the discreteness of the monads (into which the individualistic ideal of personality had withdrawn itself) to the continuity of the mathematically comprehended science-ideal and vice versa.

The mathematical antinomy of actual infinity is hidden in the metaphysical concept of the monad.

The differential number is actually only an approximative one. It derives all its definiteness exclusively from the principle of progression. But as the infinitesimal it can never possess an actual existence. LEIBNIZ himself has constantly pointed out the merely methodological origin of his concept of the infinitesimal [1].

Viewed mathematically, the infinitesimal in LEIBNIZ is not a smallest part of spatial matter. This was imagined in the atomism of GASSENDI, but this conception, formerly adhered to by LEIBNIZ himself, was intrinsically contradictory [2]. The infinitesimal must be viewed as an ideal $\dot{v}\pi \delta \vartheta \varepsilon \sigma \iota \varsigma$ for the mathematical process of

---

[1] CASSIRER II, 155 ff.

[2] "Mais les a t o m e s d e m a t i è r e sont contraire à la raison: outre qu'ils sont encore composés de parties; puisque l'attachement invincible d'une partie à l'autre, (quand on le pourrait concevoir ou supposer avec raison) ne détruiroit point leur diversité," *Système Nouvelle* 11 (ERDM., p. 126). ["But the atoms of matter are contrary to reason — not considering that they are still composed of parts — because the invincible attachment of one part to the other (if one could conceive or suppose it reasonably) would not destroy their diversity."]

thought in which reality is created as a logically continuous coherence — which is its *noumenal essence.*

In the face of empirical reality, the differential is a mathematical fiction. It does not possess any factual individual existence. In a letter to JOHANN BERNOULLI, LEIBNIZ characteristically expressed it as follows: "the differential is not present in the parts of matter. Its place is in the ideal grounds through which things are regulated as through their laws."

Nevertheless, LEIBNIZ' metaphysics elevated the differential to actual reality in the concept of the monad. His metaphysics needed this hypostasis in order to reconcile the science-ideal with the still individualistically conceived ideal of personality.[1].

Now the logicist principle of continuity must in the final analysis come into conflict with the discreteness of the monads. This is the intrinsic antinomy in LEIBNIZ' mathematical idealism, in which he wished to overcome naturalism, as well as dualism.

This antinomy acquired a Humanistic religious meaning. In his Theodicy the actual infinity of the cosmic monads (as differentials) must be finite in contrast to that of the divine monad (the infinite analysis of the divine creative mathematical thought). And their imperfection and the metaphysical evil of the world lies in this finitude. The cosmos is only possible in a metaphysical-logical sense, if it consists of such finite and therefore imperfect beings.

"Metaphysical evil" as an eternal necessary truth in creative mathematical thought.

The monads *must be* finite substances which are autarchical

---

[1] Compare *Réflexions sur l'essai de Locke* (ERDM. p. 138): "...ainsi le véritable i n f i n i ne se trouve point dans un tout composé de parties. Cependant il ne laisse pas de se trouver ailleurs, savoir dans l' a b s o l u, qui est sans parties, et qui a influence sur les choses composées, parce qu'elles résultent de la limitation de l'absolu.

Donc l' i n f i n i p o s i t i f n'étant autre chose que l'absolu, on peut dire qu'il y a en ce sens une idée positive de l'infini, et qu'elle est antérieure a celle du fini." ["...consequently the veritable i n f i n i t e is not to be found in a totality composed of parts. However, it is found elsewhere, namely in the a b s o l u t e, which is without parts and has influence over the composed things, because they result from the limitation of the absolute.

Consequently, because the p o s i t i v e i n f i n i t e is nothing but the absolute, one can say that in this sense there is a positive Idea of the infinite, and that this Idea precedes that of the finite."]

with respect to each other. They *must be* confined within their
own borders. For if this were not the case, everything in the
cosmos would flow together into a formless whole. This can only
be prevented by the finite discreteness of the monads. The spiritual soul-monads participate in mathematical thought and as
such, together with the deity, they constitute a part of the civitas Dei. With respect to them LEIBNIZ observes, that if they were
not limited, at least in as much as they encounter a definite
limit for the mathematical analysis in sensory perceptions, everyone of them would itself be the unlimited deity [1]. On account
of its participation in mathematical reason, however, the finite
spiritual monad is only "une petite divinité dans son département" [2] (a little deity in its department).

Metaphysical evil in the cosmos — i.e. the discrete limitation
and finiteness of the created monads — is *necessary*, if a cosmos
is to be *possible*. In this way "the metaphysical origin of evil"
is derived from creative mathematical analysis itself: the origin
of evil lies in the eternal truths of mathematical thought [3].

It is extremely interesting to notice the ground on which
LEIBNIZ rejects the conception of ancient philosophy which
sought the origin of evil in "matter". The ground for this rejection is that the ancients viewed matter as uncreated and independent of God [4].

This conception is in conflict with the creation-motive in
LEIBNIZ' mathematical ideal of science, which here clearly discloses its secularization of the Biblical creation-motive. The
cause of evil must also in a metaphysical sense be derived from

---

[1] *Théodicée*, Partie I, 64 (ERDM. 520): "l'âme serait une Divinité, si elle n'avoit que des perceptions distinctes."

[2] *Monadologie* 83 (ERDM. 712).

[3] *Théodicée*, Partie I, 20 (ERDM. 510).

[4] *Théodicée*, Partie I, 20 (ERDM. 510): "Les Anciens attribuoient la cause du mal à la matière, qu'ils croyoient incréée et indépendante de Dieu; mais nous qui dérivons tout Être de Dieu, où trouverons-nous la source du mal? La réponse est, qu'elle doit etre cherchée dans la Nature idéale de la créature, autant que cette Nature est renfermée dans les vérités éternelles qui sont dans l'entendement de Dieu, indépendant de sa volonté."
["The ancients ascribed the cause of evil to matter which they thought to be uncreated and independent of God; but we, who deduce every being from God, where shall we find the source of evil? The answer is, that it is to be sought in the ideal nature of the creature, in so far as this nature is included in the eternal truths which are in the understanding of God, independent of His will."]

God, als absolute thought, bound to the *"vérités éternelles"*. Even sensory matter is rationalized by the analysis of the infinite completed in the divine mind.

The human spiritual monad is limited in its thought, it is not omniscient, and therefore it can err in thinking and fall into moral faults.

Metaphysical evil as the root of physical and moral evil (sin!).

LEIBNIZ distinguishes evil in a physical and moral sense from metaphysical evil. Physical evil consists in suffering and moral evil is "sin".

Physical and moral evil are not necessary, as is metaphysical evil. But, because of the eternal truths, they are *possible*. And this is sufficient to explain their origin. They are a possible consequence of the necessary metaphysical imperfection. And the latter is itself nothing positive; it is a privatio, a mere lack of perfection.

The metaphysical cause of evil is not a *causa efficiens*, but a *causa deficiens*, according to LEIBNIZ' scholastic formula. And the activity of God is directed solely toward the positive, toward perfection and the good.

It is true that physical and moral evil are not *necessary* in themselves. But they are a negative *condicio sine qua non* for the realization of the good. This good manifests itself physically as pleasure, and ethically as the freedom of personality. And because of this freedom the latter is a member of the "Kingdom of Grace", the *"société de la raison"*. A cosmos without physical suffering and sin would have been possible, but then it would be very inferior to the one existing now. Such a cosmos would not leave any room for the free rational personality of man, nor for an organic union of soul- and material monads, i.e. a union of body and soul under the direction of the latter as central monad. And this would be a deficiency, because in this case the continuity in the species of substances would not be actualized, and a breach of the principle of continuity would imply a "vacuum formarum" [1].

---

[1] *Théodicée* I, 13 and 14 (ERDM. 507).

How LEIBNIZ attempted to resolve metaphysical evil into the continuity of infinite mathematical analysis.

Ergo, the moral freedom of personality is required by the principle of continuity of the mathematical science-ideal. And the same principle of continuity requires relative physical and moral evil, because the relative imperfection, as implied in the gradual diversity of clarity in the representations of the monads, is a pre-requisite for the ever greater perfection in the mathematical order of development of the cosmos.

Physical and moral evil possess empirical but not metaphysical reality: they belong to the obscure, sensory confused representations.

The analysis of the universe is accomplished *uno intuito* in the creative mathematical thought of the deity. Therefore, in the actual infinity of this analysis, the individual evil of the monads disappears in the relative perfection of the total cosmos, as the latter is conceived of in the spaceless continuity of creative mathematical thought. The kingdom of nature, the "phenomenon", is identical in its root with the kingdom of grace, the intelligible world of the clear and distinct concept. The "*causae efficientes*" are brought into perfect correspondence with the "*causae finales*" by the "*harmonia praestabilita*". They are brought into complete harmony with *the appetitions* in the continuous transition of the representations of each monad. And these appetitions originate in the metaphysical nature of the monads and have as a goal the realization of good and evil.

In this way LEIBNIZ attempts to solve theologically the basic antinomy in his transcendental ground-Idea between the ideal of science and that of personality.

But in spite of its ingenious design, this attempt was bound to fail. In his *Theodicy* LEIBNIZ entangled himself in constant contradictions. On the one hand, he made individual metaphysical evil to be something logically negative, i.e. a mere lack of pure analysis, and, on the other, he elevated it as the condicio sine qua non for the metaphysical reality of perfection, i.e. the good of the cosmos.

Thus the finite discreteness of the monads, as the metaphysical differentials of the cosmos, becomes both an actual metaphysical reality and a logical negative.

Even in its metaphysical form the concept of actual infinity continues to be intrinsically *antinomic*. The continuity of the movement of thought must necessarily break through the discreteness of the monads and, vice versa, the discreteness of the monads must necessarily contradict the lex continui.

LEIBNIZ and BAYLE.

The basic problem in LEIBNIZ' theodicy is, as we saw, that of the reconcilitation between the Humanistic ideal of science and that of personality. This is still more evident, when we remember that the voluminous and popular theological work of LEIBNIZ was pointed directly against PETER BAYLE. By means of his sceptical arguments against the Cartesian cogito and the mathematical axioms, the latter had undermined the very founations of the mathematical science-ideal.

BAYLE's nominalist doctrine of the two sorts of truth[1] set forth an absolute cleft between Christian faith and natural reason. This view did not interest LEIBNIZ, because of his concern with the absoluteness of the Christian religion. In fact, he always conceived of the Christian "dogmas of faith" as contingent truths, bound to the sensory representation. Mathematical thought must transform them into the eternal mathematical-metaphysical truths of the religion of reason! It was indeed a quite different aspect of BAYLE's scepticism that disturbed LEIBNIZ.

In his sceptical attitude toward the Cartesian ideal of science BAYLE indeed granted primacy to the ideal of personality in natural reason, the so-called "practical reason". He had tried to show that moral commandments do not derive their intrinsic value from the Christian religion but from "practical human reason". Thereby "practical reason" had been completely emancipated from the Humanistic science-ideal.

BAYLE considered the Christian religion to be independent of, or rather in open conflict with human reason. He had sharply opposed the Idea of a "Vernunftreligion". His intention had been to retain a place for Christian religion in the "heart". This could only appear to LEIBNIZ as blasphemy against sovereign reason[2]. He wrote his *Theodicy* in order to bring the ideal of personality

---

[1] One can say that, with respect to the intensification of the antithesis between the Christian faith and the Humanistic science-ideal, BAYLE filled a similar rôle as had been played in the disruption of the Christian faith and Aristotelian metaphysics by WILLIAM OF OCCAM, and even more strongly by the Averroist SIGER OF BRABANT. BAYLE laid bare this antithesis in its sharpest form; he accepted a positive conflict between the Christian faith and Humanistic thought.

[2] This LEIBNIZ continually evidences in his polemics with BAYLE.

again under the domination of the mathematical science-ideal. He wished to reduce the Christian religion again to a lower function of the "religion of reason".

But the extremely refined antinomies which lay hidden in LEIBNIZ' haughty metaphysics, and which can be traced back to the basic antinomy in the transcendental ground-Idea of Humanistic thought, were soon to be subjected to the scrutiny of KANT's *Critique of Pure Reason* in order to break the primacy of the ideal of science at its very root.

Compare, *Theodicy* III, 353 (ERDM. 606) where he attacks BAYLE as follows: ;"Il s'accommodoit de ce qui lui convenoit pour contrecarrer l'adversaire qu'il avoit en tête; son but n'étant que d'embarrasser les Philosophes, et faire voir la foiblesse de notre Raison: et je crois que jamais Arcésilas ni Carnéade n'ont soutenu le pour et le contre avec plus d'éloquence et plus d'esprit." ["He availed himself of what suited him to cross the adversary which he had in view; for his goal was only to confuse the philosophers, and to show the weakness of our reason: and I believe neither Arcesilaus nor Carneades ever have defended the pro and con with more eloquence and more genius."]

And especially the introductory *Discours de la conformité de la foi avec la Raison*, 71—82. See no 81: "Mr BAYLE poursuit: "qu'il faut alors se moquer de ces objections, en reconnoissant les bornes étroites de l'esprit humain." Et moi, je crois que bien loin de-là, il y faut reconnoître des marques de la force de l'esprit humain, qui le fait pénétrer dans l'intérieur des choses." ["Mr BAYLE continues: "that one ought to mock at these objections, when one acknowledges the narrow boundaries of the human mind." And I believe, on the contrary, that one ought to acknowledge in these objections marks of the power of the human mind which makes it penetrate into the very interior of things."]

CHAPTER III

THE IDEAL OF PERSONALITY AND THE IDEAL OF SCIENCE IN THE CRITICAL TRANSITION TO THE PRIMACY OF THE IDEAL OF PERSONALITY

§ 1 - THE PSYCHOLOGICAL TURN IN THE SCIENCE-IDEAL AND ITS TRANSCENDENTAL IDEA OF ORIGIN

Rationalist mathematical dualism, rationalist mechanical naturalism and rationalist mathematical idealism prove to be the chief types in which the transcendental ground-Idea of Humanist thought was specified during the first phase of its development since the rise of the new science-ideal. The latter had built a new metaphysics and it was in the cadre of this metaphysics that the dialectical tension between the nature — and the freedom-motives displayed itself.

As long as the primacy of the mathematical science-ideal was maintained, it made no sense to oppose rationalism to empiricism. HOBBES was doubtless an empiricist in the epistemological sense. Nevertheless, his empiricism was of an extremely rationalist stamp, since it conceived of the process of knowledge itself in terms of the mechanical laws of movement.

The psychological turn in the ideal of science in empiricism since LOCKE.

Since LOCKE, however, empiricism brought a psychological turn into the science-ideal. The latter retained its primacy, nevertheless, the turn toward psychologism was highly significant. The science-ideal began to liberate itself, in an epistemological sense from metaphysics. It no longer sought its common denominator(s) for the different aspects of reality in one or two metaphysical concepts of substance. It now sought it within the functional apparatus of human knowledge itself, and at least its

The development of the basic antinomy etc. 263

inner tendency was to seek it in the psychical function of feeling and sensation alone.

The "substance", the "Ding an sich", became the epistemological X, the unknown and unknowable background of the "empirical world" which is given only in psychical impressions and perceptions.

According to the subject-object-relation in the psychical aspect of human experience, there is to be distinguished an outer world, given only in objective sensations, and an inner world of the subjective operations of the mind which are to be *psychically perceived* in the so-called "reflection" or "internal sense" only [1]. According to LOCKE experience is exhausted by these two "sources".

The understanding or the logical function borrows all "Ideas" from them. Just as the "external material things" are the objects of psychical sensation, the operations of the mind (including passions and feelings) are the object of inner perception or reflection [2]. For the rest, LOCKE's division of the whole of human experience into "sensation" and "reflection", or *as it was later to be called,* the distinction between outward and inner experience („aüszeren" and „inneren Sinn" in KANT), is' the perfect counterpart of DESCARTES' dualistic separation of "extensio" and "cogitatio". Although LOCKE denies the possibility of theoretical metaphysics, his psychological dualism between "sensation" and "reflection" remains grounded in the conviction that behind these two realms of experience, a material substance and a spiritual one must be present. And the latter are the causes of the external sensible and the internal spiritual impressions of experience. In DESCARTES these substances are supposed to possess the sharpest possible independence in respect to each other, although he was not able to maintain this dualism in an integral way. LOCKE agrees, except that he no longer considers the substances to be knowable. And if the material sub-

---

[1] In his *Essay concerning human understanding,* vol. I, Bk 2 ch. I § 4 LOCKE observes as to the latter: "This source of Ideas every man has wholly in himself; and though it be not sense, as having nothing to do with external objects, yet it is very like it, and might properly enough be called internal sense. But as I call the other sensation, so I call this r e f l e c t i o n, the ideas it affords being such only as the mind gets by reflecting on its own operations within itself."

[2] Ibid. in fine.

stance can be only an unknown X to human knowledge, then, in the nature of the case, the monistic materialist metaphysics of HOBBES must also lose its foundation.

Nevertheless, LOCKE, too, did not maintain his dualistic position in an integral sense. Although he attempted to oppose sensation and reflection as two entirely independent sources of experience, he did not ascribe to both of them an equal originality. According to him, the inner perception of the operations of the mind is not possible unless the mind by sensations of the outer world has first been stimulated to a series of operations which are the first content of its reflection.

This is the very reason why in the new empiricist school of LOCKE the same polar tensions were present as in the metaphysical rationalism of the Cartesian one.

Both HOBBES and LEIBNIZ had sought to free themselves of the Cartesian dualism. In like manner empiricist-nominalist trends arose which sought to remove the psychological dualism. The new psychologism turned in the mechanistic association-psychology (already stimulated by HOBBES) of a HARTLEY, BROWN, PRIESTLY, DARWIN et al., to the *naturalist* and *materialist* pole. It turned to the *idealist* pole in the spiritualism of BERKELEY. The latter, however, does not belong to the closer community of Humanistic thought, because of his scholastic accommodation of the new psychologism to authentic Christian motives. MALEBRANCHE had done the same with Cartesianism.

The inner antinomy in LOCKE's psychological dualism.

LOCKE's psychological dualism involved itself in yet sharper antinomies than did the metaphysical dualism of DESCARTES.

Indeed, although he acknowledges innate faculties of the soul, LOCKE contests from the empiricist standpoint the "innate Ideas". The point at which he differed in principle from DESCARTES in this matter consisted in his view that the understanding owes *all its content to the simple or elementary psychical representations* ("Ideas") given in sensation and reflection. Thought can obtain no knowledge beyond the reach of these representations. LOCKE even refuses to conceive of mathematical thought as purely logical, as DESCARTES and LEIBNIZ had done.

The *simple* sensible and "spiritual" impressions of psychical experience which the mind must receive purely passively, are sharply distinguished by LOCKE from the complex representations ("Ideas"). In the latter, thought is actively and freely operative, but still remains constantly bound to the material of the "simple Ideas".

The "simple Ideas" owe their origin to sensation and reflection and they not only include pleasure, pain, joy, and grief, but also the representations of force, causality, unity and reality.

The "complex ideas", in which LOCKE includes also the "universalia", i.e. the universal generic concepts acquired by abstraction, are freely formed by the understanding out of the combination of "simple" ones. Among these complex Ideas, the number of which is infinite, LOCKE investigates in particular the concepts of number, space, infinity, the concept of identity (chiefly that of personal identity), that of power (especially in connection with the problem of the freedom of the will) and that of substance.

Thus psychological analysis dissolves the entire content of knowledge into simple psychical impressions. Consequently, even the mathematical science-ideal with its Idea of free creative mathematical thought must be given up, if the analysis is to be carried through consistently. But this consequence was entirely contrary to LOCKE's intention. He continued with DESCARTES to view mathematical thought, with its strict deductive coherence, as the mainstay of the ideal of science. The total *psychologizing* of scientific thought was first carried through by BERKELEY and HUME. And so LOCKE's psychological dualism necessarily involved itself in the following antinomy: on the one hand it must reduce the concepts of mathematical thought, with respect to their proper mathematical meaning, to passive psychical impressions of experience; and at the same time, it continues to ascribe a free creative power to reflection in its active character of scientific thought. This antinomy originated from the attempt to furnish a psychological foundation for the mathematical science-ideal.

From LOCKE's travel-diary it appears that he originally gave up the mathematical ideal of science in the interest of absolutized psychological analysis[1]. In his *Essay*, however, this radical psychological standpoint is abandoned and he tried on the one hand to bind mathematical thought to the psychical representations, and on the other hand to maintain the concepts of mathematical thought as the very foundation of the reality of experience. The psychological point of view predominates in the first

---

[1] See CASSIRER *op. cit.* II, p. 243 ff.

two books; in the fourth book, however, the mathematical science-ideal predominates. Almost imperceptibly LOCKE's psychological dualism is transformed into a radical dualism between psychical experience and creative thought. This dualism, however, was threatened at the root by LOCKE's absolutized psychological startingpoint.

And this also explains why in the further development of the psychologizing trend of thought the attack was launched in the first place against the dualistic separation between "sensation" and "reflection".

In his psychological analysis the world of experience is dissolved by LOCKE into atomistic psychical elements, which as such exhibit no orderly inner coherence, but nevertheless are irresistably related by the consciousness to a common, though unknown, bearer (substance).

Reflexion may possess the capacity to join these given elements in an arbitrary manner, as the 24 letters of the alphabet [1]; but such freedom to unite remains arbitrary. And an orderly coherence between the simple Ideas of experience cannot be based on arbitrariness. Unlike HUME, LOCKE had not yet attempted to reinterpret this orderly coherence in a psychological manner. His concept of order was still that of the mathematical science-ideal.

Thus psychological analysis necessarily led to the conclusion that no scientific knowledge of empirical reality is possible.

And at the same time it led to the conclusion that the necessary orderly coherence in the joining of concepts, without which science is not possible, cannot find its origin in the psychical impressions of experience.

LOCKE asserted that exact science would be impossible, if there were no necessary relations between the Ideas. According to him, these relations are elevated above the temporal process of the psychical impressions of experience and possess an eternal constancy. Otherwise one could never pass universally valid propositions. A man would ever remain bound to the psychical perception of the individual impressions of experience [2].

---

[1] *Essay concerning human understanding* II, 7 § 10. The Idea of an alphabet of logical thought has here acquired a psychological rather than a mathematical sense.

[2] *Essay* IV, 1 § 9: "If the perception that the same Ideas will eternally have the same habitudes and the same relations be not a sufficient ground

We saw, however, that LOCKE did not in the least intend to approve of the drawing of this sceptical conclusion from his psychological resolution of all the content of knowledge into isolated psychical "elements". On the contrary, he remains true to the mathematical science-ideal, and affirms his belief in the super-temporal necessary coherence of the concepts of thought. True science, according to him, is possible wherever we deal only with the necessary connection of concepts, rather than with the "empirical reality of things". Such is the case in mathematics and in ethics.

LOCKE maintains the mathematical science-ideal with its creation-motive, though in a limited sphere.

Here it is the understanding itself that creates its objects, i.e. the necessary relations between the Ideas. The mind forms the archetypes, the original patterns to which the things in the experience of reality must conform. A triangle possesses in an empirical form the same sum of its angles as does the universal triangle in the mathematical concept. Moreover, according to LOCKE, what is valid for the mathematical complex Idea is just as valid for "moral Ideas". These Ideas too are absolutely independent of empirical reality, independent of the question whether or not human actions are really directed by them. "The truth of CICERO's doctrine of duties does not suffer any injury by the fact that no one in the world exactly follows its precepts or lives according to it in its portrayed example of a virtuous man."

Therefore, according to LOCKE, exact proofs are as possible in ethics as in mathematics.

The thesis: "where there is no property, there is no injustice either," is no less accurate than any thesis in EUCLID. Mathematical science and ethics furnish us with apriori knowledge, infallible, true and certain.

Thus it is clear that in spite of the epistemological-psychologi-

---

of knowledge, there could be no knowledge of general propositions in mathematics; for no mathematical demonstration would be any other than particular: and when a man had demonstrated any proposition concerning one triangle or circle, *his knowledge would not reach beyond that particular diagram.* If he would extend it farther, he must renew his demonstration in another instance, before he could know it to be true in another like triangle and so on: by which means one could never come to the knowledge of any general propositions."

cal turn of his investigation, LOCKE retains completely the fundamentals of the mathematical science-ideal. In his transcendental ground-Idea the latter still possesses the primacy over the ideal of personality.

With a tenacious faith, equal to that of DESCARTES and LEIBNIZ, LOCKE clung to the Idea that human personality can only maintain its freedom of action by being obedient to sovereign mathematical thought.

However, because of the psychological turn which the Cartesian cogito had acquired in LOCKE's epistemological research, there arose an insoluble inner antinomy in the foundation of the mathematical ideal of science.

This antinomy is produced by the fact that the "sovereign reason", in which the Humanistic ideal of personality had concentrated itself, refused to accept the dogmatic theory concerning the "Ideae innatae" in their Cartesian sense [1].

The tendency toward the origin in LOCKE's opposition to the innate Ideas, and the transcendental Idea of origin in LOCKE's epistemology.

For LOCKE's opposition to innate Ideas can only be explained in terms of the internal tendencies of the psychological ideal of science. The latter will not permit any restriction upon its sovereign freedom. LOCKE, like HOBBES, could only view the innate Ideas as an arbitrary restriction placed upon the sovereignty of thought. DESCARTES, as we have seen, viewed these Ideas only as *potentially* innate. In fact, for him they served to check the postulate of the continuity of the science-ideal so that, in due time, the autonomy of creative mathematical thought might be saved. So little did DESCARTES account for the possibility of

---

[1] RIEHL, *Der Phil. Kritizismus*, supposes that no antinomy may here be indicated in LOCKE's system. This statement contains several errors. In the first place, in the Prolegomena we have pointed out the untenability of an opposition between the genetic and critical view-point. Nevertheless, in RIEHL's argument this distinction plays its confusing rôle. He does not see that the question about the origin of our logical concepts is a transcendental-critical one, because it cannot be solved without a transcendental Idea of the origin and the mutual relation of the different modal aspects of reality. In the second place, RIEHL forgets that LOCKE in the first two books of his essay had considered unity, force and causality as simply Ideas, and that he proceeds upon the assumption that all complex Ideas possess the simple Ideas as their elements. LOCKE did not yet know KANT's doctrine of the apriori forms of intuition and understanding.

mathematical thought, that he permitted it to become a static "res cogitans". LOCKE was the first Humanist thinker to grant to psychology the central task of explaining the origin and limits of human knowledge and of critically examining the validity of its foundations. Therefore, he could only view the dogmatic acceptance of innate ideas as an attack upon the very sovereignty of thought.

If the psychological origin [1], the psychological ἀρχή, of mathematical thought with its creative concepts is not shown, then, according to LOCKE, the ideal of science does not proceed from the sovereign self-consciousness, but from a dogmatical faith in authority. And it is just this latter that the "Aufklärung" intended to combat with all the means at its disposal: "The way to improve our knowledge is not, I am sure, blindly and with an implicit faith, to receive and swallow principles; but is, I think, to get and fix in our minds clear, distinct and complete Ideas, as far they are to be had, and annex them to their proper and constant names." So LOCKE writes in the fourth book of his *Essay concerning human understanding* (Ch. 12, sect. 6).

The antinomy in LOCKE's thought which we must establish between the psychologized Idea of origin and the mathematical ideal of science, was disguised by his limiting scientific knowledge to the sphere of the non-real.

> The distinction between the knowledge of facts and the knowledge of the necessary relations between concepts.

For this purpose LOCKE introduced a fundamental distinction between the knowledge of *empirical facts* and the scientific knowledge of the *necessary relations between concepts*.

A distinction which had previously been made by HOBBES and

---

[1] LOCKE himself qualified his *Essay concerning human understanding*, as an enquiry "into the original, certainty and extent of human knowledge, together with the grounds and degrees of belief, opinion, and assent." (I, 1 § 2). And in book II, 1 § 24, he writes, *after having established* sensation and reflection, sensory perception and internal introspection as the only sources of our knowledge: "All those sublime thoughts which tower above the clouds, and reach as high as heaven itself, take their rise and footing here: in all that good extent, wherein the mind wanders, in those remote speculations, it may seem to be elevated with, it stirs not one jot beyond those Ideas which sense or reflection have offered for its contemplation."

would later be taken over by Hume. We shall see that it no longer could have any critical value for the latter.

In opposition to Descartes, however, Locke maintained the view that mathematical and moral judgments are synthetical and not merely logical. From the standpoint of his psychologism no possibility existed to ground synthetic judgments otherwise than on the single psychical impressions of experience.

This is exactly what Hume later did in a very consistent manner. Now Locke, in the fourth book of his *Essay*, introduced, in addition to "sensation" and "reflection", a new faculty of cognition, namely the *intuition* of the "cogito". This faculty was proclaimed to be the indubitable foundation of all exact scientific knowledge and was thought of as the basis of mathematical proof ("demonstratio"). But by introducting this faculty he really turned away from the paths of his psychologizing epistemology.

Descartes had also founded the certainty of mathematical knowledge on the intuitive certainty of the thinking self-consciousness. But he considered that mathematical knowledge originated in creative logical thought alone, apart from any assistance from sensory perception.

It was precisely against this purely analytical conception of scientific thought that Locke directed his thesis that, if thought is to lead us to knowledge, it must always remain joined to the material of psychical sensations.

Locke recognized that the continuity and infinity of space and time go beyond the perception of particular empirical sensations. Nevertheless, his analyses, in the second book of his *Essay*, of the complex Ideas of number, space, time, and infinity are invariably joined to the simple impressions of experience.

Thus the ultimate termination of Locke's psychological analysis of knowledge in the face of mathematical thought signifies a capitulation of his critique which is replaced here by the dogmatic proclamation of the primacy of the mathematical science-ideal.

The psychological epistemology had only caused a rupture in this latter, because Locke no longer deemed it possible to grant to mathematical thought domination over empirical reality. Physics and biology are, according to him, entirely dependent upon sense perception and cannot be subject to any mathematical method of demonstration: "Certainty and demonstration are things we must not in these matters pretend to"[1].

Nevertheless, we can observe in the epistemological turn of LOCKE's philosophy the germ of a critical self-reflection regarding the root of the science-ideal. This self-reflection was soon to cause a radical reaction against the rationalism of the "Enlightenment". It was to lead to the granting of primacy to the ideal of personality. For LOCKE irrevocably rejected the Cartesian deduction of "Sum res cogitans" from "Cogito ergo sum". In other words to mathematical thought was denied the competency to identify itself with the "sovereign personality", as the root of the science-ideal.

Similarly LOCKE refused to resolve the will into a mode of mathematical thought.

Thus the science-ideal was critically emancipated from the domination of a metaphysics, in which, in the last analysis, mathematical thought had been exalted as the origin and root of the cosmos. This emancipation was to have a radical significance for the further development of Humanistic philosophical thought.

The emancipation of the mathematical ideal of science from the rationalistic metaphysics of nature opened the way to the insight that the root of reality is not to be discovered by scientific thought. And it now became possible to see that the science-ideal must have its fundamentals in the ideal of personality.

The consciousness of the absolute *autonomy* and *freedom* of personality was not clearly expressed in Humanistic philosophy, as long as the root of reality was sought in a material substance. Nor was it clearly expressed as long as a material substance was opposed to a "res cogitans".

§ 2 - THE MONISTIC PSYCHOLOGICAL TYPE OF THE HUMANISTIC TRANSCENDENTAL GROUND-IDEA UNDER THE PRIMACY OF THE SCIENCE-IDEAL

However, before the transcendental Humanist ground-Idea could acquire this final turn and before Humanistic thought could really follow the transcendental direction which is pecu-

---

[1] *Essay* iv, 3 § 26, As is known, LOCKE retracted this statement with respect to physics after he learned from NEWTON the method of scientific physics. See RIEHL, *Der phil. Kritizismus* (3e Aufl. I, p. 89).

liar to KANT's *"Critiques"*, it had to endure a serious crisis in which it would appear, that a radical psychologism in epistemology must undermine the foundations both of the ideal of science and of the ideal of personality.

The credit for having performed this preparatory critical work must unquestionably be given to HUME. This keen thinker had inwardly outgrown the spirit of the "Enlightenment". Nevertheless he continued to accept the primacy of the science-ideal in its psychological turn. LOCKE had previously undermined the metaphysical conceptions of nature and human personality. By means of his psychological critique of knowledge, HUME reduced them to absurdity.

The fact that HUME in his psychologism proceeded from the standpoint of the Humanistic science-ideal is evident from the announcement of the aim of his research in the second book of his main work, *Treatise upon Human Nature*. Here he states, that he desired to achieve the same result in the field of the phenomena of human nature as had been attained in astronomy since COPERNICUS. He desired to reduce all phenomena to the smallest possible number of simple principles [1]. The principle of the economy of thought took a central position in this ideal of science. This same principle had been praised by LEIBNIZ, in his essay on the philosophical style of NIZOLIUS, as one of the treasure troves of Nominalism [2].

> The psychologized conception of the science-ideal in HUME. Once again the nominalistic trait in the ideal of science.

The science-ideal, however, now received a radical objective-psychological turn. All abstract concepts, which are expressed in general symbols of language must in the last analysis be reduced to individual sensory "impressions" as the simplest elements of consciousness. There may not remain a rest in our supposed "knowledge" which is not resolved into these simple psychological elements. If it does, the psychological ideal of science is still subjected to a dogmatic limitation. And the latter must be overcome by sovereign analysis.

---

[1] *A Treatise of Human Nature* II, Part I, Sect. III, p. 81. I am quoting from the 4 vol. edition of GREEN and GROSE.

[2] This principle has in itself nothing to do with nominalism. ARISTOTLE referred to it in his criticism of the Platonic ideas. And ARISTOTLE, to be sure, was not a nominalist.

In this is evident the strong nominalistic tenor of HUME's psychologism. I would here like to point out once more the misconception in the traditional opinion which presumes that modern nominalism manifests itself only in this so-called empiricist form. That this view is erroneous is apparent, if we remember that the so-called "rationalism" desired as much as "empiricism" to discover by analysis the simplest elements of knowledge. It was just by this method that rationalism thought it had found the guarantee for the creative continuity of mathematical thought.

The difference between HUME and LEIBNIZ consists only in the basic philosophic denominator chosen by "sovereign reason" to bridge over the diversity of the modal aspects of our cosmos. In LEIBNIZ the ultimate origin of empirical reality is creative mathematical thought, in HUME it is to be found in psychological analysis.

As we have seen before, a moderate nominalism is quite compatible with the recognition of a necessary and foundational function of universal concepts (according to the ideal significance of symbols). The only condition is that universal concepts and their mutual relations must be recognized as having their origin in creative thought itself. They may not be thought of as having a foundation "in re", outside of mind [1]. HUME, however, is not a moderate nominalist but rather a radical one.

In an individualist manner he resolved the "universal representations" into "impressions", as the simplest elements of consciousness. Nevertheless, this resolution was actually the exact psychological counterpart of the resolution of complex concepts into the simplest conceptual elements by mathematicism [2].

---

[1] With respect to this, BERKELEY's *Alciphron* furnishes a convincing proof. In it he overcame the extreme sensationalist nominalism of his earlier writings. He even recognizes the logical conformity to laws in the relations between the Ideas, although, in a nominalistic fashion, the function of universality is only ascribed to the signs. But the signs, which constitute the material and instrument of all scientific knowledge, are now for BERKELEY no longer arbitrary names. On the contrary the representative character of symbols has now become the foundation of the possibility of our knowledge. They represent the validity of the relations in our thought.

[2] Compare in particular LEIBNIZ' exposition in his *Meditationes de cognitione, veritate et ideis* (1664) (ERDMANN, p. 79) of the relation of the primitive (that is simple and basic) concepts to the complex.

What Hume viewed as the "simplest elements" of consciousness, and therefore as "data", no more belongs to the real data of our experience than a single mathematical concept does.

In his penetrating critique of the "abstract Ideas" which Locke still maintained, even Berkeley had overlooked the fact that the concept of a "simple psychical element of consciousness" is itself no less abstract than that of a "triangle in general".

Hume began by demolishing the barriers which Locke in his dualistic conception had raised between "sensation" and "reflexion". This dualism in Locke was in the last analysis founded on his belief in the existence of a material and a spiritual substance. For without the latter the entire distinction between external and internal experience in his epistemology would lack a foundation.

But even Berkeley, from his "idealist" psychologistic standpoint, had completely resolved "nature" into the sensory psychical impressions. His well-known thesis *"esse est percipi"* became the psychological counterpart of Leibniz' mathematical idealism in respect to the world of phenomena. Therefore, he must also discard the distinction between primary and secondary qualities of matter that had been made by Locke in accordance with Galileo's and Newton's physics.

Hume subsumed all of cosmic reality, in all of its modal aspects of meaning, under the denominator of sensation. In a much more radical sense than in Locke, psychologism began to resolve the cosmos into the sensory contents of psychical consciousness, into perceptions [1]. It must be granted, however, that in this respect Hume's *Treatise* proceeds in a much more radical line than his *Enquiry*.

---

[1] *Treatise* I, Part II, Sect. VI p. 371): "To hate, to love, to think, to feel, to see; all this is nothing but to perceive.

Now since nothing is ever present to the mind but perceptions, and since all Ideas are deriv'd from something antecedently present to the mind, it follows, that 'tis impossible for us so much as to conceive or form an Idea of anything specifically different from Ideas and impressions. Let us chase our imagination to the heavens, or to the utmost limits of the universe; we never really advance a step beyond ourselves, nor can conceive any kind of existence, but those perceptions, which have appear'd in that narrow compass. This is the universe of the imagination."

HUME and Pyrrhonic scepticism. SEXTUS EMPIRICUS.

This radical psychologism had an outward point of contact in ancient philosophy, just as Humanist metaphysics had. The Pyrrhonic scepticism which had been transmitted to modern thought especially in the writings of SEXTUS EMPIRICUS: *Pyrrhonic Hypotyposes* and *Against the Mathematicians*, had methodically turned down the same path. But it had a purely negative tendency and the ultimate intention of denying every criterion of truth [1]. Recent investigations have made it very probable, that HUME was strongly influenced by the method of SEXTUS EMPIRICUS, even though his defective knowledge of Greek presumably kept him from reading the *Hypotyposes* in the original [2]. However, in 1718, SEXTUS EMPIRICUS' work had been published in a Latin translation and in 1725 it was published anonymously in a French translation which is now ascribed to HUART.

During this period HUME studied in Edinburgh, where much of his time was occupied with the study of classic writers. In addition, a noteworthy harmony has been discovered between HUME and the connoisseur of Pyrrhonism, CROUSAZ, in the theory of perceptions, in the psychological treatment of logic, in the doctrine of imagination and of habit in the association of impressions. CROUSAZ was professor of philosophy and mathematics at the University of Lausanne, and had devoted an extensive work to Pyrrhonism [3].

Sceptical doubt in HUME, as in DESCARTES, has only methodological significance.

Nevertheless, HUME did not have the slightest intention of following MONTAIGNE and BAYLE by ending in a destructive Pyrrhonistic scepticism.

On the contrary, in him scepticism had no other significance than it had in DESCARTES; it was only intended to be methodological, that is to say, methodological in the sense of the psycholo-

---

[1] The Pyrrhonic thesis taken over by HUME and BERKELEY: "Being is appearance" can be found in SEXTUS EMPIRICUS, *Pyrr. Hyp.* Ic. XIV, 8th trope.

[2] B. M. LAING, *David Hume* (1933), p. 74 f. I refer to this book also for the following particulars. In his *Dialogues concerning natural religion* (W.W. II, 376 ff) HUME repeatedly mentions the sect of the Pyrrhonists.

[3] *Examen du Pyrrhonisme, ancien et moderne*, 1733.

gical ideal of science, which in order to carry through its principle of continuity must also repudiate the dualistic division between "sensation" and "reflection"[1]. Reflexion with its impressions and their corresponding "ideas" (representations, which, in HUME, are identical with "concepts") must be reduced to a dependent function, to a mere image of "sensation" with its sensory "impressions".

It is precisely this reduction which, according to HUME, makes it possible to conquer scepticism by discovering an unassailable criterion of truth.

The criterion of truth.

HUME seeks this criterion of truth in the demonstration of the "original impression" from which the idea is derived[2]. In him *"impressions"* include all sensations, passions and emotions as they originally appear in the psychical function[3]. But they are not conceived of by him in their subjective actuality; rather, in the line of the ideal of science, they are comprehended according to their objective content, as the elements of phenomena.

The "impressions" are the sole data in human experience. By "Ideas" or "thoughts", HUME understands only the apperceptions of thought and reasoning which are derived from sensory impressions; they are nothing but copies of impressions, which in their elementary forms only distinguish themselves from the latter by a decreased sensory intensity. Even "Ideas" which at first sight do not appear to have any connection with "impressions", upon closer examination give evidence that they have arisen from them. How, according to HUME, does a false Idea come into being? The answer is that either the original sensory impression is related to an Idea, which is the image of an other impression, or, vice versa, an idea is brought into relation with an impression of which it is not the copy.

With respect to the Ideas which he considered to be false,

---

[1] See *Treatise* I, Part I Sect II (p. 317): "...the impressions of reflexion are only antecedent to their correspondent ideas; but posterior to those of sensation, *and deriv'd from them*." (I am italicizing).

[2] *Enquiry concerning human understanding*, Sect. V, Part i.

[3] *Treatise* I, Part 1, Sect. I (p. 311). Thereby, passions, desires and emotions are conceived of by HUME as impressions of the "reflections". The latter themselves arise from ideas of pleasure and displeasure, and these Ideas, in turn, are copies of sensory impressions of hot, cold, hunger and thirst, etc.

HUME set himself the task of discovering the sensory impressions, from which these Ideas are actually derived.

Now, according to him, there are two methods of uniting impressions and Ideas. In the one case they are united by a purely reproducing memory, and in the other by the free combining and variegating of fantasy or imagination.

The Ideas of memory are much stronger and livelier than those of fantasy, but the former are bound precisely to the same order and position as the impressions from which they were derived, whereas fantasy, in contrast, can freely combine and vary its Ideas, and is entirely independent of the original order of impressions [1].

However, the Humanist science-ideal does not allow this activity of fantasy to be conceived of as completely arbitrary. Even in its psychological form it possesses a concept of order which excludes any Idea of arbitrariness [2]. And as we shall subsequently demonstrate, this concept of law serves in HUME, as well as in LEIBNIZ or DESCARTES, as the ὑπόθεσις, as the foundation of empirical reality. In HUME it is the concept of necessary connection or association (relating to impressions as well as to the Ideas).

To understand in HUME's nominalist course of thought this transition to the psychological concept of order, we must remember, that HUME, following in LOCKE's footsteps, divides Ideas into simple and complex. The latter are connections between simple Ideas. In part at least, they are grounded in sensorily perceived relations between impressions. For HUME also divides the *impressions* into simple and complex.

The natural and philosophical relations. The laws of association.

HUME thought, that he could reduce all associations in the succession of Ideas to three basic laws, namely, the law of resemblance, the law of spatial and temporal coherence (contiguity), and the law of cause and effect.

---

[1] *Treatise* I, Part I, Sect. III. Of the *Ideas of the Memory and Imagination*.

[2] Cf. *Treatise* I, Part I, Sect. IV (p. 319): "As all simple Ideas may be separated by the imagination, and may be united again in what form it pleases, nothing would be more unaccountable than the operations of that faculty, were it not guided by some universal principles, which render it, in some measure, uniform with itself in all times and places."

These laws of association are thought of as being purely mechanical, and concern only the so-called natural relations between the Ideas by which "two Ideas are connected in the imagination and the one naturally introduces the other," when a natural succession of ideas takes place. In his *Treatise* (I part 1 sect. vi) HUME writes: " This we may establish for a general rule, that wherever the mind constantly and uniformly makes a transition without any reason, it is influenced by these relations" (i.e. by resemblance, contiguity and cause and effect).

These natural associations, according to HUME, cannot be perceived in a sensory manner. They do not connect *impressions*, but *Ideas*. The product of these associations are the complex Ideas of relations, substances and modi, which are the ordinary objects of our thought and judgments. It is true, that these complex Ideas are founded in sensory relations of resemblance and contiguity or coherence between the impressions. But the associations, which the faculty of imagination produces upon the basis of these sensory relations, exceed that which is given; they are an "order of thought." And they can lead thought astray, because they go beyond that which is directly given in the "impression".

HUME distinguished the "natural" from the "philosophical" relations. The latter do not determine the associational transition of one "Idea" to another, but simply compare "Ideas" or impressions which are not connected by association [2].

It is very confusing, that HUME in summarizing the seven classes of philosophical relations, mentions causality once again. When we put aside this natural relation which, incorrectly, is mentioned in this connection, we can list the following six classes of philosophical relations:

---

[1] HUME called them (Ibid. sect. iv) a sort of law of attraction "which in the mental world will be bound to have as extraordinary effect as in the natural."

[2] *Treatise* I, Part 1, Sect. V: "The word *Relation* is commonly used in two senses considerably different from each other. Either for that quality, by which two Ideas are connected together in the imagination, and the one naturally introduces the other, after the manner above explained; *or for that particular circumstance, in which, even upon the arbitrary union of two Ideas in the fancy we may think proper to compare them*. In common language the former is always the sense, in which we use the word relation; and 'tis only in philosophy that we extend it to mean any particular subject of comparison, without a connecting principle" (p. 322).

1 - Resemblance, a relation, which is the foundation of all the other philosophical relations. No impressions or Ideas can be compared with each other which do not display a certain degree of resemblance. As a mere philosophical relation it does not produce any association of Ideas or any sequence in the Ideas, but is rather related to a simultaneous sensory relation of resemblance.
2 - Identity, the most universal relation. It is concerned with constant and unchangeable objects.
3 - The relations of space and time, which are the origin of an infinite number of comparisons, such as distance, contact, above, below, before, behind, etc....
4 - The relations in quantity or number.
5 - The degrees in common quality; thus two objects can both possess the common quality of weight, yet one can be lighter than the other. Thus in the same colour, e.g. red, two shades can be compared with each other etc.
6 - The relation of contrast, a relation, which only seemingly affords an exception to the rule that there cannot be any philosophical relation, unless a certain degree of resemblance exists between the impressions or Ideas; for in reality, this relation, as well, always pre-supposes a point of resemblance, if a comparison is to be possible. In his *Enquiry* HUME reduces this relation to a combination of the relations of resemblance and causality.

The reader observes, how in this table of relations not only are the basic mathematical principles reduced to psychological ones, but also the laws of logic (i.e. the principles of identity and contradiction).

HUME divided the philosophical relations into two classes: the variable and the invariable. The invariable include the relations of resemblance and contrast, and the degrees in quantity and quality. They are the ground of certain knowledge.

According to HUME, this certainty rests upon the fact that the relations in question are unchangeable and at the same time are directly sensorily perceivable together with their terms; and such without reasoning, which always consists in a succession of Ideas. They are "discoverable at first sight, and fall more properly under the province of intuition than demonstration."

The same also holds good for the variable philosophical relations of identity and time and place. The latter do not go beyond that which is actually given in the sensory impressions. The reason why we say, that an object A is at a distance from object B, is that we perceive them both at that distance. Here the relation itself is given in the complex sensory impression.

It is entirely different, however, in the case of the natural relations. The latter rest upon a veritable association in the sequence of Ideas. According to HUME, it is only on the ground of the relation of causation that the relations of time, place, and identity can really exceed that which is directly given by the senses and can play their part in an associational process of thought [1]. But we will explain this point later.

§ 3 - THE TRANSITION OF THE CREATION-MOTIVE IN THE SCIENCE-IDEAL TO PSYCHOLOGICAL THOUGHT. HUME'S CRITICISM OF MATHEMATICS

Proceeding from the four invariable philosophical relations as the only possible foundation of certain knowledge, HUME began first of all with his criticism of mathematics. In the latter the adherents of the Humanistic science-ideal (including LOCKE) had till now sought their fulcrum. In HUME, however, the science-ideal has changed its basic denominator for the different modal aspects of reality. This appears nowhere clearer than here.

HUME is even willing to abandon the creative character of mathematical thought in order to be able in his epistemological inquiry to subject all the modal aspects to the absolute sovereignty of psychological thought. However, this interpretation of his criticism of mathematics has been called in question.

Contradictory interpretations of HUME's criticism of mathematics.

In particular RIEHL and WINDELBAND believe, that HUME, together with all his predecessors since DESCARTES, shared an unwavering faith in mathematics as the prototype and foundation of all scientific thought.

WINDELBAND, however, has overlooked the distinction between natural and philosophical relations, which is extremely fundamental in HUME. Consequently, WINDELBAND completely mis-

---

[1] *Treatise* I, Part III, Sect. II (p. 376): "'Tis only *causation*, which produces such a connexion, as to give us assurance from the existence or action of one object, that 't was follow'd or preceded by any other existence or action; nor can the other two relations be ever made use of in reasoning, except so far as they either affect or are affected by it."

represents HUME's conception of the certainty of mathematical knowledge [1]. RIEHL, too, did not touch the real content of this conception.

Beyond any doubt HUME displays in his *Treatise* a sceptical attitude with respect to the claims of mathematics to exact knowledge. RIEHL, however, tries to deprive this attitude of its sharpness by limiting it to "applied geometry", which refers the standards of "pure geometry" to "empirical reality". According to him, HUME never meant to dispute the universal validity of "pure geometry" itself. Moreover, he thinks, that even in this limited sense, HUME's criticism only affected a single point, namely the possibility, presumed by geometry, of dividing space to infinity.

RIEHL believes, that the appearance which HUME gives in his *Treatise* of having denied the exactness of pure geometry is only due to his unfortunate manner of expression. According to him, the inexactitude which HUME thought he had discovered in "pure geometry" is not concerned with the proofs of the latter, but only with their relation to the objects in "empirical reality" and with the *concepts* upon which these proofs are based [2].

To support his view, RIEHL appeals to the distinction that HUME also made between knowledge of facts (matters of fact) and knowledge of the relations between Ideas. For in HUME mathematics indubitably belongs to the latter. Besides, RIEHL can, indeed, appeal to some statements even in the *Treatise* which seem to support his point of view. And, if his interpretation is adopted, the anomaly between the appreciation of mathematical knowledge in the *Treatise* and in the *Enquiry* would be overcome.

For, in HUME's *Enquiry* which he published after the *Treatise*, we encounter the statement: *"That three times five is equal to the half of thirty,* expresses a relation between these numbers. Proportions of this kind are discoverable by the mere operation of thought, without dependence on what is anywhere existent in the universe. Though there never were a circle or triangle in nature, the truths, demonstrated by EUCLID, would forever retain their certainty and evidence"[3]. In other words, HUME here

---

[1] *Geschichte der neueren Phil.* I, 340 ff. WINDELBAND thereby entirely overlooks the *problem* of mathesis in HUME.
[2] RIEHL, *Der phil. Kritizismus* (3e Aufl.) I, 180.
[3] *Enquiry,* Part I, Sect. IV.

appears to have returned completely to the logicist conception of pure mathematics which lay at the foundation of the mathematical ideal of science. And, as we have seen, even LOCKE's psychologizing epistemology had capitulated in favour of the latter. Nevertheless, RIEHL's interpretation is rejected by GREEN and CASSIRER [1]. In keeping with our view, they hold that at least in his *Treatise*, HUME's psychologism had undermined the foundations of mathematical knowledge as such.

The method of solving this controversy.

In order to take sides correctly in this controversy, we must not base our opinion upon incidental statements in HUME concerning mathematical knowledge. For it is firmly established that especially HUME's *Treatise* contains very contradictory statements on this point.

The problem can only be solved by answering the preliminary question as to whether or not the fundamentals of HUME's epistemology actually leave room for an exact mathematical science. Only on the basis of the answer given to this question are we able to examine critically the mutually contradictory statements concerning the value of mathematics.

In the first place we must notice that the contrast in HUME between "matters of fact" and "relations of Ideas" can no longer have the same fundamental significance as it possessed in LOCKE. From the very beginning HUME abandoned the Lockian dualism between "sensation" and "reflection", which gradually changed into a fundamental dualism between creative mathematical thought and sensory experience of reality.

In HUME reflection is no longer "original". It is only a mere image of "sensation". True "Ideas" also have become images of "impressions": the true complex "Ideas" are mental images of complex "impressions" (connected by sensory relations). And the true simple "Ideas" are such of simple "impressions".

Now, to be sure, HUME observes that not all our Ideas are derived from impressions. There are many complex Ideas for which no corresponding impressions can be indicated, while vice versa many of our complex impressions are never reflected exactly in "Ideas" [2].

---

[1] See GREEN's *Introduction* to the first part of HUME's works; CASSIRER II, 345.
[2] *Treatise* I, Part I, Sect. I (p. 312/3).

Nevertheless, when RIEHL appeals to this statement, to demonstrate the fundamental distinction between "matters of fact" and "relations of Ideas", he distorts it, and ascribes to it a meaning which is quite different from what HUME had intended. For the latter illustrates his thesis with an instance taken from the activity of our fantasy, in which, according to him, the truth and universal validity of "Ideas" are entirely excluded: "I can imagine a city like the "New Jerusalem", he writes, "whose pavements are of gold and whose walls are of rubies, although I have never seen such a city. I have seen Paris; but can I maintain, that I can form such an Idea of this city which completely represents all its streets and houses in their real and exact proportions?"

In fact all judgments, in which the "Ideas" are no longer pure copies of the original impressions, must in the light of HUME's criterion of truth, abandon their claim to certainty and exactness.

> HUME drew the full consequences of his "psychologistic" nominalism with respect to mathematics.

Thus even mathematical knowledge can never go beyond the limits of possible sense impressions without losing its claim to universally valid truth.

With respect to mathematics, HUME drew the full consequences of the extreme psychological nominalism to which he adhered, and which he also ascribed to BERKELEY [1]. He considered it to be one of the greatest and most valuable discoveries of his time that—as BERKELEY had established—all universal ideas are nothing other than particular ones, which by universal names acquire an extended meaning, and thereby evoke other individual ideas in the imagination which exhibit a resemblance with the first.

Even abstract mathematical "Ideas" are always individual in themselves. They can represent a great number of individual Ideas by means of a general name, but they remain mere "images in the mind" of individual objects.

The word triangle, for instance, is in fact always connected with the Idea of a particular degree of quantity and quality (e.g. equal angles, equilateralness). We can never form a universal concept of a triangle that would really be separate from such individual characteristics. Our impressions are always entirely

---

[1] As we saw above, BERKELEY has later on abandoned this extreme nominalism.

individual: "'tis a principle generally receiv'd in philosophy that everything in nature is individual, and that 'tis utterly absurd to suppose a triangle really existent, which has no precise proportion of sides and angles. If this therefore be absurd in *fact and reality*, it must also be absurd *in Idea*; since nothing of which we can form a clear and distinct Idea is absurd and impossible"[1].

This was the radical sensationalistic nominalism LEIBNIZ combated from the very beginning. He knew that it must necessarily undermine the foundations of the mathematical ideal of science. We shall subsequently see, however, that HUME did not draw the sceptical consequences of this nominalism in respect to his *psychological* ideal of science.

The entire view in HUME's *Treatise* concerning the Ideas of space and time and their infinite divisibility must be understood in the light of this radical sensationalism.

In HUME the certainty of mathematical knowledge remains stringently connected with the sensory impressions and their mutual sensory relations. If mathematicians seek to find a rational standard of exactness, which transcends our possible sense impressions, they are in the field of pure fictions. These fictions are as useless as they are incomprehensible and, in any case, they cannot satisfy the criterion of truth.

HUME's psychologistic concept of space. Space as a complex of coloured points (minima sensibilia).

HUME's conception of space and time is entirely in this line. The concept of space can only be the copy of sensory impressions of "coloured points". The basic denominator, which HUME chose to compare the modal aspects of reality does not allow any meaning to be ascribed to the concept of space other than a visual and tactual one.

If this psychical space is a complex sensory impression, it must exist in the sensory relation between simple impressions. In that case the "coloured points" — as the smallest perceptible impressions of extension or *minima sensibilia* — function as such simple impressions, and the concept of space is a mere copy of them. And these points must ever possess a sensory extension which itself is no longer divisible.

In this view the concept of the original mathematical point,

---

[1] *Treatise* I, Part I, Sect. VII (p. 327).

that never can have any extension, is untenable. Even in the "order of thought" it cannot have any truth or universal validity. For, according to Hume, anything which is absurd "in fact and reality" — that is to say, anything which cannot be given in sensory impressions — is also absurd "in Idea".

Psychologizing of the mathematical concept of equality.

The concept of mathematical equality is treated in the same way: "The only useful notion of equality or inequality is derived from the whole united appearance and the comparison of particular objects" (read: particular sensory impressions). On the other hand the so-called exact standard of equality between two magnitudes in "pure geometry" is plainly imaginary. "For as the very Idea of equality is that of such a particular appearance corrected by juxta-position or a common measure, the notion of any correction beyond that we have instruments and art to make, is a mere fiction of the mind, *and useless as well as incomprehensible*" [1].

The same holds for mathematical definitions of straight lines, curves, planes, etc.

Hume admits, that the fictions concealed in such exact definitions are very natural and usual. Mathematicians may with ever more exact measuring instruments try to correct the inexactitude of the sensory perceptions which take place without the aid of such instruments. From this the thought naturally arises that one should finally be able to reach an ideal standard of accuracy beyond the reach of the senses. But this Idea lacks all validity. The measuring instruments remain sensory instruments whose use remains bound to the standard of sensory perceptions. "The first principles" (viz. of mathesis) "are founded on the imagination and senses: The conclusion, therefore, can never go beyond, much less contradict these faculties" [2].

In contradiction to Riehl's interpretation, it is evident from the following statement, that this thesis is not restricted to the question as to whether or not space is infinitely divisible, but is actually concerned with the entire claims of "pure geometry"

---

[1] *Treatise* I, Part II, Sect. IV (p. 353/4).
[2] This entire course of thought is misunderstood by Riehl when he thinks that Hume recognizes an exact standard for "pure geometry" independent of sense experience.

to ideal exactness: "Now since these Ideas (i.e. of exact standards) are so loose and uncertain, I wou'd fain ask any mathematician, what infallible assurance he has, not only of the more intricate and obscure propositions of his science, but of the most vulgar and obvious principles? How can he prove to me, for instance, that two right lines cannot have one common segment? Or that 'tis impossible to draw more than one right line betwixt any two points?... The original standard of a right line is in reality nothing but a certain general appearance; and 'tis evident right lines may be made to concur with each other, and yet correspond to this standard, tho' corrected by all the means either practicable or imaginable" [1].

All that HUME taught here with respect to the concept of space applies even more strongly to the concept of time. For in similar fashion, he gave only a sensationalist sense to the latter. The Idea of time is formed out of the sequence of changing sensory "impressions" as well as "Ideas". As a relation of sensory succession it can never exist apart from such successive sensory Ideas, as NEWTON thought of his "absolute mathematical time". Five notes played on a flute, give us the impression and the concept of time. Time is not a sixth impression which presents itself to our hearing or to one of our other sense organs. Nor is it a sixth impression which the mind discovers in itself by means of "reflection". Therefore, a completely static and unchangeable object can never give us the impression of "duration" or time [2].

All false concepts in mathematics, which pretend to give us an ideal exactness beyond the testimony of the sense organs, arise through the natural associations of resemblance, contiguity, and causality. And, according to HUME, the first of these three is "the most fertile source of error."

---

[1] *Ibid.*, p. 356/7: The statement in question to which RIEHL appeals is certainly not clear, when HUME writes further: "At the same time we may learn the reason why geometry fails of evidence in this simple point" (i.e. the pretended infinite divisibility of space) "while all its other reasonings command our fullest assent and approbation." For it is just this very point which strikes in its entirety the claim of mathematics to exactness!

[2] *Treatise* I, Part II, Sect. III, p. 342—344.

cosmonomic Idea of Humanistic immanence-philosophy 287

The position of arithmetic in Hume's sensationalism.

Now it may appear that Hume still granted the standard of ideal mathematical exactness at least to algebra and arithmetic. He writes in part III, sect. 1 of his *Treatise*: "There remain, therefore, algebra and arithmetic as the only sciences, in which we can carry on a chain of reasoning to any degree of intricacy, and yet preserve a perfect exactness and certainty. We are possest of a precise standard, by which we can judge of the equality and proportion of numbers; and according as they correspond or not to that standard, we determine their relations, without any possibility of error. When two numbers are so combin'd, as that the one has always an unite answering to every unite of the other, we pronounce them equal; and 'tis for want of such a standard of equality in extension, that geometry can scarce be esteem'd a perfect and infallible science" [1]. But has the meaning of number in Hume's system in fact escaped from being rendered psychological? Not in the least. The logicistic conception of arithmetic (held to by Descartes and Leibniz) is here only seemingly maintained.

In Hume's thought, arithmetical unity as an abstract concept can only be the copy of a single impression. Number as unity in the quantitative relations is a fiction. The real unity, which alone has real existence, and which necessarily lies at the foundation of the abstract concept of number, "must be perfectly indivisible and incapable of being resolved into any lesser unity" [2]. Number can only be composed of such indivisible unities. Twenty men exist, but only because there exist one, two, three men.

What then is the true unit? In Hume's system it can only be an impression which is perceived separately and cannot be resolved into other impressions. As Laing has correctly observed, this was the conception of unity which is to be found in Sextus Empiricus [3]. Let us now return to the "minima sensibilia", the coloured points of space.

A sum of units can in Hume's system only be grounded on a sensory relation between individual impressions [4]. Hume does

---

[1] *Ibid.*, p. 374.
[2] *Treatise* I, Part II, Sect. II, p. 338.
[3] Laing, Op. cit., p. 107.
[4] In Part 1, Sect. vii (p. 330) Hume introduces a virtually adequate concept of number: "when we mention any great number, such as a

not see the inner antinomy in which such a reduction of the original modal meaning of number to that of sensory impression must necessarily involve itself. He does not see that sensory multiplicity pre-supposes the original multiplicity in the modal sense of the numerical aspect, and that in a sensory multiplicity as such no arithmetical meaning can hide. In his system the arithmetical laws which rule the necessary quantitative relations among all possible numbers, must be reduced to psychical laws ruling the relations of the sensory impressions. Thus, even arithmetic must abandon all claim to being an exact science. Not only the irrational, the differential and the complex functions of number, but also the simple fractions have no valid ground. Even simple addition, subtraction, and multiplication of whole numbers lack a genuine mathematical foundation in his system. It appears from the exceptional position which he ascribes to arithmetic in contradistinction to geometry, that HUME did not expressly draw this conclusion. It seems he did not dare to draw it [1]. Moreover, his entire exposition with respect to number must be judged extremely summary, vague, and intrinsically contradictory.

Nevertheless, the destructive conclusion here intended, lay hidden inexorably in his psychological starting-point.

> HUME's retrogression into the Lockian conception of mathematics remains completely inexplicable on the sensationalistic basis of his system.

The position which HUME in his later work, *Enquiry concerning human understanding,* assumes with respect to mathematics, is actually a relapse into the Lockian standpoint; it is a capitulation in face of common opinion concerning the exactness of mathematical thought.

Locke, however, could base his view upon his dualism between sensation and reflection. But in HUME's sensationalistic nominalism, no single tenable point of contact is to be found

---

thousand, the mind has generally no adeaquate Idea of it, but only a power of producing such an Idea by its adeaquate Idea of the decimals, under which the number is comprehended." But even the concept of the decimals in HUME's system only permit themselves to be maintained as the copy of a sensory multiplicity of simple impressions.

[1] GREEN, op. cit., p. 254, thinks that HUME saw the impossibility of reducing arithmetic to sensory relations.

for the traditional conception with regard to the creative character of mathematical thought.

At the utmost, the claims of mathematics to exactness and to independence of all sensory impressions can be judged valid in a pragmatic sense. For in the final analysis in both his *Treatise* and *Enquiry*, HUME did not wish to contest the practical utility of mathematics in natural science.

And, as it will subsequently appear, *faith* in the exactness of mathematics and in the objective universal validity of the causal judgments of physics can be explained by him from imagination and the psychical laws of association of human nature. By means of the latter he finally intended to arrest the radical Pyrrhonist scepticism. There is, however, in his system no room for the real mathematical science-ideal.

§ 4 - THE DISSOLUTION OF THE IDEALS OF SCIENCE AND OF PERSONALITY BY THE PSYCHOLOGISTIC CRITIQUE

In HUME the creative function has actually been transferred from mathematical to psychological thought. In the latter he thought he had found his Archimedean point which needs "nulla re extra mentem ad existendum".

HUME's criticism of the concept of substance and his interpretation of naïve experience.

In the rationalistic metaphysics both the ideal of science and that of personality had been founded on a concept of substance. It is against this metaphysical concept that HUME, on the basis of his new psychological view of the science-ideal, now directs his penetrating criticism.

As his starting point he took the belief of naïve experience in the existence of things in the external world — things which have a continuing reality independent of our consciousness. We shall later show in detail that his interpretation of naïve experience is a falsification of the latter by the realistic "*Abbildtheorie*" (image-theory). Generally speaking, contemporary Humanistic epistemology has still not gone beyond this false conception of naïve experience. HUME at least does not *intend* to impute to the naïve experience of reality a theory concerning the relationship between consciousness and reality. He observes that the faith of naïve man in the existence of a reality which is independent of our consciousness cannot rest upon a theory. It must rather be explained in terms of a natural impulse of human feeling [1].

HUME thinks naïve man does not distinguish between his "impressions" and the "things in the external world", he identifies the latter with the former.

It was philosophy that originated the distinction between the reality of sensory impressions, which are real only in appearance, and the true reality of "things in themselves", the reality of the "substances". On theoretical grounds it rejected the misunderstood naïve conception of the external world.

HUME deemed this philosophical view to be false and dogmatic. In contradistinction to scepticism and the false mathematical metaphysics, he wished to give an account of naïve experience by explaining it in terms of the psychical laws of association inherent in human nature.

Although this interpretation is basically erroneous, and must undoubtedly falsify naïve experience in a functionalistic way, yet, in the face of the rationalistic metaphysics of the mathematical ideal of science, it affords us the important critical point of view, that naïve experience is no *theory* of reality [2].

HUME starts from his psychological basic denominator for all the modal aspects of meaning. In our impressions there is not a single one which gives us a ground to form any concept of a constant "thing in itself", which would be independent of our consciousness [3]. Nothing is given in experience but the mul-

---

[1] *Treatise* I, Part IV, Sect. 1 (pag. 474/5): "Nature, by an absolute and uncontrollable necessity has determin'd us to judge as well as to breathe and feel;"

"...belief is more properly an act of the sensitive part than of the cogitative part of our nature." *Treatise* I, Part. IV, Sect. I (pag. 475). From this it is clearly evident, that HUME reduces the modal function of faith to that of feeling.

[2] Cf. especially *Treatise* I, Part IV, Sect. II (p. 483): "And indeed, whatever convincing arguments philosophers may fancy they can produce to establish the belief of objects independent of the mind, 'tis obvious these arguments are known but to very few, and that 'tis not by them, that children, peasants, and the greatest part of mankind are induc'd to attribute objects to some impressions, and deny them to others. Accordingly we find, that all the conclusions, which the vulgar form on this head, are directly contrary to those, which are confirm'd by philosophy." These remarks are excellent!

[3] *Treatise* I, Part IV, Sect. II (p. 479): "To begin with the senses, 'tis evident these faculties are incapable of giving rise to the notion of the

tiplicity of the sensory impressions which continually arise and fade away.

Like BERKELEY, HUME abandoned the distinction, still made by LOCKE, between the primary qualities (extension, motion, solidity) which belong to the things themselves, and the secondary qualities (colour, sound, odour, taste, heat, etc.) which have only a subjective character [1]. But while BERKELEY could seek an explanation for the belief in an external world in his metaphysical conception of God, this escape was not open to HUME. The positivistic psychologism of the latter had no room for a metaphysical theology.

There is nothing to be found in our impressions which gives us any right to assume that the "primary qualities", independent of our consciousness, belong to things of the external world. The belief in the *"Ding an sich"* can only be explained in terms of the natural laws of the imaginative faculty.

The "natural associations" are here active and they rest upon the temporal succession of Ideas. They necessarily lead fantasy beyond that which is given. They lead metaphysics to its false concept of substance.

The task of true philosophy is to indicate the impressions which furnish naïve experience ("common sense") with a basis for its belief in the independent world of things. HUME supposes that in this way he has explained the origin of the false concept of substance. Metaphysical philosophy actually did nothing else but relate the natural associations to a false concept. So HUME wishes to show that his philosophy is in agreement with naïve experience ("the vulgar view"), while, in contrast, metaphysics has from this very experience drawn a false concept of substance.

He supposes that there are two characteristic relations to

---

continu'd existence of their objects, after they no longer appear to the senses. For that is a contradiction in terms..."

"That our senses offer not their impressions, as the images of something *distinct*, or *independent*, and *external* is evident; because they convey to us nothing but a single perception, and never give us the least intimation of any thing beyond. A single perception can never produce the Idea of a double existence, but by some interference either of the reason or imagination."

[1] Ibid., p. 482: "Now 'tis evident, that, whatever may be our philosophical opinion, colours, sounds, heat and cold, as far as appears to the senses, exist after the same manner with motion and solidity!"

be indicated in our impressions, namely the constancy and the coherence of impressions, which actually give the foundation for the naïve faith in the existence of an independent world of things. Constancy indicates a temporarily continuous uniformity or resemblance in specific impressions in spite of their fluctual character in temporal succession.

The trees, mountains, and houses, which I see before me at the moment, have always appeared to me in the same resemblance of impressions. Once I have turned my head or closed my eyes, no longer retaining them in my field of vision, I see them before me immediately afterward, without the least alteration, when I again hold them in view [1].

But this first relation of my sensory impressions is not yet enough to establish the belief in a constant empirical reality of things. If it were to be decisive, this faith would be bound to the unchangeability of impressions. There arises a problem, however, from the fact that naïve experience accepts the constant reality of things in spite of all changes in their properties and mutual relations.

Therefore, only in conjunction with the law of their coherence can the constancy of impressions supply a sufficient foundation for the belief in the constant reality of things. It is a law of association, namely that of the contiguity or coherence of impressions in time, through which we fill up by our imagination the impressions, actually given in a gradual discontinuity, so that they become a constant and continuous reality of things. The imagination (not logical thought) leaps, as it were, over the gaps in the temporal sequence of sensory impressions and fuses together the successive similar impressions, so that they become identical and continuously existing things.

The creative function of imagination and the way in which the creation-motive of the Humanistic ideal of science is transmitted to psychological thought.

This fusion of impressions is executed (by a natural necessity) through the influence of relations. It is executed through the relations of resemblance and coherence between impressions. The imaginative faculty follows the separate impressions, and on the basis of the resemblance between them passes from the one to the other. Thereby, it creates a continuous bond between

---

[1] *Treatise,* Part IV, Sect. II (p. 484).

the impressions, and this bond has been incorrectly interpreted by metaphysics as being a substantial connection within the things themselves.

We speak of an identical thing, whereas actually the only data that we have, are similar impressions, separated in time, but united by associational relations.

So the creative function is shifted in HUME's theory from mathematical to psychological thought. At every point he attempts to give a purely psychological explanation of our naïve experience of reality, by means of the laws of association ruling our sensory impressions. The sensory aspect of this experience is absolutized in a psychologistic way [1].

He rejected the attempt, undertaken by the metaphysics of the mathematical science-ideal, to construct a noumenal world of things out of "creative" mathematical thought.

Mathematical rationalism had sought to defend the foundations of the science-ideal against the consequences of the postulate of continuity by means of the doctrine of innate Ideas. The latter is rejected by HUME in a much more radical way than by LOCKE. In his entire analysis of "human nature" HUME was primarily concerned with the vindication of the absolute sovereignty of psychological thought. In favour of the latter he abandoned all the dogmas of the mathematical ideal of science. And I would especially call attention to the fact that he desired to explain the claims to logical exactness of the supposed creative mathematical thought in terms of the same psychological principle which he had employed in the construction of the world of things of naïve experience, namely, the creative function of fantasy: "I have already observ'd in examining the foundation of mathematics", so he writes in this context, "that the imagination, when set into any train of thinking, is apt to continue, even when its object fails it, and like a galley put in motion by the oars, carries on its course without any new impulse. This I have assign'd for the reason why after considering several loose standards of equality, and correcting them by each other, we proceed to imagine so correct and exact a standard of that relation, as is not liable to the least error or variation.

---

[1] *Translator's Note:* As we shall see in more detail in Vol. III naïve experience is characterized by *total structures of individuality*, which are never to be explained in terms of the association of separate sensory impressions.   D. H. F.

The same principle makes us easily entertain this opinion of the continu'd existence of body. Objects have a certain coherence even as they appear to our senses; but this coherence is much greater and more uniform, if we suppose the objects to have a continu'd existence; and as the mind is once in the train of observing a uniformity among objects, it naturally continues, till it renders the uniformity as complete as possible"[1].

In other words, psychical imagination or fantasy is the creator of the world of things of naïve experience. It is also the origin of the claims of mathematical thought to exactness. However, this is true only *in appearance*.

For it is *sovereign psychological thought* by which HUME wishes to account for this situation of things, and which is placed as such above the "creative" fantasy. It is the "creative" power of this thought which is imputed to the faculty of imagination, since the latter is not able to isolate itself in a theoretical way.

So it is actually psychological thought that is elevated by HUME to the position of ἀρχή, origin and lawgiver of the cosmos of experience.

The fact that he failed to account for this transcendental Idea of origin, the fact that he degraded logical thought itself to a dependent image of sensory fantasy only proves that HUME had not yet arrived at a transcendental critical self-reflexion.

The laws of association of his psychological ideal of science serve indeed the same purpose as the mathematical *lex continui* in LEIBNIZ. In an analogous manner HUME employed them as an ὑπόθεσις, as the foundation of the reality of experience. Only the basic denominator of the science-ideal was changed. In HUME, too, constant reality is resolved into a process which conforms to fixed laws. But in him this process is a psychological one.

HUME destroys the metaphysical foundation of the rationalist ideal of personality.

Unlike BERKELEY, HUME did not restrict his radical criticism of the concept of substance to the concept of the material substance of nature. He extended it to the metaphysical concept of a spiritual substance in which the rationalist ideal of personality sought its sole foundation. In a really superb critical

---

[1] *Treatise*, Part IV, Sect. II, p. 487/8.

manner HUME demonstrated that (from the standpoint of immanence-philosophy) the whole conflict between materialism and idealism is only a conflict between "brothers of the same house". The idealists called SPINOZA an atheist, because he did not accept a soul-substance. HUME correctly observed that both of these standpoints are rooted in the same metaphysical principle. Consequently, if one calls SPINOZA an atheist, then with equal reason one must label the idealistic metaphysics of the immortal soul as atheistic. The idealists arrive at their metaphysical theory of the immateriality, simplicity, and immortality of the soul by the same sort of rational speculations: "It appears, then, that to whatever side we turn, the same difficulties follow us, and that we cannot advance one step towards establishing the simplicity and immateriality of the soul, without preparing the way for a dangerous and irrecoverable atheism" [1].

HUME arrived at this conclusion on the basis of his psychologistic standpoint, according to which the *universe* of our experience is in the final analysis resolved into impressions, and into Ideas which are derived from them. From this standpoint the opposition between *idealism and materialism must, in the nature of the case, be a relative one.*

HUME had brought the different modal aspects of temporal reality under a psychological basic denominator. Therefore, in keeping with his honest critique, he must also reject the soul-substance. In DESCARTES and LEIBNIZ the ego, the personality, was identified with mathematical thought and was hypostatized as a thinking substance. Seeking after the origin of this concept HUME states that the ego is not itself an impression, because it is always conceived of as something to which are related all impressions and ideas [2]. The "ego is in truth nothing more than a collective concept of the different series of Ideas which are ordered constantly in accordance with the laws of association. HUME observes: "Nowhere in my experience do I encounter myself apart from an Idea and I can never perceive anything other than Ideas." There is in the soul no single faculty which in time remains unchangeably the same: "The mind is a kind of theatre, where several perceptions successively make their appearance; pass,

---

[1] *Treatise* I, Part IV, Sect. V (p. 527).
[2] "self or person is not any one impression, but that to which our several impressions and ideas are supposed to have a reference." *Treatise* I, Part IV, Sect. VI (p. 533).

re-pass, glide away, and mingle in an infinite variety of postures and situations"[1].

But, even this comparison of the mind with the theatre of our "perceptions" is misleading. For the mind itself consists of nothing other than "perceptions".

Even the illusion, which, in spite of everything, ever causes "the ego" to appear to us as a constant and self-sufficient entity, must be explained in terms of the associational law of the resemblance and coherence of impressions. Because the contents of the Ideas of a particular moment are only imperceptibly different from those of the following moment, our imagination easily passes over from the one phase of our "spiritual existence" to the following.

This continuity in the associational process causes the illusion of an absolutely identical and singular personality or "selfhood": "From thence it evidently follows, that identity is nothing really belonging to those different perceptions, and uniting them together; but is merely a quality, which we attribute to them because of the union of their ideas in the imagination, *when we reflect upon them*"[2]. (I am italicizing).

The radical self-dissolution of the ideals of science and of personality in HUME's philosophy.

In a truly radical manner, the psychological science-ideal has here conquered the ideal of personality by destroying its supposed metaphysical foundation. In his psychological method HUME could no longer find a way back to the "free and sovereign" personality.

The ideal of science had in fact no other foundation for the „sovereign personality" than the metaphysical concept of substance. In HUME's philosophy, however, even the science-ideal in its claim to conceive "nature" in the sense of "the outer world", dissolves itself in a really radical manner. This is evident from the famous critique of the principle of causality, which received its clearest formulation in the *Enquiry*. We shall see that in this critique HUME not only undermined the foundations of mathematical physics, but at the same time those of his own associationism in which the science-ideal had acquired its psychological turn.

---

[1] *Treatise* I, Part. IV, Sect. VI (p. 534).
[2] *Ibid.*, p. 540.

§ 5 - CONTINUATION: THE CRITICISM OF THE PRINCIPLE OF CAUSALITY AS A CRITIQUE OF EXPERIENCE

At the outset the principle of causality had been elevated by the metaphysics of the mathematical science-ideal to the rank of an eternal logical truth. LEIBNIZ broke with this purely logical conception, and conceived of causality as a "factual verity". But he, too, held to its ideal logical foundation (viz. on the principium rationis sufficientis) in our judgment.

HUME's criticism of this principle became a critique of experience in the sense later on ascribed to it by KANT. It aimed at an investigation of the ground of validity of all theoretical synthetic judgments which claim to be universally valid and necessary, and this on the supposition that experience has no other data than sensory impressions.

Like KANT, HUME did not make any fundamental distinction between naïve experience and natural science!

According to HUME, all "experience" goes beyond the sensory impressions which alone are given. We can only speak of experience when epistemological judgments of supposed universal validity and necessity are given with reference to the sensory impressions and when from a sensorily given fact we conclude to another fact that is not given.

This is only possible with the aid of the principle of the connection of cause and effect. Through this principle alone can the relations of identity and of time and place transcend that which is given in sense data. "Here then it appears, that of those three relations, which depend not upon the mere Ideas, the only one, that can be trac'd beyond our senses, and inform us of existences and objects, which we do not see or feel, is *causation*" [1].

If the principle of causality with its kernel, the necessity in the relation of cause and effect, is really to possess an established validity, then a basis in the sensory impressions must be indicated for the Idea of causality. The foundation in question can only be sought in the relations of impressions.

An analysis of the Idea of causality shows that two relations, viz. that of contiguity and that of the priority in time of one event before an other, are essential elements of the relation of causality. And these relations are in fact sensorily given [2].

---

[1] *Treatise* I, Part III, Sect. II (p. 377).
[2] *Ibid.*, p. 397.

But the Idea of causality very decidedly goes beyond this sensory relations. For the judgment of causality does not state a mere *post hoc*, but pretends to be able to indicate a *propter hoc*, a necessity.

> The problem pertaining to the necessary connection of cause and effect is to HUME the problem of the origin of natural laws as such.

To HUME the problem with respect to the foundation of the relation of cause and effect becomes in the final analysis the problem of the origin of natural laws as such.

Mathematical physics had based the certainty of its results upon the law of causality as a functional law of physical relations. DESCARTES called this law an "innate idea". LEIBNIZ saw in it the foundational principle of all judgments of experience, an ideal rational ground by means of which we can give an account of empirical phenomena, but which remains bound to the "factual verities". To HUME, however, this very principle of causality became problematical, insofar as it was conceived of as *the principle of a necessary connection between a prior and subsequent event in the outer world.*

HUME rejected as sophisms the attempts made by HOBBES, CLARKE and LOCKE to demonstrate the logical necessity in the inference from cause to effect. There is no object that as a "cause" would logically imply the existence of any other object. The denial of a necessary connection between cause and effect does not lead to a single logical contradiction.

Only by experience can we conclude from the existence of any object to the existence of another. With respect to this experience the situation is as follows: We remember that, after certain sorts of facts in space and time, we have constantly seen other facts follow. For instance we rember that, after the sensory perception of fire, we have regularly experienced the sensation of warmth. Thereby, a new relation is discovered which constitutes an essential element of the connection between cause and effect, namely, the constant connection of two sorts of impressions which follow each other in time [1].

In this relation there is nothing that in itself implies a necessity which would possess an objective validity: "From the mere repetition of any past impression, even to infinity, there never

---

[1] *Treatise* I, Part III, Sect. VI (p. 389).

will arise any new original Idea, such as that of a necessary connexion; and the number of impressions has in this case no more effect than if we confin'd ourselves to one only" [1].

> According to HUME, the law of causality is only to be maintained as a psychical law of association. Nevertheless, every legitimate foundation for the ideal of science in a mathematical physical sense is lacking.

HUME thought that he could only maintain the law of causality in the sense of a psychical law of association, which through habit compels the mind to proceed without any reasoning from that which is given to that which is not given.

In his *Treatise* he still took the trouble to indicate an impression as the psychological origin of the concept of causality. Here his argument is as follows: It is of course true, that from the mere repetition of similar events subsequent to previously perceived similar antecedents, nothing objectively new arises which is in fact sensorily perceived in each instance. But the constant resemblance in the different instances does raise a new subjective impression in the mind, namely, a tendency to pass over from an instantly given impression to the Idea of another impression which in the past repeatedly occurred after the former. This is then the impression which corresponds to the Idea of causality [2].

In his *Enquiry* HUME no longer took the trouble to bring his theory of the concept of causality in agreement with his doctrine concerning the relation between "impressions" and "Ideas". In fact this was impossible, because repetition can by no means give a new impression. Therefore HUME immediately introduces *habit in connecting Ideas* as a *natural law*.

> The way in which HUME's *Critique* finally undermines the foundations of his own psychological science-ideal.

It is only *habit* which compels us to join the Idea of an event B, which repeatedly followed the same event A, with the Idea

---

[1] *Treatise* I, Part III, Sect. VI (p. 389).

[2] *Treatise*, Part. III, Sect. XIV (p. 459: "Tho' the several resembling instances, which give rise to the Idea of power, have no influence on each other, and can never produce any new quality *in the object*, which can be the model of that Idea, yet the *observation* of this resemblance produces a new impression in the *mind*, which is its real model."

of the latter. Habit, in the constant perception of like consequences after like antecedents, is the only foundation for the judgment of causality. The subjective sequence of Ideas is incorrectly interpreted as an objective necessity in the relations between the contents of the Ideas.

The "propter hoc" — and with that the entire necessary coherence of phenomena — can never be demonstrated or understood rationally. It can only be believed [1]. This faith is only "some sentiment or feeling" that accompanies our Idea. But implicitly, this acknowledgement destroys the foundation of the psychical laws of association, as psychical laws of "human nature". For in these laws, too, there is implied a necessary connection between Ideas in temporal sequence: "nature by an absolute and uncontrollable necessity has determined us to judge as well as to breathe and feel" [2].

HUME even admits that he cannot account for these psychical laws of nature and he appeals to them in a purely dogmatic fashion as to "a principle of human nature, which is universally acknowledged, and which is well-known by its effects" [3]. Thus he not only undermined the Humanistic metaphysics of the rationalistic mathematical science-ideal and of the ideal of personality with its three themes: deity, freedom and immortality, but through his psychologistic epistemology he also shook the ground-pillars of the ideals of personality and of science, as such.

HUME disregards the synthesis of logical and psychical meaning in his psychological basic denominator.

In keeping with the postulate of continuity of the ideal of science in its psychologized sense, HUME levelled the modal boundaries of meaning between the law-spheres, and thereby involved himself in evident antinomies. He was not conscious of the fact that his reduction of the entire given reality

---

[1] "All these operations are a species of natural instincts, which no reasoning or process of the thought and understanding is able either to produce or to prevent." *Enquiry*, Sect. V, Part. I.

[2] *Treatise* I, Part. IV, Sect. 1 (pag. 474/5).

[3] *Enquiry*, Sect. v, Part. 1. It is true, that again and again in the *Enquiry* the insight appears, that the law of causality must be postulated as the foundation for all events. (See WENTSCHER, *Geschichte des Kausalproblems*, 1921, p. 102). But HUME's psychologism compels him to seek the *ground* of the Idea of causality exclusively in subjective associations.

to a psychological basic denominator rests upon a fundamental rational abstraction; he did not understand that only theoretical thought, by synthesizing analytical and psychical modal meaning, is in a position to isolate the psychical aspect of reality. That he failed to acquire this insight is evident from his attempt to obliterate, in the face of the psychical aspect of sensation, the original sense of the logical aspect and to reduce the concept to a mere copy of the psychical impression of feeling.

HUME had sharply recognized the antinomy (previously analyzed by BAYLE and BERKELEY) of the metaphysical concept of substance, an antinomy, which originates from the fact that a product of thought is proclaimed to be absolutely independent of thought, and to be a "thing in itself" [1].

But he did not see the inner antinomy which lay in his own absolutizing of the psychical (feeling-)aspect of reality. He was unconscious of the antinomy which arises from the attempt to reduce the meaning of the logical aspect to the psychical "in itself". In truth his basic denominator for all given reality was a *psycho-logical* one, and not merely *psychical*.

In empirical reality the psychical aspect of meaning only exists in the full coherence of all the modal aspects. Only theoretical thought can abstract it, and within its modal cadre isolate the objective sensory impressions, the subjective emotions and the images of sensory phantasy. How then can the logical concept itself be comprehended as a mere image of a sensory impression? Whoever attempts to do so, is guilty of undermining the logical criterion of truth, and necessarily involves himself in logical contradiction. Where only psychical laws of association rule, there is no room for a veritable normative criterion of truth, there every concept of natural law becomes meaningless.

---

[1] This antinomy is excellently characterized by FICHTE in his *Zweite Einleitung in die Wissenschaftslehre* (Sämtl. Werke 1, S. 491), when he remarks in opposition to those who have accepted the "Ding an sich": "Ihr Ding ist durch ihr Denken hervorgebracht; nun aber soll es gleich darauf wieder ein Ding an sich, d.i. nicht durch Denken hervorgebracht seyn. Ich verstehe sie wahrhaftig nicht; ich kann mich weder diesen Gedanken denken, noch einen Verstand denken, mit welchem man diesen Gedanken denkt..." ["Their "thing" has been produced by their thought; nevertheless it should immediately after that again be conceived of as a "thing in itself", i.e. as not being produced by thought. Truly, I don't understand them; I can neither think this Idea, nor can I think of an understanding by means of which this Idea is thought..."].

Thus, in his naturalistic psychologized system, HUME has also undermined his own theory's claim to truth.

§ 6 - THE PRELUDE TO THE SHIFTING OF PRIMACY TO THE IDEAL OF PERSONALITY

The extension of the psychologized science-ideal over the modal boundaries of the aesthetic, juridical, moral and faith-aspects.

Even though HUME accepts psychological "feeling", in its modal subject-object-relation (emotion-sensation), as the basic denominator for all modal aspects of reality, yet he recognizes a relative modal diversity of meaning in the cosmos. Within the absolutized psychical law-sphere, the aesthetic, juridical, moral and faith aspects of experience were distinguished by him from the logical one (which he had also psychologized). Nevertheless, the science-ideal, with its psychologically conceived law of causality, arbitrarily exceeds these modal boundaries.

In LEIBNIZ all modal aspects of meaning are made to be modi of mathematical thought. In HUME they become modi of his psychological basic denominator. So the aesthetic aspect, too, becomes a modus of psychical feeling: "Pleasure and pain... are not only necessary attendants of beauty and deformity, *but constitute their very essence*" [1]. The same can be stated in respect to the remaining normative modal aspects of experience. HUME presented a mechanistic theory of human emotions, entirely in accord with the tradition handed down by DESCARTES, HOBBES and SPINOZA, and directly connected with LOCKE. On this point the latter had reproduced HOBBES' theory in the form in which it acquired its great influence in the English, French, and Scottish philosophy of the Enlightenment. For HUME — as it had been for HOBBES — this theory was the foundation of his ethical philosophy and of his theoretical view of faith: "in the production and conduct of the passions, there is a certain regular mechanism, which is susceptible of as accurate a disquisition, as the laws of motion, optics, hydrostatics, or any part of physical nature" [2].

The laws of association are the sole explanatory principles which HUME will here employ. They are grounded on the principle of the uniformity of human nature at all times.

---

[1] *Treatise* II, Part. I, Sect. VIII (p. 96).
[2] *Diss. on the Passions*, Sect. VI.

The psychologically comprehended science-ideal that lies at the foundation of this entire explanatory method, is clearly formulated by Hume in the following statement: "We find in the course of nature that though the effects be many, the principles from which they arise are commonly but few and simple, and that it is the sign of an unskilful naturalist to have recourse to a different quality, in order to explain every different operation. How much more must this be true with regard to the human mind" [1].

We saw that the emotions form a second class of impressions next to those which belong to the sensory function of perception and to the corporeal feelings of pleasure and pain [2]. Hume designated the first mentioned impressions as "reflective" and deemed them to be derived from the original sensual impressions either directly or indirectly through the intermediary of an Idea of a sensory impression. He therefore called the emotions "secondary" impressions, in contradistinction to the "original" ones of "sensation".

He divided the "secondary impressions" into two classes, the calm and the vehement ones. He considered the emotions of beauty and ugliness as "calm" impressions. Under the "vehement" he subsumed all such passions as love and hate, sorrow and joy, pride and humility.

The "passions" themselves were further divided into "direct" and "indirect". Under the former he understood all such which arise directly out of the elementary feelings of pleasure or pain, such as desire, aversion, sorrow, joy, hope, fear and despair; under the latter, all such which, although originating from the same source, nevertheless, do so only by combining other qualities. Pride and humility, ambition, vanity, love, hate, jealousy, compassion, generosity, malice, and so on, are considered to be "indirect" passions.

All these emotions appear in human nature in connection with certain Ideas and objects; moreover, they do so in a regular conformity to natural laws. Hume sharply distinguishes the causes of emotions from their objects. The selfhood can never be the cause, but can only be the object of a passion [3]. For in Hume's criticism of the concept of substance the selfhood was

---

[1] *Treatise* II, Part. I, Sect. I (p. 81).
[2] *Ibid.* (p. 75).
[3] *Treatise* II, Par. I, Sect. II (p. 77).

resolved into a collective concept of the associational series of ideas. In the case of pride and humility, one's own selfhood is the object of the emotions, whereas in the case of hate and love, the emotion has other selves for its object.

The cooperation between the associations of Ideas and those of passions.

All the various causes of the "passions" are now reduced to the simple natural principles of association.

The impressions are as much associated as the Ideas, but with the fundamental difference that the former in the temporal sequence combine only in accordance with the natural associational law of resemblance, whereas the Ideas are, in addition, connected according to the associational laws of contiguity and causality [1].

Because the emotions are always accompanied in a natural way by certain Ideas, also the associations of the Ideas and the associations of the passions combine in the same object: "Thus a man, who, by any injury from another, is very much discompos'd and ruffled in his temper, is apt to find a hundred subjects of discontent, impatience, fear, and other uneasy passions; especially, if he can discover these subjects in or near the person, who was the cause of his first passion. Those principles, which forward the transition of Ideas, here concur with those, which operate on the passions; and both uniting in one action, bestow on the mind a double impulse. The new passion, therefore, must arise with so much greater violence, and the transition to it must be rendered so much easy and natural" [2]. A mere association of Ideas is consequently not sufficient to originate passions. In the sphere of the emotional or secondary impressions, the laws of association are only valid on the basis of a natural and original connection between an Idea and a passion [3].

---

[1] *Treatise* II, Part. I, Sect. IV, p. 82: "'Tis evident, then, there is an attraction or association among impressions, as well as among Ideas; tho' with this remarkable difference, that Ideas are associated by resemblance, contiguity, and causation; and impressions only by resemblance."

[2] *Ibid.*, p. 83.

[3] *Ibid.*, Sect. IX (p. 101): "From this reasoning, as well as from undoubted experience, we may conclude, that an association of Ideas, however necessary, is not alone sufficient to give rise to any passion.

'Tis evident, then, that when the mind feels the passion either of pride

The way in which HUME's *psychologized ideal of science destroys the conception of the freedom of the will in the sense of the mathematical ideal of science.*

In this entire psychological mechanism of "human nature" there remains no room for the freedom of the will. HUME's standpoint in this respect is quite different from that of LOCKE and LEIBNIZ.

LOCKE could leave some room to the freedom of the will in the indeterministic sense of a "liberum arbitrium indifferentiae" or "liberum arbitrium equilibrii", since he did not dissolve human self-hood and personality into a mechanism of psychical associations, and held to the dualism of reflection and sensation [1]. In HUME's psychologized system, such an Idea of freedom must be discarded equally with the conception, according to the mathematical science-ideal, that the freedom of the will consists in the fact that it is determined by clear and distinct thought.

The metaphysical bulwark of the rationalistic Humanist ideal of personality, i.e. the selfhood, concentrated in its mathematical thought, as a substance, as "res cogitans", had been destroyed by HUME's psychological criticism. And with equal force, the content of this ideal of personality (autonomous freedom) had to be sacrificed to the psychologized science-ideal. The "will" is therefore conceived of as a mere inner impression which we feel, when we consciously execute a new corporeal motion or produce a new Idea in our mind [2].

This psychical impression which we call "will" is as necessarily determined as are the movements of psychical phenomena. There is a necessary causal connection between human actions

---

or humility upon the appearance of a related object, there is, beside the relation or transition of thought, an emotion or original impression produc'd by some other principle."

[1] In his *Essay concerning Human Understanding* II, 2. Sect. 51, LOCKE found a place for the moral freedom and responsibility of personality in the "power a man has to *suspend his desires* and stop them from determining his will to any action, till he has examined, whether it be really of a nature in itself and consequences to make him happy or no." And he taught: *"The care of ourselves that we mistake not imaginary for real happiness, is the necessary foundation of our liberty."* In his Introduction (p. 16) to book II of HUME's *Treatise*, GREEN correctly observes, that this concession to the ideal of personality again evokes an intrinsic antinomy with LOCKE's ideal of science.

[2] *Treatise* II, Part. III, Sect. I (p. 181).

and their motives and the circumstances in which they arise. This necessity, however, is only comprehended in the sense of the natural laws of association, in the sense of constant sequences of similar motives and actions. It is not thought of in the sense of any hidden mechanical force or compulsion which proceeds from the impulses.

Hume was of the opinion that his psychological determinism could in no way be called materialistic, nor could be at all in conflict with religion. Rather he deemed his doctrine of the psychological necessity of human actions to be essential both for morality and religion[1]. Every other conception altogether destroys the Idea of law, not only of human laws, but of the divine as well.

It must be granted that on the basis of Hume's psychologized cosmonomic Idea no other solution is possible!

The prelude to the shift of primacy to the ideal of personality.

We have seen that Hume's psychologized epistemology dissolved the very foundations of the ideal of science and that of personality. Nevertheless, the fact that Hume subordinated theoretical mathematical thought to the absolutized psychical function of feeling and sensation can be considered as the prelude to the shift of primacy from the nature-motive to the freedom-motive.

In the beginning of his exposition concerning the motives of the will, Hume states in the clearest possible manner the contradiction which exists between his own ethical standpoint and that of the mathematical science-ideal: "Nothing is more usual in philosophy, and even in common life, than to talk of the combat of passion and reason, to give the preference to reason, and assert, that men are only so far virtuous as they conform themselves to its dictates. Every rational creature, 'tis said, is oblig'd to regulate his actions by reason; and if any other motive or principle challenge the direction of his conduct, he ought to oppose it, 'till it be entirely subdu'd, or at least brought to a conformity with that superior principle... In order to show the fallacy of all this philosophy, I shall endeavour to prove *first*, that reason alone can never be a motive to any action of the

---

[1] *Treatise* II, Part III, Sect. II (p. 189 ff.).

will; and *secondly*, that it can never oppose passion in the direction of the will" [1].

Reason, in the sense of the mathematical ideal of science of DESCARTES and LEIBNIZ, is expelled completely from its sovereign position as the ultimate rule of human actions: "reason is and ought to be, the slave of the passions, and can never pretend to any other office than to serve and obey them" [2].

Mathematics is of course useful in all mechanical technique, and arithmetic is utilized in nearly every art and in every occupation: "But 'tis not of themselves they have any influence...

A merchant is desirous of knowing the sum total of his accounts with any person: Why? but that he may learn what sum will have the same *effects*, in paying his debt, and going to market, as all the particular articles taken together. Abstract or demonstrative reasoning, therefore, never influences any of our actions but only as it directs our judgment concerning causes and effects" [3].

Even the causal natural scientific thought in which the mathematical ideal of science found the method to extend its postulate of continuity over the entire reality of experience cannot in itself influence nor activate the will. Reason only *discovers* the causal relations between the phenomena, but "where the objects themselves do not affect us, their connexions can never give them any influence; and 'tis plain, that as reason is nothing but the discovery of this connection, it cannot be by its means that the objects are able to affect us" [4]. Reason cannot motivate an action, because experience demonstrates, that action only arises from an emotion: "nothing can oppose or retard the impulse of passion but a contrary impulse."

Thus the rationalist prejudice is abandoned that the decisions of the will are determined by theoretical Ideas (whether clearly distinguished or confused).

> HUME withdraws morality from the science-ideal.
> Primacy of the moral feeling.

Now it is this which paves the way to HUME's own moral philosophy. It is not correct to say that HUME denied the normative

---

[1] *Treatise* II, Part III, Sect. III, p. 193.
[2] *Ibid.*, p. 195.
[3] *Ibid.*, p. 193/4.
[4] *Ibid.*, p. 194.

sense of ethics. On the contrary, no other Humanist philosopher before KANT[1] had pointed out so sharply the necessity of the distinction between that which "is" and that which "ought to be". And, even in HUME, this distinction implies the contrast between scientific thought and ethical action [2].

From this very distinction HUME drew the consequence that ethics is not capable of being proven logically-mathematically, thereby dealing a new blow to the mathematical ideal of science. His argument in support of this view is extremely interesting, since in his own way HUME laid bare the antinomy existing between the mathematical ideal of science and that of personality.

If logical mathematical thought is to be in a position to establish the norms of good and evil, then, according to HUME, either the character of virtue and vice must lie in certain relations between the objects, or they would have to be "matters of fact" which we would be able to discover by our scientific reasoning.

According to the dominant (Lockian) conception, the necessary

---

[1] To be sure, LEIBNIZ, too, makes a sharp distinction between what "is" and what "ought to be". Cf. his *Méditation sur la notion commune de la justice* [Meditation concerning the common notion of justice] in jur. vol. IIIa, Fol. 72—87; here he remarks against HOBBES: "Car autre chose est, ce qui se peut, autre chose ce qui se doit." [For what is possible is quite different from what ought to be].

However, in LEIBNIZ this does not mean, that ethical action would be independent of clear and distinct thought. On the contrary, as we have seen, he agrees in principle with DESCARTES' rationalist view of ethics, although in him this rationalism is mitigated by a mystical motive due to his conception of a "supra-natural" participation of human reason in the creative thought of God, which produces "love" and "piety". See KURT HILDEBRANDT, *Leibniz und das Reich der Gnade* [Leibniz and the kingdom of grace] (The Hague, Nijhoff, 1953), especially p. 299 ff.

I fear, however, HILDEBRANDT has exaggerated this mystical motive at the cost of a just valuation of LEIBNIZ' mathematical rationalism.

[2] *Treatise* III, Part. I, Sect. I (p. 245): "In every system of morality which I have hitherto met with, I have always remarked, that the author proceeds for some time in the ordinary way of reasoning, and establishes the being of a God, or makes observations concerning human affairs; when of a sudden I am surprised to find, that instead of the usual copulations of propositions, *is*, and *is not*, I meet no proposition, that is not connected with an *ought*, or an *ought not*. This change is imperceptible; but is, however, of the last consequence. For as this ought, or ought not, expresses some new relation or affirmation, it is necessary that it should be observed and explained;" cf. LAING on this point, op. cit. pp. 189 ff.

relations between the Ideas must be sharply distinguished from "matters of fact".

Thus, if it were true that virtue is discoverable through thought, it would have to be an object either of mathematical science which examines the relations between Ideas, or of empirical natural science. There is, according to Hume, no third activity of thought.

According to the dominating rationalist conception, however, only the first possibility can receive consideration. For it pretends that the norms of ethics are capable of being proven apriori, "more geometrico". And a mere "matter of fact" is not susceptible of such proof. When it is conceded, however, that virtue and vice consist in relations concerning which certainty can be attained or for which mathematical proof can be given, then only the four invariable philosophical relations of resemblance and contrast, and the grades in quantity and quality can be taken into consideration. Now, in this case one is immediately involved in inescapable absurdities. For since there is not a single one among the four relations just mentioned which could not just as well be applied to animals and plants, or even to lifeless objects, the consequence would be inescapable that even such things would have to be capable of being judged as moral subjects: "Resemblance, contrariety, degrees in quality, and proportions in quantity and number; all these relations belong as properly to matter, as to our actions, passions and volitions. 'Tis unquestionable, therefore, that morality lies not in any of these relations, nor the sense of it in their discovery" [1].

Hume was too keen a thinker to be blind to the fact that with the same sort of reasoning one could also indicate the intrinsic antinomy in his own psychologized view of morality.

In his system virtue and vice are derived from feelings of pleasure and pain, which have nothing to do with normative properties. He attempts to rescue himself from this antinomy by pointing out that the feeling of pleasure is only a general term which signifies very different "feelings". So the aesthetic feeling and the sensory feeling of taste are not mutually reducible the one to the other [2]. Nevertheless, Hume forgets that his theory of the mechanism of human nature destroys the foundation for all normative imputation. If the normative ethical distinctions

---

[1] *Treatise* III, Part. I, Sect. I (p. 241).
[2] *Ibid.*, p. 248.

are not to be derived from mathematical reason, the question arises, in what must their basis be sought? HUME answers: in the moral sense, an explanation which clearly betrays the influence of HUTCHESON. In HUME's system moral Ideas, just like other ideas, must be derived from "impressions". Each feeling has its particular impressions. If a particular moral feeling exists, there must also exist moral impressions which cannot be reduced to other sorts of impressions. What is the character of these moral impressions? "To have the sense of virtue is nothing but to feel a satisfaction of a particular kind from the contemplation of a character. The very *feeling* constitutes our praise or admiration. We go no further; nor do we inquire into the cause of the satisfaction. We do not infer a character to be virtuous, because it pleases; but in feeling, that it pleases after such a particular manner, we in effect feel that it is virtuous" [1].

Good and evil, therefore, are nothing but feelings of pleasure and pain of a particular moral character. This special character lies in the feeling of approval or disapproval that an act provokes in ourselves or others. However, in the final analysis, the motives of acts, even of moral acts, in HUME still remain a-normative. Acts are not performed on the ground of their morally good or bad character; they are hedonistically determined. But the *contemplation of the act* creates a particular satisfaction or feeling of pleasure, which is approbation or the feeling of virtue, from which the Idea of virtue is the copy. In consequence, it may be that the psychologized ideal of science still absorbs the personal moral freedom; but the *ratio*, in the sense of mathematical thought, is in any case rejected as the foundation of ethics and as the basis for the ideal of personality. The tendency to withdraw the ideal of personality from the stiffening grasp of the Humanistic science-ideal is clearly perceptible. Yet KANT was to be the first to undertake the *actio finium regundorum*.

> HUME's attack upon the rationalistic theory of Humanist natural law and upon its construction of the social contract. VICO and MONTESQUIEU.

HUME's break with the mathematical ideal of science of his rationalist predecessors is also evident from his noteworthy criticism of the entire rationalistic-Humanist doctrine of natural

---

[1] *Treatise* III, Part. I, Sect. II (p. 247).

law, and in particular from his criticism of its conception that the state was to be construed by means of one or more contracts between pre-social individuals. From the very beginning the nominalistic trait of the Humanistic ideal of science in its mathematical form manifested itself very clearly in this construction. According to its adherents, the political community is not to be founded on the substantial form of human nature, as the Aristotelian-Thomistic doctrine of natural law had done. Nominalist natural law can no longer ascribe ontological reality to the state, not even in an accidental sense. Even in HUGO GROTIUS, who externally follows the Aristotelian-Thomistic doctrine of the *appetitus socialis,* authority and obedience have no natural foundation. Both must be construed "more geometrico" out of the simplest elements, the free and autonomous individuals.

The construction of the social contract seemed to be the sole method to reconcile the postulate of the mathematical ideal of science and that of the Humanistic ideal of personality. For, whereas the former must lead to a construction of the state as an instrument of sovereign domination, the latter must require a justification of the modern concept of sovereignty, introduced by JEAN BODIN, in the face of the autonomous freedom of human personality. And the construction of the social contract seemed to satisfy both postulates. While for the rest HUME took a radical nominalistic standpoint, he nevertheless exercised a sharp criticism of this construction, because he correctly thought that by so doing he was able to strike a blow at the mathematical ideal of science. Thereby, in contradistinction to Cartesianism, HUME, by virtue of his historical-psychological method, came to stand on the side of VICO and MONTESQUIEU. And since the Whigs based their political views upon the mathematical doctrine of natural law, HUME's political affinity with the Tory party is also noteworthy in this connection. Over against the contract-theory HUME appealed to the psychical condition of primitive people. The latter certainly cannot comprehend obedience to political authority in terms of an abstract contract of individuals. Moreover, it bears witness to HUME's deeply penetrating insight into the weak side of the contract theories, when repeatedly he pointed out, that the obligation which arises out of an agreement is not of a natural but of a conventional character [1]. The contract,

---

[1] As I indicated in my series of treatises *"In the Struggle for a Christian*

therefore, cannot precede the establishment of an ordered community and the institutions of the state.

The historical side of HUME's criticism as he developed it in his *The Original Contract* and in his *An Enquiry concerning the Principles of Morals*, naturally did not strike at the heart of the contract theory. The latter — at least in its general tendencies — always wished to construe the justification for the state along the mathematical logical path. HUME, however, had repudiated the mathematical ideal of science. In keeping with his psychological ideal of science, the mathematical conception of the natural state is replaced by a psychological one corresponding to his theory of "human nature". In his treatise *The Original Contract* (in sharp contradistinction to his conception in the *Enquiry* [1]) HUME assumed, to be sure, an original equality of men, from which he concluded that there was an original consent of individuals by which they subjected themselves to authority. But this agreement is not to be understood — in the sense of the mathematical science-ideal — as a universal continuous basis for the authority of the rulers. According to HUME's psychologized conception of mathematics, exact concepts which go beyond sensory impressions (e.g. the concept of an exact measure of equality, the concept of the infinitesimal, the mathematical point etc.) are ungrounded. The same conclusion must be drawn with respect to the search for mathematically exact foundations for the state and the legal order. In HUME's psychologized theory of state and law the original agreement can only be understood psychologically and intermittently in terms of the impressions of necessity and utility which arise in a given situation for the sake of subjecting oneself to someone of eminent qualities. Such situations occur again and again, and, in direct proportion to the frequency of their re-occurrence, a custom of obedience is born out of the impression. In the further development of the state, however, the psychologically comprehended agreement of the

---

Politics", the contract theory was the very seed of dissolution within the rationalist doctrine of natural law. The conflict between the absolutist concept of state-sovereignty and the principles of natural law concerning freedom and equality of all men as such, was a document to the inner antinomy between the ideal of science and the ideal of personality within the Humanist theory of natural law. See also my *The Contest about the Concept of Sovereignty in Modern Jurisprudence and Political Science* (publ. by H. J. Paris, Amsterdam 1950).

[1] *Enquiry concerning the principles of Morals*, Sect. III, Part. II.

subjects is of no use as an explanatory principle. The factual basis of authority is only to be found in continually exercised force.

In answer to the question concerning the right of authority HUME points to the influence of time upon the human soul. From the feeling of utility arises the first psychical impulse to obey. When, however, a government has retained its power long enough to create constancy and stability in political life, there arises in the human soul an impression or custom which forms the foundation for the Idea of the right of the government, and personal interest and advantage are reduced to a subordinate value [1].

Thus HUME's psychologism conquered the strongest position in which the mathematical ideal of science had hitherto thought it could defend the freedom of the individual in the sense of the ideal of personality. Even the Humanistic doctrine of natural law caves in under his critique.

§ 7 - THE CRISIS IN THE CONFLICT BETWEEN THE IDEAL OF SCIENCE AND THAT OF PERSONALITY IN ROUSSEAU

In ROUSSEAU's philosophical world of thought the tension between the ideal of science and that of personality reached a religious crisis. In 1750, in answer to the question posed by the Academy of Dijon, which offered a prize for the best response, the Genevan autodidact sent in his treatise entitled *"Discours sur les sciences et les arts"*. This writing at one blow established his European renown. It signified a passionate attack upon the entire Humanistic civilization which was dominated by the rationalist science-ideal, and had trampled the rights of human personality to a natural development. From the very beginning the Humanistic ideal of science had implied a fundamental problem with respect to the relationship between scientific thought, stimulated by the Faustian passion for power,

---

[1] *Treatise* III, Part. II, Sect. X (p. 319): "Time alone gives solidity to their right" (viz. of the usurpers) "and operating gradually on the minds of men, reconciles them to any authority, and makes it seem just and reasonable... When we have been long accustom'd to obey any set of men, that general instinct or tendency, which we have to suppose a moral obligation attending loyalty, takes easily this direction... 'T is interest which gives the general instinct; but 't is custom which gives the particular direction."

and the autonomous freedom and value of human personality. In the soul of ROUSSEAU this problem attained such a tension, that he openly proclaimed the antinomy between the two polar motives of Humanist thought. He did not eschew the consequence of disavowing the science-ideal, in order to make possible the recognition of human personality as a moral aim in itself.

"If our sciences are vain in the object proposed to themselves, they are still more dangerous by the effects which they produce." So runs the judgment passed by ROUSSEAU on the science-ideal in his *Discours sur les sciences et les arts* [1]. And his writing ends with the pathetic exhortation to return into ourselves in all simplicity. Freed from the burden of science, we may learn true virtues from the principles which are inscribed in the heart of everybody. "O virtue! sublime knowledge of simple souls, should we need so much trouble and intellectual apparatus to know thee? Are not thy principles engraved in all hearts and does it not suffice for us in order to learn thy laws to return into ourselves and to hear the voice of conscience in the silence of the passions?" [2]

This was the passionate language of the re-awakened ideal of personality that called Humanistic thought to ultimate self-reflection, to reflection upon the religious motive of the freedom and autarchy of personality, through which the ideal of science was itself called into being.

In his *Discours sur l'origine de l'inégalite parmi les hommes* (Discourse on the origin of inequality among men) ROUSSEAU rejected the conception which sought the difference between man and animals primarily in thought. Only the consciousness of freedom and the feeling of moral power proves the spiritual character of the human soul: "Every animal has ideas, because it has senses; it even combines ideas up to a certain point... Consequently it is not so much the understanding which among the animals makes the specific distinction of man, but rather man's

---

[1] *Oeuvres compléts de J. J. Rousseau*, 1855 (ed. H. Bechold) II, p. 126: "Si nos sciences sont vaines dans l'objet qu'elles se proposent, elles sont encore plus dangereuses par les effets qu'elles produisent."

[2] *Ibid.*, p. 138: "O vertu! science sublime des âmes simples, faut-il donc tant de peines et d'appareil pour te connaître? Tes principes ne sont-ils pas gravés dans tous les coeurs? et ne suffit-il pas pour apprendre tes lois de rentrer en soi-même et d'écouter la voix de la conscience dans le silence des passions?"

quality of a free agent. Nature commands every animal, and the beast obeys. Man experiences the same impression, but he is aware of his freedom to yield or to resist; and it is especially in the consciousness of this freedom that the spirituality of his soul manifests itself; for physics explains in some fashion the mechanism of the senses and the formation of Ideas, but in the power of willing or rather choosing, and in the feeling of that power one finds only purely spiritual acts which in no single part are to be explained in terms of mechanical laws"[1].

Thus human thought was in a sensualistic sense degraded to a mere higher level of the animal associations of sensory Ideas, in order to permit all value of human personality to be concentrated in the feeling of freedom.

Nevertheless, in his democratic-revolutionary political philosophy, ROUSSEAU did not abandon the mathematical pattern of thought. By means of the latter he sought to maintain the natural rights of human personality in the face of the despotism of HOBBES' Leviathan, although the latter was philosophically construed by the same means of mathematical-juridical thought, namely the social contract.

ROUSSEAU sharply distinguishes the *"volonté générale"* from the *"volonté de tous"*, because the former can only be directed towards the common good. But in this "general will", in which "each of us brings into the community his person and all his power, in order that we may receive every member as an indivisible part of the whole"[2], personal freedom is again absorbed by the principle of majority[3]. The state-Leviathan

---

[1] *Oeuvres* II, p. 30/1: "Tout animal a des idées, puisqu'il a des sens; il combine même des idées jusqu'à un certain point... Ce n'est donc pas tant l'entendement qui fait parmi les animaux la distinction specifique de l'homme que sa qualité d'agent libre. La nature commande à tout animal, et la bête obéit. L'homme éprouve la même impression, mais il se reconnait libre d'acquiescer ou de résister; et c'est surtout dans la conscience de cette liberté que se montre la spiritualité de son âme, car la physique explique en quelque manière le mécanisme des sens et la formation des idées; mais dans la puissance de vouloir ou plutôt de choisir, et dans le sentiment de cette puissance, on ne trouve que des actes purement spirituels, dont on n'explique rien par les lois de la mécanique."

[2] *Du Contrat Social (Oeuvres* II), p. 274: "chacun de nous met en commun sa personne et toute sa puissance, afin que nous recevons encore chaque membre comme partie indivisible du tout."

[3] Op. cit., p. 325: "Hors ce contrat primitif, la voix du plus grand nombre oblige toujours tous les autres; c'est une suite du contrat même." [Except

construed both in HOBBES and in ROUSSEAU in accordance with the mathematical ideal of science which respects no limits, devours free personality in all its spheres of life. The introduction of the Idea of the "volonté générale" was actually meant in a normative sense. And in it personality was to regain its natural autonomous freedom in a higher form construed by mathematical thought. In fact, its introduction implied the absorption of free personality into a despotic construction issued from the condemned ideal of science. It was the picture of Leviathan, with its head cut off that formed the frontispiece of the first edition of *The Social Contract!*

Meanwhile — and this is the point in which ROUSSEAU had decidedly outgrown the spirit of the Enlightenment — the accent in his philosophy is definitely shifted to the ideal of personality. And the latter can no longer be identified with mathematical thought.

In HUME's philosophy the ideal of personality had already begun to revolt against the science-ideal by making moral feeling independent of the theoretical Idea. In ROUSSEAU feeling became the true seat of the Humanistic ideal of personality which had been robbed of its vitality by the hypertrophy of the science-ideal.

ROUSSEAU's religion of sentiment and his estrangement from HUME.

ROUSSEAU's bitterest attacks were directed against the rationalistic view of religion of the "Enlightenment". In it he correctly saw an attack upon the religious kernel of the Humanistic ideal of personality.

His proclamation of the natural religion of sentiment[1] was directed just as much against the materialism of the French Encyclopedists as against the deism of NEWTON's natural philosophy. ROUSSEAU never grew weary of telling his contemporaries that religion is not seated in the head, but in the "heart". He never grew tired contending that abstract science may not en-

---

for this original contract, the vote of the greatest number obliges always all the rest; this is a consequence of the very contract.]

[1] See the famous fourth book of his EMILE, where ROUSSEAU expounded his dualistic conception of human nature (sensory nature versus the feeling of freedom). I suspect that this conception influenced KANT's dualism.

croach upon the holy contents of human feeling. He combated the rationalistic associational psychology which had excluded the "soul" from its field of investigation. And his opposition was marked by a passionateness which can only be understood in terms of an ultimate religious reaction of the Humanistic ideal of personality against the tyranny of the ideal of science. Thus not only did he necessarily become estranged from the circle of the Encyclopedists but also from his earlier friend and protector DAVID HUME. For, no matter how ROUSSEAU could feel in agreement with HUME in his emancipation of the function of feeling from theoretical thought, yet in the final analysis, in HUME's absolutizing of the deterministic viewpoint of associational psychology, the ideal of science still dominated that of the sovereign personality.

Disillusionized, the passionate defender of the freedom of sovereign personality turned away from Western culture. The freedom of the sovereign personality ought to be recognized equally in all individuals, but Western culture was dominated in all the spheres of life by sovereign science, which was not in the first place concerned with personal freedom. ROUSSEAU sought consolation in the dream of a natural state of innocence and happiness which had been disturbed by modern culture.

Optimism and Pessimism in their new relation in ROUSSEAU.

The state of nature is no longer painted, as in HOBBES, in the shrill colours of a *"bellum omnium contra omnes"*. On the contrary, in his representation of the original state of mankind, ROUSSEAU revived the Stoic Idea of the "golden age". Perhaps he was influenced by such idealistic pictures of primitive society as were current at his time. But his conviction of the value of the primitive had undoubtedly deeper grounds in his anti-rationalist conception of human nature. ROUSSEAU's optimistic view of the original goodness of the latter differed radically from the optimistic life- and world-view in which the ideal of science held the supremacy.

Science has not made good its promise to human personality, it has not brought freedom to man, but slavery, inequality, and exploitation. Optimism and pessimism are the light and shadow in ROUSSEAU's picture of the state of nature and of culture; however, their rôle is completely the reverse of what it had been in HOBBES. With respect to the culture of the science-ideal ROUSSEAU was a pessimist. He was an optimist only in his belief in the free personality which will break the strait-jacket into which it was clapped by the rationalistic culture. It will build a new culture in which the sovereign freedom of man will shine forth in greater brilliance than in the uncorrupted state of nature. This new culture will find its foundation only in the divine value of personality.

Locke and Rousseau. The contrast between innate human rights and inalienable rights of the citizen.

In the natural state all individuals were free and equal but they remained individuals. Their inalienable human rights were formulated by Locke in opposition to the absolutistic doctrine of Hobbes. Nevertheless, Locke was a genuine figure of the "Enlightenment". He held fast to the optimistic faith that the domination of mathematical thought was the best guarantee of the freedom of personality.

Just as he resolved all complex Ideas into simple ones, so to him the free individual remained the central point of the civil state. Just as the entire preceding Humanistic doctrine of natural law, Locke construed the transition from the natural state to the civil state by means of the social contract. The citizens had already possessed their inalienable rights of freedom and private property in the natural state, but they needed the social contract to guarantee them by an organized power. And this was the sole intention of this contract in the system of Locke. The civil state is no more than a company with limited liability, designed for the continuation of the natural state under the protection of an authority. It is the constitutional state of the old liberalism, the state which has as its only goal the maintenance of the innate human rights of the individual.

Rousseau broke with this liberalistic conception. Just like the Stoics he did not consider the natural state of freedom and equality to be in itself the highest ideal. This situation is forever gone. A higher destiny calls humanity to the civil state. Only within the latter can the sovereign freedom of personality completely unfold in its divine value. Natural freedom ought to be elevated to the level of a higher, a normative Idea of freedom. The innate natural rights of men must be transformed into inalienable rights of the citizens. By means of the social contract the individual must surrender all of his natural freedom in order to get it back again in the higher form of the freedom of the citizen. To that end the social contract can no longer be conceived of in a formal sense, as HOBBES, PUFENDORF and even GROTIUS had done. For with these teachers of natural law, the original contract could in the final analysis even justify the abandonment of all freedom of personality. For them the construction of the social contract was not first and foremost orientated to the ideal of personality but to the mathematical science-ideal with its domination-motive. ROUSSEAU raises his flaming protest against this subjection of the value of personality to mathematical thought: "To give up one's liberty that is to give up one's quality of man, the rights of humanity, even one's duties. These words *slavery* and *right* are contradictory, they exclude one another mutually" [1].

Freedom, just as equality, is an inalienable human right that only can be abandoned in its natural form, in order to be regained in the higher form of citizenship. There is only a single specific form of association which secures this freedom. Therefore, this form is the only lawful one.

Thus in ROUSSEAU the transition from the natural state to the civil state became the fundamental problem of guaranteeing the sovereign freedom of personality in the only legitimate form of association.

> The ideal of personality acquires primacy in ROUSSEAU's construction of the social contract.

This is the new motive in ROUSSEAU, and therefore he could rightly oppose his doctrine concerning the social contract to the earlier Humanistic theories of natural law: the ideal of personality has acquired primacy over the ideal of science. In his famous work *Du Contrat Social ou Principes du Droit Politique* he formulated the problem in question as follows: "To find a form of association which with all the common power defends and protects the person and goods of every member and by means of which each one uniting himself with all, nevertheless is only obedient to himself and remains as free as before" [1].

---

[1] *Du Contrat Social* I, chap. IV (Oeuvres II), p. 269: "Renoncer à sa liberté, c'est renoncer à sa qualité d'homme, aux droits de l'humanité, même à ses devoirs." Ces mots *esclavage* et *droit* sont contradictoires, ils s'excluent mutuellement."

[1] *Ibid.*, chap. VI (Oeuvres II), p. 273: "Trouver une forme d'association qui défende et protège de toute la force commune la personne et les biens

ROUSSEAU intended to solve this problem through his "social contract" which, in order to be valid, must include precisely the clause that each individual delivers himself with all his natural rights to all, collectively and thus through becoming subject to the whole by his participation in the "general will" gets back all his natural rights in a higher juridical form: "For in the first place, if every one gives himself entirely, the condition is equal for all; and if the condition is equal for all, nobody is interested in rendering it onerous for the others" [2].

According to ROUSSEAU, the inalienable right of freedom maintains itself in the inalienable sovereignty of the people, which can never be transferred to a magistrate. The sovereign will of the people is the general will, which expresses itself in legislation. As such it is to be distinguished sharply from the "volonté de tous".

For the "volonté générale" should be directed exclusively toward the general interest; it is therefore incompatible with the existence of private associations between the state and the individual, because they foster particularism. At this point ROUSSEAU appeals expressly to PLATO's "ideal state".

Public law, formed by the general will, does not recognize any counter-poise in private spheres of association. The "social contract" is the only juridical basis for all the rights of the citizens. Thus the construction of the general will becomes the lever of an unbridled absolutism of the legislator. "Just as nature gives every man an absolute power over all his limbs, so the social contract gives the body politic an absolute power over all its members; and it is this same power which, directed by the general will, bears the name of sovereignty" [3].

ROUSSEAU did observe indeed, that there was an inner tension between his doctrine of the "volonté générale" and the individual freedom of human personality.

WOLFF's basic law for the state: *"Salus publica suprema lex*

---

de chaque associé, et par laquelle chacun, s'unissant à tous, n'obéisse pourtant qu'à lui même, et reste aussi libre qu'auparavant."

[2] "Car, premièrement, chacun se donnant tout entier, la condition est égale pour tous; et la condition étant égale pour tous, nul n'a intérêt de la rendre onéreuse aux atres."

[3] "Comme la nature donne à chaque homme un pouvoir absolu sur tous ses membres, le pacte social donne au corps politique un pouvoir absolu sur tous les siens; et c'est ce même pouvoir qui, dirigé par la volonté générale, porte le nom de souverainité."

esto", was to be reconciled with LOCKE's doctrine of the inalienable human rights. WOLFF had openly acknowledged that there was an insoluble antinomy between these two poles of Humanistic political theory.

In ROUSSEAU's theory, therefore, the question as to the mutual relationship between the natural rights of man and the rights of the citizen became a problem of essential importance. "Besides the public person," so he observes, "we have to consider the private persons which compose it, and whose life and liberty are by nature independent of it. Consequently the question is that we should *well distinguish the rights of the citizens and those of the sovereign, and the duties which the former have to discharge in their quality of subjects from the natural right which they ought to enjoy in their quality of men*" [1]. According to him it is beyond dispute, that in the social contract every individual transfers to the state only as much of his natural power, his possessions, and freedom, as is required for "the common good" of the community.

The "common good", and so also the "general will", do not recognize any particular individuals, but only the whole.

> The antinomy between the natural rights of man and the rights of the citizen. ROUSSEAU's attempt to solve it.

Proceeding from this principle ROUSSEAU thought he had discovered the way by which "natural human rights", as private rights, could also be maintained uncurtailed in the civil state.

The first principle of the "general will' that follows from the fact that the latter only can aim at the general interest, is namely the absolute equality of all citizens with respect to the demands of the community.

As soon as the sovereign lawgiver (the people) would favour certain citizens above others, so that special privileges would be accorded (recall the privileges of forum, freedom from taxation etc. of nobility and clergy under the ancient regime), the

---

[1] *Du Contrat Social* II, IV "Des bornes du pouvoir souverain" (Oeuvres II, p. 286): "Outre la personne publique, nous avons à considerer les personnes privées qui la composent, et dont la vie et la liberté sont naturellement indépendantes d'elle. Il s'agit donc de *bien distinguer les droits respectifs des citoyens et du souverain, et les devoirs qu'ont à remplir les premiers en qualité de sujets, du droit naturel dont ils doivent jouir en qualité d'hommes.*"

"general will" would be transmuted into a private or particular will and the sovereign would exceed the limits of its competency [1].

For the clause of the "social contract", upon which all sovereignty in the state is based, contains unchangeably the principle of equality of all citizens with respect to the public interest. In other words, the "general will", because of its unchangeable inner nature, can never have a particular object. This is the significance of ROUSSEAU's concept of statute law which is quite different from the formal one. And it is also different from the so-called "material concept of statute law" in the sense of a positive juridical rule touching the rights and duties of the citizens, as understood by the positivistic German school of LABAND in the XIXth century.

According to ROUSSEAU, a real public statute *(loi)* can never regulate a particular interest. And it cannot issue from an individual by virtue of a seignorial right: "Besides, because the public statute unites in itself the universality of the will and that of the object, it is evident that an order issued by any individual whatsoever in virtue of his own right, is not at all a statute; even an order of the sovereign concerning a private object is no more a statute but a decree, nor an act of sovereignty but of magistracy" [2]. In other words, not everything which possesses the form of a statute is a statute in a material sense.

There are formal statutes which are not real ones, and conse-

---

[1] *Op. cit.* III, Chap. IV (p. 286: "On voit par là que le pouvoir souverain, tout absolu, tout sacré, tout inviolable qu'il est, ne passe ni peut passer les bornes des conventions générales, et que tout homme peut disposer pleinement de ce qui lui a été laissé de ses biens et de sa liberté par des conventions; de sorte que le souverain n'est jamais en droit de charger un sujet plus qu'un autre, parce qu'alors l'affaire devenant particulière, son pouvoir n'est plus compétent." ["From this it is seen that the sovereign power, however absolute, however sacred, however inviolable it may be, does not and cannot surpass the limits of the general conventions, and that every man can completely dispose of what these latter have left him of his goods and of his liberty; so that the sovereign has never the right to charge a subject more than another, because in this case the matter becomes a particular one and his power is no longer competent"].

[2] "On voit encore que la loi réunissant l'universalité de la volonté et celle de l'objet, ce qu'un homme, quelqu'il puisse être, ordonne de son chef n'est point une loi: ce qu'ordonne même le souverain sur un objet particulier n'est pas non plus une loi, mais un décret; ni un acte de souveraineté, mais de magistrature."

quently which are not the expression of the sovereign general will, but are only decrees, private acts of the magistrate which as such are not binding, unless they give effect to the „loi". Thus it seems that in ROUSSEAU the inalienable human rights as private subjective rights are in no way absorbed in the general will, since within the sphere of private law they cannot be assailed by arbitrary decrees or acts of a magistrate. But as we have seen, human rights in the civil state have changed their ground of validity. Now this ground lies exclusively in the social contract. In other words, the juridical source of private and public rights is, in the civil state, one and the same, and on the condition that the formal principle of equality and generality is respected, the general will is omnipotent. Consequently, in the civil state private human rights can only exist by the grace of the general will.

All limits of competency must yield to the general will of the sovereign. ROUSSEAU himself wrote that the judgment concerning what the public interest demands belongs exclusively to the sovereign people. Moreover, he accepted the well-known construction, adhered to by the nominalistic doctrine of natural law since MARSILIUS OF PADUA up until and inclusive of KANT, according to which the general will, in which every citizen encounters his own will, cannot do any injustice to any one: *volenti non fit injuria!*

The limits of the competency of the legislator which ROUSSEAU constructed are not real ones, since they are neither grounded on the inner nature and structure of the different social relationships, nor on the modal structure of the juridical aspect, but have been deduced from the abstract principle of equality and generality which neglects all structural differences in social reality.

> The origin of this antinomy is again to be found in the tension between the ideal of science and that of personality.

In his undoubtedly ingenious construction of the relation between public and private interest, it is once again the mathematical ideal of science that pretends to guarantee the value of personality. And in the final analysis the "sovereign personality" is again sacrificed to this science-ideal. ROUSSEAU's famous expression: "On les forcera d'être libre" (they must be forced to be free) soon would become the watchword under which the legions of the French revolution were to bring to the nations revolutionary freedom and equality, although ROUSSEAU himself was impatient of every revolution. But it was the expression of the unsoluble antinomy between the ideal of science and that of personality which in ROUSSEAU's doctrine of the social contract had reached its highest tension.

The reawakened ideal of personality had in ROUSSEAU's religion of sentiment reacted spontaneously against the science-ideal. Yet, finally it submitted again to the mathematical construction of the latter. The fulminant protest, however, that out of the religious depth of ROUSSEAU's contradictory personality sounded against the supremacy of scientific thought, was to summon mightier spirits than he to fight for the supremacy of the ideal of personality.

CHAPTER IV

THE LINE OF DEMARCATION BETWEEN THE IDEALS OF SCIENCE AND OF PERSONALITY IN KANT. THE (CRITICAL) DUALIST IDEALISTIC TYPE OF TRANSCENDENTAL GROUND-IDEA UNDER THE PRIMACY OF THE HUMANIST IDEAL OF PERSONALITY

§ 1 - INTRODUCTION. THE MISCONCEPTION OF KANT'S TRANSCENDENTAL IDEALISM AS THE PHILOSOPHIC EXPRESSION OF THE SPIRIT OF THE REFORMATION

In the preceding chapters we have only given a sketch of the main lines of development of the basic antinomy in the transcendental ground-Idea of Humanistic thought during the period in which primacy was ascribed to the science-ideal. Our investigation ended in an examination of Rousseau's philosophy in which the first violent reaction on the part of the religious freedom-motive manifested itself. In the light of this previous development the philosophic system of IMMANUEL KANT must be viewed as inaugurating a new phase in Humanistic thought: namely, the phase of "transcendental freedom-idealism".

This phase is typified by several characteristic features: The ideal of personality finally wrested itself free from the tyranny of the science-ideal. Primacy is now definitely acknowledged as belonging to the former and the ideal of science is limited to the world of sense-phenomena. The root of human personality is sought in the normative ethical function of its free will. In addition this new phase is marked by the growing self-reflection of Humanism upon the religious foundations of its philosophic attitude.

> KRONER's view of the relation of KANT's transcendental idealism to the Christian religion.

It is typical of the lack of a critical view of historical-philosophical connections that in the XXth century KANT has often been characterized as the first to have expressed the intrinsic spirit of the Christian faith within a so-called philosophical life- and world-view. In this respect KANT's "critical" idealism is sharply contrasted with medieval Christian thought. For example, the Hegelian philosopher RICHARD KRONER states: "The impact of Greek concepts on Medieval Christian thought in its totality was overwhelming, so that the true essence and the real depth of the Christian faith could not find here its full expression within a philosophical view of the world. It is especially KANT and German Idealism that deserve credit for having performed this enormous task, which is of unique importance in the history of the world. It was here for the first time that the idealism of the I-ness, surpassing that of the $\iota\delta\epsilon\alpha\iota$ and $\epsilon\check{\iota}\delta\eta$, was opposed to the latter. Here at last the attempt was successful to conceive of God no longer as an objective Idea, as Pure Form, as First Cause and Substance, but rather out of the depth of the ethical-religious life" [1].

> Is KANT the philosopher of the Reformation?
> PRZYWARA.

Such a statement strongly attests to a complete lack of insight into the antithesis between the really Christian and Humanistic ground-motives of philosophical thought.

It is very much to be regretted that some Roman-Catholic thinkers foster this basic misconception by seeking in German idealism since KANT the philosophical expression of the view developed by the Reformation with respect to the relation of God and His creation. It is further contended that the Roman Catholic conception, as embodied in Thomism, forms the real

---

[1] RICHARD KRONER: *Von Kant bis Hegel* I (1921) s. 45: "Während das gesamte christliche Denken des Mittelalters dem übermächtigen Anprall der Griechischen Begriffe gegenüber es nicht vermochte, das wahre Wesen, die eigene Tiefe des christlichen Glaubens innerhalb der philosophischen Weltanschauung zur vollen Geltung zu bringen, ist durch KANT und den deutschen Idealismus diese weltgeschichtliche Aufgabe gelöst worden. Hier zuerst wird dem Idealismus der $\iota\delta\epsilon\alpha\iota$ und $\epsilon\check{\iota}\delta\eta$ der ihn überragende Idealismus des Ich entgegengesetzt. Hier zuerst gelingt es, Gott, statt als objective Idee, als reine Form, als erste Ursache und Substanz, vielmehr aus der Tiefe des sittlich-religiösen Lebens heraus zu begreifen."

philosophical antipode to this idealism [1]. We shall return to this point, but in passing, it is well to note, that this view of the philosophical antithesis between the Reformation and Roman Catholicism simply stems from the immanence-standpoint. Consequently, it can not do justice to the real situation.

KANT is not the philosopher of the evangelical idea of freedom; his philosophy is separated from the Biblical spirit of the Reformation by the irreconcilable cleft between the Christian and Humanistic ground-motives. Naturally this does not exclude the fact that KANT has been *historically* influenced by Puritanism and Pietism in his ethical and theological conceptions. But the very spirit and transcendental ground-Idea of his critical idealism is ruled by the Humanistic motive of nature and freedom. And the latter cannot be reconciled to the genuine Biblical ground-motive of the Reformation. All attempts at synthesis are born out of a lack of insight into the religious foundation of KANT's philosophy, and into the integral and radical character of the Biblical ground-motive.

It cannot be denied that criticistic idealism has deeply influenced the philosophical thought of Protestantism. But this is not to be explained in terms of the religious spirit of the Reformation. On the contrary, it betrays the invasion of the scholastic spirit of accommodation, originating from the religious ground-motive of nature and grace in its dualist nominalistic conception. And we have shown that this very ground-motive has impeded the inner reformation of philosophical thought.

In KANT's philosophy, it is actually *the Humanistic ideal of personality* which awakens from its lethargy and causes Humanism to become conscious of the ὑπόθεσις of its philosophic attitude. ROUSSEAU's religion of feeling could only signify a transitional stage in this course of development.

The deepest tendencies of the Humanistic ideal of personality could not reveal themselves in the psychical sphere of feeling which in KANT belongs to the realm of "nature" and "heteronomy". They could only find an adequate expression in a fundamental freedom-idealism which transcends "nature" as the particular domain of the science-ideal.

In KANT's critical ethics the "Idea" is the expression of the subjective autonomy of the rational and moral personality. And

---

[1] See for example, the work of ERICH PRZYWARA, *Thomas oder Hegel*, in Logos Bnd. XV, Heft I, 1926, p. 12.

as the ideal subject this personality is itself the final source of the categorical ethical imperative. Henceforth, the Idea is identified in an increasingly greater degree with the religious totality of meaning and with the very origin of the temporal cosmos [1].

The Idea of freedom as both the religious totality and origin of meaning: HÖNINGSWALD.

In a pregnant statement, RICHARD HÖNIGSWALD summarized this development in the conception of the "Idea", as the embodiment of the Humanistic ideal of personality which was becoming self-conscious: "so the course of the argument always urges us again to go back to the classical concept of the Idea: the latter signifies as ἀνυπόθετον totality and process, end and beginning, content and norm, datum and task. As the point of indifference of every question and every answer the Idea embodies the highest form of necessity. But this means neither that the Idea compels something else, nor that the former is subjected to a constraint strange to itself: the Idea itself is this necessity. For this very reason, however, it signifies also in the deepest and most complex sense of the word *freedom*. The Idea is, as BAUCH in a striking fashion has called it, the Λόγος of each phenomenon; the meaning of the concept, the problem of the being of the phenomenon. As an unbreakable bond it embraces world and experience, community and truth, language and object.

"Orienting itself to the world, the Idea furnishes itself with the organon of its working and only through this working it *is*. It is the Spirit which never has been and never will be; for the Idea simply "is": that is to say, it is, as HEGEL has said, "present", consequently, "essentially *now*". It is not *in* time, and neither *outside* it. For the Idea itself *is* time; not, to be sure, the mere concept of its order, not only NEWTON's "*tempus, quod aequabiliter fluit*", but time in the fulness of its development, "standing time", time as totality, i.e. as eternity(!). In this — (and only in this conception) — the Idea means *Being* itself; Being, free from

---

[1] Strictly speaking this identification of Origin and totality of meaning cannot be correct. For, as we saw in the Introduction, the Origin necessarily transcends meaning. In the Prolegomena I pointed out, that the absolutization of the transcendental idea in idealism, actually issues from the religious *ground-motive* that makes this philosophy possible. In the transcendent religious sphere the *idea* can never maintain itself as the actual origin.

the notion of a mysterious "entity", Being as *Meaning,* grounded in itself, which eternally renews and forms itself, thereby, however, imposes and at the same time realizes — the highest conditions of the concept of the "Gegenstand". Meaning was "in the beginning"; and it stands at the end. In Meaning beginning and end are one. *For meaning is the totality"* [1].

The course of development in the conception of the Idea in this sense commences in KANT's *Critique of Practical Reason.* It continues in dialectical tension in FICHTE, SCHELLING, and in Romanticism and it reaches its completion in HEGEL's absolute idealism.

It is my intention to sketch this course of development in the light of the inner dialectic within the transcendental ground-Idea of Humanistic thought. Our discussion will center around the extremely complicated evolution of the thought of KANT and FICHTE. And from this evolution we shall seek to explain the intrinsic necessity of subsequent developments.

---

[1] R. HÖNINGSWALD: *Vom Problem der Idea* (The problem of the Idea), Logos Bnd. XV, Heft 3 (1926) p. 301: "So drängt der Beweisgang immer aufs neue zurück zu dem klassischen Begriff der Idee: Sie bedeutet als ἀνυπόθετον Inbegriff und Prozess, Letztheit und Anfang, Gehalt und Norm, Gegebenheit und Aufgabe auf einmal. Der Indifferenzpunkt jeder Frage und jeder Antwort, verkörpert die Idee die höchste Form der Notwendigkeit. Aber weder bedeutet das, dasz die Idee ein anderes bezwingt, noch auch dasz etwa sie fremdem Zwang unterliege: sie, die Idee, selbst *ist* diese Notwendigkeit. Ebendarum aber bedeutet sie auch im tiefsten und komplexesten Sinn des Wortes *Freiheit.* Sie ist, wie Bauch es einmal treffend nennt, der λόγος jeglicher Erscheinung; der Sinn des Begriffs, das Problem des Seins der Erscheinung. Ein unzerreiszbares Band, umfängt sie Welt und Erleben, Gemeinschaft und Wahrheit, Sprache und Object.

"Die Idee schafft sich an der Welt das Organ ihres Wirkens, weil sie selbst in ihrem Werk und durch dieses Werk allein ist. Sie ist der Geist, der nie gewesen ist und nie sein wird; denn sie "ist" schlechthin: d.h. sie ist, mit den Worten HEGELS, "präsent" also "wesentlich itzt". Sie steht nicht *in* der *Zeit;* aber auch nicht auszerhalb dieser. Denn sie selbst *ist* ja die Zeit; nicht freilich der blosze Gedanke ihrer Ordnung, nicht nur NEWTON's "tempus, quod aequabiliter fluit", sondern die Zeit in der Fülle ihrer Gestaltung, die "stehende" Zeit, die Zeit als Ganzheit, d.h. als Ewigkeit(!). In diesem, und nur im diesem Verstande bedeutet die Idee das *Sein* selbst; das Sein, frei von dem Gedanken an eine dunkele "Entität", als der sich ewig erneuernde und gestaltende, gerade damit aber die höchsten Bedingungen des Gegenstandsgedankens fordernde und zugleich erfüllende, in sich selbst gegründete *Sinn.* Der Sinn war "im Anfang"; und er steht am Ende. Im Sinn sind Anfang und Ende *eins. Denn der Sinn ist das Ganze."*

§ 2 - THE DEVELOPMENT OF THE CONFLICT BETWEEN THE IDEAL OF PERSONALITY AND THAT OF SCIENCE IN THE FIRST PHASE OF KANT'S THOUGHT UP UNTIL HIS INAUGURAL ORATION OF 1770

All the philosophical motives of Humanistic thought during the rationalistic and transitional periods were focused in KANT's mind. In his struggle for release it was the mutual tension of these motives that gave rise to a new conception of the Humanist transcendental ground-Idea, which aimed at saving both the ideal of science and that of personality by bringing against them the *actio finium regundorum*.

The motives of the preceding Humanistic philosophy. The manner in which KANT wrestles with their mutual tension. The influence of Pietism.

Even in his pre-critical period KANT struggled with various mutually antagonistic motives. In the main they included: the proud structure of NEWTON's system of natural science, in whose philosophic attitude the Enlightenment found the incarnation of its own spirit; the Leibnizian-Wolffian metaphysics of the mathematical ideal of science, in which the free human personality was proclaimed to be a function of creative mathematical thought and a relatively perfect stage of development in the system of monads; the epistemological psychologism of HUME, which was detrimental to both the ideal of personality and that of science; and, last but not least, ROUSSEAU's passionate plea for the liberation of the Humanistic ideal of personality from the tyrannical domination of the science-ideal.

In addition, the religious influence of Puritanism and Pietism, that had impressed itself on his entire education, continued to rule KANT's rigorous attitude with respect to sensory human nature, without having any affinity with the Biblical conception of sin. In his transition to the critical standpoint this influence was to acquire a conclusive significance.

No Humanistic thinker previous to KANT had struggled so intensely with the inner polarity in the basic structure of the Humanistic cosmonomic Idea. No one had understood the religious significance of the ideals of science and of personality as he did.

His "fondness of metaphysics" had its deepest root in the hope that he would be able to find a scientific foundation for his moral and religious convictions. Yet, even in his pre-critical period, under the influence of HUME and especially of ROUSSEAU, he acquired the insight that the speculative metaphysics of the mathematical science-ideal was necessarily incompetent to aid him in the fulfilment of his desire. Even in this phase he became confident that the sovereign freedom of human personality is not to be grasped in the categories of mathematical natural scientific thought.

In his natural scientific conception, KANT remained a faithful adherent of the ideal of science; his reverence for the spirit of the "Enlightenment".

After all, KANT was from the very beginning an enthusiastic follower of this very science-ideal. He had been so captivated by the spirit of the "Enlightenment" that even in his critical period he still spoke of it with an extreme reverence. His short answer to the question "What is Enlightenment?", given in 1784, begins with his confession of faith in the Humanistic Idea of science: "Enlightenment is the departure of man from his self-incurred blame of minority. Minority is the inability to use one's understanding without the direction of another... *Sapere aude!* Pluck up courage to use your own understanding! this is consequently the device of the Enlightenment." No church can contractually bind sovereign human thought to a dogma: "I say: this is quite impossible. Such a contract drawn up in order to keep mankind for ever from all further enlightenment, is simply null and void" [1].

Even the inception of KANT's philosophical development was characterized by a strong faith in the science-ideal in its mecha-

---

[1] KANT's Werke (Groszherzog Wilhelm Ernst Ausg.), Bnd. I, pp. 163 and 167. Henceforth I shall cite from this edition. I shall only use the edition of CASSIRER in order to supplement.

In the German text the quoted passages read as follows: "*Aufklärung ist der Ausgang des Menschen aus seiner selbstverschuldeten Unmündigkeit. Unmündigkeit ist das Unvermögen, sich seines Verstandes ohne Leitung eines Anderen zu bedienen... Sapere aude! Habe Mut, dich deines eigenen Verstandes zu bedienen! ist also des Wahlspruch der Aufklärung...*" Keine Kirche kann "berechtigt sein, sich eidlich auf ein gewisses unveränderliches Symbol zu verpflichten, um so eine unaufhörliche Obervormundschaft über jedes seiner Glieder, und vermittelst ihrer über das Volk zu führen, und diese sogar zu verewigen. Ich sage: das ist ganz unmöglich. Ein solcher Kontrakt, der auf immer alle weitere Aufklärung vom Menschengeschlechte abzuhalten geschlossen würde, ist schlechterdings null und nichtig."

nistic conception. In his hypothesis concerning the origin of the planetary system, developed in the natural scientific treatise of his first period *Allgemeine Naturgeschichte des Himmels* (1755), he extended this mechanistic conception to the most extreme consequences. Here he repeated the proud motto of Descartes' work *"Le Monde"*, in which the passion to dominate nature found its classic expression: "Give me matter, I will build a world from it" [1].

Throughout the rest of his life Kant remained faithful to this science-ideal. He never repudiated the spirit of Newton whom he admired so strongly.

Even when Hume's epistemological psychologism temporarily gained the ascendency in Kant's thought, the resulting sceptical attitude could only momentarily shake his firmly established faith in the sovereignty of mathematical and natural scientific thought over the entire "empirical" reality "in space and time".

Kant's radical doubt was limited to the sovereignty of mathematical thought insofar as it involved itself with the most profound questions of life and of the world. It arose only with respect to the *metaphysics* of the mathematical science-ideal. Kant abandoned the latter insofar as he sought a definite answer to the questions in which the ideal of personality was directly involved.

The influence of Rousseau and Hume.

At this point he was deeply moved by Rousseau's proclamation of the freedom of human personality from its subjection to science.

Windelband correctly sought in the influence of Rousseau a decisive turning-point in Kant's philosophical thought. Through Rousseau's influence, indeed, the division between the theoretical and the practical element in his philosophy was accomplished in an ever increasingly radical fashion [2].

---

[1] Preface, *Allgem. Naturgesch. des Himmels* (General natural history of the Heaven), W.W. Bnd. II, pp. 267: "Gebet mir Materie, ich will eine Welt daraus bauen." To which Kant added: "das ist, gebet mir Materie, ich will euch zeigen, wie eine Welt daraus entstehen soll" ["that is, give me matter, I will show you how from it a world is to proceed."]

[2] *Tr.'s note:* By employing our terminology, this division can be more accurately expressed as the division between the ideal of science and that of personality.   D. H. F.

The decisive influence of ROUSSEAU upon KANT's conception of the value of personality clearly appears from the famous treatise entitled *"Träume eines Geistersehers erläutert durch Träume der Metaphysik"* (Dreams of a visionary explained by dreams of metaphysics) (1766). KANT himself bore witness to the revolution in his thinking in his statement: "I myself am an investigator by nature. I feel all the force of the thirst after knowledge and the restless urge to make progress therein, but also the satisfaction at every advance. There was a time when I believed that all this could be to the honour of mankind and I disdained the mob that do not know anything. ROUSSEAU has set me right. This blind preference is disappearing; I learn how to honour men, and I would esteem myself much more useless than the common labourers, if I did not believe, that this view can give to all the rest a value on which to found the rights of the human race"[1].

It is the voice of the ethical and religious spirit of ROUSSEAU's *Discours sur les sciences et les arts"* that we hear in this remarkable writing[2].

In the *"Pratical conclusion from the whole treatise"* KANT writes: "But true wisdom is the companion of simplicity, and because with it the heart"(here taken in the sense of moral feeling) "lays down the law to the understanding, it generally renders the elaborate equipment of learning superfluous, and its goals do not need such means that can never be in the power of all men." "When science has run its course, it naturally arrives at the point of a modest distrust and, angry with itself, it says: *How many things there are which I do not understand*. But reason ripened to wisdom by experience speaks in the mouth of SOCRATES in the midst of the wares of an annual fair with a

---

[1] "Ich bin selbst aus Neigung ein Forscher. Ich fühle den ganzen Durst nach Erkenntnis und die begierige Unruhe, darin weiter zu kommen, oder auch die Zufriedenheit bei jedem Fortschritte. Er war eine Zeit, da ich glaubte, dieses alles könnte die Ehre der Menschheit machen und ich verachtete den Pöbel, der von nichts weisz. ROUSSEAU hat mich zurecht gebracht. Dieser verblendete Vorzug verschwindet; ich lerne die Menschen ehren, und würde mich viel unnützer finden, als die gemeinen Arbeiter, wenn ich nicht glaubte, dasz diese Betrachtung allen übrigen einen Wert geben könnte, die Rechte der Menschheit herzustellen."

[2] See *Traüme*, first part, chapt. 2, p. 115. (W.W. Vol. I) in which the moral motives "which move the human heart" are empirically reduced to "moral feeling".

cheerful mind: *How many things there are that I do not need at all!"* [1].

Rousseau's *Discours* also ended in this strain. With this statement the domination of the mathematical science-ideal over the ideal of personality in Kant's thought was definitely broken.

For in his humorous criticism of the "visionary" Swedenborg, Kant turned against the entire rationalistic metaphysics. He actually dealt a blow to the metaphysics of the Humanist science-ideal, as conceived of by Leibniz and Wolff and to which he himself had formerly adhered. Henceforth, to Kant, this metaphysics lost the right to speak on questions of morals and religion.

Just as in Rousseau and in Hume, the ideal of personality in Kant, though only for a time, withdrew into the function of feeling. Henceforth, under the influence of Hume, theoretical metaphysics acquired in an ever increasing degree the positive significance of a critical theory concerning the foundations and limits of mathematical knowledge of nature.

Even in the so-called "empirist" phase of Kant's philosophical development, the influence of Hume was only restricted in scope. Kant was no more capable of embracing definitively Hume's sceptical attitude with regard to the foundations of the mathematical science-ideal, than he was of following Rousseau's complete degradation of the latter.

He never took seriously Hume's attempt to establish the ground of the natural scientific judgment of causality in the laws of association which pertain to the connection of our successive psychical Ideas.

Kant was soon to assign to theoretical metaphysics the task of founding the objective universal validity of mathematical natural scientific thought in opposition to Hume's sceptical criticism.

---

[1] *Ibid.*, p. 159 and p. 155: "Allein die wahre Weisheit ist die Begleiterin der Einfalt, und da bei ihr das Herz (read "das sittliche Gefühl"!) dem Verstande die Vorschrift gibt, so macht sie gemeiniglich die grosze Zurüstungen der Gelehrsamkeit entbehrlich, und ihre Zwecke bedürfen nicht solcher Mittel, die nimmermehr in aller Menschen Gewalt sein können." "Wenn die Wissenschaft ihren Kreis durchlaufen hat, so gelangt sie natürlicherweise zu dem Punkte eines bescheidenen Mistrauens und sagt, unwillig über sich selbst: *Wie viel Dinge gibt es doch, die ich nicht einsehe!* Aber die durch Erfahrung gereifte Vernunft, welche zur Weisheit wird, spricht in dem Munde des Sokrates mitten unter den Waren eines Jahrmarkts mit heiteren Seele: *Wie viel Dinge gibt es doch, die ich alle nicht brauche!*"

At the same time, however, in opposition to rationalistic metaphysics, he sought definitely to limit mathematical and causal thinking to the sensory-aspect of experience.

I shall now endeavour to present a more detailed examination of these different phases in KANT's development up to his famous inaugural oration.

KANT's first period: KANT as an independent supporter of the metaphysics of LEIBNIZ and WOLFF. The primacy of the mathematical science-ideal in the first conception of his transcendental ground-Idea.

From the very beginning KANT was conscious of a certain discrepancy between mathematics and metaphysics in the sense in which the latter was defended by the Leibnizian-Wolffian school. Even in his *Physische Monadologie* (1756), he expounded the difference between the Leibnizian metaphysics and the mathematical conception of the problem of space.

In the discourse with which he began his career as special university lecturer in philosophy, KANT opposed WOLFF's attempt to derive the principle of causality from the logical *principium contradictionis*. This discourse, KANT's first metaphysical treatise, was entitled *de Principiorum primorum cognitionis metaphysicae nova dilucidatio* (1755). It attacked the Wolffian conception with CRUSIUS' distinction between "logical ground" and "ground of being" (Realgrund) and rejected the ontological proof for the existence of God, which concluded from logical grounds to the actual existence of a perfect divine Being.

Both these treatises were written during KANT's first period in which he still held to the possibility of a theoretical metaphysics in the Wolffian sense; a metaphysics which in a purely analytical way, would furnish apriori knowledge of reality from mere concepts and also fancied itself competent to answer questions pertaining to the ideal of personality.

Even in this period KANT had gained the insight that the "metaphysical" root and origin of reality cannot be derived from the logical unthinkableness of the opposite. Even at this time he rejected the conception of LEIBNIZ and WOLFF that a metaphysical-logical possibility lies at the foundation of metaphysical reality.

According to KANT, metaphysical being can be ascertained by logical thought only in the judgment of identity, but it cannot be proved to be necessary from the *principium contradictionis*.

That is why KANT laid great emphasis upon the logical superiority of the principle of identity to the principle of logical contradiction.

KANT's second period: the methodological line of demarcation between mathematics and metaphysics. The influence of NEWTON and English psychologism.

In his second period, which extended from 1760 to 1765, these insights were intensified, so that they led to the drawing of a provisional line of demarcation between the method of mathematics and that of metaphysics.

KANT's views in this period are characterized especially by the following writings: *Der einzig mögliche Beweisgrund zu einer Demonstration des Daseins Gottes* (1763), *Versuch, den Begriff der negativen Gröszen in die Weltweisheit einzuführen* (1763), and *Untersuchung über die Deutlichkeit der Grundsätze der natürlichen Theologie und Moral* (1763, published 1764), the last of which was written in answer to the prize question posed by the Academy of Science of Berlin. KANT noted a distinction between the mathematical and metaphysical method of acquiring knowledge on two points, namely, with respect to the significance of definitions and the form of demonstration. Mathematical definitions are synthetical in contradistinction to metaphysical definitions which are analytical. Mathematics creates its own *"Gegenstand"* in arbitrary concepts. The *being* taken into consideration by it does not arise from anything other than the mathematical concept.

Therefore, in mathematics definitions come first, whereas in metaphysics the concepts of things are given. By means of thought the latter cannot create any new reality. Metaphysics can only logically analyze the concepts of concrete facts and things given in experience into their simplest elements, in order to make them clear and distinct. In metaphysics, therefore, unlike mathematics, definitions nearly always must be placed at the end rather than at the beginning. KANT pointed metaphysics to the method of mathematical physics as it was formulated by NEWTON: "At bottom the true method of metaphysics is identical with that introduced by NEWTON in physics and which had such useful results there" [1]. By so doing he unequivocally sided

---

[1] "Die ächte Methode der Metaphysik ist mit derjenigen im Grunde einerlei, die NEWTON in der Naturwissenschaft einführte und die daselbst von so nutzbaren Folgen war."

with NEWTON against the mathematical idealism of LEIBNIZ and WOLFF. According to NEWTON, knowledge commences with sense phenomena, from which by means of induction and analysis, scientific thought must ascend to the causes of these phenomena, which are expressed in natural laws.

NEWTON's famous pronouncement: *"Hypotheses non fingo"* demanded, that the natural laws formulated with the aid of mathematical thought must in the last analysis be subjected to the test of experience. The causes of phenomena cannot be devised by thinking. Only sense experience can offer us the necessary material for knowledge. Even mathematical thought must therefore remain bound to the confines of sense experience, if it is to furnish us with veritable knowledge of reality. By the acceptance of this method of mathematical natural science for metaphysics, KANT implicitly acknowledged, that the line of demarcation, which he made between the method of mathematics and that of philosophy in his writings during the year 1763, could not be definitive and fundamental.

His opinion was only that for metaphysics the time to follow the synthetical method of geometry had not yet come. As soon as "the analysis will have furnished clear and thorougly understood concepts, the synthesis of the simplest cognitions will be able to subsume under itself the complex, just as in mathematics" [1].

In other words, the standpoint of KANT during this period is still that of the English and French Enlightenment. As also appears from the other writings of this phase, the science-ideal, at least partially, still possesses the primacy. This ideal, however, is no longer conceived of in the abstract mathematical deductive sense of DESCARTES, but rather in the sense in which it was formulated by NEWTON. In his first metaphysical treatise, it was this conception of the science-ideal which caused KANT to reject the freedom of the will, thereby manifesting its supremacy over the ideal of personality.

---

[1] *Untersuchung über die Deutlichkeit der Grundsätze der natürlichen Theologie und Moral* [Enquiry concerning the clearness of the basic principles of natural theology and ethics], W.W. Bnd. IV, pp. 299 (Conclusion of the "second consideration").

The rupture between the metaphysics of the science-ideal and moral philosophy in this period of KANT's thought.

Nevertheless, during this time, under the influence of English psychologism a break began to show between the theoretical metaphysics of the science-ideal and moral philosophy. This break reveals itself in the treatise concerning the clarity of the basic principles of natural theology and ethics which I have just cited.

Here KANT made a sharp distinction between the knowing faculty, through which we are able to represent that which is true, and the power to distinguish that which is good. And together with SHAFTESBURY, HUTCHESON and HUME, KANT sought the latter faculty in the moral sentiment: "It is a matter of the understanding to analyze the complex and confused concept of the good and to render it distinct," KANT observes, "by demonstrating how it originates from more simple impressions of the good. If once this latter, however, is simple, the judgment: this is good, is wholly incapable of demonstration, and an immediate effect of the consciousness of the feeling of the pleasure we take in the Idea of the object" [1].

The first principles of "natural theology" are indeed capable of the greatest philosophical evidence, insofar as they are metaphysical principles of knowledge, as for example, the principle that an absolutely existing perfect Supreme Being must lie at the foundation of all possible existing things, or the principle of the omnipresence of this Supreme Being.

In contrast to these, however, (like all basic principles of ethics in general) the first principles of this theology are only capable of *moral certainty,* insofar as they are concerned with God's *freedom in action,* His *justice* and *goodness.*

From this we see that in moral philosophy KANT had taken the path of psychologism. This fact is also confirmed by his *Beobachtungen über das Gefühl des Schönen und Erhabenen (Considerations on the feeling of the beautiful and the sublime),*

---

[1] W.W. Bnd. IV, S. 311 (Fourth Consideration § 2): "Es ist ein Geschäft des Verstandes, den zusammengesetzten und verworrenen Begriff des Guten auf zu lösen und deutlich zu machen, indem er zeigt, wie er aus einfachern Empfindungen des Guten entspringe. Allein ist dieses einmal einfach, so ist das Urteil: dieses ist gut, völlig unerweislich und eine unmittelbare Wirkung von dem Bewusztsein des Gefühls der Lust mit der Vorstellung des Gegenstandes."

published in 1764, where in the footsteps of SHAFTESBURY, ethics is psychologically and aesthetically grounded in the "feeling of beauty." During this period in KANT's thought, the first division began to arise between the ideal of science and the still psychologically comprehended ideal of personality, although this line of demarcation was not yet radically drawn.

In this phase, in which KANT orientated theoretical metaphysics to mathematical natural science, he also proceeded critically to examine the contradiction between the latter and the logicistic-mathematical method of CHRISTIAN WOLFF, who thought that by mere conceptual analysis he could obtain apriori knowledge of reality and its causal relations.

Influence of CRUSIUS.

The constant confusions between logical and real states of affairs in the ruling logicistic metaphysics were now analyzed with a real critical furor. KANT made CRUSIUS' fundamental distinction between the logical ground of knowledge and the ground of being into the very foundation for this critical investigation.

Following in the footsteps of his teacher RUDIGER, but with much more solid means, CHR. AUG. CRUSIUS (1715—75) had been the foremost German opponent of the geometrical method in metaphysics. CRUSIUS had related the material principles of knowledge to the sensory side of experience. Upon the same grounds he also combated LEIBNIZ' monadology with a famous argument that since has very frequently been employed: if, as LEIBNIZ taught, the essence of each monad were to consist in the fact that the latter represents to itself all the other monads, an absolute concept of the essence of any single monad is not given. If, however, nothing is absolute it is also contradictory to assume something which is relative [1].

In other words, the necessary relations may not be absolutized.

CRUSIUS' fundamental distinction between the grounds of knowledge and the grounds of being and his further division of the latter into causal ones and mere grounds of existence (whereby he simultaneously distinguished the physical from

---

[1] *Entwurf der notwendigen Vernunftwahrheiten, wiefern sie den zufälligen entgegengesetzt werden* [*Project of the necessary truths of Reason, in how far they are opposed to the contingent ones*] (3th ed. 1745) § 432.

merely mathematical ones) undoubtedly exerted considerable influence upon the further development of German philosophy.

Such men as LAMBERT and MENDELSOHN developed these distinctions further, while SCHOPENHAUER's treatise *"Über die vierfache Wurzel des Satzes vom zureichenden Grunde (Concerning the four-fold root of the principle of sufficient ground)* is practically a faithful reproduction of CRUSIUS' schema.

In his just-mentioned treatise, KANT recognized the great importance of this schema and made ample use of it. In his *Versuch den Begriff der negativen Gröszen in die Weltweisheit einzuführen (Attempt to introduce the concept of negative magnitudes in philosophy)*, he affirmed that in physics the terms negative and positive have an entirely different significance from that ascribed to them in logic and mathematics. In physics the mutual neutralizing of physical determinations (forces) leads to rest, whereas the mutual neutralizing of logical determinations leads to a logical contradiction and with that to a logical nothingness [1].

> Third period; the dominating influence of HUME and ROUSSEAU. Complete emancipation of the ideal of personality from the metaphysics of the science-ideal.

As ALOIS RIEHL has convincingly demonstrated [2], during the following period of his development KANT was for a short time very close to HUME's scepticism with respect to the foundations of the mathematical ideal of science. At the same time the influence of ROUSSEAU led him to the radical emancipation of the science-ideal from the grasp of theoretical metaphysics.

This phase in the evolution of his thought is best expressed in the writing which I have mentioned above, *Träume eines Geistersehers*.

In this period (between 1764 and 1766) KANT introduced the distinction between analytical judgments which in the predicate do nott add anything to the concept of the grammatical subject, and synthetical judgments which do so. This distinction which later on was to form the foundation of the entire *Critique of Pure Reason*, had not yet been introduced in his treatise concerning the "negativen Gröszen" (1763) [3]. To be sure, the syn-

---

[1] *Versuch den Begriff* etc. first chapt. (W.W. Vol. IV), p. 239.
[2] RIEHL, *Der phil. Kritizismus* I (3e Aufl.), S. 306ff.
[3] See CASSIRER, *Erkenntnisproblem* II, p. 612ff.

thetical method of the mathematical formation of concepts had, at this earlier stage, been placed in opposition to the analytical method of metaphysics. But this only meant to signify that mathematics creates its own "Gegenstand" in its concepts. Mathematical judgments, which develop only the content given in the definitions, were still conceived of as merely logical. In the period with which we are now dealing, however, the distinction has assumed a new sense.

Following HUME, KANT could for the present find no other solution than to reduce all synthetical propositions to the sensory aspect of experience, thus qualifying them all as "empirical judgments" [2]. Thereby, in fact, scepticism momentarily predominated with respect to the universally valid foundations of mathematical physics.

The physical principle of causality, as a "synthetic judgment", does not possess universal validity or necessity. The universality which we ascribe to it, rests upon a generalizing of the sensory perception of the sequence of causes and effects.

Nevertheless, this psychologistic standpoint was abandoned almost immediately after KANT realized, that mathematical judgments, as "synthetical", must possess an apriori universal validity which cannot be grounded in the senses. It was abandoned when he considered that scepticism with respect to the foundations of mathematical natural science would first of all touch the very foundations of mathematics [2].

Henceforth, the question arises as to whether or not apriori principles of form are included in all synthetic judgments, principles which, themselves possessing a synthetic character, lie at the foundation of all mathematical and natural scientific knowledge, and as such are the necessary prerequisites for all experience.

The transitional phase in KANT's thought until 1770.

Henceforth, the development of KANT's thought is very complicated. Its course can only be reconstructed in some degree by making use of KANT's philosophical journal, published by ERDMANN, *Reflexionen Kants zur kritischen Philosophie* supplemented by the "stray notes" of KANT of the Duisburg inheritance, first

---

[1] Cf. *Reflexionen* (ERDM.), p. 92 and 500 in CASSIRER II, p. 614.
[2] *Reflexionen* 496. See also H. J. DE VLEESCHAUWER, *L'évolution de la pensée Kantienne* (1939) p. 48.

edited by REICKE and later on by TH. HAERING [1]. But it must be granted, that every reconstruction, in view of the scarcity of available material, must retain a hypothetical moment.

From the source material in question, it appears, that by this time the problem concerning the relation of space and time to real things had been placed in the centre of KANT's interest. In a treatise entitled, *Vom ersten Grunde des Unterschiedes der Gegenden im Raume (About the first ground of the difference of situations in space)* [2], which he wrote in 1768, KANT defended NEWTON's and EULER's mathematical doctrine of "absolute pure space" against LEIBNIZ' conception, which held that space is nothing but an apriori *"ordre des coexistences possibles",* an apriori concept of relation. KANT showed, with respect to incongruent symmetrical figures, that two things in the ordering of their parts can be completely alike without the one being capable of covering the other spatially. Consequently, space cannot be the product of the relations of material parts with respect to each other, but it is rather the prerequisite for the relations of spatial things to each other.

In this writing KANT was concerned exclusively with the significance of NEWTON's and EULER's doctrine for geometry and mathematical natural science; he never wished to be held accountable for the metaphysical speculation which NEWTON joined to his theory of absolute space as *sensorium Dei*.

At the end of his treatise, he only mentioned the difficulties which are inherent in the concept of absolute space, "if one wishes to conceive its reality by means of rational concepts, whereas the inner sense is satisfied with grasping it in intuition. But this difficulty manifests itself everywhere, when we want

---

[1] I could not consult the *Reflexionen* myself and cite them from CASSIRER, *Erkenntnisproblem* II.

[2] It is not easy to translate the German term "Gegend" in the sense here intended by KANT. In his introductory considerations KANT refers to LEIBNIZ' *analysis situs;* but he remarks that he is not able to say in how far the subject of his treatise has affinity with the branch of mathematics which LEIBNIZ meant. KANT defines the "Gegend" as the "relation of the system of spatial positions (Lagen) of a thing to the absolute world-space". As the simplest examples of "Gegende" he refers to the distinctions of above and beneath, right and left, ahead and astern of us, in which our body is the point of reference in relation to three planes of the three-dimensional space which intersect each other rectangularly. I think the English term "situation" is the best I can find to translate KANT's "Gegend" in the sense here explained.

to philosophize at all about the first *data* of our knowledge, but it is never so decisive as that which presents itself when the consequences of an assumed concept contradict the most apparent experience"[1].

Thus KANT expressly removed the metaphysical side of NEWTON's doctrine in order to limit himself to the data of experience.

The problem of the mathematical antinomies. LEIBNIZ'
and NEWTON's conception of space and time.

Meanwhile, the very difficulties of this conception of space were to be of an enormous importance for KANT's further development. The thorough consideration of the problem concerning the relationship of absolute space and time to the universum of corporeal things led him to the discovery of the mathematical antinomies of actual infinity which were to play such an important rôle in the central part of the *Critique of Pure Reason*. Quite naturally, we shall deal with them later on.

By reason of these reflections, KANT finally became convinced, that space and time cannot be absolute realities in NEWTON's and EULER's sense. Therefore, for the time being he accepted LEIBNIZ' doctrine, which had proclaimed them to be apriori forms of pure thought, "*notions*" or "*conceptus intellectus puri*"; notions, however, of which we first become clearly aware on the occasion of our sensory perceptions of corporeal things[2].

For while KANT was in the middle of his reflections upon the exact relation between sensibility and the logical function of thought with respect to knowledge, the major epistemological work of LEIBNIZ, the famous *Nouveaux Essais sur l'Entendement Humain* appeared.

In it LEIBNIZ treated the same problem, and, as we have seen

---

[1] *Von dem ersten Grunde des Unterschiedes der Gegenden im Raume* (W.W. Bnd. IV) p. 325: "wenn man seine Realität, welche dem inneren Sinne anschauend genug ist, durch Vernunftideen fassen will. Aber diese Beschwerlichkeit zeigt sich allerwärts, wenn man über die ersten *data* unserer Erkenntnis noch philosophieren will, aber sie ist niemals so entscheidend als diejenige, welche sich hervortut, wenn die Folgen eines angenommenen Begriffs der augenscheinlichsten Erfahrung widersprechen."

[2] In contradistinction to the earlier view, more recent investigation has made it very likely, that we are not here dealing with a merely external influence of LEIBNIZ, but rather with an influence explainable only by the internal development of KANT's own thought.

earlier, he sought its solution in the fact that the contents of experience virtually contain the very apriori concepts of mathematical metaphysical thought. Consequently, the latter do not originate from the sensory elements of the Idea, rather they are an originally obscure and unconscious possession of the mind. Even though sense experience acts as an intermediary, the mind becomes conscious of them only in clear conceptual apperception.

Nevertheless, LEIBNIZ had given a metaphysical turn to his epistemology. The apriori concepts of the mind enable us to know the "eternal truths", the metaphysical order of the cosmos; they reveal to us the laws of the "noumenon", of the „Dinge an sich", whereas sense experience, as a lower function of knowledge, supplies us with knowledge only of the sensory world of phenomena, in which world only contingent truths hold good.

Although originally KANT had accepted LEIBNIZ' doctrine of the creative apriori concepts of mind, he could at this time no longer ascribe any value to their metaphysical application. Even in this phase of his development he had planned a schema of apriori basic concepts, although this project did not yet correspond to any specific methodical point of view. In this schema, space and time originally functioned next to the concepts of actuality, possibility and necessity, sufficient reason, unity and multiplicity, part, totality and nothing, complex and simple, change and motion, substance and accident, force and activity. In the *Reflexion* 513, written between 1768 and 1769, KANT reckoned all these concepts to ontology, in its true sense related to the rest of philosophy as *mathesis pura* to *mathesis applicata* [1]. Nevertheless, he could not remain satisfied with this view. For, as we shall see, he was driven further in his thought by the activity of the ideal of personality.

§ 3 - THE FURTHER DEVELOPMENT OF THIS CONFLICT AND THE ORIGINATION OF THE REAL CRITICAL PHILOSOPHY

The separation of understanding and sensibility in KANT's inaugural address of 1770.

In his *Prolegomena zu einer jeden künftigen Metaphysik (Prolegomena to every future Metaphysics)*, KANT declared, that it was only after long reflection that he came to the conclusion

---

[1] CASSIRER II, 623/4.

that a complete separation must be made between space and time as synthetic apriori forms of sensory intuition and the apriori pure concepts of understanding. He executed this division in his inaugural address with which he accepted a chair at the University of Königsberg: *De mundi sensibilis atque intelligibilis forma et principiis*. Nevertheless, his terminology is still vacillating insofar as sometimes he called space and time "*conceptus singulares*", and other times "*intuitus singulares puri*" [1].

By means of the term "*conceptus singularis*", KANT intended to place space and time in opposition to the "*conceptus universales*" or concepts of species which are acquired by abstraction: there exist only one space and only one time, which respectively include all limited spaces and all finite periods of time as their parts. This conception passed over unchanged into the *Transcendental Aesthetic* of the *Critique of Pure Reason*.

The deeper ground of this new conception of time and space is to be sought only in a reaction against theoretical metaphysics on the part of KANT's gradually maturing new conception of the ideal of personality.

As long as space and time were subsumed under the creative apriori concepts of logical thought, there lurked the constant danger that the relations discovered between spatial things would be tranferred to the "*mundus intelligibilis*". This would result again in a domination of the mathematical science-ideal within the realm of the free and autonomous human personality.

Ethics and religion, the kingdom of sovereign personality, may no longer be conceived of in the forms of nature-experience. For this very reason the metaphysics of the intelligible world must be strongly prohibited from the domain of natural science.

---

[1] *De mundi sensibilis* etc. (W.W. Bnd. IV), Sectio II § 12, S. 343: "Intuitus autem purus (humanus) non est conceptus universalis s. logicus, *sub quo*, sed singularis, *in quo* sensibilia quaelibet cogitantur, ideoque continet conceptus spatii et temporis." CASSIRER I, 626/7, thinks KANT conceived of time and space as "conceptus singulares" before he conceived of them as forms of intuition. In this connection he refers exclusively to "*Reflexions*" written during 1768 and 1769; but CASSIRER has apparently overlooked the fact that KANT even in his inaugural oration, in which he distinguished to the utmost possible degree the "forms of pure sensibility" from the "pure synthetical concepts of reason", still sometimes qualified space and time as "*conceptus singulares*".

Consequently, the significance of the inaugural oration of 1770 lies primarily in the sharp distinction made between the sphere of the knowledge of sensory phenomena and the intelligible world, accompanied by the recognition of the apriori synthetic forms of sensibility and logical understanding. KANT called this distinction the chief methodological basic principle of metaphysics [1].

Even in his *Träume eines Geistersehers,* he had made a division between the sphere of the experience of nature and that of ethics and religion, and thus withdrew the ideal of personality from the supremacy of natural scientific thought. Even here KANT taught that outside the sphere of sensory experience no scientific judgment is possible. Theoretical metaphysics which endeavours to acquire knowledge from pure concepts lapses into speculative mysticism. It tries to comprehend the spiritual world in the conceptual forms of sense-experience. The value of personality is, however, not dependent upon scientific thought. But during this period KANT still adhered to the sentimental religion and ethics defended by ROUSSEAU and English psychologism.

The development of KANT's new conception of the ideal of personality. Earlier optimism is replaced by a radical pessimism with respect to the sensory nature of man.

A new conception of the Humanist ideal of personality matured in KANT in proportion to the degree in which he became involved in the antithesis between sensibility and reason. As WINDELBAND has explained, this antithesis acquired an axiological character. The pietistic motives of KANT's youth, traversing the influence of ROUSSEAU, were active in an increasingly rigourous suspicion of sensory human nature. And because of this distrust it was no longer possible to seek the value of personality in the function of feeling, which function KANT considered to be only sensual.

---

[1] *De mundi sensibilis* etc. Sectio V, § 24 (S. 359): "Omnis metaphysicae circa sensitiva atque intellectualis methodus ad hoc potissimum praeceptum redit: sollicite cavendum esse, *ne principia sensitivae cognitionis domestica terminos suos migrent ac intellectualia afficiant."* ["Every method of metaphysics concerning the sensory and the intelligible is to be chiefly reduced to this precept: take great care lest principles belonging to sensory knowledge should surpass their boundaries and affect the intelligible"].

With the elimination of this possibility, KANT definitely said farewell to the optimistic life- and world-view which, after the fashion of LEIBNIZ' *Theodicy*, he had previously defended in his *Versuch einiger Betrachtungen über den Optimismus* [*An attempt at some considerations on Optimism*] (1759)[1]. KANT's gradually maturing dualistic transcendental ground-Idea made it impossible for him to harmonize with the sensory nature of man the Idea of normative autonomous freedom contained in his new conception of the ideal of personality. That caused him to adopt the pessimistic view of human nature expressed in his critical philosophy of religion, by his doctrine of the "radical evil" in man.

If sensory human nature with its sensual inclinations forms the real antithesis to the rational morality of man, then, in consequence, knowledge bound to sense-experience cannot furnish us with a knowledge of the real essence of things.

"Nature" as the sole experienceable reality is degraded by KANT to *mundus sensibilis*. In the same sense as in English psychologism[2], this *mundus sensibilis* includes both external and internal experience. Space was conceived of as a synthetical form of the *"äuszeren Sinn"* (outer sense), time as a synthetical form of the *"inneren Sinn"* (inner sense). Both space and time are already recognized as necessary transcendental conditions for all sensory experience, as universally valid subjective conditions of our sensibility, in which the material of our sensory impressions is ordered apriori[3].

---

[1] W.W. Bnd. IV, pp. 73ff. It is the metaphysics of the Leibnizian ideal of science that motivated KANT to write here (p. 81/2): "...ich bin... erfreut, mich als einen Bürger in einer Welt zu sehen, die nicht besser möglich war." Man functions as a member of a cosmos which in its totality is the best possible!

[2] *De mundi sensibilis etc.* Sectio II, § 12 (S. 343): "Phaenomena recensentur et exponuntur *primo* sensus externi in P h y s i c a, *deinde* sensus interni in P s y c h o l o g i a empirica." ["Phenomena are investigated and explained in the first place in *physics* insofar as they belong to the outer sense, afterwards in empirical *psychology*, insofar as they belong to the inner sense."]

[3] *De mundi sensibilis etc.* Sectio III, § 14, 5: "*Tempus non est objectivum aliquid et reale...* sed subjectiva condicio per naturam mentis humanae necessaria, quaelibet sensibilia certa lege sibi coordinandi, et *intuitus purus.*" ["Time is not something objective and real... but a subjective condition necessitated by the nature of the human mind in order to coordinate any sensible impressions whatever according to a

But this entire "mundus sensibilis" only reveals the phenomenon to us, the mode in which the "Dinge an sich" appear. The latter are, as such, fundamentally excluded from the sphere of experience. In this way even mathematics and mathematical natural science, the primeval domain of the ideal of science in the Cartesian conception, are in principle limited to the phenomenon. Thus NEWTON's metaphysics of space, which elevated space as "sensorium Dei", is cut off at its very root.

Mathematics furnishes us with universally valid apriori knowledge of space and time which are the apriori forms of sensibility. Consequently, mathematics only provides us with knowledge of the apriori forms of the world of appearance.

With the aid of mathematics, whose universal validity was thus secured, KANT tried in his inaugural address to uphold the foundations of mathematical natural science against HUME's psychological criticism.

Following NEWTON, he accepted the conception of corporeal things as *filling of mathematical space* (a basically false conception as we shall see in the second volume). Corporeal things are only possible in space, as an apriori form of intuition. This apriori form of sensibility is at the same time an apriori structural law of the entire experienceable world of things.

In the creation of the mathematical theory of the world of phenomena, logical understanding is still limited by KANT to the *usus logicus,* that is to the formal analysis of the phenomena given in time and space [1].

In addition an *usus realis* is postulated for logical understanding. The synthetical apriori concepts are related to the "mun-

---

fixed law, and it is a *pure intuition."*] Space is qualified in a simular way. *Ibid.,* p. 15. D.

[1] *De mundi sensibilis* etc. Sectio V § 23: "Usus autem *intellectus* in talibus scientiis, quarum tam conceptus primitivi quam axiomata sensitivo intuitu dantur non est nisi logicus h.e. per quem tantum cognitiones sibi invicem subordinamus quoad universalitatem conformiter principio contradictionis, phaenomena phaenomenis generalioribus, consectaria intuitus puri axiomatibus intuitivis. ["But the *use of the intellect* in such sciences, whose primal concepts as well as whose axioms are given in sensory intuition, is only *a logical* one, that is to say that by means of the latter we only subordinate our cognitions to one another with respect to their generality in conformity to the principium contradictionis: the phenomena to more general phenomena, the conclusions of pure intuition to intuitive axioms."]

dus intelligibilis". This intelligible world is to be sure still conceived of as that of the *"Dinge an sich"*. But even in the inaugural address of 1770 it appears that, contrary to the opinion of WINDELBAND [1], this does not indicate a relapse into the speculative Leibnizian metaphysics. It is rather *the new conception of the Humanistic ideal of personality* which now embodies itself in the Idea of the "thing in itself", at least insofar as the latter is an object of metaphysics! Our pure autonomous will, being only determined by the form of moral legislation, is itself "an example of an Idea of freedom, of an intelligible substance, namely insofar as it binds effects, which can be given in experience, to super-empirical grounds of determination" [2].

In section 11, paragraph 9 of his inaugural address, KANT assigned two different tasks to metaphysics, namely, an elenctic and a dogmatic one. In the first respect metaphysics must eliminate all sensory concepts out of the sphere of *noumena*; in the second respect it must direct all the principles of pure reason — which exceed sense experience — toward one thing only, namely the *perfectio noumenon*, that is the super-sensory perfection. And the latter, as the perfection of God, becomes a principle of theoretical knowledge; and as a moral perfection, as perfectio moralis, it becomes a principle for human action. Knowledge derived from pure concepts of the mind is only a *"cognitio symbolica"*.

The expression "symbolical knowledge" is derived from LEIBNIZ' treatise, *Meditationes de cognitione, veritate et ideis* of 1684, in which this thinker developed further the Cartesian criteria for the clarity and distinctness of knowledge. By *"cognitio symbolica"* in contradistinction to *cognitio intuitiva*, LEIBNIZ understood a *"cognitio caeca"*, in which, when we lack insight into the total character of the sensory object, we call in the help of abbreviated symbols in stead of the objects themselves. Nevertheless, it is by means of these very symbols that, according to him, we can acquire adequate knowledge, as in mathematics.

When KANT now applied this conception of the *"cognitio symbolica"* to the concepts of pure reason, and as a result denied to theoretical metaphysics every mode of intuitive adequate know-

---

[1] *Gesch. der neueren Phil.* II (4th ed.) S. 39.
[2] Cf. CASSIRER II, 635. In *Reflexion* 1156 and 1157, *"die Regel der Freiheit apriori in einer Welt überhaupt"* ["the rule of apriori freedom in a world in general"] is expressly called the *"forma mundi intelligibilis."*

ledge, he chose a position diametrically opposite to that of LEIBNIZ: according to the latter, we do acquire intuitive metaphysical knowledge derived from pure and simple concepts of reason.

KANT combated strongly the Idea of LEIBNIZ and WOLFF that sensory knowledge is only a *"cognitio confusa"*, whereas, in contrast, knowledge derived from simple concepts is clear and distinct. In *Reflexion* 414 KANT observes: "It is perfectly out of the question that the sensory intuitions of space and time are confused Ideas; rather they furnish the most distinct cognitions of all, namely the mathematical ones"[1]. As confirmed by the *"Reflexions"* of this period, the notion of metaphysical knowledge as merely symbolical is to be considered as the prelude to the doctrine of transcendental Ideas of KANT's critical period. "The *mundus intelligibilis*", he remarks in one of these *Reflexions*, "as an object of intuition, is a mere undetermined Idea; but as an object of the practical relation of our intellect to intelligences of a world in general and to God as the practical original Being of it, it is a true concept and a determined Idea: civitas Dei (the city of God)"[2].

In the *Reflexions* written during this time, the *mundus intelligibilis* was plainly identified with the *mundus moralis* and the idea of God was qualified as the "practical original Being". The identification in the cited "Reflexion" (1162) of the *mundus intelligibilis* with the Idea of the "civitas Dei" is undoubtedly formally derived from LEIBNIZ[3]. But LEIBNIZ' God was in the last analysis the deification of mathematical thought, the final hypostasis of the mathematical science-ideal. Whereas, in KANT's Idea of God, even in this phase, is expressed the moralistic ideal of personality, in the sense of supra-theoretical practical freedom and sovereign self-determination.

---

[1] "Es ist so weit gefehlt, dasz die sinnlichen Anschauungen von Raum und Zeit sollten verworrenen Vorstellungen sein, dasz sie vielmehr die deutlichsten Erkenntnisse unter alle, nämlich die mathematischen verschaffen."

[2] CASSIRER, *Ibid.*: "Der *mundus intelligibilis* als ein Gegenstand der Anschauung ist eine blosze unbestimmte Idee; aber als ein Gegenstand des praktischen Verhältnisses unseres Intelligenz zu Intelligenzen der Welt überhaupt und Gott als das praktische Urwesen derselben, ist er ein wahrer Begriff und bestimmte Idee: civitas Dei."

[3] CASSIRER II, 635.

cosmonomic Idea of Humanistic immanence-philosophy 351

*The new conception of the ideal of personality as
ὑπόθεσις in the transition to the critical standpoint.*

The last phase in KANT's development, the rise of his actual critical philosophy, can be understood only in terms of this new conception of the ideal of personality. The Idea of the autonomous self-determination of personality became the hidden ὑπόθεσις of theoretical knowledge.

It may be true that according to KANT's own testimony he was awakened from his "dogmatic slumbers" by the discovery of the antinomies of theoretical metaphysics [1]. Yet this *theoretical discovery cannot be considered to have been the deeper cause*, but only the occasion of his transition to critical idealism. The real motive of this transition was *religious* in nature.

Once the ideal of personality is recognized as the foundation of the ideal of science, the autonomy of the theoretical function of thought can be proclaimed over against the empirical determinations of the merely receptive, passive sensibility. The spontaneity of the logical function of thought acquires a new meaning in contrast to the receptivity of sensibility! The sovereign value of personality can express itself in the spontaneity of the intellect only if the latter, in its apriori synthetic functions, is elevated to the position of law-giver with respect to "nature". KANT's famous letter of February 21, 1772 to MARKUS HERZ is the first clear attestation to this new turn in his thought.

Up til now KANT had approached the problem concerning the relation of theoretical thought to reality only from the metaphysical side. In his inaugural address of 1770, he *went no further than drawing* a sharp line of demarcation between *mundus visibilis* and *mundus intelligibilis*. The *usus realis* of logical understanding with its synthetical categories was related here to the metaphysical root of reality, to the *"Ding an sich"*.

Henceforth, KANT posed the problem concerning the relation of logical understanding and reality with reference to the world of sense-experience ordered in the apriori forms of intuition, space and time.

Does not the intellect possess an *"usus realis"* in the apriori foundation of the *"mundus visibilis"*?

Henceforth, KANT concentrated his attention upon the problem of the apriori synthesis, through which in his opinion the world

---

[1] KANT's letter to GARVE of Sept. 21, 1798, Cf. RIEHL *op. cit.* I, p. 351.

of experience is first constituted as a universally valid ordered cosmos. To KANT, universally valid experience becomes identical with the *"Gegenstand"* of theoretical knowledge, and *"Gegenstand"* becomes identical with "objectivity".

In his letter to HERZ, KANT wrote, that the key to the entire mystery of metaphysics is to be found in the question: "w h a t is the basis for the relation between that which is called our representation, and the object" (Gegenstand).

The "Gegenstand" may be given to us by our senses, however, this sensory datum appears only as a chaotic mass of as yet unordered material of experience, a mass of intermingled sensory impressions, within the apriori forms of intuition, space and time in which they are received.

All of our representations of things in the external world are actually syntheses of our consciousness through which we bring under the unity of a concept a given sensory multiplicity received in the forms of space and time. The universal validity and necessity of these syntheses can never be found in the psychical laws of association of our representational activity. It can only originate from the apriori function of pure logical understanding with its synthetical categories, which understanding is not determined by sensibility, but, on the contrary, does itself define the sensory datum in a universally valid manner. It is the logical function of thought in its pure unconditioned apriori structure that synthetically constitutes the "Gegenstand" by realizing its categories in sensory experience.

The reason why we rightly assume that the things in experienceable reality conform themselves to these concepts and their combinations, is that our mind itself constitutes the apriori form of the *"Gegenstand"*, while only the sensory material is given to us in the apriori forms of intuition.

Beyond any doubt, even in this letter to MARKUS HERZ, KANT has clearly formulated the problem of his "critical" philosophy. For the first time he developed the program of the *Transcendental Analytic*, in sharp contrast to the traditional formal logic, and he introduced the name "transcendental philosophy" for the critical inquiry concerning the apriori elements of human knowledge.

In the *"Transcendental Analytic"* KANT wished to discover the system of all synthetical functions of the "pure understanding" which are related apriori to the *"Gegenstand der Erfahrung"*.

Once this task had been accomplished the key would be found for the solution of a question that he later was to formulate as the central problem of his first critical work, *The Critique of Pure Reason* (1781): *"How are synthetical judgments apriori possible?"* But it took nine years before KANT was prepared to present the elaborate system of the *Critique of Pure Reason* to the scientific world.

The discovery of the system of the transcendental categories cannot in itself explain this long delay. KANT had quickly found the principle of the "metaphysical deduction" of these categories, as it is called in the *Critique of Pure Reason*. Namely, the principle that all of these categories are founded in the logical function of judgment, so that they automatically arise from the four classes of these judgments (quantity, quality, relation and modality).

Rather it appears, as RIEHL supposes [1], that the so-called "transcendental deduction" presented KANT with his greatest difficulty. This deduction entailed the task of explaining why the categories are necessarily related to the *"Gegenstand"* of experience, and as such have universal validity for all possible experience. As B. ERDMANN has shown, we find the first utterance concerning the principle of this transcendental deduction in a letter which KANT wrote on Nov. 24, 1776.

It is also certain that it was again HUME's critique of the principle of causality which stimulated KANT to demonstrate the transcendental-logical character of the synthetical categories. In the transcendental deduction, the foundations of the mathematical and natural scientific pattern of knowledge were at stake.

The "Dialectic of Pure Reason" as the heart of KANT's *Critique of Pure Reason*.

But these foundations had an inner connection with the intrinsic dialectic of KANT's hidden transcendental ground-Idea.

According to his own testimony, the core of the *Critique of Pure Reason* is not to be found in the Transcendental Analytic or in the Transcendental Aesthetic; rather it is to be found in the Dialectic of Pure Reason, in which he develops his doctrine of the transcendental Ideas of pure reason.

---

[1] RIEHL I, (3e Aufl.) p. 371 ff.

For here the tyranny of the science-ideal over the ideal of personality must be broken. Therefore, in the transcendental deduction of the categories the foundations of the ideal of science were to be brought in accordance with the aim of KANT's dialectic of pure reason. The claims of theoretical metaphysics inspired by the mathematical science-ideal to acquire knowledge of the supra-temporal root and origin of experienceable reality were to be rejected and the way was to be opened for the apriori rational faith in the reality of the idea of autonomous freedom of human personality.

For that very reason we shall have to place the doctrine of the transcendental ideas in the centre of the *Critique of Pure Reason*.

Over and above this, in the explanation of KANT's "critical" philosophy it will become evident to us how his three main critical works: *The Critique of Pure Reason* (1781), the *Critique of Practical Reason* (1788), and the *Critique of Judgment* (1790) must be viewed as a whole, inseparably connected to his dialectical transcendental ground-Idea. In other words, we shall see, that if any one, from a Christian point of view, believes he can accept KANT's epistemology, while rejecting his ethical and religious philosophy, he is only giving evidence of a lack of appreciation of the true transcendental foundations of KANT's philosophy.

In the second volume, in our treatment of the problem of epistemology, we shall give special attention to KANT's theory of knowledge; therefore, in the present connection we shall only consider its main Idea, insofar as it is necessary in order to gain an insight into the structure of KANT's transcendental ground-Idea.

§ 4 - THE ANTINOMY BETWEEN THE IDEAL OF SCIENCE AND THAT OF PERSONALITY IN THE CRITIQUE OF PURE REASON

Actually KANT's "Copernican deed", i.e. his critical reversal of the relation between the knowing subject and empirical reality, his fundamental break with dogmatical metaphysics, in short the whole content of his *Critique of Pure Reason,* acquires its essential significance only in the light of the new relationship between the ideal of science and that of personality, in the basic structure of his transcendental ground-Idea.

If one isolates KANT's epistemology from the latter, KANT's

Copernican deed, which is usually considered to be a radical revolution in modern philosophy, is, in itself, in no wise radical.

It is quickly forgotten that since the time of DESCARTES, Humanist philosophical thought had been characterized by the tendency to seek the foundations of reality in the knowing subject only. HUME had with extreme acuteness tried to show that our experience is limited to sense phenomena. In distinction to the "objective" metaphysics of Greek and medieval philosophy, the Cartesian adage *"cogito, ergo sum,"* signified the very proclamation of the sovereignty of subjective thought. Insofar as the Humanist ideal of science, with its logicistic principle of continuity, developed without a real synthesis with medieval or ancient metaphysics, its deepest tendency was the elevation of mathematical-logical thought to the throne of cosmic ordainer. If any one doubts this, he may return to the sources of the Humanistic science-ideal and behold once again the cleft which separates modern Humanist thought, with its essentially nominalistic concept of substance, from the old objective metaphysics of substantial forms. He may examine once again the experiment of HOBBES, as presented in the preface to his *"De Corpore"*, according to which the entire given world of experience is theoretically demolished, in order that it may be reconstructed by the creative activity of mathematical thought [1].

If indeed KANT had done no more than to proclaim the sovereign transcendental-logical subject as lawgiver of empirical reality, his Copernican deed would have been nothing more than the realization of the basic tendency of the Humanistic science-ideal restricted to sense phenomena and his *Criticism* would have never become a true "transcendental idealism".

> The deepest tendencies of KANT's Copernican revolution in epistemology are brought to light by the ascription of primacy to the ideal of personality resulting in a new form of the Humanistic ground-Idea.

KANT's withdrawal of the "Ding an sich" from the domination of the mathematical ideal of science, and his limitation of all theoretical knowledge to sense-phenomena is only to be understood from the dialectical turn of Humanist thought to its religious freedom-motive, embodied in the ideal of personality.

---

[1] Cf. p. 197 of this volume.

Henceforth, the transcendent root of human existence is no longer sought in limited mathematical and natural scientific categories but rather in the rational moral function of sovereign personality, as it is expressed in the transcendental *Idea* of human freedom. This is the real cause of KANT's aversion to LEIBNIZ' logicistic cosmonomic Idea of harmonia praestabilita, by which free personality was included in a continuous mathematically construed cosmic order, and in which, in the last analysis, the distinction between sensibility and rational *freedom* was relativized by the ideal of science.

In KANT's epistemology the postulate of the sovereignty of mathematical thought remains in full force with respect to knowledge of nature, but the ideal of science (essentially pertaining only to the domination of nature) cedes its primacy to the ideal of personality. KANT had become fully aware of the polar tension between both of these ideals.

The (sit venia verbo!) *naturalistic* idealism of the mathematical concept is replaced by a normative freedom-idealism of the transcendental Idea which — in pointing to the root of human personality — transcends the limits of logical understanding.

The neo-Kantian idealism of the Marburg school, in its first critical enthusiasm, thought it could correct KANT by abolishing his limitation of the sovereignty of theoretical thought to sensory phenomena. Thus it wished to extend the logicized ideal of knowledge to the normative world. Meanwhile, we have observed in an earlier context that, in so doing, this school was simply not conscious of the fact that it violated the typical structure of KANT's transcendental ground-Idea. It supposed it could elaborate KANT's critical method more consistently by eliminating the epistemological function of sensibility. It was unaware that in so doing it substituted a new type of Humanist ground-Idea for the Kantian one!

The very transcendental critical meaning of KANT's epistemology is indissolubly linked up with the binding of the mathematical and the natural scientific categories to the sensory function of experience. For this restriction of the Humanist science-ideal was strictly commanded by KANT's critical insight into the definitive antithesis between the nature- and the freedom-motives in the religious root of Humanistic thought.

The transcendental Ideas of reason point theoretical thought regulatively to the totality of the determinations of empirical reality without logical understanding ever being able to encompass this totality. At the same time these Ideas point beyond the logical function of theoretical thought to the supra-sensory root of reality, which the Humanistic ideal of personality henceforth, in an increasing degree, would identify with the practical Idea of autonomous moral freedom.

Here the deepest tendency in KANT's proclamation of the "primacy of practical reason" manifests itself. This proclamation signified the first step in the process of concentrating philosophical thought in the Idea of autonomous moral personality.

As we observed in an earlier context, it was still only the first step which KANT's critical philosophy took in this direction. For the sharp line of demarcation between both of the basic factors in his transcendental ground-Idea, for the present, prevented the drawing of the full consequences of freedom-idealism.

The dualistic type of the Kantian transcendental ground-Idea.

The *Critique of Pure Reason* and its counterpart the *Critique of Practical Reason* break the cosmos asunder into two spheres, that of sensory appearance and that of super-sensory freedom. In the former, the ideal of science is the lord and master, the mind is the law-giver of nature, since it constitutes empirical reality as *"Gegenstand"*. But the ideal of science with its mechanical principle of causality is in no way deemed competent in the super-sensory sphere of moral freedom. It is not permitted to apply its categories outside of the domain of sensory experience. In the realm of moral freedom the *"homo noumenon"* (the humanistic ideal of personality in the hypostatized rational-moral function) maintains its own sovereignty.

KANT severed all cosmic connections of meaning which bind the normative moral function to the sensory. This hypostatization of the moral function of personality, as a self-sufficient metaphysical reality, avenges itself by a logical formalism in the treatment of ethical questions.

Here it clearly appears how the meaning of the normative functions of reality is disturbed by the attempt to loosen them from their coherence with all other modal aspects in cosmic time.

The dualism between the ideal of science and that of personality in KANT's conception of the Humanist cosmonomic Idea comes sharply to the fore in the relationship between the "transcendental unity of apperception" and the hypostatized Idea of the absolutely autonomous moral freedom. This relationship was in KANT essentially unclarified and antinomical. On the one hand the freedom-motive expresses itself in the "transcendental thinking ego", conceived of as the necessary pre-requisite for all objective experience of nature and as the apriori form of logical unity of the autonomous knowing subject. Whereas, on the other hand, opposite to it was posited the Idea of autonomous freedom of "pure will".

> In KANT's transcendental dualistic ground-Idea the basic antinomy between the ideals of science and of personality assumes a form which was to become the point of departure for all the subsequent attempts made by post-Kantian idealism to conquer this dualism.

Are we confronted here with two distinct roots in human reason? If this question were to be answered affirmatively, the unity of human selfhood (which from the outset had been sought in human reason) would be destroyed. This, however, cannot be KANT's true meaning, for he denied emphatically that the logical form of the "transcendental cogito" has any "metaphysical" meaning.

Must we then conclude that the "transcendental logical ego" itself belongs to the *phenomenon*? This supposition, too, appears to be untenable, because, in this case, this transcendental subject could never be conceived of as the *formal origin* of the world of natural phenomena.

So the basic antinomy between the ideal of science and that of personality discloses itself in the transcendental Idea of the autonomous human ego itself. This was to become the point of departure in the development of post-Kantian idealism. In FICHTE the Idea of autonomous freedom was in a radical fashion elevated as the all inclusive root and origin of the entire cosmos.

For we have seen in an earlier context, that, just as the classical ideal of science implies a postulate of continuity which requires a methodical levelling of the modal aspects, in similar fashion the ideal of personality possesses its proper *tendency to continuity* which soon was to contest the self-sufficiency of the science-ideal.

KANT conceived of the "transcendental cogito" neither as a substance nor as a phenomenon, but as a merely logical function,

cosmonomic Idea of Humanistic immanence-philosophy

as pure spontaneity of the uniting act synthesizing the multiplicity of a possible sensory intuition [1].

He tried to represent this "cogito" as a spontaneous activity, and as a final logical unity in consciousness which is ever elevated above all logical multiplicity in concepts [2].

When we deal with the problem of knowledge in the second volume of this work, we shall more closely analyze the intrinsic antinomy which lies hidden in this concept of the "unity of pure consciousness". Nevertheless, we can note in passing, that KANT cannot recognize the real unity of self-consciousness, because his hidden transcendental ground-Idea requires an unbridgeable gulf between the so-called theoretical and practical reason.

The expression of this dualism in the antithesis of natural laws and norms.

The transcendental logical subject is lawgiver of "nature"; the transcendent subject of autonomous moral freedom is lawgiver of human action (or rather is the logical form of the moral law itself)!

Natural necessity and freedom, causal law and norm, in their relationship to each other become antinomic species of laws which cannot find any deeper reconciliation in KANT's dualistic cosmonomic Idea.

If natural necessity cannot itself find its root in the Idea of free sovereign personality, it remains a counter force against the declaration of the absoluteness of the moral Idea of freedom, and this fundamental antithesis cannot be resolved by a mere axiological subordination of theoretical to practical reason.

---

[1] Kr. d. r. V. *Allgemeine Anmerkung den Übergang von der rationalen Psychologie zur Kosmologie betreffend* [*General remark concerning the transition from rational psychology to cosmology*], p. 322/3: "Das Denken, für sich genommen, ist blosz die logische Funktion, mithin lauter Spontaneität der Verbindung des Mannigfaltigen einer blosz möglichen Anschauung... Dadurch stelle ich mich mir selbst weder wie ich bin, noch wie ich mir erscheine, vor, sondern ich denke mich nur wie ein jedes Objekt überhaupt" (sic), "von dessen Art der Anschauung ich abstrahiere." ["Thought, taken in itself, is merely the logical function, consequently pure spontaneity of the uniting activity synthesizing the multiplicity of a merely possible sensory intuition... Through it I represent myself neither as I am, nor as I appear to myself, rather I think myself only as an object in general, abstracted from the mode in which it is perceived."]

[2] Kr. d. v. V. *Transsz. Logik*, 2e Abschn. §§ 15 and 16.

If philosophical thought is to avoid becoming constantly involved in intrinsic antinomies, the Archimedean point of philosophy cannot be as a house divided against itself.

The form-matter schema in KANT's epistemology as an expression of the inner antinomy of his dualistic transcendental ground-Idea.

In KANT's epistemology, too, an inner antinomy is concealed by the fact that sensibility and logical understanding are dualistically set in opposition to each other. And this antinomy is dangerous to both the ideal of science and that of personality.

In spite of the proclamation of logical understanding as the lawgiver for nature, the sovereignty of theoretical thought is seriously threatened, because sensibility as a purely receptive instance, imposes insurmountable limits upon it. The understanding ("Verstand") is the sovereign lawgiver only in a *formal* sense. Only the universally valid *form* of natural reality originates in the "transcendental cogito".

The *material* of knowledge, remains deeply a-logical, so that at this point the problem of the "Ding an sich" behind the phenomena of nature arises again in a dangerous fashion. In the traditional metaphysical way, KANT permits the purely receptive sensibility to be affected by the "Ding an sich".

This "Ding an sich" is obviously again thought of as a natural substance and cannot be compatible with the Idea of the "homo noumenon" as a free and autonomous supra-temporal being. In consequence, post-Kantian transcendental idealism necessarily must consider this to be an insult to sovereign reason. The a-logical "natural substance" threatened both the ideal of science and that of personality.

Pre-Kantian rationalism had actually conceived of the substance of nature as the creation of absolute mathematical thought, and thereby it had made the latter to be the deepest root and the origin of the cosmos. In so doing, however, it had disregarded the proper claims of the Humanistic ideal of personality.

In his dualistic delimitation of the ideal of science and that of personality, KANT permitted an a-logical *"Ding an sich"* to remain behind the phenomena of nature, a "Ding an sich" which destroys the sovereignty of thought[1] and gives rise to the pro-

---

[1] KRONER rightly observes op. cit. I, p. 103: "In den so gedachten Dingen

blem of a deeper root behind both logical thought and the metaphysical natural substance, and which on the other hand is not compatible with the postulate of continuity of the Humanistic ideal of personality; the acceptance of a metaphysical "substance of nature" did not permit the Idea of free and autonomous personality to be recognized as the deepest root of empirical (natural) reality.

KANT himself felt the antinomy in his delimitation of the science-ideal by a natural "Ding an sich". He tried, therefore, to avoid this antinomy by his construction of an *intellectus archetypus,* an intuitive divine mind, that creatively produces its "Gegenstand" in direct non-sensory intellectual intuition. This Idea is essentially derived from LEIBNIZ' notion of infinite analysis which is to be completed only in divine thought. KRONER rightly observes from the Humanist point of view: "The consequence of epistemological thought compels us to transcend the separation and to arrive at the unity of the intuitive understanding; with regard to the latter, however, the opposition between the "Gegenstand" and the ego can no longer be maintained. In the Idea both are identical, and such not as "Gegenstand", because the understanding is not produced by that which is viewed, but as understanding, since the latter produces that which is viewed... The Idea of the understanding producing its "Gegenstand" leads beyond logic as epistemology: it is a limiting concept, — a concept which limits epistemology" [1].

---

an sich tritt dem Subject ein gleichwertiges, gleichmächtiges, ja übermächtiges Prinzip entgegen, zwischen beiden aber wird keine gedankliche Vermittlung festgestellt (denn die "Affection" ist ein völlig dunkeles Wort, das nur die Stelle eines fehlenden Begriffs vertritt." ["In the things in themselves thought of in this manner, the subject is confronted with an equivalent, equipotent, nay predominant principle; but there is not established in thought a mediation between both (because "affection" is an entirely mysterious word, which only takes the place of a concept that is lacking").]

[1] KRONER, *Op. cit.* I, p. 109: "Die Konsequenz des erkenntnistheoretischen Denkens zwingt dazu, über die Trennung hinauszugehen bis zur Einheit des intuitiven Verstandes; für ihn kann dann aber auch der Gegensatz von Gegenstand und Ich nicht länger fortbestehen. In der Idee sind beide identisch, und zwar nicht als "Gegenstand", denn der Verstand wird nicht vom Angeschauten erzeugt, sondern als Verstand, denn er erzeugt das Angeschaute... Die Idee des seinen "Gegenstand" erzeugenden Verstandes führt über die Logik als Erkenntnistheorie hinaus: sie ist ein Grenzbegriff, — ein Begriff, der die Erkenntnistheorie begrenzt."

The function of the transcendental Ideas of theoretical reason.

In spite of all this, it cannot be denied that in the transcendental dialectic, by introducing the transcendental Ideas of theoretical reason, KANT took an important step in the direction later taken by FICHTE. The latter completely eliminated the natural "Ding an sich" and proclaimed practical reason, as the seat of the ethical ideal of personality, to be the deepest root of the entire cosmos.

With the synthetic determination of the "Gegenstand" by the mathematical categories of quantity and quality, and by the physical (categories) of relation, substance, causality and interaction, the logical understanding is set on an endless path; in this way alone the totality of the conditions can never be thought of as the "unconditioned" itself.

The very limitation and the restriction of the categories to the sensory phenomenon makes it impossible for the intellect to conceive of the "Ding an sich" in a positive sense as the absolute.

The "absolute" can never be given in experience, since the latter is itself determined by the mathematical and dynamical (natural scientific) categories.

For this very reason the mind can conceive of the "noumena" as "Dinge an sich" only in a negative sense. In his remarkable explanation "Von dem Grunde der Unterscheidung aller Gegenstände überhaupt in *Phaenomena* und *Noumena*," KANT wrote: "The concept of a noumenon is also merely a *limiting concept*, in order to fence in the presumption of sensibility, and it is also only to be used in a negative sense. Nevertheless, it has not been arbitrarily invented, but is connected with the limitation of sensibility, without, however, being able to set anything positive in addition to its extent"[1].

It was from this point of view that KANT began his destructive criticism of the rationalist metaphysics of the Leibnizian-Wolffian school. This criticism was pregnantly expressed by KANT

---

[1] *Kr. der reinen Vernunft* (W.W. Bnd. III) p. 243: "Der Begriff eines Noumenon ist also blosz ein *Grenzbegriff*, um die Anmaszung der Sinnlichkeit einzuschränken, und also nur von negativem Gebrauche. Er ist aber gleichwohl nicht willkührlich erdichtet, sondern hängt mit der Einschränkung der Sinnlichkeit zusammen, ohne doch etwas Positives auszer dem Umfange derselben setzen zu können." In the present connection I am quoting exclusively from the second edition. In Vol. II when we take up the problem of Epistemology I will consider the differences between the first and second edition.

in the statement that concepts without sensory intuitions are empty, as vice versa intuitions without concepts are blind. It began with the famous Appendix: "Concerning the amphiboly of the concepts of reflection by means of mistaking the empirical use of the understanding for the transcendental one" and reached its culminating point in the "Antinomies of Pure Reason".

Yet, KANT simultaneously tried to show that no contradiction is implied in the acceptance of the concept of a "noumenon" as the "Gegenstand" of an infinite intuitive intellect, even though the reality of the "things in themselves" is only secured by "practical reason" in apriori faith.

By recognizing the infinity of its task in the determination of the "Gegenstand", the intellect subordinates itself to "theoretical reason", which with its transcendental Ideas — as mere regulative principles for the use of the understanding — indicates to the latter the direction to follow in order to bring unity to its rules [1]. The transcendental idea presents to the understanding the unattainable goal: the "unconditioned", as totality of categorical determinations; so theoretical reason subjects logical thought to an infinite task. Consequently, in KANT the theoretical transcendental Idea is viewed as nothing but the logical category extended to the "absolute". This extension is made possible in pure reason by freeing the category from the inevitable limitations of possible experience and by so extending the concept beyond the limits of the sensory empirical, although still in contact with it [2].

---

[1] *Kr. d. r. Vern.*, p. 276: "Der Verstand mag ein Vermögen der Einheit der Erscheinungen vermittelst der Regeln sein, so ist die Vernunft das Vermögen der Einheit der Verstandesregeln unter Prinzipien. Sie geht also niemals zunächst auf Erfahrung oder auf irgend einen Gegenstand, sondern auf den Verstand, um den mannigfaltigen Erkenntnissen desselben Einheit a priori durch Begriffe zu geben, welche Vernunfteinheit heiszen mag und von ganz anderer Art ist, als sie von dem Verstande geleistet werden kann." ["The understanding may be a faculty of bringing unity to the phenomena by means of rules: Reason, *on the other hand, is the faculty of creating the unity of the rules of understanding under principles. Consequently, the latter is never directly related to experience or to a "Gegenstand", but rather to the understanding, in order to furnish the manifold cognitions of the latter with unity a priori by means of concepts; a unity which may be called unity in the sense of Reason and is of a quite different nature from that which can be produced by the understanding.*"]

[2] *Kritik der r. Vern.*, p. 327.

The transcendental Idea is a necessary concept of reason to which no corresponding objects can be given in the sensory aspect of experience. "Pure reason" is never related to "Gegenstände", but only to the apriori *concepts* of "Gegenstände", to the logical categories.

As KANT tried to derive his table of pure concepts or categories of the understanding from the forms of logical propositions according to the viewpoints of quantity, quality, relation and modality[1], so he also tried to construct a table of transcendental Ideas of pure reason patterned after the form of the judgments of relation: the categorical, the hypothetical, and the disjunctive.

Thus he divided these Ideas into three classes:

1 - the first is that of the absolute unity of the thinking subject as the absolute substratum of all subjective psychical phenomena;

2 - the second is that of the absolute unity of the series of synthetical determinations of the objective sensory phenomena;

3 - the third is that of the absolute unity of determinations of all the objects of thought in general or the Idea of a supreme Being, a "Wesen aller Wesen"[2]. The first point of view furnishes the *Idea of the soul* as absolute unity of the thinking subject, the second the *Idea of the world or that of the universe* as totality of all objective phenomena in the external world. The third furnishes the *Idea of Deity* as the being which includes all reality within itself (ens realissimum).

None of these transcendental Ideas are related to experience. Since in KANT's system all science is limited to the sensory aspect of experience, it is impossible to acquire scientific knowledge

---

[1] KANT's list of the logical forms of proposition is as follows:

I - *Quantity* of propositions: universal, particular, singular propositions.
II - *Quality* of propositions: affirmative, negative, infinite propositions.
III - *Relation*-propositions: categorical, hypothetical, disjunctive propositions.
IV - *Modality* of propositions: problematical, assertoric, apodictic propositions.

To this table corresponds that of the categories:
I - Categories of *quantity*: unity, plurality, totality.
II - Categories of *quality*: reality, negation, limitation.
III - Categories of *relation*: substance and accident, cause and effect, interaction.
IV - Categories of *modality*: possibility, actuality, necessity.

[2] *Kritik der r. V.*, p. 297 ff.

from such Ideas. In their speculative use, in which we conclude from the mere "Idea" to the absolute reality of its content, there arises the "dialectical illusion": theoretical thought transcends the boundaries of experience and supposes that in this way it can attain to knowledge of the "supra-empirical".

The task of the *"Critique of Pure Reason"* is to dispel this dialectical illusion and to keep theoretical thought within its boundaries, while, at the same time, it must furnish us with an insight into the fact that the speculative "dialectical conclusions" are not arbitrary, but rather spring necessarily from the very nature of pure reason itself [1].

Thereby the three metaphysical sciences are discarded in which idealistic pre-critical rationalism had attempted to carry through the primacy of the ideal of science over the ideal of personality, namely rational (metaphysical) psychology, cosmology (more exactly called: metaphysics of nature) and natural theology.

> KANT's shifting of the Archimedean point of Humanist philosophy is clearly evident from his critique of metaphysical psychology, in which self-consciousness had identified itself with mathematical thought.

In his doctrine of the "Paralogisms of Pure Reason" in which the rationalist psychology, as theoretical metaphysics, is reduced to absurdity, KANT struck at the very core of the Cartesian conclusion drawn from the intuitive self-consciousness in the *cogito*, to the *esse* [2]. From this appears most clearly the shift in the

---

[1] *Kritik der r. V.*, p. 302.

[2] *Ibid.*, p. 321: "Der dialektische Schein in der rationalen Psychologie beruht auf die Verwechselung einer Idee der Vernunft (einer Intellegenz) mit den in allen Stücken unbestimmten Begriffe eines denkenden Wesens überhaupt... Folglich verwechsele ich die mögliche *Abstraktion* von meiner empirisch bestimmten Existenz mit dem vermeinten Bewustztsein einer abgesonderten möglichen Existenz meines denkenden Selbst und glaube das substantiale in mir als das transzendentale Subject zu erkennen, indem ich blosz die Einheit des Bewusztseins, welche allem Bestimmen als der bloszen Form der Erkenntnis zum Grunde liegt, im Gedanken habe." ["The dialectical illusion in rational psychology arises from mistaking an Idea of Reason (of an intelligence) for the concept of a thinking being in general, which is undetermined in all respects... Consequently, I mistake the possible *abstraction* from my empirically determined existence for the supposed consciousness of a *separate* possible existence of my thinking self, and I believe I know the substantial in myself as the

Archimedean point which the Humanistic transcendental ground-Idea underwent in KANT's criticism.

The basic theses of metaphysical psychology: the substantiality, immateriality, simplicity, immortality and personality of the "thinking" ego and the different metaphysical conceptions concerning its relation to the things of the "external world", were pulled to bits by KANT's critique. According to him, they only rest on an unjustifiable relating of the empty logical form of transcendental self-consciousness to a supra-empirical *"Gegenstand"*. And this is done by means of the logical categories. "All *modi* of self-consciousness in thought as such, are therefore not yet logical concepts of objects (categories), but mere logical functions which neither give to thought any "Gegenstand", nor any knowledge of myself as a "Gegenstand". The object is not the consciousness of the *determining* but only of the *determinable* self, that is of my intuition (in so far as its multiplicity can be synthetized according to the general condition of the unity of apperception in thought)" [1].

As soon as the ideal of personality had freed itself from the stifling grasp of the science-ideal, Humanism could no longer seek the metaphysical root, the "substance" of personality, in sovereign mathematical thought.

Thus, even the basic problem of Humanistic theoretical metaphysics, namely, the relation of the material substance to the soul substance (in its three pre-Kantian solutions, viz. the naturalistic acceptance of an influxus physicus, occasionalism, and the Leibnizian doctrine of the pre-established harmony between material and spiritual monads), became null and void to KANT.

For him the entire problem is reduced to the relation between the subjective-psychical phenomena of the *"inner sense"* and

---

transcendental subject, while I have nothing in mind but the unity of consciousness which as mere form of knowledge lies at the foundation of all determining acts of thought".]

[1] *Kritik der r. Vernunft, Transsz. Dialektik* 2es Buch: "Beschlusz der Auflösung des Psych. Paralogism", p. 322: "Alle *modi* des Selbstbewusztseins im Denken an sich sind daher noch keine Verstandesbegriffe von Objecten (Kategorien), sondern blosze logische Functionen, die dem Denken gar keinen Gegenstand, mithin mich selbst auch nicht als Gegenstand zu erkennen geben. Nicht das Bewusztsein des *bestimmenden*, sondern nur des *bestimmbaren* Selbst, d.i. meiner Anschauung (so fern ihr Mannigfaltiges der allgemeinen Bedingung der Einheit der Apperzeption im Denken gemäsz verbunden werden kann), ist das Object."

cosmonomic Idea of Humanistic immanence-philosophy 367

the objective-psychical phenomena of the *"outer sense"*, in other words, to the question how these phenomena can be joined in the same consciousness [1]. In fact, this is the problem which concerns the relation between logical thought and psychical sensibility in the same consciousness, which problem KANT deemed to be insoluble in a *psychological* sense. For him the transcendental Idea of the soul has no other theoretical function than that of a regulative principle of pure reason for all psychological knowledge whose final goal, though never attainable, lies in the insight into the absolute unity of the functions of sensibility and logical understanding.

Nevertheless, as limiting concept, the Idea of the soul possesses an actually *transcendental* significance. In his *"General remark concerning the transition from rational psychology to cosmology"* KANT indicated the practical use of the transcendental Idea, in which it directs theoretical thought toward the *homo noumenon*, as the autonomous law-giver in the supra-sensory realm of freedom.

A principle of the supra-sensory determination of human existence is really found "through the admirable faculty that first reveals to us the consciousness of the moral law". Metaphysical psychology had vainly sought this principle in theoretical thought [2].

Thus in its practical trend, within the limits set for the Humanist science-ideal by the *"Critique of Pure Reason"*, the Kantian idea of the soul displayed itself as a transcendental foundation, even of this science-ideal itself. But KANT's dualistic transcendental ground-Idea prevented him from drawing the consequences through which the cleft between "theoretical" and "practical" reason could be bridged.

>KANT's criticism of "rational cosmology" (natural metaphysics) in the light of the transcendental trend of the cosmological Ideas.

In the analysis of the antinomies of pure reason KANT reduced to absurdity rational cosmology, in the sense of the natural metaphysics of the mathematical science-ideal.

According to him the paralogisms of metaphysical psychology cause a completely one sided dialectical illusion with respect

---

[1] See note 1 p. 366.
[2] *Kritik der r. Vern.*, pp. 324/5.

to the Idea of the subject of our thought, since there is not to be acquired the least evidence for the affirmation of the contrary through a speculative ratiocination from the pure transcendental Idea of the soul. It is entirely different, however, in the case of the "cosmological ideas of the universe". If reason desires to draw theoretical conclusions from these Ideas with respect to the *"Dinge an sich"*, it necessarily involves itself in antinomies.

If with respect to a supposed metaphysical object, one can prove with the same logical right the thesis as well as the antithesis of a speculative proposition, and consequently the logical principle of contradiction is violated, then it is evident that the supposed object cannot be a real *"object of experience"*.

Now in the first place, KANT developed the system of all possible cosmological Ideas in accordance with the table of categories. These Ideas are nothing but the pure concepts of understanding elevated to the rank of the absolute, viz. the totality of the determinations performed by the logical function of thought, insofar as the synthesis contained in the categories forms a series of determinations [1]. Thus KANT arrived at four transcendental Ideas, which, when speculatively misused, lead to a corresponding number of theoretical antinomies.

In these four cosmological Ideas the Idea of the universe is related to the categorical points of view of quantity, quality, relation and modality.

The antinomies, which arise in the speculative application of these transcendental Ideas, were accordingly divided by KANT into two mathematical and two dynamical (natural metaphysical) ones.

According to him, it can be proved with equal logical stringency that the world with respect to quantity is both limited and infinite in time and space. And, with respect to quality, the world can be shown to consist of absolutely single parts, while at the same time the opposite can be proved with equal logical force. With respect to relation (causality) it can be demonstrated, that causality through freedom in the sense of a first cause is possible. And, with seemingly the same force of argument it can be demonstrated, that such a metaphysical cause cannot exist and everything occurs in the world according to a fixed mechanical necessity. Finally, with respect to modality, the existence of an

---

[1] *Kritik der r. Vernunft*, p. 328.

absolutely necessary supreme Being can be both proved and disproved.

The actual transcendental trend which the theoretical Idea acquired in KANT is, nevertheless, also evident at this point. Here, too, the *"Critique of Pure Reason"* discloses itself only as a preparation for the *"Critique of Practical Reason"*.

> The intervention of the ideal of personality in KANT's solution of the so-called dynamical antinomies and the insoluble antinomy in KANT's dualistic transcendental ground-Idea.

KANT's Humanist ideal of personality has as its foundations causality through freedom, that is, the autonomous self-determination of personality as "homo noumenon", and the existence of God as the final hypostasis of the moral Idea of freedom. In the treatment of the so-called dynamic antinomies which are related to the categorical points of view of relation (causality) and modality (the absolute necessity), both of these foundations are called into play.

Here, in a positive sense, KANT chooses the side of the theses, in so far as they are related to the *"Dinge an sich"*, and he grants validity to the antitheses only with respect to the sensory world of appearance.

There is at this point, indeed, no longer any question of a natural *"Ding an sich"*, but rather of the intelligible root and origin of the cosmos, in the sense of KANT's conception of the ideal of personality. Thus KANT's ideal of personality is actually involved in the case that "theoretical reason" conducts with itself in the dialectic.

As soon as KANT gives to his theoretical thought this really critical transcendental turn towards the religious root of his entire critical philosophy, the insoluble antinomy in its dualistic transcendental ground-Idea is again immediately in evidence.

At every point this ground-Idea implies "purity" in the sense of the unconditionedness of "theoretical reason". Consequently, the cleft between the ideal of science and that of personality *may* not be eradicated in an actual transcendental self-reflection. But it *must* be eradicated, since actually the Idea of the autonomy of pure theoretical thought, in the deepest sense, is entirely dependent upon the Idea of the autonomous freedom of personality!

In the treatment of both mathematical antinomies KANT had

resigned in an equal rejection of thesis and antithesis insofar as both in an untenable manner treat a mere transcendental Idea as a thing of experience.

But in the treatment of the interest that reason has in the antinomies, he gives evidence of having clearly seen the stimulus of the Humanistic ideal of personality behind the rationalist-idealistic metaphysics: "That the world has a beginning [1], that my thinking self has a simple and therefore undestructable nature, that this self at the same time is free in its volitional acts and elevated above the coercion of nature, and that finally the whole order of things in the world originates from a first Being, from which everything derives its unity and appropriate connection: *these are so many fundamentals of morals and religion. The antithesis deprives us of all these supports, or at least it appears to deprive us of them*" [2] (I am italicizing).

The question arises why in the solution of the dynamic antinomies the appeal may be made to the supra-sensory sphere of human personality in favour of the thesis, whereas in the solution of the mathematical antinomies such an appeal to a "noumenon" behind the phenomena, in support of the thesis, must be excluded. KANT answers this question in the following way: "The series of conditions to be sure are all similar insofar as one considers only their *extent* with respect to the question whether they correspond to the Idea, or that they are too great

---

[1] This thesis is also orientated to the attempt of Christian scholasticism to prove rationally the creation of the world with the aid of the metaphysically applied principle of causality, although the Thomistic demonstration did not imply a *temporal* beginning of the universe. Naturally in itself this proof has nothing to do with the Humanistic ideal of personality. KANT directs one and the same blow against all rationalistic metaphysics, and in the case of "Christian" rationalistic metaphysics his task was lightened all the more, since in origin it is in nowise more Christian than Humanistic metaphysics. In fact, in the long run, Christian metaphysics joined hands with the Humanistic!

[2] *Kritik der reinen Vernunft*, p. 373: "Dasz die Welt einen Anfang habe, das mein denkendes Selbst einfacher und daher unverweslicher Natur, dasz dieses zugleich in seinen willkürlichen Handlungen frei und über den Naturzwang erhoben sei, und dasz endlich die ganze Ordnung der Dinge, welche die Welt ausmachen, von einem Urwesen abstamme, von welchem alles seine Einheit und zweckmäszige Verknüpfung entlehnt: *das sind so viele Grundsteine der Moral und Religion. Die Antithesis raubt uns alle diese Stützen, oder scheint wenigstens sie uns zu rauben.*" (I am italicizing).

or too small for it. But the concept of understanding which lies at the foundation of these Ideas, contains either merely *a synthesis of the similar* (which is pre-supposed with every quantity both in its composition and in its division) or also of the *dissimilar*, which at least can be allowed in the dynamical synthesis of the causal connection as well as in that of the necessary with the contingent. This is the reason why into the mathematical connection of the series of phenomena there cannot enter any other condition than a *sensory* one, that is such a one which itself is a part of the series; the dynamical series of sensory conditions, on the contrary, still allows a dissimilar condition, which is not a part of the series, but as merely *intelligible* lies outside the latter; thereby Reason is satisfied and the unconditioned is placed at the head of the phenomena, without thereby disturbing the series of the latter, which is always conditioned, and without interrupting it contrary to the principles of understanding" [1].

One cannot say, that this argument is very convincing. Consider for example the second mathematical antinomy [2]: the Leibnizian monadology affirmed, that the monad is spaceless, and insofar as it made this affirmation, it taught that the infinite

---

[1] *Kr. d. r. V.*, pp. 416/7: "Die Reihen der Bedingungen sind freilich in so fern alle gleichartig, als man lediglich auf die Erstreckung derselben sieht; ob sie der Idee angemessen sind, oder ob diese für jene zu grosz oder zu klein sind. Allein der Verstandesbegriff, der diesen Ideen zum Grunde liegt, enthält entweder lediglich *eine Synthesis des Gleichartigen* (welche bei jeder Grösze in der Zusammensetzung sowohl als Teilung derselben vorausgesetzt wird) oder auch des *Ungleichartigen*, welches in der dynamischen Synthesis der Kausalverbindung sowohl, als der des Notwendigen mit dem Zufälligen wenigstens zugelassen werden kann.

"Daher kommt es, dasz in der mathematischen Verknüpfung der Reihen der Erscheinungen keine andere als *sinnliche* Bedingung hinein kommen kann, d.i. eine solche, die selbst ein Teil der Reihe ist; da hingegen die dynamische Reihe sinnlicher Bedingungen doch noch eine ungleichartige Bedingung zuläszt, die nicht ein Teil der Reihe ist, sondern als blosz *intelligibel* auszer der Reihe liegt, wodurch denn der Vernunft ein Genüge getan und das Unbedingte den Erscheinungen vorgesetzt wird, ohne die Reihe der letzteren, als jederzeit bedingt, dadurch zu verwirren und den Verstandes Grundsätzen zuwider abzubrechen."

[2] The thesis reads here as follows: "Eine jede zusammengesetzte Substanz in der Welt besteht aus einfachen Teilen und es existiert überall nichts als das Einfache oder das, was aus diesem zusammengesetzt ist." ["Every composite substance in the world consists of simple parts and there exists nowhere anything but the simple or what is composed of it."]

series of spatial analysis has its metaphysical origin in a noumenon which is dissimilar to the parts of space. So it can be said with respect to the thesis of the first mathematical antinomy (the world has a beginning in time and is spatially limited) that cosmic time originates in eternity as timelessness, and with that is likewise accepted a heterogeneous "noumenon" outside the "synthetical series of temporal moments".

> Within the cadre of KANT's transcendental ground-Idea the natural "Ding an sich" can no longer be maintained. The depreciation of the theoretical Idea of God.

The truth of the matter is, that in the deepest ground of his transcendental ground-Idea, KANT had to reject the natural "Ding an sich" and could only accept the normative ethical function of personality as the very root of natural reality. This is also true in respect to KANT's theoretical Idea of God, which as *"Transzendentales Ideal" (Prototypon transcendentale)*, only had to pave the way for the practical Idea of the deity as a "postulate of practical reason", an idea, which in this practical function is nothing but the idol of the Humanistic ideal of personality.

The entire *theologia naturalis* with its speculative rational proofs for the existence of God must be destroyed by the *"Critique of Pure Reason"*, because the ideal of personality can no longer find its veritable Idea of God in absolutized mathematical thought, but only in the hypostatized moral function of free and autonomous personality. To this end even the theoretical Idea of God must be *depreciated*. As long as it concerns the "merely speculative reason", one had better speak of the "nature of the things of the world" than of a "divine creator of nature" and better of the "wisdom and providence of nature" than of the divine wisdom, since the first mode of expression "abstains from the presumption of an assertion which exceeds our competency and at the same time points our reason back to its proper field viz. nature"[1].

§ 5 - THE DEVELOPMENT OF THE BASIC ANTINOMY IN THE "CRITIQUE OF PRACTICAL REASON"

The kernel of the Humanistic ideal of personality in the

---

[1] *Ibid.*, p. 533: "die Anmaszung einer gröszeren Behauptung, als die ist, wozu wir befugt sind, zurück hält und zugleich die Vernunft auf ihr eigentümliches Feld, die Natur, zurückweiset."

typical form which it assumes in KANT's transcendental ground-Idea is the freedom and autonomy of the ethical function of personality in its hypostatization as "homo noumenon".

As we have formerly seen in another context, it is essentially the hypostatization of the merely formally conceived moral law itself which is identified with the "homo noumenon", as "pure will."

Autos and nomos in KANT's *Idea of autonomy.*
KRONER strikingly observes that "a double sense is included in the Idea of moral autonomy". The ego does not only subject *itself* to the moral law, instead of receiving as a slave the command of his master from outside, but it also acquires its own *selfhood* only through the very law. It does not become *autos* but on account of its subjecting itself to the *nomos*, it only becomes an ego when it obeys *itself*: "The (moral) law is consequently the true ego in the I-ness, it is the transcendental consciousness, the pure practical Reason, to whose rank the empirical will has to elevate itself, if it is to become an ethical one. Reason becomes only as law-giver the reason which separates itself from arbitrariness and inclination. The law which derives its legitimation from itself, and commands by its own authority, elevates Reason above all finite connections, and makes it infinite, absolute" [1].

In KANT's theoretical philosophy self-consciousness had only a hovering existence in the "transcendental unity of apperception" which is related to the phenomenon. In the *"Critique of Practical Reason"*, however, it discloses its "metaphysical root" [2].

---

[1] *Von Kant bis Hegel*, Bnd. I, p. 167: "Das Gesetz ist also das wahre Ich im Ich, es ist das transzendentale Bewusztzsein, die reine praktische Vernunft, zu der sich der empirische Wille zu erheben hat, wenn er ein sittlicher werden will. Die Vernunft wird als Gesetzgeberin erst zur Vernunft, die sich von Willkur und Neigung unterscheidet. Das Gesetz, das seinen Rechtsgrund aus sich schöpft, das eigener Vollmacht gebietet, erhebt die Vernunft über alle endlichen Zusammenhänge, macht sie unendlich, absolut."

[2] *Kritik der praktischen Vernunft* (W.W., Bnd. V), Vorrede, p. 108: "Hierbei erhält nun zugleich die befremdliche, obzwar unstreitige, Behauptung der spekulativen Kritik dasz sogar *das denkende Subject ihm selbst in der inneren Anschauung blosz Erscheinung* sei, in der Kritik der Praktischen Vernunft auch ihre volle Bestätigung, so gut, dasz man auf sie kommen musz, wenn die erstere diesen Satz auch gar nicht bewiesen hätte." [With this the critique of Practical Reason at the same time com-

We have seen that in this very dualistic conception of the selfhood once more is disclosed the unsoluble antinomy in KANT's trascendental ground-Idea: In the *"Critique of Pure Reason"* the "thinking ego", conceived of as a pure transcendental-logical subject, is made the autonomous unity of self-consciousness, whereas in the *"Critique of Practical Reason"* the ethical and faith functions of human personality are hypostatized as metaphysical root of human existence. In this way the human ego is itself broken up into two diametrically opposed roots. This remains true even though KANT rejects the conception that the transcendental selfconsciousness is a "Ding an sich".

<blockquote>The dualistic division between the ideal of science and the ideal of personality delivers the latter into the hands of a logical formalism.</blockquote>

The hypostatization of the moral and faith functions of human personality necessarily results in a logical formalization of ethics and theology, which, as we saw, leads to a disturbance of meaning of the modal law-spheres concerned. Contrary to KANT's own intention, theoretical logic dominates the ideal of personality as formulated in the categorical imperative. The sharp dualistic "either-or" between sensibility and reason, induced him to apply — though not in a theoretical epistemological sense — even to the moral principles, the same *form-matter schema* which had played a dominating rôle in his epistemology: "If a rational being is to think of his maxims as practical universal laws, it can think the same only as such principles which contain the ground of determination of the will, not in respect to the matter, but merely in respect to the form" [1].

KANT's categorical imperative: "Behave so that the maxim of your will can at the same time hold as a principle of a universal legislation," is in essence a logicistic judgment, for the very reason that it is thought of as an "absolute" principle, separated from the cosmic-temporal coherence of meaning. By its elimination

---

pletely confirms the surprising, although undisputable, assertion of the speculative critique, that even *the thinking subject in the inner intuition can conceive itself only as phenomenon*; and this confirmation is so striking, that one must even arrive at this thesis if the latter (viz. the speculative critique) had not at all demonstrated it."]

[1] *Kritik der pr. V.*, S. 136: "Wenn ein vernünftiges Wesen sich seine Maximen als praktische allgemeine Gesetze denken soll, so kann es sich dieselbe nur als solche Prinzipien denken, die nicht der Materie, sondern blosz der Form nach den Bestimmungsgrund des Willens enthalten."

from the cosmic coherence among the modal law-spheres, it lacks any true inter-modal synthesis. In our treatment of the epistemological problem, we shall have ample opportunity to demonstrate this thesis more elaborately. In KANT the religious meaning of the Humanist ideal of personality concentrates itself essentially in the absolutizing of a *function* of human personality.

The transcendental concept of freedom considered in itself is merely negative (freedom from natural causality) and is to acquire a positive sense only through the principle of autonomy, in the sense of the absolute sovereignty of Human personality as the highest legislator. But this "autonomy", too, lacks as such a meaningful content. It is in itself only a formal principle. The religious ground-motive which finds its expression in KANT's transcendental freedom-Idea implies the *self-sufficiency* of the *homo noumenon* and it is this very divine predicate which makes any moral autonomy of man meaningless.

In KANT's conception, the ideal of personality actually requires the logistic hypostatization of the "categorical imperative"; however, it destroys itself by the very fact that it can only offer "stones for bread" when challenged to disclose its full religious content. Perhaps never in the history of philosophy has the Humanist ideal of personality received a more impressive formulation than in KANT's famous eulogy of duty, but, on the other hand, this ideal of personality has never before exhausted itself in an emptier formalism. To the impressive question, "Duty! sublime and great name... what is the origin worthy of yourself, and where is the noble root to be found that proudly excludes all kinship with the inclinations, and which is the indispensable origin from which man can derive any value that he can give himself?" — the Königsberg philosopher replies: "It must be nothing less than that which elevates man (as a part of the sensory world) above himself, and connects him with an order of things only to be conceived by the understanding, an order embracing the whole world of the senses — including the empirically determinable existence of man in time — as well as the totality of all purposes... It is nothing but *personality*, i.e. the freedom and independence of the mechanism of the whole of nature. But at the same time it is to be considered as a faculty of a being to whose own peculiar — i.e. by its own reason imposed — and purely practical laws it is subjected insofar as it belongs to the sensory world. In other words the person, as belonging to the world of the senses, is subjected to his own personality insofar as he belongs to the intelligible world. It is not surprising, therefore, if man, who belongs to both worlds, looks upon his own being in relation to his second and highest destination with veneration and considers its laws with the greatest respect" [1].

The precise definition of the principle of autonomy through the Idea of personality as "end in itself".

Free personality is viewed as an end in itself, as *"absoluter Selbstzweck"*. To be sure, it is true enough that man is unholy, but "humanity" in his person ought to be sacred to him.

In the entire cosmos all that man desires and all that over which he has power may be merely used as a means, only man and with him every rational creature is *"Zweck an sich selbst."*

This "human value", however, which must be sacred to everyone as *homo noumenon*, is itself in the last analysis the empty formula of the categorical imperative. The real motive of "pure practical reason" is also none other than the "pure", that is the absolutized and therefore formalized and empty moral law [2]. Therein consists in KANT the fundamental difference between mede *morality* and *legality*.

---

[1] *Kritik der praktischen Vernunft*, p. 211/2: "*Pflicht!* du erhabener, groszer Name... welcher ist der deiner würdige Ursprung, und wo findet man die Wurzel deiner edlen Abkunft, welche alle Verwandtschaft mit Neigungen stolz ausschlägt, und von welcher Wurzel abzustammen, die unnachläszliche Bedingung desjenigen Werts ist, den sich Menschen allein selbst geben können? Es kann nichts minderes sein, als was den Menschen über sich selbst (als einen Teil der Sinnenwelt) erhebt, was ihn an eine Ordnung der Dinge knüpft, die nur der Verstand denken kann, und die zugleich die ganze Sinnenwelt, mit ihr das empirische bestimmbare Dasein des Menschen in der Zeit und das Ganze aller Zwecke... unter sich hat. Es ist nichts anders als die *Persönlichkeit*, d.i. die Freiheit und Unabhängigkeit von dem Mechanism der ganzen Natur, doch zugleich als ein Vermögen eines Wesens betrachtet, welches eigentümlichen, nämlich von seiner eigenen Vernunft gegebenen, reinen praktischen Gesetzen, die Person also, als zur Sinnenwelt gehörig, ihrer eigenen Persönlichkeit unterworfen ist, so fern sie zugleich zur intelligibelen Welt gehört: da es denn nicht zu verwundern ist, wenn der Mensch als zu beiden Welten gehörig, sein eignes Wesen in Beziehung auf seine zweite und höchste Bestimmung nicht anders als mit Verehrung und die Gesetze derselben mit der höchsten Achtung betrachten musz."

[2] *Ibid.*, p. 213: "So ist die ächte Triebfeder der reinen praktischen Vernunft beschaffen; sie ist keine andere als das reine moralische Gesetz selber, so fern es uns die Erhabenheit unserer eigenen übersinnlichen Existenz spüren läszt..." ["Such is the nature of the true motive of the

The thesis that human personality is an end in itself, can have a good meaning only in respect to the things which can become an object of human goals. That is to say it is meaningful only in the *temporal subject-object relation* in which things have modal object-functions in respect to the different modal functions of the volitive act of man.

As soon, however, as this thesis is extended to the central religious sphere, it becomes void, because it contradicts the exsistent character of the religious centre of human personality.

The true religious root of our existence is nothing *in itself*, because it is only an *imago* Dei.

As soon as it is absolutized, it fades away in nothingness and cannot give any positive content to KANT's freedom-Idea. This very absolutization is implied in KANT's conception of the ethical idea of human personality as an *absolute* end in itself.

We have learned, in an earlier context, that the antinomy in the Humanist concept of substance consists in the fact that a result of theoretical abstraction is absolutized as a "thing in itself".

In KANT's practical philosophy, the absolute freedom of the "homo noumenon" exists by the grace of the same logical understanding that he had bound in his epistemology to the chain of sensory phenomena!

Now this understanding with its analytical laws even subjects the very ideal of personality to a logical formalization, whereas one would expect that, in keeping with the primacy of "practical reason", it should, on the contrary, be subject to the latter.

This is clearly evident from the noteworthy section of the "*Analytic of Practical Reason*", in which KANT treats the subject of the pure practical judgment [1].

At this point a problem rises with respect to the categorical imperative, which runs parallel to the problem KANT had raised in the so-called "Schematism-chapter" [2], with respect to the pure concepts of the understanding. Just as these pure concepts must be capable of being applied to sensory intuition, in the same manner that which in the ethical rule is said generally *(in ab-*

---

pure practical reason; it is but the pure moral law itself insofar as it makes us aware of the sublimity of our own super-sensual existence."]

[1] *Ibid.*, p. 188.

[2] I must postpone a detailed analysis of this important part of the *Critique of Pure Reason* until the second volume in which I will discuss the problems of epistemology.

stracto) must be applied, by the practical faculty of judgment, to an action *in concreto*.

This gives rise to the difficulty that in KANT's system a concrete action is always "empirically determined", that is, belongs to the sensory experience of nature. And as KANT expressed it: It seems absurd, that one could encounter an instance in the sensory world, that, although itself subject to the laws of nature, yet is capable of being brought under a law of freedom. Naturally there can be no question of a schematization of the practical Idea of reason in the same manner as the schematization of the categories of the understanding, because the moral good ("the pure will") is something supra-sensory that never permits itself to be related to experience.

> In the application of KANT's categorical imperative to concrete actions, the dualism between "nature" (ideal of science) and "freedom" (ideal of personality) becomes an antinomy.

The antinomy which necessarily must arise from the dualistic division of nature and freedom emerges at this point. The function of moral activity is impossible outside its cosmic temporal coherence of meaning with the "natural" functions. But the recognition of that connection of meaning would have immediately destroyed the hypostatization of the moral function in KANT's conception of the ideal of personality.

The way in which KANT sought to escape this contradiction is quite typical. The transcendental idea is only to be related to concepts of the understanding and not to sensory experience. Consequently, the moral law can only be schematized by relating it, in its abstract logical formulation, to the mere form of a natural law which is then qualified as a type of the moral law.

The natural law itself can be related to the "sense-objects" in concreto. It is evident that thereby the possibility of applying the categorical imperative to concrete actions is not demonstrated. Even though in KANT's system the category of causality can be related to sensory actions in concreto, this is only possible by means of its schematization in time.

But the mere form of natural law cannot be applied to sensory experience without its schematization in time as a form of intuition of the "inner sense" [1].

---

[1] *Ibid.*, p. 191: "Es ist also auch erlaubt, die *Natur der Sinnenwelt* als

According to KANT, the rule of the judicative faculty under laws of pure practical reason is this: ask yourself whether the action which you intend to perform could be viewed as possible through your will, if it would occur according to a law of nature, of which nature you yourself would be a part. Consequently, if the subjective maxim of action does not permit itself to be *thought* of according to the form of natural law, as a universal law of human action, it is *morally impossible*.

In the final analysis, this *"Typik der reinen praktischen Urteilskraft"* is simply reduced to the judgment of the concrete actions according to the logical *principium contradictionis*. The mere form of the natural law is, according to KANT's own statement, nothing but the form of the "conformity to law in general"; for laws as such are of the same kind, no matter from where they derive their "determinative grounds".

To apply the categorical imperative, KANT has no other choice than to relate it to the logicistic generic concept of "law", which in fact is identified with the analytical principle of contradiction.

As the result of this logical formalism, the antinomy between the ideal of science and that of personality acquires its greatest sharpness in KANT's transcendental ground-Idea. The "pure will" must be comprehended as "causa noumenon", i.e. as absolute metaphysical cause of human actions in their sensory mode of appearance. Under the "mechanism of nature" — the sovereign domain of the ideal of science — KANT subsumed psychical as well as physical causality, and mockingly he called psycholo-

---

Typus einer *intelligibelen* Natur zu brauchen, so lange ich nur nicht die Anschauungen, und was davon abhängig ist, auf diese übertrage, sondern blosz die *Form der Gesetzmäszigkeit* überhaupt (deren Begriff auch im gemeinsten Vernunftgebrauche stattfindet, aber in keiner anderen Absicht, als blosz zum reinen praktischen Gebrauche der Vernunft *a priori* bestimmt erkannt werden kann) darauf beziehe. Denn Gesetze als solche sind so fern einerlei, sie mögen ihre Bestimmungsgründe hernehmen, woher sie wollen." ["It is consequently also permitted to use the *nature of the sense-world* as a *type* of an *intelligible* nature, so long as I do not transfer to the latter the sensory intuitions and what is dependent on them, but relate to it only the form of *conformity to law* in general (the concept of which is also present in the most common use of reason, but to no other end than what can be understood as destined merely to the pure practical use of reason *a priori*). For laws as such are of the same kind, no matter from where they derive their determinative grounds."]

gical freedom "the freedom of a turnspit, which also, once it is wound up, executes its movements of its own accord"[1].

KANT's characterization of LEIBNIZ' conception of free personality as "automaton spirituale."

The Leibnizian *automaton spirituale*, which through its representations is determined to its activity, is, according to him, just as devoid of real transcendental freedom as the *automaton materiale* that is nothing but a material machine. KANT remarks: "if indeed human actions, as they actually belong to the determinations of man in time, were not only determinations of man as phenomenon, but as 'thing in itself', then freedom could not be saved. Man would be a marionette or an Vauconson automaton, constructed by the highest Master of all art works, and even though selfconsciousness would make him a thinking automaton, he would be of such a nature that the consciousness of his spontaneity, when considered as freedom, would be a mere deception..."[2].

God has created man, however, only as a *homo noumenon*, not as *"phenomenon"*. So it is a contradiction to say that God, as Creator, is the cause of actions in the sense-world, while he is at the same time the cause of the existence of the acting being as *noumenon*[3].

But the "causa noumenon" of sensory actions itself appears to be nothing but the absolutized form of the law "überhaupt". This is the embodied antinomy itself.

The categorial imperative, as moral law, is itself thought of as subjective "causa noumenon". Why? Since the subjective moral volitional function (over against which the categorical imperative sets itself as a "norm", because the volitional function can exceed the law) cannot be comprehended as "free cause". For KANT views this subject-function as "empirically conditioned" and dependent upon sensory nature.

KRONER thinks he can solve this antinomy by stating, that not the "pure" (that is hypostatized) will, but only the "empirically conditioned pure will" is to be understood as "causa noumenon" of actions. However, unintentionally he gives in this way the

---

[1] *Kritik der pr. Vern.*, p. 224.
[2] *Kritik der pr. Vern.*, p. 229.
[3] *Ib.*, p. 231. At this point one can clearly see how KANT's Idea of God is determined by the ideal of personality.

most pregnant formulation to this Kantian antinomy [1]. For how can a "pure will" be "empirically conditioned" without losing its "purity", i.e. its absolute character? Speculative idealism with its dialectical method sanctions the antinomy as a transitional stage to a higher synthesis. KANT, however, did not accept antinomies and so this solution can never constitute an answer within his system.

KRONER's conception of the origin of the antinomy in KANT's doctrine of "pure will" as "causa noumenon".

KRONER has, however, penetratingly seen wherein lies the origin of the antinomy in KANT's doctrine of "pure will" as "causa noumenon". This origin is hidden in the impossibility of thinking the moral-logical *form* of reason together with its sensorily determined *material*.

As we saw before, the *"Typik der reinen praktischen Vernunft"* does not afford any escape from this difficulty. In KANT's system the "Dialectic of pure reason" could only demonstrate that the natural scientific category of causality is exclusively related to sensory experience but never to "Dinge an sich". The *"Critique of pure Reason"*, however, could not furnish us with the insight into the possibility of a real connection between nature and supra-sensory freedom, since it was itself based upon the hypostatization of the logical and psychical functions of consciousness. KANT thought he could lift these functions out of the cosmic temporal coherence of meaning without this hypostatization. But this is impossible.

The antinomy between nature and freedom in KANT's concept of the highest good.

In a final attempt KANT tried to re-establish in practical reason the coherence of meaning between nature and freedom, which he had crudely severed. To this end he used the concept of *the highest good*. Nevertheless, it has generally been acknowledged that it is just this very point in KANT's system which exhibits its weakest spot and actually resolves itself into intrinsic antinomies.

It is our intention to examine briefly this final attempt to achieve a synthesis. KANT considers the older heteronomous (non-realistic) ethics to be characterized by the fact that it sought after an "object of the will" in order to make this at the same

---

[1] KRONER, *Op. cit.* I, S. 199.

time both the material and the ground of the moral law. This was done instead of first seeking after a law, which apriori and directly determines the will and the object of the latter only through the will itself.

Thus in this heteronomous ethics the concept of the highest good became the final determinative ground of the moral will [1]. To KANT the concept of the "highest good" becomes the "unconditional totality of the object of pure practical reason", but it is never to be comprehended as the determinative ground of the "pure will" [2]. The moral law as the final determinative ground is rather pre-supposed in this concept.

In the concept of the highest good, however, virtue (as the determination of the will exclusively by the categorical imperative) and blessedness (as the motive of our sensibility) must, according to KANT, be conceived of as necessarily united. For it cannot be supposed that personality needs blessedness and is worthy of it, but nevertheless cannot possess it; this would be incompatible with the perfect will of the rational Being that at the same time is almighty (i.e. the deity). This uniting of virtue and beatitude cannot be conceived of analytically, since freedom and nature do not logically follow from each other, but rather exclude each other [3]. It can only be thought of synthetically, and then only in such a manner, that either happiness is the necessary result of virtue as "causa noumenon", or vice versa the desire for happiness is the moving cause of moral action. The latter alternative is excluded by the principle of autonomy. But the first way seems equally impossible, since all

---

[1] *Ibid.*, p. 183/4.
[2] *Ibid.*, p. 283/9.
[3] *Kr. d. pr. V.*, S. 243: "Also bleibt die Frage: *"wie ist das höchste Gut praktisch möglich?* noch immer unerachtet aller bisherigen Koalitionsversuche eine unaufgelösete Aufgabe. Das aber, was sie zu einer schwer zu lösenden Aufgabe macht, ist in der Analytik gegeben, nämlich dasz Glückseligkeit und Sittlichkeit, zwei spezifisch ganz *verschiedene Elemente* des höchsten Guts sind, und ihre Verbindung also nicht *analytisch* erkannt werden könne... sondern eine *Synthesis* der Begriffe sei." [Thus, notwithstanding all attempts at a solution, the question: *"How is the highest good practically possible?"* still remains an unsolved problem. That, however, which makes the latter a problem hardly to be solved, is given in the Analytic, namely that blessedness and morality are two specifically completely *different elements* of the highest good, so that their uniting cannot be understood *analytically*... but rather is a *synthesis* of concepts"].

practical uniting of causes and effects in the world as a result of the determination of the will is not directed by the moral inclination of the will, but rather by the knowledge of natural laws and the physical power to employ these to its purposes.

> KANT formulates the antinomy between the ideal of science and that of personality as it is implied in the concept of the highest good as the "antinomy of practical reason".

Thus arises the "antinomy of practical reason" which KANT treats in the chapter entitled *"About the dialectic of pure Reason in the defining of the concept of the highest good"*. He thought, however, the following solution would afford a satisfactory answer to the difficulty. He conceded that the judgment according to which the desire for happiness is the moving cause of moral action, must be unconditionally qualified as false. The second proposition, that happiness is the necessary result of virtue, however, is only false insofar as virtue is considered to be the cause of happiness in the *sense world*, so that only a phenomenal existence would be ascribed to rational beings. It is, however, not only quite reasonable to think of the existence of man as *noumenon* in an intelligible world, but there is even given in the moral law a pure intelligible determinative ground of the causality of free personality in the sense-world. Therefore, according to KANT, it is not impossible that by an intelligible Creator of nature, the moral inclination is set in a necessary causal coherence with beatitude as its effect in the sense-world.

Thus KANT finally felt compelled to accept a coherence between "nature" and "freedom" in order to escape the antinomical consequences of his hypostatization (and consequently logicistic formalization) of moral personality. The acceptance of such an intelligible Creator of nature (the Deity) cannot be rationally proved, but it is a *postulate* of pure practical reason that makes possible the realization of the highest good. This postulate consequently, does not rest upon a theoretical knowledge, but just as the two other postulates of pure practical reason (freedom in a positive sense and immortality), it rests upon a universally valid and necessary reasonable faith in the reality of a suprasensory, noumenal world and in the possibility of the realization of the highest good.

It is easily seen that this entire attempt to bring "nature" and "freedom" again in a deeper coherence, can only be accomplished by abandoning the Idea of the "homo noumenon" as "Ding an sich". If the free and autonomous moral function of personality is actually to be the "substance" of human being (existence), a substance, which according to Descartes' pregnant description *"nulla rē indiget ad existendum"*, then there is no possible bridge between "nature" and "freedom". Every attempt to effect a synthesis must necessarily dissolve the basic absolutization in Kant's Humanistic ideal of personality. Kroner correctly observes, that the very characteristic of pure practical reason, i.e. its autonomy, is undermined by the inclusion of happiness as material determination ("Inhaltsbestimmung") in the pure moral law. By so doing the very absolute sovereignty of the moral will is restricted to sensibility instead of maintaining its absolute independence in the face of the latter [1].

It is the concept of the highest good itself into which all of the antinomies between the ideal of personality and that of science are crowded together!

> In Kant's Idea of God the ideal of personality dominates the ideal of science.

Kant's Idea of deity as postulate of "pure practical reason" is the final hypostatization of the ideal of personality. In this hypostatization, the Idea of the noumenal world as "a nature under the autonomy of pure practical reason" [2], reaches its climax. This reasonable God is the categorical imperative itself, conceived of as *the noumenal determinative ground of sensible nature*. His will does not exceed "practical reason" with its hypostatized moral law. For the "principle of morality is not merely restricted to men, but extends to all finite beings which have reason and will, nay it even includes the infinite Being as Supreme Intelligence" [3].

The autonomous will can only recognize a command as divine insofar as it originates from "practical reason".

The philosophy of "religion" which Kant built upon his metaphysics of "reasonable faith" is the "Religion within the boundaries of mere Reason". In the writing published under the same title Kant attempts to accommodate Christian faith to his metaphysics rooted in his Humanist ideal of personality. In so

---

[1] Kroner, *Op. cit.* I, p. 209.
[2] *Kr. d. pr. V.*, t.a.p., p. 158.
[3] T.a.p., p. 143.

doing he gave a striking example of the fundamental lack of insight into the essence and starting-point of the Christian doctrine, a lack of insight, which has from the outset characterized Humanistic philosophy. The faith of pure reason is, according to him, the kernel of all religious dogmas. Mankind is not capable of conceiving this kernel in its "purity"; it must be rendered perceptible, so that it can become a living force, a "religious reality".

If this "pure ethical kernel" is selected from the Christian revelation it is wonderfully in accord with the "apriori reasonable faith". The fall into sin is then nothing but the antagonism between sensory and moral nature, between "nature" and "freedom" in man.

The "radical evil" in human nature is its tendency to subject the will to sensory inclinations, instead of directing it by the "categorical imperative". Regeneration is a free deed of our moral nature through which the good conquers the evil.

The "God-man" is the Idea of the "moral ideal man" in whom reasonable faith accepts the absolute realization of the Idea of the good; in this sense the God-man is the pre-requisite for regeneration, for the latter can only take effect insofar as we believe in the possible realization of the moral Idea.

Consequently, insofar as the God-man is the redemptive force through whom regeneration is effectuated in this moral ideal of humanity and in the striving toward its realization, individual sins are atoned!

This is the religion of the Humanistic ideal of personality clad in the stiff garb of moralistic rationalism. And this is the "pure ethical kernel" which Kant thought he could select from the Christian revelation!

§ 6 - THE DEVELOPMENT OF THE BASIC ANTINOMY IN THE CRITIQUE OF JUDGMENT

The attempt to resolve the dualism between the ideal of science and that of personality in the Critique of Judgment. The problem of individuality.

In both the *"Critique of Pure Reason"* and the *"Critique of Practical Reason"*, Kant failed to resolve the antinomy between the ideals of science and of personality. In his third main work the *"Critique of Judgment"*, Kant attempted to bridge the cleft between nature and freedom in another way. Here he surveyed the entire course which his philosophical thought had previously taken. In his famous introduction he wrote: "Now, to be sure, an immense cleft has been established between the realm of the nature-concept as the sensory, and the realm of the freedom-idea as the super-sensory, so that no transition is possible from the former to the latter (that is to say by means of the theoretical use of reason), as if there were two different worlds, the one of which cannot have any influence on the other. Nevertheless, the super-sensory *ought* to influence the sensory, that is to say the freedom-Idea ought to realize in the sense-world the goal set by its laws; consequently nature must also be conceivable in such a way, that the laws of its forms at least agree with the possibility of the goals which are to be realized in it in conformity to laws of freedom. — Consequently, there must after all be a ground of *unity* of the super-sensory which lies at the foundation of nature, with the practical content of the freedom-Idea; and although the concept of this unity neither theoretically nor practically arrives at a knowledge of the same, and consequently *does not have a proper realm*" (I italicize), "nevertheless it must make possible the transition from the mode of thought according to the principles of the one to that according to the principles of the other" [1].

The problem raised by the *"Critique of Judgment"* is, consequently, not new to KANT's system. For it is once again the possibility of subsuming nature under the freedom of reason which

---

[1] *Kritik der Urteilskraft* (W.W. Bnd. VI) pp. 19/20: "Ob nun zwar eine unübersehbare Kluft zwischen dem Gebiete des Naturbegriffs, als dem Sinnlichen, und dem Gebiete des Freiheitsbegriffs, als dem übersinnlichen, befestigt ist, so dasz von dem ersteren zum anderen (also vermittelst des theoretischen Gebrauchs der Vernunft) kein Übergang möglich ist, gleich als ob es so viel verscheidene Welten wären, deren erste auf die zweite keinen Einflusz haben kann: so *soll* doch diese auf jene einen Einflusz haben, nämlich der Freiheitsbegriff soll den durch seine Gesetze aufgegebenen Zweck in der Sinnenwelt wirklich machen; und die Natur musz folglich auch so gedacht werden können, dasz die Gesetzmäszigkeit ihrer Form wenigstens zur Möglichkeit der in ihr zu bewirkenden Zwecke nach Freiheitsgesetzen zusammenstimme. — Also musz es doch einen Grund der *Einheit* des Übersinnlichen, welches der Natur zum Grunde liegt, mit dem, was der Freiheitsbegriff praktisch enthält, geben, wovon der Begriff, wenn er gleich weder theoretisch noch praktisch zu einem Erkenntnisse desselben gelangt, *mithin kein eigentümliches Gebiet hat*, dennoch den Übergang von der Denkungsart nach den Prinzipien der einen zu der nach Prinzipien der anderen möglich macht."

is made a problem. But the manner in which this third *Critique* seeks to arrive at a solution is certainly original. The course of thought here followed constitutes a counterpart to the way that had been taken by Leibniz.

Kant's rationalistic conception of individuality.

The path taken by Kant led him to consider the problem of individuality, or rather that of the "specificity in nature"; for Kant was always concerned with conformity to a law and, as we know, within the cadre of his rationalistic cosmonomic Idea he again and again identified law and subject [1]. Only Kant's aesthetic philosophy, in its doctrine of the creative genius, attributed an independent place to subjective individuality. In the final analysis, it appeared that both the laws of understanding and those of reason can only determine their "object" apriori in an abstract-universal way. There are, however, many forms of nature, "as it were so many modifications of the universal transcendental nature-concept" which are left undetermined by the laws given apriori by the pure logical function of understanding. For these forms of nature there must also be laws, which, to be sure, are empirical and consequently, according to our rational insight, must be called contingent, but which nevertheless, if they actually can be called laws, must be viewed as necessarily originating from a principle of unity in multiplicity. And this is the case even though this latter principle may be unknown to us [2].

Now in the "class of the higher cognitive faculties" there is a peculiar connective link between understanding and reason, namely, the "power of judgment" ("Urteilskraft"). This faculty subsumes the particular under the universal laws, and as such, i.e. as "determining transcendental faculty of judgment", it is constitutive for experience; while, as the mere "reflecting power of judgment", it judges of the appropriate accommodation of the particularity in the laws of nature to our cognitive faculty

---

[1] In our later treatment of the problem of individuality we shall see, that the species as a type-concept includes only the typical law-conformedness, but does not include subjective individuality. Furthermore, we shall find that in the irreducibleness of subjective individuality to the typical law of individuality, the subject-side of our cosmos discloses very clearly its proper unexchangeable rôle with respect to the law-side.

[2] *Kritik der Urteilskraft*, p. 24.

(that can only give universal laws apriori). And in this latter function it is not constitutive for experience, but regulative only.

When compared with the determining faculty, the reflecting faculty of judgment, consequently, operates in just the opposite way. The latter judges the particular in its accommodation to the universal laws given to "nature" by the understanding in the apriori synthesis. The determining judicative faculty, on the contrary, proceeds from the very apriori universal laws and subsumes under the latter the particular empirical laws of nature. The "reflecting judgment", in contrast to the determining, does not possess objective principles apriori, but only subjective ones. It judges the particular multiplicity of nature *as if* a higher understanding than our own had given the empirical laws of nature for the benefit of our cognitive faculty, in order to make possible a system of experience according to particular laws of nature.

KANT related the reflecting power of judgment to his famous schema of the faculties of the soul. According to him, all of the latter can be reduced to three, which do not allow of any further deduction from a common basis. These faculties are the cognitive, the feeling of pleasure and pain, and the desiring power. Insofar as the former, as the faculty for the acquisition of theoretical knowledge, is related to "nature", it receives laws apriori only from the understanding. The desiring power, as a "higher faculty according to the Idea of freedom", receives its laws a priori only from reason. Therefore, in accordance with his schema, it is quite natural for KANT to relate the reflecting power of judgment to the feeling that we have when confronted with the theoretically known nature.

According to KANT's extremely rationalistic conception, every feeling is a "synthetical activity" through which we relate the representation of an object to our subjective intentional activity in which we set ourselves a purpose. In every feeling we order an imagined object under an end.

The Idea of teleology in nature.

In its empirical form the reflecting faculty of judgment, according to KANT, coincides completely with the "inner life of feeling". It is this power that permits us to recognize the higher unity between understanding and reason, because it orders a "Gegenstand" of knowledge under a goal. But these empirical reflections of the power of judgment being entirely arbitrary and subjective, are never able to possess a universally valid and necessary character. The reflecting judgment possesses, however, a universally valid principle apriori, a transcendental principle joined with a feeling which is likewise necessary and universal. This principle is that of the *"formal teleology of nature."*

For the concept of the objects so far as they are judged according to this principle, is only "the pure concept of objects of possible empirical knowledge in general" and includes no single empirical content [1].

According to this transcendental principle, the reflective power of judgment must consider nature as if it were generated after a teleological plan. As KANT himself says, "as if that which, for our human insight, is contingent in the empirical specificity of the laws of nature, is, nevertheless, generated by a higher intellect after a law-conformed unity, which unity, although not knowable to us, is, however, conceivable."

> The law of specification as the regulative principle of the transcendental faculty of judgment for the contemplation of nature.

This transcendental concept of a teleology in nature is neither a concept of nature, nor a concept of freedom. For the power of judgment, through its transcendental principle, does not dictate a law to nature, but rather to itself in order to judge nature [2]. This law can be called the "law of specification", and it is a mere regulative principle for our view of nature. "For it is not a principle of the determining, but only of the reflecting power of judgment; one wants only that the empirical laws of nature — as to its universal laws the latter may be ordered as it pleases — must absolutely be investigated according to this principle and the maxims founded therein; because only in this case can we proceed with the use of our understanding in experience and can acquire knowledge" [3].

---

[1] *Kritik der Urteilskraft*, t.a.p., pp. 26/7.
[2] KANT here speaks of the "heautonomy" of the reflecting judgment.
[3] *Kritik der Urteilskraft*, p. 32: "Denn es ist nicht ein Prinzip der bestimmenden, sondern blosz der reflektierenden Urteilskraft; man will nur, dasz man, die Natur mag ihren allgemeinen Gesetzen nach eingerichtet sein, wie sie wolle, durchaus nach jenem Prinzip und den sich darauf gründenden Maximen ihren empirischen Gesetzen nachspüren müsse, weil wir, nur so weit als jenes statt findet, mit dem Gebrauche unseres Verstandes in der Erfahrung fortkommen und Erkenntnis erwerben können."

If we momentarily overlook the task which KANT here ascribes in a general sense to the reflecting power of judgment, it is easily ascertained, that the basic problem submitted for solution to the *"Critique of Judgment"* has its root in the question which the other two Critiques had failed to solve; namely, the problem concerning the relation between the ideal of science and that of personality. *The Critique of Pure Reason* did not ascribe to the understanding the possibility of possessing knowledge of the "totality of determinations", which knowledge was supposed to have included that of the theoretical necessity of empirical laws. If such a possibility were open to the understanding, then, once again, the ideal of science would have dominated the realm of the "absolute", which KANT had once and for all intended to set apart in the supra-sensory teleological kingdom of personality as *"Selbst-zweck"* (end in itself).

The logical and psychical functions of consciousness may, consequently, only be brought to a unity in a *formal* synthesis, and the sensory material must continue to be a limit for logical thought.

The teleological mode of contemplation of practical reason, on the other hand, may not penetrate into the domain of the ideal of science, since KANT will not abandon the sovereignty of mathematical and natural scientific thought over nature. This prevented him from following the course taken by FICHTE who at the expense of the ideal of science accepted the domination of the ideal of personality over nature!

The reason why the *"Critique of Judgment"* cannot resolve the basic discord in KANT's Archimedean point.

Consequently, there remained for KANT no other way than to seek a connecting link between understanding and reason. However, this connecting link, in its subjective functional character, is actually not the absolute "supra-sensory subject beyond theoretical and practical reason", but only a third immanent function of consciousness next to and between the latter. For that very reason, it cannot effect a veritable unity between the two antagonistic factors of the Humanist transcendental ground-Idea.

According to both "sources of knowledge" which the faculty of judgment compares with one another reflecting on their mutual appropriate accord, i.e. sensory intuition and logical understanding, this faculty can display an alternative function: it can either judge a given sensory representation — before we have acquired any logical concept of it — and establish, that in its immediate visibleness it has an appropriate accommodation to our understanding; or it can, inversely, judge that the concept of an object is the ground of being of the latter and, consequently, establish that the concept has an appropriate accomodation to the visible reality of the object.

In the first case, the object is only called appropriate upon a subjective ground, since its representation is directly joined with a subjective feeling of pleasure (complacence) that never can become an objective "piece of knowledge", and this representation is itself a teleological representation of an aesthetic character. In the second case the teleological judgment is related to a specific objective knowledge of the object under a given concept; it has nothing to do with a subjective feeling of pleasure concerning things, but with the understanding in the judgment of things only. In this case we judge that the teleology is laid objectively (actually) in the thing of nature as an organism.

In the first case, the original point lies in the emotional effect of (natural) things upon us, and we become explicitly conscious of the teleological relations only by analytical investigation. In the second case, the centre of gravity of our attitude toward the things lies in the rational conception of the relations in the "object", which we judge to be appropriate. Moreover, in this case the feeling of pleasure is only secondarily united with this judgment.

It is upon these alternative functions that KANT based the division of the "*Critique of Judgment*" into the critique of the aesthetic and that of the teleological judgment: "By the former we understand the faculty to judge the formal appropriateness (ordinarily also called the subjective) through the feeling of pleasure or pain: by the latter the faculty to judge the real (objective) appropriateness of nature through the understanding and the reason" [1].

The former has to demonstrate how the universal validity of a cognitive judgment can rightly be attributed to the aesthetic judgment, even though such a judgment lacks a concept. The critique of the teleological judgment has to show, that all teleo-

---

[1] *Kr. der Urt. kr.*, p. 41.

logical contemplation of nature only possesses a regulative value for biological investigation and it must reject its possible claims to constitutive value for knowledge.

In the final paragraph of the "Introduction", KANT treated "the uniting of the laws given by the understanding and by reason through the faculty of judgment." Here, once again, the dualism between the ideal of science and that of personality is formulated with great acumen: "The realm of the nature-concept subjected to the laws of the one legislator, and that of the freedom-Idea subjected to those of the other, are completely isolated from each other, precluding all reciprocal influence which they (each according to their basic laws) might have on one another; this separation is guaranteed by the great cleft which severs the super-sensory from the phenomena. The freedom-Idea does not determine anything with respect to the theoretical knowledge of nature; just as the nature-concept does not determine anything with respect to the practical laws of freedom; and insofar it is impossible to bridge over the gulf between the two different realms" [1].

Be that as it may, the *"Critique of Practical Reason"* furnished the Idea of a causality through freedom. This causality through free will is the final goal, which itself (or the appearance of which in the sensory world) *ought* to exist, to which end the condition in nature was pre-supposed which would permit the possibility of such an effect. Now, according to KANT, the faculty of judgment is supposed to furnish us with the mediating concept between the concept of nature and that of freedom, and this in the concept of a teleology in nature: "because through the latter is understood the possibility of the final end which can only be realized in nature and in accord with its laws" [2].

KANT thought that in his system the concept of an absolute causality through freedom could be conceived of without an

---

[1] *Kr. der Urt. kr.*, p. 43: "Das Gebiet des Naturbegriffs unter der einen und das des Freiheitsbegriffs unter der anderen Gesetzgebung sind gegen allen wechselseitigen Einflusz, den sie für sich (ein jedes nach seinen Grundgesetzen) auf einander haben könnten, durch die grosze Kluft, welche das Übersinnliche van den Erscheinungen trennt, gänzlich abgesondert. Der Freiheitsbegriff bestimmt nichts in Ansehung der theoretischen Erkenntnis der Natur; der Naturbegriff eben sowohl nichts in Ansehung der praktischen Gesetze der Freiheit; und es ist in sofern nicht möglich, eine Brücke von einem Gebiete zu dem andern hinüberzuschlagen."

[2] *Ibid.*, p. 44.

intrinsic contradiction. It has, however, become apparent to us, that the concept of an unconditional "causa noumenon" is encumbered with all the antinomies of the Humanistic concept of substance.

The "homo noumenon" is supposed to be a "Ding an sich" in an absolute sense, and its moral freedom was to have an unconditional validity. This hypostatization is, nevertheless, actually determined by analytical thought in its cosmic relativity [1]. It is nothing but an absolutizing of the moral aspect of human existence, which is lifted out of the cosmic temporal coherence of the modal law-spheres by means of a false analysis, and is thus logically formalized. And in this logical formalization it destroys itself. Even the Humanistic freedom-motive is in this way almost completely reduced to the logical principle of contradiction. It is only the Idea of human personality as "*Selbstzweck*" in which the religious meaning of this motive could withdraw in order to escape its complete dissolution into a formal tautology. But we have seen, that this Idea itself, because of its absolutization, dissolves itself in nothingness.

> The same antinomy which intrinsically destroys the Idea of the "homo noumenon" recurs in the principle of teleological judgment.

The same antinomy reappears in the principle of teleological

---

[1] In the famous para. 76 of the "*Critique of Judgment*", KANT writes: "Die Vernunft ist ein Vermögen der Prinzipien und geht in ihrer äuszersten Forderung auf das Unbedingte; da hingegen der Verstand ihn immer nur unter einer gewissen Bedingung die gegeben werden musz zu Diensten steht. Ohne Begriffe des Verstandes aber, welchen objective Realität gegeben werden muss, kann die Vernunft gar nichts objectiv (synthetisch) urteilen und enthält als theoretische Vernunft für sich schleehterdings keine konstitutive, sondern blosz regulative Prinzipien." ["Reason is a faculty of principles, and in its extreme demands it points to the unconditional; *the understanding, on the contrary, is always only at the service of the former on a specific condition which must be previously fulfilled.* Reason, however, is not able to judge anything objectively (synthetically) without concepts of the understanding to which objective reality must be given, and as theoretical reason it does not contain in itself any constitutive principles, but merely regulative ones."]

But KANT has not seen that the Idea of the "homo noumenon" as the hypostasis of the moral function of personality is itself the product of a religiously founded analytical mental activity which ignores the cosmic coherence and is thus false! For the transcendental "Idea" points toward the totality of meaning and not towards an analytical abstraction, which in its hypostatization destroys the meaning-coherence.

judgment. The point here in question is the possibility to conceive of the stringent mechanical causality of the classical Humanistic science-ideal together with a teleology in nature, a teleology which can only find termination in a moral "Selbstzweck".

The critique of teleological judgment derived the justification of a teleological view of nature from the fact that in nature itself phenomena are given, namely, the living organisms, which set a limit to causal explanation and present themselves to our contemplation, as if they were constructed after a teleological plan.

A thing, which as a product of nature can nevertheless be conceived only as a natural *organism,* must be *related to itself* as cause and effect. It is a product of nature itself, and not like the beautiful, only the *representation* of a thing which is produced by nature or by art. For it gives "objective reality" to the concept of a goal. Since this is the case, the question must necessarily be raised: How is this possible according to the "transcendental conditions of objective reality" in conformity with the category of causality? Now the connection of cause and effect, so far as it is only thought by means of the understanding, is a synthetical determination of phenomena that forms a series of causes and effects and in which the effect is always subsequent to the cause. Therefore, the causal coherence, in a natural organism, can never be a *nexus effectivus,* a coherence of mechanical, efficient causes.

The organism cannot result from an external cause, but must be thought of as its own cause and at the same time as the effect of this cause; therefore, this relation of causality can be considered by the reflecting judgment in such a manner only, that it is viewed as a *nexus finalis,* in which the effect is at the same time thought of as a *causa finalis* [1]. This includes a twofold condition:

1 - the parts of the organism can only exist through their relation to the whole, and

2 - the parts are only connected to the unity of the whole through the fact that they are the mutual cause and effect of each other's form.

---

[1] *Kr. der Url. kr.,* pp. 261/2.

Cosmonomic Idea of Humanistic immanence-philosophy

The fictitious character of the teleological view of nature follows directly from KANT's transcendental ground-Idea.

Since such a teleological union of cause and effect is known to us only from our own human action, we can, to be sure, lay this teleological principle at the foundation of our judgment concerning the natural organisms, but we must always bear in mind, that by so doing we do not categorically determine the "objective reality" of the organic, but only reflect on it, in order to acquire a regulative principle for the mechanical determination of nature. We may judge the living organism, only *as if* a teleological activity lay at its foundation. KANT's dualistic transcendental ground-Idea does not permit any other view.

The principle of the inner teleology in nature leads the reflecting judgment necessarily beyond the living organism to the *"Idee der gesamten Natur als eines Systems nach der Regel der Zwecke"*, *in other words*, to the Idea of nature as a "universal organism" (an expression first employed by SCHELLING) to which Idea all mechanism of nature must be subordinated according to principles of reason: "The principle of reason has for it (viz. the teleological judgment) only subjective competency, that is to say as maxim. Everything in the world is good for something whatsoever; nothing in it is aimless; and by the example which nature gives in its organical products, one is entitled, nay called upon, to expect from it and its laws nothing but what is appropriate in its totality" [1].

The teleological view may never again be introduced as an immanent principle of the causal explanation of nature. It remains a transcendental Idea, a limiting concept for the latter and has as such the heuristic value that it constantly raises the question as to which mechanism is responsible for effectuating the particular end of nature.

On the other hand, insofar as it can discover no single "Selbstzweck", no single final goal in nature, the teleological view of nature automatically results in the supra-sensory Idea of the "homo noumenon" and with that in an *ethical teleology*. Thus it appears, that in the "reflecting faculty of judgment" a reconcilia-

---

[1] *Kr. der Urt. kr.*, p. 268/9: "Das Prinzip der Vernunft ist ihr als nur subjectiv, d.i. als Maxime zuständig. Alles in der Welt ist irgend wozu gut; nichts ist in ihr umsonst; und man ist durch das Beispiel, das die Natur an ihren organischen Produkten gibt, berechtigt, ja berufen, von ihr und ihren Gesetzen nichts, als was im Ganzen zweckmäszig ist, zu erwarten."

tion is to be really found between the ideal of science and that of personality. *This reconciliation, however, is not a real one.* In the "Dialectic of teleological judgment" KANT himself begins with the formulation of the antinomy between the mechanical view of nature of the ideal of science and the teleological view of nature which is essentially derived from the ideal of personality. The thesis in this antinomy is: "All production of material things is possible according to merely mechanical laws."

The antithesis: "Some production of the same is not possible according to merely mechanical laws" [1].

It is clear that the antinomy here formulated fits entirely in the cadre of the Humanist cosmonomic Idea, in which the antagonistic postulates of continuity of the ideal of science and of personality are involved in an irreconcilable conflict with each other.

The origin of the antinomy of the faculty of teleological judgment in the light of KANT's cosmonomic Idea.

We are not concerned here with the maintenance of the modal boundaries of meaning among the law-spheres which are anchored in the cosmic order of time, but only with the maintenance of the ideal of personality against the ideal of science that desires to erase all the boundaries of meaning through creative sovereign thought. For this very reason, the solution given by KANT to the antinomy which he formulated, rests entirely upon an analytical hypostatic division of the functions of consciousness of reflective and determinative judgment: "All appearance of an antinomy between the maxims of the properly physical (mechanical) and the teleological (technical) mode of explanation consequently rests upon this: that a principle of the reflecting faculty of judgment is taken for that of the determinative faculty and the *autonomy* of the former (which only subjectively holds good for the use of our reason in respect to the particular laws of experience) for the *heteronomy* of the latter which must conform itself to the (universal and particular) laws gives by the understanding" [2].

---

[1] *Ib.*, p. 278.

[2] *Kr. der Urt. kr.*, p. 281: "Aller Anschein einer Antinomie zwischen den Maximen der eigentlich physischen (mechanischen) und der teleologischen (technischen) Erklärungsart, beruht also darauf: dasz man

From where, however, does the antinomy of teleological judgment arise? It arises from thinking together two principles which, according to KANT, really have their origin in two entirely different and separated functions of reason.

This antinomy cannot be solved by referring either of these functions to its own apriori principles. We are here concerned with the very basic question which every transcendental ground-idea must answer in principle: Where is to be found the deeper unity and the mutual coherence of meaning of the different functions of our consciousness and of temporal reality?

This problem is not taken up again by KANT before the famous Par. 78 of his "Critique of Judgment" where he treats, "Von der Vereinigung des Prinzips des allgemeinen Mechanismus der Materie mit dem teleologischen in der Technik der Natur."

After having first established that the mechanical and teleological ways of explaining nature mutually exclude each other, KANT observes: "The principle which is to make possible the compatibility of the two in judging nature according to them, must be placed in that which lies outside both (consequently also outside the possible empirical representation of nature) but which nevertheless contains the ground of them. This is the super-sensory and each of the two modes of explanation is to be related to it" [1].

The reason why the causal and teleological views of nature are capable of coexisting harmoniously in thought is consequently sought by KANT in the supra-sensory substratum of nature, of which, however, we cannot acquire any theoretical knowledge [2].

---

einen Grundsatz der reflectierenden Urteilskraft mit dem der bestimmenden und die *Autonomie* der ersteren (die blosz subjectiv für unsern Vernunftgebrauch in Ansehung der besonderen Erfahrungsgesetze gilt) mit der *Heteronomie* der anderen, welche sich nach den von dem Verstande gegebenen (allgemeinen und besonderen) Gesetze richten musz, verwechselt."

[1] *Kr. der Urt. kr.*, p. 309: "Das Princip, welches die Vereinbarkeit beider in Beurteilung der Natur nach denselben möglich machen soll, musz in dem, was auszerhalb beiden (mithin auch auszer der möglichen empirischen Naturvorstellung) liegt, von dieser aber doch den Grund enthält, d.i. im Übersinnlichen gesetzt und eine jede beider Erklärungsarten darauf bezogen werden."

[2] *Ibid.*, p. 312, KANT wrote as proof for the necessity of thinking together natural mechanism and natural teleology: "Denn wo Zwecke als Grunde der Möglichkeit gewisser Dinge gedacht werden, da musz man auch Mittel annehmen, deren Wirkungsgesetz *für sich* nichts einen Zweck

The influence of NEWTON's view of the compatibility of mechanism and divine teleology in nature is here very evident [1].

Once again we are confronted with the concept of the *"Naturding an sich"* which is so extremely problematical in the system of KANT. Moreover, in this connection it is doubly problematical, since KANT himself began to explain, that the apriori teleological principle of the reflecting judgment may itself never be related to the objective reality of things in nature, but is only a subjective principle for judging nature, which we essentially derive from the teleology in our own human actions!

How then can the basis for the compatibility in thought of the mechanical and teleological explanation of nature suddenly be sought in a supra-sensory substratum of nature, while a little earlier, KANT himself wrote: "in conformity with the particular constitution of our understanding *we* are *obliged to consider* some products of nature with respect to their possibility as being produced after a plan and as goals; we may not pretend, however, that there actually exists a particular cause which has its determinative ground in the idea of a goal; consequently it is not permitted to deny, that another (higher) understanding than the human one can find the ground of possibility of such products also in the mechanism of nature, i.e. of a causal connection for which not exclusively an understanding as cause is assumed" [2].

Voraussetzendes bedarf, mithin mechanisch und doch eine untergeordnete Ursache absichtlicher Wirkungen sein kann." ["Where ends are thought of as grounds of the possibility of certain things, there must also be assumed means, whose law of operation in itself does not need anything which pre-supposes a goal, and consequently can be mechanical and nevertheless a subordinate cause of teleological effects."] If consistently applied, this Idea leads to the dissolution of the hypostatization of the moral function in the "homo noumenon".

[1] The rather primitive conception of divine Providence in nature after the pattern of human technics (compare the machine!) was accepted by the whole of enlightened deism.

[2] *Kr. der Urt. kr.*, p. 301: "gewisse Naturprodukte *müssen* nach der besondern Beschaffenheit unseres Verstandes *von uns* ihrer Möglichkeit nach als absichtlich und als Zwecke erzeugt *betrachtet werden,* ohne doch darum zu verlangen, dasz es wirklich eine besondere Ursache, welche die Vorstellung eines Zwecks zu ihrem Bestimmungsgrunde hat, gebe, mithin ohne in Abrede zu ziehen, dasz nicht ein anderer (höherer) Verstand, als der menschliche auch im Mechanism der Natur, d.i. einer Kausalverbindung, zu der nicht ausschlieszungsweise ein Verstand als Ursache angenommen wird den Grund der Möglichkeit solcher Produkte der Natur antreffen könne."

In this connection KANT himself expressly speaks of a "gewisse Zufälligkeit der Beschaffenheit *unseres* Verstandes" (a certain casuality in the constitution of *our* understanding), which would necessitate a teleological judgment of nature.

Furthermore, in the preceding § 76 and § 77 he had worked out this Idea more precisely in the famous contrast between the intuitive divine understanding which is creative in a *material sense* and the human understanding which is only creative in a *formal sense*.

Our understanding has this peculiarity, that it must be given sensory material which does not lie in the understanding itself, and so is not created by the latter. This material is the ground of all contingency of the particular in nature, in contradistinction to the formal and universal laws given by the understanding. For the same reasons our understanding must distinguish the possibility and reality of things. If our cognitive faculty were not assigned to the cooperation of two distinct functions, i.e. logical understanding and sensory intuition, then the distinction between possibility and reality would disappear [1]. An absolutely intuitive understanding could only know *reality*. "For an understanding in which this difference should not present itself, it would hold good: all objects which I know, are (exist)" [2] and the distinction between contingency and necessity would also disappear for such a mind (compare LEIBNIZ). Now although human reason can ascend to the transcendental Idea of the absolute necessity (in which possibility and reality are inseparably united), yet this Idea itself is only something *possible*; as an *Idea*, it is distinct from reality.

The situation which holds good for our human understanding in respect to the relation between possibility and reality, has also validity with respect to its conception of the relation between mechanism and teleology in nature. The contingency in the particular in nature is the remainder which for our understanding is not definable by the universal laws which it imposes apriori upon the phenomena. In order to subject this remainder to the understanding, we must ascend above mere possibility, above the mere universal, above the mere concept, to the transcendental Idea of reason, which requires an absolute necessity.

---

[1] *Op. cit.*, p. 300.
[2] "Für einen Verstand bei dem dieser Unterschied nicht einträte, würde es heiszen: alle Objekte, die ich erkenne, *sind* (existieren)".

It is true, that by so doing we subject the particular itself, by means of teleological judgment, to a law, namely a teleological principle, but this is only a subjective principle of reason valid for our judgment, "which as regulative (not constitutive) holds good for our *human faculty of judgment* with the same necessity as if it were an objective principle" [1].

In other words, the antinomy which in KANT's functionalistic mode of thought necessarily emerges between natural causality and natural teleology, remains in fact unsolved. For the principle of teleology in nature remains in the last analysis a fictitious one, belonging to the *"as if"*- consideration of our human reason. Consequently, we may conclude, that also his third Critique could give no real solution to the basic antinomy between the ideal of science and that of personality.

This basic antinomy is irreconcilable, since the absolutizing of reason must necessarily proceed from a rejection of the cosmic order of time, which alone can determine the mutual relation between the modal law-spheres, and which alone can maintain the cosmic coherence of meaning in the sovereignty of each sphere.

Even the appeal to an absolute intuitive mind is of no avail, because this "absolute mind" is itself the final hypostatization of the Humanistic ideal of science, and as such is not identical with the final hypostatization of the ideal of personality in the moral God of reason.

The basic antinomy between the ideals of science and of personality in KANT is everywhere crystallized in the form-matter schema. A synopsis of the development of this antinomy in the three Critiques.

If we survey KANT's three Critiques, it appears, that the basic antinomy between the ideal of science and that of personality has everywhere crystallized in the dialectical form-matter scheme. Thereby we have proved the thesis, developed in our Prolegomena, that this scheme, formally derived from the religious ground-motive of Greek thought, in KANT's philosophy has assumed an intrinsically Humanistic sense.

In the *"Critique of Pure Reason"* it violated the sovereignty

---

[1] *Kr. der Url. kr.*, p. 300: "welches als regulativ (nicht konstitutiv) für unsere *menschliche Urteilskraft* eben so notwendig gilt, als ob es ein objectives Prinzip wäre."

of the Humanistic science-ideal and, where it appealed to a natural substance, it simultaneously evoked an antinomy with the ideal of personality, that can only find its "substance" in moral law.

In the *"Critique of Practical Reason"*, it dissolved the hypostasis of the ideal of personality, the Idea of the "homo noumenon" as a "Ding an sich", by again relating this Idea to the sensory.

Finally, in the *"Critique of Judgment"*, it produced the antinomy which necessarily arises by subjecting the same sensory aspect of reality to two principles which by definition mutually exclude each other, namely, that of mechanical causality and that of teleology in nature. In KANT's system a teleology can never be a teleology of *nature*, if, as he supposes, it must be thought of as supra-sensory[2]. For how can the principle of teleology be related to sensory experience while the sensory and the supra-sensory are divided by an unbridgeable cleft?

Moreover, as soon as KANT again relates this principle of teleology to the sensory material of experience, even though only as a subjective principle for the use of the understanding, this material is subjected to two principles which mutually exclude one another. In this way the conflict between the ideal of science and that of personality is unchained in the original domain of the Humanistic science-ideal, namely, the experience of nature.

---

[1] In the second discourse of a later edition (1804) of his "Wissenschaftslehre" FICHTE observed these antinomies very clearly, where he wrote concerning KANT's three Critiques with their three absoluta: "Überdies, was noch mehr bedeutete, war über der zuletzt aufgestellten moralischen Welt, als der einen Welt an sich, die empirische verloren gegangen, zur Vergeltung, dasz sie zu erst die moralische vernichtet hatte..." ["Besides, which signified still more, with the finally projected moral world as the one world in itself, the empirical had been lost, in return for the fact that it first had destroyed the moral one..."].

[2] In his *"Critique of Judgment"* KANT thought he could continue to speak of nature-teleology by simultaneously conceiving the organized product of nature under the law of mechanical causality: "da ferner ohne allen zu der teleologisch gedachten Erzeugungsart hinzukommenden Begriff von einem dabei zugleich anzutreffenden Mechanism der Natur dergleichen Erzeugung gar nicht als Naturprodukt beurteilt werden könnte." ["because furthermore without combining the teleological conception of the mode of production with a concept of a simultaneous mechanism of nature, such a production could not at all be judged as a nature-product."] Thereby, however, only the mechanism of nature, and not the teleology of nature is saved!

Just as, on the other hand, the ideal of personality is dissolved by joining the principle of teleology (and with that in the last analysis the "homo noumenon" as the final goal) with the substratum of a mechanism of nature.

KANT's dualistic transcendental ground-Idea lacks an unequivocal Archimedean point and an unequivocal Idea of the totality of meaning.

As we observed in an earlier context, KANT's transcendental ground-Idea lacks unity in its Archimedean point and, consequently, an unequivocal Idea of totality. It is true that in its transcendental usage the Idea points very clearly towards the moral aspect of human existence and seems to absolutize it as a totality of meaning. The dualism between the ideal of science and that of personality, however, which characterizes KANT's transcendental ground-Idea, prevented him from reducing all of the functions of human existence to the moral, as the supposed root of personality. The "Ding an sich" of nature, which KANT did not definitely eliminate, continued to be a counter instance against his moralistic Idea of totality.

This is the source of all of the contradictions in his philosophy.

It must be granted that it was a really transcendental critical motive which prevented him from constructing a unity which, indeed, was excluded by his dualistic religious ground-motive [1]. Nevertheless, the very fact that, in the cadre of his transcendental idealism, he emphatically proclaimed the primacy of the ideal of personality must result with an inner necessity in the development of the post-Kantian freedom-idealism which tried to overcome the critical dualism by means of a theoretical dialectic.

KANT's transcendental Idea of freedom became the starting-point of this dialectical evolution in Humanistic thought.

---

[1] In this respect I must correct the opinion defended in the first (Dutch) edition of this work, that the maintaining of this dualism was due to a lack of critical consistency in KANT's thought.

CHAPTER V

THE TENSION BETWEEN THE IDEAL OF SCIENCE AND THAT OF PERSONALITY IN THE IDENTITY-PHILOSOPHY OF POST-KANTIAN FREEDOM-IDEALISM

§ 1 - THE TRANSITIONAL PERIOD BETWEEN CRITICAL IDEALISM AND MONISTIC FREEDOM-IDEALISM. FROM MAIMON TO FICHTE

So the inner dialectic of the religious ground-motive of nature and freedom could not come to rest in KANT's dualistic separation of the ideals of science and personality. It drove post-Kantian freedom-idealism beyond the Kantian transcendental criticism.

The critical[1] separation between understanding and sensibility, universal form and individuality, form and matter of experience, understanding and reason, had to be overcome. The freedom-motive, which since KANT was *increasingly recognized as the very root* of the Humanistic life- and world-view, called into play with a growing urgency its proper inner postulate of continuity. It must with a truly dialectical necessity transform the transcendental Idea concerning the coherence and mutual relations among the modal aspects. Thereby the whole cosmonomic Idea of Humanistic thought changed its form.

The dialectic of theoretical reason with its transcendental Ideas, by which *in* KANT reason elevates *itself* above the limits of sense experience, was to be transformed and enlarged into a new dialectical logic, as a true "organon" of freedom-idealism. Henceforth, all limits of reason ought to be abrogated and "nature" and "freedom" should be *thought together* in a dialectical way. In philosophic thought this program could be realized only by a further pushing back of the classical science-ideal and by its

---

[1] *Translator's note:* This term and the noun "Criticism" are used here to designate the Kantian philosophy as expounded in the three Critiques of the sage of Koeningsberg.   W. Y.

complete subjection to the ideal of personality. Whereas for KANT the theoretical dialectic with its insoluble antinomies was the proof of a speculative misuse of the transcendental Ideas, by which theoretical reason tries to exceed its critical boundaries, the antinomy was now sanctioned as a necessary transitional phase of dialectical thought which must continually proceed to a higher synthesis in order finally to overbridge the religious antithesis in the starting-point of Humanistic philosophy.

> MAIMON's attempt at a solution of the antinomy in KANT's form-matter scheme by means of LEIBNIZ' principle of continuity.

A first attempt at bridging over the fundamental dualism in KANT's critiques of theoretical and practical reason (with their antithetic or rather antinomic relation between "reason" and "sensibility", universally valid apriori form and sensory "empirical" matter) was undertaken by SALOMON MAIMON (1753—1800). He intended to transform KANT's antithesis between sensibility and logical understanding from a fundamental into a gradual one by introducing into Kantian epistemology LEIBNIZ' doctrine concerning the "petites perceptions". For that very reason he eliminated in a radical manner the intrinsically antinomic metaphysical concept of the "thing in itself" which KANT had maintained because he considered sensibility as merely *receptive*.

With MAIMON an absolute idealistic trend entered into the transcendental thought which issued from KANT. This trend would even have the "matter" of experience originate solely from the transcendental consciousness. But MAIMON's method for the realization of this program is to be qualified only as an apostasy from the veritable *transcendental motive* in KANT's philosophy. This qualification holds in spite of the considerable influence MAIMON exercised on the development of transcendental idealism in FICHTE.

Kantian epistemology is completely dissociated from its ὑπόθεσις, from the Idea of the autonomous freedom of human personality. The critical self-reflection on the ideal of personality, as the root of the ideal of science, had begun in KANT's philosophy only to be lost again in MAIMON.

It is essentially the mathematical science-ideal that regains the upper hand in his critical thought. LEIBNIZ' mathematical principle of continuity is introduced into Critical philosophy, to overcome, if possible, the internal antinomy of the Critical form-matter schema. As if this antinomy had a "purely theoretical" origin and could be resolved by the methods of the mathematical ideal of science!

MAIMON even reduced the "sensory matter of experience" to the creative consciousness, understood as purely *theoretical*. The matter of knowledge is produced *unconsciously* in the consciousness: its *genesis* is unknown to the latter. But if it is not to remain completely foreign to "reason", it must be understood as the "transcendental *differential*" of clear transcendental-logical thought.

> MAIMON's falling away from the veritable transcendental motive. How the transcendental Idea loses for him its direction toward KANT's ideal of personality.

The "Ding an sich" then actually loses all metaphysical meaning. Its signification is merged in that of a *theoretical limiting concept*. It indicates the limits under which our consciousness can no longer control its content by its own creative thought-forms.

This limiting concept, however, lacks all veritable *transcendental meaning*, which it had possessed for KANT. Rather it is exclusively oriented to the continuity-postulate of the mathematical science-ideal, as will appear below.

The basic problem which MAIMON encountered even in his first work, *Versuch über die Transcendentalphilosophie,* was that of the relation between the universal apriori forms of the "transcendental consciousness" and the *particular matter*. This was the same problem that KANT had tried to solve in his *Kritik der Urteilskraft* and in the year 1789 MAIMON's book had been sent by MARCUS HERZ to him for criticism even before KANT's third main work had appeared. To bridge the gap between the universal and the particular in our knowledge KANT had also used LEIBNIZ' theological Idea of the "intellectus archetypus" with its mathematical analysis completed in a single intuition (UNO INTUITO) of the whole individual reality (not to be penetrated by our finite understanding). But with him this idea remained a merely *regulative* principle for the use of the understanding, a normative Idea that obtained its transcendental turn in the teleological view of nature, insofar as the latter referred in the last analysis to the supersensible *realm of free-*

dom. On the basis of his transcendental ground-Idea, KANT must reject the metaphysical turn of LEIBNIZ' Idea of the "intellectus archetypus", resulting in a mathematical idealism that seeks both the origin and root of our cosmos in creative mathematical thought. This metaphysics of the science-ideal was incompatible with the freedom-idealism of KANT's Critical philosophy.

MAIMON's mathematical Criticism and the Marburg school among the Neo-Kantians.

MAIMON actually tried to reconcile this mathematical idealism with the Critical transcendental philosophy [1]. According to him, the Idea of the "divine understanding" in its Leibnizian sense remains "an Idea, to which any Critique of Pure Reason must be reduced, if it is to be satisfying" [2].

This was doubtless a regression into the dogmatic attitude of thought which, under the supremacy of the faith in the mathematical science-ideal, could not penetrate to the true ὑπόθεσις of the latter.

LEIBNIZ had wanted to give to phenomena in their sensory form a *foundation* in creative mathematical thought (hence his continual speaking of "phénomènes bien fondés") Similarly MAIMON seeks a mathematical basis for KANT's *matter* of consciousness, as such. This matter could no longer be relegated to the mere receptivity of sensibility, once a break had been made with KANT's doctrine of the "affection" of our subjective sensory function by the "Ding an sich".

The understanding cannot simply accept the sensory impressions of the "Gegenstand" as a *datum*; it necessarily asks after the *principles of their origin*. "Since the business of the understanding is nothing but thinking, i.e. producing unity in the manifold, it can think no object, except by indicating the rule or manner of its origin. For only thereby can the manifold of the same be brought under the unity of the rule. Consequently it can think no object as already originated, but merely as originating, i.e. flowing. The special rule of origination of an object or the nature of its differen-

---

[1] In modern times the Neo-Kantians of the Marburg School have made a similar attempt.

[2] *Über die Progressen der Philosophie*, Streifereien, p. 42, cited by CASSIRER III, p. 96: "eine Idee, worauf eine jede Kritik der reinen Vernunft zurückgebracht werden musz, wenn sie befriedigend sein soll."

t i a l makes it a special object, and the relations of different objects originate from the relations of their rules of originating or their differentials"[1].

Thus the Kantian *Idea*, or the *noumenon*, as limiting concept, gains with MAIMON the significance of a *mathematical differential concept* as the *foundation* of KANT's sensory *matter* of consciousness.

The pure categories of thought can never be *immediately* applied to sensory perceptions "but merely to their elements which are Ideas of reason concerning the mode of origination of these intuitions, and by means of these to the intuitions themselves"[2].

The Idea as such becomes the logical *origin*-principle that knows no other ἀρχή but creative mathematical thought. This was the methodical way which presently was to be taken by the *Marburg* school, much more consistently than MAIMON had done. This school began to apply LEIBNIZ' principle of continuity as a transcendental logical "principle of creation" ("Erzeugungsprinzip") to KANT's categories. The latter could no longer be analyzed as a static *datum* from the table of the forms of logical judgment; rather they must be derived in a dynamic process of creation from their logical origin, from an original synthesis of thought.

But even for this dynamic, genetic view of the "pure forms of consciousness" we find the point of contact in MAIMON's mathematical Criticism. MAIMON carries through his view of the *datum* as "transcendental differential of consciousness" not only with

---

[1] *Versuch über die Transzendentalphilosophie*, cited by CASSIRER III, p. 98: "Denn da das Geschäft des Verstandes nicht anderes als D e n k e n, d.h. Einheit im mannigfaltigen hervorzubringen ist, so kann er sich kein Objekt denken, als blosz dadurch, dasz er die Regel oder Art seiner Entstehung angibt: denn nur dadurch kann das Mannigfaltige desselben unter die Einheit der Regel gebracht werden, folglich kann er kein Objekt als schon entstanden, sondern blosz als entstehend, d.h. flieszend denken. Die besondere Regel des Entstehens eines Objekts oder die Art seines Differentials macht es zu einem besonderen Objekt, und die Verhältnisse verschiedener Objekte entspringen aus den Verhältnissen ihrer Entstehungsregeln oder ihrer Differentialen."

[2] *Ibid.*, p. 355: "sondern blosz auf ihre Elemente, die Vernunftideen von der Entstehungsart dieser Anschauungen sind und vermittels dieser auf die Anschauungen selbst."

respect to the *sensory matter* of knowledge, but also with respect to the *apriori forms* of the knowing consciousness.

<blockquote>The problem as to the relation between the universal and the particular in knowledge within the domain of KANT's apriori forms of consciousness. MAIMON's cosmonomic Idea.</blockquote>

It was the relation of the *particular* to the *universal* in knowledge which he tried to clarify by his new conception of the Idea as "differential of consciousness". The same problem, however, occurs in the apriori forms of consciousness. Here it becomes that of the relation of the transcendental logical *origin* of the theoretical cosmos to the modal diversity of formal logical, mathematical and natural scientific concepts. In other words, the basic problems which must be answered by the transcendental ground-Idea (cosmonomic Idea) here come into play.

If the origin, the ἀρχή, is to be found only in the Idea of deified creative thought, then the modal *particularity of meaning* must also be reduced to its origin, according to a logical *principle of creation*.

This modal particularity may at first sight appear as a transcendental *apriori datum* in the apriori organization of our consciousness. Nevertheless, the Critical science-ideal requires the indication of the *rule of origin* according to which this particularity is to be *created* logically.

Thus the problem of *specification* that KANT had tried to solve in his *Critique of Judgment* is now set immediately *in the frame of a cosmonomic Idea*.

MAIMON starts from the problem concerning the specification of the formal logical concepts of the understanding into the special concepts of mathematics.

Finding a point of contact in KANT's doctrine of space and time, as *forms of sensory intuition*, he conceives space as a particularity which may not remain merely a datum, as an "apriori form of intuition", a ὕλη νοητή, but must be referred to its logical *origin*. The problem broadens, however, immediately to the question concerning the principle of the origin of all so-called real thought, which comes about in *universally valid synthetic judgments of knowledge* having a special sense. MAIMON tries to answer this question in his *principle of deter-*

minability ("Satz der Bestimmbarkeit"). What is to be understood by this principle?

With MAIMON it expresses the Idea of *logical domination* (by a system of further categorical determinations) of the manifold in the *special* "Gegenstände" of thought, which may not be derived from the *merely analytic principles,* i.e. from the principles of identity and of logical contradiction alone.

As the "principium contradictionis" is the basic principle of all merely formal analytical judgments, so the "*Satz der Bestimmbarkeit*" becomes the origin-principle of all *particular* judgments of knowledge, in which thought, according to COHEN's later pronouncement, becomes "*thinking of being*" and all *being* becomes "*being of thought*". For, according to the cosmonomic Idea here laid at the foundation, reality can *hold* as reality only insofar as it is derived from its *logical origin,* in the creative process performed by theoretical thought.

> In the explanation of his "principle of determinability" MAIMON starts from three fundamentally different ways in which thought can combine a manifold of "objects of consciousness" into a logical unity.

There are three possibilities with respect to the relation between the elements of the manifold which are combined by thought into *unity*. In the first place, they can be entirely independent with respect to each other, so that each can be thought for itself separately, e.g. the sensory qualities of colour and taste, or "substances" as table and chair.

In this case, thought remains merely *formal* and arbitrary and connects the "objects of consciousness" only according to the analytic principle of contradiction. *Realiter,* however, the objects are not unified with one another according to a fixed principle.

In the second place, it is possible that the elements of the manifold, to be combined in thought, are interdependent in such a way that the one cannot be thought apart from the other. According to MAIMON, the judgment of *causality,* as a pure judgment of relation, is typical of this mode of logical synthesis, since cause and effect stand in *correlation* to one another. From this relation of thought, however, no independent "Gegenstand" can arise. Since each of its two elements supposes the other, both lack the characteristic of that independent existence, required for the "*realen Gegenstand*".

Only in the third mode of logical connection or synthesis does thought become *thought of reality,* in which the origin-principle of the "Gegenstand" can be demonstrated. In this mode of logical connection, the "subject", to be sure, can be thought in the judgment without the "predicate", but not conversely. Only a subject in the judgment that can be thought entirely independently, is a true "Gegenstand" *in* thought. Thought here ties to the concept of the "Gegenstand" an entire system of *further determinations.*

For this mode of logical synthesis the *mathematical* style of thinking is the prototype. For the totality of mathematical concepts and judgments forms a system, which, taking its beginning from an independent transcendental logical origin, is created by the continual addition of further logical determinations. Subject and predicate are constantly combined in the mathematical judgment according to the "principle of determinability" (*"Satz der Bestimmbarkeit"*).

> The break between form and sensory matter of knowledge. MAIMON's later critical scepticism with respect to KANT's concept of experience.

Not all "real thought", however, answers to this basic principle. The "empirical" judgments, which make their appeal to the sensory aspect of experience, are synthetic to be sure, but do not hang together in an apriori and systematic fashion according to the "principle of determinability". Sensory perception always affords us only a group of characteristics, which *regularly exist together,* but with respect to which it can never be proved that one characteristic is *determined* by the other. So, for example, the "complex sense-perception" which we call gold is characterized by its yellow colour, by its specific gravity, its solubility, and so on. But, the reason why these very qualities and not any others make their appearance together, remains hidden from our limited understanding. The conclusion from the *constant* perception of their *configuration* to the *necessity* of their combination rests upon the psychological association of Ideas, which HUME had previously analyzed. It is a product of the creative imagination but is not grounded in creative thought.

MAIMON has thus landed in a *critical scepticism* with respect to the actual possibility of applying the apriori forms of consciousness to the Kantian matter of sensory experience.

According to him, the category of nature-causality remains a merely *formal* synthesis of thought, *creating no actual "Gegenstand"*. It is not to be deduced according to the "principle of determinability".

The exact natural sciences do not relate the "pure categories of thought" to sensory perceptions themselves, but rather to ideal limiting concepts, to the "differentials", which they substitute for these perceptions. The sensory phenomena do not permit themselves to be connected by thought, in conformity with the logical origin-principle of determinability.

Thus MAIMON's mathematical Criticism ends in a fundamental scepticism with respect to KANT's *apriori principles of experience*, which actually intended to relate the constitutive logical *thought-forms* apriori to the *sensory material* of knowledge. The only synthetic apriori sciences which he allows to be valid are the logicized mathematics and the transcendental philosophy as science of the synthetic origin of the pure forms of consciousness.

The continuity-postulate of the mathematical science-ideal halts in MAIMON's Critical philosophy before the boundary of sensory phenomena!

How is this to be explained in view of the fact that in his first work, *Versuch über die Transzendentalphilosophie,* MAIMON had expressly maintained that the categories of thought can be related also to sensory perceptions themselves by means of the Ideas of reason (as limiting concepts in the sense of "differentials of consciousness")?

The explanation is to be found in the circumstance that in MAIMON's first work, LEIBNIZ' mathematical idealism was accepted to an extent that did not really agree with KANT's Criticism. With LEIBNIZ, in the last analysis, the sensory aspect of reality becomes a mode of mathematical thought, while the concept of the differential took a metaphysical speculative turn. It was LEIBNIZ' idea of the divine Origin as mathematical thought creating the whole cosmic coherence, that originally dominated MAIMON's entire Critical standpoint.

LEIBNIZ' conception of the relation between *phenomenon* and *noumenon* was, however, altogether different from that of KANT.

Only the *metaphysics of the science-ideal* could attempt to reduce sensory phenomena to mathematical thought as their ultimate origin and assume that, in the creative analysis of the divine thought, they answer adequately to the pure concepts of the understanding.

KANT *could not* relativize and eventually annul the boundaries between sensibility and reason in this metaphysical manner.

The way which KANT took to synthesize both antagonistic factors was eventually determined by his conception of the transcendental *Idea* of theoretical reason as *limiting concept of freedom*. That KANT thereby involved himself in insoluble antinomies was due to his dualistic transcendental ground-Idea, which did not permit a *veritable* bridging of the gap between *form* and *matter* .

MAIMON who tried to understand KANT's doctrine of the transcendental Ideas in a "purely theoretical" sense now stood before the dilemma of giving to the "Ideas" either the metaphysical speculative turn which they had possessed in LEIBNIZ' mathematical idealistic conception of the "intellectus archetypus", or of letting them shrivel up into mere fictions of the creative phantasy in the sense intended by HUME.

The first way would have carried him back irrevocably into pre-Kantian metaphysics, which he had rejected more consistently than KANT himself in his radical critique of the "Ding an sich".

> Within the limits of the Critical standpoint, the mathematical science-ideal appears unable to overcome KANT's dualism between sensibility and reason.

As in MAIMON's later works LEIBNIZ's speculative Idea of God lost positive significance and the limits of the mathematical science-ideal were drawn more sharply in the critical sense, the Ideas in MAIMON also tend more and more pronouncedly to become mere fictions [1]. To the same degree, the boundaries that KANT had drawn between reason and sensibility gain in sharpness in MAIMON's criticism. The differential-concept and the continuity-principle originating from mathematical thought halt before a boundary between sensibility and reason, which KANT, however, had drawn for the sake of his new conception of the ideal of personality. MAIMON's transcendental ground-Idea ultimately lacks unity in its Archimedean point, despite his falling back into the supremacy of the mathematical science-ideal.

Only from the personality-ideal itself, could the immediately following development of transcendental idealism attempt to overcome KANT's dualism. The science-ideal conceived according to Criticism did not prove capable of this.

---

[1] Cf. on this in detail CASSIRER III, pp. 104 ff.

§ 2 - THE CONTINUITY-POSTULATE IN THE NEW CONCEPTION OF THE IDEAL OF PERSONALITY AND THE GENESIS OF THE DIALECTICAL PHILOSOPHY IN FICHTE'S FIRST "THEORETISCHE WISSENSCHAFTSLEHRE" (1794)

The "Naturding an sich" with the doctrine (attached to it by KANT) of the *matter* of experience, altogether passively received by the sensory function of consciousness, had become the butt of the most effective criticism, in the first controversy that developed about the new critical transcendental-philosophy. Above all, the gross form which KANT's disciple REINHOLD had given to the doctrine concerning the "Affizierung" (affection) of the subjective sensibility by the mysterious "Ding an sich" had sharply exposed the antinomy inherent in it. REINHOLD conceived this "Affizierung", in fact, as a "causal process" and this conception fell prey to the annihilating attack which GOTTLIEB ERNST SCHULZE, oriented to HUME's psychologistic criticism, in his anonymously published writing *Aenesidemus* directed against the "presumptions" of the "Critique of Pure Reason". According to KANT, the category of causality is restricted to the sensory aspect of experience. How then could it be related to the "Ding an sich" beyond all experience?

MAIMON had given the sharpest form to the problem of the relation of sensibility and reason, matter and form of knowledge. In his first work he had set the requirement of explaining also the origin of the *matter* of experience from the "transcendental consciousness" itself. He had further ventured a first attempt at giving a veritable *genetic* system of the "pure forms of the consciousness" with the aid of the *origin-principle.*

All this was only a preparation for the dialectical development which the transcendental freedom-idealism was to undergo after KANT.

The ground-motive of FICHTE's first "Wissenschaftslehre". The creative moment in the personality-ideal.

Not until FICHTE's first *Wissenschaftslehre* (doctrine of science)[1] of the year 1794, does this dialectical development take

---

[1] This is the translation of "Wissenschaftslehre" in D. D. RUNES' *Dictionary of Philosophy* (1951). The terms: "Grammar of Science", "Philosophy of science" and "Science of science" usually do not have the meaning intended by FICHTE. The German term will often be abbreviated as W.L.

its start from the transcendental reflection upon the Idea of freedom as an hypothesis even of the science-ideal.

The metaphysical concept of the "Naturding an sich" (before KANT, the basic denominator for the rationalistic science-ideal, in KANT's system itself a threat to both the science- and personality-ideal) was completely abandoned. As the basic concept of "dogmatic realism", it must be abolished in the "Wissenschaftslehre" which, as the self-reflection of reason upon its own activity, refers all functions of consciousness, even the receptive sensory one, to their *absolute, transcendent root,* viz. the self-consciousness as *absolutely free ego,* determined by nothing else.

That *ego* is not itself a *being;* it is no more a given super-individual, universally valid logical unity of consciousness, as in KANT, but it *creates itself* in a free *activity* determined by nothing, by means of a free *"Tathandlung"* ("practical act").

This absolute *ego, creating itself in free activity,* is not found among the "empirical" (read "psychological"!) determinations of our consciousness and *cannot* be found among them, but is at the basis of every consciousness (which it alone makes possible) [1].

This *ego* is no longer the fundamental static form of all synthetic thought, as was KANT's "transcendental unity of apperception". *As absolutely free thesis,* it is necessarily thought of as the *dynamic totality* of activity, in itself still undifferentiated, out of which our entire cosmos must originate through a series of further acts of consciousness [2]. Nature can posses no independent root in contrast with this absolute thetic *ego.* Necessity itself in the causal coherence of nature can be understood only as a product of the free activity of the absolute I.

---

[1] *Grundlage der gesammten Wissenschaftslehre* (in J. J. FICHTE's *Sämmtl. Werke,* Bnd. I, hrg. v. J. H. FICHTE), p. 91. I cite henceforth this edition of FICHTE's works, consulted by me.

[2] *Op. cit.,* p. 99: "Auf unseren Satz, als absoluten Grundsatz alles Wissens hat gedeutet KANT in seiner Deduction der Kategorien; er hat ihn aber nie als Grundsatz bestimmt aufgestellt." ["KANT, in his deduction of the categories, has hinted at our proposition as absolute principle of all knowledge. But he has never established it definitely as a principle."]

The Archimedean point in FICHTE's transcendental ground-Idea.

What is this "absolute ego" which FICHTE makes the basis of his entire philosophy, in the first and highest *principle* of his *"Wissenschaftslehre"*: "Das Ich setzt sich selbst" (the ego posits itself)?

For a moment we might suppose, that here the deepest religious root of the whole temporal cosmos was discovered, and, as religious apriori, was made the starting-point of philosophy.

This might be supposed all the more readily, since FICHTE, in his treatise, *Über den Begriff der Wissenschaftslehre* (1th ed. 1794, 2d ed. 1798), expressly declares that his doctrine of science, with its absolute thetic principle, is not determined by logic, but, rather the reverse, provides the basis of the latter [1].

Thus even theoretical logic, the "organon" of all hypostatizing in the immanence-philosophy, is subjected to the doctrine of science.

The transcendental synthesis of the "ego" must itself be understood to be the origin of the analytic principles — a thesis, which KANT had posited in all its sharpness, if taken in a merely transcendental-*logical* sense, but to which he became unfaithful in his deduction of the categories from the analytical forms of judgment.

MAIMON had accepted a mutual dependence of analysis and synthesis, but in the *material sense* he likewise recognized the transcendental-logical synthesis as a condition of the analytical. FICHTE, however, was the first to reduce the origin of the analytic in the last analysis to the absolute "ego", which appears to be elevated above all logical determination.

But it soon turns out that in the first "Grundsatz" (principle) of the doctrine of science there is nothing embodied but the proclamation of the absolute sovereignty of "practical reason", in the sense of the Humanist ideal of moral freedom.

---

[1] W.W. I, p. 68: "die Wissenschaftslehre wird nicht durch die Logik, aber die Logik wird durch die Wissenschaftslehre *bedingt* und *bestimmt*. Die Wissenschaftslehre bekommt nicht etwa von der Logik ihre Form, sondern sie hat sie in sich selbst und stellt sie erst für die mögliche Abstraction durch Freiheit auf." ["The doctrine of science is not *conditioned* and *determined* by logic, but rather logic by the doctrine of science. The doctrine of science does not in any way obtain its form from logic, but has it in itself and only plans it through freedom for the sake of the possible abstraction."]

The first absolute "Thathandlung" (practical act) of reason originates, as FICHTE himself explains, from the *thinking* of itself on the part of the absolute ego. "This necessitates a *reflection* on that which in the first place might be taken for it, and an *abstraction* from all that which does not really belong to the same" [1].

He further grants: "The laws (of general logic) according to which that activity must be thought of absolutely as the basis of human knowledge, or — what is the same — the rules, according to which that reflection is executed, are not yet demonstrated to be valid, but they are tacitly pre-supposed, as known and established. Only below will they be derived from the principle whose formulation is correct only on condition of their correctness. This is a circle; but it is an unavoidable circle" [2].

It will have to be granted to LASK, that the "absolute ego", thus gained by *abstraction* and *reflection*, cannot be otherwise qualified than as an "hypostatizing of the *universal* concept "ego" as the *totality* of reason" [3].

> FICHTE's "absolute ego" as origin and totality of all cosmic diversity of meaning is nothing but the hypostatization of the moral function.

The "absolute ego" in FICHTE is the absolutely unlimited free activity of the *moral function,* hypostatized in the ideal of personality. As sovereign function of reason, it has the infinite task to create from itself the cosmos as the product of freedom.

The continuity-postulate inherent in the Humanist science-ideal as it was conceived of in pre-Kantian rationalism had

---

[1] *Op. cit.* I, u. 91: "Dies macht eine *Reflexion* über dasjenige, was man etwa zunächst dafür halten könnte, und eine *Abstraction* von allem, was nich wirklich dazu gehört, nothwendig."

[2] *Ib.* I, p. 92: "Die Gesetze (der allgemeinen Logik), nach denen man jene Thathandlung sich als Grundlage des menschlichen Wissens schlechterdings denken muss, oder — welches das gleiche ist — die Regeln, nach welchen jene Reflexion angestellt wird, sind noch nicht als gültig erwiesen, sondern sie werden stillschweigend, als bekannt und ausgemacht, vorausgesetzt. Erst tiefer unten werden sie von dem Grundsatze, dessen Aufstellung blosz unter Bedingung ihrer Richtigkeit richtig ist, abgeleitet. Dies ist ein Cirkel; aber est ist ein unvermeidlicher Cirkel."

[3] LASK, *Gesammelte Schriften* I, p. 88: "Hypostasierung des *Allgemein*begriffs „Ich" zur Totalität der Vernunft."

required that mathematical thought should produce a cosmic order after its own pattern.

Similarly the postulate of continuity, implied in the religious freedom-motive and first discovered by KANT in the Humanist ideal of personality, moves philosophic thought to exceed the modal boundaries of the different aspects of the cosmos and to elevate the moral function of human personality to a basic denominator of the modal diversity of meaning. To this end, natural necessity must be interpreted as a product of the hypostatized moral freedom in the "reflexive" thought of the "Wissenschaftslehre".

"Theoretical reason", "practical reason" and "faculty of judgment" may no longer remain mutually isolated "departments of reason". They must be related to the root of self-consciousness, viewed by FICHTE as *freely creative moral activity.*

This was the boundary before which KANT had halted in the interest of maintaining the science-ideal. There loomed up, in his Critical philosophy, the antinomy between moral freedom hypostatized in the Idea of the *homo noumenon,* and the science-ideal, based on the "Critique of Pure Reason", which found the scepter of its sovereignty in the category of natural causality. In the critical dialectic he tried, though fruitlessly, to "mummify" this antinomy by relegating "theoretical" and "practical reason" each within its limits.

KANT would have the understanding bow under the logical principle of contradiction. The transcendental Idea of freedom may not be related as a category of the understanding to sensory experience and thereby to nature, as little as the category of natural causality may be related to the practical Idea of the "homo noumenon".

With FICHTE, dialectical thought begins to overpass these critical limits, in order to make the cosmos originate from the free activity of the "absolute ego", from the supposed *radical unity of reason itself:* "There may be indicated something from which every category is itself derived: the ego as absolute subject. Of everything else to which it possibly may be applied, it must be shown that reality is transferred *from the ego* to it: — that it must be, insofar as the ego is" [1].

---

[1] W.W. I, p. 99: "es läszt sich etwas aufzeigen, wovon jede Kategorie

Fichte's attempt at a transcendental deduction of the Kantian forms of thought from the self-consciousness.

In the first place, the logical principle of identity is derived from the first principle of the doctrine of science. According to Fichte, it is nothing but the *form* of the conclusion from "being posited" to "being" ("vom Gesetztsein auf das Sein"), which has been abstracted from the fundamental proposition "I am", by elimination of *the content* implied in the ego. In the logical judgment "*A is A*", no possible A can be anything other than an A created and activated in the *ego*. As surely as the *ego* itself is not a static *datum*, but an infinite *activity*, so surely is *identity* not merely an immobile logical *form*, but an *infinite task* in the process of the synthetic *determination* of the cosmos in the course of reason's becoming self-conscious.

The "mode of activity of the human mind in general" ("Handlungsart des menschlichen Geistes überhaupt"), which discloses itself in the logical *form* of the judgment of identity, is the *category of reality*. "All that to which the proposition $A = A$ is applicable, has reality, *insofar as this proposition is applicable to it*. That which is posited by the mere positing of anything at all (i.e. posited in the Ego) is reality in it, is its essence" [1].

The category of reality, to Kant one of the categories of the *class of quality*, which he simply derived from the various forms of the logical judgments, is thus reduced by Fichte in the logical judgment of identity to the *absolute ego*, as actual origin of all reality. Its relationship to sensory experience can no longer be grounded in the "natural thing in itself" which affects our sensibility. Rather it is based entirely upon the "absolute ego" as the source of all reality created freely in self-consciousness. After the logical judgment of identity has received this basis, the logical judgment of contradiction (non-A is not A) is also referred to the first principle of the doctrine of science.

The first-mentioned as well as the second logical principle is

---

selbst abgeleitet ist: das Ich als absolutes Subject. Für alles mögliche übrige, worauf sie angewendet werden soll, musz gezeigt werden, dass *aus dem Ich* Realität darauf übertragen werden: — dass es seyn müsse, wofern das Ich sey."

[1] "Alles, worauf der Satz $A = A$ anwendbar ist, hat, *inwiefern derselbe darauf anwendbar ist*, Realität. Dasjenige, was durch das blosze Setzen irgend eines Dinges (eines im Ich gesetzten) gesetzt ist, ist in ihm Realität, ist sein Wesen."

found among the "facts of empirical consciousness" and must in the doctrine of science be subjected to the ultimate justification which logic itself cannot offer. In the logical judgment of the antithesis (non-A is not A), the question: "*Is* then the contrary of A posited, and under what condition *of the form of the mere* act is it then posited?" [1] remains entirely unanswered.

The logical antithesis is an absolute act of the ego. "Opposition as such is posited merely by the Ego" [2].

This act of consciousness which is enacted in the anti-thesis is possible only on condition of the unity of consciousness in its thesis and antithesis. If the consciousness of the first act did not hang together with the consciousness of the second, the second "positing" (the antithesis) would be no "*counter-positing*", but a thesis and nothing else. Only by virtue of its relationship to the absolute *thesis* does it become an *anti-thesis*.

Originally nothing is posited but the *ego*. Therefore all opposition must be made with reference to the latter. But the antithesis of the *ego* is the *non-ego*. Thus a *non-ego* is set in opposition to the *ego*, as certainly as the absolute evidence of the logical judgment, "non-A is not A", is found among the facts of empirical consciousness.

By abstraction from the content of the ego, FICHTE derives the logical principle of contradiction from the material judgment, "To the *ego* a *non-ego* is opposed." Finally, if total abstraction is made from the *act of judgment* and attention is directed solely to the *form* of the conclusion from the antithesis to *non-being*, KANT's second category of quality, that of *negation*, originates. This category also has its true origin in the free, infinite activity of the *ego;* it is not merely a static logical *form*. It is to be understood, just as all other categories of thought, only as a *dialectical point of transition* through which the ego becomes conscious of itself as infinite *free* activity.

Now there is included in the second "principle of the doctrine of science" ("Grundsatz der Wissenschaftslehre") an overt antinomy. For the *non-ego* (i.e. nature), as appears from the first principle, is to be posited only *in* the *ego* as absolute totality,

---

[1] W.W. I, p. 102: "*Ist* denn, und unter welcher Bedingung *der Form der blossen Handlung* ist denn das Gegentheil von A gesetzt?"

[2] W.W. I, p. 103: "Das Entgegengesetzsein überhaupt ist schlechthin durch das Ich gesetzt."

but at the same time, as antithesis, it *cancels* the *ego*. "Thus the second principle is opposed to itself and cancels itself" [1]. Yet, in the absolute thesis of the first principle there is implied the demand that the *ego* and the *non-ego* be thought together in the *absolute ego*. Thesis and antithesis thus require their synthesis, which is contained in the third principle: "The *ego* posits in the *ego* the *non-ego* by *limitation of itself*." If abstraction is made from the *definite* form of this judgment (i.e. that it is founded upon a basis of distinction or relation) and attention is paid only to "the universal feature of the mode of action — the limitation of the one by the other", there originates the *category of determination* (in KANT, that of *limitation*): "Namely, a positing of quantity in general, whether it be quantity of reality or that of negation, is called determination" [2].

Dialectical thought, dominated by the ideal of personality, usurps the task of the cosmic order.

What occurs in this synthesis is clear. *Dialectical thought usurps the task of the cosmic order*, which regulates the relationship of the modal law-spheres *in the cosmic continuity of time*. As we demonstrated in Part I, the cosmic order of time grounds and at the same time relativizes the sphere-sovereignty of the modal law-spheres, by bridging over their boundaries. Consequently, if logical thought in the line of *speculative dialectic* is set in place of the cosmic order, *that thought* must relativize the boundaries of the modal spheres. But since logical thought in its very principium contradictionis requires a strict maintenance of these boundaries, it can take upon itself this impossible task only by a false *logical* relativizing of its basic laws.

Logical thought, conscious of its boundaries, can never come to the point of making the meaning of the pre-logical aspects of reality — conceived of in theoretical abstraction as "nature" — originate from the moral function of free personality. Dialectic thought, however, supposes it can accomplish this magical deed by conceiving the absolutized moral aspect as an unlimited *totality*, from which by *division* (cf. the division of a geometrical straight line, an image to which FICHTE appeals again and

---

[1] W.W. I, p. 106: "Also ist der zweite Grundsatz sich selbst entgegengesetzt, und hebt sich selbst auf."

[2] t.a.p. 122/3: "Nemlich ein setzen der Quantität überhaupt, sey es nun Quantität der Realität oder der Negation, heiszt Bestimmung."

again!) the limited, finite functions are to originate: "We have united the opposed ego and non-ego through the concept of divisibility" [1]. The *limited ego* and the limiting *non-ego* of the antithesis have both originated by quantitative division or self-limitation of the absolute ego, in which, naturally, a *spatial* division is not to be thought of. Thus in the synthesis, finite "nature" and finite "freedom", sensibility and finite reason, matter and form, are thought together, after moral freedom is hypostatized by a first theoretical synthesis as a basic denominator for both! This basic denominator is again viewed rationalistically as the moral law!

FICHTE himself has formulated the moral function of law as basic denominator for temporal reality in his pronouncement: "Our world is the material of our duty, rendered sensible; this is the authentically real in things, the true basic matter of all appearance" [2].

But the absolutized moral freedom of action of the ego cannot serve as a *basic denominator* for the theoretical synthesis of meaning. By hypostatization it is torn out of the cosmic temporal coherence of the modal aspects, and becomes an abstract meaning-less *form* and no *totality of meaning*.

In FICHTE's "Wissenschaftslehre" of the year 1794, according to KRONER's excellent observation, "ethics is raised to the position of metaphysics".

Speculative dialectic, which was not to be elaborated consistently until the system of HEGEL, demands that the thesis, the "absolute ego", should not be posited as absolute in the sense of really falling *outside the dialectical system*. It requires that both thesis and antithesis should be viewed only as momenta of the synthesis which determine and mutually limit each other. But although FICHTE laid the foundations of modern speculative dialectic, his moralism prevented him from accepting this consequence.

The *absolute ego* of the thesis is separated by him from the *limited ego* of the antithesis.

---

[1] W.W. I, 110: "Wir haben die entgegengesetzten Ich und nicht-Ich vereinigt durch den Begriff der Theilbarkeit."

[2] W.W. V, 211: "Unsere Welt ist das versinnlichte Material unserer Pflicht; dies ist das eigentlich Reelle in den Dingen, der wahre Grundstoff aller Erscheinung."

To FICHTE the "absolute ego" remains outside the dialectical system. The Idea of the absolute ego as ethical task.

The dialectical system which the doctrine of science develops, does not concern the *absolute ego* of the thesis (which does not itself reflect as does the *finite* ego), but only the *finite* ego, which originates through the creation of the antithesis in the ego.

The absolute synthesis, the return of the absolute ego into itself, remains a *task* never to be realized.

Here the Idea of the absolute ego as *ethical* "task" makes its entrance into FICHTE's dialectic: "So far as the predicate of freedom can hold for man, i.e. so far as he is an absolute Subject, and not one that is represented or capable of being represented, he has nothing in common with the natural being, and is therefore not even opposed to it. In accordance with the logical form of the judgment which is positive (namely: Man is free from natural necessity), both concepts should, nevertheless, be united. Not, to be sure, in any concept, but merely in the Idea of an ego, whose consciousness is not determined by anything outside itself, but which rather determines everything outside itself by its mere consciousness. But this very Idea is not thinkable, inasmuch as it contains a contradiction. Nevertheless, it is set up for us as the highest practical goal. Man should more and more approximate infinitely the freedom which in itself is unattainable" [1].

Therefore, in the development of the dialectical system, the *final* antinomy may not be reconciled *logically*. In the process of thought, too, it may only be solved *ethically*. Therefore, FICHTE writes that, in the antitheses which are united through the first synthesis, thought has to seek after new antinomies, in

---

[1] W.W. I, p. 117: "der Mensch, insofern das Prädicat der Freiheit von ihm gelten kann, d.i. insofern er absolut und nicht vorgestelltes noch vorstellbares Subject ist, hat mit dem Naturwesen gar nichts gemein, und es ist ihm also nicht entgegengesetzt. Dennoch sollen laut der logischen Form des Urteils, welche positiv ist (scl. Der Mensch ist frei von Naturnotwendigkeit), beide Begriffe vereinigt werden; sie sind aber in gar keinem Begriffe zu vereinigen, sondern blosz in der Idee eines Ich, dessen Bewustseyn durch gar nichts ausser ihm bestimmt würde, sondern vielmehr selbst alles ausser ihm durch sein blosses Bewusstseyn bestimmte: welche Idee aber selbst nicht denkbar ist, indem sie für uns einen Widerspruch enthält. Dennoch aber ist sie uns zum höchsten praktischen Ziele aufgestellt. Der Mensch soll sich der an sich unerreichbaren Freiheit ins Unendliche immer mehr nähern."

order to unite them through a new synthesis, "until we come to opposites, which can no longer be perfectly united and we thereby pass over into the realm of the practical part"[1].

KRONER rightly compares the first absolute principle in FICHTE's first sketch of the "Wissenschaftslehre" with KANT's categorical imperative and calls the proposition of the self-creative absolute ego "the basic law of pure practical reason in its speculative use." The production of the synthesis in the dialectic is set in perfect analogy with moral activity. It is viewed as moral activity continuing itself in thought and become speculative[2]. Thus FICHTE's observation may be explained: "We accordingly begin with a deduction and go with it as far as we can. The impossibility of continuing it will doubtless show us the point where we have to break it off and to appeal to that unconditioned authoritative dictum of reason, which will result from the task"[3].

> FICHTE attempts to give an account of the possibility of theoretical knowledge by referring the latter to the selfhood. Why this attempt cannot succeed on FICHTE's immanence-standpoint.

Even in the "Wissenschaftslehre" of 1794 FICHTE ventured a serious attempt to clear up the problem of *synthesis* in epistemology, a problem which KANT had not really solved. To this end he will relate the theoretical synthesis to the root of the self-consciousness[4].

---

[1] W.W. I, p. 115: "bis wir auf Entgegengesetzte kommen, die sich nicht weiter vollkommen verbinden lassen, und dadurch in das Gebiet des praktischen Theils übergehen."

[2] KRONER I, 398.

[3] W.W. I, p. 106: "Wir heben demnach mit einer Deduktion an, und gehen mit ihr, so weit wir können. Die Unmöglichkeit sie fortzusetzen wird uns ohne Zweifel zeigen, wo wir sie abzubrechen, und uns auf jenen unbedingten Machtspruch der Vernunft, der sich aus der Aufgabe ergeben wird, zu berufen haben."

[4] op. cit., p. 114: "The celebrated question which KANT set at the apex of the Critique of Pure Reason: How are synthetic judgments possible a-priori? is now answered in the most general and satisfactory fashion. We have in the third principle performed a synthesis between the opposed ego and non-ego, by means of the posited divisibility of both, about the possibility of which nothing further may be asked, nor may a ground for the same be adduced. It is simply possible, one is authorized to it without any further ground. All other syntheses that are to be valid must be implied in it. They must at once be performed in and with it. And thus, as this is demonstrated, the most convincing proof is provided that they

On the immanence-standpoint of FICHTE's Humanistic cosmonomic Idea, however, this problem proves to be insoluble, notwithstanding FICHTE's penetrating philosophical vision. The elevation of the moral noumenal man *(homo noumenon)* as root of the self-consciousness has only the effect of rooting the synthesis in the *antinomy*, which is always the token of a breaking through the modal boundaries of meaning by hypostatizing thought!

The antithetical relation of theoretical thought here becomes a logical contradiction, in the dialectical sense!

FICHTE derives the Kantian categories of quantity [1] and quality by abstraction from the *absolute ego* (as *origin* of the Kantian *forms* of consciousness as well as of the sensory *matter* of experience).

> Transcendental deduction of the Kantian categories of relation from self-consciousness. The science-ideal is here derived from the ideal of personality.

In the further dialectical development of his system, FICHTE tries to deduce in this manner the Kantian categories of substance and inherence, causality and interaction. The synthesis between *reasonable freedom* (of the ego) and *sensory nature,* posited in the third principle, is the starting-point for this deduction. Here we shall not follow in the wake of this dialec-

---

are valid even as the former." ["Die berühmte Frage, welche KANT an die Spitze der Kritik der reinen Vernunft stellte: wie sind synthetische Urteile a priori möglich? — ist jetzt auf die allgemeinste und befriedigendste Art beantwortet. Wir haben im dritten Grundsatze eine Synthesis zwischen dem entgegengesetzten Ich und nicht-Ich, vermittelst der gesetzten Theilbarkeit beider, vorgenommen, über deren Möglichkeit sich nicht weiter fragen, noch ein Grund derselben sich anführen lässt; sie ist schlechtin möglich, man ist zu ihr ohne allen weiteren Grund befugt. Alle übrigen Synthesen, welche gültig seyn sollen, müssen in dieser liegen; sie müssen zugleich in und mit ihr vorgenommen seyn: und so, wie dies bewiesen wird, wird der überzeugendste Beweis geliefert, das sie gültig sind, wie jene."]

[1] By setting the *ego* and the *non-ego* in the third "Grundsatz" as limited parts of the absolute ego, according to FICHTE, both are united by *quantity* (vid. § 3 of the "Wissenschaftslehre"). "Just as there (viz. in § 3) the ego was first simply posited as absolute reality *according to quality*, so here *something*, i.e. something determined by *quantity*, is simply posited in the ego, or the ego is simply posited as determined *quantity*" (I, 205). ["So wie dort" (viz. in § 3) "zuvörderst das Ich, der Qualität nach als absolute Realität schlechthin gesetzt wurde; so wird hier *etwas*, d.h. ein durch Quantität bestimmtes, schlechthin in das Ich gesetzt oder das Ich wird schlechthin gesetzt als bestimmte Quantität."]

tical development, but shall simply fix our attention upon the fact that FICHTE actually sought to derive the Humanist *ideal of science* — which found its focus in the category of causality — from the *ideal of personality*. To this end his thought followed the way of dialectical *continuity*, contained as a postulate in KANT's practical Idea of freedom. In FICHTE's dialectic this domination of the *continuity-postulate* implied in the freedom-motive finds its clear expression in the transcendental deduction of the natural-scientific categories of relation (substance, causality and interaction). Here FICHTE observes: "The independent activity (as synthetic unity) determines the change (as synthetic unity) and vice versa, i.e. they determine one another reciprocally, and are themselves united synthetically. The activity, as synthetic unity, is an absolute *transition* (Übergehen); the change, an absolute *intrusion* (Eingreifen) entirely self-determined. The former determines the latter, would mean: only by virtue of the transition, is the causal intrusion of the changing terms posited; the latter determines the former, would mean: as the terms interpenetrate, the activity must necessarily pass over from the one to the other... All is one and the same. — The whole, however, is absolutely posited; it bases itself upon itself" [1]. And a little later: "Thus the activity returns into itself by means of the change; and the change returns into itself by means of the activity. Everything reproduces itself, and there is no *hiatus* possible there; from any single term one is driven to all the rest" [2].

---

[1] I, 169: "Die unabhängige Thätigkeit (als synthetische Einheit) bestimmt den Wechsel (als synthetische Einheit) und umgekehrt, d.i. beide bestimmen sich gegenseitig, und sind selbst synthetisch vereinigt. Die Thätigkeit, als synthetische Einheit, ist ein absolutes *Uebergehen*; der Wechsel ein absolutes durch sich selbst vollständig bestimmtes *Eingreifen*. Die erstere bestimmt den letzteren, würde heizen: blosz dadurch das übergangen wird, wird das Eingreifen der Wechselglieder gesetzt: der letztere bestimmt die erstere, würde heissen: so wie die Glieder eingreifen, muss nothwendig die Thätigkeit von einem zum anderen übergehen... Alles ist Eins und Ebendasselbe. — Das Ganze aber ist schlechhin gesetzt; es gründet sich auf sich selbst."

[2] I, 170: "Also die Thätigkeit geht in sich selbst zurück vermittelst des Wechsels; und der Wechsel geht in sich selbst zurück vermittelst der Thätigkeit. Alles reproducirt sich selbst, und es ist da kein *hiatus* möglich; von jedem Gliede aus wird man zu allen übrigen getrieben."

> The domination of the continuity-postulate of the ideal of personality. The Humanist transcendental ground-Idea in its transcendental monist-moralistic type.

It would be unfair to disregard the deep philosophical tendency that is present in this entire process of thought: the search for the radical unity of philosophical reflection in a *selfhood beyond the theoretical diversity of syntheses* and the insight into the continuous coherence of meaning of the cosmos. But this insight is directed into wrong channels by FICHTE's Humanistic cosmonomic Idea. It is by means of *dialectical* logical thought that the Humanistic ideal of personality attempts to carry the continuity of the freedom-postulate, which tolerates no *hiatus*, through all cosmological thought and in this attempt multiplies the basic antinomy between the ideals of science and of personality in each new synthetic phase of the dialectical thought-process. With FICHTE, the antinomy cannot be solved by *thought*, because he makes the categorical (i.e. the *hypostatized)* moral law the basis of his "Wissenschaftslehre", in its theoretical as well as in its practical part, and because — in the line of the Kantian practical Idea — he proclaims the absolute synthesis of nature and freedom to be an eternal "task" for human personality. The limits which reason sets to itself in each new antithesis, in each new antinomy between ego and non-ego, between moral freedom and natural necessity, do not lie to FICHTE in a cosmic order set by God in his creation and not to be transgressed by reason, but they rest *upon free self-limitations of reason* itself. Therefore, theoretical reason in the dialectical system can also again and again annul the limits and in each new synthesis attempt to carry through the continuity-postulate of the freedom-idealism, until, of itself, it brings to light the fact that the absolute synthesis should be effected ultimately by the hypostatized ethical thought of "practical reason", by a "Machtspruch der Vernunft" alone.

> Productive imagination is to FICHTE the creative origin of sensory matter.

Which function of reason, however, achieves this absolute synthesis, which is thought of, otherwise than in KANT, as a *material* productive synthesis, as a synthesis that creates form and content alike (though it be in the infinite task through which the ego becomes self-conscious as a productive capacity)? This function is to FICHTE the "power of productive imagination" ("productive Einbildungskraft"), which he — again different from KANT — proclaims as the free creative origin of sensory matter. It is a *theoretical* as well as a *practical* function. KANT could not really subject the sensory "matter of experience" to a transcendental deduction; rather he excluded it as the "contingent" and "empirical" from the transcendental inquiry and, for the explanation of this matter, he again appealed to the affection of our senses by the "natural thing-in-itself".

FICHTE's absolute thesis, however, requires the deduction even of sensory matter as the product of the freely creative ego, and as comprehended in the absolute ego.

To this end, he introduces the *productive imagination*, which in a transcendental sense had for KANT only the function of achieving a synthesis between the given sensory matter and the "pure forms of thought". In KANT this synthesis is performed by means of the "schematizing" of the categories in time as a "form of intuition", by the creation of a "transcendental pattern" for all empirical "Gegenstände".

The dialectical process was described by FICHTE as a transition from the free *ego* into its opposite (the non-ego) that limits the former and as the synthetic reduction of this *non-ego* to the absolute *ego* through the mutual determination and limitation of the two momenta: the *limited ego* and the *limiting non-ego*, both posited by and in the absolute ego.

The *determining* theoretical *thought*, however, that posits *rigid conceptual boundaries*, cannot bring about the highest synthesis. It remains confined in the final antinomy between the free infinite ego and the finite ego limited by the non-ego, two egos reciprocally excluding each other.

The opposed terms of the final theoretical antithesis can be synthesized only in the concept of mere *determinability (Bestimmbarkeit)*, not in that of *determination (Bestimmung)*; and here FICHTE clearly exhibits the influence of MAIMON's "principle of determinability": "For if the boundary set between the opposites (one of which is the very element that creates the opposition, while the other, in respect of its existence, lies entirely outside the consciousness and is posited merely in view of the necessary limitation) is posited as a hard and fast unchangeable limit, then both elements are united by *determination*, but not by *determinability*; then, however, the required totality in the change of substantiality would not be fulfilled either... Accordingly, that limit must not be accepted as a fixed limit"[1].

The final theoretical synthesis is thus attainable only by relativizing the boundaries which determining thought sets between the *finite* ego and the *finite* non-ego in the *infinite* ego. Dialectical thought can grasp this final synthesis only as "determinability", as "the Idea of determination which is not attainable in this way." (I, 216): "The ego is only that which it posits itself to be. That it is infinite, is to say that it posits itself as infinite: it *determines* itself through the predicate of infinity, thus it (the ego) limits itself, as substratum of infinity; it distinguishes itself from its infinite activity (both of which are one and the same in themselves). And this must be the state of affairs if the ego is to be infinite. This activity going on to infinity, which distinguishes it (i.e. the ego) from itself must be *its own* activity; it must be ascribed to it: consequently, simultaneously in one and the same undivided act which allows no further distinctions, the ego must also again take up this activity into itself (determine A + B through A). But if it takes this activity up into itself, the former is thus determined and consequently not infinite: however, it should be infinite, and thus it must be posited outside the ego."

"This change of the ego in and with itself, inasmuch as it posits itself as finite and infinite at the same time, is the faculty of imagination. It is a change which consists, as it were(!), in a conflict with itself, and thereby reproduces itself, in that the ego seeks to unite that which is incapable of being united, and at one moment seeks to take up the infinite into the form of the finite, and at another, driven back, posits it again outside of the same, and in the same moment again seeks to take it up into the form of finiteness"[2].

---

[1] I, 216: "Wird nemlich die zwischen die Entgegengesetzten (deren eines das entgegensetzende selbst ist, das andere aber seinem Daseyn nach völlig ausser dem Bewusstseyn liegt, und blosz zum Behuf der notwendigen Begrenzung gesetzt wird) gesetzte Grenze als feste, fixierte, unwandelbare Grenze gesetzt, so werden beide vereinigt duch *Bestimmung*, nicht aber durch *Bestimmbarkeit:* aber dann wäre auch die in dem Wechsel der Substantialität geforderte Totalität nicht erfüllt... Demnach muss jene Grenze nicht als feste Grenze angenommen werden."

[2] I, 214, 215: "Das Ich ist nur das, als was es sich setzt. Es ist unendlich heisst, es setzt sich unendlich: es *bestimmt* sich durch das Prädicat der Unendlichkeit; also es begrenzt sich selbst (das Ich) als Substrat der Unendlichkeit; es unterscheidet sich selbst von seiner unendlichen Thätigkeit (welches beides an sich Eins und ebendasselbe ist); und so musste

cosmonomic Idea of Humanistic immanence-philosophy 429

FICHTE conceives of the productive imagination as an unconscious function of reason.

This productive imagination (in its thetic, antithetic and synthetic activity) does not *consciously* produce the content of representations. *It is rather the case that it alone makes consciousness possible. Only reflection raises it to the level of consciousness.* It is a free act not determined by any grounds. In the deduction of the power of imagination the theoretical doctrine of science reaches its highest synthesis. Imagination is operative prior to all reflection, as pre-conscious activity, and in its antithetic activity it sets no fixed limits at all. It is only reflection that sets fixed limits, inasmuch as it is first to fix the power of imagination: "The power of imagination is a faculty which hovers between determination and non-determination, between the finite and the infinite... This very hovering indicates the power of imagination by its product; the latter is produced by imagination, as it were during its hovering and by means of its hovering"[1].

So, in order to solve the basic antinomy in his "Wissenschaftslehre", FICHTE withdraws behind reflective analysis toward a "pre-conscious" — by which is apparently meant *pre-theoretical* — *productive* imagination. He supposes that, after having arrived at this point, he has overcome all antinomies. He keenly recognizes that the antinomies arose through *thought* which

---

es sich verhalten, wenn das Ich unendlich seyn sollte, — Diese ins Unendliche gehende Thätigkeit, die es von sich unterscheidet, soll *seine* Thätigkeit sein; sie soll ihm zugeschrieben werden: mithin muss zugleich in einer und ebenderselben ungetheilten und unzuunterscheidenden Handlung das Ich diese Thätigkeit auch wieder in sich aufnehmen (A + B durch A bestimmen). Nimmt es sie aber in sich auf, so ist sie bestimmt, mithin nicht unendlich: doch aber soll sie unendlich seyn, und so muss sie ausser dem Ich gesetzt werden.

"Dieser Wechsel des Ich in und mit sich selbst, da es sich endlich und unendlich zugleich setzt — ein Wechsel der gleichsam(!) in einem Widerstreite mit sich selbst besteht, und dadurch sich selbst reproducirt, indem das Ich unvereinbares vereinigen will, jetzt das unendliche in die Form des endlichen aufzunehmen versucht, jetzt, zurückgetrieben, es wieder ausser derselben setzt, und in dem nemlichen Momente abermals es in die Form der Endlichkeit aufzunehmen versucht — ist das Vermögen der Einbildungskraft."

[1] I, 216f. "Die Einbildungskraft ist ein Vermögen, das zwischen Bestimmung und nicht-Bestimmung, zwischen Endlichen und Unendlichen in der Mitte schwebt... Jenes Schweben eben bezeichnet die Einbildungskraft durch ihr Produkt; sie bringt dasselbe gleichsam während ihres Schweben, und durch ihr Schweben hervor."

overpassed its boundaries. The productive imagination, however, sets no fixed limits, since it has "no fixed standpoint", but in its hovering nature keeps the mean between *definiteness* and *indefiniteness, finitude* and *infinitude*. And then FICHTE supposes he can conclude: "All the difficulties which presented themselves are removed in a satisfactory manner. The task was that of uniting the opposites, ego and non-ego. They can be completely unified through the power of imagination which unites contradictories" [1].

The "productive power of imagination" explicitly qualified by FICHTE as "Faktum" (i.e. present before all reflection in the human mind), is expressly announced by him as a *synthesis* and at the same time is expressly called a "Funktion des Gemüths" (function of feeling) [2].

Here it clearly appears that in his "Wissenschaftslehre" of 1794 FICHTE was still deeply involved in KANT's functionalistic way of thinking, although in his conception of the productive imagination he deviated fundamentally from his master. KANT had attempted to solve the problem of apriori synthesis by his doctrine concerning the *transcendental* productive imagination in which understanding and sensibility are united. In the last analysis, however, it was the transcendental logical function from which the apriori synthesis should issue. FICHTE saw clearly that this could not be a real solution of the problem,

---

[1] op. cit., p. 218: "Alle Schwierigkeiten, die sich uns in den Weg stellten, sind befriedigend gehoben. Die Aufgabe war die, die entgegengesetzen Ich und nicht-Ich, zu vereinigen. Durch die Einbildungskraft, welche widersprechendes vereinigt, können sie vollkommen vereinigt werden."

[2] op. cit., p. 226: "The absolute opposites (the finite subjective and the infinite objective) prior to the synthesis, are a mere object of thought and, in the sense in which we have always taken the word, ideal. As they ought to be unified by the power of thought but cannot, they acquire reality through the hovering of the feeling (Gemüth) which, in this *function*, is called the power of imagination, since by means of it they become intuitable: i.e. they acquire reality as such; for there is and can be no other reality than that which is mediated by the intuition." ["Die absolut entgegengesetzen (das endliche subjektive und das unendliche objektive) sind vor der Synthesis etwas bloss gedachtes, und, wie wir das Wort immer genommen haben, ideales. So wie sie durch das Denkvermögen vereinigt werden sollen, und nicht können, bekommen sie durch das Schweben des Gemüths, welches in dieser Funktion Einbildungskraft genannt wird, Realität, weil sie dadurch anschaubar werden: d.i. sie bekommen Realität überhaupt; denn es gibt keine andere Realität, als die vermittelst der Anschauung und kann keine andere geben."]

because the synthesis between understanding and sensibility requires a faculty which exceeds the antithetic relation of theoretical thought. But, instead of focusing his reflection towards the supra-theoretical ego, he seeks only a "pre-logical" *function of the ego as a connecting link*, not yet involved in the rigid antithetical relation of the theoretic attitude of thought. Obviously he supposes that he appeals here to the pre-theoretic attitude of naïve experience. This, however, is a fundamental error.

> In his concept of the productive imagination, FICHTE does not penetrate to pre-theoretical cosmic self-consciousness but remains involved in KANT's functionalistic view of knowledge.

A synthetic *function* of consciousness in its isolation can never be independent of theoretical thought, and certainly can never bridge the theoretical antithesis implied in the "gegenstand-relation".

Only the *cosmic self-consciousness* (to be examined later in the discussion of the problem of knowledge) can grasp the deeper unity of all aspects of reality, because in the transcendent root of the selfhood it transcends all its modal functions, which are interwoven in the cosmic order of time [1].

But how can a "function of feeling", prior to all logical reflection, accomplish an obviously *inter-functional* synthesis, and in this synthesis guarantee the unity of functions that are theoretically opposed to each other, and which consequently cannot be derived the one from the other?

In the "productive imagination" the basic antinomy of

---

[1] That self-consciousness remains an abstraction just as much to FICHTE as to KANT, should appear from the following passage (I, 244): "Das Ich aber ist jetzt als dasjenige bestimmt, welches, nach Aufhebung alles Objects durch das absolute Abstraktionsvermögen, übrig bleibt... (Dies ist denn auch wirklich die augenscheinliche, und nach ihrer Andeutung gar nicht mehr zu verkennende Quelle des Selbstbewustseyns. Alles, von welchem ich abstrahieren, was ich wegdenken kann... ist nicht mein Ich und ich setze es meinem Ich blosz dadurch entgegen dass ich es betrachte als ein solches, das ich wegdenken kann)..." ["But the ego is now determined as that which is left after the removal of every object through the absolute faculty of abstraction... (This is therefore really the apparent source of the self-consciousness which is no longer to be disregarded after it has been indicated. All from which I am able to abstract, all that I am able to think away... is not my ego, and I set it in contrast to my ego, merely by considering it as something that I can think away.)"]

Fichte's dialectic lies open and clear before us. Being pre-logical, it would make fluid all boundaries fixed by thought between "nature" and "freedom" and thereby "unify the contradictory".

The cosmic order imposed by God's sovereign creative will is set aside by the ὕβρις (pride) of "sovereign reason". The boundaries of the law-spheres in the realms of "nature" and "freedom" become a creation of reason itself and can therefore again be cancelled by the same reason.

Since by Fichte the tension between the ideal of science and that of personality is itself conceived of as an infinite ethical task [1], he rejects without hesitation the attempt at a solution of the antinomy by dialectical thought. Rather he raises this antinomy to the position of condition and basis of the whole "Wissenschaftslehre", as a necessary result of an ungrounded, preconscious *act* of the free personality bound to no laws: "We see, how that very circumstance which threatened to annihilate the possibility of a theory of human knowledge here becomes the only condition for the building of such a theory. We did not see, how we could ever unify absolute opposites; here we see, that an explanation of the occurrences in our mind could not at all be possible without absolute opposites; since that very faculty on which all those occurrences rest, i.e. the productive power of imagination, would not at all be possible, unless absolute opposites which cannot be synthesized appeared as fully unsuited to the power of apprehension... It is from this state of absolute opposition that the entire mechanism of the human mind issues; and this entire mechanism may not be explained otherwise than by a state of absolute opposition" [2]. In this manner,

---

[1] See I, 156.

[2] op. cit., p. 226: "Wir sehen, dass gerade derjenige Umstand, welcher die Möglichkeit einer Theorie des menschlichen Wissens zu vernichten drohte, hier die einzige Bedingung wird, unter der wir eine solche Theorie aufstellen können. Wir sahen nicht ab, wie wir jemals absolut entgegengesetzte sollten vereinigen können; hier sehen wir, dass eine Erklärung der Begebenheiten in unserem Geiste überhaupt gar nicht möglich seyn würde ohne absolut entgegengesetzte; da desjenige Vermögen, auf welchem alle jene Begebenheiten beruhen, die produktive Einbildungskraft gar nicht möglich seyn würde, wenn nicht absolut entgegengesetze, nicht zu vereinigende, dem Auffassungsvermögen des Ich völlig unangemessene vorkämen... Eben aus dem absoluten Entgegengesetztseyn erfolgt der ganze Mechanismus des menschlichen Geistes; und dieser ganze Mechanismus lässt sich nicht anders erklären, als durch ein absolutes Entgegengesetztseyn."

cosmonomic Idea of Humanistic immanence-philosophy

FICHTE supposes that he has cancelled *dogmatic idealism* as well as *dogmatic realism* in a higher critical idealism.

The first formal-dialectical part of the "Wissenschaftslehre" (1794) begins with the absolute principles ("Grundsätze") and ends thus with the deduction of the "productive imagination".

In the second part, described only schematically in the W.L. of 1794, and further elaborated in his *Grundrisz des Eigentümlichen der W.L. in Rücksicht auf das theoretische Vermögen* of 1795, FICHTE follows the very reverse method. The starting-point is here the "fact" of consciousness. He tries to show how the *ego* which originally experiences only sensory impressions, can rise to that philosophical abstraction and reflection with which the philosopher begins the theoretical doctrine of science. In the second part it appears still more clearly that FICHTE's *absolute ego* cannot be the supra-temporal totality of the temporal diversity of meaning [1].

The schema of FICHTE's train of thought is namely as follows: The ego unifies in itself two conflicting, irreconcilable momenta; it must distinguish itself from itself, it must set itself in opposition to itself as something foreign and contradictory — i.e. as "nature", as non-ego. Inasmuch as it produces itself, it must produce this non-ego by imagination, it must create sensory images, it must undergo perceptible sensory impressions (the Kantian "*Empfindung*"). But since the consciousness which discloses itself in the perceptible impression is only a part of the ego itself, the ego must find *itself* in it. That is to say, it must transcend the sensory function, it must make the sensory perception *its own*. This activity cannot cease until the selfhood

---

[1] From the following passage — in which he attempts to conceive the synthesis between form and matter as an interaction between ego and non-ego — it may appear that FICHTE in fact understands the *totality* of the ego as a relative one: "*Neither of the two*" (namely form and matter) "*is to determine the other, but both are to determine each other reciprocally,* means: — to come to the point in few words — absolute and relative ground of the totality-determination are to be one and the same; the relation is to be absolute and the absolute is to be nothing more than a relation" (I, 199). ["*Keins von beide*" (viz. Form und Materie) "*soll das andere, sondern beide sollen sich gegenseitig bestimmen, heisst:* — um ohne lange Umschweifungen zur Sache zu kommen — absoluter und relativer Grund der Totalitäts-bestimmung sollen Eins und Ebendasselbe seyn; die Relation soll absolut, und das absolute soll nichts weiter seyn, als eine Relation."]

has come to the consciousness that the ego has produced the non-ego *in itself*. Since consciousness proceeds continuously in this way, the original mere sensation is changed into the object of *intuition and experience,* which in turn becomes the transcendentally conceived "Gegenstand" of epistemology, until finally the ego becomes conscious of itself as the transcendental consciousness or as "theoretical reason", which itself creates this "Gegenstand" [1].

In other words, the "Wissenschaftslehre" rests entirely upon the Kantian position with respect to reality, i.e. upon the view of empirical reality as phenomenality of nature, constituted in a synthesis of sensory and logical functions, but with definitive elimination of the "*natural thing-in-itself*". The "impulse" ("Anstosz"), which the non-ego gives to the ego, and which FICHTE continues to consider necessary for the explanation of the mental *representation,* is explicitly referred to the hypostatized moral function of the free personality: "Only the question how and whereby the impulse to be assumed for the explanation of mental representation is given to the ego, is not to be answered here; for it lies beyond the limits of the theoretical part of the "doctrine of science" [2].

FICHTE's doctrine of the productive imagination and HEIDEGGER's interpretation of KANT.

It is remarkable that FICHTE, in this second part of the theoretical W.L., makes the categories, along with the sensory objects in their apriori sensory forms of space and time, arise dialectically from the productive imagination [3]. That is remarkable,

---

[1] cf. KRONER I, 487.

[2] *Grundl. der ges. Wissenschaftslehre,* Werke I, 218: "Blosz die Frage wie und wodurch der für Erklärung der Vorstellung anzunehmende Anstosz auf das Ich geschehe, ist hier nicht zu beantworten; denn sie liegt auszerhalb der Grenze des theoretischen Theils der Wissenschaftslehre."

[3] FICHTE points (I, 387) expressly to KANT's view of the matter, *without however, like* HEIDEGGER, *ascribing his own view* to KANT: "KANT, der die Kategorien ursprünglich als *Denkformen* erzeugt werden läszt, und der von seinem Gesichtspuncte aus daran völlig Recht hat, bedarf der durch die Einbildungskraft entworfenen Schemata, um ihre Anwendung auf Objecte möglich zu machen; er läszt sie demnach eben so wohl, als wir, durch die Einbildungskraft bearbeitet werden, und derselben zugänglich seyn. In der Wissenschaftslehre entstehen sie *mit den Objecten* zugleich, und, um dieselbe erst möglich zu machen, auf dem Boden der Einbildungskraft selbst." ["KANT, in whom the categories are produced originally as thought-forms and who, from his own point of view, is fully entitled to do

since MARTIN HEIDEGGER, though from an altogether different train of thought, in his interpretation of KANT's critique of knowledge (to be dealt with in vol. II), likewise supposes that he has found in this productive imagination the root of the two sources of knowledge, the understanding and sensibility.

§ 3 - THE TENSION BETWEEN THE IDEALS OF SCIENCE AND PERSONALITY IN FICHTE'S "PRAKTISCHE WISSENSCHAFTS-LEHRE" (1794)

The *guiding thesis of the theoretical "doctrine of science"* was the following: "The ego posits itself as *determined* by the non-ego." This thesis was contained in the result of the three basic theses of the entire "Wissenschaftslehre": "The ego and the non-ego determine each other reciprocally." In this latter thesis is expressed the necessary interaction between the antithetic elements in the activity of the self-consciousness, i.e. the interaction between the (free) subject and the (natural) object.

In this thesis, however, there is also implied the *"guiding principle" of the practical "doctrine of science"*: "The ego posits itself as *determining* the non-ego." The latter is meaningful only after the demonstration in the theoretical doctrine of science that the ego actually produces the non-ego as real, so that the non-ego actually possesses *reality for and in* the ego [1].

Only in the practical part is the ethical-idealistic basis even of the theoretical doctrine of science fully clarified.

FICHTE observes forthwith, on the occasion of the "Leitsatz" ("guiding thesis") of the practical doctrine of science: "For this thesis implies a main antithesis, which contains the entire contradiction between these entities as being simply posited and consequently unlimited, and compels us to assume a practical faculty of the ego for the sake of uniting them" [2]. Only in the

---

it, was in need of the schemata projected by the power of imagination, in order to make their application to objects possible; accordingly, just as we do, did he have them fashioned by the power of imagination and made them accessible to the same (power). In the "doctrine of science" they originate *along with the objects*, and on the soil of the imagination itself, in order to make the objects possible."]

[1] FICHTE observes (I, 247) significantly: "es versteht sich, *für* das Ich, — wie denn die ganze Wissenschaftslehre, als transcendentale Wissenschaft, nicht über das Ich hinausgehen kann, noch soll..." ["naturally for the ego, — in as much as the entire doctrine of science, as transcendental science, neither can go beyond the ego, nor ought to do so..."]

[2] I, 247: "Es liegt (nehmlich) in diesem Satze eine Haupt-Antithese, die

"practical" part, is an account eventually given of the reduction of the "theoretical" to the "practical" reason, and implicitly of the ideal of science to that of personality. The essence of the theoretical reason consisted in nothing but the restless dialectical movement, in which it sets limits to itself (in the "antitheses") in order to overpass them again and again by a new synthesis. It appeared dependent on "sensation" as the first *groundless* (and therefore theoretically *incomprehensible)* limit, that the ego sets to itself. The theoretical ego discovered the antinomy between the unlimited and the limited activity as the ground of its entire dialectical movement of thought, without being able to understand this ground. The first impulse for the development of the entire dialectical series, i.e. the sensory impression (Empfindung), alone makes "theoretical" reason possible, and so is not to be derived from it.

> FICHTE refers the impulse toward sensory experience to the moral function of personality, in which the ideal of personality is concentrated.

The ground of this impulse can be sought only in the fact that the ego is *"practical"*, so far as its innermost nature is concerned, and that the true root not only of personality but even of *"nature"* must be sought in the *moral* function [1]. In the "Leitsatz" of the practical doctrine of science is implied the requirement that the ego operate causally upon the non-ego. Thereby the antinomy between the independence of the ego as an absolute being on the one hand, and its dependence and limitation as *intelligence* on the other, should be overcome. In this very demand, however, an antinomy is implied. The demand that the free ego operate causally upon the non-ego is based upon the absolute essence of the ego, allowing nothing alongside of or opposed to itself. The objection against this postulated causality is grounded on the fact that a non-ego is simply opposed to the ego, and that it must remain so, if the I-ness is not to become an empty form.

---

den ganzen Widerstreit zwischen ebendenselben, als schlechthin gesetzten, mithin unbeschränkten Wesen umfasst, und uns nöthiget, als Vereinigungsmittel ein praktisches Vermögen des Ich anzunehmen."

[1] FICHTE gives to this insight pregnant expression in his *"Grundlage des Naturrechts"*: "Das praktische Vermögen ist die innerste Wurzel des Ich, auf diese wird erst alles andere aufgetragen und daran geheftet," III, 20 ff. ["The practical faculty is the innermost root of the ego; on it alone all the rest is built and affixed."]

cosmonomic Idea of Humanistic immanence-philosophy

The antinomy which is contained in the practical "Leitsatz" may be reduced to the antinomy between the ego as *unlimited and infinite* and the ego as *limited and finite activity*. Consequently, at this point, a higher discrepancy is involved in the very nature of the ego. How is this antinomy solved by FICHTE?

The infinite and unlimited ego as moral striving. Elimination also of KANT's practical concept of substance. The ego as infinite creative activity is identified with KANT's categorical imperative.

The antinomy is resolved in that the infinite and unlimited character of the ego is viewed not as an infinite *substance* at rest, but rather as an infinite *striving*. The free unlimited and infinite ego *ought* again and again to sets limits to itself as *"intelligence"* by an objective non-ego, in order to provide its infinite striving activity with a resistance to be overcome ever and anon, which alone gives content to this striving.

"Just as the ego is posited, all reality is posited; in the ego everything is to be posited; the ego is to be simply independent; everything, however, is to be dependent upon it. Consequently, there is required accordance of the object with the ego; and it is the absolute ego which for the very sake of its absolute being, does require it" [1].

In the *striving* resides the final ground of the opposing and of that which is set in opposition, the final ground of the "impulse", which the theoretical W.L. was unable to explain. Therefore, *the practical reason is at the basis of the theoretical as its condition, for without striving no object is possible* [2].

In a note to the passage just cited, FICHTE observes: "KANT's categorical imperative." Thus it clearly appears that FICHTE really seeks the deepest root of the self-consciousness in the hypostatized *moral law,* identified with the ideal subject in the rationalist conception of the cosmonomic Idea of Humanistic thought [3].

---

[1] I, 260: "So wie das Ich gesetzt ist, ist alle Realität gesetzt; im Ich soll alles gesetzt seyn; das Ich soll schlechthin unabhängig, Alles aber soll von ihm abhängig seyn. Also, es wird die Uebereinstimmung des Objects mit dem Ich gefordert; und das absolute Ich, gerade um seines absolutes Seyns willen, ist es, welches sie fordert."

[2] I, 264.

[3] WINDELBAND rightly observes, op. cit. II, 224: "Das *Sittengesetz* also, d.h. die Forderung eines Handelns, das lediglich sich selbst zum Zwecke

At the same time it appears from the sequel that the Divinity, as the absolute ego, is nothing but the result of this moralistic hypostatization. The *striving* activity of the ego, going on to infinity, is *as striving* characterized again as finite: "Even the very concept of striving, however, implies finiteness, for that which is not *counter*-acted (striven *against*), is no striving" [1].

The finite (moral, "practical") ego, however, can have no other goal for its infinite striving than again to become *absolute*.

The tension between ego and non-ego, between form and matter, consciousness and being, freedom and nature, the ideal of personality and the ideal of science, should be eliminated in the absolute ego (the Divinity), which is just so far an unthinkable Idea (unthinkable, because reason is unable to emerge beyond the antinomy). Actually, however, the absolute ego is nothing but a hypostatized, activistically conceived moral Idea of reason, which as such remains involved in the antinomy between the ideal of science and the ideal of personality; for, on the one hand, it must contain the *origin* as well as the *totality of meaning*, but, on the other hand, it is nothing but an absolutized abstraction from the cosmic temporal coherence of meaning [2]. From the Humanist standpoint, KRONER correctly observes: *"Even the absolute ego needs necessarily the 'impulse' if in any sense it is to be an ego"* [3]. In other words, even

---

hat ist der die Welt erzeugende Trieb des absolutes Ich." ["Consequently, it is the *moral law*, i.e. the demand of an acting which has only itself as its aim, that is the impulse of the absolute ego whereby the world is generated."]

[1] V, 270: "Im Begriffe des Strebens selbst aber liegt schon die Endlichkeit, denn dasjenige, dem nicht *widerstrebt* wird, ist kein Streben."

[2] FICHTE has given to his conception of the Deity as absolutized moral law a pregnant expression in his treatise *Ueber den Grund unseres Glaubens an eine göttliche Weltregierung* (WW. V, 185), where he writes: "Dies ist der wahre Glaube; diese moralische Ordnung ist das Göttliche das wir annehmen"; ["this is the true faith; this moral order is the Deity which we accept;"] and in his *Appellation an das Publikum gegen die Anklage des Atheismus* (1799; WW. V, 210), where he writes: "Erzeuge nur in dir die pflichtmäszige Gesinnung und du wirst Gott erkennen." ["Produce only in yourself the inclination in conformity to moral duty and you will know God."] The moral order, as Deity, is to FICHTE pervaded with the activity-motive of his philosophy of the ego. It is: "Thätiges Ordnen" (active ordaining), ORDO ORDINANS. Cf. WW. V, 382, *Aus einem Privatschreiben*.

[3] KRONER, I, 511: *"Der 'Anstosz' ist auch dem absolutem Ich, damit es nur überhaupt ein Ich sein könne, notwendig."*

in the "absolute ego" as a hypostatized function there is latent the basic antinomy between "nature" and "freedom".

In the practical doctrine of science, the ego is conceived of as absolute striving. With the striving there is connected a *counter-striving,* and the *theoretical ego* is now viewed by FICHTE as necessarily coherent with the *practical.* For, by reason of the *counteraction* (i.e. of "nature" as the non-ego), the ego is determined by something outside itself. Because it is an *ego,* it must *reflect* about this being-limited, it must relate itself to the "Gegenstand", as to its opposite. In the theoretical doctrine of science, in the deduction of the *representation,* the *ego* (conceiving itself as limited by the non-ego) is deduced genetically by ascending from the sensory consciousness (limited by the non-ego) to the free transcendental consciousness. Likewise, in the second constructive part of the practical W. L., beginning with par. 6, the origin of the practical ego, which conceives itself as free and determines the non-ego, is deduced from the ego that is determined merely by the "impulse". There is a strict correspondence between these two ways of deduction.

Besides, it appears in the nature of the case that the theoretical and the practical ego are *one and the same* (for we saw previously that FICHTE tries to reduce the ideal of science to the ideal of personality and to absorb the former in the latter!). "All reflection is based upon striving, and there is no reflection possible, if there is no striving" [1]. Striving is the final common root of the theoretical and the practical ego: all theoretical reflection, all sensation, all intuition stems from the practical striving, from the activity of the moral ego-function, which transcends its boundaries. In this context we will quote a passage which is very characteristic for the whole system, because it gives a clear expression to the eventual absorption of the ideal of science in the ideal of personality. We insert it here entirely on that account: "From this follows, indeed, in the clearest manner the subordination of theory to the practical; it follows that all theoretical laws are based upon *practical* ones and, as there can be only one single practical law, upon one and the same law; consequently the most complete system in the total (human) being; if the impulse should permit itself to be elevated, then also follows the elevation of the insight, and vice versa;

---

[1] "Alle Reflexion gründet sich auf das Streben, und es ist keine möglich, wenn kein Streben ist."

then follows the absolute freedom of reflection and abstraction also in a theoretical respect, and the possibility of focusing one's attention to something *according to moral duty* and of abstracting it from something else, without which no morality would be possible at all."

"Fatalism is destroyed at its very root, this fatalism based on the opinion that our acting and willing depend upon the system of our representations; for it is shown here, that the very system of our representations depends upon our impulse and our will; and this is indeed the single way to refute this view thoroughly. — In short, by this system there is brought *unity* and *coherence* into the whole man, a unity and coherence which are lacking in so many systems" [1].

The totality of meaning of the consciousness, the very root of human existence, and consequently of the entire cosmos, resides in the *absolutized moral function*. It is that which must bring unity and coherence in the whole man.

> The "fatalism" so keenly opposed by FICHTE is nothing but the science-ideal of the "Aufklärung", dominating the ideal of personality.

The "fatalism" so sharply opposed by FICHTE *is nothing but*

---

[1] I, 294/5: "Hieraus erfolgt denn auch auf das einleuchtendste die Subordination der Theorie unter das Praktische; es folgt, dass alle *theoretischen* Gesetze auf *praktische* und da es wohl nur Ein praktisches Gesetz geben dürfte, auf ein und ebendasselbe Gesetz sich gründen; demnach das vollständigste System im ganzen Wesen; es folgt, wenn etwa der Trieb sich selbst sollte erhöhen lassen, auch die Erhöhung der Einsicht, und umgekehrt; es erfolgt die absolute Freiheit der Reflexion und Abstraktion auch in theoretischer Rücksicht, und die Möglichkeit *pflichtmäszig* seine Aufmerksamkeit auf etwas zu richten, und von etwas anderem abzuziehen ohne welche gar keine Moral möglich ist.

"*Der Fatalismus wird von Grund aus zerstört, der sich darauf gründet, das unser Handeln und Wollen von dem Systeme unserer Vorstellungen abhänglg sey* (the italics are mine!), indem hier gezeigt wird, das hinwiederum das System unserer Vorstellungen von unserem Triebe und unserem Willen abhängt: und dies ist denn auch die einzige Art ihn gründlich zu wiederlegen. — Kurz, es kommt durch dieses System *Einheit* und *Zusammenhang* in den ganzen Menschen, die in so vielen System fehlt."

Vid. also I, 284, note: "Die Wissenschaftslehre soll den ganzen Menschen erschöpfen; sie läszt daher sich nur mit der Totalität seines ganzen Vermögens auffassen..." ["The doctrine of science ought to exhaust the whole man; it is consequently to be conceived only with the totality of all human faculties..."]

the Humanistic science-ideal of the "Enlightenment", which had no place for the freedom of human personality, because it was made independent of the latter.

In the polar tension between this ideal of science and the ideal of personality, FICHTE chooses unconditionally for the absolute primacy of the latter — *at the expense of the former,* as we are still to see!

In his practical doctrine of science, FICHTE consequently does not stay with the Kantian dualism between moral self-determination and sensory "inclination of nature". Just as the "sensory ego", quâ ego, is driven forward dialectically by itself *to become the ego that knows itself as intelligence,* so also the ego dominated by its sensual impulses becomes the *ego determining itself* as "pure ethical will".

So FICHTE intends to show that even in the "triebhafte Ich", the "pure will" or the "absolute impulse" is operative, and that only thereby does the ego feel itself "driven on and ahead" by natural impulses. The sensory nature must finally take its rise dialectically from moral freedom itself. In *the ego* there is an original striving to "fill out" infinity. This striving conflicts with all limitation in an object. A self-producing striving is called impulse ("Trieb").

Infinite striving requires on the other hand the resistance, the *counter-action* from an object, in order to overcome this latter. The ego has in itself the law, according to which it must reflect about itself "as filling out infinity". But it cannot reflect about itself, if it is not limited. The fulfilling of this law, or — what amounts to the same thing — the satisfaction of the "Reflexionstrieb" (impulse to reflection), is thus *determined* by the non-ego, and depends on the object (the non-ego). This impulse toward reflection cannot be satisfied apart from an object: hence it may also be described as an *"impulse toward the object"* [1]. The striving therefore requires a counter-action that holds it in *balance.*

In the limitation, which the "impulse" experiences through the object, the *feeling* arises as the expression of a suffering, a passivity, an *inability:* "The expression of impotence in the ego is called a *feeling.* In it is united most intimately an *activity* — I feel, I am the feeling subject; and this activity is that of reflection — and a *limitation* — I *feel,* I am passive and not active; there is

---

[1] I, 291.

present a constraint. This limitation necessarily supposes an impulse to go beyond it. That which wills, needs, embraces nothing more, is — naturally with respect to itself — unlimited"[1].

In its limitation by feeling, the "Reflexionstrieb" is at the same time satisfied and not satisfied:

a - It is satisfied: the ego must *reflect* on itself: it reflects with absolute spontaneity and is thereby satisfied with respect to the *form* of this operation of consciousness. So far the feeling can be related to the free *ego*.

b - It is *not satisfied* with respect to the content of this operation of consciousness. "The ego was to be posited as filling out infinity, but it is posited as limited. This, too, is now necessarily present in feeling"[2].

c - The originating of the condition of *non-satisfaction*, however, is determined by the ego proceeding beyond the limit which is set by feeling[3].

> The dialectical line of thought of the practical doctrine of science: feeling, intuition, longing, approbation, absolute impulse (categorical imperative).

The course of FICHTE's deductions is therefore as follows: the *ego*, as a limited and finite ego, is *moral striving* according to its deepest being. To be able to create itself as such, and to become aware of itself as such, it is, however, required, that it should be and *feel* itself as a *sensibly driven feeling and intuiting ego*. But conversely, it would never feel itself as *sensibly limited*, if it were not *moral striving* according to its deepest being.

In consequence of the *appropriation* by the striving ego of the feeling of *compulsion*, which arises from the counter-action of the non-ego, i.e. in consequence of the conscious *reflection* about it as the ego's own limit, there arises a new feeling, in

---

[1] I, 289: "Die Aeusserung des Nicht-könnens im Ich heiszt ein *Gefühl*. In ihm ist innigst vereinigt *Thätigkeit* — ich fühle, bin das fühlende, und diese Thätigkeit ist die der Reflexion — *Beschränkung* — ich *fühle*, bin leidend, und nicht thätig: es ist ein Zwang vorhanden.

Diese Beschränkung setzt nun notwendig einen Trieb voraus, weiter hinaus zu gehen. Was nichts weiter will, bedarf, umfasst, das ist — es versteht sich, *für sich selbst* — nicht eingeschränkt."

[2] "Das Ich sollte gesetzt werden als die Unendlichkeit ausfüllend, aber es wird als begrenzt. — Dies kommt nun gleichfalls nothwendig vor im Gefühle."

[3] I, 291/2.

which the feeling ego feels itself in the impulse which strives out beyond the limit.

So far as the drive which is formally satisfied in the reflection about the *feeling ego,* strives out beyond the limit set in reflection, as a force that strives outward, it becomes longing, ("Sehnen"), "a drive toward something completely unknown, which merely manifests itself by a want, by an uneasiness, by a void, which seeks to be filled out, and does not indicate from where." FICHTE here makes this note: "This longing is important, not only for the practical, but for the whole doctrine of science. Only by the same the ego is *in itself* driven *beyond itself:* only by the same does an outerworld disclose itself in the very ego" [1].

This longing, however, is also limited, for otherwise it would be no desire, but *fulfilment* of desire: *causality.* Through this limitation *by the non-ego* there arises a new feeling of compulsion, which again becomes the ground for the creation of an object, the production of something outside the ego through "ideal activity", the "ideal" for which the ego longs in its striving.

The object of the feeling of compulsion produced by the limitation is something real. The object of the longing, however, has no reality (since the ego in itself can have no causality, without cancelling itself as "pure activity"), "but it ought to have it in consequence of the longing; for the latter seeks reality" [2]. Both objects stand in an antinomic relation to one another ("nature" and "freedom"!).

The reality *felt* determines (limits) the ego. The ego, however, is ego only insofar as it determines *itself* (in the reflection about the *feeling).* Therefore its longing becomes the *impulse* to determine itself. Or indeed, since it feels its determination (limitation) in the reality of the object, its longing becomes the impulse to determine *this reality* for the object and thus to create the determination *in itself.*

In the "longing" arises the impulse to sensory perception

---

[1] I, 303: "einen Trieb nach etwas völlig unbekannten, das sich bloss durch ein Bedürfniss, durch ein *Misbehagen,* durch eine *Leere* offenbart, die Ausfüllung sucht, und nicht andeutet woher." "Dieses Sehnen ist wichtig, nicht nur für die praktische, sondern für die gesammte Wissenschaftslehre. Lediglich durch dasselbe wird das Ich *in sich selbst — ausser sich* getrieben: lediglich durch dasselbe offenbart sich *in ihm* selbst eine Aussenwelt."

[2] I, 306: "aber es soll sie zufolge des Sehnens haben; denn dasselbe geht aus auf Realität."

("Empfindungstrieb") and the "drive toward knowledge" in general, which strives to regain for the ego the natural object created by it, but not created with reflection on this act (and therefore not experienced as the ego's *own*); it strives to *represent* the object in the I-ness. The limit is felt *as* felt, i.e. as one created *in the ego by the ego*. The sensory feeling ("Empfinden") is changed (as the theoretical W. L. has shown) by a new reflection into an *intuition*. So far as the ego has not yet, in the self-reflection of thought, theoretically *appropriated* that which is sensibly perceived, it does not yet regard the sensory image as a product of the ego, but the image is intuited as an "objective character". Since the free spontaneity of the ego in the activity of intuition is the *driving force*, the image is, to be sure, intuited as a character belonging to the *object*, but *contingent*, determined by no necessity [1].

If, however, the object is to become an *object for the ego*, then the ego must become aware of this self-determination of the object as a *product of the ego* itself. The *feeling ego* feels itself *limited*, the *intuiting ego freely exceeds the limit*. The feeling and the intuiting ego are, however, *one and the same:* feeling and intuition must therefore be synthetically united. In themselves they have no coherence. "Intuition *sees,* but it is *empty*: feeling *is related to reality*, but is *blind*" [2]. They can be united only when the *feeling ego* no longer feels itself as such to be *limited*, when, so to speak, it keeps pace with the intuition, which views what is felt as something *contingent* in the object. This is only possible in such a way that the feeling ego *as such* exceeds its limits, and that it, as feeling ego, goes on a d i n f i n i t u m, or that it is driven on in its longing, instead of losing itself in sensuous feeling.

So the longing discloses itself, as an "impulse toward change of

---

[1] I, 317: "Würde das Ich seiner Freiheit im Bilden (dadurch, dass es auf die gegenwärtige Reflexion selbst wieder reflektirte) sich bewuszt, so würde das Bild gesetzt, als zufällig *in Beziehung auf das Ich*. Eine solche Reflexion findet nicht statt; es muss demnach zufällig gesetzt werden (*in Beziehung auf ein anderes nicht-Ich,* das uns bis jetzt noch gänzlich unbekannt ist)." ["If the ego should become aware of its freedom in its production (thereby, that it reflects again on the present reflection itself), the image would be set as contingent *in relation to the I.* Such a reflection does not occur; it is consequently to be set contingently *(in relation to another non-ego,* which up till now is still entirely unknown to us)."]

[2] I, 319.

feelings": only where the feelings change, is the primitive longing satisfied.

Feeling as such, however, cannot determine the *change of feelings*. The ego can reflect about what is felt only at a higher stage of consciousness. "Consequently, the changed situation cannot be *felt as changed situation*. This other should therefore merely be *intuited* by the ideal activity, as something other and opposed to the present feeling"[1]. The changed feeling must therefore be *intuited as changed*, if the ego is to be able to reflect about the impulse to change its feelings.

Only through this reflection does *the ego* become *an ego*, because it is an ego only insofar as it not merely longs, but insofar as it *becomes aware* that it longs to change the feelings. If the ego is to be able to arrive at this consciousness, then it must be able as *feeling ego* to relate itself to a feeling which is not itself that which is felt. And to this end *intuition* and *feeling* must be synthetically united in this feeling. This is the *feeling of longing*, which is necessarily accompanied by a *feeling of satisfaction*. The altered feeling must satisfy the longing after a change of the feeling. The synthesis here achieved FICHTE calls "approbation" ("*Beifall*").

The ego reflects about its feeling in the intuition of it. The act of determining the feeling (the *intuiting*) and the drive toward determination (the *longing*) are now one and the same[2].

The ego cannot produce this synthesis of *impulse* (longing) and *action* (intuiting) without distinguishing the two, but it cannot distinguish the two without positing some respect in which they *contradict* each other: So the feeling of approbation finds its opposite in the displeasure ("*Misfallen*"), in which the disharmony between impulse and act comes to expression. "Not every longing is necessarily accompanied by displeasure, but when it is satisfied, there arises displeasure as to the former; it becomes insipid, flat." So are "the inner determinations of the things (which are related to feeling) nothing more than degrees of displeasing or pleasing"[3].

The synthesis in the approbation, however, may not be per-

---

[1] I, 321: "Also der veränderte Zustand kann als veränderte Zustand nicht gefühlt werden. Das andere müsste daher lediglich durch die ideale Thätigkeit *angeschaut* werden, als etwas anderes und dem gegenwärtigen Gefühle entgegengesetztes."

[2] I, 325.

[3] ibidem.

formed merely by the *spectator*, i.e. only *theoretically*, but the ego *itself* must perform it. The ego must be driven on to desire approval as such; it must also be aware of the impulse which strives toward approval, and therewith towards the unity of its selfhood.

If the ego is to become *aware* of the synthesis between intuition and feeling in approbation, then the intuition and the impulse alike must be understood as *determined* and *self-determining* at the same time. Then alone is the ego aware of itself as an ego that determines itself absolutely and consequently is also absolutely determined.

If the action that satisfies the impulse is determined and self-determining *at once*, then it happens out of absolute freedom, as the self-creation of the absolute ego. If the impulse which determines this action is *absolute* in the same way, *then it is grounded in itself*. It is the impulse that has itself for its goal. The drive towards change ("Trieb nach Wechsel") is in the last analysis determined by the "drive towards mutual determination of the ego through itself" ("Trieb nach Wechselbestimmung des Ich durch sich selbst") or the drive towards absolute *unity* and perfection of the ego in itself ("Trieb nach absolute *Einheit* und Vollendung des Ich in sich selbst")[1].

The categorical imperative as the absolute impulse that is grounded in itself.

It is the impulse that has itself for its goal which strives to create itself (and thereby the harmony in the ego, of which the latter is aware): i.e. the absolute drive: *"der Trieb um des Triebens willen."* To this, FICHTE adds: "If it is expressed in terms of a law, as for the very sake of this determination at a certain point of reflection it should be expressed, then it must be established that a law for the very sake of the law is an absolute law, or the categorical imperative: — You ought unconditionally. It is easy to understand, where in such an impulse the undetermined moment lies: it drives us, namely, out into the indefinite without an aim (the categorical imperative is merely formal without any object)"[2].

---

[1] I, 326.

[2] I, 327: "Drückt man es als Gesetz aus, wie es gerade um dieser Bestimmung willen auf einem gewissen Reflexionspunkt ausgedrückt werden muss, so ist ein Gesetz um des Gesetzes willen ein absolutes Gesetz, oder der kategorische Imperativ: — *Du sollst schlechthin.* Wo bei einem

cosmonomic Idea of Humanistic immanence-philosophy 447

If now action and impulse are to determine one another reciprocally, the object produced by the action (i.e. the effect of the drive which can be intuited in the theoretically determinable sense-world) must be determined by the impulse and agree with the "ideal of longing". Conversely, the impulse must be intuited in the reflection itself, as desiring this object alone. In this case the longing striving finds its *consummation*. But since the longing and striving in their very essence *cannot be completed*, the ego must again be driven out away from the feeling of harmony and into the infinite.

The "Du sollst" remains, entirely in the Kantian line, "ewige, nimmer erfüllbare Aufgabe" (an eternal task, never to be fully accomplished).

In FICHTE's identity-philosophy, the Humanist-ideal of personality in its moralistic sense has, to be sure, absorbed the science-ideal entirely along the line of the continuity-postulate of freedom, but, as we saw continually, at *the cost of sanctioning the antinomy.*

> FICHTE's dithyramb on the ideal of personality: "Ueber die Würde des Menschen" (On the dignity of man).

Dithyrambically FICHTE sings the praise of this ideal of personality in the address *"Ueber die Würde des Menschen"* delivered at the close of his philosophical lectures in 1794: "Only from man does orderly arrangement spread around him up to the limit of his observation, — and when he extends the latter to a greater distance, order and harmony are extended too to the same degree. His observation indicates the place of all things in their infinite diversity, so that no single one may suppress the other; it brings unity into the infinite diversity.

"Through this the celestial bodies maintain themselves together, and become only one organized body; through this the suns turn in their determined orbits. Through the ego the gigantic ladder (of entities) rises from the lichen up to the seraph; in it is the system of the entire world of spirits, and man expects with reason, that the law which he imposes on himself and on this world, must be valid for the latter; he expects with reason the future universal recognition of the

---

solchem Triebe das *unbestimmte* liege, lässt sich leicht einsehen; nemlich er treibt uns ins unbestimmte hinaus, ohne Zweck (der kategorische Imperativ ist bloss formal ohne allen Gegenstand)."

same. In the ego lies the sure pledge that from it order and harmony shall be extended ad infinitum where it is lacking until now; that with the expanding human culture at the same time the culture of the universe shall expand. Everything which still lacks form and order, shall be resolved into the most beautiful order, and what is already harmonious shall — according to laws not developed till now — become continually more harmonious. Man shall bring order into the confusion, and a plan into the general destruction; through him shall putrefaction produce form, and death summon to a new glorious life. This is man, when we consider him merely as observing intelligence; what would he not be, when we think him as *practically* active power!" [1].

> The passion for power in FICHTE's ideal of personality. The science-ideal converts itself into a titanic ideal of culture.

The Faustian passion for power in the Humanistic science-ideal has dissolved itself into the passion for power in the personality-ideal. The science-ideal has converted itself into a

---

[1] I, 413: "Allein von Menschen aus verbreitet sich *Regelmässigkeit* rund um ihm herum bis an die Grenze seiner Beobachtung, — und wie er diese weiter vorrückt, wird Ordnung und Harmonie weiter vorgerückt. Seine Beobachtung weist dem bis ins unendliche verschiedenen, jedem seinen Platz an, dass keines das andere verdränge; sie bringt Einheit in die unendliche Verschiedenheit.

Durch sie erhalten sich die Weltkörper zusammen, und werden nur *Ein* organisierter Körper; durch sie drehen die Sonnen sich in ihren angewiesen Bahnen. Durch das Ich steht die ungeheure Stufenfolge da von der Flechte bis zum Seraph; in *ihn* ist das System der ganzen Geisterwelt, und der Mensch erwartet mit Recht, dass das Gesetz, das er sich und ihr giebt, für sie gelten müsse; erwartet mit Recht die einstige allgemeine Anerkennung desselben. Im Ich liegt das sichere Unterpfand, das von ihm aus ins unendliche Ordnung und Harmonie sich verbreiten werde wo jetzt noch keine ist; dass mit der fortrückenden Cultur des Menschen, zugleich die Cultur des Weltalls fortrücken werde. Alles was jetzt noch unförmlich und ordnungsloss ist, wird durch den Menschen in die schönste Ordnung sich auflösen, und was jetzt schon harmonisch ist, wird — nach bis jetzt unentwickelten Gesetzen — immer harmonischer werden. Der Mensch wird Ordnung in das Gewühl, und einen Plan in die allgemeine Zerstörung hineinbringen; durch ihn wird die Verwesung bilden, und der Tod zu einem neuen herrlichen Leben rufen. Das ist der Mensch, wenn wir ihn bloss als beobachtende Intelligenz ansehen; was ist er erst, wenn wir ihn als praktisch-thätiges Vermögen denken!"

moralistic ideal of culture that comes to full expression in titanic activity! [1]

There is, however, no longer any place for the science-ideal in its earlier sense which hypostatized "nature" in its mathematical and mechanical functions, in order to extend the continuity of natural-scientific thought across all modal boundaries of the aspects. With respect to FICHTE's system, WINDELBAND justly writes: "Nature has meaning only as material for the performance of our duty. Therefore FICHTE's doctrine does not embrace a natural philosophy in the earlier sense of the word. He could not have given such a philosophy, since — apparently because of the one-sidedness of his education as a youth — he lacked any detailed knowledge of natural science. *However, the very principles of his philosophy did not permit him to project it. The doctrine of science could not consider nature as a causal mechanism existing in itself"* [2].

FICHTE could view nature neither as a mechanistic "world in itself", nor as an organic world immanently adapted to its own end. His teleological conception of nature had no other intention than to demonstrate in the dialectical way of his "Wissenschaftslehre" that nature, as it exists, must have been created by the free ego in order to render possible a resistance against the realization of its moral task [3].

---

[1] This conversion of the authentic ideal of science into a *culture-ideal* comes pregnantly to expression in FICHTE's writing *"Die Bestimmung des Menschen"* which appeared in 1800, (W.W. vol. II, pp. 267 ff).

[2] WINDELBAND, op. cit. II, 226 f: "Die Natur hat Sinn nur als Material unserer Pflichterfüllung. Deshalb gibt es für die Fichtesche Lehre keine Naturphilosophie im sonstigen Sinne des Wortes. Er hätte sie nicht geben können, weil ihm, wie es scheint bei der Einseitigkeit seiner Jugendbildung genaue und spezielle naturwissenschaftliche Kenntnisse mangelten. *Aber die Prinzipien seiner Philosophie erlaubten sie ihm gar nicht. Als einen in sich bestehenden Kausal-mechanismus konnte die Wissenschaftslehre die Natur nicht betrachten."*

[3] For the rest, FICHTE did not abandon this standpoint, even in his *fourth metaphysical period.* Cf., e.g., his writing *"Thatsachen des Bewusztseyns"* (1810—'11), based on the *Transzendentale Logik* included in the first volume of the "Nachgelassene Werke" (W.W. vol. II, p. 663): "Die Natur ist Bild unserer realen Kraft, und so absolut zweckmässig; wir können in ihr und an ihr das was wir sollen. Ihr Prinzip ist schlechthin ein sittliches Prinzip, keinesweges ein Naturprincip (denn dann eben wäre sie absolut)..." ["Nature is the image of our real power and thus absolutely purposive, we can do in it and in respect to it what we ought

> The antinomy between the science-ideal and personality-ideal has actually converted itself in FICHTE's first period into an antinomy between Idea and sense within the personality-ideal itself.

In KANT's dualistic world-picture, the antinomy between the ideal of science and that of personality actually implied the recognition of both factors. For FICHTE this antinomy is really converted into a contradiction within the personality-ideal itself between free activity (spontaneity) and bondage to the resistance of the lower nature or between "Idea" and sense [1].

KANT too had posed the latter antinomy in his *Critique of practical Reason*. The ideal of personality *cannot* cancel the bondage to sensory nature without dissolving itself into an empty abstraction. With the hypostatization of the moral norm, this antinomy *must* be retained. WINDELBAND justly remarks in this connection: "For this very reason the world is to FICHTE the posited contradiction, and dialectic is the method to know it" [2].

---

to do. Its principle is simply a moral one, by no means a nature-principle (for in this very case it would be absolute)..."]

[1] See also the characteristic pages in *Die Bestimmung des Menschen* (The Vocation of Man) II, 313—319.

[2] Op. cit. II, 227: "Eben deshalb ist die Welt für FICHTE der gesetzte Widerspruch und die Dialektik die Methode ihrer Erkenntnis."

CHAPTER VI

THE VICTORY OF THE IRRATIONALIST OVER THE RATIONALIST CONCEPTION OF THE HUMANISTIC TRANSCENDENTAL GROUND-IDEA. THE IDEAL OF PERSONALITY IN ITS IRRATIONALIST TURN IN THE PHILOSOPHY OF LIFE

§ 1 - THE TRANSITION TO IRRATIONALISM IN FICHTE'S THIRD PERIOD UNDER THE INFLUENCE OF THE MOVEMENT OF "STURM UND DRANG" ("STORM AND STRESS")

FICHTE's development did not stop with the standpoint of the first edition of the *Wissenschaftslehre*. EMIL LASK especially deserves credit for having sharply analysed the various phases in this development since 1797. We are here not so much interested in FICHTE's second period, characterized by the *"Second Introduction into the Doctrine of Science" (Zweite Einleitung in die Wissenschaftslehre)* of 1797. In this phase we can only observe a return to and a completion of the critical transcendental philosophy in a teleological system of "the pure forms of reason". It does not open new viewpoints in respect to the dialectical development of Humanistic thought. Therefore, we shall now focus our attention on FICHTE's *third period*, in which, under the strong influence of JACOBI's *philosophy of feeling*, a new irrationalistic trend gained ground in the Humanistic personality-ideal.

FICHTE's relation to "Sturm und Drang".

FICHTE's relations with the so-called "Sturm und Drang" have recently been examined in detail by LEON[1], BERGMANN[2], GELPCKE[3] and others. GELPCKE sees from the very beginning in FICHTE the

---

[1] XAVIER LEON: *Fichte et son temps* 2 vols. Paris 1922.

[2] ERNST BERGMANN: *Fichte und Goethe (Kantstudien* 1915, Vol. 20).

[3] ERNST GELPCKE: *Fichte und die Gedankenwelt des Sturm und Drang* (Leipzig 1928).

influence of such typical representatives of this movement as Lavater, Hamann and Jacobi operative, even before he was taken up with Kantian critical idealism. The titanic activity-motive, the strong voluntaristic tendency, characteristic of Fichte's philosophy, in all the phases of its development, and which signally differentiates it from the more static Kantian system, shows indeed a veritable congeniality of spirit with the deepest motives of "Sturm und Drang", glorifying the "activity of genius". The activistic ideal of personality permeates all expressions of this transition-period and concentrates itself, as it were, in Goethe's *Faust*, with its typical utterance: *"Im Anfang war die Tat* ("In the beginning was the deed").

"Sturm und Drang", as Gelpcke observes, finds its artistic form of expression in the "ego-drama". Activity and selfhood are the two poles in this world of thought. The ideal "ego" is absolutized in a limitless subjectivism and becomes elevated to the rank of *genius* possessing in itself the perfectly individual moral measure of its action, bound to no general norm. In the foreword to his *"Räuber"*, Schiller has given the following expression to this ingenious subjectivism: "The law did not yet form a single great man, but freedom hatches colossosses and extremities"[1].

In his *"Sokratische Denkwürdigkeiten"* (1759)[2] Hamann expressed the same idea in the following form: "What replaces in Homer the ignorance of the rules of art which an Aristotle invented, and what in a Shakespeare the ignorance or violation of these critical laws? Genius, is the unanimous answer"[3].

Only in the very *deed* can this selfhood of genius render itself objective. A true enthusiasm and optimism of the deed characterizes the period of *"Sturm und Drang"*, sharply distinguishing its basic tone from the preponderatingly pessimistic one of Rousseau, nothwithstanding all its dependence upon Rousseau's philosophy of sentiment.

---

[1] "Das Gesetz hat noch keinen groszen Mann gebildet, aber die Freiheit brütet Kolosse und Extremitäten aus."

[2] "Socratic Memorabilia."

[3] "Was ersetzt bei Homer die Unwissenheit der Kunstregeln, die ein Aristoteles nach ihm erdacht, und was, bei einem Shakespeare die Unwissenheit oder Uebertretung jener kritische Gesetze? Das Genie ist die einmütige Antwort."

cosmonomic Idea of Humanistic immanence-philosophy 453

The irrationalist view of the individuality of genius.
The irrationalist turn in the ideal of personality.

This entire movement was still bound to ROUSSEAU by the naturalistic view of the personality-ideal expressed in the watchword, "natural forming of life". But for the rationalism of the time of the Enlightenment the "natural" was identical with what was "conceived in terms of natural laws". In contrast the "*Sturm und Drang*" movement ran to the other extreme: it absolutizes the *subjective individuality* in nature: the genius must realize himself in the completely individual expression of his psychical drives.

The true reality is sought in the completely irrational depths of subjective individuality and these depths of subjective reality are to be grasped not by the analysing understanding, but by *feeling*. This irrational philosophy of feeling, predominating especially in HAMANN, the young HERDER and JACOBI, and of which GOETHE makes his Faust the mouth-piece in the utterance: "Gefühl ist alles", is the true Humanistic counter-pole of the rationalistic line of thought characteristic of the "Enlightenment".

The philosophy of life of the "*Sturm und Drang*" period finds its culminating point in the demand for subjective ethical freedom. This new Humanistic postulate of freedom is averse to all universal rational norms. GELPCKE characterizes it as follows: "The regained concept of freedom becomes a dogma. It is freedom against every rule, every authority, every compulsion of the wrong society. Consequently, it implies unconditional freedom of feeling from all dependence, just as the Enlightenment had preached the unconditional freedom of reason"[1].

Tension between the irrationalist conception of freedom and the science-ideal in its Leibnizian form in HERDER. The antinomy is sought in "life" itself. The Faust- and the Prometheus-motive.

The Humanistic ideal of personality discloses itself here in an irrationalist type, still oriented to the aesthetic view of nature, but exhibiting all the more strongly its polarity with the ratio-

---

[1] GELPCKE, op. cit., p. 27: "Der neu gewonnene Begriff der Freiheit wird zum Dogma. Es ist die Freiheit gegen die Regel, gegen die Autorität, gegen den Zwang der verkehrten Gesellschaft. Freiheit also des Gefühls schlechthin von aller Abhängigkeit, wie einst die Aufklärung Freiheit der Vernunft von aller Abhängigkeit gepredigt hatte."

nalistic science-ideal from which "Sturm und Drang", despite its passionate protest against deterministic rationalism, never was able to liberate itself definitively. This is especially evident in HERDER's philosophy of history, with its naturalistic concept of development derived from LEIBNIZ. Antinomy is not shunned, but rather sought for in the very reality of life.

"Faust" and "Prometheus" become the favourite problems of this period. Faust contends with nature, from which he wished to wrest her deepest secrets, in a boundless striving toward power and infinity. Prometheus is the stormer of heaven, who in Titanic pride brings fire from heaven to earth. KLOPSTOCK has given to his Prometheus-motive the following pregnant expression: "Forces of the *other* world are contained in the Idea of God, but man feels like a second Creator, able to reflect the Idea of the universe" [1].

The irrationalist Idea of humanity and the appreciation of individuality in history.

The new ideal of humanity did not spring from mathematical thought, but from the irrational depths of feeling. It displays itself in a boundless reverence for all that man is, and, as such, possesses irrational creative individuality. It further displays itself in an appreciation of historical individuality in people (Volk), nation and state, usually strange to the time of the Enlightenment.

The conception of "Sturm und Drang" about individuality has indeed no longer anything in common with the atomistic individualism of the time of the Enlightenment. It is an irrationalist view that gains ground here, and that seeks everywhere after the irrational relations by which the individual is a part of the totality of an individual community. It is this very view which is characteristic of the philosophy of history of a HERDER, who tries to understand the voice of history by way of empathy, by feeling himself into the spirit of historical individualities. HERDER unhesitatingly accepts the polarity, the inner antinomy between this irrationalist view and the determinist conception of development, which he had taken over from LEIBNIZ. Necessity of nature

---

[1] JANENSKY, *Lavater*, p. 2: "Kräfte jener Welt hat der Gedanke an Gott, aber wie ein zweiter Schöpfer fühlt sich der Mensch, der die Idee des Universums nachzudenken vermag."

and creative freedom of the irreducible individuality come together in history and render impossible KANT's attempt at a separation of the two realms. In this philosophy of history, the science-ideal of the "Aufklärung" still discloses its influence, insofar as historical development is thought of as subject to natural laws. In accordance with LEIBNIZ' lex continui, development is here conceived of in increasingly complicated and more highly ordered series, as passing in a continuous transition from inorganic matter to organic life and human history, and as disclosing a steady progress in the evolution of culture. But this naturalistic cultural optimism is entirely pervaded and refined by the new humanity-ideal of the "*Sturm und Drang*". The impulse toward a *sympathetic understanding* of every individuality in the cultural process protected this view of history from the rationalistic construction of world-history after the manner of VOLTAIRE.

> FICHTE's third period and the influence of JACOBI. Transcendental philosophy in contrast with life-experience. The primacy of life and feeling.

In what way then did the influence of the irrationalist philosophy of life, briefly sketched above, find expression in FICHTE's third period, of which his writings: "*Die Bestimmung des Menschen*", 1st ed., 1800, and his *Sonnenklarer Bericht an das grössere Publikum über das eigentliche Wesen der neuesten Philosophie*, are most strikingly charactistic?

This influence discloses itself in the sharp cleavage, which FICHTE here sets between theoretical knowledge and real life, identifying the latter with feeling, desire and action[1], and placing the full accent of value upon *life* in opposition to philosophical speculation. In his *Rückerinnrungen, Antworten, Fragen (Remembrances, Answers, Questions)*, an unpublished writing of the year 1799, FICHTE observes: "Now the goal is *life*, and in no way speculation, the latter is only a means (an instrument) to *form* life, for it resides in an entirely other world, and what is to influence life, must itself have originated from life. It is only a means to know life"[2].

---

[1] W.W. V, p. 351.

[2] *Ibid.*, p. 342: "Nun is das *Leben* Zweck, keinesweges das Speculieren; das letztere ist nur Mittel, das Leben zu bilden, denn es liegt in einer ganz anderen Welt, und was auf das Leben Einflusz haben soll, musz selbst aus

A little further on we read: "*Life* in its true essence is *not-philosophizing; philosophizing* in its true essence is *not-life*... There is here a complete antithesis, and a point of juncture is as surely impossible, as the conception of the X that rests at the foundation of the subject-object ego..."[1].

The opposition between his own philosophic standpoint and that of his opponents who accused him of atheism (EBERHARD and others), is here formulated as follows: "The true seat of the conflict between my philosophy and the opposed doctrines, which are more or less aware of this situation, concerns the relation between (mere, objectively directed) knowledge and life (feeling, appetitive power and action). The opposed systems make knowledge the principle of life: they believe that through free, arbitrary thought they can originate some knowledge and concepts and implant them in man by means of reasoning and that thereby would be produced feelings, the appetitive power would be affected and thus finally human action determined. For them knowledge is consequently the higher, life is the lower and absolutely dependent on the former... *Our philosophy, on the contrary, makes life, the system of feelings and appetitions the highest and allows to knowledge everywhere only the looking on*" (italics are mine)[2].

---

dem Leben hervorgegangen sein. Es ist nur Mittel, das Leben zu erkennen."

[1] "*Leben* ist ganz eigentlich *Nicht-Philosophieren; Philosophieren* ist ganz eigentlich *Nicht-Leben*... Es ist hier eine volkommene Antithesis und ein Vereinigungspunct ist ebenso unmöglich, als das auffassen des X, das dem Subjekt-Objekt Ich, zu Grunde liegt..."

[2] "Der wahre Sitz des Wiederstreites meiner Philosophie und der entgegengesetzten Lehren, welche letztere sich dieses Umstandes mehr oder weniger deutlich bewusst sind, ist über das Verhältniss der (blossen, auf Objecte gehenden) Erkenntniss zum wirklichen Leben (zum Gefühle, Begehrungsvermögen und Handeln). Die entgegengesetzte Systeme machen die Erkenntniss zum Prinzipe des Lebens: sie glauben, durch freies, willkürliches Denken gewisse Erkenntnisse und Begriffe erzeugen und dem Menschen durch Räsonnement einpflanzen zu können, durch welche Gefühle hervorgebracht, das Begehrungsvermögen afficirt und so endlich das Handeln des Menschen bestimmt werde. Ihnen also ist das Erkennen das Obere, das Leben das Niedere und durchaus von jenem Abhängende... *Unsere Philosophie macht umgekehrt das Leben, das System der Gefühle und des Begehrens zum Höchsten und lässt der Erkenntniss überall nur das Zusehen.*" Vol. V, pp. 351/352.

Hegel as opposed to the philosophy of life and feeling.

In order to realize the polar distance which separates Fichte's philosophic thought in this period from Hegel's identity-philosophy, it is only necessary to compare these utterances as to the relation of the dialectical concept and the reality of life (seized immediately in feeling) with Hegel's following pronouncement in his *Encyclopaedia*: "It is wrong to suppose that the things which form the contents of our representations were first, and our *subjective* activity which through the earlier mentioned operation of abstracting and synthesizing of the common characteristics of the objects, produces the concepts of the same, would come only afterwards. The concept is rather the true first"[1].

Kant's sensory matter of experience is now the "true reality" to Fichte.

Kant's irrational "sensory matter of experience", which in the "Critique of Pure Reason" played only the negative rôle of a limit for the transcendental possibility of knowledge, acquired in Fichte's third period the positive meaning of "true reality". Only the "material of experience" accessible to immediate feeling, not yet "logically synthesized" and deeply irrational, can claim to be reality.

In the impressive conclusion of the second book of the writing *Die Bestimmung des Menschen (The Vocation of Man)*, the "spirit" says to the "ego" that wished to come to knowledge of reality through the "Wissenschaftslehre": "All theoretical knowledge is only image, and there is always something required in it which corresponds to the image. This demand cannot be satisfied by any theoretical knowledge; and a system of science is necessarily a system of mere images, without any reality, significance and aim... Now you seek after all something real which resides outside the mere image... and another reality than that which was destroyed just now, as I know likewise. However, it would be in vain, if you would try to create it through and from your knowledge and to

---

[1] Hegel's *Werke* VI, p. 323: "Es ist verkehrt, anzunehmen, erst seien die Gegenstände, welche den Inhalt unserer Vorstellungen bilden, und *dann hinterdrein* komme unsere *subjective* Tätigkeit, welche durch die vorher erwähnte Operation des Abstrahierens und des Zusammenfassens des den Gegenständen Gemeinschaftlichen die Begriffe derselben sind. *Der Begriff ist vielmehr das wahrhaft Erste*..."

embrace it with your science. If you have no other organ to grasp it, you shall never find it. However, you do possess such an organ. Vivify it only and warm it: and you shall come to complete rest. I leave you alone with yourself" [1].

In agreement with JACOBI, FICHTE now seeks this other organ in *belief,* which he, together with this philosopher of feeling, views as the diametrical opposite of cognitive thought. JACOBI had taught that the "unconditional Being" could not be demonstrated theoretically, but could only be felt immediately. And he had not restricted the truth-value of immediate feeling to the bounds of sense perception, but had proclaimed as its second basic form the certainty of supra-sensory belief. In like manner, FICHTE, too, now teaches that the true reality is discovered only by *belief,* rooted in the immediate feeling of the drive to absolute, independent activity [2].

JACOBI supposed his view to be based upon naïve experience when he identified the latter with the function of feeling. FICHTE follows suit in teaching that naïve man, even without being aware of it, grasps all reality existing for him, only by faithful feeling: "We all are born in belief; who is blind, follows blindly the secret and irresistible drive; he who sees, follows seeing; and believes because he wants to believe" [3].

This faith is no longer the a-priori practical *reasonable faith* of KANT, that elevates abstract noumenal Ideas to a practical reality "in itself". It is rather JACOBI's *emotional faith,* that this thinker set again, in the old nominalist manner, *in opposition*

---

[1] V, 246 f: "Alles Wissen (aber), ist nur Abbildung, und es wird in ihm immer etwas gefordert, das dem Bilde entspreche. Diese Förderung kann durch kein Wissen befriedigt werden; und ein System des Wissens ist nothwendig ein System bloszer Bilder, ohne alle Realität, Bedeutung und Zweck... Nun suchst du denn doch etwas, ausser dem blossen Bilde liegendes Reales... und eine andere Realität, als die soeben vernichtete, wie ich gleichfalls weiss. Aber du würdest dich vergebens bemühen, sie durch dein Wissen, und aus deinem Wissen zu erschaffen, und mit deiner Erkenntniss zu umfassen. Hast du kein anderes Organ, sie zu ergreifen, so wirst du sie nimmer finden. Aber du hast ein solches Organ. Belebe es nur, und erwärme es: und du wirst zur vollkommensten Ruhe gelangen. Ich lasse dich mit dir selbst allein."

[2] W.W. II, p. 249 fl.

[3] "Wir werden allen in Glauben geboren, wer da blind ist, folgt blind dem geheimen und unwiderstehlichen Zuge; wer da sieht, folgt sehend; und glaubt, weil er glauben will." Cf. the entire sensualistic conception of naïve experience explained in the context of the cited passage (p. 255).

to the understanding in his famous expressilon: "Heathen with the head, Christian with the heart" [1]. It must, however, be borne in mind that JACOBI supposed he found true Christianity in the well-known postulates of the Humanistic ideal of personality: belief in the personality of God, in moral freedom and autonomy, and in the immortality of human personality, whereas FICHTE, who identified the Deity with the "moral order of the universe", abandoned the belief in a personal God. It was this that brought upon him the charge of atheïsm.

The relationship which FICHTE here accepts between "faith" and reflective thinking also diverges diametrically from that which he accepts between the two in his *Staatslehre* of 1813.

In the last mentioned work all progress in history is seen as a methodical victory of the understanding over faith "until the former has entirely destroyed the latter and has brought its content into the more noble form of clear insight" [2].

Yet a great mistake would be made, if the agreement between the philosophy of feeling and FICHTE's standpoint in his third period were interpreted as a complete surrender to the former.

Even LASK, who for the most part clearly indicates the points of difference, goes too far in imputing to FICHTE a radical depreciation of the "Wissenschaftslehre" in his third period [3]. He has overlooked that the same writing in which FICHTE ascribes the discovery of true reality to *vital* feeling alone — allowing to philosophy only the "Zusehen" (looking on) — concludes with a veritable eulogy of the "Wissenschaftslehre": "In short: by the acceptance and universal propagation of the doctrine of science among those to whom it is appropriate, the whole of mankind shall be freed from blind chance and fate shall be destroyed for the same. All mankind becomes its own master under the control of its own concept; it makes henceforth itself with absolute

---

[1] "Heiden mit dem Verstande, Christen mit dem Gemüt."

[2] IV, p. 493: "so lange bis der erste den letzten ganz vernichtet und seinen Inhalt aufgenommen hat in die edlere Form der klaren Einsicht." Essentially the same motive of thought is to be found in the *Grundzüge des gegenwärtigen Zeitalters*, (1804—5) VII, pp. 1—15 and passim.

[3] LASK, op. cit., pp. 105/6: "Genauer konnte des Glaubensphilosophen JACOBI Beurteilung der Wissenschaftslehre nicht bestätigt werden." ["The judgment of the doctrine of science by the philosopher of faith JACOBI could not be affirmed in a more precise manner."]

liberty into everything, into which it can only want to make itself"[1].

JACOBI was never able to recognize the value of the "doctrine of science". To FICHTE, on the contrary, even in his closest approach to the philosophy of feeling, it remained the only way to conceive the full consequences of the freedom-motive, just as, even at this time, he never abandoned the transcendental moralistic standpoint and never fell into the aestheticism of the philosophy of life and feeling[2].

> Recognition of the individual value of the empirical as such. FICHTE's estimation of individuality contrasted with that of KANT. Individualizing of the categorical imperative.

In this period the recognition of the *value* of "empirical" individuality goes hand in hand with the recognition of "feeling" as an immediate source of knowledge of reality. In his frequently cited writing LASK has given a keen analysis of the fundamental difference between KANT's transcendental-logical concept of "empirical" individuality and the conception developed by FICHTE in his third period concerning the epistemological individual value of the "empirical" as such.

KANT was not able to ascribe any value to empirical individuality as such, and could qualify it only as contingent in contrast with the norms of reason which alone have value. For FICHTE, on the contrary, empirical individuality has now acquired an inner value as being rooted in the individuality of the moral ego itself. Even in FICHTE's *System der Sittenlehre (System of Ethics)* of 1798 this recognition of the value of individuality discloses itself in his supplement to the formal principle of Ethics. KANT's "universally valid" categorical imperative is in-

---

[1] *Sonnenklarer Bericht*, p. 409: "Mit einem Worte: durch die Annahme und allgemeine Verbreitung der Wissenschaftslehre unter denen, für welche sie gehört, wird das ganze Menschengeschlecht von dem blinden Zufall erlöst, und das Schicksal wird für dasselbe vernichtet. Die gesammte Menschheit bekommt sich selbst in ihre eigene Hand, unter die Botmässigkeit ihres eigenen Begriffes; sie macht von nun an mit absoluter Freiheit Alles aus sich selbst, was sie aus sich machen nur wollen kann." LASK has apparently paid no attention to this whole dithyramb on the *"Doctrine of Science"*.

[2] In all writings of this period "feeling" and "drive" remain *oriented* to the activistic and moralistic consciousness of duty.

dividualized. It comes now to read as follows: "Act in conformity with your individual destination, and your individual situation" [1].

The individuality of the empirical world, incomprehensible in a theoretical way, acquires practical significance for the personality, insofar as the material of our individual duty discloses itself in it [2]. In each individual act of perceiving and knowing is concealed a "practical" *kernel of feeling*, in spite of its theoretical function [3].

In this connection, too, the estimation of individuality is fastened to the immediate evidence of feeling: "whether I doubt or am sure, it does not originate from argumentation... but from immediate feeling... this feeling never deceives" [4].

In the *Wissenschaftslehre* of 1801 the principle of individuation *(principium individuationis)* is explicitly sought in feeling as the concentration-point of knowledge *(Konzentrationspunkt des Wissens)* [5].

No radical irrationalism in FICHTE's *third period.*

Thanks to the influence of the transcendental critical line of thought, which never completely disappeared from the "Wissenschaftslehre", there never was, in the case of FICHTE himself, a complete victory of an irrationalist philosophy of feeling. The moralistic law of reason is not abrogated, even where, in his third period, the recognition of the value of what is individually experienced in feeling makes itself increasingly operative in his moralistic and activistic ideal of personality. FICHTE seeks only to individualize its *content* within the cadre of its universally valid *form*.

---

[1] IV, p. 166: "Es ist daher für jeden bestimmten Menschen in einer jeden Lage nur etwas bestimmtes pflichtmässig..." ["Therefore for every individual man in every (individual) situation there is only some individual conduct in conformity with duty"].

[2] This motive continues to be maintained even in FICHTE's fourth metaphysical-pantheistic period. Cf. *Die Thatsachen des Bewusstseyns* (1810—1811) II, 641: "Nur in der individuellen Form ist das Leben praktisches Prinzip" (Life is a practical principle in the individual form only).

[3] IV, 166/7.

[4] IV, 169.

[5] II, 112.

§ 2 - AESTHETIC IRRATIONALISM IN THE HUMANISTIC IDEAL OF PERSONALITY. THE IDEAL OF THE "BEAUTIFUL SOUL". ELABORATION OF THE IRRATIONALIST FREEDOM-MOTIVE IN THE MODERN PHILOSOPHY OF LIFE AND ITS POLAR TENSION WITH THE SCIENCE-IDEAL

So much the stronger does the irrationalist turn in the Humanistic ideal of personality assert itself in the feeling-philosophy of "Sturm und Drang" and in early Romanticism. From the outset, this tendency proceeds in an aesthetic direction. Here, KANT's *"Critique of Aesthetic Judgment"*, with its orientation of the aesthetic judgment to free feeling and with its recognition of the absolute individual value of the genius, offered an immediate point of contact.

SCHILLER and KANT's *"Critique of Aesthetic Judgment"*. Aesthetic idealism. The influence of SHAFTESBURY.

SCHILLER transformed this theory into an *aesthetic idealism*, in which the aesthetic aspect of meaning is elevated to the rank of the deepest root of reality. Behind KANT's influence on this point, there was here at work SHAFTESBURY's *aesthetic ethics of virtuosity*. As CASSIRER[1] has shown, SHAFTESBURY's aesthetics had a decisive significance for KANT's own aesthetic views. Even in SHAFTESBURY (1671—1713), the Humanistic ideal of personality, in an irrationalist transformation of the Greek ideal of καλοκάγαθον, was converted into the principle of aesthetic morality of the genius, turning against every supra-individual norm and law. True morality does not consist in the rule of general maxims, nor in the subjection of subjectivity to a universal norm, but in a harmonious, aesthetic self-realization of the total individuality.

The highest disclosure of the sovereign personality in the moral realm is *virtuosity*, which allows no single power and instinctive tendency in the individual talent to languish, but brings them all into aesthetic harmony by means of a perfect practice of life, and thereby realizes the happiness of the individual as well as the welfare of the entire society. In the nature of the case, this ethics of virtuosity cannot find the source of moral knowledge in the rational functions directed to general laws, but only in the subjective depths of *individual feeling*.

---

[1] CASSIRER, *Die Philosophie der Aufklärung* (1932), p. 426 ff.

Accordingly, morality was brought under a subjective and aesthetic basic denominator. The morally good was regarded as the beautiful in the world of practical volition and action: according to SHAFTESBURY, the good, like the beautiful, consists in a harmonious unity of the manifold, in a complete unfolding of that which slumbers in the individual nature as subjective talent. It is, just like the beautiful, the object of an original *approbation*, rooted in the deepest being of man: thus *"taste"* becomes the *basic faculty* for ethics as well as for aesthetics.

This aesthetic philosophy of feeling has acquired a profound influence, even though HUTCHESON and the *Scottish school* replaced the absolutism of individuality in SHAFTESBURY by the absolutism of law, characteristic of the rationalistic types of the Humanistic cosmonomic Idea. As we saw before, the turn that ROUSSEAU gave to the Humanistic freedom-motive, in the emancipation of personality from the grip of the science-ideal, rests essentially on a mobilizing of the undepraved natural feeling against the sober analysing understanding of the Enlightenment-period.

With the Dutch philosopher, FRANZ HEMSTERHUYS, and the philosophers of life of the "Sturm und Drang" this philosophy of feeling recaptures its original, irrationalist character, disclosing itself in an absolutizing of the aesthetic individuality.

The ideal of "the beautiful soul".

In SCHILLER's aesthetic Humanism, the irrationalist and aesthetic conception of the ideal of personality embodies itself, though within the formal limits of transcendental idealism, in the Idea of the "beautiful soul". *The philosophical basic-denominator of reality is shifted to the aesthetic aspect of meaning viewed exclusively from its individual subjective side.*

Beauty is, according to SCHILLER's definition, "freedom in appearance (phenomenon)"[1]. In the aesthetic play-drive ("Spieltrieb"), the fulness of human personality, and therein of the cosmos, becomes evident. Man is really *man* only where he is playing, where the conflict between sensuous nature and rational moral freedom in him is silent. KANT's rigorist morality holds only for the man who has not yet matured to full harmony, in whose innermost being the moral impulse must still wage war with sensuous nature. In the "beautiful soul", however,

---

[1] See the so-called Kallias-letters to KÖRNER of February 1793.

there is realized the harmony that no longer knows this combat, for its nature is so ennobled, that it does good out of natural impulse. Only by aesthetic education does a man acquire this refinement. In this way alone is the discord between sensuous and super-sensuous functions in human nature reconciled.

WINDELBAND has keenly fathomed the attempt at a solution of all antinomies between the ideals of science and personality undertaken by this aesthetic Humanism, in which the second German Renaissance attains its point of culmination. As to this point he remarks: "This second Renaissance of the Germans is not only the completion of the former, which had been broken off in the midst, but it contains also the first consciousness of the basic drive which inspired the whole European Renaissance. Not before this aesthetic Humanism had there been the awareness of the deepest meaning of all contrasts in whose reconcilation modern culture finds its task. The two sides of the human being, whose harmonical reconciliation is the very content of culture, have assumed manifold proportions in the historical movement. In antique culture the sensuous prevails, in Christian culture the supra-sensuous man. From the very outset it was the tendency of modern culture to find the full reconciliation of these two developments. The sensuous nature of man rules his scientific knowledge, the supra-sensuous determines his ethical consciousness and the faith fastened to the latter. It is the continuous striving of modern thought to find the synthesis of this "twofold truth". However, the sensuous supra-sensuous nature of man discloses itself as complete totality only in its aesthetical function. Therefore, the whole Renaissance was in the first place artistically moved...! This was the very greatness of the epoch, that at the same time this synthesis of the sensuous and the supra-sensuous man was living in the modern *Greek*, in GOETHE. And it is the immortal merit of SCHILLER that he has understood this moment in its deepest signification and that he has formulated it according to all its directions. He is truly the prophet of the self-consciousness of modern culture" [1].

WINDELBAND supposes, that he can identify the antinomy between sensuous nature and the supra-sensuous moral consciousness in the Humanistic freedom-idealism with the tension between Greek and Christian culture. This testifies to a fun-

---

[1] *History of modern Philosophy (Geschichte der neueren Philosophie)* II, 267/8.

damental lack of insight into the fact that the Humanistic ideal of personality in its moralistic conception is not essentially Christian, but rather a secularization of the Christian Idea of freedom implying an apostasy from the latter.

The "morality of genius" in early Romanticism.

In SCHILLER's more mature period, aesthetic irrationalism was still held within the limits of transcendental idealism. In the "morality of genius" of early Romanticism, however, where the morality of the "beautiful soul" becomes religion, this irrationalism discloses itself in its *radical* sense [1]. By way of SCHELLING, it would dig itself a wide channel in the most recent philosophy of life, with its fundamental depreciation of the science-ideal and its absolutizing of "creative evolution".

The tension of the ideals of science and personality in NIETZSCHE's *development. Biologizing of the science-ideal (*DARWIN*).*

The Humanistic ideal of personality in its irrationalist turn was confronted with a new development of the natural science-ideal which, since the second half of the nineteenth century under the mighty influence of DARWIN's evolution-theory, pervaded the new "historical mode of thought". As we shall presently show, this new "historical mode of thinking" originated in the irrationalistic turn of the Humanistic freedom-idealism. This dialectical struggle between the two basic factors of the Humanistic transcendental ground-Idea in their new conception discloses itself in a truly impressive manner in the dialectical development of NIETZSCHE, whose final phase, as we observed in an earlier context, is the announcement of the beginning of the religious uprooting of modern thought as a result of a dialectical self-destruction of the Humanistic ground-motive in a radical Historicism.

We have only to compare NIETZSCHE's first romantic-aesthetic period, influenced strongly by SCHOPENHAUER and RICHARD WAGNER, with the second positivistic phase beginning in 1878,

---

[1] Cf. the statement of NOVALIS: "Gesetze sind der Moral durchaus entgegen" (laws are absolutely opposite to morality) and: "Gesetze sind das Komplement mangelhafter Naturen und Wesen" (laws are the complement of defective natures and entities), cited in W. METZGER, *Gesellschaft, Recht und Staat in der Ethik des Deutschen Idealismus* (1917, p. 207 note 3).

in which the biological ideal of science gains the upper-hand, and the last period of the culture-philosophy of the "Superman", beginning in 1883. In this last period, the science-ideal has been entirely *depreciated*. Henceforth, science is viewed as a merely biological means in the struggle for existence, without any proper truth-value. BERGSON and other modern philosophers of life took over this pragmatist and biological conception of the theoretical picture of the world, created by scientific thought.

It would be false to suppose that the irrationalist philosophy of life preached chaos. On the contrary, it does not *intend* to abandon *order. But, as the rationalist types of Humanist philosophy make the concept of the subject a function of the concept of the law in a special modal sense, and thus dissolve the former into the latter, so, in a reverse manner, the irrationalist types reduce the "true" order to a function of individual subjectivity.*

> The relationship of αὐτός and νόμος in the irrationalist ideal of personality. Dialectical character of the philosophy of life. Modern dialectical phenomenology.

In KANT's formulation of the Humanistic ideal of personality, the true αὐτός discovers itself only in the νόμος; in the irrationalist conception of autonomy the νόμος (nomos) is rather a reflex of the absolutely individual αὐτός.

Rationalism and irrationalism in their modern sense are merely polar contrasts in the basic structure of the Humanistic cosmonomic Idea.

The tension, the inner antinomy that originates for the irrationalist types between absolutized subjective individuality and law, led HAMANN and early romanticism to a dialectical conception of reality which ascribed the character of absolute reality to logical contradiction.

In the modern dialectical phenomenology, issuing from DILTHEY's irrationalist historical philosophy of life, "dialectical thinking" has this same irrationalist character; it is sharply to be distinguished from HUSSERL's *rationalist* phenomenology [1].

In this dialectical trait of irrationalism, we can once again

---

[1] See the detailed analysis of this irrationalist phenomenology in my work, *De Crisis der Humanistische Staatsleer (The Crisis of the Humanistic Theory of the State)*, publ. Ten Have, Amsterdam, 1931, pp. 47 ff.

cosmonomic Idea of Humanistic immanence-philosophy

find the proof of the thesis that in the last analysis, even the irrationalist types of Humanist philosophy are rooted in an absolutizing of the theoretical attitude of thought.

An antinomy is always the product of the failure of theoretical thought to recognize its boundaries. In pre-theoretical naïve experience theoretical antinomies are out of the question. The sanctioning of a theoretical antinomy bears the stamp of a subjective attitude of thought directed against the cosmic order and the basic logical laws functioning in the latter. This attitude of thought is indubitably a component part of sinful reality, but only insofar as its anti-normative meaning is determined by the cosmic order and by the logical norms within this order, against which it turns itself in revolt. Sanctioning antinomy in the identification of dialectical thought with irrational reality, signifies a meaningless negation of the law-side of reality founded in the cosmic order. This negation is meaningless, because subjectivity without an order that defines it *can have no existence and meaning.*

The types of the irrationalist cosmonomic Idea of Humanistic thought.

As rationalism in the Humanist philosophy is shaded into various mutually antagonistic types of cosmonomic Ideas, so is irrationalism. In principle we can think of as many types of irrationalism as there are non-logical aspects of temporal reality.

§ 3 - THE GENESIS OF A NEW CONCEPT OF SCIENCE FROM THE HUMANISTIC IDEAL OF PERSONALITY IN ITS IRRATIONALIST TYPES. FICHTE'S FOURTH PERIOD

The Humanistic ideal of personality, having become aware of its own deepest tendencies, must in the long run transfer its tension with the mechanistic science-ideal to the realm of special scientific thought. The continuity-postulate of the Humanistic freedom-motive could not finally accept the Kantian identification of scientific thought with that of mathematical natural-science. It could not finally abandon in this way its claims to the knowledge of temporal reality.

Humanistic philosophy had in its pre-Kantian rationalist types proclaimed the supremacy of the mathematical science-ideal over the normative aspects of temporal reality.

KANT brought, as we saw, the antinomy between the ideals of science and personality to a pregnant formulation, and established between the two the ACTIO FINIUM REGUNDORUM. FICHTE had begun to deprive the mechanical science-ideal of its independence with respect to the ideal of personality and to deduce the former from the latter. The moment must come in which this carrying through of the primacy of the personality-ideal would make itself felt in special scientific thought and contend the exclusive dominion of the mathematical-physical conception of science.

The stimulus to this development could only issue from the irrationalist currents which had absolutized the subjective side of the normative aspects of human existence in its complete individuality under this or that basic denominator, and had resolved the rationalist Idea of the lex into an irrationalist Idea of the subject.

Where else but in the individual subjectivity could the freedom-motive of the irrationalist Humanistic ideal of personality have made its dominion over "empirical" reality felt? If subjective individuality is no longer proclaimed with KANT as a merely negative logical limit of mathematical causal knowledge, but rather as empirical reality κατ' ἐξοχήν, the whole view of human experience must be altered in principle. Natural-scientific thought, suited only for the discovery of universally valid laws, could then no longer raise the pretension of providing us with genuine knowledge of the whole field of empirical reality.

Orientation of a new science-ideal to the science of history.

From the outset we see the irrationalist types in Humanistic philosophy concentrating their attention upon the *science of history*, which by the coryphaei of the Enlightenment period was denatured to a crypto-natural science with strong ethicizing tendencies (the ideal of the necessary progress of mankind through the illumination of thought!).

It must immediately become evident that the method of natural science cannot grasp the proper "Gegenstand" of historical research, as soon as the ban of the mathematical science-ideal was broken by the antagonistic pretensions of an irrationalistically conceived ideal of personality. KANT's transcendental critique of teleological judgment had still only cleared the way for a *philosophy* of history, oriented, to a certain extent at least, to the personality-ideal, still conceived of in essentially rationalist terms. His teleological view of historical development, as explained in his treatise *On Eternal Peace (Vom ewigen Frieden)* did not lay claim to a scientific character. In order to wrest *special scientific historical* thought from the supremacy of the rationalistic science-ideal, there was needed first and foremost a fundamentally different *evaluation* of subjective individuality.

It was originally an aesthetic irrationalism that even in HERDER's *Ideen zur Philosophie der Geschichte der Menschheit* (1784—1791) — although here still checked by LEIBNIZ' rationalist Idea of development — cleared the way for an irrationalist method of cultivating the science of history: an empathetic and sympathetic treatment of the historical contexts in their incomparable individuality. Presently, SCHELLING's organological idealism was to provide the philosophical equipment for the view of history held by the *Historical school,* with its doctrine of the originally unconscious growth of culture from the historical "Volksgeist" in the individual nationalities.

The spirit of restoration which acquired the upper hand after the liquidation of the French revolution and the fall of Napoleon, naturally favoured the rise of the historical mode of thought. The apriori constructions of state and, society by the Humanistic school of natural law were replaced by the historical insight that state, society, law and culture in general cannot be "created" from mathematical thought after a pattern valid for all times and for every people, but are rather a result of a long historical evolution of a people whose "spirit" has an irreducible individuality.

The rise of the science of sociology in the early part of the nineteenth century was also an important factor in the development of a new historical mode of thought; this sociology, however, intended to perform a synthesis between the latter and the natural scientific pattern of thought, which synthesis presently was to lead to an invasion of Darwinist evolutionism in historical science.

FICHTE in his fourth period and the South-West-German school of Neo-Kantianism.

In the present connection, however, we will restrict ourselves to an inquiry after the contribution given by FICHTE, in his fourth metaphysical period, to the methodology of historical thought. From this context, a clear light falls over the epistemology of historical thought, propagated in recent times by the South-West-German school of the Neo-Kantians, especially by its two leading figures, RICKERT and MAX WEBER.

LASK's researches in particular have shown that it was essentially the fundamental change in the valuation of individuality which brought FICHTE in his fourth period to a speculative metaphysics completely different from the identity-philosophy which we find in the "*Wissenschaftslehre*" of 1794.

FICHTE's later development is indeed to be seen in full connection with the rather general opposition arising at this time against the abstract Kantian criticism, brought to a head in the opposition between form and matter, and hostile to the true valuation of individuality.

The so-called "critical" method had concentrated all value in the universally valid forms of reason and had depreciated the individual, as the transcendental *irrational*, as "only empirical", as the merely contingent instance of formal conformity to the law of reason. The irrationalistically orientated metaphysical idealists of this period, who had all passed under KANT's influence, now supposed they had to reject the entire critical method. To be sure, KANT, in his *Critique of Judgment*, had *raised* the problem of *specification*, but here too, only *within the framework of the form-matter schema*. Only in Aesthetics was he in a position to appreciate subjective individuality as such.

The irrationalistically conceived freedom-motive demanded a new speculative method for the knowledge of individuality, and eventually it was under the inspiration of *problems of the philosophy of culture* that this motive began its contest against the old rationalist science-ideal.

HEGEL's supposed "rationalism".

The new metaphysics of the *absolute Being, as totality of individuality,* is nothing but a metaphysics of the irrationalist ideal of personality. The later formal rationalizing of this irrationalism in HEGEL's so-called "pan-logism" is only a typical specimen of the inner polarity of the transcendental Humanistic ground-Idea; but it never warrants the neglect of the fact that this apparent rationalism is the very antipode of the rationalism after the pattern of the classical Humanistic science-ideal, oriented to mathematics and natural science.

SCHELLING became the recognized leader in the controversy against formalistic transcendental idealism. The conception of knowledge in terms of the abstract Kantian form-matter schema — in which, as we saw previously, all antinomies between the ideals of science and personality were crowded together — was to be abrogated. Philosophy was to be understood as "the absolute knowledge of the absolute". Here an association was made with the old speculative motive of an intuitive divine understanding, to which there were also allusions in KANT's *Kritik der Urteilskraft*. But it was now liberated from the mathematical ideal of science. It was not the Idea of the *uno intuito* perfected mathematical analysis (LEIBNIZ) that inspired the new "idealism of the spirit".

"Intellectual intuition" in SCHELLING.

In contrast to the dualistically separated sources of knowledge in the Kantian critique of knowledge, SCHELLING posits the "intellectual intuition" in which the absolute totality of meaning is comprehended by a single all-embracing glance. KRAUSE elevates the knowledge of the arch-essential *(das ur-wesentliche)*, the intuition of essence, above the relative knowledge from concepts. TROXLER, with explicit appeal to JACOBI, sets the arch-consciousness or immediate knowledge in opposition to reflecting and discursive thought, and SOLGER contests the dualism of the universal and particular.

In his *Lectures on the Method of Academic Study*, delivered in 1802 at the university of Jena, SCHELLING appealed to a method of genius for scientific insight [1] and in so doing he simply gave expression to the whole spirit of this time, which was deeply inspired by the irrationalist ideal of personality. Everywhere it is the value of absolute individuality that one hoped to grasp

---

[1] SCHELLING, *Vorlesungen über die Methode des academischen Stadiums* (Stuttgart und Thübingen, 3e Ausg. 1830), p. 15: "Von der Fähigkeit, alles auch das einzelne Wissen, in den Zusammenhang mit dem ursprünglichen und Einen zu erblicken, hängt es ab, ob man in der einzelnen Wissenschaft mit Geist und mit derjenigen höhern Eingebung arbeite, die man wissenschaftliches Genie nennt!" ["It depends on the ability, to view everything, also special knowledge, in the context with the original and the Unity, whether one is able to work in the special science with spirit and with that higher inspiration which is called scientific genius!"]

by a speculative metaphysical method of intellectual intuition immediately grasping the absolute.

In opposition to the irrationalism of feeling on the part of "*Sturm und Drang*", all attention is now directed to the individual disclosure of the "*Spirit*", of the "*Idea*".

> Hegel's new dialectical logic and its historical orientation.

In his younger days, Hegel himself had lived in the sphere of the irrationalist philosophy of feeling. In his mature period, he rationalized the irrationalist thought of Romanticism by his new dialectical logic, which in its kernel is nothing but an antirationalist, universalistic logic of historical development. Lask correctly observes that the very structure of the individual totality, as exhibited for example in the transpersonalistic-universalistic conception of the state as a "moral organism", becomes the pattern for Hegel's conception of the structure of the logical concept. The break with the logic of the naturalistic ideal of science — a logic which had led to an atomistic individualism in the field of philosophy of culture — was indeed inescapable after the victory of the irrationalist ideal of personality. Hegel's positive work was the creation of a new speculative metaphysical logic of individuality, by which he sought simply to replace the natural scientific logic of the Humanistic ideal of science, along the entire line of human knowledge. With Hegel the irrationalist and idealist conception of the ideal of personality creates its own metaphysical logic. Thereby it sets itself sharply in opposition to critical idealism, which in spite of its ascription of the primacy to the ideal of personality, nevertheless, in its method of forming concepts had remained entirely oriented to the logic of the naturalistic science-ideal.

Fichte's "metaphysics of spirit", which speedily gained the upper-hand in his thought after the brief period of his approach toward the philosophy of life, also originated essentially from the irrationalistic and universalistic conception of the freedom-motive with its orientation to problems of the philosophy of culture.

In contrast with the problem of the universally-valid transcendental ego of the first sketches of the "doctrine of science", there emerged even in his *System der Sittenlehre* (1798) the question of the *individual ego*. This compelled him to proceed beyond the immanent transcendental analysis of consciousness and to raise the question as to the metaphysical foundations *in being* for the spiritual life [1].

To the essence of self-consciousness of one's own ego belongs, as FICHTE clearly realizes, the consciousness of the other ego, the Thou. Concrete freedom and autonomous determination of the will arise only in the immediate connection of the individual ego with other "spiritual beings". It is no longer satisfactory to deduce my knowledge of *other* egos, as a necessary activity of consciousness, from the transcendental self-consciousness. The other egos, the plurality of spiritual beings outside myself, have an altogether other mode of being with respect to myself than the material external world ("nature").

The problem of the "Realität der Geisterwelt" (reality of the world of spirits).

The problem of the reality of the "Geisterwelt" (world of spirits) emerges and it arises from the moral foundation of the ego itself, from the duty to recognize every free individual as an independent moral "end in himself". The ego must not only *think or intuit* the other egos in itself (as if they were natural things), but it stands also in a real spiritual contact, in a living spiritual exchange with them. Consequently, the syntheses performed by the transcendental ego of the critical doctrine of science did not exhaust the development of the syntheses of the system of reason. The latter urgently demand a conclusion in a metaphysical "synthesis of the real world of spirits" (HEIMSOETH).

In the "*Wissenschaftslehre*" of 1801 this highest metaphysical synthesis is viewed as a synthesis of the absolute Being with infinite freedom. The individual ego is one of the many concentration-points of the "Absolute Spirit", of the Origin of the cosmos. It has the *form* of existence ("Dasein") from the *absolute Being*, but *definite, concrete, individual being* from the interaction of its freedom with the totality of the spiritual world [2].

Consequently, FICHTE seeks the original, essential reality of all finite individual selves in a transpersonally conceived life of reason. The individual egos are not substances, but individual differentiations and "forms of manifestation" of the one infinite

---

[1] On this see further H. HEIMSOETH: *Metaphysik der Neuzeit* (1929), p. 120 ff.
[2] W.W. II, 112, 113.

life of reason; the "bond of union" in the world of spirits is not a joining afterwards of isolated ego-monads; it is much rather the fundamental communion of all individual egos as appearance of the infinite Origin, from which the free spiritual beings, with all their spiritual interactions, originate by a metaphysical ACTUS INDIVIDUATIONIS in which time itself acquires individual points of concentration [1]. Thus, even in FICHTE's fourth period, the ideal of personality acquires that *trans-personalist* turn which was to find its consummation in HEGEL's identity-philosophy of the absolute self-developing Idea.

Trans-personalist turn in the ideal of personality. The new conception of the "ORDO ORDINANS" in FICHTE's pantheistic metaphysics.

The *being* of the "Spirit" is a *transpersonal being of freedom*, which, in the totality of individual spiritual life, realizes its infinite actual freedom, still preceding all thought. The "moral order of the world", as the infinite active ORDO ORDINANS, or the "infinite will", now becomes the trans-personal bond of union for all finite spirits in their individual moral destination. It has become the true antipode, irrationalist in its deepest root, of KANT's abstract "universally valid categorical imperative." The ethical individuality of the ego, in FICHTE's irrationalist conception of it, leads through itself to a *trans-personal community of free spirits*. Only from this totality of the community may

---

[1] W.W. II, 113: "Was ist nun also — dies ist eine *neue* Frage — der Charakter des wirklichen Seyns? Durchaus nur ein Verhältniss von Freiheit zu Freiheit zufolge eines Gesetzes. Das *Reale*, das nun daliegt und vor allem wirklichen Wissen vorher das Wissen trägt, ist ein Concentrationspunct zuvörderst aller Zeit des Individuums, und es ist begriffen als das was es ist, nur inwiefern diese begriffen ist; — aber sie wird immer begriffen und nie. Es ist ein Concentrationspunct aller wirklichen Individuen in diesem Zeitmomente, ferner, vermittelst dessen, aller Zeit dieser und aller noch möglichen Individuen; — das Universum der Freiheit in *einem* Puncte und in *allen* Puncten." ["What is therefore — this is a *new* question — the character of the real being? Absolutely only a relation of freedom to freedom in consequence of a law. The *real*, which now presents itself and which bears knowing prior to all real knowing, is a concentration-point first of all of the whole time of the individual and it is understood as such only insofar as this whole of time is understood; — but the latter is always and never understood. It is a point of concentration of all real individuals in this moment of time, furthermore, by mediation of this moment, of all time of this and all still possible individuals; — the universe of freedom in *one* point and in *all* points."]

spiritual individuality be understood. The concept of "material freedom" consequently gains in FICHTE a trans-personal character which, from the start, was tuned to the grasping of the objective cultural coherences, in which the individuals are interwoven [1]. FICHTE's philosophy of history is only to be understood in the framework of this transpersonalist and, at least in its root, irrationalist metaphysics of the spirit.

Meanwhile, this metaphysics finds its conclusion only in a final hypostasis; the *absolute Being,* raised above all becoming and change, of the impersonal, because actually infinite Divinity. This absolute Being is eternally *transcendent* to all reflection, to all *knowledge,* and it is not an external "Ding an sich", but the *inner real ground of the possibility of rational freedom* with all its finite manifestations. As such, however, it is at the same time the *absolutely irrational,* the completely incomprehensible. All life is only manifestation, image or *schema* of God, the finite "existence" (Dasein), the finite form of manifestation of the absolute Being. But only in the moral freedom of human personality does the appearance of this absolute Being have immediate "Dasein" (existence).

"Nature" in the sense of the naturalistic science-ideal is only the appearance of the reasonable *ethical appearance of God.* This latter discloses itself in the trans-personal individual life of the free ethical world of spirits. Nature continues to lack independent meaning with reference to the ethical aspects of the cosmos. Not in "nature", but in ethical activity only does God reveal himself in the "appearance".

The earlier rationalist deification of the moral law is now replaced by an entirely irrationalist idea of God. God has become the absolute hypostasis of the creative, subjective ethical stream of life, which is the trans-personal bond and totality of the individual free subjects.

---

[1] See e.g. W.W. IV, 584: "Die durch Vernunft *a priori* eingesehene Voraussetzung ist nemlich die, dass jedem unter den freien Individuen im göttlichen Weltplane angewiesen sey seine bestimmte Stelle, die nicht sey die Stelle irgend eines anderen zu derselben Zeit in demselben Ganzen Lebende..." ["The pre-supposition, perceived apriori by reason, is namely this, that in the divine worldplan to each of the free individuals must be indicated its individual place which may not be the place of any other individual living at the same time in the same totality..."]

FICHTE's basic denominator for the aspects of meaning becomes historical in character. FICHTE's philosophy of history.

Yet — and this is of the highest importance in this new metaphysics of spirit — the moral basic denominator, to which FICHTE apparently still reduces all aspects of temporal reality and which finds its final hypostasis in the irrationalist Idea of God, is, nevertheless, under the influence of the irrationalist ideal of personality, itself transformed into an *historical* basic denominator.

HEIMSOETH correctly observes: "For the first time in the history of philosophy, the specific reality of historical existence is not only conceived of as an original reality of metaphysical rank, but it is even interpreted as the final mode of being of finite existence as such... The modern pathos of the "book of nature" is replaced by the metaphysical-religious conception of history as the proper mode of appearance of the Absolute or the divine Spirit. The world presents itself to FICHTE as an infinite active chain of "challenges", of freedom-evoking and spirit-cultivating interaction of self-acting life-centres, in creative freedom producing new and new faces as it were from nothing" [1].

The absolute ethical Idea, the absolute Being, assumes a purely historical mode of appearance in its manifestation in the "spiritual life" of the temporal human community. It schematizes itself in the infinite movement of the development of history, in which the Deity, in creative irrational fashion, continually assumes new spiritual forms of manifestation. The theme of history for FICHTE, just as for KANT, is that of striving upwards to *freedom*. But in FICHTE's fourth period, the higher ethos of the spiritual life is no longer, as in KANT, conceived rationalistically in the formalistic Idea of autonomy, in which the *autos* only comes to itself in the *nomos*, i.e. the formal categorical impera-

---

[1] "Zum ersten Male in der Geschichte der Philosophie wird die spezifische Realität des geschichtlichen Daseins nicht nur als eigenwüchsige Realität von metaphysischem Rang erfaszt, sondern sogar als die entscheidende Seinsweise endlichen Daseins überhaupt gedeutet... Das neuzeitliche Pathos vom "Buche der Natur" schlägt um in die metaphysisch-religiöse Fassung der Geschichte als der eigentlichen Erscheinungssphäre des Absoluten, oder des Göttlichen Geistes. Als eine unendliche Wirkenskette der "Aufforderungen", des freiheitsweckenden und geistgestaltenden Ineinandergreifens selbsttätiger Lebenszentren steht die Welt vor FICHTE, in schöpferischer Freiheit neue und neue Gesichte wie aus dem Nichts hervorbringend."

tive. It is rather conceived in the irrationalist sense of the "creative" historical process, in which the one absolute metaphysical Idea, through the concentration-points of the great leading personalities, realizes itself in the diverse forms of cultural Ideas: in the Ideas of art, state, science and religion. The inner value of the latter corresponds to their precedence [1]. In this period, FICHTE is deeply convinced of the irrationality of the absolute Idea in its inexhaustible creative fulness of life [2].

Only in the spiritual originality of great individuals, of creative geniuses, does the divine image immediately break through into appearance. History, as an immediate manifestation of the ethical Idea, is essentially made by great personalities. So FICHTE himself expresses it: "All that is great and good, upon which our present existence is based, from which it starts, and which is the only supposition under which it can display its essence in the manner it does display it, has only been realized by the fact that noble and vigorous men have sacrificed all enjoyment of life for the sake of Ideas; and we ourselves with all that we are, are the result of the sacrifices of all previous generations, and especially of their most worthy fellow-members" [3]. "The original divine

---

[1] WW. VII, 58 ff. As to the conception of beauty as the lowest form of manifestation of the *Idea*, cf. *Die Anweisung zum seligen Leben* (1806), WW. V, 526.

[2] Cf. also FICHTE's letter to SCHELLING from May 5 to August 7, 1801 (*Aus Schelling's Leben* I, 345) where he emphatically speaks of the "root'" of the world of spirits as "irrational".

[3] *Die Grundzüge des gegenwärtigen Zeitalters (The principal traits of our present period)*, WW. VII, p. 41: "Alles grosse und gute, worauf unsere gegenwärtige Existenz sich stützet, wovon sie ausgeht, und unter dessen alleiniger Voraussetzung unser Zeitalter sein Wesen treiben kann, wie es dasselbe treibt, ist lediglich dadurch wirklich geworden, dass edele und kräftige Menschen allen Lebensgenuss für Ideeën aufgeopfert haben; und wir selber mit allem, was wir sind, sind das Resultat der Aufopferung aller früheren Generationen, und besonderes ihrer würdigsten Mitglieder." "Die ursprüngliche göttliche Idee von einem bestimmten Standpunkt in der Zeit läszt gröszten Teils sich nicht eher angeben, als bis der von Gott begeisterte Mensch kommt und sie ausführt... Im allgemeinen ist die ursprüngliche und reine göttliche Idee... für die Welt der Erscheinung schöpferisch, hervorbringend das neue, unerhörte und vorher nie dagewesene." "Von jeher war es Gesetz der übersinnlichen Welt, dasz sie nur in Wenigen Auserwählten... ursprünglich herausbrach in Gesichte; die grosze Mehrzahl der übrigen sollte erst von diesen Wenigen aus... gebildet werden." "In der Geisterwelt ist Jedwedes um so edler, je seltener es ist;... in äuszerst Wenigen spricht die Gottheit sich unmittelbar aus."

Idea of a definite standpoint in time is for the greater part not to be indicated before the (elected) man comes, inspired by God, and executes it... The original and pure divine Idea is in general... creative for the world of appearance, originating that which is new, unheard of and never had existed before." "From time immemorial it was a law of the super-sensory world that it only in few elected men... originally broke forth in visions: the great majority of the rest should only be cultivated by mediation of these few..." "In the world of spirits the nobility of everything becomes greater according to its rareness... in extremely few (personalities) the Deity expresses itself immediately"[1].

Natural individuality must be annihilated in the historical process by the individuality of the spirit.

The value of the individuality of genius, which FICHTE sets here so emphatically in the foreground, is not that of the merely sensuous individuality of nature. Just as "nature" as such possesses for FICHTE no meaning of its own, so also must the individuality of nature (natural individuality) be *annihilated* for the sake of the disclosure of the absolute Idea. In a clear manner FICHTE says that his "unconditional rejection of all individuality" exclusively relates to the "personal sensory existence of the individual", but that, on the contrary, his philosophy postulates that "in each particular individual in which it comes to life, the one eternal Idea absolutely exhibits itself in a new figure which never existed before; and this quite independent of the sensory nature, through itself and its own legislation, consequently by no means determined through the sensory individuality, but rather annihilating the latter and purely from itself determining the ideal individuality, or, as it is called more exactly, the originality"[2].

Individuality and Society.

As this "spiritual" (historical) individuality is further thought

---

[1] Compare the German text in footnote 3 of the preceding page.

[2] WW. VII, 69: "die Eine ewige Idee im jedem besonderen Individuum, in welchem sie zum Leben durchdringt, sich durchaus in einer neuen, vorher nie dagewesenen Gestalt zeige; und dieses zwar ganz unabhängig von der sinnlichen Natur, durch sich selber und ihre eigene Gesetzgebung, mithin keinesweges bestimmt durch die sinnliche Individualität, sondern diese vernichtend und rein aus sich bestimmend die ideale Individualität, oder, wie es richtiger heisst, die Originalität."

of only as a point of concentration, in which the absolute Idea makes itself concrete in the historical supra-personal stream of life, there is automatically a break with the atomistic natural-scientific view of history. According to FICHTE, individuality can only be understood from the individual *communities*, in which alone it has temporal existence. Even in his *Reden an die deutsche Nation* (1808), FICHTE has made a serious attempt to conceive the individuality of a nation as an historical totality.

The remarkable feature of this whole metaphysical conception, typical at the same time of its irrationalist root, is the nominalistic view, which denies both the reality of abstract general concepts (universalia) and the possibility of a derivation of subjectivity from a law. FICHTE's absolute transcendent Idea is not a *universal*, but a *totality*. He rejects unconditionally every hypostatization of general concepts in the sense of Platonic ideas. In my opinion, it is also entirely incorrect to characterize FICHTE's metaphysics as monistic Eleaticism, as LASK does[1], The static Eleatic conception of "absolute being" has nothing in common with FICHTE's view of the absolute Idea as a totality of being, which unfolds itself in the historical process. The Eleatic being, as I have shown in the first volume of my trilogy *Reformation and Scholasticism in Philosophy*, is not to be understood apart from the religious form-motive of Greek thought. It is the indivisible, supra-sensory and divine form of being, as such, which can be intuited only in "theoria", and which cannot have any relation to the "matter-principle", the principle of becoming and declining. This "form of being" is thought of as a purely geometrical one, corresponding to the immaterial shape of the sphere, which in Greek philosophy was viewed as the most perfect.

FICHTE's "divine Being", on the contrary, although in itself supra-historical, has an essential relation to the historical process. It is the divine origin of all activity and cultural individuality, and is thus by no means to be characterized as a static "universal".

Abandonment of the Critical form-matter schema.

In FICHTE's metaphysical conception of the Idea (as closed totality of its individual disclosures in historical development), the Critical form-matter schema is in principle broken through

---

[1] WW. I, p. 175.

and abandoned. Within the framework of the latter schema, the totality of individual determinations could only be an *Idea* in the sense of a limiting-concept, by which transcendental thought is driven forward without being able to realize its demand because of its limitations in comprehending the empirical material of experience. The recognition of these limitations is here the point of departure. FICHTE's irrationalistic metaphysics, on the contrary, follows the reverse course from the absolute totality as "absolute Being". The "Idea" is not thought of here as an eternal task for bridging over the cleavage between the form and matter of our knowledge, but rather as a metaphysical totality of all individuality.

In proceeding from the absolute totality in this metaphysical sense, there is a constant threat of an apriori construction of historical development. Such a construction abandons the temporal material of experience, which, as *merely* empirical, as only simple *phenomenon*, is reasoned away in FICHTE's metaphysics of history.

To this metaphysical passion for apriori construction, FICHTE fell victim in his first work on the philosophy of history, the *Principial Traits of the Present Era ("Grundzüge des gegenwärtigen Zeitalters"*, 1804—'05). Here he observes: "if the philosopher has the task to deduce the phenomena, possible in experience, from the unity of his supposed Idea, then it is evident, that for the fulfilment of this task he does not at all need experience; and that he, merely as a philosopher, and strictly paying attention to his limitations, can do his work without allowing for any experience, and simply *apriori*, as it is called with the technical term, and that — in relation to our subject — he must be able to describe apriori the whole of time and all possible periods of it" [1].

Thus the Idea of an historical world-plan is construed apriori. FICHTE defines it in a teleological sense: *"the aim of the earthly*

---

[1] WW. VII, 5: "hat der Philosoph die in der Erfahrung mögliche Phänomene aus der Einheit seines vorausgesetzten Begriffs abzuleiten, so ist klar, dass er zu seinem Geschäfte durchaus keiner Erfahrung bedürfe, und dass er blosz als Philosoph und innerhalb seiner Grenzen streng sich haltend, ohne Rücksicht auf irgend eine Erfahrung und schlechthin *a priori*, wie sie dies mit dem Kunstausdrucke benennen, sein Geschäft treibe, und, in Beziehung auf unseren Gegenstand, die gesammte Zeit und alle möglichen Epochen derselben *a priori* müsse beschreiben können."

cosmonomic Idea of Humanistic immanence-philosophy 481

life of mankind is this, that the latter should arrange all its relations within the same with liberty according to reason" [1].

"This world-plan is the Idea of the unity of the whole of human earthly life" [2].

Out of this apriori Idea FICHTE deduces, once again apriori, his five chief periods of world-history. It is not the individual, but rather the "human race" as a whole that functions as the subject of the latter.

In this entire philosophical conception, there appears to be no point of contact for a methodological concept of history, as a condition for the cultivation of the *science of history*. The empirical science of history appears rather to be handed over to the "Chronikmaker" (annalist), whereas the systematics of history is reserved entirely for the apriori metaphysics of history as "Vernunftwissenschaft" (science of reason).

LASK, however, has pointed out, that in the *Grundzüge* another motive in the philosophy of history announces itself alongside of this metaphysical one. The two motives may not entirely be brought into agreement. The latter is to be explained in terms of the continued operation of Critical-transcendental motives even in FICHTE's last period. This second motive may be characterized as follows: our thinker by no means made the task of the philosophy of history to consist entirely in the construction of the world-plan, but he sets also the requirement that it should make a thorough logical analysis of the general conditions of "empirical existence", as the *material of historical construction.*

FICHTE's logic of historical thought.

In this requirement of a "logic of the historical mode of enquiry", not to be found in KANT, the *irrational character* of the historical material of experience is placed in the foreground.

It is especially the important ninth lecture of the *Grundzüge,* in which FICHTE set himself the task of a "transcendental logical" delimitation of the concept of the historical field of investigation,

---

[1] WW. VII, 7: *"der Zweck des Erdenlebens der Menschheit ist der, dass sie in demselben alle ihre Verhältnisse mit Freiheit nach der Vernunft einrichte."*

[2] *"jener Weltplan ist der Einheitsbegriff des gesammten menschlichen Erdenlebens"* (italics mine!).

and describes this task explicitly as a *philosophical one*. It is not the task of the historian to consider empirical existence and its conditions as such. Both belong to his pre-suppositions: "The question which are these conditions of empirical existence — what is to be pre-supposed for the mere possibility of a history as such, and what in the first place must be (present), before history can merely make a beginning — belongs to the competence of the philosopher, *who has to guarantee to the historian his basis and foundation*" [1].

With "timeless Being" or "divine life" plunging into earthly existence, or into the "flowing of life" in time, *infinity and irrationality* are joined for knowledge. *Physics* is the science that investigates empirically the constant objective and periodically recurrent features of temporal existence, i.e. "nature". Investigation directed toward the contents of the flowing time-series is called the science of history: "Its 'Gegenstand' is the always inconceivable development of knowledge concerning the incomprehensible" [2]. While the historian accepts his "facts" (FACTA) simply as such, the task of the philosopher of history, who sees through their logical structure, is "to comprehend them in their incomprehensibility" and to render intelligible the appearance of their "contingency" out of their character which is incomprehensible to the understanding. It is, consequently, the task of philosophy to indicate the boundary between speculation and experience in the study of history. At this point, the influence of Criticism on FICHTE's view of history exhibits itself very clearly, where he opposes every attempt to deduce the historical facts themselves from the infinite understanding of the absolute *Being*. "Consequently: the *timeless* being and existence is in no way contingent; and neither the philosopher nor the historian is able to give a theory of its origin: the *factual* existence in time appears as contingent because apparently it can be otherwise; however, this appearance originates from the

---

[1] WW. VII, 131/2: "Das empirische Daseyn selber und alle Bedingungen davon setzt er daher voraus. Welche nun diese Bedingungen des empirischen Daseyns seyen — was daher für die blosze Möglichkeit einer Geschichte überhaupt vorausgesetzt werde und vor allen Dingen seyn müsse, ehe die Geschichte auch nur ihren Anfang finden könne, — ist Sache des Philosophen, *welche dem Historiker erst seinen Grund und Boden sichern muss*" (italics mine!).

[2] *Ibid.*, p. 131: "Ihr Gegenstand ist die zu aller Zeit unbegriffene Entwickelung des Wissens am Unbegriffenen."

fact that it is not comprehended: the philosopher can, to be sure, say in general *that* the One inconceivable, just like the infinite comprehending of the same, is such as it is, for the very reason that it is to continue being understood to infinity; he can, however, not at all deduce it genetically, and define it from this infinite comprehending, because then he would have *conceived* infinity, which is absolutely impossible. Here consequently is his limit, and, if he desires to know something in this department (realm), he is referred to experience. As little can the historian point out genetically this inconceivable (infinity) as the original beginning of time. His calling is to expose the factual successive determinations of empirical existence. Empirical existence itself and all the conditions of it are consequently presupposed by him" [1].

In this way FICHTE comes to the conclusion that neither the philosopher nor the historian can say anything about the origin of the world or of mankind: "for there is no origin at all, but only the one timeless and necessary Being." The philosopher has only to account for the *conditions* of factual existence "as lying beyond all factual existence and all experience."

What FICHTE had in mind with this actually epistemological task of philosophy with respect to the science of history, appears clearly from his statement: "It acquires a definite concept of what is truly asked for by history and what belongs to it, besides a logic of historical truth; and so, even in this infinite territory, the groping about at random is replaced by the sure proceeding according to a rule" [2].

---

[1] *Ibid.*, p. 131: "Also: das *zeitlose* Seyn und Daseyn ist auf keine Weise zufällig; und es lässt sich weder durch den Philosophen, noch durch den Historiker eine Theorie seines Ursprunges geben: das *factische* Daseyn in der Zeit erscheint als anders seynkönnend, und darum zufällig; aber dieser Schein entspringt aus der Unbegriffenheit: und der Philosoph kann zwar wohl im Allgemeinen sagen, *dass* das Eine Unbegriffene, sowie das unendliche Begreifen an demselben, *so ist, wie* es ist, eben weil es in die Unendlichkeit fortbegriffen werden soll; er kann es aber keinesweges aus diesem unendlichen Begreifen genetisch ableiten und bestimmen, weil er sodann die Unendlichkeit *erfasst* haben müsste, was durchaus unmöglich ist. Hier sonach ist seine Grenze, und er wird, falls er in diesem Gebiete etwas zu wissen begehrt, an die Empirie gewiesen. Ebensowenig kann der Historiker jenes Unbegriffene, als den Uranfang der Zeit, in seiner Genesis angeben. Sein Geschäft ist: die factischen *Fort*bestimmungen des empirischen Daseyns aufzustellen. Das empirische Daseyn selber und alle Bedingungen davon setzt er daher voraus."

[2] "Sie erhält einen bestimmten Begriff davon, wonach die Geschichte

FICHTE also mentions more precisely the relationship in which the components of historical development to be known *apriori* stand in his opinion to those to be known *aposteriori*. History is beyond doubt conceived of by FICHTE as the development of culture which does not begin before the *"Normalvolk"* postulated by him, was dispersed over the "seats of rudeness and barbarism." This *"Normalvolk"* is supposed to have been in a situation of perfect "Vernunftkultur" and such "through its mere existence, without any science or art." "Now for the first time something new and remarkable presented itself that stimulated the remembrance of men to retain it: — now for the first time could begin the true history which can do nothing more than notice factually, by means of mere experience, the gradual cultivation of the true human race of history, originated from a mixture of the original culture and the original barbarism"[1].

The metaphysically conceived apriori component of historical development is the formerly discussed *world-plan* that leads mankind through the five periods of world-history. Without any historical experience the philosopher can know that these periods must follow one another: "Now this development of the human race does not make its entrance in the general manner in which the philosopher paints it in one single survey, but gradually, disturbed by forces strange to it, at definite times, in definite places, under definite circumstances. All these particular surroundings do by no means originate from the Idea of this world-plan; they are the non-understood in it, and, as it is the only Idea for this world-plan, the non-understood in general; and here the pure empiricism of history makes its entrance, its *a posteriori:* the history proper in its form"[2].

---

eigentlich frage, und was in sie gehöre, nebst einer Logik der historischen Wahrheit; und so tritt selbst in diesem unendlichen Gebiete das sichere Fortschreiten nach einer Regel an die Stelle des Herumtappens auf gutes Glück."

[1] WW. VII, 138: "erst nun gab es etwas neues und merkwürdiges, das das Andenken der Menschen reizte, es aufzubehalten; — erst jetzt konnte beginnen die eigentliche Geschichte, die nichts weiter thun kann, als durch blosse Empirie factisch auffassen die allmählige Cultivirung des nunmehr durch Mischung der ursprünglichen Cultur und der ursprünglichen Uncultur entstandenen, eigentlichen Menschengeschlechtes der Geschichte."

[2] ib., p. 139: "Nun tritt diese Entwickelung des Menschengeschlechtes nicht überhaupt ein, wie der Philosoph in einem einzigen Überblicke es schildert; sondern sie tritt allmählig, gestört durch ihr fremde Kräfte, zu

cosmonomic Idea of Humanistic immanence-philosophy 485

The irrational, new element, not to be repeated, that can be discovered only empirically, fills the time-series of historical development and arises in the subjection of raw nature through rational and free cultural activity of the human race in the various *forms* of the absolute Idea. In this is seen the "transcendental-logical" criterion of history in FICHTE's first main work on the philosophy of history.

FICHTE's new hstorical concept of time.

Remarkable to a high degree and yet scarcely observed up to now is the fact that FICHTE *has paid special attention also to historical time.* He distinguishes *the true historical time* from *empty* time.

In the latter, there moves only dream and show, all that which serves only for pastime or for the mere satisfaction of a curiosity that is not grounded in a serious desire for knowledge: "The pastime is truly an empty time which is placed in the midst between the time filled up by serious business." In the "true and real time", on the contrary, something happens, "when it becomes a principle, a necessary ground and cause of new phenomena which never before existed. Then for the first time a living life has arisen which originates other life from itself" [1].

We see here how FICHTE in a typical manner anticipates the historical conception of time of the modern philosophy of life. Its distinction of *true* and *apparent* time is still to engage our attention in detail in our further discussion of this problem.

Yet, in spite of everything that is offered in the *"Grundzüge"* for the development of an irrationalist logic of the science of history, the fundamental dualism between the merely empirical

---

gewissen Zeiten, an gewissen Orten, unter gewissen besonderen Umstände ein. Alle diese besonderen Umgebungen gehen aus dem Begriffe jenes Weltplanes keinesweges hervor: sie sind das in ihm Unbegriffene, und da er der einzige Begriff dafür ist, das überhaupt Unbegriffene; und hier tritt ein die reine Empirie der Geschichte, ihr *a posteriori:* die eigentliche Geschichte in ihrer Form."

[1] WW. VII, 245: "Der Zeitvertreib ist ganz eigentlich eine leere Zeit, welche zwischen die durch ernsthafte Beschäftigungen ausgefüllte Zeit in die Mitte gesetzt wird;" in the "true and real time", on the contrary, something happens "wenn es Princip wird, nothwendiger Grund und Ursache, neuer und vorher nie dagewesener Erscheinungen in der Zeit. Dann erst ist ein lebendiges Leben geworden, das anderes Leben aus sich erzeugt."

individuality and the individuality of value in history is not yet bridged over here. Consequently, at this stage the historical logic exhibits a fundamental hiatus.

Indeed, the true science of history remains restricted to the "Sammlung der blossen Facten" (collection of mere facts); the professional historian remains one "who in collecting historical facts has no other criterion but the external sequence of the years and centuries "ohne alle Rücksicht auf ihren Inhalt" [1] (without any regard to their content) even though his work is called "useful and honourable."

Now LASK has demonstrated, that in the writings between 1805—9, this dualism between empirical individuality and value, not yet overcome in the „Grundzüge", is removed *in fact*, by reason of the explicit ascription of *value-character* to that which is recognized as irrational with respect to its logical structure. Not until the last phase of all (namely in the *Staatslehre* of 1813) is the ascription of value-character to the historical material of experience (logically recognized as irrational) made a problem, which was possible only by means of a deepening of the methodological inquiries begun in 1805.

Indeed we find for the first time in the important considerations on the *Deduction of the "Gegenstand" of the History of Mankind* in the *Staatslehre* of 1813, properly speaking an elaboration of the task set in the *Grundzüge*: the discovery of the logic of historical truth.

> In the "Staatslehre" of 1813, FICHTE anticipates the "cultural-historical" method of the South-West German school of Neo-Kantianism. The synthesis of nature and freedom in the concept of the "free force".

Here for the first time a serious attempt is made to find a synthesis between nature and freedom within the transcendentally analysed historical field of inquiry. The manner in which FICHTE tries to reach this synthesis is characteristic of the irrationalist motive which is operative behind the critical form.

FICHTE begins his views with setting a sharp antithesis between the "realm of nature" (as the domain of the naturalistic science-ideal) and the "realm of freedom" (as the domain of the ideal of personality).

These two realms are now synthetically unified by an inter-

---

[1] WW. VII, 140.

mediate concept, i.e. that of the *free force*: "Nature is *death* and *rest*: freedom only must vivify and stimulate it again; according to a concept; and this is the very character of the free force, that it can only be moved according to a concept" [1]. "Consequently — and that is the point here — we acquire in that which is possibly given, besides that which is given in nature, also a world of freedom-products, constructed through absolute freedom on the basis of the former, however, not at all grounded on this nature which was closed with this dead force." "From this (originates) the sphere of the freedom-products, as being possibly given and under a particular condition: *these (freedom-products) are contingent for the intuition, however qualified for the very history as a description of what in this way is given*" (italics mine) [2].

The following dilemma presents itself directly in FICHTE's world-picture, which knows no modal law-spheres: The realm of "dead nature" is ruled by the mathematical and mechanical laws imposed by the understanding; the realm of living actual freedom by the autonomous moral law. To which laws is now subjected the third realm, that of history as the synthetical realm of visible, cultural freedom?

FICHTE emphatically observes: "The ethical (realm) is purely spiritual and without figure, it is a *law* without any image. It acquires its concrete figure only from the ethical matter" [3].

Consequently, history in its individual figures and its "free forces" which produce culture, must be characterized as "lawless". To FICHTE there is no other solution possible: "The state

---

[1] WW. IV, 461: "Die Natur ist *Tod* und *Ruhe*: die Freiheit erst muss sie wieder beleben und anregen; nach einem Begriffe: und das ist eben der Charakter der freien Kraft, dass sie nur nach einem Begriffe bewegt werden kann."

[2] WW. IV, 462: "Wir erhalten sonach, worauf es ankommt, ausser dem in der Natur Gegebenen, in dem möglicherweise Gegebenen auch noch eine Welt der Freiheitsproducte, aufgetragen durch absolute Freiheit auf die erste, in dieser aber, die mit jener todten Kraft geschlossen war, durchaus nicht begründet." "Daraus die Sphäre der Freiheitsproducte, als eines möglicherweise und unter einer gewissen Bedingung gegebenen: *diese sind für die Anschauung ein Zufälliges, also aber eben zur Geschichte, als einer Darstellung des also Gegebenen, sich qualificirend*" (italics mine!).

[3] "Das Sittliche ist rein geistig und gestaltlos, *Gesetz*, ohne alles Bild. Seine Gestaltung erhält es erst aus dem sittlichen Stoffe" (p. 464).

of affairs is therefore as follows: by far the greater part of the freedom-products present in a period of time of the intuition, have not come about according to the clear concept of the moral law, consequently not according to this law; no more have they come about by the law of nature, since the latter is closed to the creation of these products which have originated from freedom. Since there is no legislation besides these two, this (originating) occurs quite *lawless*, at random. This is truly, as is well known, the object of human history as it has developed until now..." [1].

The "hidden conformity to law" of historical development. The irrationalist concept of the law.

Thus the historical aspect is brought into explicit opposition to that which is conformed to a law: "a particular historical matter is to be understood only through history in general; the latter again is only to be understood through its opposite, that which happens in conformity to laws and is, consequently, to be known in a strictly scientific way" [2].

Nevertheless, to this statement, FICHTE immediately adds the remark that the freedom which discloses itself in historical development must possess a *hidden conformity to a law* which is nothing other than the providence of the moral deity. But this *conformity to a law* is not to be known from rational concepts. It is rather a hidden *telos* in the displaying of the *given freedom* in the irrational development of culture which makes the transcendent values visible in the individual temporal formations of culture.

Here, in a Humanistic perversion of the Christian faith in the Divine Providence, the law is very clearly made a simple

---

[1] WW. IV, 462/3: "So darum steht die Sache: Bei weitem das Meiste der etwa in einem Zeitraume der Anschauung vorliegenden Freiheitsproducte ist zu Stande gekommen nicht nach dem deutlichen Begriffe vom sittlichen Gesetze, also nicht nach diesem Gesetze; ebensowenig aber ist es zu Stande gekommen durch das Naturgesetz, indem dieses geschlossen ist vor dessen Erzeugung, und es zu Stande gekommen ist durch Freiheit. Da es nun ausser diesen beiden keine Gesetzgebung gibt, erfolgt sie ganz gesetzlos, von ohngefähr. Dies nun eigentlich und notorisch der Gegenstand der bisherigen Menschengeschichte..."

[2] *Ibid.*, p. 458/9: "ein besonderes Geschichtliches ist verständlich nur durch Geschichte überhaupt; diese wiederum nur verständlich durch ihren Gegensatz, das Gesetzliche, streng wissenschaftlich zu Erkennende."

reflection of the individual free subjectivity, disclosed in the "irrational process" [1].

The irrational historical conformity to law, which FICHTE accepts, is the very negation of veritable historical norms. It is the precipitation of the irrationalist ideal of personality, in which the νόμος is nothing but the reflection of the individual αὐτός [2]. Only by conceiving the individual in its turn as a member of an individual community whose historical tradition and "common spirit" is an inner constitutive factor of the individuality of all of its members, can this irrationalism escape the anarchistic view of history. Therefore, it must result in a universalist conception of temporal human society which — in polar opposition to individualism — views society according to the schema of the whole and its parts; not considering the inner nature of the different social relations.

Irrationalizing of the divine world-plan.

The divine world-plan, that FICHTE in his *"Grundzüge"*, still tried to deduce rationalistically in a purely apriori fashion, apart from the historical material of experience, is now, on the contrary, sought in the very individuality of the historical matter which cannot be comprehended in rational concepts: "However, is there not in this inconceivable incomprehensible element at

---

[1] Which unfortunately also passed over into Fr. J. STAHL's philosophy of history under the influence of SCHELLING's romanticism. "God's guidance in history" is now irrationalistically conceived of as an unconscious operation of God's "secret counsel", which nevertheless is accepted as a complementary norm for human action! Thus irrationalism penetrated even into the Christian view of history! The so-called "Christian-historical" trend in political theory in Germany and the Netherlands is undoubtedly influenced by this irrationalist view of history.

[2] Compare FICHTE's statement: "Only the formal concept, formed in pure science, is finite, since it is the concept of a law. The judgment of the given facts, on the contrary, is infinite: for it proceeds according *to the law which rules in this judgment itself and remains eternally hidden*; it springs up eternally new and fresh. From every point indeed through taking part from the side of the law develops eternity and so in every following moment of time." ["Nur der formale, in der reinen Wissenschaft aufgestellte Begriff ist endlich, denn er ist der Begriff eines Gesetzes: die Beurteilung des faktisch gegebenen aber ist unendlich; denn sie geht einher nach *dem in ihr selbst herrschenden, ewig verborgen bleibenden Gesetze*: quilt ewig neu und frisch. Aus jedem Punkte entwickelt sich ja durch Hinzutritt des Gesetzes die Ewigkeit und so in jedem folgenden Zeitmomente."]

the same time a world-plan, therefore undoubtedly a Providence and an Understanding? So what is the law of the world-facts, i.e. of that which gives to freedom its task? This question lies very deep; until now I have helped myself by ignoring and denying! I might there indeed arrive at a deeper, truly *absolute* Understanding, giving the inner support to the infinite modifiability of freedom. Therefore, that which I posited as absolutely factual, might perhaps yet be posited by an *Understanding*"[1].

It is clear, that in this final phase of FICHTE's thought, the *principium individuationis* has shifted to the historical realm, as the synthesis of value and temporal reality, whereas, in his first rationalistic period, he had sought it — in accordance with KANT — only in the sensory matter of nature-experience.

The apriori conformity to a law which the *"Staatslehre"* assumes for historical development, i.e. the gradual conquest of faith by the understanding, is merely a *formal* one.

It is only the qualitatively individual, moral nature, which, as *given freedom*, produces the *material* of history, since it becomes an individual *paradigm* for the producing by freedom.

Its first appearance is a creative wonder of Providence, transformed by FICHTE into a "transcendental-logical condition" of the possibility of history: "Consequently: the concept of a moral procreation or nature of man has replaced Providence (as a Miracle), which is the ground of the truly historical material of history. According to our Idea we have immediately taken up this morality of nature into the necessary form of appearance"[2].

As the very "transcendental-logical" condition for the possibility of an historical experience, the presence of a "moral

---

[1] *Politische Fragmente aus den Jahren 1807 und 1813*, WW. VII, 586: "Aber ist in diesem Elemente des Unbegreiflichen, Unverstandenen nicht zugleich ein Weltplan, drum allerdings eine Vorsehung und ein Verstand? "Welches ist denn das Gesetz der Weltfacten, d.i. desjenigen, was der Freiheit ihre Aufgaben liefert? Diese Frage liegt sehr tief; bisher habe ich durch Ignorieren und Absprechen mir geholfen! Ich dürfte da allerdings einen tieferen, eigentlich *absoluten* Verstand bekommen, an der unendlichen Modificabilität der Freiheit, und dieser den inneren Halt gebend. Was ich daher als absolut factisch gesetzt habe, möchte doch durch einen *Verstand* gesetzt seyn."

[2] WW. IV, 469: "Also: der Vorsehung (als Wunder), dem Grunde des eigentlich geschichtlichen Stoffes des Geschichte, ist substituiret worden der Begriff einer sittlichen Erzeugung oder Natur des Menschen. Nach unserer Idee haben wir diese Sittlichkeit der Natur gleich aufgenommen in die nothwendige Form der Erscheinung."

nature" may not be accepted further than is necessary for the explanation of the development.

The concept of the "highly gifted people" (das geniale Volk).

FICHTE takes a further step in the development of his irrationalist methodology of history by transferring the concept of the miraculous from the individual to social groups or communities viewed as "individual totalities". Just as an individual paradigm is postulated for the historical development of the morality of the individual, the social paradigm of an entire people is postulated for the moral development of the human race: "However, since we must conceive the appearance of freedom as a totality absolutely closed in time, we must assume some society which compels and instructs without itself having needed both, since, by its mere existence, it possessed this very morality to which it leads the society coming after it and originating from it, by means of compulsion and instruction: because it was by nature that to which others have to educate themselves in freedom under its cultivating power"[1].

In this way the hypothesis (introduced for the first time in the *"Grundzüge"*) as to a primeval people that is in possession of a morality, given in an individual moral nature, is now rendered serviceable to the methodology of history.

By virtue of its very *non-recurrent individual and "lawless" realization of value,* the historical development receives in FICHTE a higher value-accent than that which recurs periodically according to the uniformity of natural laws. The historical is no longer, in a rationalistic fashion, set in opposition to the law of reason and in this opposition conceived of as the value-less (because law-less) material of experience; but it is rather understood as totality of what is new and creative individual in opposition to the merely *"stehende Sein"* (static being) of nature [2].

FICHTE's conception, in sharp opposition to that of KANT, is

---

[1] WW. IV, 470: "Da wir aber doch die Erscheinung der Freiheit schlechterdings als in der Zeit schlechterdings geschlossenes Ganze auffassen müssen, so müssen wir irgend eine Gesellschaft annehmen, die da zwingt und belehrt, ohne selbst beides bedürft zu haben, weil sie durch ihr blosses Daseyn das schon war, wozu sie die nach ihr und aus ihr entstehende Gesellschaft mit Zwang und Belehrung erst bringt: von Natur das war, wozu Andere unter ihrer Bildung sich machen mit Freiheit."

[2] LASK, *op. cit.,* p. 293, also for the following.

now to the effect that the framing of "final ends" of historical development, such as: "education for freedom", "education for clarity", etc. can have only the significance of a general descriptive formulation: "Both, however, are only formal. For the infinite content of this freedom, the moral task, remains in fact something incomprehensible, the image of God, for this very reason that the latter is absolutely incomprehensible, and is to be experienced only in the revelations of history" [1].

The concept of revelation in the sense of a synthesis of irrationality and originality is now expressly taken up in the "transcendental-logical" structure of history.

In this way the religious life in the historical-empirical form of Jesus is characterized as immediate individual revelation of the Idea of God in the appearance [2].

It will, consequently, have to be conceded to LASK, that in FICHTE there has actually been developed a *transcendental logic of history* in contrast with the *metaphysics of* HEGEL. The concept of science here developed finds, as we believe we have demonstrated in detail, its transcendental root in a cosmonomic Idea inspired by the irrationalist ideal of personality.

The inner antinomies in this irrationalist logic of history.

If this conception is thought through consistently it must resolve itself into inner antinomies. For, on the one hand, by reason of its immanent continuity-postulate, it knows cosmic boundaries of meaning as little as the concept of science that originated from the naturalistic science-ideal; consequently it brings all normative subject-functions of temporal reality under a historical basic denominator. On the other hand, by its denaturing of historical conformity to law into a mere reflection of individual subjectivity, it must deny all knowable historical determination of facts. For de-termination can only issue from a law, which cannot be a mere reflection of individual subjectivity, but which regulates and limits the subject-functions in their infinite individual diversity. In our discussion of the

---

[1] "Beides aber ist nur formal. In der Tat bleibt nämlich der unendliche Inhalt jener Freiheit, die sittliche Aufgabe, etwas Unbegreifliches, das Bild Gottes eben darum, weil dieser schlechthin unbegreiflich ist, und nur zu erleben in den Offenbarungen der Geschichte."

[2] WW. V, 483 f. 567—674.

modal structure of the historical aspect in the second volume we shall return to this point.

Law and individuality.

Notwithstanding all its concreteness and individualization, a real law can never acquire the function of a mere register of the subjective facts in their complete individuality. The concept of a *hidden, eternally incomprehensible conformity to law is contradictory* and establishes in scientific thought only endless confusion, since it elevates to the status of law the temporal individual subjectivity itself which cannot really exist unless it is bound to a supra-individual order.

Even the circumstance that FICHTE does not view historical development as a uniform progress but rather as a process with hindrances and reactions, exhibits the impossibility of carrying through the irrationalist concept of history. For hindrances and reactions are to be recognized scientifically only under the test of a *supra-subjective* standard.

The dangerous historistic tendency in FICHTE's so-called "spiritual-scientific" thought discloses itself in its pregnant sense at the same point at which it has won permanent gains for the science of history, namely, in the discovery of the national community of a people as an individual historical totality in contrast with the atomistic cosmopolitan view of the *"Aufklärung"* (Enlightenment).

Attention has been drawn sufficiently to the great gain of this discovery in modern FICHTE-literature. In KANT's time, individualism was willing to acknowledge, beyond the atomistic individual conceived in natural-scientific terms, only the abstract universal concept of *humanity* in an ethical sense.

Surely under the influence of Romanticism, which also is to be observed in SCHLEIERMACHER's principle of *"Eigentümlichkeit"* (singularity), FICHTE breaks radically with this individualistic point of view: "The form of a people itself is from nature or God: a certain highly individual manner to advance the aim of reason. Peoples are individualities with particular talents and character for it." "This then is a people in the higher sense of the word taken from the view-point of a spiritual world in general: the whole of men who continue living together in society and originate continuously themselves from themselves naturally and spiritually, a whole that is subject to some particular law of development of the divine from it. It is the common bond of this particular law that in the eternal world, and for that very reason also in the temporal, joins this multitude to a natural and self-conscious totality" [1].

The "historical nationality" as "true reality" contrasted with the state as conceptual abstraction.

FICHTE now shows clearly his historistic view of society. He opposes the nationality — which he conceived as a *purely historical* entity — to the *state*. The former is, according to him, a *full* and *true temporal* reality, the state, on the contrary, a mere *conceptual abstraction*. He thereby paved the way for the most recent historistic-phenomenological theory of human society. The newly discovered historical aspect of reality is forthwith absolutized as the basic denominator for all aspects of human society and the national community of the people is elevated to the rank of "true historical reality" which has an "earthly eternity": "People and fatherland in this signification, as bearer and pledge of earthly eternity, and as that which down here can be eternal, lies far above the state in the ordinary sense of the word, — above the social order as it is conceived in a mere clear concept, and à propos of this concept is established and kept up" [2].

---

[1] *Reden an die deutsche Nation,* WW. VII, 381: "Die Volksform selbst ist von der Natur oder Gott: eine gewisse hochindividuelle Weise, den Vernunftzweck zu befördern. Völker sind Individualitäten, mit eigentümlicher Begabung und Rolle dafür." "Dies nun ist in höherer, vom Standpuncte der Ansicht einer geistigen Welt überhaupt genommener Bedeutung des Wortes, ein Volk: das Ganze der in Gesellschaft mit einander fortlebenden und sich aus sich selbst immerfort natürlich und geistig erzeugenden Menschen, das insgesammt unter einem gewissen besonderen Gesetze der Entwickelung des Göttlichen aus ihm steht. Die Gemeinsamkeit dieses besonderen Gesetzes ist es, was in der ewigen Welt, und eben darum auch in der zeitlichen(!) diese Menge zu einem natürlichen und von sich selbst durchdrungenen Ganzen verbindet."

[2] "Volk und Vaterland in dieser Bedeutung, als' Träger und Unterpfand der irdischen Ewigkeit, und als dasjenige, was hienieden ewig seyn kann, liegt weit hinaus über den Staat, im gewöhnlichen Sinne des Wortes, über die gesellschaftliche Ordnung, wie dieselbe im bloszen klaren Begriffe erfaszt, und nach Anleitung dieses Begriffes errichtet und erhalten wird." I will here by no means ignore the influence of the historical-political situation in which FICHTE wrote his *"Reden an die deutsche Nation"*, and in which his entire concern was the awakening of the national consciousness against the French usurper of his fatherland. However, his construction of the relationship between *nation* and *state* is doubtless more deeply based upon his historic view of temporal social life."

Insofar as FICHTE here directs his polemic against the abstract individualistic conception of human society in the school of natural law he is again right to a certain extent. But his intention goes much further. Nationality is absolutized as the true historical revelation of the eternal spiritual community of humanity. The Humanistic ideal of personality here shows a most dangerous irrationalist and transpersonalist turn.

FICHTE's conception concerning the relation of nation and state is in principle the same as that of the "Historical School".

In the most recent times it has been elaborated in detail in the irrationalist and so-called "pluralistic" sociology of GEORGES GURVITCH [1].

---

[1] Compare his *Sociology of law* (1947), where the nation is characterized as a super-functional, all-inclusive community, whereas the state is only a functional super-structure.

PART III

CONCLUSION AND TRANSITION TO THE DEVELOPMENT OF THE POSITIVE CONTENTS OF THE PHILOSOPHY OF THE COSMONOMIC IDEA

CHAPTER I

THE ANTITHETICAL AND SYNTHETICAL STANDPOINTS IN CHRISTIAN PHILOSOPHICAL THOUGHT

§ 1 - A SYSTEMATIC PRESENTATION OF THE ANTITHESIS BETWEEN THE BASIC STRUCTURE OF THE CHRISTIAN AND THAT OF THE VARIOUS TYPES OF THE HUMANISTIC TRANSCENDENTAL GROUND-IDEA

From the previous part of our inquiry we have seen how the basic antinomy in the transcendental ground-Idea of Humanistic thought develops into polar antitheses within and between the various systems. By continually returning to the common basic structure of this transcendental Idea we have disclosed the deeper unity in the foundations of all Humanistic philosophic thought. It is now evident that the development of this thought into apparently diametrically opposed systems, in fact, is only the development of an internal dialectic of the same religious ground-motive, namely, that of nature and freedom. The latter determines the general framework of the Humanistic transcendental ground-Idea.

In the final analysis the motive of freedom is the religious root of this basic Idea and (as we have shown in Part II, ch. 1 par. 3) by its ambiguity it evokes the opposite motive of the domination of nature. Before the rise of transcendental philosophy, this root still remained hidden under the primacy of the science-ideal, born out of the ideal of personality.

The transcendental trend in Humanistic philosophy was the first to penetrate to the foundation of the science-ideal, viz. the ideal of sovereign personality. It was not before FICHTE that this foundation was openly recognized, which recognition implied a break with KANT's dualistic conception of the transcendental Humanistic ground-Idea. However, the immanence-standpoint itself remained the ultimate obstacle in Humanism for a radical transcendental critique of philosophic thought.

In critical self-reflection Humanistic transcendental philosophy does not attain anything higher than the *Idea* of the sovereign freedom of personality, which it persistently identifies with the religious root of the cosmos. It seeks the transcendent root of reality in particular immanent normative aspects of the cosmos, abstracted and absolutized in its transcendental ground-Idea. It cannot attain the insight that the free personality of man cannot be identified with its moral aesthetic or historical functions.

It is true that in HEGEL the free personality became a dialectical phase in the logical self-unfolding of the all-embracing metaphysical "Idea". But this metaphysical standpoint implied the abandonment of the critical transcendental attitude of Humanistic thought, which FICHTE had preserved, at least in his first period.

In HEGEL's absolute Idealism, philosophical thought once again became identified with absolute divine thought. Not recognizing any critical limits with respect to belief and religion, it intends to solve the religious antinomy of its ground-motive by a theoretical dialectic. The same must be said of SCHELLING's "absolute thought".

The preservation of the critical-transcendental standpoint in Humanistic thought implies the rejection of this absolutizing of theoretical dialectic. But in this case FICHTE's critical moralism seems to be the ultimate degree of critical self-reflection possible in Humanistic immanence-philosophy during its florescence. Therefore, in the last analysis, even in its most profound systems, critical Humanistic transcendental philosophy lacks insight into the final *transcendent* determination of philosophical thought. Even when it thinks it has made the ego its Archimedean point, it has not focused its vision upon the religious root of personality, as the concentration-point of all temporal existence, but upon an hypostatized function of personal existence.

This is the limit of all immanence philosophy. If the thinker would cross over these boundaries, he would see through its religious root in its *apostasy from the true Origin and the full selfhood*. This radical religious criticism, however, is only possible from the Biblical transcendence-standpoint. Humanism cannot surpass its own religious starting-point.

From the Humanistic immanence standpoint it is easy to consider the internal dialectic of Humanistic philosophical thought as an innerly necessary polar course of development, originating from the very nature of philosophical theory, as such.

When Christian philosophy accepts this view-point and permits Humanism to force its method of thinking and problems upon itself, then it is not surprising that the crucial problem of Christian synthetical philosophy, the conflict between philosophical thought and Christian faith, remains forever insoluble.

>Schema of the basic structure and the polar types of the Humanistic cosmonomic Idea, in confrontation with the Christian ground-Idea.

In parts I and II of this volume we have examined in detail the antithesis between the basic structure of the Humanistic transcendental ground-Idea in its various types and that of the Christian one. We will now give a parallel schematical presentation of both ground-Ideas and their different implications. A cursory glance will suffice here to show the impossibility of any real compromise.

A - Basic structure of the Humanistic ground-Idea.

a - Archimedean point
: is the selfhood in its apostasy to the immanence standpoint, in its conscious or unconscious absolutizing of the theoretical attitude of thought (the "cogito" in rationalistic and irrationalistic conceptions).
The insight that theoretical thought has been made absolute is completely lost in that irrationalistic conception of the Archimedean point according to which the cogito is replaced by the "vivo", or the "exsisto", respectively.

b - Religious ground-motive of philosophic thought:
: Nature and freedom. This dialectical motive originated from a secularization of the Christian Idea of creation and freedom, emancipating human personality from its religious dependence upon the God of Revelation.

c - Basic problem:
: The intrinsically contradictory relation between the ideals of science and of personality with their different basic denominators.

d - Polar tensions:
: 1 - The Faustian passion to dominate reality,

manifesting themselves within particular types of antinomies:	expressing itself in the Idea of creative scientific thought, versus the Titanic notion of practical freedom expressing itself in the idea of absolute sovereign personality. 2 - Pessimism versus optimism. 3 - Rationalistic individualism versus irrationalistic trans-personalism. 4 - Universal validity versus individuality, form versus matter, theory versus life. 5 - Speculative metaphysics of the science- or personality-ideal versus scepticism as the result of an unbridled extension of the ideal of science over its own foundations; concept of function versus concept of substance.
e - Idea of origin (1) with hypostatizing of modal laws (rationalism in all variegations, from naturalism under the primacy of the science-ideal to freedom-idealism under the primacy of the ideal of personality, with its hypostatizing of the categorical imperative):	"Reason" as lawgiver. 1 - Under the primacy of the science-ideal: absolutized special scientific thought (mathematical, mechanical, biological, psychological etc.); 2 - Under the primacy of the ideal of personality: transcendental thought in its apriori syntheses, directed towards the Idea of freedom. a) With the dualistic-transcendental type of ground-Idea (KANT): transcendental thought in its relation to the experience of nature, as the formal origin of the laws of nature, and transcendental thought as "practical reason" in its direction toward the Idea of autonomous freedom, as the origin of the norms of moral freedom. (b) With the speculative metaphysical conception of the ideal of science or ideal of personality: "reason" (in a theoretical or in a practical sense) is, in a final hypostatization, identified with the deity.
(2) with hypostatizing of the individual subjectivity (irrationalism in all its variegations, from biologistic vitalism to irrationalistic dialectical spiritualism and historicism):	the dialectical, or the hermeneutical thought which absolutizes the subjective side of reality in one of its modal aspects, and rejects the conception of general laws; in a speculative metaphysical trend of this irrationalistic Idea of origin the ἀρχή is called "spirit" (Geist), with the idealistic, and "Lebenstrom", with the naturalistic and historicist types. Usually "Lebens-philosophie" lacks insight into the theoretical character of its Idea of origin.

f - Idea of the totality of meaning (1) with hypostatizing of modal laws:	1 - Under the primacy of the science-ideal: the mathematical or natural scientific system of functional relations within the absolutized aspect of temporal reality, considered as an infinite task for scientific thought; thereby all other aspects are conceived of as modi of the aspect which has been absolutized in theoretical thought (e.g. the mathematical, mechanical, biological or psychical). In the metaphysical-speculative trend of the science-ideal the Idea of the totality of meaning is grasped in the metaphysical concept of substance, (dualistic, pluralistic and monistic systems have been elaborated in this sense). 2 - Under the primacy of the ideal of personality: the Idea of the "homo noumenon" as a categorical imperative (FICHTE in both of his earlier periods etc.). (a) The dualistic-transcendental ground-Idea of KANT lacks an unequivocal circumscription of the Idea of totality of meaning. The latter should here also be conceived in a dualistic sense. But KANT holds to an agnosticism in respect to the metaphysical background of "nature", the "Ding an sich"! The theoretical Idea of totality is exclusively conceived of in its relation to natural science, but does not refer to the root of reality. The practical Idea of totality is conceived of in the moralistic sense of moral autonomy and freedom. (b) In the modern idealistic value-philosophy the transcendental trend continues to recognize the primacy of the ideal of personality. The Idea of totality is here grasped in the Idea of the "totality of values" (in which theoretical and a-theoretical values are united into a hierarchical order to be established by human personality in autonomous freedom).
(2) with hypostatizing of modal aspects of the individual subjectivity (irrationalism):	Under the primacy of the ideal of personality: (a) in a metaphysical vitalistic trend: the creative "Lebenstrom" (vital stream) with its infinite succession of individual forms (BERGSON). (b) in a psychological trend: the totality of feeling (feeling-philosophy: compare GOETHE: "Gefühl ist alles"!).

(c) in a historicist trend: the historical stream of experience (DILTHEY, SPENGLER etc.);
(d) in an absolute idealist trend: the absolute Idea in its dialectical development through the totality of creative individuality under the common denominator of the absolutized aspect (aesthetic, moral, historical irrationalism, etc.): a formal limitation is possible through the system of transcendental thought forms.

g - Idea of the inter-modal coherence of meaning between the modal aspects of reality
(1) with hypostatizing of modal laws (rationalism):

1 - Under the primacy of the science-ideal: the continuity of the movement of thought within the absolutized aspect of meaning is made the philosophical basic denominator of reality (therefore, different types of this idea of continuity: mathematicism, mechanism, biologism, psychologism): recognition of a relative diversity of meaning as to the other aspects of reality in the continuous coherence of thought.

2 - Under the primacy of the ideal of personality: the continuity of the Idea of freedom which intends to establish a deeper coherence between the different modal aspects by means of a common denominator chosen in a normative aspect of temporal reality; in value-philosophy: the axiological hierarchy of values, established in autonomous freedom.

(2) with hypostatizing of modal aspects of the individual subjectivity (irrationalism):

Under the primacy of the ideal of personality:
(a) In the metaphysical, psychological-vitalistic trend: the continuous coherence of the creative stream of life in which all individual moments permeate each other in a qualitative duration.
(b) In the relativistic-transcendental trend within historicism: the continuous dialectical historical stream of experience (the transcendental "vivo").
(c) In the absolute idealistic trend: the logical-dialectical continuity in the self-development of the absolute Idea in its dialectical passage through the totality of its individual forms in historical time.

Observation concerning section g: the Humanistic Idea of the coherence of the different modal aspects of the cosmos is at every point incompatible with the acceptance of a divine cosmic order which would abolish the sovereignty of reason or of theoretical consciousness.

h - The modal concept of law and subject (1) with hypostatizing of the law-side of the cosmos:	1 - Under the primacy of the science-ideal: A law is a general concept of function, in which the genetic coherence of reality is created by theoretical thought; individual subjectivity is a dependent "exemplary" instance of this law, it is a particular function of it. 2 - Under the primacy of the ideal of personality in the transcendental idealism of KANT: the law in the sense of the universal law of nature is a transcendental thought-form, through which the sensory material of experience is determined; the law in the supersensuous realm of autonomous freedom is a "categorical imperative" identical with the pure will of human personality; all prelogical functions of reality are objects of consciousness, not subject; the only subject is the transcendental consiousness and the "homo noumenon" as lawgiver, respectively. [Objectivity is identified with universally valid law-conformity, and then both are identified with "*Gegenständlichkeit*"]. (a) in the dualistic-transcendental type of cosmonomic Idea (KANT): there is an unbridgeable cleft between two types of laws: laws of nature and norms of freedom; (b) in the monistic-transcendental type, the law of nature is deduced from the ethical norm (FICHTE).
(2) with hypostatizing of modal aspects of the individual subjectivity:	Laws, as mathematical natural scientific concepts, are technical symbols which denaturalize reality in order to dominate nature for the benefit of the biological adaptation of man: (NIETZSCHE, BERGSON, HEIDEGGER, and others). The subject is the creative actual individuality which is not subject to a universally valid law; it has its individual and irrational law in itself, in nature as well as in culture and ethics.

General observation: The preceding schema includes the most prominent types of the transcendental Humanistic ground-Idea in its pure basic structure. The synthesis of the ground-motive of this basic Idea with the ground-motives of the cosmonomic Idea of Greek or scholastic-Christian thought, gives rise to new complications and tensions. This requires a special investigation.

The ideal of science and the ideal of personality as a secularizing of the

Christian Idea of creation and freedom is foreign to pre-Humanistic systems.

B - Basic structure of the Christian transcendental ground-Idea as theoretical expression of the pure Biblical religious ground-motive.

a - Archimedean point
: Christ as the new religious root of the temporal cosmos, from which regenerate mankind receives its spiritual life, in subjection to the central religious meaning of the law: the love of God and one's fellow man with all one's heart.

 Although in this Archimedean point philosophical thought is emancipated from the obscuring influence of sin, yet, in time, it continues to be subject to error, through the activity of the apostate root of existence.

 Christian freedom is only guaranteed in constant subjection to the Word of God which reveals us to ourselves.

 The heart in its pregnant Biblical sense as religious root and centre of the whole of human existence may never be identified with the function of "feeling" or that of "faith", neither is it a complex of functions like the metaphysical concept of soul which is found in Greek and Humanistic metaphysics; it is alien to any dualism between the body (as a complex of natural functions) and the soul (as a complex of psychical and normative functions).

 The heart is not a blind, or dumb witness, even though it transcends the boundary of cosmic time with its temporal diversity of modal aspects, and temporal thought within this diversity. For it is the fulness of our selfhood in which all our temporal functions find their religious concentration and consummation of meaning; "Ego, in Christo regeneratus, etiam cogitans ex Christo vivo", versus the Cartesian "cogito ergo sum", and the irrationalistic "vivo in fluxu continuo, etiam cogitans".

b - Religious attitude in philosophic thought:
: By belonging to Christ the Christian is in a daily fight, also in philosophical thought, against the "flesh", in its Biblical sense, against our apostate ego, which absolutizes the temporal and withdraws it from God.

c - Religious ground-motive:	The Biblical motive of creation, fall into sin, and redemption in Jesus Christ in the communion of the Holy Spirit. This implies the conflict between the Kingdom of God and the kingdom of darkness in the root and the temporal coherence of our cosmos. It implies, too, the recognition of the checking of the disintegrating activity of sin by common grace, because of the regenerate human race that is accepted and hallowed by God in Christ as the Head (particular grace). This basic motive does not lead to antinomies in philosophical thought, but rather to an absolute antithesis with all philosophy which is dominated by apostate ground-motives. It also leads to a thankful recognition of all the gifts and talents that God has left to fallen humanity.
d - Idea of the Origin:	The origin of the Law and of individual subjectivity, according to their religious unity and temporal diversity in the coherence of meaning, is God's holy sovereign creative will. Our cosmos is equally the creation of God with respect to its law- and subject-side; the law is the absolute boundary between God and His creation, that is to say all creatures are by nature subject to the law, God alone is "legibus solutus" (*sed non exlex*, as in nominalism).
e - Idea of the totality of meaning:	The direction of philosophical thought toward Christ as the root and fulness of meaning of the cosmos; Christ fulfilled the law and in Him all subjective individuality is concentrated in its fulness of meaning; nothing in our temporal cosmos is withdrawn from Him, there is no sphere of "indifferent things" [1] (adiaphora).
f - Idea of the coherence in the modal diversity of meaning with respect to the law- and subject-side of temporal reality:	The inter-modal coherence of meaning is not a construction of philosophical thought but is rather sustained by the divine temporal world-order which is also the condition of theoretical thought. The modal aspects of meaning have with respect to each other, as law-spheres, sovereignty in their own sphere. Each aspect points in its own structure toward and is an expression of the temporal coherence of meaning which

---

[1] Compare St. Paul's statement: "Whatsoever ye eat or drink, do to the glory of God."

points beyond itself toward the fulness of meaning in Christ. The cosmic order of time guarantees the *integral* coherence of meaning between the modal aspects. A pre-logical natural reality *"an sich"*, apart from the normative aspects of reality, does not exist.

g - T h e m o d a l c o n- c e p t o f l a w a n d s u b j e c t:
The law in its modal diversity of meaning is the universally valid determination and limitation of the individual subjectivity which is subject to it. The subject is *sujet*, that is subjected to the law in the modal diversity of the law-spheres. There is no law without a subject and vice versa.

§ 2 - THE ATTEMPTS TO SYNTHESIZE CHRISTIAN FAITH WITH IMMANENCE-PHILOSOPHY BEFORE AND AFTER THE REFORMATION

The consequences of the synthetic standpoint for Christian doctrine and for the study of philosophy in patristic and scholastic thought.

As we have seen in part I, Christian philosophy, at its very inception, sought the aid of ancient philosophy even in formulating its transcendental basic Idea.

Consequently, patristic and especially medieval scholastic thought developed into a compromise-philosophy. Both held to a synthetic standpoint with respect to the relation between Christian faith and Greek philosophy. There are, however, two types of this synthetic standpoint, and they should be sharply distinguished from each other. The first deemed it necessary to bind philosophical thought to the Word-revelation, whereas the second proclaimed the autonomy of the "naturalis ratio" in the sphere of natural thought. This latter standpoint prevailed under the influence of the scholastic ground-motive of nature and grace. As soon as Christian scholasticism thought it had found its real starting-point in the naturalis ratio, the increasing decay of Christian philosophy could not be checked.

The Christian religion cannot tolerate any theoretical conception of cosmic reality which is emancipated from the pure Biblical religious ground-motive, because such conceptions are actually dominated by wholly or partly apostate motives and seek in the last analysis a deceitful restpoint for thought. The Christian religion does not tolerate any hypostatization which ascribes independent being to dependent *meaning*. It does not permit these absolutizations, even if they disguise themselves in the garb of a speculative "theologia naturalis". The speculative Aristotelian Idea of the "unmoved mover" as "pure form" is not, as Thomistic scholasticism taught, a natural preamble to the revealed knowledge of God. The self-revelation of God in Christ is, in the full sense of the word, a consuming fire for all apostate speculation in which human ὕβρις thinks it can create God after its own image!

The consequences of the synthetic scholastic standpoint have also left a deep impression in Christian theology. With the penetration of neo-Platonic, Aristotelian, Stoic, and other philosophical motives into the patristic thought and scholasticism of the Middle Ages, immanence-philosophy even infected the Christian doctrine of faith and paved the way for the rise of a speculative "theologia naturalis".

Scholastic philosophy had a particularly devastating influence on Christian theology in respect to the pure Biblical religious conceptions of "soul", "heart", "spirit" and "flesh". The latter were replaced by abstract concepts of dualistic Greek metaphysics, in keeping with the dualistic religious basic motive of form and matter.

> The cleft between "faith" and "thought" is only a cleft between the Christian faith and immanence-philosophy.

As soon as Christian philosophy, under the influence of this metaphysics, began to seek the concentration-point of human existence in "reason", it blocked the way to an intrinsic penetration of philosophy by the Biblical ground-motive. An unbridgeable cleft arose between speculative philosophy and genuine Christian faith. Scholastic theology presents a true *"spectaculum miserabile"* of controversial theological questions, which are completely alien to the Biblical sphere of thought and originate in Greek metaphysics. What had a really Biblical theology to do with such problems as the conflict concerning the primacy of the will or intellect in the "essentia Dei"; what did it have to do with the attempt to support individual immortality of the soul philosophically upon the basis of the realistic Aristotelian view which sought the "principium individuationis" in matter? Of what concern to it was the controversy concerning the question which "parts" of the soul possess immortality (a question which even CALVIN still took seriously in his *Institutio*) ? Of what interest to Biblical theology were the curious problems inherent in "psycho-creationism", i.e. a scholastic transformation of the Platonic doctrine seth forth in the dialogue TIMAEUS and of the Aristotelian doctrine about the origin of the active intellect νοῦς ποιητικός) in the human soul? (according to ARISTOTLE this intellect does not proceed from nature but from outside; according to PLATO the divine Demiurge himself has formed the immortal human *nous* only). Such problems are pseudo-problems and make no sense in a Biblical theology.

The false conception concerning the relationship between Christian revelation and science. Accommodated immanence-philosophy as ancilla theologiae.

The counterpart of the scholastic effort to accommodate immanence-philosophy to Biblical revelation, was the rise of the false idea that Holy Scripture offered certain solutions to scientific problems, at least to the problems discussed in scholastic theology on the basis of Aristotelian metaphysics, physics and psychology. These supposed Biblical theories were, with the full authority of divine revelation, brought into play against scientific investigations which deviated from tradition.

One only needs to recall the position of the Church in the conflict concerning the astronomical theory of COPERNICUS, which position, although historically understandable, was not, therefore, less reprehensible!

The attempt at a synthesis between the Christian religion and immanence-philosophy was a source of confusion which led to intrinsic contradictions; it was equally oppressive to the Christian faith and to honest scientific investigation.

Nothing characterized the scholastic standpoint more sharply than the attempt to employ Scripture in the sense of a scientific "*deus ex machina*".

Because theoretical thought was not itself reformed in a radical Christian sense, scholastic theology as the "*regina scientiarum*", deemed itself called to control the "*scientiae profanae*". Since this theology had accepted an accommodated Aristotelian philosophy, Holy Scripture was itself interpreted in an Aristotelian manner, and could in its turn confirm the Aristotelian theses against the Copernican and, later on, against the Cartesian conceptions.

This was the result of the scholastic notion of philosophy as "ancilla theologiae". The handmaiden was soon to break her chains and became mistress!

The consequence of the Reformation for scientific thought.

The Reformation supplied the first receptacle capable of producing a conception radically different from the scholastic one with respect to the relationship between the Christian religion and scientific thought. As we have seen, the nominalism of late scholasticism demolished every bridge between the Christian faith and Greek metaphysics.

The rise of the modern Humanistic life- and world-view, which preceded the Reformation, placed sharply before the eyes of the Reformers an inescapable dilemma. They were confronted with the antithesis between the attitude of the Christian religion with respect to temporal life and the secularization of this attitude in the Humanistic ideal of personality.

A return to the medieval synthetic standpoint in order to oppose Humanism with the aid of a scholastical philosophy must necessarily contradict the very nature and spirit of the Reformation. For the latter could show no other credential than its claim to a pure Biblical conception of Christian doctrine. This must imply a return to the integral and radical ground-motive of Holy Scripture, as the only religious motive of its theological and philosophical thought and of its whole life- and world-view. By virtue of this religious ground-motive the Reformation should have led to an inner reformation of philosophical thought.

The fact that this did not directly happen, but that after an original promising start, Protestantism fell back upon the scholastic compromise-standpoint, can only be explained as an after-effect of a very old tradition in Christian thought. This tradition found fertile soil, especially in Lutheranism, and, under the influence of MELANCHTON, proceeded to infect also the Calvinistic idea of science. In the final analysis it was the dialectical scholastic motive of nature and grace that in this way kept its influence on the philosophical standpoint of orthodox Protestantism.

The after-effect of the nominalistic dualism in LUTHER's spiritualistic distinction between the Law and the Gospel.

LUTHER confessed the central significance of God's Sovereignty in the Biblical sense. He possessed the insight that divine grace in Christ must intrinsically penetrate temporal life in all spheres. Yet, in spite of this, he never fully escaped the nominalistic influence of the Occamist University of Erfurt and of his later studies in an Augustinian monastery (*"Ich bin von Ockam's Schule"*). This influence is evident from his dualistic conception of the relation between the Law and the Gospel. LUTHER considered a person in the sinful state to be bound to temporal ordinances. A Christian person in the state of grace, on the contrary, is not intrinsically subject to the Divine Law, but lives in evangelical freedom according to love. In "this earthly valley of tears" he only bows to ordinances out of obedience to the will of God with respect to the natural state of sin. And, by so doing he tries to penetrate them with the spirit of Christian love. But intrinsically this spirit contradicts the severity of the Law. This dualism between the Law and the Gospel must, with respect to the relationship between the Christian religion and philosophy, again lead to the nominalistic separation of faith and science, with the usual Occamistic depreciation of the latter. At this point we can observe the after-effect of the scholastic nature-grace-motive in its antithetical Occamistic conception. We find, to be sure, in LUTHER a fulminating judgment against ARISTOTLE and the medieval scholastic philosophy; we find in him a passionate opposition to the Biblical Humanism which in Germany and Holland (ERASMUS) tried to effect a new synthesis between the Christian faith and the spirit of Greco-Roman antiquity. But, nowhere do we discover the conviction that the religious root of the Reformation requires a radical reformation of philosophy itself.

LUTHER never had an inner contact with the Humanistic spirit. In his attitude toward human knowledge he remained a prisoner to the medieval spirit of Occamism. The spiritualistic trend in his character was strongly nurtured by the German mysticism of ECKHART and by the Augustinian-Franciscan spirit. Moreover, his *"Welt-offenheit"*, which caused him to reject the monastic ideal, continued to be broken by a dualism, unexplainable in terms of the Biblical doctrine concerning the corruption of nature due to the fall. LUTHER never wrested himself loose from a nominalistic dualism in his view of the church. He considered the regulation of the "visible church" to be a matter of relative indifference and sought support from the governing prince for an ecclesiastical reformation. In addition, this dualism displayed itself in his subsequently abandoned distinction between official and personal morality. His attitude towards scientific thought continued to be burdened in the same manner with the dualistic prejudice concerning the relation of faith and natural reason.

One can recognize this without in any way being deficient in love and appreciation for the great reformer. The recognition of his faults does not obliterate the fact that LUTHER's Biblical faith became the impulse to a continuous reformation of his thought and the cause of his later abandonment of many previous errors.

The scholastic philosophy of MELANCHTON. MELANCHTON and LEIBNIZ.

MELANCHTON did have close literary contact with German and Dutch Humanism, without having any affinity with the new ideal of personality. When he undertook the gigantic task of establishing a relation between the Reformation and modern science, he fell back upon the scholastic standpoint of accommodation.

Throughout the next centuries the influence of MELANCHTON was therefore instrumental in preventing the development of a philosophy consistent with the spirit of the Reformation. This influence was enormous. It dominated philosophic instruction at the Protestant universities in Germany and Holland, until the spirit of the "Aufklärung" penetrated the latter and Protestant theology itself fell a victim to its alliance with MELANCHTON's philosophical scholasticism.

LEIBNIZ, too, the genius of the German "Aufklärung", grew up in this school-philosophy, and his own thinking is indebted to it for various motives [1]. But we have seen how these scholastic motives were transformed by him in a rationalistic Humanistic sense.

The scholastic tradition was not beneficial to the Reformation. Accommodated immanence-philosophy, temporarily clothed in pious garments, was soon to cast aside its sober pastoral garb and display its true character!

MELANCHTON, the *"praeceptor Germaniae"*, grew up in a circle of German humanists. He admired AGRICOLA, and, at an early age, because of his close connection with his second cousin, REUCHLIN, he enjoyed the friendship of ERASMUS and WILLIBALD PIRKHEIMER. In August, 1518, at the age of twenty one, he was

---

[1] Cf. E. WEBER, *Die philosophische Scholastik des deutschen Protestantismus im Zeitalter der Orthodoxie*, [*Philosophical Scholasticism of German Protestantism in the Age of Orthodoxy*], Abh. zur Phil. und ihrer Geschichte, hrg. von R. Falckenberg, 1e Heft 1907.

appointed professor of Greek at the University of Wittenberg. His inaugural address, *De corrigendis adolescentiae studiis*, was a vigorous attack upon the ruling scholastic barbarisms and in general upon the mutilation of the Greek and Latin languages and philosophy in the era of the "seraphic and cherubic doctors". But this iron-clad declaration of war with respect to the scholastic corruption of the Classics was only an expression of a philological humanism. It did not signify a break with the religious starting-point of scholastic thought.

The reformation of academic study which MELANCHTON promised remained within the framework of the scholastic encyclopaedia; the subjects of the old trivium (grammar, dialectic and rhetoric) formed its preparatory foundation.

The chief aim of MELANCHTON was to reform dialectic after the fashion of AGRICOLA in the nominalistic sense of an art of reasoning. In addition he wished to endow the youth with an excellent philological humanistic [1] training, so that they would be able to read ancient philosophers and poets in the original. It is the spirit of AGRICOLA and ERASMUS that inspired the young MELANCHTON. The program that he proposed in his inaugural address only aimed at the type of philological and at the same time moral and ecclesiastical reform that would be in accord with the desires of these men. The reform-program of the latter, although it possessed a Christian-Stoical coloration, was actually preponderantly motivated by the spirit of Humanistic nominalism. They aimed at an accommodation of the Humanistic ideal of personality to the program of a supposedly "simple, Biblical Christianity". Yet their synthesis between Humanism and Christianity only amounted to a "humanizing" of the radical Christian doctrine by laying stress upon the moral view-point.

LUTHER differed very much from MELANCHTON in character and disposition. The electrifying contact with the passionate champion of faith raised in MELANCHTON the antithetical spirit of the Reformation.

---

[1] The adjective "humanistic" does not imply here the religious meaning of the term "Humanism" as we used it in our transcendental critique of Humanistic thought. Here it is only related to the study of the "humaniora". Therefore, it is not written with a capital. Nevertheless, we shall see, that even the conception of this "humanistic" studies was penetrated by a Humanist spirit.

Melanchton did not break radically with immanence-philosophy.

But a penetrating examination makes it clear that even during this period MELANCHTON did not break radically with immanence-philosophy. In essence, his opposition was only directed against speculative realistic metaphysics, with its doctrine of universalia, its "formalitates", its theory of the infinite, and so on. Even at this time MELANCHTON tenaciously retained the nominalistic dialectic. Meanwhile, his apostasy from the ideals of humanism caused a break with his sponsor REUCHLIN, and ERASMUS turned away from him in disappointment. After this break occurred, MELANCHTON's old love for antiquity again awoke within him and a new phase in his development began.

This period commenced in 1536 when he brought about a definitive synthesis between the Lutheran faith and a nominalistically interpreted Aristotelian philosophy. We observed that even in his short antithetical period MELANCHTON never abandoned the nominalistic dialectic derived from AGRICOLA. This dialectical method, which he had applied to Lutheran doctrine, intrinsically necessitated his return to ancient immanence-philosophy. This is substantiated by the unsuspected testimony of HEINRICH MAIER in his important study of MELANCHTON's philosophy [1].

Why a radical Christian philosophy can only develop in the line of CALVIN's religious starting-point.

CALVIN also passed through an early Humanistic period during

---

[1] *Philipp Melanchton als Philosoph* (in *An der Grenze der Philosophie*, Tübingen 1909, S. 47), where he writes: "Die humanistische Erudition bleibt auch damals Bildungsideal. Und in das Gewand der Eloquenz werden auch die neuen Glaubensgedanken gekleidet. Die lehrhafte Bearbeitung des religiösen Stoffs erfolgt in den Formen und mit den Mitteln der humanistischen Methodik. Aber es ist klar, dasz diese Formen aufs engste mit der Weltanschauung verbunden sind, auf der die Realphilosophie ruht... So treibt die Entwicklung mit immanenter Notwendigkeit zur Restitution der Physik, Metaphysik und Ethik" (i.e. of ARISTOTLE, interpreted in a nominalistic sense). ["In this period too the humanistic erudition remains the ideal of education. And also the new Ideas of faith were clothed in the garments of eloquence. The didactic elaboration of the religious material occurs in the forms and with the means of humanistic methodology. But it is evident, that these forms are closely connected with the world- and life-view on which the material philosophy rests... So the development with an inner necessity leads to the restitution of the" (nominalistically interpreted Aristotelian) "physics, metaphysics and ethics."]

which he wrote his well-known commentary on SENECA's *De Clementia*. But when he reached the turning-point of his life, he broke radically with the nominalistic dualism that more or less continued to flourish within LUTHER's world of thought and that was dominated by the scholastic ground-motive of nature and grace.

In CALVIN's Biblical view-point this scholastic motive is eliminated. He maintained that the true nature of man cannot be opposed to grace. Nature is in its root corrupted by the fall, and is only restored or (as CALVIN more pregnantly states) "renewed" by God's grace in Jesus Christ[1]. This was also AUGUSTINE's conception. The Bible does not permit any view of nature, in distinction to grace, in which human reason in its apostasy from God, becomes the main stay of a *"philosophia et theologia naturalis"*. It does not sanction any view in which the νοῦς τῆς σαρκός (that is to say, the intellect which is apostate from Christ in the sense of thinking according to the "flesh") is declared to be sovereign.

God's revelation must take hold of the heart, the root of our entire existence, that we may "stand in the truth". CALVIN hits rationalistic scholasticism at the root of its apostasy from a Christian attitude towards knowledge, when he writes: *"Nec satis fuerit mentem esse Dei spiritu illuminatam, nisi et eius virtute cor obfirmetur ac fulciatur. In quo tota terra Scholastici aberrant, qui in fidei consideratione nudum ac simplicem ex notitia assensum aripiunt, praeterita cordis fiducia et securitate"* [2].

---

[1] See *Institutio religionis Christianae* (1559), II, 1, 9: "Unde sequitur partem illam, in qua refulget animae praestantia et nobilitas, non modo vulneratam esse, sed ita corruptam, ut non modo sanari, sed novam prope naturam induere opus habeat." ["From this it follows that that part upon which shines the excellence and nobility of the soul, not only is wounded, but as much corrupted that it not only needed to be healed, but nearly to assume a new nature."]. Also see II, 1, 6, where the radical character of sin is sharply set forth.

[2] "And it will not have been sufficient that the mind is illuminated by the Spirit of God, unless also by its virtue the heart is made firm and is strenghtened. In this matter the scholastics completely deviate, which in a superficial way conceive the motive of faith as a mere and simple assent by virtue of the understanding, whereas the confidence and surety of the heart is completely neglected." This statement only gives expression to the pure Biblical conception which considers knowledge — and in the first place knowledge furnished by faith — to be rooted in the heart from

CALVIN radically rejected the speculative natural theology. He called it an "audacious curiosity" of human reason that seeks to intrude upon the "essentiae Dei", which we can never fathom, but can only worship [1]. Again and again he warned against the *vacua et meteorica speculatio* on God's essence apart from His revelation in His Word [2]. CALVIN expressed the true critical religious attitude concerning knowledge of God, an attitude grounded in the humble insight into the essential boundary between the Creator and the creation, in timidity with respect to the deep mystery of God's majesty.

The scholastic motive of nature and grace is not found in CALVIN's thought, nor is there any trace of the spiritualistic contrast between the divine Law and the Gospel, found in LUTHER. God's divine Majesty does not tolerate the blotting out of

---

which proceed the issues of life. This is characteristically misunderstood by Roman Catholics as "sentimentalism". In 1931 A. J. M. CORNELISSEN wrote a meritorious comparative study concerning the *Doctrine of the State of "Calvin and Rousseau"*. In this thesis which he defended at the Roman Catholic University of Nijmegen, he wrote (page 25): "If faith does neither require a praeambula furnished by reason, but the reverse, rational knowledge is strengthened by faith, then, if one is consistent, the act of super-natural "knowing" is only an act of feeling. CALVIN drew this conclusion and thus fell into sentimentalism."

Under the influence of Thomistic-Aristotelian epistemology the insight into what the Bible means by the "heart", as the religious centre of life, has been so completely lost sight of that there remains nothing else to do but identify it with the temporal function of feeling and then place it in opposition to theoretical thought.

[1] *Inst.* I, 5, 9: "Unde intelligimus hanc esse rectissimam Dei quaerendi viam et aptissimam ordinem; non ut audaci curiositate penetrare tentemus ad excutiendam eius essentiam, quae adoranda potius est quam scrupulosius disquirenda; sed ut illum in suis operibus contemplemur, quibus se propinquum nobis familiaremque reddit ac quodammodo communicat." ["Hence we understand, that this is the most correct way and appropriate order to seek God; not that in an audacious curiosity we try to penetrate into an examination of His essence, which is rather to be adored than scrupulously to be examined; but that we contemplate Him in His works by which He comes near to us, makes Himself familiar to us and in some way communicates Himself."]

[2] *Ibid.* I, 10, 2: "deinde commemorari eius virtutes quibus nobis describitur non quis sit apud se, sed qualis erga nos; ut ista eius agnitio vivo magis sensu, quam vacua et meteorica speculatione constet." ["Moreover we must remember His virtues by which is described to us not what He is in Himself, but how He is in respect to us; in order that this knowledge about Him may rather consist in a lively consciousness than in a void and meteoric speculation."]

the boundary between the Creator and the creation. In view of this boundary, LUTHER's elevation of Christian liberty beyond the limits of the lex divina cannot be accepted.

The cosmonomic Idea of CALVIN *versus the Aristotelian-Thomistic one.*

We have already referred to one of CALVIN's statements that occurs several times in his writings: *"Deus legibus solutus est"* [1]. This statement necessarily implies that "all of the creation is subject to the Law."

Christ has freed us from the "law of sin" and from the Jewish ceremonial law. But the cosmic law, in its religious fulness and temporal diversity of meaning, is not a burdensome yoke imposed upon us because of sin, but it is a blessing in Christ. Without its determination and limitation, the subject would sink away into chaos. Therefore, CALVIN recognized the intrinsic subjection of the Christian to the decalogue, and did not see any intrinsic antinomy between the central commandment of love as the religious root of God's ordinances, and the juridical or economic law-spheres, or the inner structural law of the state. Anabaptists lost sight of the religious root of the temporal laws, and consequently placed the Sermon on the Mount, with its doctrine of love, in opposition to civil ordinances. CALVIN strongly opposed this error. He proceeded from the radical religious unity of all temporal divine regulations and could therefore radically combat each absolutization of a temporal aspect of the full Law of God, as well as every spiritualistic revolution against the state and its legal order: "Christo non est institutum legem aut laxare aut restringere, sed ad veram ac germanicam

---

[1] Cf. *De aeterna praedestinatione* (1552) C.R. 36, 361: "Non vero commentum illud recipio, Deum quia lege solutus sit quidquid agat reprehensione vacare. Deum enim exlegem qui facit, maxima cum gloriae suae parte spoliat, quia rectitudinem eius ac iustitiam sepelit. Non quod legi subiectus sit Deus, nisi quatenus ipse sibi lex est." ["I truly do not acccept that device that God's acts are exempt from reprehension because He is not bound to the Law. For he who renders God "exlex", deprives Him of the principal part of His glory, because he annuls His equity and justice. Not that God should be subjected to the Law, *unless in so far as He is a law to Himself.*"]

Cf. *Comm. in Mosis libros* V (1563) C.R. 52, 49, 131: "atque ideo legibus solutus est, quia ipse, sibi et omnibus lex est," ["and therefore He is above the laws, because He is the Law to Himself and to everything."] (Contra the nominalistic *ex-lex*!).

intelligentiam reducere, quae falsis scribarum et Pharisaeorum commentis valde depravata fuerant" [1].

This fundamental Idea of the Divine Law does not go with a falling back upon the Aristotelian-Thomistic conception of the "lex naturalis". For this latter proceeds from the religious form-matter motive of Greek thought, and therefore necessarily conflicts with the Biblical conception. The speculative Idea of the "lex aeterna" provides the foundation for the speculative "lex naturalis" with its teleological order of "substantial forms". In this construction human reason thinks it can prescribe what is law to God. And in the final analysis the Aristotelian conception of the world-order is deified, because in the Idea of the lex aeterna it is identified with the "rational essence" of God. In opposition to it, the Reformation was forced to preach the doctrine of Christian liberty. In this, both CALVIN and LUTHER were prominent, but CALVIN succeeded in enunciating a purer position. In his conception of the Divine Law, he lost nothing of the Biblical Idea of freedom in Christ. LUTHER did not escape falling into a spiritualistic antinomianism against which must be proclaimed the Biblical conception of the Divine Law, grounded in the central confession of God's sovereignty as Creator. This was necessary for the sake of maintaining the Biblical ground-motive of the Reformation.

<blockquote>CALVIN's Idea of the Law versus BRUNNER's irrationalistic and dualistic standpoint.</blockquote>

This Biblical view of Law is at the present time rejected by EMIL BRUNNER. He seeks to replace it by an irrationalistic ethics of love which must break through the temporal divine ordinances. For, according to him, the latter are not the true will of God [2]. In a typically spiritualistic fashion, BRUNNER fulminates against the Idea of a Christian science, philosophy, culture,

---

[1] *Inst.* II, 8, 26. ["Christ has not received the mandate to loosen or to unbind the Law, but rather to restore the true and pure understanding of its commands which had been badly deformed by the false devices of the Scribes and the Pharisees."]

[2] See *Das Gebot und die Ordnungen* (1932) ["The Commandment and the Ordinances"], p. 108 and following, in connection with BRUNNER's treatment of *Das Einmalige und der Existenzcharakter* in *Blätter f. deutsche Philosophie* (1929). The command of love, as "*Gebot des Stunde*" or "*des Augenblicks*" (a typically irrationalistic expression) is here opposed to the law in temporal ordinances.

politics, etc. As to philosophy this is indicative of a new attempt to effect a compromise with the immanence standpoint (namely, with Kantianism and modern irrationalistic existentialism). This compromise does not proceed from the spirit of CALVIN. It is rather born from LUTHER's dualism and cannot have a fruitful future.

BRUNNER attempts to accommodate the after-effect of the Lutheran nominalistic dualism between "nature" and "grace" to CALVIN's view of the Law. But just as this dualism is incompatible with the Biblical ground-motive, it is also irreconcilable with CALVIN's standpoint. The Word of God reveals to us the root of temporal existence; within this root it lays bare the unbridgeable cleft between the Kingdom of Christ and the Kingdom of darkness; it drives us with inexorable seriousness to an "either-or".

If a Christian philosophy, Christian jurisprudence, politics, art etc. are not possible, then these spheres of temporal life are withdrawn from Christ. Then once again the un-Biblical dualism between "nature" and "grace" or between the Law and the Gospel must be accepted, and once again, in order to bridge the dualism, the path of scholastic accommodation must be followed.

In this case one may reject the synthesis of Christian faith with the rationalistic cosmonomic Idea of ARISTOTLE or of the Stoics, but modern Humanistic irrationalism or Criticism are not an iota more Christian.

For, by following this way one arrives with BRUNNER at a depreciation of certain aspects of reality. BRUNNER absolutizes love at the expence of justice; he irrationalistically misinterprets the central religious commandment of love. As a consequence of his dialectical standpoint he treats the Idea of justice in a neo-Kantian fashion [1]: it is denatured to a "purely formal value". BRUNNER sets forth a thesis which denies the fulness of meaning of the Cross; he holds that complete justice is in itself a contradiction and that love, although it must pass through formal

---

[1] See *Das Gebot und die Ordnungen* ("The Commandment and the ordinances"), S. 675, where it is said of the Critical Kantian conception of the Idea of juridical order, that it "*erfahrungsgemäsz und aus guten Grunden nur von solchen Juristen verstanden wird, die mit der reformatorischen Glaubenstradition in Zusammenhang stehen*" (for example, STAMMLER and BURCKHARDT) ["that, according to experience and for good reasons, it is only understood by such jurists who stand in connection with the tradition of faith of the Reformation"]. Thus the synthesis with Kantian immanence-philosophy is completed.

justice, nevertheless does abrogate the latter [1]. If we follow BRUNNER along the path of synthesis, we must also tumble into the same pitfall. In this respect Christian philosophy has no more choice than has immanence-philosophy.

The synthesis with ancient immanence-philosophy led Christian thought into complicated antinomies; the synthesis with Humanistic immanence-philosophy does the same. It not only involves Christian thought in the basic antinomy between "nature" and "freedom", but above all it leads to a radical collision between the hidden apostate ground-motive of this philosophical thought and the central Biblical motive of the Christian religion. Dialectical theology is only the expression of the religious dialectic born out of this collision.

---

[1] See *Das Gebot und die Ordnungen*, S. 436: "Gerade vom Christlichen Glauben aus gibt es keine irgendwie faszbare Idee der volkommenen Gerechtigkeit. Denn Gerechtigkeit ist an sich unvollkommen." ["From the Chritian faith itself there cannot in any conceivable way proceed an Idea of perfect justice. For justice is in itself imperfect."] I would like to suggest that justice "an sich" does not exist but is a meaningless absolutization. The same is true of love "an sich". Cf. p. 437: "Die Liebe ist konkret, persönlich, nicht-vorausgewuszt, nicht allgemein, nicht gesetzlich. Die Gerechtigkeit ist gerade allgemein gesetzlich, vorausgewuszt, unpersönlich-sachlich, abstrakt, rational." ["Love is concrete, personal, not foreknown, not generalizing, not legal. Justice, on the contrary, is general, legal, foreknown, impersonal-real, abstract, rational."] From the Biblical point of view our answer is simply that the opinion of BRUNNER is not in keeping with the Biblical conception of the Law but stems from a semi-Humanistic point of view. A Christian must learn to bow before God's majesty and justice, which is not different from His love. God is the *origin and original unity* of all modal aspects of human experience which are to be distinguished only in the temporal order, but coincide in their religious root and a fortiori in their Divine Origin.

In his later work *Gerechtigkeit* (1943), BRUNNER did not essentially change his earlier position. He now spoke of "the justice of faith" in contradistinction to the justice in the sphere of ordinances, but the former *does not have any intrinsic connection* with the latter. "Justice of faith" is identical with the Love of the Gospel and it abolishes justice in the sense of retribution. And the latter is also true of Divine Justice. Divine Justice is diametrically opposed to earthly justice in the sphere of ordinances. Although earthly ordinances and justice oppose the *command of love*, yet the former aid in the life of love. This conception is typically Lutheran. In addition compare REINHOLD NIEBUHR, *The Principles of Ethics*, chap. V and VI and the *Nature and Destiny of Man* II, chap. IX. If earthly justice is *diametrically opposed* to Divine Justice, and nevertheless the former belongs to the sphere of Divine ordinances, there is accepted a dialectical dualism in the Divine Will which betrays the influence of the dialectical ground-motive of nature and grace.

When we consider this whole situation and recall that CALVIN was the first to formulate a purely Biblical conception of the lex in its origin, radical religious unity and temporal diversity, we arrive at the conclusion that a real reformation of philosophic thought cannot historically proceed from LUTHER but only from CALVIN's point of departure.

Do not misunderstand this conclusion. The reformation of philosophy in a Christian sense does not signify the inauguration of a new school-philosophy such as Thomism which binds itself to the authority of a philosophical system and thinker. It does not signify the elevation of CALVIN to a *pater angelicus* of reformed philosophical thought. It does not mean, that we will seek a philosophical system in CALVIN that is not there. It does mean, however, that we will relate philosophical thought in its entire foundation, starting-point, and transcendental direction, to the new root of our cosmos in Christ. We will reject every philosophical standpoint that leans upon the "naturalis ratio" as a supposed self-sufficient Archimedean point. Our aim is an inner reform of thought which is born from the living power of God's Word, and not from an abstract and static principle of reason. Therefore, in the development of a Christian philosophy which is actually stimulated by the Biblical ground-motive of the Reformation, there must be a constant striving after the reformation of philosophical thought. This precludes the canonizing of a philosophical system.

Christian philosophical thought cannot be led by a spiritualistic mysticism of faith that fancies itself to be elevated above Divine law. It can only be led by the vivifying spirit of God's Word. In spite of the fact that the temporal cosmos is shattered by sin, since God has maintained its structural order, and since the fulness of meaning is not to be found in time; it is possible to accept the cosmos, in its many-sided richness of meaning, as God's creation, concentrated in its new religious root: Jesus Christ.

The Christian transcendental ground-Idea embraces the religious antithesis [1] between the apostasy of nature and its destiny according to creation: it does not seek a dialectical synthesis after the fashion of "natura praeambula gratiae". But it re-

---

[1] In Vol. II we shall show more completely that this is something entirely different from a "cult of antinomies" as CORNELISSEN, apparently under the influence of dialectical theology, misinterprets CALVIN's thought.

cognizes in "common grace" a counter force against the destructive work of sin in the cosmos, because the antithesis between sin and creation is *really* abrogated by the redemption in Jesus Christ.

> There is no dualism between "gratia communis" and "gratia particularis".

Common grace may not be dualistically opposed to particular grace. If this is done, the dualistic motive of nature and grace is permitted to enter reformed thought under another name. CALVIN himself subordinated "gratia communis" to "gratia particularis" and to "the honour and glory of God" [1].

Common grace is meaningless without Christ as the root and head of the regenerated human race. Meaningless without Him, because it only manifests itself in the temporal cosmos. And the latter is necessarily related to its religious root and does not have any existence apart from it. Gratia communis is grace shown to mankind as a whole, which is regenerate in its new root Jesus Christ, but has not yet been loosened from its old apostate root. This is the meaning of JESUS' parable of the tares among the wheat. The wheat and the tares must grow together until the harvest.

For the present, I cannot explain this point any further, but, must postpone its development until we treat the *opening process* in the cosmos in the general theory of modal law-spheres in Vol. II.

> ABRAHAM KUYPER and his often misunderstood Idea of antithesis.

The philosophy of the cosmonomic Idea, from the beginning of its development to its first systematic expression in this work, can only be understood as the fruit of the Calvinistic awakening in Holland since the last decades of the XIX century, a movement which was led by ABRAHAM KUYPER.

But, this philosophy is not to be understood as the exclusive thought of a small *clique of Calvinists*. On the contrary, according to its basis, by reason of its transcendental ground-Idea, it includes within its range all of Christian thought, as such.

No Christian can escape the dilemma that it sets forth, if he really takes seriously the universality of the Kingship of Christ

---

[1] Compare *Inst.* I, 17, 7 and 11; I, 5, 14; II, 2, 16; III, 3, 25; III, 20, 15 and 24, 2.

and the central confession of God's sovereignty over the whole cosmos as Creator. He cannot avoid its impact unless he seeks to escape by employing such idle words as "Christian freedom" requiring the "freedom of thought". Idle words, indeed, because "Christian freedom" cannot imply a freedom in thought which is stimulated by an anti-Christian ground-motive!

It is in this universal sense that we must understand KUYPER's Idea of the religious antithesis in life and thought. Many peace-loving Christians have made this very point the victim of numerous misunderstandings. They do not recognize that this antithesis does not draw a line of *personal* classification but a line of division according to fundamental principles in the world, a line of division which passes transversely through the existence of every Christian personality. This antithesis is not a human invention, but is a great blessing from God. By it He keeps His fallen creation from perishing. To deny this is to deny Christ and His work in the world.

Why I reject the term "Calvinistic philosophy".

It may be clear from the preceding that I definitely reject the term *"Calvinistic"* as being appropriate to name the *Philosophy of the Cosmonomic Idea*. I reject the term Calvinistic, even though I fully acknowledge that this philosophy was the fruit of the Calvinistic re-awakening in the Netherlands [1].

Because of its religious basic motive and its transcendental ground-Idea, however, this philosophy deserves to be called *Christian philosophy* without any further qualification. For it would be impossible for an intrinsically Christian philosophy to be based on any other ground-motive than the integral and radical one of Holy Scripture which does not depend on man.

Thomistic philosophy has constantly rejected the name "Christian". It is true that certain neo-Thomists such as GILSON and MARITAIN have begun to depart from this tradition. But this departure is more readily explained as the result of an Augustinian rather than a Thomistic influence.

We can speak of a re-formed Christian philosophy in contrast to a particular neo-scholastic-Christian one, which has aban-

---

[1] Therefore, I regret the fact that the philosophical association, which was formed in Holland [after the appearance of the Dutch edition of this work], chose the name "The Association for Calvinistic Philosophy." But I will give due allowance for the fact that I, myself, in an earlier stage of my development, called my philosophy "Calvinistic".

doned the dogma concerning the self-sufficiency of philosophic thought.

It is permitted to do so only if we mean that in the former the Biblical ground-motive of the Christian religion is operative in an inner reformation of philosophic thought, whereas the latter remains bound to the scholastic ground-motive of nature and grace and within this cadre only seeks to break through the boundaries between the natural and the super-natural spheres in order to show the insufficiency of natural philosophical thought in respect to the Christian faith.

The philosophy of the Cosmonomic Idea and Blondelism.

One of the neo-scholastic trends of thought which follow this latter way has entirely broken with Thomism. It is born out of French spiritualism founded by MAINE DE BIRAN and developed in an increasingly antirationalist sense by RAVAISSON, LACHELIER, BOUTROUX and others. It wants to continue the Augustinian tradition in Christian thought. But by virtue of the dialectical ground-motive of nature and grace it cannot permit itself to return to the authentic Augustinian conception which rejected in a *radical sense* the autonomy of philosophical thought, but made philosophy the handmaid of Christian theology.

The main representative of this neo-scholastic Christian philosophy, MAURICE BLONDEL, a disciple of the neo-scholastic thinker OLLÉ LAPRUNE, starts with the immanence-standpoint in philosophy in order to show the deficiency of philosophic thought by means of an irrationalistic and activistic metaphysical interpretation of thought and being. This interpretation was strongly inspired by the Leibnizian Idea of the immanence of the universe in the representations of every metaphysical being, and by the irrationalist and universalistic turn which this latter conception had taken in SCHELLING's "concrete and absolute thought", and later on in BERGSON's philosophy of life. It was also inspired by the idea of MALEBRANCHE concerning a "visio omnium rerum in Deo". But by no means can BLONDEL's Christian philosophy be considered as an intrinsically *reformed* mode of thought. It lacks in principle a transcendental critique of philosophical thought as such. And its inner dialectical character is clearly shown by the fact that this Roman-Catholic thinker intends to break through the immanence-standpoint and to arrive at a Christian view by means of an activistic, irrationalist and universalistic metaphysics which in principle is ruled by the Humanistic ground-motive, in its accommodation to the scholastic motive of nature and grace [1].

The opinion of FERDINAND SASSEN, professor of philosophy at the University of Leyden, that there is an inner connection between the philosophy of the cosmonomic Idea and BLONDEL's voluntarism [2], consequently rests upon a misunderstanding.

The significance of the philosophy of the cosmonomic Idea for a philosophic contact between the different schools.

The significance of the philosophy of the cosmonomic Idea may not be limited to Christian thought as such. For in its transcendental critique this philosophy has raised new problems, which must be considered by every philosophy irrespective of its starting-point. Moreover, it has approached each philosophical system from the standpoint of its own ground-motive and deepest pre-suppositions. Therefore, as we have shown in the Prolegomena, this philosophy has opened the way for a better mutual understanding of the various philosophic trends. Under the influence of the dogma of the autonomy of theoretical thought the various schools had isolated themselves in a dogmatic exclusivism and had propagated their supra-theoretical *prejudices* as theoretical axioms.

The significance of the philosophy of the cosmonomic Idea is not at all negative for other philosophic schools. It has a positive contribution to make. In the next two volumes I have to show the importance of its theory of the modal structures of the aspects, and of its theory about the structures of individuality and the *enkaptic interlacements* between the latter. I have to show that these two theories disclose states of affairs which hitherto had not

---

[1] This dialectical synthesizing of the Humanist and the scholastic ground-motives in BLONDEL's thought is clearly explained by his disciple HENRY DUMÉRY in his treatise *Blondel et la philosophie contemporaine* (Études Blondéliennes, 2, 1952, p. 71 ff.). See my two lectures entitled *Le problème de la philosophie chrétienne. Une confrontation de la conception Blondélienne et de l'idée nouvelle concernant une réformation de la pensée philosophique en Hollande,* delivered at the University of Aix en Provence-Marseille (May 1953), which will be published in the quarterly review "Philosophia Reformata" of this year.

[2] See F. SASSEN, *Philosophy of the present time* (Wijsbegeerte van dezen tijd), 2nd ed., sect. V § 2.

been subjected to philosophical examination. These "states of affairs" belong to the structure of empirical reality and we have observed in the Prolegomena that, just as the laws of theoretical thought, they are the same for every philosophical standpoint. The only question is: Which philosophy is in a position to give a satisfactory theoretical explanation of these data? We have established in the Prolegomena, that no single philosophy may claim to have a monopoly. Each philosophy may strive in a noble competitive manner to work at a common task. But this cooperation can only take place on one condition. The schools of immanence-philosophy must be ready to abandon their theoretical dogmatism and they must take seriously the transcendental critique of philosophic thought set forth in our *Prolegomena* [1].

What we have said is in the first place applicable to our theoretical view of empirical reality. Because of the inner structure of theoretical thought our view of empirical reality is dependent upon the transcendental ground-Idea which directs our philosophic inquiry. And the content of every ground-Idea is determined by super-theoretical motives. If this is not acknowledged, then any philosophic exchange of Ideas is condemned to failure in advance. Philosophical discussion is possible between schools which do not have the same starting-point, if, and only if, a sharp distinction is made between authentic theoretical judgments (concerning which philosophic discussion is possible) and the necessary *pre-theoretical prejudices* which lie at the foundation of such theoretical judgments.

Philosophical discussion about the theoretical judgments is to be based on the undeniable states of affairs in the structures of theoretical thought and of empirical reality which precede all *theoretical interpretation* and are to be established with ἐποχή of the latter. They are to be confronted with the different philosophical views in order to investigate whether these views, each from their own super-theoretical starting-point, are able to account for them in a satisfactory way.

---

[1] I am happy to be able to say, that during recent years, the critical significance of this philosophy has been better understood in Holland, both in Thomistic and Humanistic circles. However, I do not want to pretend, that this is always the case.

CHAPTER II

THE SYSTEMATIC PLAN OF OUR FURTHER INVESTIGATIONS AND A CLOSER EXAMINATION OF THE RELATION OF THE PHILOSOPHY OF THE COSMONOMIC IDEA TO THE SPECIAL SCIENCES

§ 1 - THE SO-CALLED DIVISIONS OF SYSTEMATIC PHILOSOPHY IN THE LIGHT OF THE TRANSCENDENTAL GROUND-IDEA

With this we have come to the end of our critical examination of the significance of the transcendental ground-Idea for all philosophical thought. We have reached the point where we can begin to develop the positive content of our philosophy. To this end we must first give an account of the plan which will determine the course of our future investigations.

The question arises as to whether or not we can employ the basic divisions of philosophic problems as they are made by immanence-philosophy.

The reply is in the negative. And this denial rests upon the fact that also the classification and formulation of problems in immanence-philosophy is intrinsically connected with its transcendental ground-Idea.

With respect to the systematic development of Humanistic philosophy we can state, that the foundation of all systematic attempts at a classification of problems is rooted in both polar basic factors of the Humanistic ground-Idea: the ideal of science and that of personality, with their inherent postulates of continuity.

> The fundamental significance of the transcendental ground-Idea for all attempts made in Humanistic immanence-philosophy to classify the problems of philosophy.

We have seen that both of these basic factors have dominated Humanistic philosophy since the Renaissance. Before the critical philosophy of KANT, however, they were not clearly isolated as a regulative principle for the systematic classification of philosophical problems. The *Critique of Pure Reason* fenced the first main field of philosophic inquiry: the epistemological foundation and limitation of the classic ideal of science (which is directed toward the "domination of nature"). The second main field of philosophical investigation is indicated by the *Critique of Practical Reason*, i.e. the critical foundation of autonomous ethics, according to the Humanistic ideal of personality. In connection with this latter *Critique*, KANT treats the philosophical problems of jurisprudence ("*Metaphysische Anfangsgründe der Rechtslehre*") and of theology. The *Critique of Teleological Judgment* (Kritik der teleologischen Urteilskraft) investigates the philosophical problems of biology, history [1] and aesthetics and is thought of as a subjective synthesis between the two other critiques.

In FICHTE we find a re-occurence of this basic division. He classified philosophy into a "*Wissenschaftslehre*" with a "theoretical" and a "practical" section. Upon this foundation was subsequently constructed the pantheistic metaphysics of absolute Being. In HEGEL's dialectical division of philosophy into logic, natural philosophy, and the philosophy of Spirit, it is not difficult to detect the influence of the same Humanistic ground-Idea.

As we have seen, pre-Kantian rationalistic Humanistic philosophy was completely under the influence of DESCARTES' program of a *mathesis universalis*. In the naturalistic branch (HOBBES) this program could only lead to an encyclopaedical systematizing of the sciences in a successive continuous procession, from the simple to the complex spheres of knowledge. This was done upon the basis of a mathematical logic and a so-called "prima philosophia". The method of thought of mathematical natural science was maintained in every field of philosophical investigation, in accordance with the con-

---

[1] In my treatise *Norm and Fact*, published in the Dutch juridical quarterly "*Themis*" (1932), I have shown in detail that KANT's philosophy of history, particularly developed in his treatise *Idee zu einer allgemeinen Geschichte in weltbürgerlicher Absicht* (1784), must be explained from the view-point of the "Critique of teleological Judgment" (published a few years after).

tinuity-postulate of the science-ideal. The same can be ascertained again in COMTE's positivism. In spite of their maintenance of the primacy of the science-ideal, we saw that, in the dualistic types of pre-Kantian metaphysics, a fundamental metaphysical cleft was made between natural philosophy, on the one hand, and metaphysical psychology and ethics, on the other.

CHRISTIAN WOLFF divided philosophy into two main fields: theoretical philosophy or metaphysics (including natural theology, psychology and physics), and practical philosophy.

Pre-Kantian empiristic philosophy could also accept a division into theoretical and practical sections. JOHN LOCKE, for example, considered philosophy (as a scientific system) to possess three main divisions: "physica" or natural philosophy, "practica" whose principal part constitutes ethics, and "semiotica", whose principal element consists of nominalistic logic [1].

Even in the philosophy of the XXth Century, attempts at a systematic division continue to be made in accordance with the foundational structure of the Humanistic transcendental ground-idea.

Thus we find that COHEN, the father of the neo-Kantian Marburg school, divides philosophy into three principal realms: *"Logic of pure Knowledge"*, *"Ethics of pure Will"* and *"Aesthetics of pure Feeling"*. Obviously this classification receives its orientation from KANT.

The neo-Kantian philosophy of values (RICKERT) divides the sphere of real nature from the sphere of ideal values. We have seen in part I, that it seeks to effect a subjective synthesis between the two spheres in the intermediary sphere of culture. The system of values which philosophy must give, according to this standpoint, is grounded in the fundamental distinction between theoretical and practical values. It is not difficult to recognize in this distinction the dualism between the science-ideal and the ideal of personality. Theoretical philosophy becomes a transcendental critique of natural science, practical philosophy a "Weltanschauungslehre".

---

[1] *Essays on Human Understanding* IV, 21, § 1 ff.

WINDELBAND's opinion concerning the necessity of dividing philosophy into a theoretical and a practical section.

In his *Introduction into Philosophy*, WINDELBAND divided the philosophical material into theoretical problems (Wissensfragen) and the axiological ones (Wertfragen). In this context he observes: "The connection of both moments (i.e. of the theoretical and practical) is characteristic of philosophy to such a degree, that the division of its historical manifestations into different appropriate periods can be gained in the best manner from the change of the relations between these two. We see how with the Greeks that which is called philosophy originates from purely theoretical interest and methodically comes under the influence of the practical need, and we follow the triumph of the latter in the long periods during which philosophy essentially aims at being a doctrine of the redemption of man. With the Renaissance once more there comes to rule a preponderatingly theoretical striving and the Enlightenment again makes the results of the latter subservient to its practical cultural-ends: until in KANT, with impressive clarity, the intimate coherence between both sides of philosophy is realized and made understandable" [1].

WINDELBAND summarily tries to justify this "foundational" distinction between theoretical and practical philosophy by conceiving it as founded upon the two sides of human nature, considered here as a "thinking" and "volitional-acting" being. But this explanation is not serious. For the so-called "practical" philosophy is as much theoretical as the "theoretical" one, and thinking can be either a practical or a theoretical act.

---

[1] *Einleitung in die Philosophie*, 2e Aufl., 1920, S. 19/20: "Die Verknüpfung beider Momente (i.e. "des theoretischen und praktischen") ist für die Philosophie so charakteristisch, dasz aus dem Wechsel der Beziehungen zwischen ihnen die Gliederung ihrer historischen Erscheinungen in sachgemäsz unterschiedene Perioden am besten gewonnen werden kann. Wir sehen das, was sich Philosophie nennt, im Griechentum aus rein theoretischem Interesse erwachsen und allmählich unter die Macht des praktischen Bedürfnisses kommen, und wir verfolgen den Triumph des letzeren in den langen Jahrhunderten, während deren die Philosophie wesentlich eine Lehre von der Erlösung des Menschen sein will. Mit der Renaissance kommt vom neuem ein vorwiegend theoretisches Bestreben zur Herrschaft, und dessen Ergebnisse stellt wieder die Aufklärung in den Dienst ihrer praktischen Kulturzwecke: bis dann in KANT der intime Zusammenhang zwischen beiden Seiten der Philosophie mit eindrucksvoller Deutlichkeit zum Bewusztsein und zum Verständnis gebracht wird."

532 *Conclusion and transition to the development of the positive*

We quoted the preceeding statement of WINDELBAND to demonstrate how completely dominating the division of philosophy into theoretical and practical is thought to be; it is viewed as not being peculiar to the Humanistic, but to the entire western immanence-philosophy.

It is, however, the polar tension between the ideal of science and that of personality, in the basic structure of the Humanistic ground-Idea, that gives this division its particular Humanistic sense.

The distinction between theoretical and practical philosophy in Greek thought.

The distinction between theoretical and practical philosophy was in fact already present in ancient Greek philosophy. It played a fundamental rôle since ARISTOTLE, and in the Middle Ages it was in many respects accepted without further reflection.

The reason for its adoption is readily understood, if we examine the Socratic trend in Greek thought. The path of the latter had been paved by the sophists.

As we have seen in our transcendental critique, Greek thought was dominated by the religious form-matter motive. And this motive determined the central content of the various forms of its transcendental ground-Idea.

In the Ionic natural philosophy the matter-motive of the old religion of life had the primacy up until ANAXAGORAS. In the transcendental Idea of Origin, the divine ἀρχή was conceived of as the formless and impersonal stream of life. And in most instances it was identified with what was later called a mobile element (e.g. water, air, or fire). In ANAXIMANDER, however, it was simply referred to as the invisible ἄπειρον (the formless or unlimited). Under the influence of this transcendental *Idea of Origin*, man and his culture were viewed under the same perspective as the rest of things, arising in a specific form out of the womb of the eternal flowing stream of life. Man and all things are condemned to death and decay because "form" is ungodly and perishable.

In opposition to the matter-motive the Eleatic school posited its counter pole, viz. the principle of form. It developed a metaphysical ontology in which the all-inclusive form of being was qualified as the only true, eternal, and unchangeable entity. However, the form-motive is here still orientated to the old ouranic [1] religion of nature. As a result, this dialectical trend did not lead Greek thought to critical self-reflection concerning the central position of man in the cosmos. This latter did not occur until the form-motive of the culture-religion acquired the primacy in Greek thought. Under its leadership interest was directed to human culture and in particular to the Greek *polis* as the bearer of the Olympian culture-religion. In PROTAGORAS, the father of Sophistic, this dialectical trend was accompanied by a sceptical criticism of natural philosophy and metaphysical ontology, a criticism which involved the whole of theoretical knowledge. It drew the most extreme conclusions from the matter-motive of the older nature-philosophy [2].

If everything is in a constant state of flux and change, this is also true of theoretical truth. There is no fixed norm for the latter. Individual man in his constantly changing subjectivity is the measure of all things. This devaluation of theoretical knowledge of nature had its back-ground in the shift of interest to human culture and in particular to the Greek polis as the sphere of human action. In opposition to theoretical philosophy, which is valueless in itself, was posited a practical philosophy, not concerned with truth, but with what is useful and beneficial to man. In particular its task was to furnish practical knowledge necessary for politics. For by means of its *paideia*, the polis, as the bearer of the culture-religion, gives form to human nature, which in itself does not posses any law or form, because it is entirely subjected to the ever flowing stream of becoming and decay.

The sophistic distinction between theoretical and practical philosophy in the light of the Greek motive of form and matter.

Thus, for the first time, a fundamental opposition was introduced between theoretical and practical philosophy, and this

---

[1] "Ouranic" (derived from "Ouranos") means what is related to the celestial sphere (the "celestial Gods", i.e. the sun and the stars).

[2] Neither the Ionic philosophy of nature, nor HERACLITUS had done this. For in the *physis*, i.e. the process of growth and decay, they had always accepted a fixed norm and proportion. They derived the latter from the motive of form. In other words, they did not eliminate the form-motive, but merely ascribed primacy to the motive of matter.

opposition was entirely dominated by the dualistic Greek ground-motive. The question as to whether primacy was to be ascribed to the motive of form or to that of matter was expressly viewed by SOCRATES in the light of critical self-knowledge. According to the testimony of PLATO in the dialogue PHAEDRUS — which, if not authentic, nevertheless suits the Socratic spirit perfectly — SOCRATES wished to know, if his ego was related to TYPHON, the wild and incalculable God of destructive storms (a genuine mythological symbol of the matter-motive), or whether he was in possession of a simple (Apollinian) nature, to which form, order, and harmony are proper.

Just as PROTAGORAS, SOCRATES ascribed primacy to the form-motive of the culture-religion. His interests also were entirely directed to culture, ethics, and politics. He was solely concerned in human action. But before everything else he wished to regain fixed norms in philosophical *theoria* as to the good, the true, and the beautiful. These had been undermined by the critique of the sophists, a critique exclusively inspired by the matter-principle and loosened from the principle of form. The criterion of utility, which PROTAGORAS had accepted for practical philosophy, was in the last analysis itself caught in the matter-principle of eternal flux and change.

Therefore, SOCRATES wished to elevate practical philosophy to an *epistèmè*, a science. The virtues must be comprehended in a *concept*. Every concept of an ἀρετή, however, remains enclosed in the theoretical diversity of the normative aspects. It must therefore be concentrically directed toward the divine *Idea* of the good and the beautiful, as the origin of all form in the cosmos. This orientation of the scientific method in ethics to the divine form-principle gave a teleological direction to practical philosophy.

All temporal laws and ordinances and all things in the cosmos must in the last instance aim at expressing the Idea of the good and beautiful, according to which the divine *nous* formed the cosmos.

A concept is valueless, if it does not inform us of the good of the thing being defined. A concept has value in SOCRATES' practical philosophy only, if it informs us of the ἀρετή, the use of a thing. This Socratic Idea of *aretè* implies in the last analysis the teleological relation to the divine Idea of the good and beautiful.

Meanwhile, SOCRATES sharply emphasized the theoretical character of his "practical" philosophy. He did not countenance the sophistical opposition of theoria and praxis [1].

The distinction between theoretical and practical philosophy is not again significant until PLATO and ARISTOTLE. For even though they took full cognizance of SOCRATES' contribution to thought, they again became interested in the problems of metaphysics and natural philosophy.

Since primacy was now ascribed to the form-motive of the culture-religion, the motive of matter was deprived of all divine attributes and the deity was now conceived of as pure *nous* ("pure form" in ARISTOTLE).

The Socratic influence on Greek thought directed the latter toward the self-hood. And as soon as this critical self-reflection appeared in Greek philosophy, the characteristic of man, which distinguishes him from other beings bound to the principle of matter, was now sought in the *nous* (reason). This *nous* was conceived of as *theoretical thought*.

Besides ethical and political questions, the theoria was again concerned with ontological problems and with those of nature. Consequently, the need arose to introduce a distinction in human reason itself. Henceforth, the misleading opposition between *theoretical* and *practical* reason was introduced. This distinction is really misleading here! For by "practical reason" (*phronèsis* in PLATO, *nous praktikos* in ARISTOTLE) was not in the least understood pre-theoretical naïve thought, insofar as it is concerned with practice. In principle, both PLATO and ARISTOTLE held to the Socratic view that only theoretical insight into the good can protect human action from being dominated by sensory passions and desires, which originate in the "matter" of human nature. From this view-point the distinction between theoretical and practical reason cannot be founded in the subjective act of thought, but exclusively in the *Gegenstand* of its logical function.

The philosophical ethics and political theory of PLATO and ARISTOTLE intend to give theoretical insight into objective norms for ethics and politics. It is indifferent to the inner nature of philosophic investigation that it intends to give theoretical information to practical life. For every theoretical investigation can be utilized by the praxis. This even applies to mathematics and physics which do not have any normative aspects as their "Gegenstand".

---

[1] According to XENOPHON, *Memor.* 3, 9, 4, SOCRATES himself did not yet distinguish the theoretical *sophia* from the practical σωφροσύνη (morality).

The Sophists referred theoretical knowledge to the matter-principle and thus denied any universally valid standard for theoretical truth. Consequently, only on this standpoint could the antithesis between theoretical and practical philosophy have a fundamental significance *for the mode of thought as such*. PROTAGORAS maintained a pragmatic standpoint with respect to philosophy: *Theoria* does not have any value in itself. Its value lies solely in the practical aim that it serves, namely, in politics.

Naturally, this extreme nominalistic standpoint cannot recognize norms for praxis which are not conventional. PROTAGORAS' sophistic criterion of utility is purely subjective, but not individualistic, as in his epistemology. The *nomos*, established by the polis, is the *common* opinion about good and evil, not that of an *individual*. It has the task to give cultural form to human *physis* through its *paideia*. But, as we have seen, the principle of form is subject here to the matter-principle of the eternal flux and change. PROTAGORAS' evolutionary philosophy of culture is a clear proof of this. The *nomos* is here only a higher phase of development of the lawless *physis*.

Only with this background in mind can a proper understanding be gained of the realistic standpoint of PLATO and ARISTOTLE.

The axiological turn of this distinction. The primacy of theoretical philosophy versus the primacy of practical philosophy.

In addition to distinguishing between them, Greek thought immediately arranges theoretical and practical philosophy in an axiological order. In the realist-idealistic systems of PLATO and ARISTOTLE a higher value was ascribed to theoretical philosophy. On the contrary, the naturalist-nominalistic systems which proceeded from the Sophistic standpoint, though they were also influenced by SOCRATES' Idea of virtue, depreciated pure *theoria* and ascribed exclusive value to practical philosophy.

In the last analysis, this axiological ordering of theoretical and practical philosophy was connected here with the transcendental ground-Idea of Greek philosophy. For, as we have seen, the distinction acquired an entirely different sense in modern Humanistic philosophy.

According to SEXTUS EMPIRICUS (*Adv. Math.* 7, 16), the first explicit division of philosophy into *ethica*, *physica* and *logica* was made by PLATO's pupil XENOCRATES who directed the academy after SPEUSIPPOS.

In his *Topica*[1] ARISTOTLE provisionally took over this method of classification. He subsumed all philosophical problems that are related to the *universal* under λογικαί. The specific physical or specific ethical do not receive any attention in this general branch of philosophy. According to this point of view, in addition to including formal logic, λογικαί encompasses metaphysics.

If we observe the place here accorded to logic in this wide sense, the influence of the metaphysical (speculative) immanence-standpoint is clearly visible. It is evident insofar as it is related to the metaphysical-universal in its supposed elevation above the cosmic diversity. Metaphysical logic is foundational both for natural and ethical philosophy.

In a later part of his *Topic* and in his *Metaphysics* ARISTOTLE introduced the main division between practical and theoretical philosophy next to which he placed the *Poiètikè*, a third main division of philosophy. According to this new division, metaphysics, as the science of the first grounds of being[2], became theoretical philosophy κατ' ἐξοχήν. ARISTOTLE ascribed to theoretical metaphysics a higher value than to the other branches of philosophical inquiry; he did so, according to the object of knowledge[3]. Practical and *"poetical"* philosophy possess less value; the former is directed toward ethical and political human activity and the latter toward human creation in technique and art. How is this higher appreciation of metaphysical *theoria* to be understood?

Insofar as metaphysics investigates the absolute "formal" ground of being, it is theology (θεολογική). Theoretical reason furnishes us with knowledge of the pure *nous* as divine "actus purus". And the latter, as *Archè*, is considered to be the final "formal" ground of being of the cosmos, whereas "pure matter" is the original principle of becoming and continuous change. Theoretical metaphysics, therefore, takes axiological precedence of all practical and "poetical" knowledge. Practical philosophy has its foundations in theoretical philosophy in this metaphysical sense. With this is closely connected the distinction made in

---

[1] *Top.* A 14, 105b. 199 sq.

[2] In this later division ARISTOTLE did not give any place to the Analytica. The Peripatetici explained this by saying that Logic only functions as an organ of philosophy proper.

[3] Metaph. K 7, 1064b, 5b: βελτίων δὲ καὶ χείρων ἑκάστη λέγεται κατὰ τὸ οἰκεῖον ἐπιστητόν.

ethics between the "dianoetic" and the ethical virtues. The former point to theoretical and the latter to practical life. The "dianoetic" virtues are the highest, because they are directed toward theoretical knowledge itself. A life devoted only to sensory enjoyment is bestial. An ethical-political life is human, but a life devoted to theory is divine. In it the divine in man, the *nous poiètikos* (which is planted in him ϑύραϑεν, that is to say, from outside) reveals itself in its purest form. It is evident that this whole appreciation of pure theory depends upon the religious primacy of the Greek form-motive. Pure *theoria* is the only way to a real contact with the divine "forma pura". The transcendental Idea of Origin has two poles: pure Form versus pure matter.

This Aristotelian axiological view of theory and practice was accepted by THOMAS AQUINAS. He also placed the "dianoetic" virtues above the practical and ethical ones.

The primacy of practical knowledge in the naturalistic-nominalistic trends of Greek immanence-philosophy.

In giving pre-eminence to theoretical philosophy, the metaphysical-idealistic systems of Greek philosophy held to the reality of the ideal forms. In contrast, naturalistic-nominalist Greek philosophy, influenced by the sophistic subjectivism and the Socratic Idea of virtue, ascribed primacy to practical philosophy. Perhaps it is better to say that they rejected all pure "theoria". The Megaric, Cynic, and Cyrenaic schools apparently did not distinguish between theoretical and practical philosophy, nor does one find in them the division of philosophy into physics, ethics, and logic. Nevertheless, they concentrated their entire philosophical interest on ethics, to which logic (dialectic) was made subservient.

EPICURUS divided philosophy into a canonic (logical), a physical and an ethical section. The philosophy of nature was treated only for the sake of its ethical utility, namely, insofar as it could liberate the soul from the terrors of superstition and could prepare it for the hedonistic enjoyments of cultural life in wise self-restriction. It accomplishes this task by furnishing an insight into the rigid mechanical coherence of the events of nature, considered as an interaction of atoms in the void. In my *Reformation and Scholasticism in Philosophy* (1949, vol. I) I have shown that this Greek atomism has nothing to do with the modern atomistic view of matter, but originated from the Greek form-matter-motive. The systems of the Stoics also followed the traditions of the Academy in dividing philosophy into logic, physics, and ethics. Primacy was, here too, ascribed to practical philosophy[1], even though the philosophic physics (which, in a nominalistic strain, had replaced Platonic and Aristotelian metaphysics) occupied the highest position among the theoretical sciences, because as "physical theology" it should lead to knowledge of God[2]. The old Stoic view of nature and deity was also completely dominated by the Greek form-matter motive. God is the ever flowing life-stream in its dialectical identity with the form-principle: he is the primal fire and the *Logos* of nature. It is the task of ethics to teach us how to live according to this *Logos*.

In Stoic ethics the primacy of practical philosophy is clearly revealed, where — in sharp contrast to the Aristotelian view — it teaches, that the highest human task is found in moral action rather than in theoretical contemplation. All virtues are practical and moral in nature; there is no place for pure "*dianoetic*" ones as in ARISTOTLE. ZENO traced them back to Φρόνησις.

According to PLUTARCH, CHRYSYPPUS opposed the philosophers who viewed theoretical life as an end in itself. He contended, that such a view was basically a refined hedonism. It was only agreed that in moral life the correct πρᾶξις, in conformity with reason, rests upon the θεωρία and blends with it.

> In Greek immanence-philosophy, the necessity of ascribing primacy to the theoretical or to the practical reason is connected with the dialectical form-matter motive.

Our discussion should disclose the fact, that the modern Humanistic ideals of science and personality did not play a rôle in the Greek distinction between theoretical and practical philosophy, but that the latter originated from the religious form-matter motive in its dialectical development within philosophic thought. As we saw, this distinction made its entry in Sophistic under the influence of the dialectical opposition of *physis* and

---

[1] Cf. WINDELBAND, *Gesch. der alten Phil.*, 2e Aufl., S. 184.
[2] This theological preference for theoretical philosophy of nature is maintained by POSIDONIUS in the middle Stoa, and by SENECA in the late Stoa.

nomos, as a dialectical antithesis of pure matter and cultural form (due to the *paideia* of the *polis* as the bearer of the cultural religion). It appeared that the further development of the distinction, and the question about the primacy of theoretical or practical philosophy, is closely connected with the dialectical antithesis between the realist-idealistic and the nominalist-naturalistic elaboration of the form-motive, conceived in conformity with the cultural religion. The *nous* is elevated to the rank of the form-principle of human nature.

This *nous*, as a pseudo-Archimedean point, is imprisoned in the modal diversity of meaning. Realist-idealistic attempts to surmount the modal diversity in a transcendental Idea of the Origin of all forms, theologically leads to an absolutizing of theoretical thought as divine nous, and the latter is then thought of as "pure form without matter". "Practical reason", because bound to the aim of conducting temporal human behaviour, is always related to the matter-principle of human nature. Therefore, it lacks the perfection of pure theoretical thought. The primacy of theoretical reason cannot be maintained unless this hypostatization of theoretical thought is made.

Naturalistic nominalism does not join in this metaphysical hypostatization of "pure thought" to "pure form" lifted out of the cosmic coherence of meaning. Yet, if it did not wish to abandon the Socratic trend toward the ethical form of the selfhood, nor to accept the Sophistic nihilism as to theoretical truth, it could only escape the extreme dualism between theoretical and practical reason by axiologically subordinating theoretical philosophy to practical ethics. But the basic antinomy between theoretical and practical reason in Stoic and Epicurean philosophy testifies to the fact that the two poles in the transcendental ground-Idea of Greek thought were no more reconciled in naturalistic nominalism than in idealistic realism.

Why we cannot divide philosophy into a theoretical and a practical.

Our conclusion is, that the basic division of philosophy into a theoretical and practical section, as well as the division between nature- and spirit-philosophy, are intrinsically connected with the immanence standpoint and its conception of the human selfhood. This division points to an inner dissension in the Archimedean point, a discord, which necessarily leads to the ascription of primacy to theoretical or practical philosophy.

From the standpoint of re-formed Christian philosophy, in view of its transcendental ground-Idea, this distinction must be discarded in all of its many forms. Our rejection is not made, because we will not have anything to do with immanence philosophy, but because the division in question is incompatible with the Biblical ground-motive of our philosophical thought.

We have seen, that the human selfhood as the religious root, as the heart of our entire existence, transcends the temporal limits of our cosmos. It transcends all the modal aspects. Philosophy, directed toward the totality of meaning, in the whole of its activity, is necessarily of a theoretical character. From a Christian point of view, therefore, it is meaningless and even dangerous to take over a basic classification, employed by immanence philosophy, which is rooted in the intrinsic dissension of its Archimedian point.

Upon a re-formed Christian standpoint "practical reason" cannot bridge over the fundamental diversity of the normative modal aspects of our cosmos. And neither a theoretical, nor a practical reason, in the sense of immanence philosophy, is identical with our veritable transcendent selfhood.

§ 2 - THE SYSTEMATIC DEVELOPMENT OF THE PHILOSOPHY OF THE COSMONOMIC IDEA IN ACCORDANCE WITH INDISSOLUBLY COHERING THEMATA

In the light of our transcendental ground-Idea, philosophical investigation ought to be carried out in accord with the following fundamental, but mutually inseparably cohering *themata* (themes):

1 - The transcendental criticism of philosophical thought implying the investigation of the religious ground-motives which determine the contents of the transcendental ground-Ideas.
2 - The investigation directed toward the analysis of the modal aspects of temporal reality in order to discover their functional structure. This is the general theory of the modal aspects and their proper law-spheres.
3 - The theory of knowledge with respect to naïve experience, the special sciences, and philosophy, or the transcendental self-reflection on the universally valid conditions of naïve experience and of the theoretical analysis and synthesis of modal meaning, in the light of the transcendental ground-Idea.

4 - The examination directed towards the data of naïve experience in order to investigate the typical structures of individuality of temporal reality, and their mutual intertwinements.
5 - The investigation of the structural unity of human existence within cosmic time, in the light of the transcendental Idea of human self-hood; this is the theme of philosophical anthropology. It can only be developed on the basis of all former themes of investigation.

The problem of time cannot be a particular theme, since it has a universal transcendental character, and as such embraces every particular philosophical question. It is the transcendental background of all our further inquiries.

In this volume, we have concluded the discussion of the first theme, the transcendental criticism of philosophy. We are left with the task of applying this ὑπόθεσις to the four remaining themata. But the fifth, that of philosophical anthropology, will be treated separately in our new trilogy *Reformation and Scholasticism in Philosophy*, especially in the third volume.

> The philosophy of the cosmonomic Idea does not recognize any dualistic division of philosophy. The themata develop the same philosophical basic problem in moments which are united in the transcendental ground-Idea, in its relation to the different structures of cosmic time. These moments are inseparably linked together.

This thematization is not intended to be a division of the philosophical fields of investigation in the sense of a delimitation of self-sufficient spheres of problems. We consider such a division to be in conflict with the essence of philosophical thought, as theoretical thought directed toward the totality of meaning. Our entire work is concerned with the religious self-reflection in philosophical inquiry; we cannot allow any single philosophical problem to be viewed in isolation.

The psychologized as well as the so-called Critical epistemology sought to set up the problem of knowledge as an independent isolated basic problem. We cannot accept this absolutization of the epistemological questions, viewed as purely theoretical ones, because a really critical transcendental epistemology depends upon religious self-knowledge and knowledge of God which transcend the theoretical sphere. Epistemology is theory directed towards the totality of meaning of human knowledge. It is the theory in which our selfhood, having attained the limits of philosophical thinking, returns into itself and thereby reflects upon the limits and supra-theoretical suppositions of temporal knowledge.

Thus viewed, what is all of philosophy other than epistemology? But it is evident, that with such a conception of the problem of knowledge, we might at the same time ask: What is all philosophy other than philosophy of the structures of temporal reality or of time? For in all of its dimensions, philosophical investigation signifies the structural theory of temporal reality, directed toward the totality and Origin of meaning in religious self-reflection. Nay — without religious self-reflection upon the meaning of our temporal cosmos, a veritably critical theory of knowledge would be unattainable for philosophy, because our temporal knowledge, in theory as well as in naïve experience, only has meaning in the whole coherence of meaning of temporal reality.

Our further investigations will be carried on in accord with the four remaining themata which we have just enumerated. These themata are to be understood as a methodical explication in different respects of one and the same basic problem. They develop this problem in its relation to the different structures of cosmic time and temporal reality, according to the moments which are contained in our transcendental ground-Idea: the transcendental Ideas of Origin, super-theoretical totality and temporal diversity of meaning in its modal aspects (opposed to each other in the theoretical "gegenstand-relation", but coherent in cosmic time) and in its temporal structures of individuality.

Only the transcendental ground-Idea gives an account of the method of thematization of philosophy.

> The philosophy of the cosmonomic Idea does not recognize any other theoretical foundation than the transcendental critique of philosophical thought.

Immanence-philosophy very often recognizes particular philosophical basic sciences as the self-sufficient foundation of the special branches of science and philosophical inquiry. Our transcendental ground-Idea does not permit us to accept any other *theoretical* foundation for philosophy than the transcendental critique of philosophical thought as such. We do not acknowledge as a true foundation of philosophy a "phenomenology" as developed by HUSSERL or SCHELER, nor a "prima philosophia" as in speculative metaphysics. A "logic of philosophy", as is found in LASK, a critique of knowledge as developed by HUME or KANT, as well as the critical ontology of NICOLAI HARTMANN or a symbolic logic in the sense of the Vienna school, are also unacceptable to us as the basis for all philosophical investigation, because they lack a really critical foundation. Nor do we agree that a philosophy of values, or a philosophy of mind may furnish an adequate basis for all cultural sciences, whereas an epistemology may be the exclusive foundation of the natural sciences. The very notion that philosophy is founded upon self-sufficient basic sciences is rooted in the immanence standpoint. And this is true whether or not philosophy is taken as a coherent whole, or — in the case of a dualistic main division of its field of investigation — in its separate parts. Immanence-philosophy withdraws philosophical thought from a radical transcendental critique.

The transcendental critique of theoretical thought, which we have presented in this volume, is, to be sure, the ultimate theoretical foundation of philosophy. This critique is, however, not to be considered as a self-sufficient philosophical basic science, since it gives a theoretical account of the supra-philosophical ὑπόθεσις of all philosophical thought.

Philosophical thought, in accordance with its immanent limitations, remains enclosed within the temporal diversity of meaning, within which no single specific synthesis can be the common denominator of all the others, or of a complex of other syntheses. The philosophy of mathematics, physics, biology, psychology, logic, history, language, sociology, economy, aesthetics, jurisprudence, ethics, and theology, as "philosophia specialis", fall under the third and fourth theme. That is to say, they belong to the particular theory of modal aspects and to the theory of the structures of individuality, insofar as the latter express themselves within the modal aspects of reality which delimit the specific fields of inquiry of the different branches of science.

In the sense just specified, no single "philosophia specialis" can function as a philosophical basic science. The particular philosophical pre-suppositions of a special science exert their apriori influence in the most concrete problems of any particular science. We shall later show this in detail. But the particular philosophy of a special science only exists as philosophy, insofar as it examines this foundation in the light of a total theoreti-

contents of the philosophy of the cosmonomic Idea 545

cal vision of temporal reality. And the latter is ruled by the transcendental ground-Idea and the religious basic motive. A *philosophia specialis* only exists to set forth the basic problems of the special sciences in the all-sided coherence of meaning of temporal reality and to relate these problems to the supertemporal fulness of meaning and to the *archè*. An isolated *philosophia specialis* is a contradiction in terms.

§ 3 - A CLOSER EXAMINATION OF THE RELATIONSHIP BETWEEN PHILOSOPHY AND THE SPECIAL SCIENCES

At this point, however, the question arises once again as to whether or not the special sciences can operate independently of philosophy. Although our transcendental critique of theoretical thought has led to a negative answer, a closer examination is not superfluous. For the prejudice concerning the independence of special science in respect to philosophy seems to be nearly unconquerable. It is argued that the special sciences wrested themselves free from philosophy with great difficulty. The Renaissance and the period following are marked by this struggle. Mathematical physics had to fight in order to free itself from the bonds of the Aristotelian philosophy of nature whose doctrine of substantial forms and especially whose non-mathematical conception of natural events was supposed to impede exact physical investigation. In the XIXth century jurisprudence had to struggle against the rationalistic philosophy of natural law (WOLFF c.s.). Even to-day, especially for the students of natural science, the example of "Hegelianism" demonstrates the dangers of a philosophy which tries to meddle in the problems of the special sciences.

It may be that our transcendental critique has shown the impossibility of the autonomy of philosophical thought in respect to faith and religion. Its argument, however, that even the special sciences lack in principle this autonomy, because they necessarily are founded upon philosophical pre-suppositions, will meet with much more resistance, especially from the side of the exact sciences. And, at least nowadays, we have no occasion to ascribe this resistance merely to a conceited attitude with respect to philosophical reflection as such.

Logic, ethics, and aesthetics are generally considered as being parts of philosophy [1]. In addition, the concession is made that

---

[1] I can not agree with this opinion; Only the special *philosophy* of

there must be room for a philosophy of the special sciences and for a general epistemology. But according to the generally held opinion, philosophy and science must remain separate, in order to insure the "objectivity" of the latter. When special sciences operate within their own sphere and employ their own scientific methods, they are to be considered as being independent of philosophy.

The separation of philosophy and the special sciences from the standpoint of modern Humanism.

Nowadays, Humanism generally concedes that the special sciences are autonomous with respect to philosophy [1].

In the positivistic period of the second half of last century, speculative philosophy was completely discredited. It has been extremely difficult for philosophy to regain general recognition. Therefore, Humanist thought now seeks to guard against its old errors and grants complete autonomy to the special sciences within their own sphere [2].

Even many adherents of the so-called Critical epistemology have changed their attitude in this respect.

---

logic, ethics and aesthetics does have this character. But, here too, philosophy permeates special scientific thought.

[1] In modern metaphysical Humanistic philosophy, however, there can be observed some reaction against the tendency of the special sciences to look upon philosophy as something quite indifferent from the view-point of their own empirical research. HANS DRIESCH, for instance writes: "sie (i.e. die Naturphilosophie) will nicht nur den Naturwissenschaften eine Lenkerin sein, die ihnen sagt, welche Wege sie gehen müssen, und welche Wege sie nicht gehen dürfen, sondern sie will auch für die Philosophie den einen von jenen Sammelpunkten bedeuten, in welche alle möglichen Wege des Denkens über Gegebenes zusammenlaufen, und welche ihrerseits Wege ausstrahlen lassen in jenes Gebiet, das das Ziel aller Philosophie ist, in die Lehre vom Wirklichen, vom Nicht-blosz-für-mich-sein: in die *Metaphysik* (*Zwei Vorträge zur Naturphilosophie*, Leipzig 1910, S. 21/2. ["It (i.e. the philosophy of nature) does not only want to be a guide of the natural sciences, telling them which roads to choose and which not; but it also wishes philosophy to be one of these central points into which all possible ways of thought about the data meet. From this centre there are roads leading into the sphere that all philosophy aims at, i.e. the theory of reality, of the being that does not exist merely for me, viz. metaphysics. *(Two Lectures on Nature-philosophy)*]. DRIESCH recognizes that he opposes the commonly held view.

[2] On this standpoint it is pre-supposed that "empirical reality" does not have normative aspects, so that there is no room for "normative sciences".

In his critical period, KANT proclaimed three-dimensional space, as an intuitional form, to be a transcendental condition of geometry [1]. On this ground, several of his followers (L. RIPKE KÜHN and others) opposed EINSTEIN's theory of relativity. The Marburg school of neo-Kantians, however, hastened to accommodate the Kantian theory of knowledge to the non-Euclidean geometries (GAUSZ, LOBATSCHEWSKY, RIEMANN, BOLYAI and others). The same can be said about the Kantian apriori conception of causal natural law, which was orientated to the classic physics of NEWTON, but could not be maintained against the modern quantum-physics.

An independent philosophical critique of the method and theoretical constructions of mathematical natural science is, however, impossible when epistemology is exclusively orientated to the *"Factum"* or (as the Marburg school prefers to say) to the *"Fieri"* of this science, which must be accepted as it is.

The universal validity and autarchy of scientific theory must in this case be accepted apriori, since, in rationalistic immanence-philosophy, natural scientific thought occupies the same position in the sphere of "natural reality", as the divine world-order has in Christian philosophy. Epistemology has simply to follow in the footsteps of the special sciences and is thus safe from being in conflict with scientific progress. Philosophy does not guide or give advice but merely reflects upon the course which the special science has followed. It is consequently assured of the good graces of the latter. And the special sciences need take no cognizance of the way in which philosophy seeks to explain epistemologically the course of scientific investigation. The special sciences think they can remain philosophically and religiously neutral. Which sciences can be more neutral than mathematics and physics? When the other special sciences follow the same method, they will need no more philosophical guidance.

Even when the methodological monism of the classical-Humanistic ideal of science is called into question, the neutrality of the special sciences is generally permitted to go unchallenged. In this connection we need only recall the views of RICKERT

---

[1] In his pre-critical period KANT had admitted the conceivableness of a non-Euclidean space. Cf. his *Gedanken von der wahren Schätzung der lebendigen Kräfte* (1747, 9 ff) ["Considerations on the true appraisal of the living forces"] and his *Allgem. Naturgeschichte des Himmels* (1755, IIIth chap.) ["Natural History of the Heavens"].

and LITT with respect to the relationship between philosophy and the special sciences.

Nowadays, such conceptions are so deeply rooted in philosophical and scientific circles that very often any divergent opinion is quickly branded as an unscientific return to an antiquated conception of the task of philosophy. Yet we must not be frightened by an overwhelming "*communis opinio*". We must not hesitate to criticize the current distinction between philosophical and special scientific thought, when it appears to be incompatible with a really critical standpoint.

We are not blind to the danger of apriori speculative metaphysics, if it concerns itself with the specific problems of science. It is not necessary to parade before our eyes this past spectaculum miserabile, because we reject in principle every speculative metaphysics and demand an *integral empirical* method in philosophic investigations.

The intrinsic untenability of a separation between science and philosophy.

It is impossible to establish a line of demarcation between philosophy and science in order to *emancipate the latter from the former*. Science cannot be isolated in such a way as to give it a completely independent sphere of investigation and any attempt to do so cannot withstand a serious critique. It would make sense to speak of the autonomy of the special sciences, if, and only if, a special science could actually investigate a specific aspect of temporal reality without theoretically considering its coherence with the other aspects. No scientific thought, however, is possible in such isolation "with closed shutters". Scientific thought is constantly confronted with the temporal coherence of meaning among the modal aspects of reality, and cannot escape from following a transcendental Idea of this coherence. As we have shown in the *Prolegomena*, even the special sciences investigating the first two modal aspects of human experience, i.e. the arithmetical and the spatial, cannot avoid making philosophical pre-suppositions in this sense.

The impossibility of drawing a line of demarcation between philosophical and scientific thought in mathematics, in order to make this special science autonomous with respect to philosophy.

Is it possible that modern mathematics would escape from philosophical pre-suppositions with respect to the relationships and coherence of the arithmetic aspect with the spatial, the analytic, the linguistic and sensory ones? Is it permissable to include, with DEDEKIND, the original spatial continuity- and dimensionality-moments in our concept of number? Is mathematics simply axiomatical symbolic logic whose criterion of truth rests exclusively upon the principium contradictionis and the principium exclusi tertii? Does the "transfinite number" really possess numerical meaning? Is it permitted, in a rationalist way, to reduce the subject-side of the numerical aspect to a function of the principle of progression (which is a numerical law) and can we consequently speak of an actually infinitesimal number? Is it justified to conceive of space as a continuum of points? Is it permitted to designate real numbers as spatial points? Is motion possible in the original (mathematical) sense of the spatial aspect?

This whole series of basic philosophical questions strikes the very heart of mathematical thought. No mathematician can remain neutral to them. With or without philosophical reflection on his pre-suppositions he must make a choice. The possibility of effecting a complete separation between philosophy and mathematics is especially problematical with respect to so-called pure ("non-applied") mathematics, because it is conceived of as an apriori science and its results cannot be tested by natural-scientific experiments [1]. Is it not the very task of the philosophy

---

[1] The opinion that pure mathematics would be apriori in this sense, that it may proceed from fully arbitrary axioms, is incompatible with the Christian conception of the divine world-order as the ultimate foundation of all scientific investigation. From our view-point the apriori-character of pure mathematics cannot mean that the latter would be emancipated from the modal structures of the mathematical aspects which are founded in the temporal order of experience.

The investigation of these structures can only occur in an *empirical* way, since they are not created by human thought and are no more apriori "thought-forms", but rather are included in the "modal horizon" of our experience as apriori *data*. They must be *discovered* in reflection upon our experience of the mathematical aspects. The Kantian conception of the apriori and the empirical moments in human knowledge identifies the "empirical" with the sensory impressions. We have again and again

of mathematics to investigate the modal structures of the mathematical aspects on which depend all well-founded judgments in pure mathematics?

Is it possible to separate the task of mathematical science from that of the philosophy of mathematics by saying that the latter only seeks to explain the epistemological possibility of apriori mathematical knowledge, whose methods and contents must be accepted without any critique?

But, by such an attempt at demarcation, mathematics is made a "factum", a "fait accompli", and the possibility of a real philosophical criticism of the latter is precluded.

Such an attitude toward the special sciences may be acceptable in the cadre of a transcendental ground-Idea in which the Humanistic ideal of science has a foundational function, but, in the light of our transcendental critique of theoretical thought, it must be rejected as false and dogmatical.

It is true that philosophy can only explain the *foundations* of mathematics, but this does not warrant the ascription of autonomy to mathematical thought, which reaches its focal point in the technique of reckoning, construction, and deduction. Philosophy cannot attribute this autonomy to it, because the mathematician must necessarily work with subjective philosophical pre-suppositions, whose consequences are evident in mathematical theory itself, as we have explained in the *"Prolegomena"*.

The positivistic-nominalistic conception of the merely technical character of constructive scientific concepts and methods.

The truce between philosophy and the special sciences formulated in the statement that each is to remain in its own sphere, in the final analysis signifies the sanctioning of the positivistic-nominalistic manner of thinking in the sphere of the special sciences. The theoretical scientist is inclined to maintain that — at least in his constructive work — he operates only with technical concepts and methods which are independent of philosophical and a fortiori of religious pre-suppositions.

Thus a mathematician, for example, will say: In our profession, when we employ the concept of the actual continuity of the series of real numbers, we do so without any philosophical prejudice. We utilize such concepts merely, because we find them

---

to establish that this sensationalistic conception of the "empirical" is incompatible with our integral conception of human experience.

practical and instrumental in the acquisition of satisfactory results.

Similarly, a jurist will say: we use the concept "corporation" (Rechtsperson) as a construction of thought under which we include a whole complex of legal phenomena. We do so from a purely technical juridical consideration, because it is useful and "denkökonomisch", that is to say, in conformity with the principle of logical economy. Behind this technical construction we grant philosophy complete freedom to seek a social reality, a collection of individuals, or a super-individual "person". Or if we formally reduce all positive law to the will of the state and declare the law-giver to be juridically omnipotent, then we do so, detached from each standpoint which is dependent upon a philosophy of law; we are equally detached from every political state-absolutism. We employ the concept of the source of law in a purely formal sense and thereby only express the fact that all positive law derives its formal validity from the state. We grant to the philosophy of law the complete freedom to criticize a specific statute as being erroneous and in conflict with justice. It is quite free to oppose a political state-absolutism by insisting upon the freedom of personality.

The positivistic view of reality versus the jural facts.

In spite of such contentions, however, the truth of the matter is, that behind such would-be technical concepts are hidden very positive philosophical postulates. This is especially the case with the appeal to the principle of "logical economy" in order to defend the use of theoretical fictions which do not correspond to the true situation of things within the modal aspect of reality, that forms the specific field of theoretical research. This appeal is characteristic of a nominalistic-positivism. In the general theory of the modal aspects we shall show in detail, that the principle of logical economy has a logical sense only in indissoluble connection with the *principium rationis sufficientis,* which implies that we really *account for* the theoretical states of affairs in a sufficient way. It can never justify theoretical fictions, which are only introduced in order to mask the antinomies caused by a false theoretical conception of empirical reality.

The ruling positivistic conception in jurisprudence identifies empirical reality with its physical-psychical aspects, that is to say with an absolutized theoretical abstraction.

In this naturalist image of empirical reality there is no room for modal aspects of an intrinsically normative character. The juridical aspect completely loses its irreducible modal meaning if — in the line of the modern so-called "realistic" jurisprudence — it is reduced to physical-psychical phenomena. The juridical *facts* are the *juridical aspect* of *real* facts and within this aspect the latter cannot be established without jural norms to which they are subjected. As soon as in theoretical jurisprudence which maintains the normative character of the legal rules, this structural state of affairs is lost sight of and the "facts" within the juridical aspect are conceived of as "physical-psychical" ones, there originate theoretical antinomies which are usually masked by the introduction of "theoretical fictions". And again and again it is the principle of "logical economy of thought" which is called into play to justify these fictions.

We shall return to this state of affairs in the second volume when we engage in a detailed investigation of theoretical antinomies.

In the present context we want only to stress the fact that behind the so-called "non-philosophical" positivist standpoint in jurisprudence there is hidden a *philosophical view of reality*, which cannot be neutral in respect to faith and religion.

The modal-functional and the typical structures of reality.

Under the mask of philosophical and "weltanschauliche" neutrality, the technical pragmatic conception of scientific thought has done a great deal of mischief, especially in the branches of theoretical research which find their "Gegenstand" in modal aspects of temporal reality whose laws are of a normative character.

To make this clear I will briefly indicate the difference between the typical concept of a structure of individuality and the modal concept of function, which difference is set forth in detail in the second and third volume. In every modal aspect we can distinguish:

1 - a general functional coherence which holds in mutual correspondence the individual functions of things, events, or social relationships within a specific modal law-sphere; this coherence exists independently of the typical differences between these things, events or social relationships which function within the same modal aspect.

2 - the typical structural differences manifesting themselves within a modal aspect and which are only to be understood in terms of the structures of individuality of temporal reality in its integral inter-modal coherence.

Some states of affairs taken from the juridical and physical aspects may suffice for the present to make clear this distinction. As we have observed in the Prolegomena, the structures of individuality embrace all modal aspects without exception and group them together in different typical ways within individual totalities. However, they also express themselves within each of their modal aspects by typicalizing the general modal relations and functions.

In the juridical aspect of reality, all phenomena are joined in a jural-functional coherence. Viewed according to the norm-side of this aspect, this means, that constitutional law and civil law, internal ecclesiastical law, internal trade law, internal law of trade-unions and other organizations, international law, etc. do not function apart from each other, but are joined in a horizontal-functional coherence, a coherence guaranteed by the modal structure of the juridical aspect itself. When we view only this universal functional coherence between the various sorts of law, we abstract it from the internal structural differences which the latter display.

This general functional view-point is highly abstract; it only teaches us to recognize the modal functions within the juridical aspect apart from the typical structures of individuality which are inherent in reality in its integral character. It is absolutely impossible to approach the internal structural differences between the typical sorts of law, solely with a general juridical concept of function. Therefore, it must be clear that the general modal concept of law can never contain the typical characteristics of *state*-law.

Similarly, the general functional coherence between phenomena within the physical aspect is to be abstractly viewed as indifferent in respect to the internal typical differences displayed by reality within its structures of individuality. To discover the general laws of physical interaction, physics views all physical phenomena under the modal functional denominator of energy.

The physical concept of function [1] is a systematic concept "par

---

[1] It will be evident that we do not mean here the concept of function

excellence", because it possesses the capacity of grasping the universal horizontal coherence of all possible physical phenomena within this modality.

As long as this functional view dominates exclusively, scientific thought does not view the actual things of nature with their internal structures of individuality. A tree, an animal, and so on (as well as an "atom", a "molecule", and a "cell") undoubtedly have physical-chemical functions in their internal structure as a thing of nature; but an exclusively functional view of the physical aspect of reality reveals nothing within the energy-relations of the universum that could eventually delineate itself as the typical structure of an individual totality. Such a functional view only discloses external relations of abstract "energy" or "matter", relations, which exceed any internal structural difference, and which are grasped according to the functional aspect of physical law. This functional view was from the outset evident in the formulation of Newton's law of gravitation, which law is independent of the typical structures of "things", and actually dominates the physical universum. A pencil falling to the ground is subjected to this law just as much as the motions of the planets.

But there is no single science, except pure mathematics, which is not confronted with reality in its typical structures of individuality. Chemistry essentially investigates the same modal law-sphere as physics, but it can no longer operate solely with a general concept of function, no more than physics itself, since the discovery of the internal atom-structures. Free fluttering electrons may only display bare functional properties of mass and charge, of motion, attraction, and repulsion, but as soon they function, bound within the structure of an atom or molecule, they display specific properties in which internal structural differences enforce themselves.

The distinction between modal-functional and typical structures of reality which we have just shown to be present in the juridical and physical modalities, can also be discovered within all the remaining modal aspects. We shall later demonstrate this in detail.

---

in the specific sense of the infinitesimal calculus. It is used here only in the sense of *modal* function, abstracted from the typical structures of individuality.

The absolutization of the concept of function and the illegitimate introduction of a specific structural concept of individuality as a functional one.

What have we seen take place under the influence of the positivistic view of the task of science? In keeping with the postulate of continuity of the Humanistic science-ideal, the concept of function was absolutized in order to eradicate the modal diversity of meaning which exists between the modal aspects. At the same time the attempt was made to erase completely the typical structures of individuality which reality displays within the modalities investigated. But, especially in the so-called "pure theory of law" (reine Rechtslehre) and in "pure economics", there often can be observed a curious confusion of the modal-functional and the typical structural view-points. Often unintentionally, under the guise of a general concept of function, a specific concept of a typical structure of individuality is introduced in order to level all other typical differences of structure within the investigated aspect of reality.

Consequently, the supposed merely general modal concept of function is in truth transposed into a typical structural concept.

Under the guise of an abstract purely functional view-point the so-called Austrian school in its "pure economics", absolutized free market relations at the expense of the other typical structures of society, which manifest themselves within the economic aspect of reality.

In the same way the so-called "pure theory of law", developed by HANS KELSEN and his neo-Kantian school, tried to construe a merely functional-logical coherence between all typical spheres of positive law, either from the hypothesis of the sovereignty of state-law or from the hypothesis of the sovereignty of international law. In the first case, all the other typical juridical spheres were in a pseudo-logical way reduced to state-law, in the second case, to law of a supposed international super-state (civitas maxima). The confusion between modal-functional and typical-structural view-points was completed by the pseudo-logical identification of law and state, or of law and super-state, respectively.

But if state and law were identical, it makes no sense to speak of *state*-law. And if — as KELSEN thinks — from a purely juridical view-point all positive juridical norms are of the *same formal nature,* and *typical material* differences should be considered as *meta*-juridical, then it is contradictory to introduce into this modal-functional conception of law the typical characteristics of *state*-law or *super-state*-law.

Just as all other spheres of human society, the state possesses an internal structure of individuality which functions in all modal aspects of temporal reality. This is precisely the reason why the state cannot be grasped in an abstract concept of function, no more than its typical juridical sphere.

The modal concept of function is falisified, if under the guise of a merely functional view of law, the whole problem of the sources of law is orientated toward the state or the international community of states, respectively [1].

Setting aside this aberration, it is advisable to make the following clear: The absolutization in scientific thought of the functionalist view-point is not neutral with respect to philosophy or religion. Rather it must be viewed as the fruit of a nominalist view of science which is grounded in the Humanistic science-ideal, although nowadays this latter has undergone a degeneration in consequence of its purely technical conception, especially in the positivist school of ERNST MACH and the younger logical positivism of the Vienna school. In modern times psychology and the cultural sciences have reacted against the complete domination of this functionalistic science-ideal. In the main this reaction comes from the side of the irrationalistic antipode of this functionalism.

> The dependence of empirical sciences upon the typical structures of individuality. The revolution of physics in the 20th century.

I do not deny that experimental and descriptive sciences are strongly bound to empirical reality in its modal-functional and in its typical structures. In other words I do not deny the fact

---

[1] In biological theory there is often found a confusion of the modal-functional concept of organic life with a concept of substance, referring to a living *being* as an individual totality. Compare DRIESCH' conception of "organic life" as an entelechy, or WOLTERECK's conception of organic life as a material living "substance" (matrix), which has an outer material constellation and an inner side of life-experience. Cf. my treatise *The concept of substance in recent natural philosophy and the theory of the enkaptic structural whole* ("Het substantiebegrip in de moderne natuurphilosophie en de theorie van het enkaptisch structuurgeheel") publ. in the quarterly review *Philosophia Reformata* (15th year p. 66—140).

that the insufficiency or incorrectness of rationalistic levelling methods can appear in the course of empirical research by the discovery of stringent facts. In the twentieth century physics, for example, underwent a revolution and had to abandon its classic functionalistic concept of causality, matter, physical space and time. The theory of relativity and the quantum-theory have reduced NEWTON's physical conception of the world to a mere marginal instance.

In keeping with the Humanist ideal of science, the classic mechanical concept of causality aimed at an absolute functionalization of reality in a strictly deterministic sense. This concept of causality could not explain the micro-structure of the physical side of reality, disclosed by continued investigation. PLANCK's discovery of the quantum-structure of energy and HEISENBERG's relations of uncertainty made it no longer possible to reduce the physical processes to a bare continuous causal coherence. On experimental grounds, the quantum theory and the theory of relativity radically broke with NEWTON's conception of matter as a static substance filling absolute space and subject to completely determined causal processes in "absolute time".

The discovery of radio-activity taught the physicist to recognize an autonomous physical change which takes place entirely within the internal structure of the atom, and which cannot be explained in terms of any external functional cause. But the discovery of phenomena which cannot be comprehended in a classical concept of function does not in any way insure that they will be interpreted correctly and in a manner that is philosophically and religiously neutral. On the contrary, it is quite obvious, that the scientific attitude of the leading investigators of nature is profoundly influenced by their theoretical total view of reality. It is evident, for instance, that MACH's and OSTWALD's opposition to the acceptance of real atoms and light waves, and their attempt to resolve the physical concept of causality into a purely mathematical concept of function, was dependent upon their positivist sensualistic standpoint in philosophy. B. BAVINK pointed out that the modern trend in physics which, following HEISENBERG and JORDAN, declared itself to be in favour of a fundamental abandonment of the concept of causality in physics, did so on the basis of philosophical considerations which it owed to MACH and AVENARIUS [1].

---

[1] *Ergebnisse und Probleme der Naturwissenschaften* ("Results and

558 *Conclusion and transition to the development of the positive*

The conflict concerning philosophical foundations is not alien to the heart of special sciences. In fact it is the physicist who is in danger of uncritically accepting positivist and nominalist pre-suppositions. By blindly contemplating the "technical" side of his field, he is soon inclined to accept, without even being aware of their philosophical implications, a nominalistic view of physical problems and a merely technical-constructive view of physical methods and concepts.

From the standpoint of physics alone, may a physicist accept the thesis that a mathematically formulated theory must be considered as correct, if it explains in the simplest way possible the phenomena known up until the present time by bringing them in a functional coherence? In other words is the principle of logical economy in the positivist and so-called empirio-critical sense, in which it is conceived of by MACH and AVENARIUS, the only criterion of correctness in physics?

Recall the conflict concerning EINSTEIN's theory of relativity which was not only conducted in philosophical circles but also in natural-scientific ones.

Recall the controversy between PLANCK, v. LAUE, LENARD and other physicists on the one hand, and SCHRÖDINGER, HEISENBERG, JORDAN on the other, in which the question was discussed as to whether or not the physical concept of causality could in principle still be maintained in the further development of the quantum theory.

Was the former situation in classical physics a matter of indifference to the Christian examiner of nature? Was it of no consequence to him, that classical physics adopted an essentially rationalistic view of empirical reality in which the entire individual factual side of the physical aspect was fundamentally reduced to the purely functionalistically conceived of law-side? In other words ought we to accept physical determinism as

---

Problems of the Natural Sciences") (9th ed. 1948, p. 233 fl.). In my opinion it is not permitted to identify this fundamental concept with the deterministic one, which has originated from the classic mechanical image of reality. The concept of causality has a so-called *analogous* character. Every empirical science must conceive it in the special modal sense of its field of inquiry. The mechanistic-deterministic conception has turned out to be incompatible with the very nature of physical phenomena. But this does not prove that every physical concept of causality has become meaningless.

correct with respect to the situation of physics in the 19th century, because it could arrange most of the then known phenomena in a systematic functional coherence?

And is it immaterial to the Christian physicist, whether or not physics may be identified with the conventionalist conception that the Vienna school has of it? If it really was indifferent to physics to choose a position in this question, the term "science" might become meaningless. For science pre-supposes a theoretical view of reality [1], because it must continually appeal to it.

The defense of the autonomy of the special sciences from the so-called critical realistic standpoint.

From the standpoint of so-called critical realism [2], B. BAVINK, the famous German philosopher of nature, has tried to make clear that natural science is autonomous with respect to philosophy: "The principal point is not at all with what methods and means of thought we should approach things, but rather what resulted and probably will result further from this approach which for centuries we have executed with the greatest success without any epistemology. The whole question is not at all a question of epistemology, but rather of ontology, that is to say, it does not

---

[1] BAVINK (op. cit., p. 271) remarks: *"Für die Physik sind vielmehr die Moleküle und die Lichtwellen, die Felder und ihre Tensoren" u.s.w. von genau derselber Wirklichkeitsart wie Steine und Bäume, Pflanzenzellen oder Fixsterne."* ["For physics the molecules and light-waves, the electromagnetic fields and their tensors etc. are rather of exactly the same sort of reality as stones and trees, vegetable cells or fixed stars]. But he overlooks the fact that physics has eliminated the naïve view of reality!

[2] "Critical" realism (Ed. v. HARTMANN, ERICH BECKER, RIEHL, MESSER, KÜLPE, and others) proceeded from KANT's critical conception of human knowledge. But, in contradistinction to KANT, it acknowledges, that the categories of thought sustain a relation to the *"Dinge an sich"*: It repudiates the Kantian view that the "thing in itself" is unknowable. Thus it falls back upon the metaphysics of the Humanistic ideal of science, which in BAVINK is accommodated to scholastic realism (universalia in re et ante rem; see his cited work, p. 264). In opposition to KANT's transcendental idealism it accepts a metaphysical conception of the categories.

BAVINK thinks that the categories can only be derived aposteriori from a scientific investigation of nature. He rejects KANT's categories of relation as being in conflict with the present state of physics. In contrast, he ascribes to KANT's teleological view of nature a real rather than a fictitious significance in respect to "nature in itself". Because of its starting point, "critical realism" must misconstrue and reject the naïve experience of reality. In volume III we shall develop this point at greater length.

matter how I ought to think the world or can or must think it, but how it really is"[1].

This statement seems to be philosophically neutral, but it really depends upon a sharply defined apriori philosophical view of the cosmos. It is only meaningful on the condition of our accepting a constellation of reality in which the physical universum is opposed to human thought as a "world in itself", a constellation in which reality is shut off in its pre-sensory natural aspects[2]. There is a connection between this view of the cosmos and BAVINK's agreement with the epistemological conception of the merely subjective character of "secondary qualities" (the objective sensory properties of colour, smell, taste, etc.)[3].

If it is true, however, that cosmic reality, as a universal and temporal coherence of meaning, does not permit itself to be

---

[1] *Op. cit.*, 5th ed. 1933, p. 204: "*Es handelt sich gar nicht zuerst darum, mit welchen Denkmethoden und Denkmitteln wir an die Dinge heran zu gehen hatten, sondern darum, was bei diesem Herangehen, das wir ohne alle Erkenntnistheorie seit Jahrhunderten mit grösztem Erfolge ausgeübt haben, herausgekommen ist und mutmaszlich weiter herauskommen wird. Die ganze Frage ist gar keine Frage der Erkenntnistheorie, sondern eine Frage der Ontologie, d.h. es kommt nicht darauf an, wie ich mir die Welt denken soll oder kann oder musz, sondern wie sie wirklich ist.*" In the 9th ed. the first sentence has been omitted, but the standpoint itself has not been changed.

[2] BAVINK does not consider "nature" and "reason" as two absolutely distinct and uncrossable spheres, but considers "nature" as being "rational" in its deepest foundation (op. cit., p. 273 fl.). This is in keeping with critical realism, especially in its scholastic accommodation to the Augustinian doctrine of the divine Logos. It does not contradict the metaphysical conception of a physical world "in itself", independent of the mutual coherence of all modal aspects in cosmic time. It does only imply that in this physical world "in itself" is expressed the "divine Reason" which is also the origin of human reason. According to this view "nature in itself" must be "rational" in an absolute *objective* sense. This objective rationality of physical order is quite independent of and has in itself no relation to the logical subjective function of man. But the latter has a relation to the former.

[3] *Op. cit.*, p. 59. In this connection I am speaking of "objective" as related to possible adequate subjective sensory perception or sensation. BAVINK does not see the modal difference between the physical electromagnetic waves with their different frequencies and the objective sensory qualities which are founded upon the former. But his opinion is in keeping with the current physiological and psychological conception which lacks an insight into the modal structures of the different aspects.

enclosed within its pre-sensory sides, then BAVINK's view of reality and his conception of the autonomy of science is false. In other words, if the physical aspect of the cosmos is not separate from the psychical-sensory and logical, and, if subject-object-relations exist in reality, then it is meaningless to speak of a "nature in itself".

The physical modality of reality does not permit itself to be comprehended by scientific thought apart from a subjective insight into the mutual relation and coherence of the modalities within the cosmic temporal order.

> Experiments do not disclose a static reality, given independently of logical thought; rather they point to the solution of questions concerning an aspect of reality which, under the direction of theoretical thought, is involved in a process of enrichment and opening of its meaning.

The physical aspect of reality does not represent itself in sensory perception as upon a sensitive plate in a photographical apparatus, nor is it arranged *"an sich"* according to theoretical categories. But, because of the very intermodal coherence of the aspects, physical phenomena have an *objective analogon* in the sensory ones; they must be subjectively interpreted in scientific thought and thereby *logically opened*. In this connection the question as to how the physical aspect ought to be understood in its relation to the other aspects of reality is extremely important.

The experimental method is essentially a method of isolation and abstraction. Experiments do no more disclose to us the physical aspect of phenomena as a fixed or static reality in itself, independent of theoretical thought, but rather as an opened aspect of meaning, which, in its cosmic coherence with the logical one, is enriched and unfolded by disclosing its logical anticipations under the direction of scientific thought. For, as we have observed repeatedly, every modal aspect of temporal reality expresses its cosmic coherence with all the others in its modal structure.

Experiments are always pointed to the solution of theoretical questions which the scientist himself has raised and formulated.

BAVINK's opinion that in the course of centuries physics has been able to achieve its greatest results without any aid from epistemology is unworthy of a thinker who is trained in the history of science and philosophy. The truth is that modern physics rests upon epistemological pre-suppositions which have had to wage a sharp fight against the formerly ruling Aristotelian conception of nature [1], and which only little by little have been generally accepted since the days of GALILEO and NEWTON. Most physicists carry on their investigations without being conscious of their philosophical implications and accept the fundamentals of their science as axioms. This sort of philosophical naïvety is very dangerous for a Christian scientist.

For in addition to the gains that it reached in physics, GALILEO's and NEWTON's epistemology implied a purely quantitative and functionalistical view of reality. The latter was not restricted to physics and became the very content of the rationalistic Humanistic science-ideal.

BAVINK's arguments in defence of the philosophical neutrality of physics, which at first glance seem to be strong, on second thoughts appeared to be not free of pre-suppositions which exceed science. Although he rejects apriori rationalism and the nominalist conventionalism of the Vienna circle, his own opinion concerning the philosophical neutrality of science depends upon a specific philosophical view of reality which to a high degree rests upon an absolutization of the functionalistic view-point of natural science [2], which has no room for naïve experience.

The appeal to reality in scientific investigation is never philosophically and religiously neutral. Historicism in science.

The appeal to "reality" in scientific investigation is never free from a philosophical and religious prejudice. Allow me this time to choose the example of the science of history. RANKE said of the latter, that it only has to establish how the events have really happened (*"wie es wirklich gewesen ist"*). But in the word *"wirklich"* (really) there is a snare. For it is impossible for a particular science to grasp an event in its full reality. History, as all other special sciences, can only examine a particular aspect of the latter. Consequently, it groups and arranges historical material in a theoretical modal analysis of temporal reality,

---

[1] One need only think of the application of the mathematical concept of function and the introduction of the exact method of experimentation without which modern physics would be impossible.

[2] Compare especially op. cit. p. 272 fl.

without which it could not focus its attention upon the historical aspect.

In the second volume we shall analyze in detail the modal structure of the latter in order to delimit the true "Gegenstand" of historical investigation. This branch of science pre-supposes a theoretical view of reality which has a philosophical character, since historical investigation can only comprehend the historical aspect in its theoretical coherence with the remaining aspects. Now it is extremely easy for Historicism to gain adherents among historians. Historicism, as we know, is a view of reality which eradicates the boundaries between the modalities and subsumes all other aspects of temporal reality under an historical common denominator. In Part II of this volume we have seen how, since the beginning of the 19th century, Historicism exerted an enormous influence upon the foundation of scientific thought.

The Historical school of jurisprudence proclaimed positive law to be an "historical phenomenon". At the same time it had a great influence on the current view of society and on the theory of the state.

If the state is viewed historically, then it is especially considered in its modal aspect of power. As we shall show in the second volume of this work, power is the central moment in the modal structure of the historical aspect. Under the influence of Historicism this fact has given rise to the idea that the state, in its *total reality*, is an organization of power. The empirical reality of the state is, in this way, theoretically identified with its historical aspect.

As a matter of fact, the integral typical structure of the state is in this way completely misrepresented. It cannot be enclosed in its historical aspect of power, no more than it can be comprehended as a purely juridical, economical, or psychological phenomenon. Its typical structure embraces all these modal aspects, but cannot be identified with any of them.

The attempt to comprehend the state purely in its historical aspect of power, accompanied by a claim to religious and philosophical neutrality, results in a view which offers a false theoretical abstraction instead of the state as it veritably exists.

The conflict between the functionalistic-mechanistic, the neo-vitalistic and holistic trends in modern biology.

Biology also offers many examples of a functionalistic view of reality in which a specific modal aspect is absolutized. The theory of evolution developed a mechanical genetic concept of species that eradicated the internal structural principles of individuality. It was believed, that this did not exceed the limits of biological thought.

Modern biology has become the scene of a sharp internal controversy due to the different theoretical views of empirical reality. The holistic school has sought to reconcile the conflict between the mechanists and the neo-vitalists. The former operated with a mechanical concept of function, and attempted to reduce the modal aspect of organic life to the physical-chemical which was conceived of in the obsolete mechanistic sense.

The neo-vitalists, following Driesch, have seen that the mechanistic method is insufficient to grasp the material examined by biology. Driesch, however, did not attack the mechanistic conception of matter as a purely physical-chemical constellation which should be enclosed in itself and completely determined by mechanical causality. He only denied that organic life can be reduced to a physical-chemical constellation of matter. He did not see that organic life is nothing but a modal aspect of reality. Consequently, he proclaimed it to be a reality in itself: an immaterial entelechy, a substance which would direct the material process without derogating from the principle of conservation of energy. Thus the attempt was made to correct an absolutized concept of function by means of a concept of substance, understood in a pseudo-Aristotelian sense. But this "immaterial substance" was itself the result of a new absolutization. And the latter was destructive for the theoretical insight into the typical temporal coherence between the biotical and the physical-chemical aspects, within the total structure of individuality of a living organism.

Holism made the attempt to conquer the antinomical dualism of Driesch's conception. It had the intention to bridge this dualism by a conception of structural totality. The typical structures of individual totalities, however, cannot be grasped in theoretical thought without a correct theoretical insight into the mutual relations between its different modal aspects. The holistic school lacked this insight. Consequently it fell back upon the functionalist attempt to construe a conception of the whole of a living organism by levelling the modal boundaries of meaning of its different aspects. Whereas mechanism tried to reduce the biotical aspect to the physical-chemical one, holism followed the reverse procedure.

The philosophical conflict concerning the foundations of biology intervenes in the centre of scientific problems [1], and up to now, it is exclusively conducted within the cadre of a Humanist view of science. Can the Christian biologist choose sides in the sense of a mechanistic, a vitalistic or an holistic view of the living organism? Or will he consider it safer to hide behind the positivist mask of neutrality? For it is a naïve [2] positivism that has caused the idea of philosophical neutrality to dominate the special sciences. Our conclusion is, however, that the positivistic conception of special science cannot be reconciled to a Christian cosmonomic Idea.

As soon as a special science was born, it was confronted with philosophical problems concerning the modal structure of the special aspect which has to delimit its field of research.

It makes no sense to say that special science can neglect these problems, because it has to do with the investigation of empirical phenomena alone. Empirical phenomena have as many modal aspects as human experience has. Consequently it cannot be the phenomena themselves which constitute the special scientific fields of research. It is only the theoretical gegenstand-relation between the logical aspect of our thought and the non-logical aspects of experience which gives rise to the fundamental division of these fields and to the philosophical problems implied in it.

No more can philosophy neglect the results of special scientific research of the empirical phenomena, because exactly in these phenomena the inter-modal coherence between the modal structures of the aspects is *realized*. And the typical structures of individuality can be studied only in their *empirical realization*, on condition that their modal aspects are correctly distinguished.

Therefore an interpenetration of philosophy and special science is unescapable, although the former cannot restrict itself to the

---

[1] Any one who wants to acquire a sharp view of this state of affairs, should read the work of Prof. Dr R. WOLTERECK, *Grundzüge einer allgemeinen Biologie* (1932) ["Principal Traits of a General Biology"].

[2] *Translator's note:* Naïve in the sense that the thinker is ignorant of his own philosophical pre-suppositions.   D. H. F.

philosophical problems implied in the special sciences, since it has also to give an account of the data of naïve experience.

The relationship between special science and Christian philosophy has up until now only been provisionally considered. It has been treated here within the general cadre of our transcendental critique of scientific thought. What I am suggesting concerning the mutual penetration of Christian philosophy and science, can only be presented in a more concrete fashion after the development of our general theory of the modal aspects and of the typical structures of individuality. With respect to jurisprudence and sociology I have done this in detail in my *Encyclopaedia of Jurisprudence* (3 vols.), which will soon be published. With respect to the biological problems I may refer to the second volume of my *Reformation and Scholasticism in Philosophy*. Furthermore, I may refer to many special investigations by others who adhere to this philosophy. For the present our only concern was to show that, in the light of the Biblical ground-motive of the Christian religion, the modern Humanistic division between science and philosophy cannot be maintained. In fact, even upon the Humanistic standpoint this division cannot hold its own against a serious immanent critique.

CPSIA information can be obtained
at www.ICGtesting.com
Printed in the USA
LVHW041038131218
600247LV00004B/34/P